The Old-House Journal

Guide to Restoration

The Old-House Journal

Guide to Restoration

Edited by
PATRICIA POORE

Project Editor
LOUISE QUAYLE

A DUTTON BOOK

DUTTON
Published by the Penguin Group
Penguin Books USA Inc., 375 Hudson Street
    New York, New York 10014, U.S.A.
Penguin Books Ltd, 27 Wrights Lane,
    London W8 5TZ, England
Penguin Books Australia Ltd, Ringwood,
    Victoria, Australia
Penguin Books Canada Ltd, 10 Alcorn Avenue,
    Toronto, Ontario, Canada M4V 3B2
Penguin Books (N.Z.) Ltd, 182-190 Wairau Road,
    Auckland 10, New Zealand

Penguin Books Ltd, Registered Offices:
Harmondsworth, Middlesex, England

First published by Dutton, an imprint of New American Library,
a division of Penguin Books USA Inc.
Distributed in Canada by McClelland & Stewart Inc.

First Printing, November, 1992
10 9 8 7 6 5 4 3 2 1

REGISTERED TRADEMARK—MARCA REGISTRADA

LIBRARY OF CONGRESS CATALOGING-IN-PUBLICATION DATA:
The Old-house journal guide to restoration / edited by Patricia Poore.
        p.   cm.
    Includes index.
    ISBN 0-525-93551-7
    1. Dwellings—United States—Conservation and restoration.
    2. Dwellings—United States—Remodeling.   I. Poore, Patricia.
    II. Old-house journal.
    NA7205.0625   1992   92-52881
    728′.028′80973—dc20   CIP

Printed in the United States of America

Set in ITC Garamond

Design: Libra Graphics / Dorothy L. Gordineer

ACKNOWLEDGMENTS

Many thanks to the following contributors to *Old-House Journal* whose work was adapted for this book:

David Baker
Gordon Bock
William Ward Bucher
Kenneth D. Collister
Katharine Conley
Brian D. Conway
J. Randall Cotton
John Obed Curtis
James Martin Denver
Ron DiDonno
Gary Feuerstein, P.E.

John Crosby Freeman
John Mark Garrison
Allen Charles Hill
Larry Jones
Walter Jowers
Clem Labine
Roland A. Labine, Jr.
Roland A. Labine, Sr.
John Leeke
James C. Massey
Shirley Maxwell

Dr. Roger Moss
Bill O'Donnell
Jonathan Poore
Jeremy Robinson
Joseph V. Scaduto
Jonathan T. Schechtman
Susan M. Tindall
Andy Wallace
Jeff Wilkinson
Kathleen Wolsiffer
Gregory S. Woroch

CONTENTS

PART ONE

AN
APPROACH
TO
OLD
HOUSES

CHAPTER 1

Evaluating the Property

An old house is a way of life—and old houses aren't for everyone. Pipes may leak; space isn't laid out efficiently; wiring isn't adequate . . . the list of sensible reasons why one shouldn't buy an old house goes on and on. Yet there are growing numbers who would live nowhere else. They are truly Old-House People. Why endure the extra headaches of owning an old house for the privilege of living in a structure that sometimes behaves like a cantankerous spouse? First, there is the romance: An old house is part of the collective memory of the human race, a living relic from the past. Long-forgotten joys and sadness linger in old rooms and on dark staircases. An old house continually reminds us that people have lived before, and through the house we share an experience with those people from other times. Keeping up an old house is keeping faith with the past. Also, there is something reassuring about the unmistakably handmade flavor of old houses in this increasingly mass-produced world.

Yet old-house living means plaster falling from above and water rising in the basement below. It is truly a labor of love. It confers a joy and fulfillment that no tract house or apartment can provide. Of course, joy and fulfillment may not be your immediate feelings as you dodge falling plaster or wade through the basement. But working on an old house is an adventure that you'll come to regard with satisfaction. You will have made a home while cherishing a piece of history—all without destroying the beauty of your old house or compromising the unique story it has to tell. Rather, you will have enriched that story and made it part of your own.

The *Old-House Journal* set out to answer the practical needs (and questions) of these quirky old-house lovers back in 1973 before preservation and restoration was fashionable. We focus on information you can't get anywhere else: how to fix up and keep your pre-1939 home without sacrificing its charm and character. Other handy-man magazines show you how to put aluminum siding on your house; the *Old-House Journal* tells you why that's a bad idea. At heart, the *Journal* is about preservation in the midst of a throw-away society. You won't find slap-dash remodeling here, or any misguided fascination with the newest renovation fads. In this book we've collected the best restoration, maintenance, and decoration techniques—whether they're historically proven methods or recently developed innovations—collected over our many years of old-house living.

Like many do-it-yourself publications we believe in economical self-sufficiency. But we go a step further. We believe that old houses are part of our national heritage. Every old house has a special history, its own story to tell. The ornamental detail, the evidence of past generations, the historical style—it's all part of your home's story. When you learn to hear what the house is telling you, the joy of old-house living really begins. At the same time we, like our readers, live in a modern world. That's why you'll find that our emphasis is on *sensitive* rehabilitation, not only to the house's historical details but to its inhabitants' daily needs. If you want to do a "gut renovation" and make a starkly modern statement, you won't find any help or encouragement in these pages. You will find ways to sensitively incorporate modern technology and materials without sacrificing your house's historical heritage.

Sometimes we stir up controversy. In a special issue focusing on approaches to kitchen design in 1987, readers wrote us about the "rightness" and "wrongness" of putting a modern kitchen into an old house. There are few rules in residential rehabilitation. Respect for the past, along with good taste and common sense, demand that you not destroy good old work; that what you add at least be up to the quality standards of the existing work; that nothing you do be violently jarring in the context of existing conditions. Yet self-appointed preservationists criticize the addition of anything new in an old house, arguing that anything old is always better than anything new. If that's true, what of *our* work in the late twentieth century will be worth preserving fifty or two hundred years from now?

Yes, we should preserve good old work, and yes, we should respect the intention of the original builders. But the purists would have us freeze time and turn our dwellings into museums. They forget that these houses were built by people who had everyday concerns with economy, comfort, and function—just as today. And the purists also forget that plenty of examples of *bad* old work plague old-house owners today. We don't subscribe to the idea that being involved with restoration and preservation means negating the present and future, the way architects have been known to negate the past. Are we so incapable of doing work that is both a product of our own time and lives up to the standards of the past? We don't think so.

Old-house lovers are a special breed. There is tremendous discipline involved in restoration work. Existing conditions must be dealt with; the good work of the past, the historic elements that we respond to, the sense of age—all must be respected. Creative license (and sometimes ego) must take a back seat to context.

The architects, builders, and planners who have done sensitive rehabilitation work have learned valuable lessons. Those lessons become part of the knowledge they will draw on in their work on new construction. And in *The Old-House Journal Guide to Restoration* we've tried to relate some of these lessons.

WHAT'S OLD?

Unless "old" is a pejorative word in your vocabulary (in which case, you should put down this book right now!), determining what is old *and* significant is a somewhat subjective process. In general, we cover the preservation and restoration of pre-1939 houses. But these days it's tough to find an unspoiled antique house. As likely as not someone else got there first and made some disastrous changes that have harmed or destroyed its character. (Even if you do find an undisturbed house, the owner frequently has an inflated idea of its value, and with no knowledge of the real-estate market, he or she may well be asking an exorbitant selling price.) Sometimes the house's previous owners have made additions to the house that add to its character and charm, while not keeping strictly within the historical and aesthetic bounds of the house's original period. You're left with an eclectic piece of early American farmhouse flavored with Victorian embellishment. This is where old-house restoration challenges your creativity. For example, over the years the owners of your circa 1840 farmhouse added modern conveniences like running water and electricity, not to mention rooms to keep up with a growing family, and so on. Do you tear everything away to restore the house to its original building plan? More likely, you'll make choices—

based on history and aesthetics—to keep some of the newer elements while restoring the house's historical integrity at the same time. Otherwise, you'd find yourself creating a museum house that probably wouldn't meet your needs for liveability and comfort.

There are few examples of "pure" styles. Some houses and buildings show tendencies and influences that allow them to be assigned to a particular school or style. Others show the effects of compromises by designers and builders that make them candidates for those classic weasel words *transitional* and *eclectic*. Still other buildings bear the idiosyncratic stamp of the original designer and are a style unto themselves.

This raises the question of what makes an old house "significant." What of the thousands of vernacular houses that aren't architecturally or historically significant? What determines whether such a structure is "worthy" of preservation? While we'll discuss the principles of sensitive rehabilitation in more detail later in this chapter (including federal standards for accurate historic preservation), basically there are three yardsticks you can apply to vernacular structures:

• Is the building in sound physical shape? In an era of limited resources, we can ill afford to waste sound buildings.

• Is it connected in people's minds with a landscape, streetscape, or neighborhood? Would people miss it if it disappeared? The architectural significance of a building can be understood by a handful of architectural historians. But the people who live near or pass by a building can tell you if they *like* it. Isn't that enough? These vernacular landmarks give stability and a framework to our daily routine.

• Is it beautiful or visually entertaining? Given the sterility of so much modern construction, we should cherish beautiful old buildings that bring joy to our lives.

Ultimately, the choices you make about what to retain and what to modify are yours. You won't find definitive answers here, but you will find guidelines to help you sensitively rehabilitate your old house. As we said, there are obviously limits to how little change one can make and still have a habitable house. Modern kitchens and bathrooms are essential, as are measures to reduce fuel consumption. Careful thought can usually lead to good solutions: incorporating the "moderns" into secondary space or newly built additions, inconspicuous heat-saving means that will not damage the building now or in the future, and so on. If you intend to treat an old house with respectful regard for its age and what it represents, then you must take care that the very qualities that give it its value are not needlessly damaged or destroyed. Taking the trouble to determine what is important about a house before charging ahead and pouring money into a complete rehabilitation is the critically important first step in treating just an "old" house as a "significant" antique house.

RESEARCHING YOUR
──────HOUSE HISTORY──────

Knowing what your house looked like in the past can help you make informed decisions about how to proceed with your own rehabilitation of the structure. Among other resources, you can make use of local museums and historical societies, old magazines and newspapers, physical artifacts, and city maps. But your first step should be a title search in the local real-estate transaction records. The search enables you to plot the "chain of title" to your house: when it was built, by whom, who owned it and for how long, how much it sold for over the years. All transactions, whether mortgage, sale, or conveyance by inheritance, are recorded and accessible (as long as the records still exist).

Every community has a Recorder's Office or Deed Office. It stores the permanent records of all transactions involving real property. You'll have to unravel the idiosyncracies of the local filing system for yourself, but you can be certain that the office is open to the public and that its information is indexed according to the names of both buyers and sellers of the property.

If you know either end of the chain of title, either the current or the original owner, you can recreate the chain of title using what is known as the "grantee," or buyer, and "grantor," or seller, index. You certainly know one end of the chain: your own name, when you bought the house, and from whom.

Start your search with the grantee index for the year in which you bought the property, and go backward through each year of indexes. Look for the name of the people who sold you the house, to find out when they bought the house and from whom. When you find their name, read the actual deed to be sure it refers to your property. Take the name of the seller from that deed and use the grantee index to find out who sold *them* the house, and so on.

If by chance you're doing this from the original owner on, use grantor indexes to determine who sold the house each time, and then go forward to find out who that person sold to, and so on. Keep in mind that indexes, especially for earlier years, are not bound individually but rather in groups of years.

Each of these transactions can provide valuable clues to the early life of your house. A sizable increase in price, for example from $1,200 in 1860 to $8,000 in 1865, suggests a capital improvement like a new building. A mortgage on a property may coincide with the construction of a new wing or outbuilding. You can often confirm your guesses with a visit to the Building Department in your town. Building- and alteration-permit files may include the owner's name, date of construction, architect, builder, cost of construction, roof covering, dates of alterations, plans, even working drawings.

The Office of Taxation or comparable municipal departments in your area may also yield clues. Increases in tax assessments from year to year may indicate improvements on the property. Be cautious, however, in making assumptions based on these increases. A city-wide reassessment may have doubled everyone's taxes in one year. Inflation, real-estate booms, and other factors affect property values as well, so it is important to know something about the economic history of your town. Visit your local museum and historical society to see if you can learn something about your area's (and your house's) history.

In searching backward through the grantor index you may find that there had been a *reconveyance,* meaning that someone gave back an interest in land. Translated, this generally means that the owner of a piece of property has paid off the mortgage. A reconveyance also allows the house historian to skip many years of indexes.

Make sure you examine the reconveyance document itself. These documents are usually housed in the same building as the grantor-grantee indexes. The reconveyance will refer to the deed or mortgage it is extinguishing. The year in which the deed or mortgage was executed is crucial. For example, if the reconveyance occurred in 1950 and the deed was executed in 1944, you can skip the indexes for 1944 through 1950 since the property was held by the same owner during this period.

You may run across sales conducted following legal proceedings known as "probate," which means the owner died. In this case you'll find the phrase "order of sale" or "decree of distribution." The documents contained in probate files frequently offer the house historian a fascinating detour and can provide useful clues for restoration. A will may indicate which family member inherited a lot, a house, or a piece of property. With luck, you may find descendants who might have old photographs. If the property was not willed, the administrator's records will show if the house was sold to pay expenses; often these records include correspondence or affidavits that afford insights into the personality and activities of the deceased. The file may also contain inventories of personal property drawn up when the estate was divided or sold. Lists of possessions and home furnishings can assist researchers in piecing together the life and circumstances of the property owner and his or her family. The probate office may reveal a list of the descendants of the deceased owner. You also may find a will listing the contents of the house.

A probate index is organized like a telephone directory. By looking up the name of the person who died, you can determine whether there was a probate proceeding on his or her estate. If such a proceeding took place, the index will list a court file number.

Look in past city directories for more information about the owners and their descendants. Directories often listed the occupations of residents, along with their business and home addresses. Public libraries and historical societies maintain these directories.

Federal census information is available for years prior to 1880. Your nearest center that houses federal archives may have questionnaires filled out by people who lived in your house.

You may find also obituaries of the house's inhabitants that will tell you more about their lifestyles and descendants. Visiting the cemetery where they are buried may reveal more relations. Checking the state death registry (available at the county seat) and probate records that named heirs, you may track down living descendants with photographs or other records of the house.

A probate index, while helpful in many regards, may not state categorically that a certain owner built your house. To be on the safe side you should continue working back until you reach the first deed that describes your property accurately but does not mention your house, or that conveys your property as part of a larger, buildingless tract. Presumably, then, your house was built between the sale of the unbuilt land and the sale of the built-on land. Even so, you should check the next deed back in the chain, to make sure no building is mentioned.

Also keep in mind that there may have been a succession of structures on the property, so make sure the building described matches yours, or that its construction date makes sense for your house.

Title searching is not simply a technical exercise. With luck, it will round out the history of the house's first inhabitants. Once you have immersed yourself in the history of your home, it takes on a new personality. Often the desire to remodel diminishes and the wish to restore increases; it becomes more and more difficult to make dramatic changes in a house that has meant so much to so many. Somehow its history strengthens your desire to improve it.

Maps

You can find out much useful information about your town's history by taking advantage of the Library of Congress's Geography and Map Division in Washington, D.C. The New York Public Library is similarly well equipped (Map Division, 42nd Street and Fifth Avenue, New York, New York 10018).

The Library of Congress boasts the world's largest cartographic collection. Among its 38,000 atlases are 1,500 atlases of U.S. counties and states dating from the 1870s. Many of them, particularly for larger communities, are profusely illustrated with prints and engravings of local points of interest, such as elegant houses. Some atlases contain small maps of towns within a county; main streets are labeled, and buildings, shown in silhouette, are marked with the owner's name.

Fire-insurance maps, also known as Sanborn maps (the Sanborn Map Company has been producing them since 1876), can be an information gold mine. The Map Division's 600,000 large-scale fire-insurance maps, dating back to 1884, cover more than 10,000 U.S. towns. Some cities are contained in one volume or on a single sheet, while New York City requires 80 volumes. (Local libraries also sometimes carry these maps.)

The maps were used, beginning in the mid-nineteenth century, to provide underwriters with detailed fire-risk information. They show a property's location, function, street address, dimensions, construction and roofing material, number of storeys, porches and other exterior features, and location of outbuildings and wells. The maps use a simple color code to indicate construction materials, and symbols to represent number of storeys, porches, and the like.

Panoramic maps, while they can aid in locating and dating buildings, often suffer from the creator's exaggeration. Popular during the late nineteenth and early twentieth centuries, panoramic maps were usually rendered from the perspective of someone looking down at the town from a hill top.

Chambers of commerce and other civic groups often commissioned these maps, and they appealed greatly to house-proud Victorians. Communities depicted were always thriving: smoke pours from factory smokestacks, people throng the streets, trains chug merrily on tracks. Often the artist would draw two trains running on the same track, one on each side of town, blissfully unaware of the impending collision. Sometimes a single-storey porch turned into a double decker, or bountiful hedges and gardens were added to a barren lot. In other cases, maps were drawn so painstakingly and accurately that windowpanes and porch-railing spindles can be counted. Whenever possible, panoramic-map information should be double-checked with other sources.

The Geography and Map Division of the Library of Congress is open to the public and all materials are available for viewing. Upon written request, the Library will provide a list of maps of your area and itemize charges for reproduction and postage.

Before contacting the Library, you should:

1. Check your local library's map holdings, particularly if you live in an area that panoramic mapmakers often portrayed.

2. Ask if your local library has these guides: *A List of Geographical Atlases in the Library of Congress,* U.S. Library of Congress Map Division (8 vol.); *United States Atlases: A List of National, State, County, and Regional Atlases in the Library of Congress,* U.S. Library of Congress Reference, compiled by Clara Egli LeGear (2 vol.).

When you are ready to contact the Map Division, make your request as concise as possible. State either the exact map you want if you have located it in the two guides listed above, or give the area of which you would like a map, including your complete address, lot number, or other information that may help identify the property (a list or sketched map of nearby landmarks and streets, a plan of the building, even a photo). Indicate which kind of map you would prefer.

TWO GOLDEN RESTORATION RULES

The confusion in nomenclature about preservation gives a lot of well-meaning old-house owners needless guilt feelings. If you feel that you are "restoring" your house, then you should use "restoration" procedures. But let's say you read an article about restoration written by a preservation professional who has a museum house in mind. You begin to feel inadequate and guilty because you aren't using paint microanalysis and the documentary research that the author advocates.

Most people fixing up an old house probably aren't working with a museum-grade structure. Most old-house owners are doing something between a sensitive rehabilitation and an interpretive restoration rather than an "historic restoration" that most professionals talk about. While some of the procedures involved in historic restoration can be helpful to the average old-house owner, they can give you the guilts unless you observe our two golden rules:

- **Thou shalt not destroy good old work**
- **To thine own style be true**

Basically this means that as you approach the task of fixing up your old house, be sensitive to the details in the house. Every time you destroy or "fix" something, you change the character of the building. If we think of a building as a collection of individual details, then changing the character of one changes the character of them all. It is better to repair rather than replace original elements and materials whenever possible. And when replacement is necessary, the replacement should resemble the original as closely as possible in terms of proportion, texture, and material. Beware the contractor who wants to rip out lots of old "unsalvageable" detail. Many materials a contractor might deem unusable are in fact recyclable with a little creative restoration work.

How do you determine if the old work is "good"? In general, it's good if 1) it is fabricated from good quality materials; 2) the workmanship is good; and 3) the design typifies a particular style or works in harmony with the rest of the structure. You may find newer additions to the house good, too. It is best to leave additions if they pass the test for good work and they don't interfere with the operation of the structure as you intend to use it.

The second golden rule—To thine own style be true—will save you from needless professional preservation (i.e., you don't need to "over-historicize"). Your house represents a specific architectural style (or a combination of styles). Be proud of it and don't try to make it into something it isn't. Learn everything you can about that style, then let your rehabilitation or restoration bring out the character and flavor of that style.

A few years back, many people made the mistake of trying to "antique" their old homes. Victorian houses were never meant to look "Colonial" with fake shutters, pedimented doorways, and the like. Similarly, trying to "Victorianize" a turn-of-the-century house can produce disastrous stylistic results.

Every house had an original design concept. This is true whether it was designed by a famous architect or constructed by an anonymous carpenter-builder. Your

work should enhance and clarify this original design concept. Or, at the very least, it should not detract from it.

To sum up the golden rules, your attitude about the rehabilitation or restoration will mean the difference between a "remuddled" job (see page 10) and a sensitive treatment. When you have sensitivity, everything else falls into place. (A quick look at the remuddling examples later in this chapter will give you a rough idea of your sensitivity quotient.) Sensitivity implies an attitude of respect toward the good work of others and an attitude of frustration with the obvious examples of ugly work on a building that detracts from the beauty of the streetscape.

RESTORATION *VS.* RENOVATION: DEFINITIONS ———————MEAN A LOT———————

Part of the confusion in working on your old house may involve using the right terms for the work you intend to do. Throughout this book, we'll use similar sounding words that deal with fixing up old houses. Here's how we define them:

Adaptive reuse refers to the recycling of an old building for use other than that for which it was originally constructed. This can involve a sensitive rehabilitation that retains much of a building's original character, or it can involve extensive remodeling.

Preservation means keeping an existing building in its current state by a careful program of maintenance and repair.

Reconstruction involves recreating an historic building that has been damaged or destroyed by erecting a new structure that resembles the original as closely as possible. A reconstruction may be built with new or recycled building materials.

Rehabilitation means making a structure sound and usable again, without attempting to restore any particular period appearance. Rehabilitation respects the original architectural elements of a building and retains them whenever possible. Sometimes also called "reconditioning."

Remodeling involves changing the appearance and style of a structure, inside or out, by removing or covering over original details and substituting new materials and forms. Also called "modernizing."

Renovation is similar to rehabilitation, except that in renovation work there is a greater proportion of new materials and elements introduced into the building.

Restoration is the repair or re-creation of the original architectural elements in a building so that it closely resembles the appearance it had at some previous point in time. As compared with rehabilitation, restoration implies a more active approach to reproducing architectural features that may have been removed.

Historic restoration requires that the re-creation duplicate the appearance at some previous point in time as closely as current scholarship allows. This often means that the additions from later periods must be removed. Historic restoration also usually couples a restoration of the structure with a restoration of the interior spaces—both decoration and furnishings. This rigorous approach is usually restricted to museum houses.

Interpretive restoration is less scholarly than historic restoration. It involves keeping all of the original architectural features intact, and reconstructing missing elements as faithfully as budget allows. Decoration and furnishing of interior spaces are appropriate to the style of the house without attempting to duplicate what was in the house originally. Restored houses that function as homes are usually of the interpretive variety.

Depending on the condition of your house, you will have to decide between restoration or renovation—it is a basic design decision. Remember, renovation means just putting the house back into sound mechanical condition without regard to any particular style. Restoration involves putting the house back into a state that resembles its condition in an earlier period. And it involves attention to detail, both interior and exterior. By preserving detail, you are not only conserving a cultural resource, but also insuring the long-term market value of the house. The restoration of damaged or neglected detail is well within the capabilities of most home craftspersons; the basic ingredients are sensitivity, time, and patience.

The third-floor addition to this row of houses has destroyed their distinguishing architectural feature.

A Colonial doorway on a late Victorian brownstone adds a discordant element to the building's facade.

TEN BASICS FOR SENSITIVE REHABILITATION

Old-house rehabilitation creates many more difficult choices than either a pure restoration or total preservation. That's because an infinite range of possibilities present themselves during rehabilitation. The only absolute requirement is that a rehabilitation leave a building functional.

Here are the ten basic principles from the Secretary of the Interior's Standards used to enforce the Federal Rehabilitation Incentive Tax Program. (They are followed by over 100 specific dos and don'ts.) Though the wording is "legalese," the principles offer sound advice.

1. Every reasonable effort shall be made to provide a compatible use for a property which requires minimal alteration of the building, structure, or site and its environment, or to use a property for its originally intended purpose. In other words, it's always best to use an old building for its originally intended purpose.

2. The distinguishing original qualities or character of a building, structure, or site and its environ- ment shall not be destroyed. The removal or alteration of any historic material or distinctive architectural features should be avoided when possible. This echoes the first of our golden rules—don't destroy good old work. And if you have to add to an old building, do it in a way that doesn't destroy its existing distinctive characteristics.

3. All buildings, structures, and sites shall be recognized as products to their own time. Alterations that have no historical basis and which seek to create an earlier appearance shall be discouraged. Need we say more?

4. Changes which may have taken place in the course of time are evidence of the history and development of a building, structure, or site and its environment. These changes may have acquired significance in their own right, and this significance shall be recognized and respected. Many old houses have additions that you may not find aesthetically pleasing. Yet even those additions that can't be called a triumph of architectural design may have a claim to being a cultural artifact. It may embody the aspirations and workmanship of past generations.

5. Distinctive stylistic features or examples of

skilled craftsmanship which characterize a building, structure, or site shall be treated with sensitivity.

6. **Deteriorated architectural features shall be repaired rather than replaced, whenever possible. In the event replacement is necessary, the new material should match the material being replaced in composition, design, color, texture, and other visual qualities. Repair or replacement of missing architectural features should be based on accurate** duplications of features, substantiated by historic, physical, or pictorial evidence rather than on conjectural designs or the availability of different architectural elements from other buildings or structures. If you must make repairs with new materials, be sure they match as closely as possible the original features.

7. **The surface cleaning of structures shall be undertaken with the gentlest means possible. Sandblasting and other cleaning methods that will**

A rambling farmhouse illustrates the fourth principle of sensitive rehabilitation. Much of the architectural merit is concentrated in the Greek Revival wing on the left. The gabled wing on the right has its own rustic charm. The middle section, however, cannot be called a triumph of architectural design. Nevertheless, it does have a role as a cultural artifact. Because it embodies the aspirations and workmanship of past generations, it merits thoughtful treatment. On a purely practical level, it provides useful living space.

The exterior wood—especially on the porch—is in bad repair. Removing the porch and the bad woodwork would rob the house of much of its visual interest, to say nothing of its historic appearance. This is a repair job that requires sensitivity to the characteristic features of the building's design.

Rather than scrap these rotting wood balusters, replace the square elements at the base where most of the rot is concentrated. To replace the missing turned work on the baluster at left, build it up with epoxy putty.

damage the historic building materials shall not be undertaken.

This brick wall was cleaned by sandblasting. While blasting, the contractor left a piece of electrical conduit on the wall, which was removed later. You can see where the bricks were protected by the conduit; they still have their smooth, hard surface and small, neat, concave mortar joints. The blasted bricks are badly pitted (having lost about 1/8 inch of their surface), and the mortar joints (after a sloppy repointing job) are about twice the width of the original joints.

8. Every reasonable effort shall be made to protect and preserve archeological resources affected by, or adjacent to, any project. The ground around old buildings is often the resting place for significant historical artifacts. If major excavation is conducted without professional advice, priceless artifacts may be lost.

9. Contemporary design for alterations and additions to existing properties shall not be discouraged when such alterations and additions do not destroy significant historical, architectural, or cultural material, and such design is compatible with the size, scale, color, material, and character of the property, neighborhood, or environment. New additions need not mimic the old style, but new construction can reflect the design philosophy of its time. New construction should blend harmoniously with the older section.

10. Whenever possible, new additions or alterations to structures shall be done in such a manner that if such additions or alterations were to be removed in the future, the essential form and integrity of the structure would be unimpaired. Ideally, any work that we do on old buildings should be reversible. That is, at some point it should be possible to remove our work and leave the original building intact.

——————— REMUDDLING ———————

In the October 1981 issue of the *Old-House Journal* we introduced an opinion page that invited readers to share with us their best "found" examples of house reha-

bilitation or renovation gone awry. In "improving" the house, it was "remuddled." Since then we've featured a "Remuddling of the Month" in every issue, showing structures that were robbed of their original charm and character by insensitive renovation.

Homeowners want to "do the right thing" to their houses but often are paralyzed by the welter of conflicting information hurled at them: "Don't tell me what the problems are," the well-intentioned homeowner cries. "Tell me what I should *do!*" But every house—and every homeowner—is different. There are no definitive answers when it comes to sensitive rehabilitation and restoration, but we believe that negative examples can be a powerful teaching tool. By showing mistakes that already have been made, we hope to encourage better treatment of buildings that haven't yet been hopelessly remuddled.

Some of the remuddlings sent in by our readers elicit a painful groan, while others give us a giggle for the absurdity of the "creative" addition. The lack of sensitivity for visual continuity can be astonishing. Yet what to some is an obvious remuddling is to others an acceptable solution to adorning a neglected old house. As we've pointed out, inappropriate architectural embellishment of an old house, as with "Colonial" details on a Victorian house, constitutes remuddling. But sometimes embellishment can work. For example, in one issue we featured a "Home Made Gingerbread" house. At least one reader thought the gingerbread house was no different from the "Colonial" supermarket or the "Victorian" hamburger stand. We disagreed. The Colonial supermarket stands as an example of the sort of disregard for architectural continuity and historical detail that constitutes remuddling. Our basic belief is that, when working on old houses, you should not destroy the good work of past generations. That rule was observed with our gingerbread house: No woodwork was destroyed; no trim discarded. Rather, this was a case of adding appropriate and tasteful architectural ornament to an existing house. However, in this case what was "right" was less clear cut.

The house shown was a "plain" house—an unornamented, functional box with minimal architectural detail. These kinds of houses are common in rural areas where they were built as farmhouses. They present a more complex problem than historically significant houses (designed by a famous architect or lived in by someone famous, for example) or architecturally distinctive houses (those with a clear architectural style and/or detailing that gives them character). We felt that the plain house could be architecturally enhanced. Because architectural indifference or a lack of money prevented the original owner from building a more distinctive house, does that mean that every subsequent owner should feel duty-bound to preserve the plainness?

As long as the work is done in good taste and in keeping with the spirit and style of the house, we advocate this type of interpretive restoration. In the mid-nineteenth century, many plain farmhouses were enriched with vergeboards, brackets, gable ornaments, and porch

For some, the addition of gingerbread detail to this originally plain, unornamented structure constitutes egregious "remuddling." For others, the ornamentation enhances the building's architectural features.

scrollwork. Today's preservationists would argue that this embellishment should be preserved as part of the architectural history of the house. Should we argue that plain farmhouses can no longer be ornamented because this is the twentieth century rather than the nineteenth?

Other remuddlings challenge our sensitivity to style, materials, visual appeal, and functional appropriateness. Two once-identical houses in Fort Scott, Kansas, got new porches. On each the porch was remodeled—updated around 1910. Do we call any modification "remuddling," or only those changes that alter functions or degrade what we perceive as quality?

In this example, the classically inspired porch addition makes a big statement. But the workmanship is good, the details (dentils, pediment) are taken from the existing

building; the grand scale of the original has not been compromised.

In the other Kansas house, the worst sin is that the porch is no longer the porch. Instead of being a buffer between public and private spaces, an entry to the house, it's as solid and closed as can be. (It is now the casket showroom of this funeral parlor.)

The classical addition stems from the same architectural roots as the Italianate house. But the American Prairie references in the brick addition have no basis on the original structure. Maybe that, too, contributes to its jarring presence.

Remuddling takes many forms, and through it we've tapped into a vast reservoir of Americana. We've accumulated thousands of photos showing amazing, imagi-

The porch is marked as a later addition by its materials— concrete blocks and concrete columns.

The addition is out of character in terms of proportion as well as in architectural precedent.

This house illustrates the Callous Conversion. Feeling no cultural responsibility or emotional attachment to the building, the owner chose the cheapest—at least in the short run—repair.

native ways to mutilate old buildings. Recognizing that our remuddling archive is of priceless value to scholars, we engaged a team of cultural demographers, social histographers, and statistical phychographers to analyze, codify, and interpret our collection. Here are a few of the categories they came up with: Modernist Mania; Asinine Additions; Mega-Buck Monopoly; Creative Chaos; Technological Trashing; Callous Conversions. You can test your sensitivity quotient by matching our experts' categories to the remuddlings shown here, or you can come up with your own nomenclature.

HOUSE STYLES

American house styles developed as a result of available building materials and the builder's cultural (and architectural) heritage. In addition to the commonly known features distinguishing a house as, say, Georgian rather than Federal, or Greek Revival from Gothic Revival, examples of American vernacular architecture abound that distinguish one region from another, one cultural heritage from another. We can't pretend to cover all American house styles in one short section of a chapter, but we

This old house suffers from Technological Trashing. When solar power was in vogue, old houses everywhere were trashed with solar panels and trombe walls. Now it's satellite dishes.

The opposite of a Callous Conversion: The building becomes the vehicle for the owner's bold personal statement, resulting in Creative Chaos.

According to Webster's, asinine means ''marked by an inexcusable failure to exercise intelligence or sound judgment.'' The square addition to the front of this house, together with the stairs to the second floor, need no further explanation.

do illustrate and describe some of the most common examples of old houses found today. Your old house, like many old houses, probably possesses features or detailing of more than one architectural style. The important thing is to develop your architecture vocabulary so you can identify and describe the detailing on your house to an impatient contractor as you plan your rehabilitation.

Colonial Houses

For simplicity's sake, we'll define Colonial architecture as those typical American buildings constructed before about 1780. (Colonial characteristics, however, persisted well into the nineteenth century in many areas and in many building types.) Though the Swedes, Germans, Dutch, French, and Spanish all left their marks in Colonial American architecture, the buildings we most likely label "Colonial" or "Early American" are those whose antecedents are in English architectural traditions. Usually the houses of Massachusetts and Virginia first come to mind.

Colonial houses encompass a number of different styles, from the saltbox and the Cape Cod Cottage to the copies of Medieval and Tudor cottages found in Virginia. Different approaches to building, and quite different social and environmental circumstances in the New World, led to distinctive building styles in the Massachusetts Bay and Virginia colonies. Despite using the same materials and having similar architectural and structural understanding, the northern and southern colonies wound up with strikingly different buildings.

New England farmers tended to live in town, away from their fields, in the safety and community of the village. Within the villages, the houses were clustered on small lots; two-and-one-half- and three-storey houses were common. Cape Cod houses, however, which became a type unto themselves, were ordinarily found in relatively isolated settings, though they do appear in village lots.

In Virginia, where farms were larger, farmers often lived in the midst of their fields, far apart from each other but generally near rivers or other waterways that linked them to the commerce and culture of other places.

In general, New Englanders built wood houses, whereas Virginians preferred brick. New Englanders didn't have the same large supply of good lime that Virginians did, and a wood house was more comfortable in the damp climate. Wood was abundant, easy to work with, and relatively easy to make watertight. The new-comers also had experience in building "half-timbered" dwellings: frames of hewn timber filled in with brick and plaster "nogging." Covered in clapboard (riven boards) or weatherboarding (sawn boards) on the outside, buildings of this sort made cozy, watertight homes. Stone and brick were used for the grander houses, especially as lime for mortar became available, as it had been from the beginning in Rhode Island.

In the Virginia Tidewater, the makings for brick and mortar were readily found, so brick became the material of choice for more substantial dwellings; all-wood build-

This typical Colonial Massachusetts house built about 1715 is two-and-a-half storeys high, and has a five-bay front and a center hall plan. Though most New England Colonials were built of wood, they sometimes had brick end walls, usually with interior end chimneys. The gable roof is accented with pedimented dormers and a modillion cornice. The windows are 12/12 double-hung sash and, on the side of the house, have a segmental arch lintel. Note also the door treatment: segmental pediment on consoles with pilasters.

The Virginia Colonial house was more often than not built with brick. This one, built some time during the mid-eighteenth century, is one-and-a-half storeys high on a raised basement. Like the New England example, it has a five-bay front with a center hall plan. Like the Massachusetts house it has tall interior end chimneys but the roof is jerkin-head gable. The pedimented dormers are taller and narrower with 6/6 light double-hung sash while its Massachusetts counterpart has 8/8 double-hung sash in the dormers. The windows on the first storey are 9/9 double-hung sash with a flat or jack arch. While this example is all brick, other Virginia Colonial houses had brick end walls with clapboard siding on the front and rear.

ings were common too. Sometimes, in both New England and the South, brick-end houses (usually with chimneys at each end) had wooden fronts and backs.

Colonial Virginia houses are often noted for their brickwork. Flemish bond, an elaborate pattern in which headers are alternated with stretchers, became standard for at least the main facades of better residences. English and common bond, in which rows of headers alternate with rows of stretchers, were used for side and rear facades and for utilitarian buildings. The latter bonding patterns require far fewer bricks to form a strong wall. Scholars now agree that, despite local legends to the contrary, virtually all of the bricks were made at or near the building site—not shipped as ballast across the ocean from England. In German-settled areas, such as Pennsylvania and western portions of Virginia, log construction was used.

New England houses tended to be compact, designed to enclose a maximum amount of space in an energy-efficient way. They typically had huge central chimneys that absorbed heat from daytime fires and radiated it back into the house at night. Their massing was blocky and low-slung compared to Southern examples, which were more likely to feature high basements (with above-ground windows), or to be built on pilings. The difference in building height may also be attributed to higher ceilings inside Virginia houses, high-ceilinged rooms being cooler in summer. In Virginia, single-pile (one-room deep) and double-pile houses built around central halls allowed good cross-ventilation.

In both Virginia and Massachusetts gable roofs were most common, often with the ridge running parallel to the front of the building, sometimes facing front. Ordinarily, the steeper the gable, the earlier the house; the pitch of the roof tended to become less pronounced as the eighteenth century progressed. Often, an extension of the main roofline to cover a one-storey addition at the rear of the house would accentuate the verticality of the roof. In Massachusetts, this form is the saltbox house; in Virginia, the same configuration is called a catslide. The jerkin-head roof, or hipped gable end, is unique to Virginia. The jerkin is a peculiar variation on the gable, sloping backward toward the main roof. Hip roofs, sloped on all four sides, were widespread in both areas. Gambrels, which have two different slopes on each side of the center ridge, may have developed from the French mansard; they are somewhat more common in New England than in Virginia.

Massachusetts houses favored central chimneys while in Virginia they were more likely placed at either end of the house, dissipating unnecessary heat and allowing for a center-hall plan. The chimneys might be interior or exterior, or even partly inside and partly outside. Exterior chimneys are found almost exclusively in Virginia—and they are frequently tall, large, decorative features. In Massachusetts, chimneys placed near the ends tended to stay well within the walls.

The entrances and windows of Massachusetts houses tended to be more elaborate: pediments above doors, pilasters on either side. Virginia concentrated generally on more subtle decorative forms worked into the brick bonding patterns.

In Massachusetts the favored floor plan was the "hall-and-parlor." The first floor was divided into two rooms, frequently of unequal size, usually with matching sleeping chambers on the floors above. This plan took full advantage of the big central chimney, which served as many as four fireplaces. The hall was actually an all-purpose work and living room, somewhat like the "great room" so beloved of today's country-style home designers. The small parlor served as a combination master bed room/guest room/formal reception room. A tiny interior "porch" at the front entrance sometimes set off the stairs from the two main rooms. Often, a one-storey lean-to addition across the back of the house continued the steep slope of the main room, forming the well-known saltbox. The lean-to provided space for a separate kitchen and, under the slope of the roof, perhaps for a couple of small bedrooms.

In Virginia, symmetrical center-hall plans, with one room on either side of a central corridor running from front to rear, provided effective ventilation. For similar reasons, the kitchen in southern houses was frequently in the basement or in a separate building altogether.

Often, it is possible to "see" the floor plan of a building from the outside. For instance, the presence of end chimneys and a carefully centered entrance door often implies a center-hall plan. A house with an off-center entrance and a chimney located near the middle is likely to have a hall-and-floor plan.

Special features of Massachusetts houses included jetties, or second-floor overhangs. These are never found on more than three sides of a house, so they were probably a result of structural or aesthetic considerations rather than a defense against attack, as has sometimes been suggested. Ornamental pendants sometimes hung from the corners of the jetty.

The modern exterior porch was uncommon in both New England and Virginia. Most entry doors faced the elements unsheltered, except perhaps for an overhanging hood above the entrance door and small stoop to ease the transition from ground to entrance level.

Georgian and Federal Styles

Colonial-era architecture was much indebted to vernacular European forms. With the Georgian and, subsequently, the Federal styles, Americans adopted a more formal approach to architecture. Of course, Colonial building features continued to be used in Georgian buildings; typically, Georgian features were added to buildings that were basically Colonial. While the builder's vocabulary changed slowly, change it did. Certain concepts are more typical of one period than another, and these are the ones we'll emphasize.

The Georgian style is named for the reigns of the three Georges of England (1714–1811). The style is best illustrated in buildings built from about 1740 until the Ameri-

can Revolution, when building in the Colonies came virtually to a stop. After the war, Americans were eager to create an architecture of their own. Although they turned to British sources for inspiration—particularly to the Scottish architects Robert and James Adam—their ideas began to assume a distinctly American shape in the Federal style, popular from about 1790 to 1820.

With no professionally trained architects until the nineteenth century, Americans relied heavily on architectural pattern books compiled in England. In both countries, revivals of the styles of Italian Renaissance architects, particularly Andrea Palladio, stirred enormous interest among well-educated and affluent Americans. Other British volumes were aimed at builders and carpenters. Not until 1806, when Asher Benjamin published *The American Builder's Companion: or A New System of Architecture Particularly Adapted to the Present Style of Building in the United States,* did a native volume become available. Even this book derived from British sources.

Although Colonial, Georgian, and Federal building styles were British imports, they had been modified for American use. Even designs for elaborate American buildings were simplified for the less affluent and builders less skilled than their British counterparts.

With the reliance on pattern books, regional variations in style began to fade in the Georgian-Federal period, though they certainly didn't disappear. Unlike functional Colonial buildings, Georgian and Federal architecture exhibit a rigid design symmetry, emphasizing form over function. In both styles main entrances are centered and window openings and other elements are evenly spaced on the facade.

Symmetry aside, however, the differences between the two styles are striking. The Georgian style is sometimes described as "masculine," meaning that the houses are likely to be blocky, robust, and assertive in design. The main entrance is frequently contained within a projecting central section (pavilion) that reaches up through the full height of the house, generally two-and-a-half or three-

and-a-half storeys above a raised basement. The grandest houses have two-storey entrance porticoes, with large pediments supported by columns.

The ultimate expression of the Georgian style is the freestanding, five-part "Palladian" mansion: a sturdy main block flanked by hyphens (an appropriate term for these low, connecting units), leading to smaller flanking wings (flankers or pavilions). The hyphens may be fully enclosed or merely covered walkways. They may extend straight out on axis or curve, with the pavilions at right angles to the mansion, as at Mount Vernon.

The Federal house, if not exactly "feminine," is more formal and restrained in both outline and detail. The style was largely a reaction to the boldness of its Georgian predecessor. Federal lines are simpler, surfaces smoother, decoration more attenuated. Where the Georgian might have a bit of swagger, the Federal leans toward refined understatement, frequently expressing an even more sophisticated geometry. Federal houses often include curving or multisided bays, elliptical rooms, semicircular or octagonal bays or porticoes, domed and arched ceilings. They are more likely than the Georgian to be three full storeys high—or conversely, much more likely to have only a large single storey above a raised basement. The five-part form was also used for Federal mansions, even for one-storey buildings.

Throughout the late eighteenth and early nineteenth centuries there was a trend toward more substantial masonry buildings and more carefully finished surfaces. Brick was favored in both periods. Georgian houses were more likely (especially in the mid Atlantic states) to be built of stone than Federal houses. In either period, fine ashlar stonework (laid with evenly cut blocks rather than irregular "rubble" chunks) is rarely found except on great public buildings. In frame construction (often used in New England Georgian houses), the wood cladding might imitate ashlar stonework, sometimes with simulated quoins (corner blocks). Similarly, the use of stucco on exterior walls, often scored to imitate ashlar stonework, is common in the Federal period, although it is occasionally found on earlier houses. Stucco was used with brick decorative work at Mount Pleasant (1761–1762), a great Georgian mansion in Philadelphia. Whereas mortar joints in the Georgian house were thick and often decoratively tooled, those of the Federal period were thin, sometimes almost to the point of being invisible.

The steeply sloped Colonial roofline gradually flattened during the Georgian and Federal years. Although gable roofs (with a steeply pitched angle forming a triangle) remained most common, lower slopes were much more fashionable, and hip or deck-on-hip roofs became *de rigeur* on the finest houses. (There were even some leaky attempts at truly flat roofs, but these experiments would not prove successful until the mid-nineteenth century.) Metal as a roofing material began to come into its own during these years, and some very fine buildings were given copper roofs.

Entryways starred in both Georgian and Federal years, but the effect was very different in the two periods. Georgian doorways were showy, gorgeously trimmed, with lots of carved and moulded wood. They might be topped with formal pediments flanked by pilasters and supported by elaborate consoles, or brackets. Semicircular fanlights with thick, straight, radiating muntins above the doors provided both decoration and natural illumination. Federal doorways, less given to self-advertisement, displayed far less wood; columns and pilasters were slim and light. They often had semicircular fanlights, but elliptical fans with delicate tracery in wood or lead are a distinctive Federal feature; muntins were thin, flat, and delicate, even when they were ornamental. Sidelights and, where there are no curved fanlights, transoms are also frequently seen in Federal buildings. In both periods, six- or eight-panel, single- or double-leaf doors were common, but the raised panels of the Georgian period gave way to a flatter look in the Federal.

The Palladian window, a three-part construction with a tall arched center section and shorter, narrower, rectangular sidelights, became almost commonplace among better American homes of the Georgian and Federal periods. Jib windows, which doubled as doors that opened from the floor up to head height, were a convenience of the Georgian dwelling. Federal houses often featured double- or triple-sash, floor-length windows. Windows and windowpanes are larger in Federal houses than in Georgian ones, but the overall ratio of window to wall actually decreases in the later Federal. A typical Georgian window may be twelve-over-twelve panes, separated by thick muntins and set within a thick frame. Both frame and muntins grew thinner as the eighteenth century drew to a close, however, and six-over-six windows were common at the beginning of the new century. Pilaster trim, with circular mouldings in corner blocks, is first found as exterior trim on Federal windows and doors. Taken indoors, it became the most common interior trim during the nineteenth century.

As we have seen, Georgian ornament is large in scale, elaborate in execution. That of the Federal period is smaller and infinitely quieter. Under the influence of Robert Adam, who developed a refined interpretation of decorative motifs from classical antiquity, the noisy splendor of Georgian woodworking was gradually muted. Where heavy masonry string courses wrapped around blunt Georgian facades, the plain surfaces of Federal buildings were likely to be broken only by shallow recessed or applied panels.

The rather sedate evolution from the Colonial and Georgian to the Federal style marked the end of a long continuum in architectural development. The nineteenth century would shortly field a lively architectural battle, as architects revived, one after another, a rich panoply of styles from other times and other places.

Greek Revival

The first of America's great Romantic revivals wore classical garb. Most of the new "Greek" buildings were not intended to be replicas of ancient structures. This new architecture was perceived less as a revival than as an innovation—a modern, "National Style," as it was called during its heyday between 1830 and 1860. Based on patterns taken from books by Minard Lafever, Asher Benjamin, and others, and modeled after structures designed by American architects such as Benjamin Henry Latrobe, Ithiel Town, Andrew Jackson Davis, Robert Mills, William Strickland, Isaiah Rogers, and Thomas U. Walter, Grecian-inspired buildings for public and private use sprang up in every corner of the land.

Decorative elements were taken from any of dozens of builder's pattern books. Pieces could be copied by any skilled carpenter or simply chosen from a catalog. A mix-and-match attitude developed, which explains the numerous, free-wheeling variations of the supposedly rigid Greek Revival format. In no section of the country was the Greek style more enthusiastically adopted than in the newly developing states of Indiana, Illinois, Ohio, Michigan, Wisconsin, and Minnesota—the Old Northwest Territory.

The basic model for Greek Revival architecture was the

ancient Greek temple, in which a series of columns supported a horizontal superstructure, called an entablature, or a triangular pediment. In the United States, the style was based—usually rather loosely, only sometimes rigidly—on the Greek "orders," sets of building elements determined mainly by the type of column used—Doric, Ionic, or Corinthian. Doric columns feature a fluted shaft and capital shaped like an inverted double scroll, or volute, while Corinthian columns are noted for their elaborately carved capitals. The Tuscan, a simplified Roman version of the Doric order (with no fluting on the column) was part of the American repertoire as well. The problem of correct proportions was often passed over lightly in American building practice. The gabled house with its massive portico was the *sine qua non* of American Greek Revival, but the most common examples looked more like traditional colonial boxes with a few Greek details pasted on.

When the columns and pediment were set out from the body of the building, they formed a covered walk or porch called a portico. The innovation of the period was turning the gable end to face the street. This gives a pediment effect which could then be extended forward to rest on a classical colonnade. More modest adaptations still had the gable face the street but eliminated the colonnade in favor of a small, two-columned entry porch, or a flat

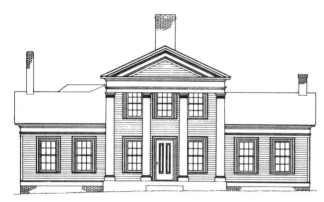

This Greek Revival house was built about 1834 in New Carlisle, Indiana. It has a three-part facade with a two-storey central pavilion and portico flanked by one-storey wings.

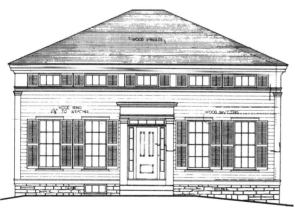

A mid-nineteenth-century house in Plainfield, Illinois, is a simple Greek design with one-and-a-half storeys, pilasters, and a doorway with a frontispiece.

front with no porch at all. A triangular pediment could be simulated at minimal cost with the judicious application of strongly moulded cornice trim; pilasters could represent the more costly columns. Fortunately for Americans of lesser means, the columns could vary almost infinitely in size, shape, number, placement, and decoration and still look Greek. They could be round or square; freestanding or engaged (attached to the building); Tuscan, Doric, Ionic, or Corinthian; fluted, reeded, or plain; with or without bases; squat and heavy or tall and tapered. In the Greek tradition there is always an even number of them (generally four or six), but Americans felt free to use five when it suited their purposes. The columns could be placed in front of the building only (prostyle) or all around it (peristyle). They could be beefed up with antae, square columns also called piers or pilasters, at the side of the building, or with engaged pilasters almost anywhere.

Another innovation, especially in smaller homes, was the off-side doorway. This departure from classical symmetry allowed a narrow three-bay house to have an adequate parlor; the traditional center hall created rooms on either side that were too small to be usable. Builders of the period were also quick to note that the three-bay, gable-to-street house used less street frontage, and suited narrow city lots.

Even the most conservative and simple Greek Revival homes were distinguished by their front doors, as in the Georgian and Federal eras. Solid-wood mouldings in a rectilinear arrangement, suggesting the fundamental column-and-architrave (post-and-beam) construct of Greek architecture, replaced the delicate arched transoms and leaded sidelights of Federal homes. Front doors were either single or paired, and featured anywhere from one to eight panels, with four the most common. In a popular variation, the entry door was set back several feet from the front wall of the house, with paired, freestanding columns placed in the plane of the front wall.

The six-over-six double-hung window of the Federal era remained popular. In some cases, a six-over-nine configuration was used on the lower storey to go with higher ceilings in the parlors. Later, improvements in glass-making technology made larger panes of glass possible, as in the two-over-two, double-hung windows popular in late Greek Revival and Italianate houses.

While the three-part Palladian window passed out of fashion, the elliptical gable window of the previous period remained popular: Its elongated shape fit neatly into shallow Greek pediments, as did the new rectangular gable window with its narrow horizontal and vertical muntins.

The most common cladding for Greek Revival houses was narrow clapboard, but flush boards were also used on the front. These flat, wide boards could be gessoed and scored to resemble blocks of marble.

Brick was another standard material, and sometimes it too would be stuccoed and scored to look like stone. Communities with access to marble or stone quarries often used the real thing.

Elaborate cornices were among the most decorative elements of the Greek Revival house. Heavy moulding framed the entire pediment; in vernacular versions, it was left incomplete along the bottom. One or two wide boards beneath the cornice represented the architrave and frieze of a Greek temple. The lower band, the architrave, was often divided into three horizontal rows; the upper band, or frieze, was left plain or divided into triglyphs and metopes, in traditional Doric manner. The wide frieze board was often pierced by those narrow, horizontal, "ear to the ground" windows. This wide board also defined the triangular gable, and in many cases featured a row of small dentils.

Hipped or flat roofs were frequently hidden from street view by low, paneled parapets ornamented by Greek motifs. Post-1850 versions of the Greek Revival have large, curvilinear brackets under overhanging cornices, influenced by the Italian Villa style.

On balance, it hardly seems surprising that so versatile a style, and one that satisfied the emotional needs of so many people, should have lasted for so long. Indeed, it never has completely disappeared from the American scene. Probably the most enduring legacy of Greek Revival is the gable-front house, the standard form of the nineteenth-century American farmhouse; it was also a predominant form for detached city houses in the Midwest and the Northeast until well into the twentieth century.

Still, it's the nature of styles to come and go, and Greek Revival had heavy competition from the Gothic style even before the Civil War. After the war, picturesque and revival styles of other times and places finally loosened Greek Revival's grip on the American imagination.

Gothic Revival

Gothic Revival sprang primarily from two philosophical trends. The first was the interest in wilder, more naturalistic and picturesque landscapes, which cried out for a romantic building style. The second was the search for an architectural form for churches that was more "Christian" than the classical temple. The architecture of medieval England seemed to satisfy both needs.

In the 1830s, English architect A. W. Pugin, considered the father of the Gothic Revival movement, attempted to define its principles in his books. John Ruskin, the prominent British art historian and social critic, added force to the argument for Gothic architecture by equating architectural "goodness"—embodied in the vertical, asymmetrical, picturesque, naturalistic designs of Gothic church architecture—with morality.

Although leading American architects like Alexander Jackson Davis, Richard Upjohn, Andrew Jackson Downing, and John Notman strove for "correct," fully integrated Gothic designs in their high-style buildings, in less sophisticated hands Gothic Revival became a style of decorative details, more often than not applied to plain boxes. Most homebuilders neither knew nor cared about the style's philosophical underpinnings. Just as they had done with Greek Revival forms, they used what they liked and ignored the rest.

The fact that the buildings they copied were most frequently constructed of masonry, usually stone, perturbed American builders not a whit. They were perfectly content to use good old abundant American wood for simple cottages and to leave the stone and brick for grander structures. Although horizontal siding was common, board-and-batten construction (closely spaced sheets of wood with thinner strips of wood nailed over the gap between the underlying sheets of wood) achieved more of the desired vertical effect while still honestly expressing the humble building materials and construction techniques used. And most homebuilders had no need in their light, balloon-framed wooden houses for flying buttresses, vaulted arches, and the other structural inventions

The Gothic Revival cottage is picturesque and romantic, informal and asymmetrical. Quintessentially domestic, it was widely available in pattern books. This cottage has the classic steep gable with pendant and finial and a decorative Gothic bargeboard (or vergeboard).

that enabled thirteenth-century stonemasons to build their soaring churches, but they liked the simpler forms of Gothic ornament very much indeed.

Two main types of Gothic house emerged: The pointed or rural Gothic features very steep gables, ornate bargeboards, and abundant use of the pointed, or lancet, arch; battlements, parapets, and square towers dominate the castellated, or castle-like, Gothic. The pointed Gothic form, whether cottage or mansion, was found most often in rural settings, since it did not lend itself to closely set urban sites. The castellated Gothic was somewhat better suited for city living but far from commonplace.

The most popular Gothic feature in houses was a very steeply pitched gable (or gables), often trimmed with a wooden scrollwork bargeboard, or vergeboard, pierced with such Gothic motifs as trefoils, quatrefoils, or rows of little pointed arches. Diamond-paned casement windows were frequently used. Small, fancifully trimmed one-storey entrance porches, large, striking chimney tops, clustered columns with chamfered edges, Tudor arches, finials, and pendants were all icing on the cake. Elaborate cast-iron ornament was a hallmark of high-style Gothic.

In rural areas, heavy, carved stone bargeboards were replicated by wooden scrollwork produced by a new machine, the scroll saw, in the thoroughly American treatment now called Carpenter Gothic. This distinctive American style featured vertical board-and-batten siding and fancy scroll-sawn bargeboards. In fact, the style was heavily influenced by the romantic landscapes turned out by painters of the Hudson River School, and Downing, Davis, and other proponents first designed cottages with such Hudson River settings in mind.

The Gothic Revival lingered until nearly the turn of the century. But despite its extraordinary longevity in various forms, from cottages to churches to skyscrapers like the Woolworth Building in Manhattan (1910–1913), Gothic Revival eventually did lose steam. It was eclipsed as the dominant force in American architecture by the Italianate style, which blossomed just before the Civil War.

Italianate

This label refers to any house or commercial building that combines Italian-style shapes and details, although often in an exaggerated fashion. Renaissance Revival details were applied to picturesque villa shapes, for example. Italianate houses were first built after villa styles were already established, and continued to be popular until the "High Victorian," late-nineteenth-century era.

The Italianate in America was actually based on the Italian style in England. The English Italian style was only the latest version of a style popular in England since Shakespeare's time, that of classical Rome. It was revived in the early nineteenth century not in its pure form but as it was translated by the Italian Renaissance. And it increased in popularity partly as a result of the growing popularity of the Romantic movement in literature and art. Italian-style houses as we think of them were built in England in the 1830s and 1840s, and these are the houses that most influenced American architecture. As with Gothic Revival, A. J. Downing, a proponent of the picturesque in landscaping and architecture, included several Italian-style villa designs in his book *The Architecture of Country Houses.*

Italian-style houses were made of all available materials, from brownstone to wood. But all the materials were used in such a way as to simulate the stone of the Italian villa and palace models. One common method was to stucco over brick, often on a wooden frame, although plain brick was not uncommon.

Renaissance-revival commercial buildings of the 1850s, however, were often decorated with a relatively new material: cast iron. The country villas were usually brick with wooden floors and roofs, although many illustrations—a "Suburban Villa" in *Godey's Ladies Book,* for example—

This Italianate house with campanile demonstrates that the porch is often the most expressive element, even on a grand house. Its piazza offers paired, turned colonnettes, a fan-motif balustrade, turned newels, and ball finials. Also note the porte cochere *to the right.*

The mansard roof distinguishes the Second Empire style. Remove the roof, and there is a good Italian house with many classic details, including a Palladian window.

show sheet metal roofs. Slate roofs were also used on Italianate houses.

Precision in defining stylistic details of any Italianate house built in America during the nineteenth century is almost impossible. Because it was such a popular style, and because it remained popular for such a long time, the Italian style manifests itself in many variations. The features of the villa and the "palazzo," or palace, are often so jumbled that the only way to recognize an Italianate house is through recognition of the details.

Second Empire/Mansard Style

Second Empire—also called Mansard for its distinctive, double-pitched mansard roofline—shouts "Victorian!" to the twentieth-century house-watcher. A house belongs to this style if it has the French-inspired mansard roof. A Second Empire house may have Italianate eave brackets or an Eastlake porch; it may be made of stone or swathed in shingles. Its windows may have moulded hoods or scrolled sides, or they may be straight and unadorned. No matter whether the house is I-shaped, four towering storeys high, or a single storey plus an attic: If the roof is a mansard, the house will be called Second Empire.

About the same time the Italianate style was popular—roughly 1855 through 1885—this related style swept across the Atlantic. Named for the seventeenth-century architect Francois Mansart, the mansard roof consists of a very steep lower slope and a gently angled, almost flat top portion. The mansard was a practical way to inject a full storey of space into the attic level, since the steep slope doesn't create leftover bits of unusable floor area. It was a relatively cheap and easy means of enlarging and modernizing old buildings, especially in cities where lot size was limited. It also helped make these buildings look a little less bulky or a little less ready to fall on their faces onto the street. Best of all, it was extremely chic.

While a boxy, straight-line roof was the most common, the trendiest thing in Second Empire was the curve—bulging outward (convex), scooping inward (concave),

or looping about in a giant S (ogee-shaped). Large houses with towers and wings often combined several different roof shapes; only porches were exempt (usually) from the mansard craze.

Slate was the preferred roofing material. Tin and wood were also popular, but not just any shingle was used: Fashion dictated that the shingles had to be multi-colored, fancifully shaped, and laid in intricate patterns. Large dormer windows almost always pierced the roofs to light the extra storey. Ornate cast-iron cresting marched along the roof ridge or around a central deck, and towers were likely to be topped by cast-iron pinnacles or finials. Tall, elaborate brick chimneys completed the impressive Second Empire roofline.

High-style Second Empire houses were usually large masonry piles, classically decorated with columns and pilasters, ornamental stone quoins at every corner, and projecting towers, bays, and pavilions. But such pure examples of the style are few and far between. Americans had too many choices in their architectural grab bag just then—a lot of Italianate, some Gothic, a little leftover Greek Revival, a powerful bit of Romanesque, and strong hints of the Shingle, Queen Anne, and Eastlake styles to come. It was much more interesting to mix things up and see what developed.

A good way to demystify the complicated house shapes of this period is to play a little game of architectural strip poker. Off with the porches, towers, bays, and wings and you almost always come up with a box. Second Empire houses are almost always two or three storeys high, sometimes four, not counting the attic storey. While masonry—stone but more often brick—was the preferred building material for mansions, most mansard-roofed houses were of light balloon-frame construction with wooden siding. The desired weighty look was achieved through the judicious use of dark, stonelike paint colors. Occasionally, corners were finished with counterfeit stone quoins made of wood, but usually they were covered by simple vertical boards painted in even darker shades for contrast. These corner treatments served to make the house look sturdier, and to draw the eye upward to—what else?—the roof.

Where does the Italian style leave off and the Second Empire begin, and when did that style fall out of fashion? Since Americans of the mid- to late-Victorian era never really made such distinctions, it's sometimes hard to tell. The Second Empire came into vogue at an unusually eclectic period in American architecture, a time when new ideas lurked behind every pilaster and there was a rich mix of ornamental influences. It's safe to call any nineteenth-century building with a mansard roof Second Empire. But to see what else is going on, a useful test is to remove the roof (mentally, please) and take a look at what's left. It could be Italian, Greek Revival (or even Federal), Romanesque, Queen Anne, or Shingle style.

Queen Anne

Popular from about 1875 through the early 1900s, the Queen Anne house is usually a two-storey structure distinguished by asymmetrical massing and a variety of shapes and textures—all of which combine to produce a highly picturesque effect. Vertical surfaces are divided into a series of horizontal bands through the use of various siding materials, such as stone, brick, clapboards, and shingles with differing end cuts. Steep gables, towers, dormers, balconies, and verandahs further enrich the surfaces. There often is a gable in the verandah roof over the entrance. Windows often have art glass, providing a surface richness that echoes the richness of the siding materials. Porches frequently display elaborately turned spindlework and prominent gables. Multiple roofs make a complex skyline, which is further accentuated by tall chimneys with decorative brickwork that is sometimes inset with terra cotta panels. Queen Anne houses often have classical details, such as swags, garlands, and classical porch columns.

Colonial Revival

Victorian America found living in an age of rapid industrial and technological change wonderful but also wearing, fascinating, and frightening. Although popular sentiment called for a return to the simple English, German, and Dutch dwellings of our colonial past, Americans still wanted to enjoy the conveniences and delights afforded by the Queen Anne style.

Queen Anne houses suited contemporary needs well with their expansive spaces, flexible floor plans, interesting building shapes, and big verandahs. While real colonial homes were inspirational, they struck the Victorian eye as small and plain. No question about it: A new style was to evolve.

Colonial Revival was helped along by a reawakened interest in classicism among many of America's young architects, who were being trained in or greatly influenced by the rigorous tradition of France's Ecole des Beaux Arts. They learned to apply the concept of architectural historicism to American building—specifically the Georgian and Federal style buildings being rediscovered in towns such as Newport, Rhode Island, and Salem, Massachusetts.

The first Colonial Revival houses were much bigger than their colonial antecedents, but the shapes were simpler and more rectangular than Queen Anne houses, closer to the boxy look of the originals. Off came the towers, and the exterior trim became restrained, classical in form. Adamesque swags in gabled pediments and modillion and dentil trim at the cornice line were used. Porches were likely to be supported in the unadorned Doric or Ionic mode. Rooflines were streamlined, and hardly anybody saw the need for more than one kind of roof to a building anymore; gables or gambrels, or a subdued hipped or pyramidal roof, served this less flamboyant era well. One or two building materials—wood,

The Early Colonial Revival house was a picturesque collection of assembled parts of early to late eighteenth-century architectural features and ornament all put together in a "new" way.

brick, or stone, simply handled—seemed more suitable than multiple siding materials.

Once again, doorways became the focal point of the facade. Larger-than-life broken pediments, rare in real colonial buildings, often appeared above six-panel doors, along with elliptical fanlights with fanciful tracery. Double-hung, six-over-six window sash, or even nine-over-nine or twelve-over-twelve, gave just the right colonial flavor in the broader window openings of the new day. Often, small panes were used only in the upper part of the window, while the bottom sash was fitted out with a single larger pane. Bulls-eye or small oval windows added interest to upper storeys, and the arched Palladian window never lost its appeal.

The Prairie School

Moving into the twentieth century, architects began designing an entirely new architecture—one that we still call "modern." On the outskirts of Chicago, a group of young architects led by Frank Lloyd Wright was rethinking American building for the twentieth century. Having helped produce the ultimate symbol of life in the industrial age, the skyscraper, these Midwesterners were ready to redefine the most basic building type—the house.

Though the Prairie School was the first American architectural effort to be taken seriously in Europe, it was short-lived in the United States, flourishing from 1900 until the beginning of World War I. It then lost out to the fashion for revival styles, particularly the "Early American" Colonial Revival. Prairie never became the predominant style, although it had plenty of middle-class followers, particularly from Minnesota to Iowa.

The new, low, earth-hugging Prairie house did not spring up unheralded. Its designers had studied English art and the work of John Ruskin and the neogothicists, were well acquainted with the British Arts and Crafts movement, and were alert to the Japanese aesthetic that became popular late in the nineteenth century. Gustav Stickley's magazine, *The Craftsman,* was also part of their design diet. But Louis Sullivan, builder of the first skyscrapers, was the teacher that guided the young generation of architects to develop a truly regional style. He tirelessly promoted a creative, individualistic approach to architecture, not tied to style but to a way of thinking about buildings and building. He wanted to foster an architecture of democracy in the Jeffersonian tradition.

The Prairie School emphasized fitting architecture into the environment. It is not surprising that, because prairies were flat, Prairie School houses would be built low to the ground. Horizontal lines were punctuated by vertical elements—big chimneys, masonry piers, and tall casement windows—just as the prairie's horizon was broken by an occasional tree. The low roofline might be hipped, flat, or gabled, but it usually had wide overhanging eaves and enclosed rafters, which provided shelter from the harsh prairie winds. There was no basement (unhealthy) or attic (inefficient). The general effect was likely to be that of a "high-waisted" building with the visual emphasis placed on the top half of the second-floor level, accentuated by string courses or horizontal wood trim. The sturdy, square pillars that anchored the entrance and the corners of the building became almost a cliché of Prairie style design.

Like Craftsman houses, Prairie houses claimed honesty in the choice of building materials. In contrast to the picturesque jumble of materials found in Queen Anne buildings, Prairie architects strove to use a single building material whenever possible. Although wood and stucco were often employed for economy's sake, masonry was preferred—particularly the new, streamlined Roman brick in bright colors.

Despite its distinctive exterior appearance, the real achievement of the Prairie house lay in its freed-up floor plan and the way it made walls, inside and out, seem to disappear. At its best, the Prairie house was not a collec-

Prairie School houses are distinguished by their low, sweeping horizontal planes that cling to the landscape, accented by vertical massing and projecting planes, which provide counterpoint to the wide sweep of the house.

The Builder Style is the American Vernacular—plain and simple, functional and practical homes for "everyman."

tion of walls defining empty spaces but flowing space that deemphasized the surrounding walls. Windows were no longer simply holes punched into walls but "light screens" that invited in the outdoors. Interior walls gave way to head-high movable partitions that allowed air, light, and people to circulate freely. Without walls, one centrally located chimney was enough to warm the whole house, physically and psychologically. The Prairie house was more than a "style"; it was a call to revolution in the design of living spaces.

The Prairie style spread as more architects developed the ideas first realized by Frank Lloyd Wright. Articles began to appear in popular magazines and the Prairie-house concept was also spread by pattern books. Published in the Midwest and distributed nationally, they offered plans at low prices. Many pattern-book houses (or houses designed by local architects) are scattered about the country, especially in the Midwest. The favorite vernacular form was a Foursquare with an off-center entrance and hipped roof, but gable roofs were also common.

Prairie houses shared some general characteristics with Stickley's Craftsman homes and Greene & Greene's California Bungalow: simple exteriors, functional floor plans, integration of house and environment, and an emphasis on horizontal lines and wide eaves. There was also a common interest in carefully finished interiors featuring natural woods, often set into panels on plastered walls; large fireplaces, frequently surrounded by richly colored, unpatterned tilework; and an overall emphasis on human scale.

Builder Style: The Homestead, Foursquare, Bungalow, and Cottage

Most houses have very little to do with "style" and a great deal to do with having a comfortable, affordable roof over one's head. These are the workers' homes of the late nineteenth and early twentieth centuries. Built for the middle and lower classes, without the direct involvement

of architects, these houses are long on function and short on stylistic effects and architectural grandeur. Related visually by their small size and their plain finishes, they also share a common social context: They were the starter houses of the up-and-coming homeowner class.

These houses are plentiful on the American streetscape because they are relatively recent. But why the name "Builder Style"? We chose the term because it pays tribute to the crucial role that speculative developers, plan-book designers, and mail-order houses played in putting homes on the new building lots of America's suburbs. Also, the term suggests the mechanization of construction methods and materials, which made home ownership possible for millions of Americans from 1895 to 1925.

This period was one of intense innovation, with the development of new techniques and new materials and vastly improved transportation facilities to deliver materials anywhere they were in demand. For example, from the 1870s on, after the introduction of cast concrete, it was possible to build sturdy houses that were capable of giving reasonable imitations of stone at only a fraction of the cost of stone. Stucco installed on top of wood or man-made sheathing was a new technique, and asbestos and asphalt shingles for roofs and siding was introduced.

Based on their form or layout, we have sorted Builder Style houses into four subcategories for discussion.

The Homestead

The Homestead is generally tall, narrow, and deep, with a pitched roof and a gable front. It is sometimes called a "temple house" because the gable is often treated as a Classical Greek pediment. The Homestead was well suited to narrow city or suburban lots; in fact, many of the city lots on which Homesteads today stand were suburban lots when these houses were built. It is also well known in the country. In fact, it never entirely disappeared from the countryside after the nineteenth-century Greek Revival made it the farmhouse of preference. It is most often two storeys tall, but one- and one-and-a-half-storey versions are not uncommon, especially in the workmen's homes provided in company towns.

The Foursquare

The Foursquare (one Midwestern version is variously titled the Cornbelt Cube) may be seen as a stripped-down version of a couple of late eighteenth- and mid-nineteenth-century forms, including the Georgian block and the square Italianate house. The Foursquare was generally roomier than the Homestead; in fact, the plan was a sort of double Homestead. The roofline is invariably pyramidal, or hipped, however, and not gabled. In its most elemental form, a Foursquare is simply four rooms on each of two floors, arranged one on each corner with no through hallway. It usually has a front porch, which may turn the corner on one side.

The simplest Foursquares have two single windows on the second floor, while more elegant houses may have two double or triple windows, or even a third set of windows. There may be a low, small dormer with a flat or pyramidal roof. As the style becomes more elaborate, the dormer arrangement moves from one or two to three sash within each of the dormers, and in some houses there may be dormers on all four sides of the main roof.

Foursquares were most commonly built in frame and stuccoed frame, but they are also found in stone or brick. "Shirtwaist" Foursquares typically have a belt course below the windows of the second floor, separating the different materials used on the first and second floors (stone below and stucco above, for example).

The Bungalow

From 1900 until World War I, no house excited the American homeowner's imagination more than the Bungalow. It seemed the perfect small house, and it was tirelessly promoted and enthusiastically built even in areas where its warm-weather origins were not particularly apt. (The name seems to have come from "bangala" or Bangali, and originally indicated a form of summer house used by colonists in India.) Architects such as Charles and Henry Greene in California made it high style, and Prairie School architects embroidered on bungalow characteristics, but it was the American public who made it, with its open floor plan and one-floor living, a mainstay of early twentieth-century suburbs.

The Bungalow is a relatively long, low, one- or one-and-one-half-storey building with a conspicuous roof, overhanging eaves, and an ample front porch included under the main roof structure. Built snug to the ground, it was intended to relate in scale and color to the surrounding shrubbery and trees. Ideally, indoors and out were blended to encourage relaxed communication between the inhabitants and nature.

The bungalow is usually covered either with shingles or shakes (large rough shingles) in natural colors. Sometimes clapboard and/or stucco was used. The bungalow reached its highest expression in the well-wrought Arts and Crafts interiors, but most houses of the type used lesser, machine-made trim of cheap materials, along the lines of inexpensive Mission furniture.

The Cottage

There is often a fine line between the Bungalow and Cottage. Both are one- or one-and-a-half-storey buildings, although there is frequently a larger upstairs in the Cottage, and Cottages are more vertically oriented than Bungalows. They are a traditional vernacular building type, here updated and simplified, but sometimes showing ornament from an earlier period.

Most often built in frame or stucco over frame, Cottages were sometimes made using brick and even stone. Front porches are standard, but may not extend across the entire front of the building. Roofs are usually gabled as in the Bungalow, but they may take other forms as well: They may be very low, enclosing only a crawl space or they may cover nearly an entire floor. There may or may not be dormers. Porte cocheres are rarely found. The plan may be rectangular or L-shaped, always with an informal and picturesque effect. When there is ornament, it may be in the style of Queen Anne houses. Windows are varied, tending to be more vertical than horizontal.

Old houses come in many shapes and styles, and the one you choose will depend entirely upon your own tastes and, of course, budget. And what's really old depends a bit on you, too. For example, don't dismiss a house built in the 1920s just because the previous owners have renovated and made many additions. With some careful digging around, you may find that you have an historical gold mine. With the *Old-House Journal* philosophy and standards described in this chapter, together with a basic knowledge of different historical architectural styles, you should be able to follow the most important old-house golden rule when thinking about buying a house or when approaching restoration or renovation: To thine own style be true.

CHAPTER 2

Buying an Old House

Increasing numbers of people dream of buying an old house. Aesthetically, you may have a particular style or period in mind. Perhaps you want to find an old house in a particular area. You're probably the sort of person to whom a Queen Anne house in the old part of town is preferable to a brick ranch in the suburbs. Shopping on Main Street is more fun than going to the mall, working in the warehouse district more interesting than commuting to a modern office campus.

No matter what your dream old house may be, making an informed decision to buy an old house depends on many factors. This chapter will take you step-by-step through the necessary practical considerations that will help you find the old house as close to your dream as possible. Realistically, you may have to sacrifice location for budget, or style for size. One house may be just the one you envisioned, but you may discover that the cost of renovation and restoration is prohibitive.

Before you rush into buying any house, carefully weigh all the factors outlined in this chapter. You'll find a review of potential tax breaks and incentives for people who buy houses with historical designations, as well as an "Inspection Checklist" for evaluating the condition of an old house and making an informed purchase decision.

Weigh your dream against the realities of your budget and the degree of inconvenience you and your family will experience during the renovation. Every old house has its own idiosyncracies and personality; no one can predict what problems you'll encounter once you've started work. Old houses are full of the unexpected; these guidelines will help you avoid some pitfalls.

RESTORATION INCENTIVES AND PRESERVATION REGULATIONS

Over the past two decades development of historic buildings has become big business—a reasonable way to make money. Preservationists motivated by a deep appreciation for history or for architectural quality are no longer alone in their desire to preserve old buildings. Driven by the seemingly insatiable demand for "historic" places in which to live, work, and play, big-time developers as well as small-time entrepreneurs have joined the ranks of preservationists; they have discovered that restoring an old building can have financial as well as aesthetic rewards.

But good restoration work is expensive and labor intensive. Many commercial restoration projects succeed only because they tap into an array of preservation incentives that help defray the costs of major rehabilitation. Tax easements and deductions are also available to private homeowners, and although tax laws change periodically, you'll find they contain major incentive programs. Before you can take advantage of them, however, your old house must meet certain eligibility requirements.

Historical Designations

Virtually every incentive program requires that the building be officially designated as historically or architecturally significant. Incentives differ according to the historic designation the building receives. This designation might come from the federal government, the various state preservation offices, or from local governmental agencies.

The first step in a restoration project is finding what level of historical designation the building has, or could have. This determines not only what incentives you're eligible for but also what preservation controls you may have to obey.

The federal government maintains the best known historical register: the National Register of Historic Places (often referred to as the Register or NR). When first instituted in 1966, the Register offered a limited degree of protection to what was essentially an honor roll of struc-

Pulling the siding off this house revealed an earlier remuddling of the porch and hidden decorative detail.

Here the house's porch and decorative detail are restored.

tures historically important to the country. Since then, listing in the National Register has become essential for eligibility for the popular Rehabilitation Investment Tax Credit (RITC).

Getting a property listed in the Register is not an easy job. The eligibility requirements can be stringent and the application process long and arduous. You'll probably need the help of an experienced preservation consultant.

Fortunately, most State Historic Preservation Offices (SHPOs)—which handle the initial Register review for the Department of the Interior—can give you a faster (and cheaper) *preliminary determination of eligibility* for a particular property.

The SHPOs also conduct systematic surveys of historic resources. Check with your SHPO: Your property may already be listed as potentially eligible as the result of survey work done in your county, city, or town.

Historic-resources surveys also identify those properties that can be included on state or local historical registers. These registers may have less stringent requirements than the National Register. Yet it is usually local designation, not National Register listing, that provides the most protection and control over the fate of historic properties.

Whether in national, state, or local registers, historic properties can be listed two ways: either individually, or as part of a historic district. In the latter case, the property must be a "contributing element" of the district to qualify for the various restoration-incentive programs.

Commercial Restorations: The Investment Tax Credit

In 1981, as part of the Economic Recovery Tax Act, Congress passed tax legislation that had a profound effect on the preservation/restoration movement in this country. Part of the Economic Recovery Tax Act, the Rehabilitation Investment Tax Credit (the RITC or ITC) is a complex tax law, involving some perplexing rules and conditions. Basically, it says that if the restoration of an eligible, income-producing, historic building qualifies for the RITC, then for every five dollars you spend on the restoration, the federal government will give you back one dollar in the form of a credit on your income tax. This is a tax credit, a dollar-for-dollar reduction of your taxes due, not just a deduction taken from your taxable income. It effectively reduces the costs of restoration by 20 percent.

The RITC is available only for income-producing properties. Owner-occupied residential buildings (private homes) don't qualify. Rental properties (including apartments), and those used in a trade or business such as stores, offices, industrial buildings, and the like, do.

The RITC was one of the very few tax credits to survive the 1986 Tax Reform Act (albeit with modifications that make it somewhat less useful for taxpayers in certain income brackets). Although unused credits can be carried over to future years, in essence the 1986 Tax Reform now puts a limit on the amount that can be taken in a particular year. The RITC's survival through the recent reform is a testimony to its effectiveness and perceived importance. By turning the tide on demolition, it has promoted preservation and reuse, and raised the country's awareness of historic buildings.

The RITC was the major reason for an explosive growth in the number of restoration projects. From huge projects running into the tens of millions of dollars to relatively small rental properties, the RITC has made the difference, not only in whether the projects would be done at all but also in the quality of restoration work.

The facts are impressive. Since 1981, over 15,000 RITC projects have been completed. The total private invest-

ARE TAX CREDITS WORTH THE EFFORT?

There's no doubt that federal income tax reforms of 1986 spelled trouble for those who hoped to benefit from rehabilitation tax credits. For many, restoration to meet the Secretary of the Interior's Standards seems hardly worth the effort in the face of stringent "passive loss" income requirements, reduced tax credits, and substantially longer property depreciation terms. Then there's the ever more rigorous interpretation of the Standards.

And in fact, the National Park Service (which administers the program) recently reported a 35 percent decrease in both the total amount of money invested in RITC projects and the number of such projects approved since 1986. The number of new projects initiated since 1985 has declined even more steeply. The Park Service thinks a lot of people have been scared off unnecessarily. Prodded by Preservation Action, the national preservation lobby, the NPS's report evaluating the impact of the original tax act was intended to encourage Congress to rethink the more damaging provisions of the 1986 act. Bills have been introduced in both the House and Senate to do just that.

Legal and economic questions of who can qualify or benefit from an RITC have been raised. Decisions about the buildings themselves are also tougher now. The Standards and their accompanying guidelines are being more stringently interpreted by the regional offices and the Technical Preservation Services branch of the Park Service. Thus, complying with the Standards may cost more than it used to. Adapting any given building for commercial use may be unexpectedly difficult or impossible. The existing building and any additions must be handled with great care, and adjacent new construction must also meet NPS approval. It used to be that only the exterior needed approval; now the interior must pass NPS muster as well. Time is critical, because the sort of rehab likely to win NPS approval is rarely the fastest way to go about the job. Unanticipated delays in the state or federal review process, which take several months at their speediest, may result in higher materials and labor outlays and lost rental income.

However, owners continue to go the RITC route because it's still a direct return—a tax credit, not merely a deduction—of 20 percent of qualified costs. Most rehabs for tax credits are under $100,000, tailor-made for groups of small investors who have only $25,000 or so qualifying for sheltering under the passive-loss rules. There is also a certain amount of prestige (often translatable into economic terms) attached to a certified historic property. And some people just like to know they've done right by an old building. Finally, although the rules are indeed stricter, chances of securing certification for a carefully planned and executed project are still very good. The NPS certification approval rate is still around 90 percent, down from about 95 percent prior to 1985.

---

ment in these restorations has reached over $10.4 billion. In some cities, money spent on rehabilitation has outstripped investments for new construction.

Owners of comparatively small "Main Street" commercial buildings or of rental properties have been the largest group to use the RITC. Their rehabilitation projects might be in the $50,000 to $200,000 range. Large projects—over a million dollars—are also good candidates for using the RITC, particularly those that are funded by large public offerings or corporate investments.

The basic ground rules for using the RITC state that

1. The property to be restored must be a qualified building; that is, it must—
- be individually listed in the National Register of Historic Places, or
- be listed as a contributing element in a National Register historic district or certified local district, or
- have received a preliminary determination of positive eligibility for the Register.

 (*Note:* A 10 percent RITC is available, too, for non-designated buildings built before 1936.)

2. For the rehabilitation project (the restoration work itself) to qualify for the RITC, it must—
- be a substantial rehabilitation—that is, the amount of money spent on the rehabilitation must be greater than the depreciated (adjusted) value of the building (minus the value of the land) and be at least $5,000 [for example, if the depreciated value of your building is $40,000 and you spend $39,999 to fix it up, you can't get the RITC, but if you spend $40,001, you're eligible for an $8,000 tax credit (20 percent)], or
- be rehabilitated according to the Secretary of the Interior's Standards for Rehabilitation (a.k.a. "the Standards").

The Secretary's Standards are, by and large, common-sense rules for appropriate and sensitive rehabilitation, very similar to the guidelines advocated by *The Old-House Journal.* Those interested in restoration will want to do the rehab work the right way anyhow. (You should be familiar with the Standards—get a copy from your SHPO. The Standards is a ubiquitous document in this field. "Even if you decide not to use the RITC, you may find yourself dealing with the Secretary's Standards because many communities use them to evaluate applications for building and repair permits in historic districts," advises preservation consultant Shirley Maxwell. "Interpretation at the local level may vary from that of the National Park Service," however.)

MEETING "THE STANDARDS"

If you're looking at old houses and hope to get approval from the National Park Service, watch out for some of the major "red flags" that the NPS will reject.

Abrasive cleaning of masonry, otherwise known as sandblasting, is the hottest button you can push. The NPS notes that it isn't happening nearly so often now that word has gotten out on its effects: it's harmful to the building and a shoo-in for rejection by the NPS. Before you strip or clean masonry—even with plain water—discuss the method you plan to use with your SHPO. Water pressure and adding chemicals or grit raises questions that should be answered before you proceed.

Masonry pointing should closely match the original in every respect. Gray portland cement is usually a no-no.

Windows and doors present sticky problems when you try to conform to the Standards. Yes, wooden sash deteriorates inexorably, single-thickness glass is an energy waster, doors are often in the wrong places (or not in the *right* places). Ah, but go slowly when you think to meddle. These are considered *design determining features.* Mess with them, and the Park Service will not fail to notice. If you're convinced that windows must be replaced, be prepared to make a

strong case and to provide exact reproductions of the originals in the same materials. So adamant is the Park Service on this point that they hold highly technical workshops on window rehab to educate SHPO staff, developers, and architects.

Decorative details such as wood trim (cornices, brackets, window parts) are also design determinants, as are porches and rooflines. It is never wise to alter any of these without very good reason, and certainly not without the prior approval in writing from your SHPO. If you want to replace any of these elements, it's essential that they be reproduced in form, size, location, and material. Remember, too, that these elements need not be as old as the original building to have acquired historical significance in their own right. (In other words, don't think you can tear it off just because it post-dates the building.)

Synthetic siding can hide damage to the siding beneath it as well as mask decorative details.

New construction must be readily identifiable as new construction, whether it's a wing attached to the old building or something adjacent. This is a confusing and, from the developer's point of view, an inconvenient aspect of the Standards. Design must meet the approval of NPS. Talk to your SHPO, submit detailed plans, and don't stray from the plans.

Changes to **the interior** will be scrutinized by the Park Service. Removing partitions (even relatively recent ones), changing the location of staircases, and taking out trim or flooring may get you in trouble. Obviously, it's often necessary to rearrange the interior of a building that is being converted to a new use. Don't count too heavily on your intended new use being a persuasive argument, however, as the NPS will also look at the *appropriateness* of use. Mechanical systems (heat, plumbing, etc.) are also subject to NPS approval.

The Review Process

Two agencies must review the project: your State Historic Preservation Office and the National Park Service. The SHPO is your strongest ally in dealing with the Na-

tional Park Service, as it's assumed that the state office, being closer to the property, is better able to evaluate your property in its context and to keep a closer watch on the project. Though not the last word, the SHPO's recommendations carry a lot of weight with the Park Service. That's why Shirley Maxwell warns, "It is very important to keep [the SHPO] informed if you decide to make any changes in the project. They are likely to react very badly indeed to last-minute surprises! Any changes must, of course, be approved through the same lengthy process."

Three forms have to be filed with the SHPO. They are commonly known as Parts I, II, and III. Part I documents that the building is a qualified historic structure. (If the property is already individually listed in the Register, you don't need to file Part I.) Part II explains the precise nature and scope of the rehabilitation work to be done; governmental reviewers will use the Secretary's Standards as their guideline in reviewing your plans. Ideally, Part II should be filed before restoration work actually begins because the NPS typically requires some changes. Part III documents the finished work—in other words, have you done what you said you would do?

As you can see, undertaking an RITC project is a complex process, but one that has the potential for saving a significant amount of money, while still demanding quality work and conferring prestige. It is particularly valuable for large, adaptive reuse projects.

Private and Commercial Restorations: Preservation Easements_____

Unlike the RITC, the benefits derived from donating a preservation easement are available to owners of both income-producing historic properties and noncommercial ones, including private residences. An easement tax deduction is one of very few preservation incentives available to private homeowners.

A preservation easement is a legal agreement between the property owner (donor) and an easement-holding organization (donee). In essence, property owners give up part of their "bundle of rights"; in this case the right to demolish or unsympathetically alter the building. Thus a historic structure is legally preserved in perpetuity.

What does this property owner get in return? Well, as you might imagine, placing these preservation restrictions on a property decreases its fair market value. The dollar-value difference between the fair market value of the property, and its value after deed restrictions are placed on it, is considered the same as a charitable donation by the IRS, and thus can be deducted from the owner's federal income tax. Typically, an easement ranges from 7 to 13 percent of fair market value, the exact figure established by a qualified real-estate appraiser. Thus a historic building worth $200,000 might have a potential easement value ranging from $14,000 to $26,000, an amount fully tax deductible.

To be eligible for the tax deduction, the property must be listed in the National Register, either individually or as a contributing part of a historic district. There are some additional conditions. For example, the property owners must—

- own the property outright.
- give up forever their right to demolish the building.

- submit, for approval by the easement-holding organization, any plans to alter or improve the building (a condition that usually applies to the exterior only).
- in some cases restore the building to a more accurate historic condition (again, exterior only).
- maintain the property in good condition.

Generally, the easement-holding organization must—

- be a not-for-profit or governmental agency.
- be willing and able to enforce the easement, usually through yearly inspections (sometimes the donee requires an endowment from the property owner in order to administer these inspections).
- review and approve requests for alterations or improvements to the property (the Secretary of the Interior's Standards are commonly used as the guidelines).

Typically, easement-holding organizations are private, statewide preservation groups, local historical societies, or the SHPO. Contact any of the major easement-holding organizations in your region (see box).

If you want to retain full control of your property, donating an easement is not for you. Remember, the preservation deed restrictions last in perpetuity, and subsequent owners must comply even though they can't get any of the tax benefits. But if you're motivated for altruistic or economic reasons—if you'd like to see the building preserved for future generations to enjoy, or if you could benefit from a significant tax deduction—it's something to consider.

Other Incentives_____

RITCs and preservation easement donations are probably the best known and most widely used restoration-incentive programs. There are others, listed below, offered mostly by the individual states and local governments through their preservation agencies.

Tax deferrals. Local property taxes can increase dramatically when a major restoration project is completed because the property is usually reassessed. To offset this disincentive, some municipalities are empowered to defer property-tax increases. The deferral might be a freeze on increases for a set number of years—usually three to seven—or a gradual phasing-in of the tax increase. Tax deferrals are commonly targeted at large commercial buildings whose restoration and reuse will benefit the economy of the community.

Tax rebates. Some preservation ordinances allow municipalities to reduce property taxes on properties listed as local landmarks. (North Carolina, for example, allows a 50 percent reduction of property taxes for landmark buildings.) In exchange for the rebate, property owners are usually required to submit to preservation regulations that restrict their right to demolish or develop the property, or require adherence to design and maintenance guidelines for alterations and improvements.

Restoration grants. Although less common than in years past, many SHPOs still administer a variety of restoration-grant programs. Often the grants are restricted to historic buildings owned publicly or by nonprofit organizations. The grant amount usually must be matched by the property owner. Your SHPO is the best source for information on the availability of these programs.

Some states—New York and New Jersey are notable examples—have passed special bond acts to create funds for qualified restoration projects. Competition for restoration grants is stiff, and the funds are usually restricted to certain kinds of projects.

Community- & economic-development programs. Restoration is now recognized as a vital part of rebuilding the nation's cities and towns. Therefore many federal, state, and regional development programs subsidize or provide below-market-rate financing for restoration projects if they contribute to the economic vitality of the community, improve deteriorating neighborhoods, or relieve housing needs.

The Department of Housing and Urban Development (HUD), for example, has several programs that aid the rehabilitation of historic structures, including residences. They include urban homesteading, Community Development Block Grants (CDBGs), and Urban Development Action Grants (UDAGs). Contact the National Trust for Historic Preservation for information. As many rehabilitated historic buildings house low- and moderate-income families, they can benefit from federal "Section 8" subsidies. Regional development agencies often have local versions of these programs as well.

Preservation Regulations

So far, we've addressed the various mechanisms that encourage owners to restore their historic properties. The restorer then must comply with various ordinances, which protect and preserve historic resources for the benefit of the public good. In that sense they're akin to zoning regulations.

Most of the ordinances affect properties in local historic districts. Sometimes the commission's role is advisory, and the municipality's legislative body (e.g., a city council) actually puts into law the commission's recommendations. In its other major role, a historic commission reviews applications for alterations and improvements to (or demolition of) historic buildings. The applications will be reviewed by a Historic Architectural Review Board, or HARB.

The HARB will approve or deny the request based on its own guidelines. These are often based on the Secretary's Standards, but there is a great range in the scope of the guidelines from one commission to another. Some HARBs are stringent and may dictate the proper exterior paint colors that are acceptable for historic buildings, or even the appropriate design for a fence. Other HARBs will do little else than try to stall demolitions.

More commonly, HARBs deal with such issues as the configuration of replacement windows, the design sensitivity of new additions such as porches, the removal of historic elements, or requests to allow aluminum siding. (The response to the last is easy to predict.)

If you are contemplating a major restoration, particularly of a large, income-producing building, you will likely encounter many of the issues discussed in this section. The project may need to be reviewed by a HARB. To make the project feasible, you may decide to use the RITCs, donate a facade easement, utilize one or more of the government subsidies, secure a preservation grant, and procure low-interest financing through an economic- or community-development program. As we said, restoration is now big business.

If you simply want to restore an old house for you and your family to enjoy, some of the historical designations and tax breaks outlined here still may apply. Check with the SHPO in the area where you plan to buy to see if any of the houses you're considering qualify for a historic designation. Also talk over your plans with a tax consultant, who can help you determine what your longer-term tax breaks might be. And, of course, the Department of Housing and Urban Development may offer a program that will help you rehabilitate the old house you want to buy.

SHOPPING AROUND

Old houses hold many secrets, some of which are better discovered before you sign a purchase-and-sale agreement. Before making your final purchase decision, shop around. Check each house thoroughly using the inspection checklist below—it takes you step-by-step through a building, guiding you to a rational evaluation of the structure and systems and will help you estimate the approximate cost of restoring the house. Later, you can use the checklist as you discover the idiosyncracies of the house you've chosen, since an old house's secrets may not reveal themselves for months or years after you move in. You can also use the checklist for annual maintenance checks.

Before you buy, a professional should inspect the house to help you make the purchase decision, and to formulate a plan and budget for rehabilitation. By using this checklist, however, you can eliminate a few potential purchases yourself.

Inspection Checklist

Make multiple copies of these pages for future use.

When setting out on an inspection, be prepared to climb around in the cellar and under the porch. Bring a flashlight, small magnet, plumb line (a string with a small weight will do), a penknife, a marble, binoculars, a pad and pencil, and this checklist.

Move through the building from roof to cellar if possible, following the order of the checklist. Whether you begin with the exterior or the interior doesn't matter, as long as you correlate what you see on the outside with what you see on the inside (and vice versa). For example, the sagging ridgeline of the roof should prompt you to look closely inside the attic, where you may discover missing collar beams.

Give each individual category a grade, from A through F; then assign overall grades to each part of the house. Average these to come up with a final grade for the building. It's impossible to assign an absolute grade in each case; many times it comes down to a judgment call.

Don't worry about the absolute value of the grade you assign. An asphalt-shingle roof in tip-top, "A" condition may get a "B" for its relatively shorter lifespan. Measure current condition against long-term maintenance and factor in the immediate work you'll need to do. Try to use the same criteria with each building you evaluate. Consistency with the grades you assign will lead to a confident and well-planned purchase decision. By grading consistently, the relative value assigned to each building will tell you what you need to know.

EXTERIOR ✓

I. ROOF

A sound, tight roof is the first line of defense against the number one enemy of an old house: water. If the roof is in bad shape, you should plan on repairing or replacing it right away.

Note: Binoculars can give you a good close-up view, if it's impossible to get up onto the roof.

A. ROOFING MATERIALS

1. Type of roof on house (arranged in approximate order of longevity):

Slate	Asbestos Tile	Asphalt Shingles
Copper	Wood Shakes	Roll Roofing
Ceramic Tile	Wood Shingles	
Tar and Gravel	Galvanized Steel	

2. Pitched Roof: Any sign of missing, broken, or warped shingles or tiles? (Will the roof need to be replaced soon? Damaged shingles may indicate water damage inside.)

3. Asphalt Shingles: Are the mineral granules getting thin? Do edges of shingles look worn? Does the roof look new but lumpy? (A new roof may have been applied directly over old shingles. Beware of sins, which are difficult to detect, that may have been covered over.)

4. Flat Roof: Any sign of bubbles, separation, or cracking in the asphalt or roofing felt? (Roofing should be flat and tight to roof; it shouldn't feel spongy underfoot.)

5. Are there any signs of ponding (standing water)—either actual water or water marks? (If so, there may be structural deflection in the roof members.)

6. Check the flashing. Usually made of thin sheets of copper, aluminum, or galvanized steel, flashing covers

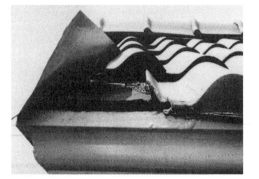

areas susceptible to water penetration, such as those around a chimney or where a porch or dormer meets the roof. Any sign of rusty, loose, or missing flashing around chimneys and valleys? (Flashing is the weakest part of any roof. Copper is the best flashing and will show a green patina.)

Roofing Materials Grade _____

B. CHIMNEYS

1. Is the masonry cracked or crumbling? Is the parging (if any) cracked or peeling?

2. Do the old chimney flues have a tile lining? (If not, they could be a fire hazard if you use a wood-burning fireplace.)

3. Is the chimney leaning? (If it is, it may have to be rebuilt from the roof up.)

Chimney Grade _____

C. ROOF STRUCTURE

1. Does the ridge or any other part of the roof sag? (Sagging may occur with age as the building settles—or it may result from rotted rafters or other structural problems. Check further!)

2. Is there badly peeling paint on the cornice, especially the underside? (This can be a sign of a roof leak spilling water into the cornice.)

3. Are there loose, rotted, or missing gutters?

4. Is the attic ventilated with a soffit vent, gable vent, ridge vent, or other type of vent?

Roof Structure Grade _____
Overall Roof Grade _____

II. WALLS

A. STRUCTURE

1. Do exterior walls seem plumb? (If you can't tell by "eyeballing" them, check with your plumb line. Out-of-plumb walls can indicate serious foundation problems. See "The Crack Detective" in chapter 3.)

2. Sight along exterior walls. Any sign of major bulges? (This could signal major structural flaws.)

3. Do doors and windows line up squarely in their frames? (Out-of-square doors can be another sign of possible foundation trouble.)

4. Does the siding undulate? (This can indicate differential settlement.)

Wall Structure Grade _____

B. WATER AND TERMITE DAMAGE

1. Are there any signs of veins of dirt on exterior walls? (These are termite mud tunnels. Look for them on foundation, steps, and cellar walls, as well as under porches. Always make purchase contingent upon a termite inspection!)

2. Does wood near the ground pass the "penknife test"? (Test wood by probing with a penknife to determine its soundness. Wood is bad if it feels soft or lifts up in short, rather than long, splinters [see page 138]. Check areas such as cellar window frames, sills, siding, porches, and steps.)

Note: Unsound wood can be caused by either termites or rot. Rot can be arrested by eliminating the source of moisture; termites call for chemical warfare. If you can't identify the cause of bad wood, call in the experts.

3. Is all exterior wood at least 6 to 8 inches above the ground? (If not, you have an inviting target for termites and/or rot.)

4. Is there any vegetation close to the house? (Vegetation holds moisture in wood; be sure to check behind it for rot.)

Water/Termite Damage Grade _____

C. SIDING, TRIM, AND FINISHES

1. Are there many loose, cracked, or missing clapboards? (This is an open invitation to water—and rot.)

2. Are shingles thick and well nailed? (You may have to replace thin, badly weathered shingles.)

3. Do shingles have a natural finish? (Natural finishes require less preparation than paint, and are easier to reapply to shingles.)

4. Is decorative woodwork firmly attached to the house and tightly caulked to prevent water penetration?

5. Is exterior paint fresh and in good condition?

6. If paint is not new, is it chalking to a dull, powdery surface? (Chalking paint requires a little extra preparation before repainting.)

7. Is the paint peeling, curling, and blistering? (This could mean a serious water problem—either a leak or an insufficient vapor barrier in the wall.)

8. Are there open joints around door frames, window frames, and trim? (If so, they will have to be caulked.)

9. Are joints between dissimilar materials (e.g., wood and masonry) well protected with flashing or caulk?

10. Is there mold or mildew on siding or trim, especially on the north side or other shady areas? (This indicates a moisture problem.)

11. Has any of the original trim or siding been covered over or replaced with vinyl or aluminum siding? (If so, it may be hiding rot or other damage underneath. Siding should be removed, if possible.)

Siding/Trim/Finishes Grade _____

D. DOORS AND WINDOWS

1. Do the doors and windows fit properly?

2. Is any of the wood rotted, especially around sills and lower rails?

3. Are the doors and windows weather-stripped?

4. Is the glass intact and properly glazed, with the glazing putty painted?

5. Are the storm and screen windows or doors in serviceable condition?

Doors/Windows Grade _____

E. FOUNDATION AND MASONRY

1. Are there any signs of cracks in masonry walls? (Horizontal or hairline cracks in mortar are usually not a problem; cracks that run vertically through bricks may be more serious.)

2. Is the mortar soft and crumbling? Are bricks missing or loose? (Loose masonry is vulnerable to water damage—repointing a masonry wall with fresh mortar is expensive.)

3. Sight along the walls. Are there any bows or bulges?

4. Has masonry been painted? (If so, it will have to be repainted about every five years, or else stripped—a major task.)

5. Is there any sign of spalling, cracking, or crumbling of stonework? (This can be expensive to repair.)

6. Is there an adequate (continuous) foundation, or is the building resting on posts or masonry piers? (A continuous foundation lessens the likelihood of differential settlement.)

7. Is ground water and downspout water properly diverted away from building with correct grading and splashblocks under leaders?

Foundation/Masonry Grade _____
Exterior Walls Grade _____

INTERIOR

I. CELLAR

A. FOUNDATION

1. Is there a dug cellar with wood sills resting solidly on a masonry foundation well above ground level? (Some old structures have "mud sills" or heavy beams resting directly on the ground. These eventually have to be replaced, which is an expensive, complicated undertaking.)

2. Again, is the mortar in the foundation soft and crumbling? (This may not be serious if there's no sign of sag in the structure; ditto for foundation walls laid dry—without mortar. See pages 42–51 and chapter 5 to determine if you have serious structural damage.)

3. Are there any vertical cracks in the foundation wall? (This could be serious, or it could be from settling that stopped ages ago. Have an engineer check it out.)

Foundation Grade _____

B. GENERAL CONDITION

1. Does the cellar smell damp or moldy? (This may indicate moisture problems.)

2. Do sills (the wood beams at the top of the foundation walls) show signs of rot or termites? (Probe with penknife.)

3. Is there any sign of dampness on the underside of floors around the pipes? (If leaks have gone undetected for some time, there could be wood rot.)

4. Does basement show signs of periodic flooding? (It's a good sign if the current owner stores important tools and papers on cellar floor. Bad signs: rust spots, efflorescence or mildew on walls, material stored on top of bricks to raise it above floor level.)

5. Are there any signs of sagging floors, cracked headers or beams, rotted support posts, or jury-rigged props to shore up weak flooring?

6. Is there asbestos board on the ceiling? (It's usually identifiable by an embossed pattern or texture and manufacturer's name in face of board. If it's there, it must be removed by a licensed asbestos-removal contractor—at considerable cost.)

7. If there's only a crawlspace instead of a cellar, does it have any insulation or a vapor barrier?

General Basement Grade _____

C. HEATING PLANT

1. Was heating plant originally designed to burn coal? (If so, it's probably more than thirty years old and may be a candidate for replacement; old converted boilers are usually leaky and inefficient.)

2. Is the fuel tank inside or outside? What is its capacity? Are the fuel lines in good condition?

3. Is the boiler encased in an asbestos jacket (whitish gray, cloth-covered material similar to crumbly cardboard)? Are heating pipes encased in this material? (If so, asbestos may have to be removed by a licensed removal contractor.)

4. With the owner's permission, run this test on the heating system:

    a. Turn on emergency switch.

    b. Move thermostat setting above room temperature.

    c. Boiler/furnace should fire immediately after burner kicks on, without any loud initial rumbling or back puffing. Heating plant should run steadily and cleanly; intermittent firing or smoking are not good signs.

    d. Look for any obvious blockage or leakage in the breaching (the flue pipe that leads to the chimney).

    e. For *forced-air systems,* heat should be evident at hot-air registers in a matter of minutes.

    f. For *hot-water or steam systems,* radiators should warm up in about fifteen to twenty minutes.

    g. All pipes in a steam system should be pitched back to the boiler; otherwise, system will knock and bang where pipes are improperly pitched.

    h. Look for signs of leakage (i.e., rust spots) on heating pipes.

    i. If you are still unsure about the condition of the heating system, have a heating contractor inspect it and test its efficiency.

5. Is the yearly heating cost reasonable for your budget? (Ask to see a season's heating bill.)

6. Is domestic hot water heated by a boiler or a separate hot-water heater? (The best system has the boiler heating water in the winter, and a separate water heater doing the job in summer.)

7. Is the capacity of the hot-water heater at least forty gallons? (That's the minimum required for a family of four.)

8. Are there rust spots indicating leaks anywhere on the tank?

9. Is the flue in good condition?

10. Are either the hot-water or heating systems multizone? (Important in a two-family house.)

Heating Plant Grade _____

D. PLUMBING

Check whether the water is supplied from city main, deep well, or spring. If the supply is from a well, have the water tested; if from a spring, you probably will have to drill a well.

1. Is the water main coming into the house made of lead? (If so, it may have to be replaced.)

2. Does the main shutoff valve function properly?

3. Type of distribution piping (arranged from best to worst):

    Copper, brass (For brass and copper, bluish green stains indicate old pipes, which should be replaced.)

    Galvanized iron (Use a magnet to test for iron.)

    Lead (Pipe is lead if soft and silvery when scratched with a penknife. Replace pipes to eliminate health hazard.)

4. Do you smell gas in the cellar? (If so, inspect gas main and distribution pipes for leaks.)

5. Is sewage disposal tied into city sewer? (If you have an on-site system, talk to the last person who serviced it to find out if it's adequate.)

Note: Waterfront properties sometimes dump raw sewage directly into water. Make sure it is possible to install a legal septic system, and find out what it would cost.

6. Are the waste pipes in good condition and properly pitched? (Look for evidence of leaks, especially at joints. Look for patches or other makeshift repairs. If waste pipes look heavily rusted, tap pipe lightly with a hammer—a ringing sound means the pipe has some life left in it; a dull thump means it is almost rusted through.)

7. Is there a dry well or sump pump in cellar? (These may point to water problems in the cellar.) Where does the sump pump discharge? (It should discharge into a sewer, or well away from the house.)

8. Is there a trap and a vent where the waste pipe exits the house? (Trap and vent prevent sewer gases from entering the house.)

Plumbing Grade _____

E. ELECTRICAL

Check the electrical service: 100 amps is usually the minimum for the average single-family house. A modern panel box will have the total capacity marked on it. If there is an old fuse box with only three or four fuses, it may mean it has only 30 to 50 amps.

Note: Many city codes require that wiring be shielded in flexible cable or rigid conduit, whereas nonurban areas often permit unshielded cable. Familiarize yourself with local electrical codes, or bring a licensed electrician along when you inspect the house.

1. Is power brought in overhead rather than underground? (If so, look for trees or other hazards that could cause problems.)

2. Are you comfortable with the general condition of the wiring and its installation? (If there is frayed insulation or exposed wiring, or if the wiring appears to be haphazard and amateurish, have an electrician look at it.)

3. Are all connections made in fully enclosed junction boxes? (This is an essential safety consideration.)

Electrical Grade _____
Overall Cellar Grade _____

II. FINISHED SPACES

A. GENERAL CONDITION

1. Are there any signs of damp plaster? (This means leaks, either from roof or internal pipes. Check especially top-floor ceilings, the inside of exterior walls, and ceilings and partitions under bathrooms.)

2. Is there any loose plaster on walls or ceilings? (Some cracks in plaster are par for the course, but plaster that crumbles or flexes when you push on it will have to be replaced. See "The Crack Detective" in chapter 3.)

3. Jump on the staircase. Is there a noticeable bounce? Are there any noticeable gaps between treads, risers, and stringers? Is the stair pulling away from the wall? (Substantial vibration may mean structural problems that will be quite costly to correct.)

4. Is flooring original and in good repair? (Floors covered with carpeting or linoleum can harbor many problems—especially if you want to restore the original flooring.)

5. Do floors have a pronounced sag or tilt? (Simple test: Place a marble on the floor and see if it rolls away. If so, check for the cause—this could be a serious structural flaw or just normal settling.)

6. Do floors vibrate and windows rattle when you jump on floors? (This indicates inadequate support. Among possible causes are undersized beams, inadequate bridging, cracked joists, or rotted support posts in the cellar.)

7. Check the windows. Do sashes move up and down smoothly?

8. Do window frames show signs of substantial water leakage? (Look for chipped and curling paint at bottom of sash and sills. Although quite unsightly, this can be cured with caulk, putty, and paint.)

9. Is bath tile and grout in good condition? (Missing caulk or grout around the edge of a tub can cause extensive water damage below.)

General Finishes Grade _____

B. FIREPLACES

1. Is the fireplace active with an unobstructed flue running all the way to the roof?

2. Does the firebox have a firebrick liner with a 1 1/2-foot hearth in front?

3. Is there an operable damper?

4. Is the flue lined with a clay-tile liner to prevent fire and fume leakage into the building?

Note: All of the above items are essential for a safe, efficient wood-burning fireplace.

5. Is the masonry cracked or crumbling? Is the fireplace in good cosmetic condition?

Note: Clean and inspect all flues and chimneys before using any fireplaces or wood stoves.

Fireplaces Grade _____
Overall Finishes Grade _____

III. MECHANICAL SYSTEMS

A. HEATING

1. Are there enough radiators or diffusers to heat all rooms adequately? (Sometimes additions or alterations are made without due consideration for upgrading the heating system.)

2. Is there evidence of water staining around radiators? (This can indicate radiator leakage.)

3. Shine a light into the hot-air register. Is there any evidence of deteriorating ductwork?

4. Are the steam radiators dead level or pitched toward the condensate return pipe? (A radiator pitched away from the return is usually noisy.)

Heating Grade _____

B. INSULATION

1. Is there any sidewall insulation evident? (Look near electrical outlets or other openings into sidewalls. It may be difficult to detect sidewall insulation. Ask owner. If possible, ask for work receipt.)

2. Type of insulation (arranged from most problem-free to least effective):

Fiberglass	Cellulose
Rockwool	Foam

Insulation Grade _____

C. PLUMBING

1. Is there adequate water pressure at the tap? (Inadequate pressure may mean the pipes are full of rust and scale.)

2. Does the water look rusty or smell unpleasant? (Find out if this is due to the poor quality of the city water supply or to some other cause.)

3. Do toilets or faucets run continually? (If water is allowed to run long enough, it will wear out the fixture and begin eroding the waste pipe.)

Plumbing Grade _____

D. ELECTRICAL

1. Are there enough outlets (at least one per wall)? Are they grounded?

2. Are the outlets in the bath ground-fault-interrupted (GFI)? GFI means that outlets are three-wire grounded (see chapter 10). (No unrenovated old house will have GFI outlets, but they should be installed as they are essential for safe power in a wet environment.)

3. Is there any surface wiring or regular extension cords tacked to the wall? (These are hazardous conditions.)

4. Are there any pull-chain fixtures? (It is expensive to install wall switches for these fixtures. Note that pull-chain fixtures are not to code in most instances.)

5. Is there a functioning exhaust fan in the kitchen?

Electrical Grade _____
Overall Systems Grade _____

IV. ATTIC

A. GENERAL CONDITION

1. Are there any signs of leaks (such as dark water stains) on the underside of the roof, especially around chimneys, valleys, and eaves?

2. Is the attic adequately ventilated? (Check especially for signs of mildew on underside of roof boards.)

3. Are there any broken or missing collar beams?

4. Are there any cracked or sagging rafters?

Attic Condition Grade _____

B. INSULATION

1. Is there any loose-fill insulation visible between attic floor joists? (This is the best place for attic insulation.)

2. Has insulation been blown into sidewalls? (You may have to take the owner's word for this. In cold weather, you can tell how good wall insulation is by feeling the inside of an exterior wall and comparing with temperature of an interior partition—they should feel about the same.)

Insulation Grade _____
Overall Attic Grade _____
House Grade _____

As the years pass in your old house, use this checklist again and again—a yearly check is a good idea—to help you determine which repairs need immediate attention and which can wait for the time being. A house shifts and changes over time, and you may find that your ideas for restoration change, too. You won't know a house's quirks until you live in it for a few years and your initial plans for a complete overhaul of the third floor may have to be revised with the addition of a new family member or a change in your living habits. So while this checklist can help you make an informed purchase, allow you and your house some time to get to know each other before making any hasty restoration or repair decisions.

CHAPTER 3

Getting Started

Once you've made the commitment to a house, you and any contractors you work with should come up with a comprehensive overall plan for restoration. Most people will phase the job, spreading the work out over months, and sometimes years. An all-at-once restoration will mean that you can't enjoy the house as it's being restored. Most people live in their houses while the job's being done. Carefully planning the work will maximize your comfort at home.

Obviously, you must first stabilize and secure the structure if necessary. Before you jump into a plan, take a look at "The Crack Detective" later in this chapter. It will help you decide which bulging or sagging floors and walls indicate major, costly rehabilitation and which indicate normal settling.

PLANNING THE RESTORATION

To avoid working haphazardly (and the potential for doing the same job twice), think about how to phase the jobs you want to do. Are you in for major structural repairs like jacking up the house and replacing a leaky roof? How can you stabilize the house and make it liveable without regretting your decisions later and creating more work for yourself?

You probably want to settle in as soon as possible. Before you make a hasty decision, remember that much work needs to be done: Take your time. Setting your priorities and making a plan depends on budget, available time, and the scope of the work. Your plans also depend on whether you plan to live in the building. Most people do, so the following guidelines assume that you will live in the house during renovation or restoration. Use them to identify the *when* as well as the *why*.

Before you begin, be sure to

• Obtain all necessary permits before starting work to

avoid expensive and frustrating delays in mid-stream. Building inspectors inevitably pay surprise visits.

• Hire an architect and/or general contractor if the job involves more than cosmetic work. They know how to sequence a job, what permits to get, and who to hire. Professionals can save you time and will probably save you money in the long run.

An architect can help you plan your restoration, even if you do the work in phases. For structural repairs, you may want an engineer, especially for major jobs.

Exterior and Stabilizing

One: Stabilize, protect, and secure against ongoing and potential property damage or personal injury. In other words, protect your investment. Start with any exterior deterioration before going on to the interior.

A. *Stabilize* or *repair* ongoing damage or deterioration.

  1. "Stabilize" is quite different from "repair." To stabilize is to arrest deterioration. To repair is to eliminate previous damage. Decide in every case whether to stabilize only (stop further damage) and defer repair—or whether it makes more sense to go ahead with a complete and proper repair.

      a. Inspect exterior for the number one enemy—water penetration. Exterior leaks eventually cause interior damage.

      b. Fix obvious leaks and water penetration, including downspout problems and the like.

      c. Inspect for and exterminate termites and other wood-destroying insects.

  2. Be sure that a temporary repair does not cause more damage over the long term than it prevents in the short term. If the temporary repair will be expensive—or if it could cause additional damage—do a proper repair immediately. For example, a leaking roof presents potential for continuing and increasingly serious damage due to water penetration. The condition can be *stabilized* with temporary methods, such as removable caulking and cheap aluminum or asphalt flashing. *But,* roof cement on salvageable slates will ruin the slates, though it may temporarily stop the leak. A temporary repair should always be reversible.

B. *Protect* building elements and occupants from *potential* damage.

   1. Eliminate fire hazards such as
      a. Exposed or otherwise improper wiring
      b. Overloaded electrical circuits (if you have any questions, have a thorough electrical inspection by a licensed electrician)
      c. Inspect and repair boiler and chimney (to prevent carbon monoxide buildup, chimney fires, etc.)

   2. Eliminate additional personal injury hazards such as
      a. Broken steps
      b. Electrical shock hazards
      c. Badly bowed or falling plaster; falling building elements
      d. Immediate, blatant health hazards such as friable (loose, crumbly) asbestos, airborne lead dust from chipped paint.

C. *Secure* against the loss or damage of historic elements.

   1. Secure loose building parts such as stained glass panels, ornamental plaster.

   2. Secure building against break-in, vandalism, theft of architectural elements.

   3. Completely mask floors and unpainted woodwork before the dirty work starts.

Two: Make a record and clean first before removing anything or making changes.

A. *Document* the entire building before you change anything.

   1. Take photographs of all exterior and interior conditions. Be sure to get all views of each facade and of each room.

   2. Important: You will want a full account of all your work—not only to look back on the job when it's done, but also for clues to reassembly, decoration, and the like during the course of the project.

   3. If you decide to nominate the building for listing in the National Register, this documentation will be required.

B. *Clean* everything before you make any decisions regarding what's "unsalvageable."

   1. Cleaning takes care of your need to "do something" to make the house your own—without getting you into trouble. It is almost always a necessity. It's an excellent way to get intimate with the building. Go over every inch and get to know the details.

   2. Cleaning an object or area and its surroundings often changes your opinion about what should stay and what should go. Quite often your initial reaction to a material or condition is colored by the dirt and disrepair you find it in. It's tempting to just "get rid of it." But once the area is clean and the general surroundings have been brought up to a consistent level of cleanliness and repair, what was once old and dirty becomes old and interesting.

For example, that mud room in your 1930s house with its original inlaid linoleum floor is dirty and out of date—it has to go. Wait! Don't tear out the floor yet. It looks dismal in a room with crumbling, institutional-green walls, the grease-stained painted woodwork, the filthy windows. Nevertheless, mask the floor before you strip woodwork, patch and paint walls, and clean windows. Now uncover the floor. It doesn't look nearly as bad. Remove the years of dirty, yellowed wax, scrub the floor, and give it a thin coat of a good wax. The old-fashioned, richly colored linoleum has a patina (almost like aged leather). You've learned that the inlaid border is a period detail that can't be reproduced today. Once you see the overall effect, you realize that this linoleum floor is exactly what should be in a 1930s mud room.

   3. *Don't rush, think ahead,* and don't make any irreversible decisions until you've lived in the house a while. Learn what the house has to offer. See if your tastes begin to change.

   4. Under no circumstances should you throw money at the house. Hire a general contractor after you've completed the Inspection Checklist and know what you want to do. Don't rush to buy replacement materials and objects. People strapped for money very often do a better restoration job because they have time to think.

Three: Make a master plan now that you and the house are in no immediate peril—and you've unearthed character from beneath the soot and filth.

This is the single most important step: *If you don't plan ahead, it will cost you to change your mind.* You probably will regret your early work on the house and waste time and money. Do not start in on a room or a project, no matter how limited it may seem, before you've got an overall plan.

If you need help with the sequence or plan, design work, mechanical systems, structural problems, or finding and scheduling outside contractors, this is the time to hire an architect.

The goal is to save money over the long haul, to be as efficient as possible with your money and time, and to have as little of your life disrupted at any one time.

The following areas of work must all be considered in making a plan. They are interrelated and they overlap. For that reason, you must think through each phase of work before you can finalize the master plan and complete the work in a logical sequence.

A. *Structural work* is high on the list of priorities:

   1. It represents a relatively major cost.

   2. It requires that conditions be open and quite often

affects more than just the immediate area of work. Plaster, woodwork, door, and window operation may be affected by jacking, sill replacement, footings, and so on.

3. Repair of structural deficiency may also be important for personal safety.

4. Start with the foundation and sills and work your way up through the building, correcting structural conditions. Don't fix a structural problem at the roof and then jack the house up from the cellar—everything will shift.

5. Structural work is hard to do in phases—this is not recommended.

B. *Reduce operating costs* if you can get a substantial or fast return on your investment.

1. Energy savings
   a. For old buildings, cost-effective measures involve tightening the envelope against infiltration: caulking, weather stripping.
   b. Deal with the old windows: repair, double-glazing, storms, night insulation. Replacement windows may be necessary, but consider their payback period (probably a long time) and the aesthetic impact of replacements.
   c. Evaluate heating plant and system. Upgrade or replace depending on efficiency and ongoing maintenance costs.
   d. Evaluate domestic hot-water system.
   e. Insulation may be cost-effective (attic or roof surely; side walls and basement in some cases).
      Note: Energy upgrading is difficult to do in phases (with the exception of weatherstrip and windows) because it involves whole systems, rather than individual pieces, and because it often requires opening up walls. Therefore, energy upgrading should be done early, and a good-size budget must be allowed.

2. Think ahead to maintenance cycles (especially for exterior materials).
   a. Before making fundamental decisions such as repainting the exterior, consider the cost-effectiveness of changing the system. Instead of scraping and repainting a bad surface, would it be better to strip to bare wood and perhaps change to a heavy-bodied, nonpeeling stain?
   b. Anticipate and avoid unnecessary future cost. If you want to save a slate roof, but the steel nails are rusting, don't wait for the slates to begin falling to the pavement.
   c. When replacing materials, match lifespans within a system. For example, don't use ten-year flashing with your twenty-five-year roofing; don't fasten siding that could last seventy-five years with steel fasteners that last fifteen.

C. *The roof* is primary protection from the weather.

1. After you've fixed the foundation and after you've made temporary stabilization repairs to stop leaks, deal with the roof permanently before going on to interior finishes.

2. Although the roof is expensive and not particularly glamorous, it will save you money and tremendous time in the long run to fix it first. One of Murphy's Old-House Laws is that an old roof *will* leak without warning as soon as you've completed interior plaster restoration.

3. Consider the time of year. If the roof starts leaking from an ice dam in the middle of winter, you can't do much about it until spring.

4. Site work. While you fix the roof and related water-directing components (gutters, etc.), attend to regrading, drainage, and foundation waterproofing as necessary.

D. *Mechanical systems*—plumbing, heating, and electrical—rank high on any priority list for several reasons.

1. They are central to the comfort and practicality of the house.

2. Systems repair or replacement are high-ticket items that must be paid for early on, to help determine what's left in the budget for finishes.

3. Work on mechanical and electrical systems requires that walls, floors, and ceilings be opened up, so they must be tackled before any finish work. ("Finish work" means more than decorative finishes—it means anything that covers the framing, including plaster.)

4. It is best not to work on mechanical systems in phases. It is often inefficient and adds cost for contractor call-backs. But if budget dictates, or if you are doing all the work yourself, consider phasing it this way: Do all the roughing for mechanical systems first so that you can close up walls. Install plumbing and electrical risers in this first stage. Once the systems are in the walls, add bathrooms or kitchens (designed earlier, installed later) as budget allows.

For example, you may want a small guest suite in the unused third floor someday. A bathroom up there will require a new plumbing riser to run up all three storeys, making a mess on all floors. Better to do it now, and close up the walls. The bathroom fittings and fixtures can be installed later without any disturbance in the rest of the house.

5. Think ahead to *lighting*. So often lighting is overlooked until the end of a project, when it is thought of as part of furnishing the room. Consider placement of chandeliers and sconces before the plaster is repaired.

E. *Liveability,* or *health, safety, and sanity* are crucial issues if you live in the house during renovation. In planning, consider measures that improve the liveability of the house, even before demolition or repair begins on the inside.

1. Health
   a. Do whatever is required to avoid eating and sleeping in a dusty atmosphere.
      i. Do the work all at once to avoid prolonged exposure (rather than letting it drag on).

ii. Hire a contractor if necessary to expedite this work.

b. Avoid chemical fumes such as paint strippers, paints, finishes, and cleansers.

c. If the work cannot be finished quickly, then try to isolate the work area from eating, sleeping, and active living areas. Hang heavy plastic tarps, tape up doors, build temporary partitions, and hang temporary doors.

d. If necessary, plan a phased approach that will allow you an undisturbed living area at all times.

2. Safety

a. Do any work that creates a new hazardous condition quickly, especially if you have children in the house. For example, replacing porch decks, reconstructing stairs and rails, and rehabilitating windows.

b. Build or provide temporary decking, safety rails, and the like required for safety.

3. Sanity. Remember, you and other members of the household have to live through this renovation. Weigh priorities accordingly.

a. Try to complete demolition all at once as this is usually the dirtiest, dustiest, most physically disruptive, and most psychologically disturbing part of any job. This is especially true for interior plaster demolition—get it over with.

b. Start with those areas that are most important to you emotionally. Renovation always takes longer than you ever imagined, so don't set yourself up to "do without." If cooking at home is central in your life, finish the kitchen first.

Four: Sequence for exterior restoration. Not all of the following will apply in every case; every general principle has exceptions. This list is the standard order for proceeding with work on the outside of the building—after inspection, stabilization, and planning.

A. *Demolition* and removal of debris.

B. *Stabilization* of deterioration and repair of serious damage, including wood, masonry, and metal. (Stop further deterioration; see page 38.)

C. *Structural work* from the bottom to the top, including chimneys and masonry. Insulate or waterproof as required while conditions are open.

D. *Site work* including regrading, drainage, waterproofing.

E. *Roof repair or replacement,* flashing, gutters, vents.

F. *Paint stripping* of masonry, wood, and metal.

G. *Masonry repairs* and repointing; large-scale wood and metal repairs and replacement.

H. *Window, sash, and door repairs.*

I. *Staining* or priming.

J. *Caulking,* glazing, puttying.

K. *Painting.*

L. *Clean-up* and labeling; storage of maintenance items.

Interior

Interior renovation is more complicated and fussy than exterior work. With exterior and structural repairs you salvage existing elements without damage to the materials and character of the building. In other words, you "fix it."

Interior work is more complicated because all your decisions are interrelated. Interior work also directly affects your comfort in the house while the work is being done. You may have to modify or update areas such as kitchens and baths just to make them functional. In other words, you are faced with "changing it" while you "fix it."

Remember, even if you're facing a one-room-at-a-time job, the master plan for the whole building must be scripted first—and adhered to. There's nothing worse (or more expensive) than going backward.

Five: Phased approaches for interior renovation. You've come a long way. The building has been stabilized, leakage has been stopped, you've got a grip on an overall plan, and the exterior restoration is well under way.

Before you can finalize the sequence for interior work, you must make a fundamental decision: Will you bring the entire building along in the most logical and efficient way, or will you phase the work by breaking it down in deference to liveability or budget?

A. *Unoccupied Building*

1. For an unoccupied building, the fastest and most cost-effective procedure is for each area to be brought along at the same rate. All the demolition, all the mechanical systems, all the replastering, all the stripping, all the painting, and so on.

2. Although it is by far more efficient to work this way—because there is virtually no contractor call-back and no steps backward and little time wasted on interim cleanup—it means that the entire building will be in the same degree of mess. It is nearly impossible to live in a building that is undergoing this kind of restoration.

B. *Occupied Building—The Phased Job*

• You will almost surely want to phase your restoration work if you are living in the building. Phasing is also necessary when there is not enough money in the budget to do everything at once. Some things, of course, are impossible to phase. You can't reroof this year and pay for flashings next year. But you can certainly tackle roofing one year and clapboards the next.

• Beware of gray areas that cost you extra in the long run. For example, it is possible to rebuild a chimney after the roof has been replaced, but there will probably be some damage to the new roof during the masonry work. If budget had allowed, it would have been better to have the mason come before the roofer.

• Always try to sequence the work so that there is minimal disruption to adjacent areas.

• Whenever a wall, ceiling, or floor is opened up, always think ahead and take advantage of the opportunity to get into the building's guts. For example, if an exterior wall is opened up, consider installing insulation, electrical or plumbing risers, nailers for built-ins, and so on. If a stair soffit is open, listen for squeaks: tighten wedges and make repairs from below while you can.

Several approaches to sequencing work can help:

1. The *living-without-finishes* approach—completing a room or area up to the point of liveability but without any finishes or decoration. You can move into a room that has mechanical systems installed, sound plaster, and a fairly clean floor. (Items you can hold off on until the rest of the interior is finished are installation and finish on baseboard and most trim; light fixtures; final floor treatment; priming, painting, and wallpaper; all decorating.)

   a. The disadvantage to this approach is that you have to live without the aesthetic satisfaction of finishes, sometimes for quite a while. There is time wasted in moving into an area and then moving out again for final finishes, but this is almost unavoidable to some degree if you're living on a job site.

   b. Advantages to this approach:

   i. The house will ultimately function fastest this way.

   ii. You don't have to commit to colors, furnishings, style, or decorating until the whole house is restored, at which point you'll have a better overview of its true character.

   iii. Any minor damage that occurs in the finished room when adjacent areas are being renovated will be easy to repair. For example, heavy work in the next room may cause hairline cracks in the already-patched plaster of the finished room. With no paint or paper on the walls, it's quite easy to tape or patch later.

2. The *zone-by-zone* approach—one suite of rooms, a floor, or a wing is brought up to a consistent level of finish before going on to the next area.

   a. This won't work in a small house or one with an open floor plan. It requires a more flexible budget than the room-by-room approach, because you'll be biting off more in each phase.

   b. Logical breaks can often be made, but be sure that plumbing, heating, and electrical risers are brought to deferred areas before any finishing is done elsewhere. You don't want to break into a papered plaster wall in the parlor because you put off even *thinking* about the third-floor mechanicals.

3. The *room-by-room* approach.

   a. The only advantage is a psychological one. You get to savor a truly finished room, which gives you a hiding place and the imagination to go on. (Some people elect to completely finish just the kitchen or a bedroom before tackling the rest of the house; the bedroom is easier.)

   b. The disadvantages are obvious. You will undoubtedly mar or dirty finishes when work proceeds on each subsequent room. Also, it's a very difficult approach to budget.

Note: Do not procrastinate over major messes. It is tempting but unreasonable to think you will "go backward" and make a mess after some or all of the house has been finished. If you know that someday you'll want the hall wainscot stripped, don't succumb to battle fatigue and put it off until you "get over stripping the dining room." Once all the major work is done and you're into selecting wallpapers, you will *never* go back to stripping.

Six: Sequence for interior renovation. Some items here will not apply to you as there are always exceptions. However, professionals approach jobs, whether it's the entire interior or one room, in this sequence.

A. *Demolition* and removal of debris.

B. *Structural work.*

C. *Framing or alteration* of partitions (nonbearing walls). Installation or closure of soffits, pipe chases. Sub-floor repair. Installation of nailers for built-ins, plumbing fixtures, chandeliers, and so on.

D. *Plumbing and electrical* roughing.

E. *Drywall* installation; lath and plaster repair or installation; taping and skimming.

F. *Underlayment* for new flooring or tile.

G. *Ceramic tile* repair or installation.

H. *Installation of fixtures,* including plumbing, radiators, electrical receptacles. Set fixtures before any additional finishes are added to avoid damage to floors, walls, trim, by outside contractors.

I. *Finish floor* repair or installation.

J. *Woodwork, window, door* repair or installation. Refinish if clean and in good condition.

K. *Finish* in appropriate sequence—no matter which order you choose, there will be overlap and some touch-up work.

   1. Install prefinished woodwork, trim, built-ins.

   2. Prime, paint, and wallpaper.

   3. Refinish floors (sand/stain/finish or scrub/wax).

L. *Touch-ups* of paint and clear finishes.

M. *Hardware,* electrical coverplates, and the like installed.

N. *Clean up* and wash windows.

O. *Gloat.* Wander into finished rooms and stare happily into space.

THE CRACK DETECTIVE

All old houses have cracks in common. Sometimes they are just part of the charm of an old house, and sometimes they mean trouble. By playing Sherlock Holmes, you can decide which cracks are important, what is causing them, and what to do about them. You'll want to take a close look at cracks before you start work. First identify and correct the cracks that indicate structural flaws and instability using the guidelines for crack repair in this chapter and in chapters 5 and 7; other cracks you'll watch over time, correcting as the need arises.

All cracks are caused by movement of the parts of a house. As a crack detective, you use the cracks as clues to find the cause of the movement. Then you can judge whether or not it is necessary to try and stop the movement.

You may decide to live with symptoms of movement and age, cracks and all. More problems have been created by quickie crack repairs than by benign neglect. Gather information over a few years until you are certain about the cause. Wait until you have the money and knowledge to make the right repair.

Detective Tools

Eyes are the most important tool for this part of the investigation. Careful observation uncovers the cracks, tells you what direction they are going, and where they are widest. Also look at the overall pattern of cracks in the room and throughout the house. Evidence that shows the house has moved over time includes suspects such as sloped floors, bulging walls, and doors that don't fit.

For information on suspects, the enterprising detective looks for "telltales" to decipher the seamy underworld of cracks. Telltales appear wherever cracks appear, especially where cracks have been plastered. Using glass or plaster telltales help Sherlock determine whether the crack still moves, and at what rate.

To make a simple telltale, draw parallel lines at each side of the crack. Measure the distance every six months. Chart your measurements on a graph to estimate how fast the crack will grow, or if it promises to remain fairly minor. Cracks occur over time, sometimes many years. Use a ruler marked off in small increments (64ths of an inch) to gauge the slowest movement possible.

Glass and plaster make excellent telltales. Neither one can take much tension before breaking, so a crack will give itself away more quickly. You'll have your suspect if a glass telltale breaks or a new crack appears in a plaster telltale.

Telltales Inside and Out

For sleuthing cracks indoors, plaster offers the most telling clues. Fill a portion of the crack with plaster or spackling compound. Write the date on the dried plaster to remind you when you applied the telltale.

Make a note of when and where walls have been patched. Later, if you see cracks in plaster, then you know the building has moved since the patch was made. Some cracks may have been patched several times. Some of these you'll just have to live with, others may mean structural repair.

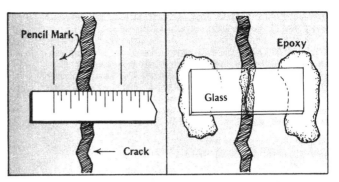

Inside use pencil marks on the wall to track a crack's movement. Outside, epoxy a piece of glass over a crack.

Outdoors, use a glass telltale. Epoxy a single-strength piece of window glass about the size of a microscope slide over the crack. You won't want to do this in a conspicuous spot as epoxy can be hard to remove. Beware the wants of a telltale—on wood, the epoxy may pull paint off the wall before the glass breaks because of a crack.

Evidence: Measuring the Crack

When investigating cracks and their causes, compare all your evidence before judging what movement causes the cracks. Measure the severity of the cracks by their size. You shouldn't worry about very small cracks, but large ones may mean you should move out until the structure gets repaired. With some cracks you won't want to wait six months or more to figure out how fast it's growing. Get severe cracks checked out by a contractor or engineer right away.

To measure the true width of a crack, you must measure the distance between two points that were originally touching. The temptation is to measure the width perpendicular to the sides of the crack, but this is rarely the right distance. Often the sides of the crack will slide relative to one another while making only a narrow crack. Measure the total distance of travel by marking two easily identifiable places (for example, where the crack makes a sharp turn).

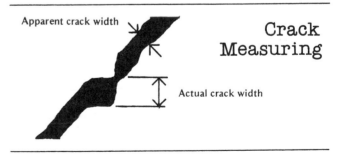

Cracks that have already been patched are sometimes difficult to measure. When possible, try to identify the original sides of the crack before it was patched. Then the total distance that the building has moved can be measured rather than just the width of a fresh crack.

The crack width will help you determine the severity of the building's problem. Small cracks up to 1/64th of an inch are of no concern structurally, and, unless they are extensive, will probably not even be noticed. Cracks this small cause only aesthetic problems on the interior, while on the exterior will allow water penetration. Water, of course, will eventually cause a structural problem. This size crack is easy to spot on the outside of a brick building, but very difficult to see on a wood one. As the cracks increase in size to a quarter of an inch, think about structural repairs.

Notice the shape of the crack. Cracks frequently taper from open on one end to closed on the other. When using the crack chart, measure the widest part of a tapered crack.

Evidence: Measuring a Crack's Moves

A small crack that has just appeared is of more concern than a large crack that hasn't moved for fifty years. Both the length and width of a crack change as parts of the house move. This is why it's important to chart the rate of movement—you'll want to know if it is getting faster or slowing down.

Cracks that don't move are clearly not a structural prob-lem. Often the best way to treat them is to leave them alone. The same is true of *decelerating* cracks, those that move more slowly as time goes by. Eventually a decelerating crack will stop moving and then it can be patched. A crack that is moving at a *constant* rate is more difficult to deal with. If it is moving so slowly that it won't become dangerous for one hundred years, then it is often best to leave it alone.

Sometimes the movement of the building is spread over the length of the wall or floor rather than just happening at one spot. When this occurs, many small cracks will appear rather than one large crack. You can assume the building is still moving if new cracks appear parallel to the old ones. The total width of all these small cracks should be used to chart the rate of movement.

However, if the crack is lengthening and/or widening rapidly, try to discover the reason for the crack and take corrective action. *Accelerating* cracks indicate that the structural stability of the house is being threatened and that the problem will continue to get worse. Action should be taken before the acceleration approaches that of a falling object (for example, the plaster ceiling in the dining room).

A fourth type of movement is *cyclical,* where the crack

Class of Crack	Crack Size		Degree of Damage	Effect on Structure & Building Use
C-0	HAIRLINE		INSIGNIFICANT	NONE
C-1	HAIRLINE TO 1/64"		VERY SLIGHT	NONE
C-2	1/64" TO 1/32"		SLIGHT	MOSTLY AESTHETIC; ACCELERATED WEATHERING ON THE EXTERIOR
C-3	1/32" TO 1/16"		SLIGHT TO MODERATE	
C-4	1/16" TO 1/4"		MODERATE	
C-5	1/4" TO 1/2"		MODERATE TO SEVERE	PLASTER BEGINS TO FALL AND BUILDING BECOMES UNSTABLE AS SIZE INCREASES
C-6	1/2" TO 1"		SEVERE TO VERY SEVERE	
C-7	GREATER THAN 1"		VERY SEVERE TO DANGEROUS	BUILDING IS DANGEROUS

© 1980 Wm. Ward Bucher, Architect

opens and closes in different seasons. The solution here again is to do as little as possible since this type of crack rarely causes structural problems.

The Plot Thickens: Shear Cracks

The direction of a crack is another good clue to its cause. Horizontal and vertical cracks of small size (C-3 or less; see chart) are rarely any cause for concern. Diagonal cracks always indicate that the house is, or has been, in movement—one part of the house has shifted relative to another part.

A diagonal crack in an old house is almost always at a 45-degree angle to the floor or wall. Diagonal cracks indicate a phenomenon called *shear,* which results from either tension or compression. When a solid material is pulled or pushed enough, it shears or breaks along a 45-degree angle and slides to a new position. Brick walls, plaster-covered stud walls, and plaster ceilings all can act in this way.

By observing which way diagonal cracks slant and which end of vertical or horizontal cracks is wider, you can determine the part of the house that has moved from its original position. The key to finding the cause of a crack is discovering the movement pattern of the house.

Though it's hard to imagine a wall being pulled apart, *tension shear cracks* are very common in old houses. Tension results from one part of the building staying in place while another part sinks. For example, a column may rot at its base and sink while an outside wall stays in place. One end of the wall above will then drop relative to the other end. Since the plaster on the wall can't move far without breaking, it shears along the familiar 45-degree angle.

The top of a tension shear crack points toward the end of a wall that has dropped from its original position. If, instead of the column sinking, the outside wall had settled, the crack would have slanted the opposite way.

Tension cracks may also appear because of lintel failure in brick or stone walls. If the arch or piece of stone or wood at the top of a door or window stops doing its job,

such as the mortar weakening, the brick above the lintel starts to drop. As the brick is pulled down by gravity, the wall on the side of the opening is pushing up. This tension creates two shear cracks that run from the top corners of the opening to form a triangle above the door or window. Since the mortar is often softer than the bricks, the cracks tend to follow the pattern of the brickwork, creating a stepped pyramid appearance.

When one part of the building pushes down on another part, *compression shear cracks* appear. Less common than tension shear cracks, they are easily identified because there will be some crushing of the material along the line of the crack.

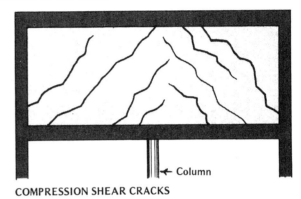

COMPRESSION SHEAR CRACKS

One kind of compression shear crack occurs when the outside of a building settles into the ground while an interior bearing wall or column stays in its original position. In this case, the column is pushing up while the exterior walls are pushing down. A wall that is above the column will shear in compression, causing 45-degree diagonal cracks whose tops slant toward the column.

Both tension and compression shear cracks set up an overall pattern that can be readily observed. Frequently these cracks come in groups that literally point to the cause of the problem. Since houses are usually divided up into many rooms, it is not possible to see the entire pattern at one time. The direction of cracks should be noted in each room and mentally added together like a jigsaw puzzle. Start at the top of a house and walk down floor by floor, checking rooms and halls on the way. One of the best places to look for cracks is in closets, since they are often not patched and painted with the other spaces.

When your mental picture of the crack pattern is complete, you should be able to determine the location of the cause. Sometimes the cracks will only be found in one corner of one room. This would indicate a localized abuse, such as a rotten beam end. Other times every room in the house may have been affected by cracking.

False Leads

There are some cracking patterns that do not necessarily indicate structural problems. The first is *alligatoring* of plaster walls and ceilings. This pattern is an interconnected grid of small cracks in a roughly rectangular form. On close inspection, one direction of the cracking follows the lines of studs in the wall, or joists above the ceiling;

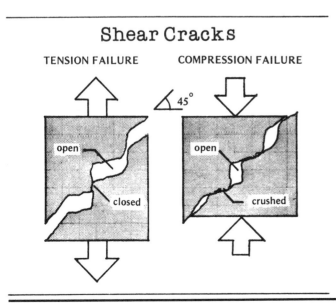

Shear Cracks

TENSION FAILURE   **COMPRESSION FAILURE**

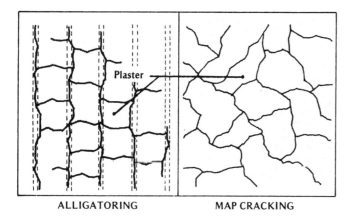

ALLIGATORING | MAP CRACKING

the other direction of cracking is a bit more random, but follows the line of the spaces between the wood lath behind the plaster.

The alligator pattern may develop after the plaster has been in place fifty or sixty years. As cracking continues, the plaster will eventually fall down. The solution is to replace the plaster or repair it. This type of cracking is caused by a failure of the plaster finish material, not by a structural problem. A similar pattern is called *map cracking*. Here, the cracks form enclosed areas surrounded by cracks, like a map with a lot of countries on it. This may be caused by the plaster's finish coat flaking off the base coats of plaster. This is, again, a failure of the finish, not the structure of the house.

Map cracking is sometimes seen on an outside wall, or on a ceiling that has had a water leak. The cracks have a puffy deposit of plaster sticking above the original surface, and are usually accompanied by peeling paint. Before you patch, the water penetration must be stopped. Although this map cracking pattern is not directly caused by a structural problem, the area around the cracking should be checked for possible wood rot due to the water.

Corroborating Evidence

Further clues to understanding cracks are found by observing the way the building has changed shape. In most cases, older houses were made as straight as their builders could manage. Over time, though, they bend, bulge, and sag. Even when the builder wasn't able to make things truly square or rectangular or circular, he usually could manage to make them reasonably straight and plumb and level: The walls were parallel, and the floors were perpendicular to the ground. Over time, many houses move out of plumb, which then causes cracks.

To check the plumb of walls, use one of the world's oldest measuring devices—a plumb line. This is essentially just a weight on a string. You can find a plumb bob (the weight) at any hardware store, but any small heavy piece of metal will do in a pinch.

While standing on a ladder, hold the plumb line next to the wall. To check exterior walls, hang the plumb line from the roof or out a window on a windless day. Sight along the string to see if the wall leans outward or inward. Measure the distance between the string and the wall at both the bottom and top to determine the amount of lean. Generally, the most important thing is to note the direction of lean.

Look around room perimeters to check the levelness of floors. There is often a space below the baseboard trim where the floor has dropped. Sometimes this gap is so large, a new shoe moulding has been used to cover it up. Note which way the floor slopes. Drop a marble at several places around the room to see which way it rolls. The levelness can also be checked with a carpenter's level: Set it on a long board, and lift the low end of the board until the bubble is in the center of the level. Measure the distance between the end of the board and the floor to determine the slope of the board.

Look at other parts of the house that were originally horizontal to see if they are still level. The easiest to see are the tops of doors, window sills, and stair treads. You can identify the general pattern of movement by noting that all of the doors slope down toward the center of the house, or perhaps toward one side of the house. This knowledge helps the detective uncover the culprit causing the cracks.

Don't Overlook the Obvious

Generally, the newer the building is, the straighter it started out in life. This is the result of greater and greater use of machines in the manufacturing process. Lumber from the sawmill, milled steel, and machine-made bricks all are much straighter than broadaxed beams, wrought iron, and sand-cast bricks. It's a good idea to keep the age of the house in mind when evaluating movement clues.

The age of the building is important for another reason. Brick and wood are relatively stiff materials that don't react if you try to bend them quickly, but after carrying the load of a building for long periods of time they act differently. Beams can sag or deflect incredible distances under continuous heavy loads without ever breaking. Brick walls can slowly bow outward without cracking on the outside. The older the building, the more likely it will bend under its own weight.

The weight on a floor or roof makes the joists or rafters sag in the middle. A small amount of sag always happens, but too much can cause falling plaster, and in extreme cases, collapse of the floor. By sighting along the ceiling you can often see a visible sag, usually in one direction. Holding a flashlight next to the ceiling will create a shadow if the ceiling bends.

Ideally, the amount of floor sag when the building is full of furniture and people will be small enough that the plaster ceiling below will not crack. Over the short term (one day) the amount the floor deflects divided by the length of the joists should be less than 1/360. For example, this would be a deflection of about 3/8-inch over a 12-foot length. Ceilings with drywall can sag more without cracking (1/240). House floors with this amount of deflection (or less) are usually very safe.

Over the long term, a loaded floor can continue to sag very slowly without cracking the plaster on the ceiling below. Eventually this deflection can be so great that you feel like you're running down hill as you enter the room. Unfortunately, there is no easy rule to determine if such a floor is safe. Contact an architect or engineer familiar with old houses for advice. After measuring the length and size of the joists, an architect can determine whether they are stiff enough and strong enough to carry the weight.

Finding the Source: Checking the Foundation

Now that you know your cracks, take a look at the exterior (e.g., foundations and porches) and walls to determine the root of the problem. You'll see more cracks as you move in to repair faulty foundations, wet basements, and sagging beams. For now, you need to identify problems that need immediate attention. Until you uncover the culprit that caused the cracks, you don't know how serious the condition is. Until you have a suspect, you can't take corrective action. Start your search with the major offenders:

- Ground and foundation erosion and settlement
- Material decay—rotting wood or seeping cement
- Renovation vandalism
- Structural failure
- Change in materials or geometry
- Moisture and temperature changes

Ground settlement is probably most often indicted, but not as often convicted. We often say that parts of a house that have moved from their original position have "settled." However, individual parts of the house moving downward isn't the same as the whole house sinking into the ground.

Different parts of the house settle before other parts. If the entire house sank into the ground at the same rate after it was built, it would experience little stress and little or no cracking. It might be hard to tell that the house even settled. Check the bottom stair on the front of the house. If it has a shorter riser than the rest, then you have a clue that your house has settled.

Most cracks appear when parts of the house settle at different rates. This is known as *differential settlement.* The very shape of the house is a frequent cause of differential settlement cracks. Many an old house is like a rectangular box with all sorts of projections: steps, porches, bays, wings, and so on. It's as if the heavy central box sinks into the soil faster than the projections. The projections are "ripped" off the main box. Naturally, cracks tend to develop at the places where projections are joined. These cracks are usually tapered—open at the bottom and closed at the top.

Exactly the opposite movement sometimes occurs. A heavy set of stone steps that has no foundation may settle faster than the main building, causing cracks where the steps join the wall. (These cracks would be open at the top and closed at the bottom.) A similar cracking pattern

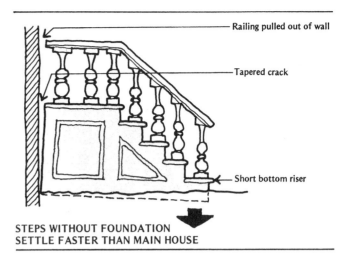

STEPS WITHOUT FOUNDATION SETTLE FASTER THAN MAIN HOUSE

Labels: Railing pulled out of wall; Tapered crack; Short bottom riser

can develop when the house is added to many years after it was built. The main house will have settled a bit for a few years after its construction. A new addition is built at the same level as the original, settled house. As the *addition* settles, cracks will develop between the two parts of the structure. These cracks should be decelerating or stationary a year or so later.

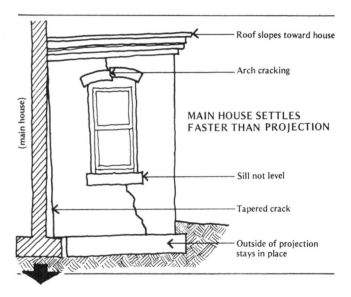

MAIN HOUSE SETTLES FASTER THAN PROJECTION

Labels: (main house); Roof slopes toward house; Arch cracking; Sill not level; Tapered crack; Outside of projection stays in place

Differential settlement occurs most often when the house sits on two different kinds of earth. Imagine one end of a house built directly on solid rock while the other end floats on swampy mush. The end on the rock will stay in its original position while the other end rapidly looks for the bottom of the swamp. A brick house would literally be torn in two by this kind of differential settlement. A crack in the exterior wall from bottom to top would develop above the point where earth changes from harder to softer.

In a wood frame house, crack evidence isn't as obvious. Wood framing and clapboards tend to bend rather than crack. Nevertheless, you can trace a general pattern of cracks from the foundation to the roof in such a case. Whether the house is brick or wood, these cracks will tend to be wider at the top of the building than at bottom.

Underground Crimes

The foundations and footings (or lack of them) may also be a cause of differential settlement. Until after the First World War, there was very little standardization of materials and methods for building foundations. An older house may have a foundation of brick, wood, stone, concrete, or mud. There are two truths about any traditional foundation: It deteriorates and it can't bridge soft spots in the soil.

In swampy parts of the country, wood piles or rafts were often used as the foundation for both wood and masonry homes. As long as the wood foundation stayed completely below water level, it didn't rot. (It is said that there are several stone buildings in New Orleans that are "floating" on cotton bales.) With modern improvements in drainage, unfortunately, the water table often drops below the top of the wood foundation. This causes rapid decay. In this case, the entire building drops down somewhat unevenly and cracks appear almost everywhere.

A foundation is designed to spread the weight of the walls over a larger area to support the house. It was not designed to act as a beam to bridge over holes that might develop from either heavy water flow or soft spots in the soil. It has a lot of weight to carry.

A heavy underground water flow will produce a cracking pattern similar to the failure of a window lintel. Above the point where the support for the foundation has washed away, there will be a stepped pyramid cracking pattern. As the erosion of the soil continues, the pyramid will get larger and larger. Cracking from this cause should be given attention right away.

Suspect water when other kinds of foundations deteriorate too. For instance, the soft lime mortars in older houses can be washed away over the years by water seepage. If the foundation is exposed to running water from an underground spring, this could result in actual collapse of the wall above. But more often the foundation settles gently as small particles of sand wash away. There may be no cracking in the foundation wall, but cracks will appear in the plaster walls above.

Settlement cracking can also be caused by the nature of the soil underneath. During construction, a trench is often dug deeper than the bottom of the foundation. Even though the hole is filled later, that soil is not as compact as the stuff that was undisturbed for centuries. The weight of the foundation compresses the disturbed soil after the house has been built, causing settlement cracks above. Since this type of settlement has usually stopped within five years of construction, it is usually not a problem for the old-house owner.

Another construction problem arises when foundations and footings are too small for the loads on them. Sometimes a builder may have guessed badly or cheated to save money, when laying the foundation. When foundations are too small, the load above them isn't distributed enough and causes localized soil compression. The foundation should adequately carry the whole load of the house.

On clay soil, cyclical cracks may appear, indicating settlement problems. Many clays expand when wet. Since the ground directly under the house is usually much dryer than the earth at the outside walls, the edge of the house will rise in damp weather and fall in dry weather. The movement causes the cyclical cracks, which open and close depending on the season and moisture levels.

Expansive clays will also cause cracks when a permanent change is made in the water table. Improvements in drainage or a new well can lower the underground water level. This dries out the clay soil—causing short-term settlement of the house above.

Checking foundation size may involve pick and shovel work to find out what's below ground. Typically, the bottom of walls and footings below columns will be six to twelve inches wider than the load-bearing structure above them. However, there is tremendous variation in the footings required on different types of soil. On hard clay, walls built without any footings at all may not show any noticeable settlement in one hundred years. But in general, undersized or missing footings *below settlement cracks* should be considered a prime suspect.

Concentrated loads over inadequate footings can also cause settlement. Such loads are found at the end of a beam supporting several floor joists, and at the bottom of a column. When the beam end rests on a wall, it can cause local settlement below, which results in a pyramid cracking pattern. Heavy loads on a column may cause it to sink relative to the rest of the house.

Foundations also can be too shallow. In northern and mountainous parts of the country, the ground freezes several feet below the surface. This will cause the foundation to move unless its bottom is below frozen soil—below the frost line. The effect of frost heaving is uneven

Footings

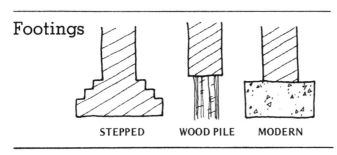

STEPPED   WOOD PILE   MODERN

Eroded Foundation

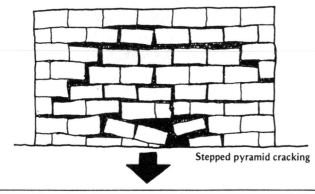

Stepped pyramid cracking

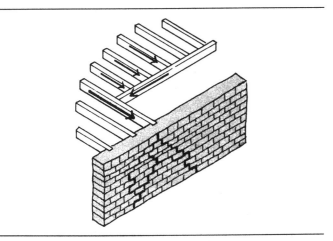

settlement of the foundation. Foundations of dry laid (mortarless) stone may actually take on a wavy appearance over the years. This problem is most common in pre-Victorian and rural houses where the builders were not able to benefit from a local craft tradition.

The Case of the Bowed Wall

An inadequate foundation is also the culprit in the case of the bowed wall. The weight of the wall causes the footing to settle unevenly, which allows the bottom of the wall to tilt outward. If the wall is tied in to the top of the building it will bow outward in the middle. At the corners, vertical tapered cracks will appear that are widest in the middle of the house and closed at top and bottom.

On the other hand, the wall may *not* be attached at the top. This occurs when the front wall of a townhouse was built after the party walls were constructed. The entire front wall can tilt outward; this results in cracks at the corner of the house that are wide at the top and closed at the bottom.

Settlement is the culprit when the structural parts of the house are basically sound but the cracking pattern indicates that parts of the house have dropped from their original level.

Decay of Materials

Nothing lasts forever, and material decay is another common suspect. Decay may cause both local cracking of finish materials and major failure of structural materials. All old houses are made of wood. Even in brick and

adobe houses, wood holds up the roof or floors. The decay of walls, beams, and columns causes loss of strength and/or size, which results in minor and major cracking patterns.

Suspect rot fungi when cracking patterns indicate failure of the wood structure. Look for deep cracks (especially across the grain), musty smells, a dead sound when you tap the wood, and fuzzy white fungus. Common rot fungi prefer dark areas for initial growth, so you may need to remove plaster or other finish materials to definitely identify it. Look in places wherever hidden moisture may be present such as the top of foundation walls, below bathrooms, in basements and crawl spaces, below built-in gutters, and below roof joints. Keep in mind that the cracking may be a long way from the rot that causes it. Decay fungi viciously consume wood and create cracks—kill it on sight.

direction of crack	THERMAL	MOISTURE	SETTLE-MENT	ROT	BEAM FAILURE	JOIST FAILURE	COLUMN FAILURE	BOWED WALL	ARCH FAILURE
HORIZONTAL	✓	✓		✓		✓	✓	✓	
VERTICAL	✓	✓			✓			✓	
DIAGONAL			✓	✓	✓	✓	✓		✓

Insects also cause wood decay. In most parts of the United States this group includes termites and carpenter ants. Both types of insects cause cracks by eliminating so much wood that the strength of the beam or column becomes negligible.

Chemical attack, freezing weather, and erosion are all accessories to masonry decay. Although we think of stone and brick as permanent materials, they decay too. As wood is eaten by its attackers, masonry decays because of its physical properties. Chemical attack includes such common phenomena as salt deposits and acid rain. Unless there is extensive visible damage to the masonry or mortar in a foundation wall, it's unlikely that relatively slow-acting chemical attack is the cause of cracking.

The freeze-thaw cycle in northern climates is easier to convict. As water freezes in masonry crevices, it expands and creates cracks. This type of damage is most often found where poor quality materials were used in the original construction and where there are many freeze-thaw cycles during the winter. One type of brownstone used on Victorian-era townhouses in the New York City area provides a notorious example. New York has numerous freeze-thaw cycles during a long winter. Spaces between the blocks of brownstone veneer provide the perfect place for water to collect, and, to make matters worse, the brownstone (sandstone) was laid up with its natural grain running the wrong way.

The appearance of masonry damaged by salt decay and freeze-thaw decay is quite similar. In tracing down the suspect, see how the cracks are distributed. The salt decay will be limited to those areas where there is a flow of moisture in the masonry. Check the base of walls,

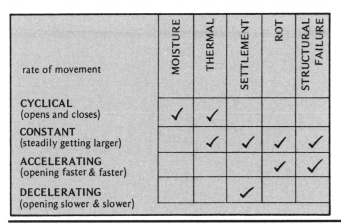

rate of movement	MOISTURE	THERMAL	SETTLEMENT	ROT	STRUCTURAL FAILURE
CYCLICAL (opens and closes)	✓	✓			
CONSTANT (steadily getting larger)		✓	✓	✓	✓
ACCELERATING (opening faster & faster)				✓	✓
DECELERATING (opening slower & slower)			✓		

below windows, and around leaking downspouts. You will find freeze-thaw cracking wherever a particularly susceptible material is used.

Rust is also associated with masonry decay. As iron corrodes it expands in volume, creating pressure where it is embedded in stone or brickwork. In some cases this is easily detected, such as where an iron railing was placed in a hole in a stone step. Shear cracks will radiate from the base of the post toward the edge of the step.

Hidden iron fasteners, called cramps, offer one of the most difficult situations to detect. Cramps hold the masonry work to a bearing wall and may have been covered up. For example, a limestone-faced house may exhibit a peculiar pattern of half-moon-shaped cracks in the stone blocks along every joint. In this case, the stone facing was attached with iron cramps to a brick-bearing wall. The moisture in the wall caused the cramps to rust and expand, thereby cracking and spalling the limestone at nearly every cramp.

Renovators: Victims or Perpetrators?

Suspects who often commit their crimes undetected are the renovators themselves. With great energy and good intentions, they inadvertently vandalize the fine old houses they're trying to improve. *The plumber did it!* If there are cracks anywhere around a bathroom, immediately suspect the plumber. The average plumber has absolutely no respect for the structure of a house. He will drill down and through, saw notches, and leave beams hanging in midair. Brick walls will be bashed out to make the largest possible hole for the smallest pipe. Anything in the way of his pipes will be removed, no matter what the consequences for house or owner.

The plumber often has accessories to his crimes. The electrician, the heating-duct installer, the mason, and the do-it-yourselfer are all guilty of house vandalism on occasion.

You will detect vandalism easily in parts of the house where the original structure has been removed. Even seemingly small changes can create large cracks. Notches and holes in beams can seriously weaken them. Holes that are drilled in the center one-third of the depth of the beam will generally not cause a problem. However, holes or notches near the top or bottom of the beam, or vertical notches, will definitely weaken the structure, especially when they appear at the center of the beam. Notches and

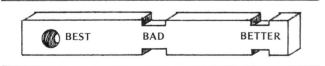

holes at the center of the beam length weaken the beam more than ones near the ends. A weakened beam will deflect or fail, creating cracking patterns in the house above.

Walls, too, can be seriously weakened by holes. Studs are often notched so deeply that less than a quarter of their original thickness is left in place. A house can often accommodate the notching of one stud, but when several studs have been notched in a bearing wall, cracks are bound to result.

Likewise, masonry walls may be damaged by holes. A small hole in a solid brick or stone wall is not likely to have much impact. However, when the hole is located in a relatively thin wall or near an opening, the effect can be much greater. In one case, a renovator had knocked out a few bricks at the end of an arch to install a four-inch dryer vent. Unfortunately, those few bricks were helping to hold the weight of the wall above, and a good part of the brickwork cracked. For the time being, the wall is held in place by the wood window frame, but it could give at any time.

The more that's removed, of course, the more likely cracking will occur. In an effort to "brighten things up," door and window openings are often enlarged. Sometimes these enlargements cause problems because not enough thought is given to what is going to hold up the wall above. For example, a new window may be placed in a wood-frame house without provision of a header over the window. In other cases, the enlargement means that the wall *between* openings becomes so small that it can no longer hold up the weight of the house above.

Moving or removing walls can also create cracking problems. Just because the house doesn't fall down immediately when a wall is removed doesn't mean that the wall wasn't part of the support of the house. When walls that hold up floors (bearing walls) are removed, there will always be deflection of the joists. In addition, removing walls that don't appear to be supporting floor joists can cause cracking. These walls may have served two different functions: stiffening the structure and holding up other walls. The stiffening function reduces "bounce" even when it is not necessary to carry the load of the building and furnishings. Interior walls weigh a lot—a plastered wall weighs about fifteen pounds per square foot. Old houses were frequently designed so that this weight was carried to the ground by "nonbearing" partitions, rather than by the floor joists and wall they bear on directly.

Moving a bearing wall even a few inches should be considered suspicious if you see new cracking patterns. The house is still structurally sound, but it will deflect a little bit differently than before the wall was moved. Cracking will generally stop after a new breaking-in period.

Disastrous things can result from removing apparently unimportant parts of a building. Beam ends may be supported by chimneys and walls in ways that are not immediately obvious. A church group in Washington, D.C., was removing some "unnecessary" brick flues and didn't notice that the brick was supporting a small beam. That small beam was holding up the end of a large beam, which in turn was supporting a brick wall at the fourth-floor level. The entire wing of the house collapsed.

Similar changes in deflection can result from just making repairs to the house. Replacing plaster on lath with drywall reduces the weight of the house considerably. This may cause the floors to deflect upward, causing ceiling and wall-finish cracking.

A particularly serious—and common—form of renovation vandalism involves the removal of the foundation footings. There are many reasons for this move, including wanting to lower the basement floor to put in an apartment, making a basement window into a door, or running a new sewer or water line. Since the footing is only cut off on one side, the weight of the wall begins to tilt the foundation. The results are the same as those with ground settlement: tilted or bowing walls, arch failure, and floor and wall settlement.

An unexpected cause of cracks can be the strengthening of parts of a house. A stiffer beam or wall may actually carry more weight than before it was strengthened. This may reroute the stresses in the house, resulting in a new cracking pattern.

New cracks can also appear when more weight is added to part of the house. This weight is sometimes obvious, as when another storey is added to the top. More commonly, the extra weight comes from small improvements. These include putting on a new type of roof, adding a fire escape, or tiling the kitchen floor. A common weight increase comes with the installation of a new bathroom. In addition to the weight of the plumbing fixtures, the eight hundred pounds of water in a full tub is likely to bend the floor joists below.

A minor, and perhaps unavoidable, kind of renovation vandalism creates cracked plaster as well: The vibration of pounding hammers and buzzing saws can break the bond of plaster to the lath quite a distance from the actual construction work. This eventually creates an alligator cracking pattern.

Now that you've been introduced to the various cracks in your house, you can begin to think about coming up with a comprehensive restoration and repair plan. But old-house restoration rarely proceeds from step one to step five without some undiscovered nuisance—or what is worse, some undiscovered structural problem—that changes your plans entirely. Be sure you fully evaluate the structural condition of your house, particularly the sills and foundation, roof, and walls before planning your repairs. While you should consider all factors and map out a plan, restoring old houses is a bit like making homemade soup—adding a pinch of this and throwing in a taste of that produces a fuller-bodied soup than simply following a recipe by rote.

CHAPTER 4

Tools to Get You Started

Like most people, you're probably planning to take a hands-on role in the restoration of your old house. Before you get started, think about the variety of tools you'll need for the various jobs, from heavy structural work to finishing work. You may have many of the tools described in this chapter on hand, but you may not want to rush out and buy all of them at once if you don't. Think about the work you'll be doing today, tomorrow, or in the next month and start from there. We offer a few words on putting tool kits together for various jobs as well as basic power tools and tools for rough stuff just to get you started.

THE KIT ADVANTAGE

Demolition debris, new materials, tools, and equipment tend to spread out into an increasing jumble the longer you concentrate on the work at hand. Getting organized will do as much as anything to make a remodeling or preservation project successful.

Keeping the clutter under control has two important benefits. The first is saving time and money. When you need a different size screwdriver, you can jump over the sawhorse and pick your way through a tangle of extension cords and electric hand tools, or walk directly across the room and select it from a row of sizes in your tool box. The second benefit is that you and your old house will be safer the more you keep things in order. Accidents happen where there is disorder.

Try using a system of tool kits to bring order to your job sites. Keep all the tools and supplies needed for a particular task, such as painting, in a "kit" or box. When you grab the paint kit, you'll have just about everything required to complete a painting task.

Collect a variety of boxes and crates in which to store your kits. You don't have to take the time to make fancy boxes. Fruit lugs—what your grocer gets his cherries and plums delivered in—are perfect for heavy tools and cans of supplies. Fruit lugs are lightweight, about the right size and shape, and usually free.

Is it worth it to take this kit approach when working on an old house? After all, you'll probably end up with more than one of the same tool. For some tools, the extra investment can be worth it. For example, if you had just one 1 3/8-inch putty knife, you might lose more than an hour of your time hunting for it. Good putty knives cost about $4.50. Five putty knives represent $22.50 worth of putty knives. $22.50 is worth just a little more than an hour of a professional renovator's time. With five putty knives, you're saving time as well as money. The kit approach definitely makes sense in a commercial setting, and often will in private settings too.

For do-it-yourself homeowners the kit approach will make sense if you are doing your whole house, even if the work is spread out over several years. You might need only two putty knives—an appropriate investment for the return you would get. On the other hand, separate kits for upstairs and downstairs in a large house might save miles of running between floors.

To put together a kit, just start doing the work. Then, take whatever tools you have gathered up by the end of the job and put them in a box. Of course, there may be a few tools that are too expensive to own more than one of, such as a saber saw or skill saw. Just make a note of these tools on the side of the box, and store the tool in the shop. The next time you pull out the kit, you'll see quickly what you need to make the kit complete.

Although we're talking mostly about tools here, the kits also include supplies that go along with the work, such as paint thinner in the paint kit. And you could have job boxes that hold special tools, materials, or parts such as hardware for each job you have going.

Safety Considerations

There are three important items not included in any of the kits listed here. The first is a pair of welder's goggles with clear shatter-proof lenses to protect the eyes. The second is a pair of earplugs to protect ears from noisy machinery. The third is a respirator, good against dust and fumes, to protect your lungs.

BASIC KITS

You may practice a wide variety of trades as you do the work—carpentry, brick masonry and plastering, and painting. Here are a few tool kits to get you started:

—PAINT KIT—

Brush, 2-inch natural bristle
Sash brush, 2-inch
Round brush, 3/4-inch
Small artist's brush
Paint thinner, 1/2 gallon
Brush cleaner, 1 quart (second-hand thinner)
Brush comb
Brush spinner (cleans brushes with centrifugal force)
3-pound and 1-pound coffee cans for cleaning brushes
Several 1-pound coffee cans for paint pots
Clean rags
Pack of newspapers
Masking tape
Paint shield (6-inch × 12-inch aluminum flashing, to keep paint off adjacent surfaces)
Hornet- and wasp-killer spray can

—PAINT REMOVAL KIT—

One of the most useful paint removal tricks is to grind and shape special scrapers to match moulding and turning profiles. So this kit includes tools for making special scrapers.

Hot-air gun
Electric heat plate
3 kinds of chemical remover (one with a spray-on applicator)
Several ordinary hook-type scrapers with packs of fresh blades
2 sets of hook-type scrapers with replaceable shaped blades
Files—flat, curved, round (for sharpening scrapers)
Small power grinder (for shaping scrapers to match mouldings)
3-pound coffee can with cover (for paint chips)
1-pound coffee can (used as pot to hold chemical remover)

—MASONRY KIT—

This kit includes tools for brick masonry, including tuck pointing and chimney repairs. Tools for hand plastering and plaster repairs are included too.

Pointed trowels (10-inch, 4 1/2-inch)
Straight trowel, steel (4 1/2-inch × 11-inch)
Concave trowel, steel, for taping wallboard (4 1/2-inch × 14-inch)
Convex trowel, steel (4 1/2-inch × 11-inch)
Pointing trowel (1/2-inch × 6-inch)
Browning brush (natural bristle, for splashing water on plaster)
Brick hammers (14 ounce, 20 ounce, for cutting brick)
Scrub brushes (natural bristle, for cleaning brick)
String and cord
Abrasive block (for smoothing cut bricks)
Joint rake (for cleaning soft mortar out of brick joints)
Level (14-inch)
Set of wood blocks (for spacing quarry tiles)
Toothed trowel (for spreading mastic adhesive)
Hand lotion
Alum (for controlling the set of plaster)
Cans (a variety of sizes for measuring proportions)
Plastering hawk (this may be too big for the kit, but keep it nearby)

—CARPENTRY/WOOD KIT—

Hammers (16-ounce framing; 12-ounce regular claw)
Combination square
Framing square
Nail puller (ram-pinch type)
Crosscut saw (20-inch × 10-point)
Rip saw
Dovetail saw
Coping saw
Keyhole saw
Sharpening stone and oil
Wood chisels (1/2-inch, 1/4-inch)
Gouge (3/4-inch)
Paring chisel (1-inch)
Awl or ice pick
Thin prybar
Level (2-foot)
Angle copier
Compass or dividers
Wood rasp (flat and round, 12-inch)
Rattail file
Nail sets (2 or 3 sizes)
Utility knife
Linoleum knife
6-foot folding wood rule
25-foot steel tape

—MECHANICAL/METAL KIT—

Ball peen hammer (16-ounce)
Hacksaw
Small hacksaw (blade-in-handle type)
Slotted screwdrivers (3 sizes)
Phillips screwdrivers (2 sizes)
Adjustable (Crescent) wrench
Vise-grip wrenches (big and small)
Wire brush
Large channellock wrench
Pliers (regular and needle-nose)
Medium-size bastard metal file
Plumber's cold chisel
Diagonal cutters
Tinsnips
Putty knife (2-inch)
Paint scrapers

—POWER TOOLS—

3/8-inch reversible variable speed electric drill
7 1/4-inch builders' saw (Skilsaw)
Electric sander (optional)
Electric scroll (saber) saw

PORTABLE POWER TOOLS

Portable power tools can be the greatest time-savers for homeowners doing their own renovation work. Unfortunately, power tools are not cheap, so it's important to decide which tools are indispensable and which can be postponed or omitted. Set priorities about which tools are the most versatile and will pay for themselves the quickest. Many companies now rent a variety of power tools. Be sure the tools you rent are in good working order before leaving the store. Check your local yellow pages under "Tools" for rental outlets. Most of the tools here are for carpentry, though some tools such as drills and sanders may certainly be used for more than just woodworking. With a few basic power tools, a homeowner can even do some simple cabinet and millwork; more sophisticated cabinet and millwork, such as frame and panel doors, and the like may require more elaborate equipment.

The most important consideration in selecting which types of power tools to buy, of course, is what kind of work is being done. For example, if you're planning to do a lot of trim work, you'll want a tool that will make quick, accurate crosscuts. Basically, any woodworking task that can be done with a power tool can also be done with hand tools. Often it takes a little more skill to do something by hand, but the major difference is in the amount of time it takes. So figure out what kind of projects you'll be spending the most time on, and focus on the tools you need to expedite the work.

Basic Portable Tools

All power tools come in various grades, no matter what the brand. Usually the range runs from home-handyman grade to professional-contractor grade, often with various models somewhere in between. To determine the right grade for you, consider how often you'll be using the tool and how heavy duty the work is. Within reason and budget, buy the best grade of tool available. Unless you're prone to losing tools, you'll have that tool for a very long time; unlike computers, tools don't become obsolete. If you're fairly sure that you'll use a certain tool very occasionally and for fairly light-duty work, then purchase the homeowner grade. The higher-grade tools are designed to take more abuse, and they also often have more powerful motors, making the task go faster with less effort. A higher-grade tool also may have better bearings for longer life, more accurate and easily adjustable guides and controls, and a better feel and balance in your hand.

When comparing the power rating of different models and different brands, look at the amperage rating of the motor, not the horsepower rating. The amperage rating is the most accurate indication of the motor's power. The higher the amperage, the more powerful the motor is. It's important for the motor to have adequate power for the job; an undersized motor will not only slow down the work but will also, under continuous use, tend to overheat and burn out prematurely.

Circular Saws

Just about every power tool collection includes a circular saw. The most popular size is 7 1/4-inch, which refers to saw-blade diameter. With the right blade, a circular saw will crosscut or rip any piece of wood up to about 2 1/2 inches thick, thicker if the cuts are made from opposite sides. Smaller and larger saws are available as well, but these are designed for fairly specific work. There are *10-inch framers saws* that are ideal for cutting large pieces of framing lumber and heavy timbers. These are powerful, heavy-duty saws, but they can be somewhat heavy and unwieldy for regular use. Little *trim saws* for fine cabinet work range in size from about 3 to 6 inches, and some are even cordless. Trim saws are excellent for fine work but are limited in power and depth of cut when working with larger pieces of lumber.

A circular saw is only as good as the blade that's in it, so don't scrimp on the blade. A good quality carbide-tipped blade will work much better than the one that's supplied with the saw. Be sure to suit the blade design and number of teeth to the task at hand.

Drills

An electric drill tops the list of Must Haves. If you're doing more than hanging a few shelves or towel racks, get a *3/8-inch drill*. A *1/4-inch drill* is limited to 1/4-inch or smaller drill bit shanks (the part that gets clamped in the chuck). A 1/4-inch drill also has limited power. If you think you'll be doing a lot of heavy-duty drilling, such as drilling holes for plumbing and electrical work, consider a *contractor-grade 1/2-inch drill*. The type with the extra side-mounted handle gives you two hands' worth of leverage.

Most drills are variable speed, an essential feature because it allows you to go slowly to get a hole started, and because each different type of material you drill through requires a different speed to maximize the speed of cutting and minimize the build-up of heat in the drill tip. (It also pays to buy a reversible model that enables you to back out screws and mired bits.) Variable speed is also useful when you use the drill for other purposes. A wide range of attachments are available for electric drills, everything from screwdriver tips to sanding disks.

Screw Gun

Screw guns were designed to drive drywall screws for hanging sheetrock, but they have many more uses than this, especially in renovation work. If you have ever tried nailing around crumbly old plaster, you know how quickly the plaster lands on the floor. A screw gun can be used to fasten things through the plaster, as well as refastening the plaster itself. Plaster that has come away from the lath, and plaster and lath that has come away from the studs, can be refastened by using plaster washers in conjunction with drywall screws. The screw gun does not jar the plaster the way a hammer and nails do, and so it offers a far less destructive process. It's also useful for attaching sheetrock patches in areas of missing plaster.

A screw gun is indispensable for building and installing cabinets. Even though you can put a screwdriver bit into an electric drill and drive screws, a screw gun is far more effective. The screw gun's magnetic tip holds the screw in place while starting it. More important, an adjustable clutch mechanism automatically stops driving the screw when it reaches the right depth. This has two major advantages: It allows you to drive the screw very rapidly to the right depth and also allows the motor to spin free as the clutch disengages, instead of forcing the motor to grind to a halt the way a drill has to. This ensures longer motor life as well as allowing you to drive screws at a very rapid rate. Screw guns were designed as a contractor's tool, so most of them are fairly heavy duty. As with other tools, compare motor amperage. Also check to see how easy the clutch is to adjust.

Driver Drill

A driver drill, a hybrid between a screw gun and a drill, is generally used for heavy jobs. It can be used as either a drill or a screwdriver, though unlike a screw gun, it has the power to drive a screw straight through a wall. It has a regular drill chuck with an adjustable internal clutch that releases when it reaches a certain preset torque (twisting force). This differs from a screw gun in that a screw gun stops when the head of the screw reaches a certain depth regardless of the torque required. Driver drills are also usually cordless with a rechargeable battery pack. If you intend to use a driver drill for construction work, be sure it has a powerful battery pack. The battery packs vary from 6 to 12 volts. For heavy service, 12-volt is preferable. The more torque settings the tool has, the more you'll be able to control the depth to which the screws are set.

Reciprocating Saw

When you work on an old house, it will invariably require some demolition, even if just for installing plumbing and heating. A reciprocating saw (sometimes called a sawzall, which is really a brand name) is the fundamental power tool for demolition. When used carefully, it can allow you to sneak pipes through tight places, move entire partitions intact, or neatly cut out rotted framing members. When used carelessly, it can destroy the structural integrity of a house in a few short hours. Because a reciprocating saw is a contractor's tool, most are fairly heavy duty. They are also rather expensive, but if you're doing a lot of major demolition and construction, the time savings may justify the cost.

Shop Vacuum

A vacuum is not really a construction tool as such, but it is essential if you're going to do any interior work while living in the house. If you attempt to use a household vacuum to clean up construction dust, especially plaster dust, it will last only a few months. Shop vacuums come in a variety of sizes with a wide range of attachments. It's better to buy a major brand than a department-store type. If you're going to vacuum plaster dust, be sure to buy the type with replaceable bags and filters, and replace them often.

ROUGH STUFF

Before getting down to the picky finish jobs, there's always rough carpentry and basic production work to do. For the rough stuff, have the following tools on hand.

Staple Hammer When you have a lot of non-precision stapling to do, staple hammers are a whole lot faster and easier to use than a staple gun. They are *the* tool for putting down felt or rosin paper. They're indispensable for roofing jobs. They're also excellent for installing foil- or paper-backed insulation. Try to buy the manufacturer's staples too—"also fits" brands tend to jam.

Holesaws Holesaws are extremely versatile if you buy the top-quality *bi-metal* type. These types are welded together from several pieces of steel rather than stamped from a single plug, and have much harder teeth. Holesaws that thread on to individual arbors (the rotating shaft of the saw) are also a plus.

Good holesaws can cut through all kinds of wood, metal, and plastic; with a little care, they usually work on slate, marble, and ceramic tile, too. With bits up to about 2 inches in diameter, you can drive them safely with a 3/8-inch electric drill, but go any larger than that and you'll need the power and chuck of a 1/2-inch machine.

There are two big points to remember when working with these tools: (1) Holesaws do not "chip" well; you have to clean the kerf out regularly or the saw will just spin without cutting; (2) for large holesaws, work slowly and carefully with two hands on the drill—these tools grab easily and develop tremendous torque that can spin the drill out of your hands and damage the work (or break a wrist!).

A favorite trick of some is to gang two holesaws on a single arbor to accurately enlarge an existing hole (for instance, when changing locksets in a door). Start with an individual-type arbor and mount a holesaw the diameter of the existing hole in the normal manner. This will be the "pilot bit." Then remove the locking ring and nut from the back of the arbor and mount a holesaw the size of the new hole here. Thread on the locking nut and tighten it behind the second holesaw. Now you have a hybrid tool that will cut perfectly concentric holes.

Ship Augers When you have to bore deep holes in lumber thicker than 6 inches, you need a ship auger. These tools look like rejects—they have no feed screws or side cutters, and only a single twist—but they burrow through wood long after other bits dull or break. No feed screw means you can pull the auger out of the hole to clear chips without stopping or reversing the drill. To start a ship auger accurately, you have to bore a pilot hole with another bit or use a guide (like a washer or some pre-bored scrap).

Cobalt Twist Bits If you're trying to bore through tough metal such as stainless steel, and regular high-speed steel bits don't suffice, use cobalt bits.

Combination Carbide Circular Saw Blade Use simple, stamped-steel saw blades for some work (they can be ground razor sharp), but for rough carpentry use a carbide-tipped combination blade. Carbide blades dull with usage as any blade will, but they keep a moderately sharp edge many times longer than plain steel. They can also take a lot of abuse—like slicing through roof decking and a little flashing or hitting a nail or two. A *combination blade* means one that works adequately for a variety of cuts and materials.

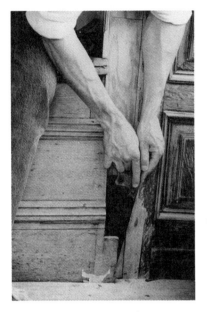

A small crosscut saw is tailor-made for trimming woodwork in tight or hidden places.

A blade with a set that cuts a wide kerf is good for notching without a chisel. Set the saw blade to the depth of the notch desired, then make successive cuts through the lumber the full width of the notch. After kerfing away about 35 percent of the notch like this, it looks like a comb, and you can usually clean the rest out with a few swipes of a hammer.

Hatchet A carpenter's hatchet—not a Boy Scout's hand axe—makes quick work of trimming or splitting lumber for framing (new work and demolition), scaffolding, shoring, masonry forms, and stakes of all kinds.

Sledgehammer You don't have to be John Henry to find a use for a sledgehammer. In fact, the best way to handle one is like a putting iron. A 10-pound head is a good all-purpose size, useful for heavy carpentry tasks like tapping wedges into place or "adjusting" the position of timbers or whole carpentry assemblies. A sledgehammer is also handy for demolition of cast-iron soil pipes or radiators. Believe it or not, this metal cracks like an eggshell if you strike it repeatedly in the same spot or where it has been scored.

Vise-Grip Pliers Vise-grips have many uses, particularly for trimming the tails on bolts and nails. When bolts are 1/4 inch or under, just clamp the pliers on tightly a thread or two after the nut and work them back and forth. The bolt will break almost as cleanly as if it was hacksawed off. You can do the same with nails when the ends are in the way (when altering framing, for instance) but you can't pull or hammer out the entire nail.

Wrecking Bar The list of uses for a "gooseneck" wrecking bar in a hefty size (2 feet long or better) is endless:

- Prying up flooring or sheathing
- Pulling lath and plaster off a wall
- Pulling nails
- "Plowing" up shingles or roofing
- "Pinching" (levering) heavy items
- "Whackin'" stuff

"Shorty" Saw A little 12-inch crosscut saw is light and small so it's never a chore to carry from job to job, and it fits in tight places—like wall cavities—where you can't work with a regular saw. Always keep it sharp (which is easy since there aren't many teeth), especially the toe, which you'll probably use for starting blind cuts in floor repairs and the like.

We've described just a few of the tools you'll need in restoring your old house. As you work, you will undoubtedly discover others. Before beginning any job, think ahead and collect the tools you will need. Throughout this book you'll find notes on more specialized tools as the need arises. (For example, you'll find tips on woodworking tools in the chapter on woodworking.)

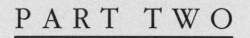

PART TWO

RESTORING THE EXTERIOR

CHAPTER 5

Sills and Foundation

With exterior repairs, most experts recommend starting at the top of your house and working down. You first want to secure the house from water damage by repairing the roof and gutters. You then may need to tackle major repairs to the foundation and sills. Your next step involves securing the rest of the exterior from the elements without remuddling. However, there are no hard-and-fast rules in old-house restoration; you'll have to assess the condition of the house overall. You may need to make minor repairs to the roof to stop water from pouring in and get right to major structural work on the sills and foundation.

Though your first line of defense will be a proper drainage system from roof to ground level that diverts water away from the house, one big job starts at the bottom. Without a secure foundation and proper drainage, the house will bend and bow under relentless moisture and the effects of soil movement. There are no miracle cures: Waterproof coatings and patches slopped onto interior basement walls will probably fail miserably. Examine the foundation, inside and out, thoroughly. While moisture creates problems from both inside and out, make sure you first stop the rain from coming in.

The foundation of a house is intended to act as a waterproof envelope similar to the hull of a ship, allowing the building to float in a sea of mud and wet earth. When a boat leaks, you can seal the openings on the outside with caulk, or you can bail furiously in the bilge. There are various solutions, too, when a foundation allows water to pour in. The remedies vary in effectiveness—and in investment of labor, materials, and dollars.

Because buildings, construction methods, materials, locations, and climate all differ, there is no one correct answer. The successful method of stopping water intrusion, therefore, may be chosen by trial and error, by economic limitations, by comparing notes with a neighbor who has a similar problem, or by consulting an experienced architect or contractor. The condition of your house will be a factor too. Obvious structural problems should be dealt with immediately.

Approaches to correcting the wet basement problem fall broadly into two categories: indoor and outdoor solutions. For the most part, resort to indoor solutions when the plumbing is bad or moisture is trapped in the structure. Outdoor solutions present a messier job and securing the actual foundation itself. If you're unsure, consult an engineer or contractor for advice. Since water's deleterious effects usually begin from the outside and work their way in, you'll find both indoor and outdoor solutions in this chapter. Before you begin major structural work on the foundation, check the house's plumbing, note the peak damp periods in the basement, and other clues to see what's causing the problem. Will a new interior drainage system do the trick or will you need to excavate the foundation and regrade and install new gutters?

In many cases, the only answer lies in excavating down to the bottom of the foundation wall. Out comes the shrubbery, grass, walks, and everything else in the way. It may feel like digging the Erie Canal! You'll have to parge and waterproof the foundation walls, install drain piping and gravel, and cover it all up again. In severe wet-basement conditions, it's the best, most cost-effective technique for permanently reducing ground-water seepage through foundation walls.

THE ADVERSARY: WATER

Assess the capabilities of the enemy well before you settle into a strategy for battling incoming water. If you try interior solutions such as parging interior basement walls and still have a wet basement, you need to go directly to the source of the problem.

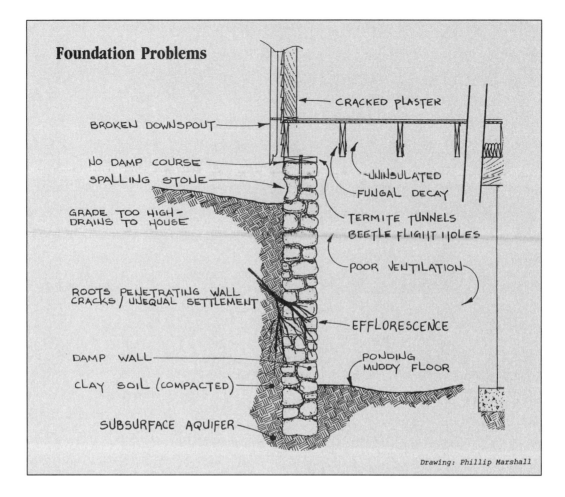

Foundation Problems

CRACKED PLASTER

BROKEN DOWNSPOUT

NO DAMP COURSE
SPALLING STONE

GRADE TOO HIGH—
DRAINS TO HOUSE

UNINSULATED
FUNGAL DECAY

TERMITE TUNNELS
BEETLE FLIGHT HOLES

POOR VENTILATION

ROOTS PENETRATING WALL
CRACKS / UNEQUAL SETTLEMENT

EFFLORESCENCE

DAMP WALL

PONDING
MUDDY FLOOR

CLAY SOIL (COMPACTED)

SUBSURFACE AQUIFER

Drawing: Phillip Marshall

Water moves through buildings and soil in a constant effort to balance itself. *Hydraulic pressure* exerts some of the strongest mechanical forces known. Floods, the shattering of dams, or the carving of the Grand Canyon all represent water's destructive effect when allowed to go unchecked. Water relentlessly seeks its own level, and few obstacles long withstand its action. Thin coats of cement or paint may stop water from intruding into the cellar or crawl space temporarily, yet any dam eventually needs shoring up or repair. Even the legendary Danish King Canute could not stop the tides from advancing when he commanded them to cease in an attempt to prove his great power.

Water seeping through foundation walls by *hydrostatic pressure* exerts force against any impervious barrier. It breaks the adhesion between the masonry and its coating material, and eats away at the mortar. Parging and cementitious or latex- and oil-based waterproofing treatments will slough off when moisture accumulates behind it. Settling or heaving will crack these coatings, regardless of their thickness, allowing the water in. Sealants that stop up pores in masonry can cause water pressure and subflorescence to build up behind the interior face. Thus, coatings can promote spalling and deterioration—conditions as harmful as the problem they were meant to solve.

Cracks, fissures, gaps, or voids in the masonry walls act as open spigots, bringing water pouring into the basement. Unless your house needs major structural repair,

you should do these repairs on the inside, even though their cause comes from the outside. Foundation walls can breach due to shifts in the soil caused by compaction, frost heaving, or expansion of water-saturated earth, especially in older houses built without footings. Voids can be created by masonry units deteriorating or merely falling out of place due to mortar failure. Rubble walls constituting the foundations of some buildings were often dry-laid, with mortar used only on the interior face to give a finished appearance. Fissures in these walls often lead directly to the outside, and must be stopped up.

Voids one-quarter to one-half inch can be patched with high-performance sealers, such as butyl or polysulphide caulk or latex masonry filler. These are all available in cartridges for gun injection. The cracks must be brushed clean and be dry for successful results. If the crack exceeds its width in depth, then it must be packed with screening or oakum or plastic filler rods first. Epoxy mortar can also be troweled into the spaces or, if the crack is wet at the time of repair, then a water-plugging patching mortar can be used. These are formulated with hydraulic cement, which expands in place and cures even when wet.

It must be stressed that these procedures may work permanently—or then again, for only a short time. In addition, the water that would have flowed through the repaired crack may merely have been rerouted, and will enter at another weak spot in the wall.

POINTING MASONRY

While brick, stone, and concrete all can absorb and conduct moisture, the outright flow of water through a seemingly solid masonry wall most often occurs at the mortar joints. Constant saturation by ground water can cause dissolution and deterioration of lime mortar. Repair these joints by *tuck-pointing* from the inside.

When a wall leaks due to faulty mortar, it is virtually impossible to determine the defective areas accurately by visual inspection. In this case, point all joints adjacent to the trouble spot. It will save labor and money to be complete and thorough from the start in this process, as too much is better than too little.

Preparation for tuck-pointing entails removing the old mortar to a depth of 1 inch; this assures adequate bonding between the new mortar and existing masonry. In cases where the joints are less than 3/8-inch thick, only a 1/2-inch slot is needed (as long as the mortar beyond that depth is sound). This procedure should be done with hammer and chisel. Power tools won't help you with this job, as they can easily damage the edges of the masonry. This is especially important in the case of old brick. Removing the hard, high-fired exterior exposes the softer, porous interior, which will more easily absorb water and dissolved mineral salts—thus causing spalling. All loose material must be removed, usually with a stiff fiber or wire brush, then hosed with a stream of water or air.

Water and Masonry

In each of its physical states, water has a deleterious effect upon interior masonry. As a liquid, water is drawn into brick or stone walls by capillary action, being conducted from moist soil into the masonry. This condition is known as *rising damp.* The slightly acidic nature of precipitation allows the water to react with the lime in the mortar, causing deterioration after a number of years. In addition, the water can serve as a vehicle for bringing dissolved mineral salts (as from fertilizer) into the masonry units. When the water evaporates, the salts remain inside the wall and cause *subflorescence;* or salts are deposited as a whitish stain on the surface, which is called *efflorescence.* The crystalline salts remaining inside the masonry exert mechanical pressure, which causes *spalling,* the crumbling or flaking of the masonry face. Finally, water trapped in fissures or pores in stone or brick can cause serious cracking of mortar, masonry units, or sections of wall through expansion as it changes from a liquid into its solid state, ice.

Mortar Specifications

New mortar should be carefully formulated to closely duplicate the proportions of the original mortar. Modern premixed bagged mortars contain too great a percentage of portland cement, thus creating a hard, inflexible high-strength mortar that stresses the masonry. This in turn leads to spalling and even cracking of bricks or stones.

High lime mortar is easier to work, more durable, can self-seal small cracks, has the least volume of change due to climate conditions, and is the traditional mortar used in early buildings.

The materials making up the mortar used in repointing an old masonry wall should have the following specifications:

- Cement—ASTM C 150 Type I or II portland cement. Gray is acceptable for areas that won't be seen, but non-staining white will provide better color for visually prominent areas. You will need one 94-pound bag per cubic foot.
- Lime—ASTM C 207 Type S Hydrated Lime for masonry purposes. Use one 50-pound bag per 1 1/4 cubic feet.
- Sand—ASTM C 144, clean, well-graded sand of medium to fine particle size. It should match original sand as closely as possible. Use one 80-pound bag per cubic foot.

General formulations for mortar vary, but a local mason can assist in duplicating the original mix. The following specifications have been used by the sources cited for varied situations. They can serve as a starting point, at least, for the concoction of the appropriate mortar for your situation.

All ingredients must be dry-mixed thoroughly, raked and turned over until there is an even, consistent appearance indicating that the cementitious material is evenly distributed throughout the mass. Then the mixture should be prehydrated to prevent shrinking when it dries and to improve its workability.

To prehydrate, mix again, adding only enough water to make a damp, stiff mortar that will retain its form when pressed into a ball. Keep it in this damp condition for one or two hours, then remix, adding sufficient water to make

FORMULATION OF MORTAR
Proportions by Volume

	TPS*	CS**	CS**	TPS*
Cement	1	1	1	1
Lime	5	3	2	2
Sand	12	2	9	6
	For masonry walls of high lime mortar, consisting of brick or soft stone.	For stone or rubble walls of durable masonry units.	For walls whose mortar contained a high cement content, or for applications with extreme weathering.

*Technical Preservation Services, Heritage Conservation and Recreation Service, U.S. Department of the Interior.
**Consulting Services, Society for the Preservation of New England Antiquities.

FILLING A JOINT

Chisel a narrow groove at the joint of the floor and the wall, 1/2-inch to 3/4-inch wide, and extend it down through the slab. This is an awkward, knuckle-bruising operation, and to make it even more difficult, undercut the floor slightly in a modified dovetail to keep the repair in place.

After the joint has been brushed and vacuumed, fill it with hydraulic cement, which will cure in the presence of water, or a tar-based joint filler. With cement, pack it into the joint, making sure all voids are filled, and build it up in thin layers until it's flush with the surface. If you use tar-based (bituminous) joint filler, a good trowel-on waterproofing mastic, apply it as you would cement. Finally, pour a concrete curb measuring about 4 × 4 inches in place over the joint. Be certain all surfaces are free of loose particles, and add a bonding agent to the concrete mix to improve adhesion.

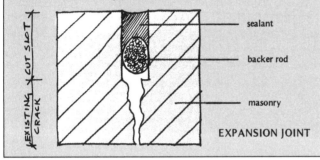

sealant

backer rod

masonry

EXPANSION JOINT

up the proper consistency (which is somewhat dryer than conventional mortar for new work).

To ensure a good bond for the actual tuck-pointing, wet the cleaned joints thoroughly before applying the mortar. Allow any freestanding water to soak into the wall, as the joints should not be visibly wet. Begin by packing mortar into the deepest voids. Then fill the back of the entire joint with a 1/4-inch layer of mortar. When it and each successive layer have reached thumb-print hardness, apply another coat of mortar of the same thickness. Several applications will be necessary to fill the joint. When flush with the wall face, tool it to a smooth, slightly concave surface.

DRAINAGE

Water that does enter the foundation must be collected, channeled, and conducted out of the building in order to minimize damage. Some old houses were constructed with a basement slab that sloped to a floor drain. Regardless of its source, water entering the cellar flowed by gravity to the drain and was conducted to a dry well buried under the floor or to a storm sewer or disposal site beyond the foundation. If water today failed to drain from the floor, the dry well might be full of water, caved in, or silted; the pipe might be frozen somewhere along its length; it might be occluded by roots, debris, a dead rodent, and so on. Remedy occlusion by unclogging with an electric auger.

Water can also make its way into a basement through the joint between a concrete floor and the foundation wall. This inflow may result from poor contact between these surfaces caused by faulty construction or shifting soil, or from an overburdened exterior drainage system.

Diverting Surface Runoff

Surface runoff is a major source of water that finds its way into a foundation. The ease with which precipitation leaves the vicinity of your building depends on soil permeability, depth of the groundwater table, and the topography of your lot. Many interior water problems can be fixed by exterior grade changes and surface drainage. After a rainstorm, look around the building for puddles of standing water, and determine whether they correlate with wet spots on your inventory sheet. (In some soils, it may take up to twelve hours for the water to percolate into the house.)

Any concavities in the terrain close to the house should be filled with soil and lightly tamped, while the height of the soil abutting the foundation may have to be increased so that it slopes away from the walls to deflect surface runoff. In severe cases, the topography of the entire building lot may have to be altered so that it is level and grades away from the house.

If an area is prone to persistent moisture, install an open drainage system near the house to conduct water from the chronically damp areas. These ditches can measure 18 to 24 inches wide by 12 to 15 inches deep, sloping 1 inch in 16 feet. Fill them to just below grass level with clean gravel, and allow them to remain open. These drains should conduct water away from the building to a dry well, collection pond, or storm sewer.

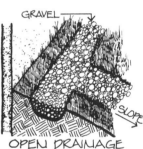

GRAVEL

SLOPE

OPEN DRAINAGE

Dirt and Vegetation

Landscaping has a tremendous effect on how well water drains away from the house. Historical research into landscape architecture reveals that, traditionally, vegetation was kept well away from the building. Plantings at the foundation will stop sunlight from striking the masonry and adjacent soil, keeping them damp.

Vegetation can also block the cellar vents and windows, obstructing air circulation. Root systems and mulch near the foundation improve the soil's water retention—another negative factor. You want the water to move away from the house with the greatest ease. In addition, roots from trees and larger shrubs can invade damp masonry walls in their search for water, often cracking or shifting the foundation. Finally, when conscientious gardeners fertilize their plants liberally, the masonry absorbs the dissolved nutrients, which crystallize, causing efflorescence, subflorescence, and spalling.

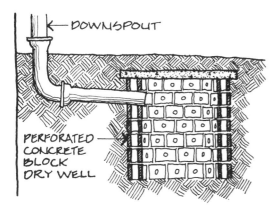

DOWNSPOUT

PERFORATED CONCRETE BLOCK DRY WELL

Over the long history of an older house, increases in the historic grade or the original soil level may accumulate against the masonry walls, threatening the integrity of the foundation. Accretions of refuse or compost from continuous habitation, silt from flooding, fill from excavation, or topsoil from landscaping improvements may have increased the ground level by several feet.

EXPANSION FORCE OF FROZEN GROUND

These volumes of earth may be compacted by settling over time, saturated by precipitation, or frozen by a winter's cold, actions that create internal expansive pressures. Such forces are transmitted as lateral thrusts to the foundation, which was constructed to accept only downward, compressive loads. This may result in cracked or inwardly bowed walls that admit water through the breaches.

To remedy the condition, simply remove the accumulated soil until you reach the original grade. Careful detective work is needed to determine where the original ground level actually was. Old photographs, the location of steps, thresholds, foundation vents, fence posts, and discoloration on building walls can aid in the investigation. Removing the cause, however, will not fix a problem that already exists, so the fill around the foundation may have to be dug up if the walls need to be repaired.

Soil Stability

The soil under a building has some bearing on the building's internal water problems. For instance, highly organic soil acts like a sponge, holding vast quantities of water and keeping masonry walls wet. As the water drains or evaporates from the soil, or the organic matter decomposes, the soil shrinks and the building settles.

On the other hand, earth with a high clay content has a low permeability and is unstable, expanding when wet, shrinking when dry, sometimes with a differential of 50 percent of its volume between extremes. This can alternately create great pressure against walls and shift stone footings, then create air pockets in the earth that will fill with water during the next wet spell.

The top 5 inches of earth on a 1/3-acre lot weigh over 250 tons. To alter the composition of a clay soil, for instance, would require adding tons of sand at great expense. A simpler way of dealing with this is to install subterranean drainage.

Footing Drains Outside

Groundwater in soil around foundations can build up sufficient hydrostatic pressure to force seepage entry through masonry or concrete walls. When a foundation is not too far below the water table, this water can be controlled and carried off by the use of footing drains placed around the outside perimeter of the building. A trench alongside the walls is excavated to the depth of the footing. It need only be as wide as a shovel or backhoe bucket.

Then, perforated PVC pipe or open-jointed clay drain tiles are placed in the bottom. The excavation is backfilled to within a foot of the surface with clean-washed gravel. (This serves as a filter, so any organic material left in the crushed stone will not clog the pipes.) A 6-inch layer of clay soil follows, capped with 6 inches of topsoil graded away from the walls. The low permeability of clay soil discourages surface runoff (i.e., rain) from seeking drainage intended for groundwater only. The pipes should slope about 1 inch in 20 feet and conduct the water by gravity to a suitable collection site located downslope from the building, such as a holding pond, dry well, or storm sewer.

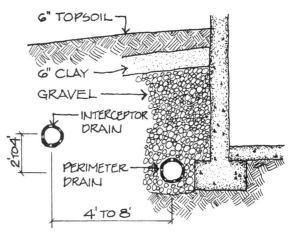

6" TOPSOIL

6" CLAY

GRAVEL

INTERCEPTOR DRAIN

PERIMETER DRAIN

2' TO 4'

4' TO 8'

In instances where the water table is very high or the present foundation drain is overburdened, the system can be augmented by an interceptor drain. It is constructed about 4 to 8 feet beyond or outside of the other drain in the manner just described. Its depth, however, is at an elevation 2 to 4 feet above the footing in order to lower the water table in stages.

SHORING UP THE FOUNDATION

The walls are the last remaining defense against water entering the house's subterranean cavity. Your inspection of the house may lead you to conclude that footings need to be replaced or portions of the foundation need to be repoured. Sometimes the problem lies with the original foundation. You may have rotted or shifting footings, which will need to be reinforced or replaced.

Shoring refers to any temporary support system you use to take the load of the building. *Jacking* simply refers to the actual lifting of a building. The shoring and jacking system you choose will depend on the type of soil underneath and around the house, the type of framing, the amount of settling, and the underlying cause of the problem. Each method must be tailored to the specifics of the building.

Settlement of part of the building will be your first indication of trouble below. In some cases, the location of failure may be obvious; in others, you'll have to dig around a bit. Not all building settlement indicates serious structural problems. However, settlement that is continuous or accompanied by other worrisome symptoms is probably serious.

As the soil settles, it may destroy the foundation. Interior piers or posts may have been set directly into the dirt, where they are subject to rot and insects. In other cases, a post may lay on a thin slab of basement floor that can't support the transmitted load from both the house and soil.

Building timbers near the ground may suffer from moisture, rot, and bugs. Probe the sill, floor joists, and even lower sections of wall studs carefully. Try to find out what caused the failure in the first place and fix the underlying cause. Where did the water come from? If foundations have failed and you are unsure about the proper size and depth for replacement, consult with a reputable contractor or engineer. Other jobs you'll find you can do yourself.

Before you start digging and jacking up the house, carefully consider the temporary support you will use. A building is a series of parts linked together to transfer loads safely to the ground. If any link fails, it creates a dangerous situation. In all forms of woodframe construction, the wall loads are transferred by vertical members (*posts* or *studs*) to a horizontal member (the *sill*) resting on the foundation. In some cases, the sill is a relatively light piece of timber requiring continuous support from below. Or, it can be a heavier piece capable of acting as a beam, which means it can support loads across a span. When the sill timber acts as a beam, it can rest on piers or cap a continuous foundation wall.

If floor joists rest on the sill and are fastened to the sides of the studs, the house has *balloon framing*. Occasionally, joists are mortised into the sill, or rest on a shelf in the foundation. With *platform framing*, the studs do not extend all the way to the sill, but rest instead on a separate piece (the *sole* or *plate*) on the first floor subfloor. Here, the ends of the first floor joists are covered on the outside with a header, which may or may not take some of the load. This arrangement is called a *box sill*. On the interior of the house, floor joists are often supported at midspan by a girder, a heavy beam at right angles to the joists, which is in turn supported on posts or piers.

Foundations themselves must be of adequate size and strength to support the accumulated loads above. Under ideal conditions, foundations should extend below the frost line to prevent heaving. They should rest on footings wider than the foundation wall itself (usual foots are 18 to 24 inches). Footings spread the transmitted load over a larger ground surface. Interior posts or piers should have similar footings, too, as they usually transmit the loads from a large area of the building above through a single post or column. This is called a *concentrated* or *point load*.

Before you start jacking, know the important support links in the house. Find out what connects to what and how the load is distributed. Be especially careful with additions, the most frequent victims of structural failure. You don't want to find part of the building left behind as you raise a section. It's better to do a little demolition now to see what's what than to face an emergency later.

Excavate your jacks first. Don't place them at ground level and then undermine them by digging a hole 3 feet

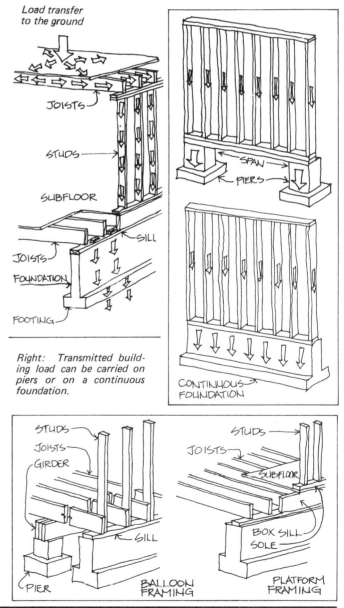

Right: Transmitted building load can be carried on piers or on a continuous foundation.

deep a foot away. If you don't place your jacks on cribbing, put them far enough away so further digging won't disturb them.

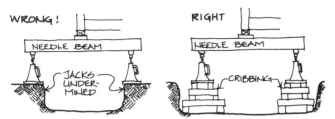

WRONG!

NEEDLE BEAM

JACKS UNDERMINED

RIGHT

NEEDLE BEAM

CRIBBING

When shoring, the weight of the load is transferred to the ground somewhere—you're not actually lifting and nothing is "floating." You can use one of three techniques for transferring the load of the building off the sill or foundation:

- Jacking or shoring from directly below
- Jacking or shoring from under a transverse beam
- Needling through the walls of the building

Jacking or Shoring from Directly Below

If your foundation is insufficient or needs rebuilding, but the rest of the structure is sound, dig out a section at a time and support the house directly from below.

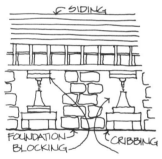

SIDING

FOUNDATION BLOCKING

CRIBBING

Disassemble a small section of the deteriorated wall; dig down to the full depth of the new foundation; locate a jack and tighten it just till it relieves the load on either side of it. (Build the jack up on cribbing, if necessary.) This method makes it possible to dismantle the foundation section by section. Leap-frogging the jacks ensures that too much of one area isn't undermined all at once. Leaving sufficient masonry to support what's above, move three or four feet away from the first jack and insert another one, then go back and remove the section of foundation between them.

If you have a heavy sill in a post-and-beam house, jacks spaced every few feet should support it. If you have a lighter sill designed for continuous support from below, you'll need to spread the support of the jacks with an additional beam beneath the sill. It doesn't have to be a continuous piece, but may also be installed in sections. Never proceed to a new section until you are sure that the first is adequately supported.

Jacking or Shoring Under a Transverse Beam

If you plan to replace the sill, or the bottom of the studs or joint ends are rotted, you'll have to support the weight of the building from a point above the damaged area. You can fasten a beam across the wall and anchor it firmly to the studs or posts. This beam must be stiff enough to carry

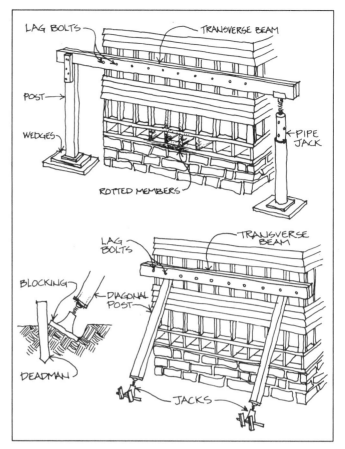

LAG BOLTS

TRANSVERSE BEAM

POST

WEDGES

PIPE JACK

ROTTED MEMBERS

LAG BOLTS

TRANSVERSE BEAM

BLOCKING

DIAGONAL POST

DEADMAN

JACKS

the whole span of the section being worked on. It should be fastened with screws or bolts capable of supporting each vertical member.

A section of siding has to be removed for direct access to the studs. Heavy lag screws should be used to fasten the beam to the studs. On a short wall, this beam can be continued out beyond the corners of the building, then supported with posts to the ground on either end. On a longer wall, intermediate posts may be placed at an angle at intervals along the wall, resting on jacks or driven up with wedges. The post bottoms have to be brought far enough away from the wall so that they don't interfere with the work, but the posts should be as close to vertical as possible to provide the maximum lift with the minimum lateral push. If jacks are used under the posts, their bases should be set at the appropriate angle with blocking, and firmly fastened with deadmen to prevent slipping.

Be sure you know your framing system before lifting a wall this way. If you have balloon framing—and if the bottom of your studs and the joist ends are sound—lifting the studs will lift the floor, allowing access to the sill. But if you have platform framing, or if the floor joists are supported independently on the foundation, the joists must be lifted separately.

Needling Through the Wall

Needling consists of placing a series of beams through the wall to carry the load of the building above. The method can be used by itself to support the sill for foundation replacement, or it can be combined with the transverse-beam method to support the wall from higher up.

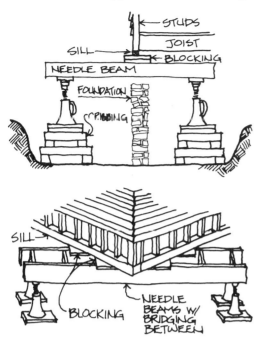

STUDS
SILL
JOIST
BLOCKING
NEEDLE BEAM
FOUNDATION
CRIBBING

SILL
BLOCKING
NEEDLE BEAMS W/ BRIDGING BETWEEN

In the latter case, additional beams are placed under the transverse member at right angles to the wall, each in turn supported by posts on either side of the wall. (That's instead of supporting the transverse member from the ends or with slanted posts.) This procedure means having posts inside the house, which normally must be carried right down to the basement. If that requires a lot of otherwise unnecessary demolition, it's obviously a procedure that has its disadvantages. On the other hand, floors may already be damaged or scheduled for replacement. The advantage of this system is that, while it usually involves

CHECKING FOR CRACKS

While the house is on jacks, check for signs of settlement or separation. Watch corners of plaster walls and trim around door frames. You're the rare one if you don't discover at least a few new cracks. Shear cracks appear when the end of a beam carrying too much weight begins to sag at the wall, creating pressure on the wall around it.

Connections between beams may also be bad, the beam may be too small for the load, or the beam may carry too many joists, creating cracks as you raise the house and the load on beams shifts. That's why it's better to do a little demolition to check the framing before jacking the house.

having more vertical supports, it carries them further away from the foundation, thus allowing more uninterrupted working space.

If needle beams are merely supporting the sill, the interior jacks, being below the first floor, do not require interior demolition of that floor. Here again, take care to avoid point-loading on the sill. Each needle should have blocking to spread the load as far as possible along the wall. Corners of the building may be needled on the diagonal, passing under each wall with jacks on the outside. It is standard to double the needles in this location due to the doubled load of the two walls.

Preventing Lateral Movement

You want to transfer the load of the building in as straight a line as possible to the ground. Lateral pressure occurs as you put the building on jacks; think of it as lifting a boat out of water. In the water, stress on the beam is different. So, too, with a house. The way it behaves to

USING A JACK

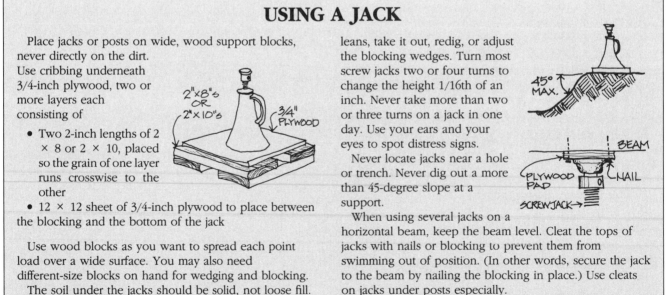

Place jacks or posts on wide, wood support blocks, never directly on the dirt. Use cribbing underneath 3/4-inch plywood, two or more layers each consisting of

- Two 2-inch lengths of 2 × 8 or 2 × 10, placed so the grain of one layer runs crosswise to the other
- 12 × 12 sheet of 3/4-inch plywood to place between the blocking and the bottom of the jack

Use wood blocks as you want to spread each point load over a wide surface. You may also need different-size blocks on hand for wedging and blocking.

The soil under the jacks should be solid, not loose fill. Even so, jacks tend to dig themselves in before they settle in.

Keep all the jacks plumb as you tighten them. If one

leans, take it out, redig, or adjust the blocking wedges. Turn most screw jacks two or four turns to change the height 1/16th of an inch. Never take more than two or three turns on a jack in one day. Use your ears and your eyes to spot distress signs.

Never locate jacks near a hole or trench. Never dig out a more than 45-degree slope at a support.

When using several jacks on a horizontal beam, keep the beam level. Cleat the tops of jacks with nails or blocking to prevent them from swimming out of position. (In other words, secure the jack to the beam by nailing the blocking in place.) Use cleats on jacks under posts especially.

Inspect the jacks constantly to check that the load is distributed evenly. Differential settlement will shift the weight of the load from one jack to another.

2"X8'S OR 2"X10'S
3/4" PLYWOOD

45° MAX.

BEAM
PLYWOOD PAD
NAIL
SCREWJACK

wind loads, banging from heavy hammers or power tools, or even people walking in it, are all different from what you've been used to.

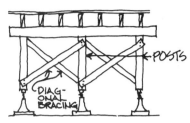

When the whole house or a section of it is supported on jacks, all the jacks or posts tend to topple in the same direction. The higher the posts, the greater the tendency this will happen. Diagonal bracing at the corners of the building or wing and between posts can help prevent this. Tighten these lateral braces just as you would the jacks.

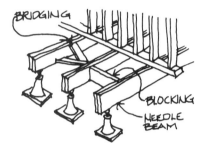

Needle beams should also be stabilized with bridging or blocking similar to that used between floor joists to prevent "roll-over." Nail needle beams to the blocking wherever possible to prevent sliding.

UNDERPINNING

If you don't want to replace the foundation, you may want to underpin it, a major task not to rush into. It basically consists of putting bigger footings under the existing house foundations. And since these foundations are holding up the entire house, it is quite dangerous to dig holes underneath them.

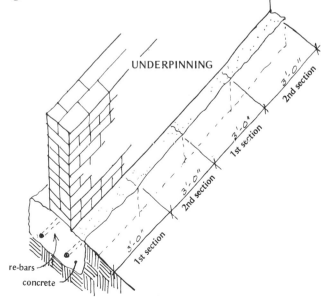

For most houses, underpinning will mean cutting out alternate 3-foot sections under the foundation, putting steel reinforcements in place, and then filling the hole with concrete. After this concrete is hard (usually about seven days), dig out the intermediate sections and repeat the process. The underpinning should be designed by a professional so that it's the right size and has the correct reinforcement for the soil conditions. Hire an experienced contractor to do the work, and if at all possible, have a knowledgeable person watching the workers the whole time they are digging.

Because of the cost and danger inherent in underpinning, it should be a last resort. Try all the other repairs first. In some settlement conditions, underpinning the foundation can be avoided by stopping underground water flow.

Water flow is also the cause of wood rot. Rot extensive enough to cause cracks in the structure will have an obvious source of water. Roof leaks, rising damp, unpainted wood, and uncaulked cracks may all have to be fixed to arrest rot.

Excavation

Some settling is charming, so you may not have to dig out completely from underneath your house. You can work at the outside of the foundation simply by excavating the building—not a do-it-yourself job—and waterproof the outside after pointing, drainage, grading, and the like have been considered. While the building is being excavated away, you can install perimeter footing drains on the inside.

Remove all the dirt abutting the foundation and inspect the outside of the walls for cracks or weaknesses that might correlate with the location of water entering the basement. A severely warped wall or places that have settled dramatically and can no longer support a load should be rebuilt. Seek a contractor's advice in this case. The probability, however, is that you'll find only cracks, voids, and failed mortar; they can be repaired by patching and tuck-pointing.

PARGING

In more severe conditions, parging the exterior of the foundation walls *after repointing* will help ensure a dry crawl space or basement. To parge, coat the masonry wall with two 3/8-inch layers of mortar, using the following formulations in the table below.

Proportions by Volume

Lime	1	—
Cement	1	1
Sand	3	3
	Gives a more flexible, plastic coat.	Gives a strong, hard coat. Add a bonding agent for greater adhesion.

Brush the wall free of all loose particles of dirt, and dampen it. Trowel the first coat on the masonry face, filling any inequities and voids. Before it hardens, scratch the surface with a stiff brush; the second coat will bond better to this rough texture. After twenty-four hours, dampen the first application and trowel on the second coat. After hardening, keep the parging damp for at least forty-eight hours to allow proper curing. Be sure to extend both coats of mortar downward over the footing, forming a cove at its joint with the wall. The parging must extend several inches above grade so that water cannot seep in behind it and loosen its grip on the wall.

COSTLY SHORTCUTS: BENTONITE WARNING

If a contractor offers to fill holes in your foundation wall with Bentonite, beware. Bentonite should seal foundation cracks from the exterior. But why fill a hole with a porous clay? Bentonite is actually weathered volcanic ash that is filled with dry sodium bentonite. According to the theory, as water flows into the cracks in the walls, it will carry bentonite with it, plugging the holes in the walls. The National Home Builders' Association and others discourage using this method. It has been found to be ineffectual and far from cost-effective.

Apply both coats so that they are thicker at the bottom than at the top. A slight difference of one-quarter to one-half inch will create a mild taper that will allow the earth to move upwards (as it tends to do when frozen) without thrusting against the wall.

Closing the Exterior Seal

The final answer to moisture problems is a bituminous (tar-based) membrane, impenetrable by water. It can be applied to any smooth masonry wall, or to the final parge coat after curing and drying. If there will be no shifting, settling, or cracking, then use a brush-on (good) or trowel-on (better) foundation-waterproofing mastic.

In a superior approach—and one which further stabilizes and protects the parging—you coat the foundation and footing (over the parging, if any) with a layer of hot roofing tar, then cover it with a roofing felt or nylon mesh. Coat the fabric with more tar, another layer of felt or mesh, and two final coats of tar. Then backfill as described in the section about exterior footing drains (see page 63). Water won't get through this barrier.

ROOF RUNOFF

Before you start digging holes or patching and parging downstairs, check the water flow from above. Up to this point, without properly routing rain water and snowmelt from the roof to the ground, your repairs to the basement will be like the Dutch boy with his finger in the dike, or the sailor bailing out a leaking lifeboat. Check the flow of water on the outside. How can you control, stop, or divert water from entering the masonry walls?

Since all water begins its cycle as precipitation, examine the condition of the roof drainage: gutters, downspouts, and leaders to the eventual disposal area. Gutters are meant to gather rainwater or snowmelt as it leaves the roof; downspouts conduct it along the side of the building away from wall surfaces; additional leaders or splashblocks divert it away from the foundation.

Without functioning gutters, roof runoff may flow down along the side of the building, soaking the walls; or plummet to the ground, splashing back and saturating the lower walls and foundation. If the earth around the building becomes saturated, hydrostatic pressure forces entry though the masonry walls. These conditions can cause paint failure, wood decay, mortar disintegration, rising damp, masonry staining, subflorescence, and spalling.

The importance of installing—and especially maintaining—an adequate roof drainage system cannot be overemphasized. It is the first line of defense against wet basements. If no gutters are in place, consider installing them. Mount the gutters so they drop 1 inch every 16 feet to allow a good flow to the downspouts. Install a leaf strainer at the ends to prevent clogging by leaves and other debris.

If there are gutters already in place, inspect their fastenings and slope. Go out and look at them during a rainstorm to confirm that the runoff is actually entering the trough, not undershooting and flowing down the wall. If the latter is the case, extend the edge of the roof with flashing or tar-backed aluminum tape to properly conduct the water.

Every six months after installing the system, clean the gutters of organic material, gravel from asphalt roofing, and the like, and make sure the downspouts are clear and fastened securely to each other and the building. Be sure the leaders direct the collected water away from the building, preferably to a storm sewer or dry well, in such a manner that the flow will not return to the vicinity of the foundation. All the labor and time spent installing gutters, downspouts, and fixing the foundation will be wasted if you don't maintain the system.

CHAPTER 6

The Roof

Water is a building's number one enemy, and the roof is your first line of defense. Roofing materials take the heaviest beating from sun, wind, rain, snow, and ice. As a result, the roof should get the most frequent inspection and attention.

In addition to its functional importance, the roof plays a major role in how the building looks. Both the type of roofing material and how it is applied can have a highly positive—or negative—impact on the building's appearance. Choose roofing materials both for their durability and for their aesthetic appeal.

Use the roofing Inspection Checklist on page 70 to determine if your roof will need repair or replacement. Generally, if more than 10 to 15 percent of the roofing material needs repair, you should replace the entire roof. Replacing the roof entirely allows you to thoroughly check the condition of roof decking, rafters, and cornice. This is the time to replace boards that have rotted from leaks and condensation. However, many roofs may only require replacing damaged sections.

Of course, you may elect to roof over the old material. We don't recommend this as it adds weight to the roof framing, which may not be adequate for the increased load. More important, you may just be papering over rot conditions that will continue undetected. You'll have to replace the entire roof in the long run anyway. Roofing over is particularly bad on flat roofs with asphalt roll roofing as moisture will be trapped between the old and new layers. Never lay new roofing over a slate roof either.

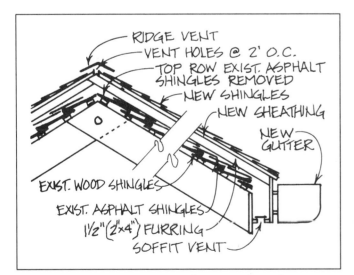

In some cases, it's possible to roof over an old roof to preserve historic building materials. Here, an existing cedar shingle roof had already been roofed over once with asphalt shingles. To save the original cedar shingles, the contractor removed a portion of the asphalt shingles at the top, installed new sheathing, and provided plenty of ventilation with a ridge vent and soffit vent.

Old cedar shingles and nailing strips are visible in the attic. Over-roofing preserved the historic materials.

INSPECTION CHECKLIST

Checking "yes" to a substantial number of items indicates major roofing problems that call for replacing the roof in the near future.

General Condition: Exterior

Yes No

Missing, broken, or warped shingles or tiles. (Pay special attention to southern roof slope; this takes heaviest beating from the sun.) — —

Active leaks that need immediate emergency repair — —

General Condition: Underside

Water stains on rafters or roof boards. (Check especially at chimney, valleys, around vent pipes, and other projections through roof, and at eaves. Investigate on a rainy day so you can tell if staining is a current or a past problem.) — —

Flat Roofs

Bubbles, separation, or cracking in the asphalt or roofing felt. — —

Roofing feels loose and squishy underfoot. — —

Water ponding on roof. — —

Mineral granules or gravel has weathered away. — —

Roofing felt looks dry and cracked. — —

Roofing Materials

Asphalt Shingles: Especially check shingles on ridge, hips, and at edges. These suffer the most wear.

Lumpiness on roof, which may mean a new roof has been applied over old shingles. — —

Mineral granules almost totally worn off shingles. — —

Mineral granules in gutters and at base of downspouts. — —

Edges of shingles look worn. — —

Nails popping up. — —

Mold or moss forming on shingles. — —

Slate and Clay Tiles

Broken or missing slates or tiles. (More than 10 to 15 percent of slates or tiles deteriorating?) — —

Rusted fixing nails. — —

Nails popping up or letting go. — —

Slate flaking apart. — —

Slate particles collecting in valley flashing. — —

Metal Roofs

Substantial number of rust or corrosion spots. — —

Signs of previous "tar pot" patch jobs. — —

Punctures in metal. — —

Broken joints and seams. — —

Wooden Shingles and Shakes

Yes No

Laid on open sheathing. (If not, provide proper ventilation in attic.) — —

Moss or mold forming on wood. — —

Cupping or warping of wood. — —

Wood uniformly thin from erosion. — —

Related Roofing Elements

Flashing

Loose, corroded, broken, or missing flashing. (Copper, the best flashing material, will show a green patina.) — —

Roofing cement on flashing. (May indicate leaks that may or may not have been corrected.) — —

Uncaulked openings at the tops of flashing. — —

Vertical joint doesn't have both base flashing and counterflashing. — —

Projections: Anything through the roof surface such as ventpipes, chimneys, TV antennae, etc.

Connections around lightning rods, finials, vents, weathervanes, and other projections properly flashed and watertight. — —

Mortar joints in chimney badly weathered. — —

Chimney flashings not tight. — —

Gutters and Leaders: Pay special attention to built-in gutters, which can feed hidden leaks directly into the cornice and down into the main structure.

Clogged, rusty, loose, askew, or tilting gutters. — —

Open or missing seams. — —

Seams broken in metal linings of built-in box gutters. (In addition to resoldering, you may need to add expansion joints.) — —

Cornice

Badly peeling paint on the cornice, especially the underside. — —

Galvanic Action

Ferrous metals touching dissimilar metals. (This causes corrosion through galvanic action.) — —

Porch Ceilings

Peeling paint, rotting, or curled boards in porch ceiling. (This usually means faulty drainage from the roof above.) — —

CHOOSING MATERIALS

Asphalt shingles offer the cheapest modern roofing material. While asphalt shingles may save you money initially, they may cost you more in the long run with replacement and maintenance. More important, a cheap asphalt shingle job can radically detract from the beauty of a building that originally had a more distinctive roof. The average roofer will recommend asphalt shingles, but you'll have to make the decision by balancing cost on one hand against longevity and appearance on the other.

If budget is the main inhibitor to choosing traditional materials, phase the job by patching the existing roof to

Program for Exterior Restoration

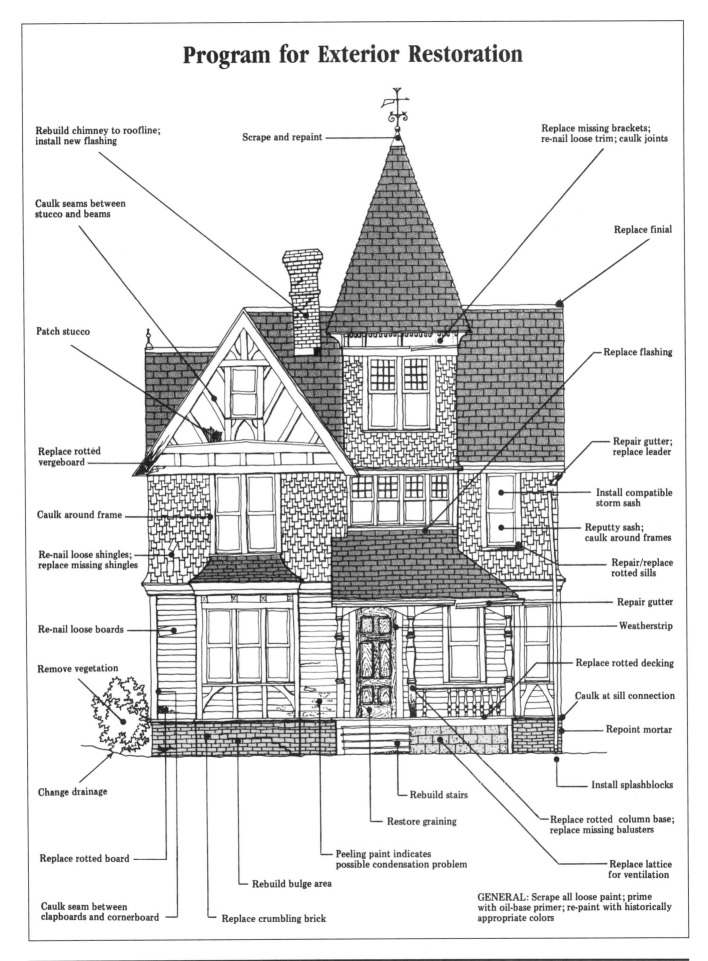

Rebuild chimney to roofline; install new flashing

Scrape and repaint

Replace missing brackets; re-nail loose trim; caulk joints

Caulk seams between stucco and beams

Replace finial

Patch stucco

Replace flashing

Replace rotted vergeboard

Repair gutter; replace leader

Caulk around frame

Install compatible storm sash

Re-nail loose shingles; replace missing shingles

Reputty sash; caulk around frames

Repair/replace rotted sills

Re-nail loose boards

Repair gutter

Weatherstrip

Remove vegetation

Replace rotted decking

Caulk at sill connection

Repoint mortar

Change drainage

Install splashblocks

Rebuild stairs

Restore graining

Replace rotted column base; replace missing balusters

Replace rotted board

Peeling paint indicates possible condensation problem

Replace lattice for ventilation

Caulk seam between clapboards and cornerboard

Rebuild bulge area

Replace crumbling brick

GENERAL: Scrape all loose paint; prime with oil-base primer; re-paint with historically appropriate colors give it another year or two of life. With the extra couple of years, build up a roof replacement fund so you can get the material of your choice.

If you choose traditional roofing materials, you'll spend extra time finding the roofer who won't insist that you use asphalt shingles. Slate roofs in particular elicit the comment, "There's no way to fix that." In many cases, the problems may be confined to flashing and a few broken or missing slates. Slate repair is not all that difficult, and replacement slate is available. Before you resign yourself to less desirable asphalt shingles, look into the feasibility of replacing the original roofing material.

TRADITIONAL ROOFING MATERIALS

Wooden Shakes

Handsplit along the wood's grain lines, shakes have a rough, textured appearance. They curl less than sawn shingles because of the natural grain shaping. Because of unevenness, however, shakes don't make a very tight roof. Shakes must be interlaid with 18-inch strips of felt, and should be installed on open sheathing.

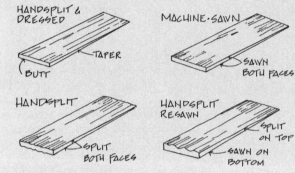

Wooden Shingles

Unlike shakes, shingles are machine sawn. Shingles also require proper air circulation and should be laid on open sheathing so the shingles can dry after rain. This allows for maximum roof life.

Slate

A properly laid slate roof should remain sound for a century or more. Vermont, New York, and Virginia slates last longer than Pennsylvania slates, which tend to delaminate from weathering and pollution.

Iron and Steel

Ferrous metal coated with tin (tin plate), zinc (galvanized), or tin and lead (terne) was popular in the nineteenth and early twentieth centuries. With proper maintenance and regular painting, these roofs will last indefinitely.

Metal Shingles

Embossed tin plate and galvanized shingles were first used during the late nineteenth century. Traditional metal shingles required regular painting. As an alternative, you can find authentic patterns made in corrosion resistant metals. Relatively inexpensive, metal shingles impart a traditional textured look to Victorian and turn-of-the-century houses.

Most of the cost of a metal roof is labor, so it makes sense to choose the best material you can afford. Copper, lead, "self-healing" alloys, and factory-finished metals don't need maintenance, but other traditional metal roofs will last indefinitely only if painted regularly.

Clay Tile

Clay tile roofs were used in this country during the 1600s. Flat tiles as well as pantiles (S-curved tiles) have been used in many variations, primarily with Italian Villa, Romanesque Revival, and Spanish Mission styles. As with slate, many roofers are unfamiliar with clay tile today and will urge the removal of a clay tile roof rather than its repair. But clay tiles are still produced, and roofs can be repaired in a manner similar to slate. Clay tiles will weather well, but are prone to breakage from mechanical shock, such as from a tree limb or people walking on them.

Spanish tile interlocks.

Barrel (Mission) tile is laid on battens.

Asphalt Shingles, Roll Roofing, Asbestos

Asphalt shingles and roll roofing were used as early as the late nineteenth century, and can be appropriate for certain types of buildings. Asbestos-cement shingles were used in the early twentieth century and can be regarded as a "traditional material" in some circumstances.

Up close, asbestos-cement shingles show a remarkable resemblance to old, weathered wood shakes.

Note: Asbestos is now known to be a highly toxic substance that can cause asbestosis (scarring of the lung tissue) and cancer. Asbestos is most dangerous when "friable," or when it is crumbled or crushed into a powder, releasing tiny airborne particles. Of all household materials made with asbestos, asbestos-cement shingles are among the safest, especially when nonfriable.

Roofing Materials Compared

MATERIAL	DESCRIP-TION	COLOR/TEXTURE	BUTT THICK-NESS	MINIMUM SLOPE (inches of rise per ft. of run)	WEIGHT/SQUARE (pounds)	FIRE RATING	COST/SQUARE (materials only)	AVG. LIFE-(years)
Asbestos-cement	Twin Lap	Green, black, white, gray, red, and cedar	5/32″	3 to 5	250–265	B	$ 60–90	25–40
	Slatelike	Convincing bevelled slate texture in gray, red, green, black	1/4″	4	500	A	$ 140	40 +
Slate	Virginia	Gray-black, micaceous luster	3/16–1/4″	4	700–800	Noncom-bustible	$ 350	175
	Vermont/N.Y.	Weathering & unfading green, light purple, mottled, gray, gray-black, red	″	″	″	″	$ 185–1200	100
	Pennsylvania	Blue-gray to blue-black	″	″	″	″	$ 250	40–50
Wood	Handsplit/resawn shakes	Rough—not tight on roof	1/2–1 1/4″	4	200–450	C (if fire retarded)	$ 50–138 $ 140–354 (fancy butt)	30
	Machine-sawn shingles	Thinner & flatter than handsplit; no "channels"	3/8″	″	200	″	$ 45–92	15
Concrete	Forms resembling Mission tile, slate, and wood shingles	Neutral and various terracotta colors; glazed and unglazed	1″ (woodlike)	2 1/2	950–1300	Noncom-bustible	$ 48–180	50–75
Asphalt	Top-of-line wood look	Three-dimen-sional appearance in variety of colors	1/8″	4	330	C (wind resistant)	$ 70	20–25
Asphalt-fiberglass	Random overlay tabs	Three-dimen-sional; mottled wood-like colors	1/8″	2″ for special applications	290	A	$ 78	20–25
Copper	Batten-, standing-, and flat seam	16 oz. and 20 oz. used	—	1/4″ flat; 2 1/2″ standing seam	125–155	Noncom-bustible	$ 200 (approx. for 16-oz. matl.)	60 +
Lead-coated copper	Batten-, standing-, and flat seam	16 oz. and 20 oz. used	—	1/4″ flat; 2 1/2″ standing seam	140–170	Noncom-bustible	$ 230 (approx. for 16-oz. matl.)	60 +
Tin/terne (coated steel)	Batten-, standing-, and flat seam	0.12–0.15″ thickness	—	1/4″ flat; 2 1/2″ standing seam	62–76	Noncom-bustible	$ 72	†

(continued on next page)

Roofing Materials Compared *(continued)*

MATERIAL	DESCRIP-TION	COLOR/TEXTURE	BUTT THICK-NESS	MINIMUM SLOPE (inches of rise per ft. of run)	WEIGHT/SQUARE (pounds)	FIRE RATING	COST/SQUARE (materials only)	AVG. LIFE-(years)
Terne-coated stainless	Batten-, standing-, and flat seam	26 gauge	—	1/4″ flat; 2 1/2″ standing seam	71	Noncombustible	$ 147	†
Metal shingles (prefinished steel)*	Victorian pattern	Interlocking, late-Victorian and early 20th cent. style	—	5	103	Noncombustible	$ 100–140	†
	"Spanish tile"	Interlocking shingle that mimics Spanish tile	—	6	120	"	$ 125	†
Clay tile	Flat Georgian shingle	To look like wood shingles; red, gray, black, moss green, cedar, and terra cotta	3/8–1″	4	1400	Noncombustible	$ 700 (large orders)	75 +
	English interlock (Williamsburg)	Flat interlocking	3/4–7/8″	4 1/2	800	"	$ 250	100 +
	Spanish	Interlocking; installed without nailing batten	1/2″	4 1/2	850	"	$ 219	100 +
	Barrel	Half-cylinders installed on nailing battens	"	4 1/2	1350	"	$ 392–432	100 +

*Approximate cost per square in other materials: Terne-coated steel, $181; Stainless steel, $375; Terne-coated stainless, $397; Copper, $516.
†Copper and lead-coated copper, as well as modern self-healing alloys such as "Galvalume," don't need to be painted. Factory-applied finishes are guaranteed by the manufacturer, usually for a period of 20 years. Traditional metals such as tin- and terne-plate will last indefinitely only if they are kept painted.

HIRING A ROOFER

There are different types of roofers: commercial, residential, those who specialize in gutters, leaders, and flashing, and roofers with specialties such as copper, slate, asphalt, or built-up roofing. If framing and sheathing need work, you might be better off with a general contractor or a carpenter for that part of the job.

Get three bids. Get more if you have serious doubts about any of the first three. Though you should avoid inexplicably low bids along with the high ones, it makes sense to take the lowest bid. First, compare bids to make sure all is equal.

Compare apples with apples. One bid may be for over-roofing alone, while another may include removing the existing shingles. The price bid by the third may include replacing flashings as well as the roof covering. Always ask whether flashing and drainage (gutters, leaders) will be repaired or replaced, and with what.

Insist on actual samples. Everything looks good in a brochure, but you won't know for sure until you see it. Know the type, color, weight, manufacturer, estimated quantity, and guaranteed or estimated life of the material.

Get references. Hire a roofer who has been in the business in your area for a good while. Ask to see a finished roof by the roofer—and one that's more than a year old. After all, all new roofs look good. Check with the Better Business Bureau and the county consumer agency to see if any complaints have been filed against your potential outfit.

Worry about insurance. The contractor should carry liability coverage, worker's compensation, and a license (if required locally). Also, you'd best have a comprehensive homeowner's policy yourself.

Sign a complete contract. A contract should include completion dates, specific materials to be used, insurance coverage, how cleanup is to be handled and by whom. If you're doing some of the work yourself and the contractor is doing the rest, explicitly spell this out in the contract. Sharing the work may save you some money, but it's the riskiest deal contractually.

HOW TO REPAIR AN OLD ROOF

If you elect to repair your old roof rather than replace it entirely, you may find you can make the repairs yourself. This way, you can add a few years to the life of your roof and save money for the total replacement job a few years later.

Finding the source of roof leaks is the hardest part of a repair job. With a flat roof, the source of the leak will usually be found directly over the spot on the top floor ceiling. But with a steeply pitched roof, water can travel many feet along roof boards and rafters before showing up as a stain on the ceiling.

If you can see the underside of your roof from the attic, observe the roof during a rainstorm. You should be able to see where the water is coming from. If there's a hole clear through the roofing or flashing, push a wire up through the hole to mark it from the top.

If you can't push a wire through the roof at the source of the leak, you'll have to mark its location by measuring from the nearest convenient reference point, such as a chimney, skylight, or vent pipe.

Roofers who are called in to make repairs often resort to "the black goop solution," a temporary remedy that eventually may lead to more repairs. Rather than find the exact source of the leak, they instead spread copious amounts of roofing cement in every suspicious area. In some cases, an entire roof will be coated with roofing cement.

A dab of roofing cement is a perfectly acceptable repair for roll roofing and built-up roofs. There, both the roofing and patching material are the same, and there's no visual

---

ROOFING DICTIONARY

Built-Up Roofing (BUR): Most often used on nearly flat roofs. Made of successive layers (plies) of roofing felt and moppings of hot tar or asphalt built up and topped by a mineral-surfaced cap sheet or gravel embedded in asphalt. It is easily patched, and a good job can last fifty years. Also called hot-tar roof, composition roofing, or multiple-ply roofing.

Butt: The bottom edge of a shingle at the widest point of taper. The butt end is the exposed part of the shingle.

Exposure: The length of a shingle, slate, or tile that is exposed to the weather, or not covered by the next course above. Exposure is expressed in inches, i.e.,

Parts of a Roof

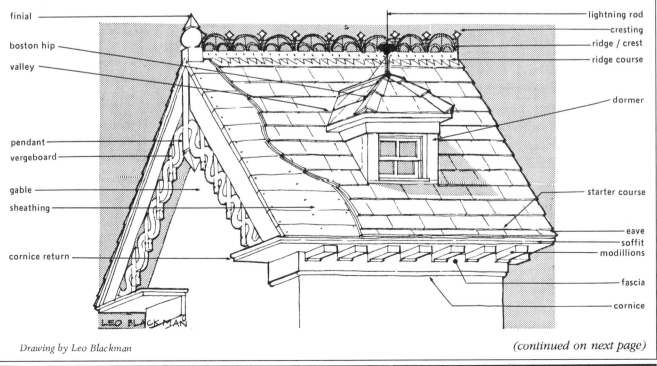

Drawing by Leo Blackman

(continued on next page)

"7 1/2-inch exposure," which means the same thing as "7 1/2 inches to the weather."

Felt: Also called asphalt-impregnated felt, rag felt, roofing felt, felt paper, and sheathing felt, it is tar-, asphalt-, or chemical-impregnated felt that is laid over the sheathing and under the roof covering to act as a dampness barrier, minor insulator, and cushion. This term is often applied to roll roofing.

Flashing: An impervious material—such as copper, tin, galvanized steel, or aluminum—placed on a roof to prevent water penetration or to provide water drainage around projections such as chimneys and vents, and wherever two surfaces having different slopes meet, such as valleys, hips, and roof curbs. Flashing for use with built-up or roll roofing is simply heavier-weight felt.

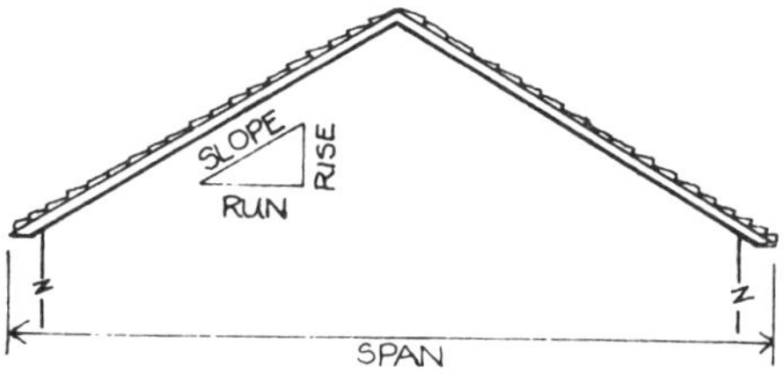

Shingle: A roofing unit made of wood, asphaltic material, slate, tile, concrete, and so on, machine-cut to stock lengths and sold in dimensional or random widths. Thickness is measured at the butt

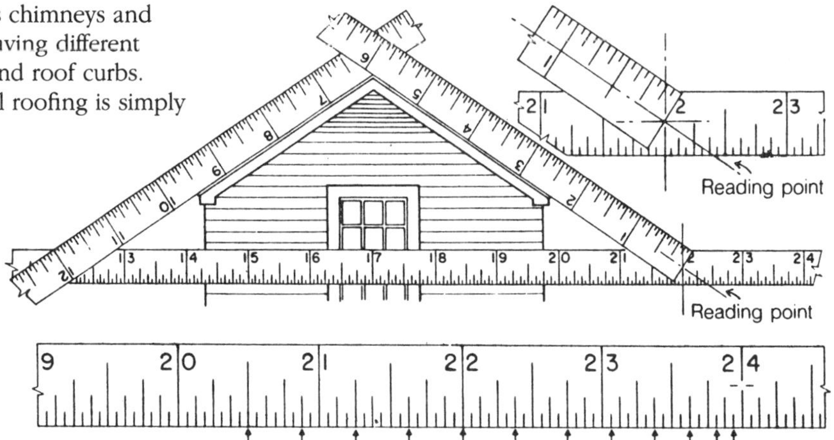

The folding rule functions like a sextant to determine roof pitch.

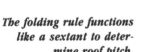

Rule reading	20 1/2	20 7/8	21 1/4	21 5/8	22	22 3/6	22 3/4	23 1/6	23 3/8	23 5/8	23 13/16	23 15/16
Pitch (fraction)	1/2	11/24	5/12	3/8	1/3	7/24	1/4	5/24	1/6	1/8	1/12	1/24
Slope (in. per ft.)	12	11	10	9	8	7	6	5	4	3	2	1

courtesy Creative Homeowner Press

Hip: The external angle formed by the junction of two sloping sides of a roof.

Lap: In shingling, that amount overlaying the shingle two courses below. Also called headlap.

Load: The weight, force, or system of forces to be carried by a roof. Roof structure must be designed to take both dead and live loads. Dead loads include sheathing and roof-covering material; live loads include snow and wind.

Red Rosin Paper: A cheap, heavy, durable building paper laid under metal roofing to provide a low-friction surface for movement due to expansion and contraction of the metal with temperature changes.

Roll Roofing: A relatively inexpensive asphaltic-felt roofing available in roll form, made by saturating felt with asphalt, then coating the saturated felt with a fine mineral, fiberglass, or asbestos. Granule-surfaced material can be used as the cap sheet for built-up roofing.

Shake: A handsplit wood shingle.

Slope (Pitch): The angle of inclination the roof makes with the horizontal. It is usually described in terms of vertical rise in inches to each foot of horizontal run, as in "8 in 1"; or it can be described in terms of the total rise (height) of the roof to its total span, as in "1/4 pitch."

Soffit: The flat board that encloses the space under the cornice. Quite prone to decay because of water leaking in from faulty gutters, worn roofing, and the like.

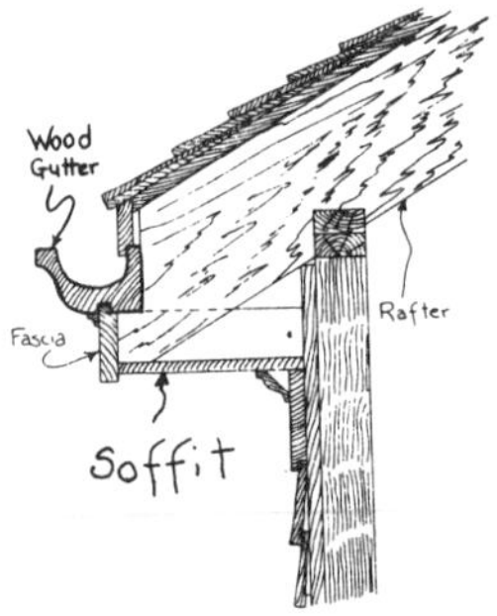

Square: The standard market measure for roofing materials. One square equals the number of slates, shingles, or tiles needed to cover 100 square feet of plain roof surface when laid with the customary lap.

Valley: The depressed (inside) angle formed by the intersection of two inclined sides of a roof. In an open valley, the metal flashing is exposed. In a closed valley, the metal flashing is covered.

clash. However, on other roofs such as slate, tile, wood shingle, and metal, black goop puts black pimples all over the roof.

Besides looking terrible, patches of roofing cement are only temporary. Roofing cement will dry, crack, and curl after exposure to the sun. Once the patch loosens, water can get trapped under the roofing cement and actually hasten roof deterioration. In addition, some asphaltic materials can corrode certain metals.

Roll and Built-Up Roofing

Most city row houses have mineral-surfaced roll roofing. A few still have the older type of built-up roofing. The mineral granules on roll roofing reflect the sun's rays and prolong the life of the asphalt felt underneath.

Most leaks in flat roofs occur where the roof meets a vertical element, such as a parapet wall, skylight, or vent pipe. Cracks and tears in asphalt flashing can be fixed as shown in the illustration.

The lapped joints in roll roofing sometimes open. Frequently it's possible to force some flashing cement under the seam and reseal it by stepping on it. If the seam won't stay bedded and keeps popping up, slit it and nail on both sides of the slit. Then cut a patch of 90-pound roofing felt that overlaps the nailheads at least two inches.

REPAIRING A CRACK IN ASPHALT FLASHING

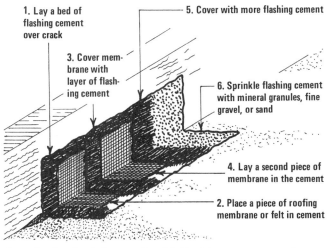

1. Lay a bed of flashing cement over crack

3. Cover membrane with layer of flashing cement

5. Cover with more flashing cement

6. Sprinkle flashing cement with mineral granules, fine gravel, or sand

4. Lay a second piece of membrane in the cement

2. Place a piece of roofing membrane or felt in cement

Coat the back of the patch with flashing cement and press it in position. Secure by nailing with roofing nails one inch apart. Cover the nailheads with flashing cement, and sprinkle fine gravel or sand over the patch.

Built-up roofing costs about 25 to 30 percent more than roll roofing. Yet built-up roofs last about twice as long—about thirty or forty years. If there are bare spots where the gravel has weathered away, sweep the area clean, then apply a layer of brushable roof coating. Sprinkle the coating with a layer of gravel. (You can usually scavenge gravel from another part of the roof where it has piled up.)

Slate

Although slate is long-lasting, a few slates may break from freeze/thaw cycles, or from the weight of a falling tree branch or someone walking on the roof. Slates may

Replacing a Damaged Section in Built-Up or Roll Roofing

1. Cut out damaged area with a knife. Do not slice away any of the underlying roofing felts. On a built-up roof, scrape away gravel with a shovel before cutting. Pick a cool day so the gravel doesn't stick to the roofing.

2. Force flashing cement under all edges of the cut. Coat the entire cut-out area with flashing cement. Cut patch from 90-pound roofing felt that just fits into the cut-out, and press firmly into the cement.

3. Cut a covering patch from 90-pound roofing felt that overlaps the cut-out by two inches on all sides. Coat bottom of the patch with flashing cement and press it into place. For additional security, fasten the edges with roofing nails every inch.

4. Cover the nailheads with a coating of flashing cement. For longer service life, sprinkle the flashing cement with mineral granules, fine gravel, or sand. The mineral coating reflects the sun's rays and helps prevent cracking.

also fall if the nails are rusting away. If the installer used galvanized or iron nails instead of copper, the only satisfactory solution is to take all the slates down and relay them using copper nails. Only when a significant portion of the slates are delaminating from pollution or weathering will you need to replace the entire roof.

Working on a slate roof can be tricky. To avoid breaking any slates, put an old blanket down first and place a ladder on top of it. Use a ridge hook, which attaches to the top of the ladder and hooks over the ridge, to secure the ladder. (Roofers use scaffold brackets or other equipment. Never let a roofer leave supporting metal straps in the roof; the metal will rust and stain the slates.)

Slate granules washed off the roof can erode metal flashings. You can solder patches on metal flashing, but you're probably better off replacing the flashing entirely. You'll have to lift some slates when you replace the flashing. Use the special nail-and-cover technique: You can

SLATER'S TOOLS

Ripper: Cast-steel tool 24 inches long used for removing damaged slate. Thin blade is slipped under broken slate and hooked around nail shaft. The other end of the ripper is struck sharply with a hammer; the end hook cuts and withdraws the nail.

Slater's Hammer: Cast-steel, one-piece tool. One end is pointed for punching slate; other end is a hammer head for driving nails. On each side of the shank is a shear edge for cutting slate.

Stake being used as a straightedge to cut slate.

Slate Cutter: A simple tool similar to an office paper cutter, convenient for cutting quantities of slate on site.

Slater's Nail: A heavy-gauge copper wire nail with a large, flat head.

Stake: T-bar (18 inches long) with the short arm pointed for driving into plank or scaffold. Long arm acts as rest for slate during punching and cutting operations, or as a straightedge.

make a temporary, short-term repair for eroded flashings by inserting a piece of 15-pound roofing felt under the slates and bedding it in flashing cement. The felt should project far enough over the flashing so that it covers the holes.

To replace slate, remove any of the remaining broken slate using a slate ripper. Slip the thin end under the broken slate and hook it on one of the two nails holding that slate. By hammering down on the handle of the ripper, you should be able to cut through the nail. Cut the other nail in similar fashion. All of the broken slate should now slide out. If the adjacent slates are bearing too heavily for you to get the slate ripper into place, force nails gently under the edges of the slates to wedge them up. (Or, try using the ripper like a shoehorn.)

Now slide the replacement slate into position. After carefully aligning it, use a nailset to punch a hole right below the slot of the two covering slates. Make sure that

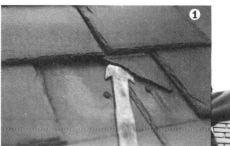

❶

❷

Slip the pointed end of the ripper under the broken slate to remove the nail.

Pry up the surrounding slates.

you punch the hole above the double coverage; you want a hole *only* in the new slate—not in the one below it. If you are hesitant about punching slate, mark it and drill it on the ground.

Replace the broken slate.

Align the slate and use a nailset to punch a hole right below the slot of the two covering slates.

Hold the new slate with a slater's nail. Its length should be twice the thickness of the slates plus one inch. 1 1/4-inch, or "3d," nails are appropriate for standard-thickness slates. *Do not* use common wire nails or shingling nails. Drive the nail between the covering slates. Clip the head of the nail to allow it to pass between the slates. Alternately, you could chip a little out of each adjoining slate. Use a nailset to drive the nail down to the surface of the new slate. The slate should hang on the nail; if you drive the nail too tightly you may break the slate.

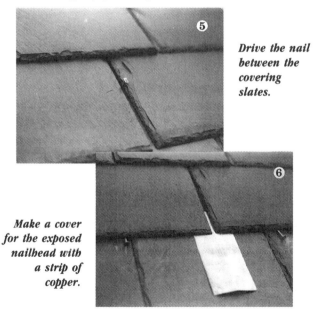

Drive the nail between the covering slates.

Make a cover for the exposed nailhead with a strip of copper.

Bend a strip of copper about 2 inches wide and 6 inches long into a slightly concave shape to make a cover for the exposed nailhead. (Some roofers call this cover a "baby.") Slide the cover up so that its bottom edge is 2 inches below the nailhead. If necessary, tap a screwdriver against the cover to push it up, or use nails as wedges. Friction holds the cover in place, keeping rain out of the

nail hole. If the cover is placed concave side up, it will channel rainwater better than placing the convex side up.

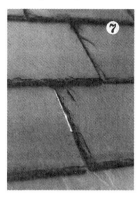

Friction holds the cover in place.

You also may hold a replacement slate with the copper tab method, particularly if only random slates are breaking. The copper tab method involves nailing a strip of copper in the area of the missing shingle. You then insert

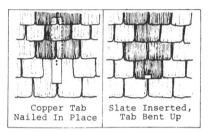

Copper Tab Nailed In Place   Slate Inserted, Tab Bent Up

the new slate, and bend the tab up to hold it in place. Trim off any excess so sliding ice and snow won't loosen the tab.

Asbestos-Cement Shingles

Asbestos-cement shingles (also called mineral-fiber shingles) are made from asbestos fibers embedded in portland cement. They make an attractive and durable roof that can last fifty or more years. Because they are gray, they are sometimes mistaken for slate.

Butt and cut edges on asbestos-cement shingles give the appearance of wood shingles.

Old asbestos-cement shingles absorb a fair amount of water during rain, and thus stay damp for a while. As a result, you'll find moss and other organic growth on some asbestos-cement roofs. Normally, this won't be a problem until the moss builds up to a point where it acts as a dam, causing backup of water on the roof. Remove these accumulations by hand-scraping.

Like slate and tile, asbestos-cement shingles are brittle, and will break from time to time. Use the same replacement technique used for slate, being careful not to break additional shingles. When removing asbestos-cement shingles, take them out as whole units, if possible. If they appear to be at all porous, soak them with a fine spray or mist of water before handling. If it's feasible—and it can be staggeringly expensive—hire a trained professional or attend an asbestos-removal training program.

Ceramic Tile

While replacing broken ceramic tiles is fairly easy, the toughest part is doing so without breaking more shingles. Remove any damaged tile by breaking it up with careful hammer blows. Cut the nail with a slate ripper or insert a hacksaw blade under the covering tile. Hold the replacement tile with a copper tab. Use a double thickness of copper at the end of the tab. This extra stiffness helps

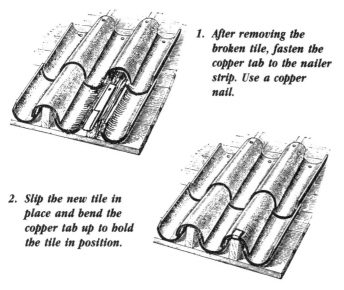

1. After removing the broken tile, fasten the copper tab to the nailer strip. Use a copper nail.

2. Slip the new tile in place and bend the copper tab up to hold the tile in position.

keep the tab from getting unbent from the weight of the tile or the force of descending ice and snow.

To find replacement tiles you may get lucky and locate

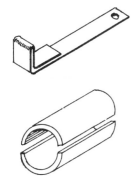

Use a double thickness at the bent end of the copper tab. Replacement barrel tile can be made by splitting a section of PVC pipe.

a dealer in salvage roofing. If you just need a couple of pieces of barrel tile, you can fake it. Get a piece of PVC drain pipe, slice it in half, and paint to match.

Wood Shingles

From the colonial era until well into the nineteenth century, wood shingles made of eastern white cedar, cypress, pine, spruce, hemlock, and oak were handsplit from logs and then tapered and dressed smooth with a drawknife, sometimes into unique shapes or patterns. By the late-nineteenth century, shingle-making machines were being perfected, and after 1900 the sawn shingle became common.

Today, western red cedar is widely used, and roof products made from this type of wood are categorized as either shingles or shakes, depending on how they are manufactured. Red cedar shingles are sawn on both faces, and are available in standard lengths (16-inch, 18-inch, and 24-inch) and several grades. These shingles closely resemble those produced by the first shingle-making machines. Red cedar shakes are a type of shingle that is hand- or machine-split. They are then either resawn to produce a textured face on one side and a smooth back on the other, or simply split on both faces. Shakes became popular in the 1950s with the fashion for a contemporary rustic look on roofs.

Less common wood roofing products are shingles cut in decorative patterns (often used in the Victorian era) or steam-bent into curves (for the "thatched" shingle roofs in vogue in the 1920s). There are also a few specialty manufacturers making historical shingle types once again in white oak and eastern white pine. Lately, a completely new industry based on preservative-treated yellow pine shingles has appeared as an alternative to the rising costs of red cedar products.

A new wood-shingle thatch roof on an English cottage–style house.

To give your wood-shingle roof as long a life as possible, use long-lasting materials and install them correctly. Lay shakes and shingles on open sheathing or nailers—not a solid deck. This is not possible in a heated building that has no headroom or attic upstairs and therefore must be insulated at the rafters. If you must use closed sheathing for insulation, do not use wood shingles unless you can replace the roof every decade or so.

Shingles and shakes come in three grades. Always get #1 Blue Label for residential roofs; these are 100 percent

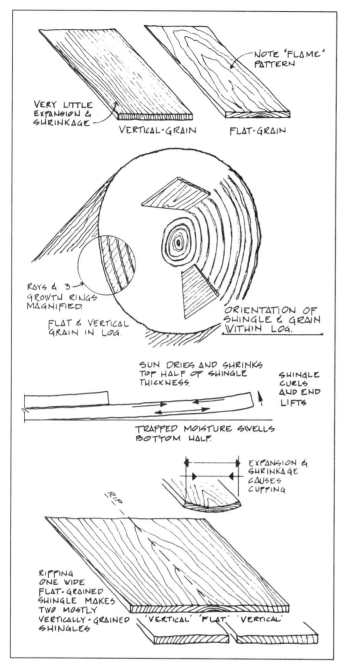

VERY LITTLE EXPANSION & SHRINKAGE

VERTICAL·GRAIN

NOTE 'FLAME' PATTERN

FLAT·GRAIN

RAYS & 3 GROWTH RINGS MAGNIFIED.

FLAT & VERTICAL GRAIN IN LOG.

ORIENTATION OF SHINGLE & GRAIN WITHIN LOG.

SUN DRIES AND SHRINKS TOP HALF OF SHINGLE THICKNESS.

SHINGLE CURLS AND END LIFTS

TRAPPED MOISTURE SWELLS BOTTOM HALF.

EXPANSION & SHRINKAGE CAUSES CUPPING

RIP

RIPPING ONE WIDE FLAT·GRAINED SHINGLE MAKES TWO MOSTLY VERTICALLY·GRAINED SHINGLES

'VERTICAL' 'FLAT' 'VERTICAL'

Open sheathing, or nailers, are best for wood-shingle roofs.

clear edge-grain heartwood. Shingles should be vertical-grain with a minimum of sapwood and defects. Use shingles no wider than 6 inches. Wide shingles split with age and service.

Use hot-dipped, galvanized nails. They are the most rust-resistant and their rough coating helps anchor the nail. Aluminum or stainless-steel nails are acceptable but expensive and, unless ribbed, do not grab the wood as well. Never use electro-coated nails; when the coating fails, the heads rust off leaving the shingles unsecured. Copper nails and flashing will fail too, as the tannins in the wood corrode the copper. Some literature recommends using nails as short as 3d (1 1/4-inch), but many restoration roofers prefer 5d box nails (1 3/4-inch), especially for a quality, four-ply job.

To properly install wood shingles, use a maximum of two nails per shingle (so that the shingle lies flat), positioned no more than 3/4 inch in from each edge. Nails should be driven so that the head comes close to the wood, but does not crush or dimple the surface. Shingles should "hang" on the nails, keeping the shingles free to shrink and swell with weather conditions. Shingles nailed too tightly will

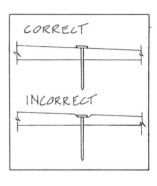

CORRECT

INCORRECT

split. The best jobs are still hand-nailed; pneumatic nailers are designed to drive nails in deeply and can actually punch through a shingle if set incorrectly. It is common practice to nail shingles roughly 1 inch higher than the butt line of the course above. With some exposures and shingle lengths, it also may be possible to nail two courses up, so that the nailheads are completely protected from the weather.

To replace a wood shingle, remove the damaged unit by splitting it with a chisel into several smaller pieces until all parts are free of the nails. Cut the heads off nails, either with a slate ripper or with a hacksaw blade inserted up under the shingles. The replacement can be held with a copper tab or by the hidden nail technique. Let the replacement shingle protrude 1/4 inch below other shingles. Toenail two finish nails immediately below the upper course. With a hammer and wooden block, strike the end of the new shingle, driving it up level with the other shingles. This bends the nails and puts heads below upper shingles.

Wood shingles require sufficient *spacing* (also referred to as the *keyway*). As the shingles swell in wet weather, these gaps nearly close. If they are laid up tight when conditions are dry, they will buckle and roll up on each other in wet weather. In earlier times, roofers were known to have soaked their shingles first in warm water (in an old bathtub, say, over an open fire) to swell them to full size before laying them up tight. Barring this technique, one should try to judge the moisture content of the shin-

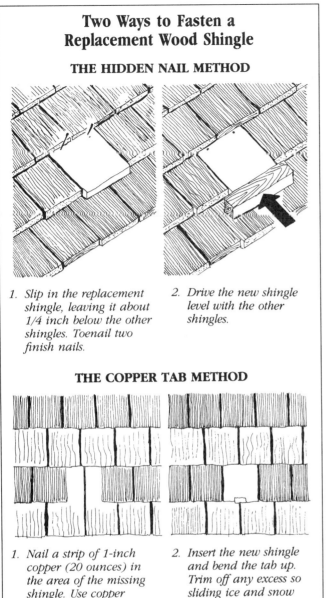

Two Ways to Fasten a Replacement Wood Shingle

THE HIDDEN NAIL METHOD

1. *Slip in the replacement shingle, leaving it about 1/4 inch below the other shingles. Toenail two finish nails.*

2. *Drive the new shingle level with the other shingles.*

THE COPPER TAB METHOD

1. *Nail a strip of 1-inch copper (20 ounces) in the area of the missing shingle. Use copper roofing nails.*

2. *Insert the new shingle and bend the tab up. Trim off any excess so sliding ice and snow won't loosen the tab.*

When determining spacing, you should also consider the overall climate and whether the sun is shining on the roof as the work is done.

Make the *sidelap,* the distance between the edge of a shingle and the space between the two shingles in the course above it, at least 1 1/2 inches. The joints between shingles should be offset in succeeding courses by no less than 1 1/2 inches, and for a quality job should be "three-stepped"—that is, not in line for at least three courses. The better the sidelap, the slimmer the chances water will ever find its way through the roof. In addition to avoiding the use of any flat-grain shingles, joints should not fall over any semblance of "flame-pattern" grain in the shingles below as the water channeled over this weak spot increases the odds that the shingle will deform or split.

Maximum weatherface *exposure* is generally a function of the pitch of the roof and the length of the shingle, as well as the "look" of the roof. However, using smaller exposures can improve the roof's integrity by not only reducing the amount of shingle exposed to the elements, but by increasing the "ply" of the roof as well. For example, 4-inch exposure with 18-inch shingles will yield a 4-ply roof (four shingle layers thick).

While seldom a problem on old houses, no roof shingle fares well on a low-slope roof, and wood shingles can deteriorate quickly if used on a pitch lower than 4 in 12. In addition to not shedding water rapidly, roofs lower than this pitch make capillary action possible between the sandwiched shingle faces so that water is actually drawn in under the roof.

Finally, provide adequate *air circulation* for wood shingles. Traditional wood-shingle roofs were on frameworks that allowed the shingles to breathe under the roof (through the attic space) as well as outside the building. This is known as an *open deck.* The most common systems used skip sheathing (boards 1 × 6 or wider spaced with the courses) or nailers (typically, 1 × 4 stock). When shingles are installed using either of these systems, roofing felt, building paper or housewrap products should *not* be added between shingles and roof framing. No matter how vapor-permeable these materials are, they trap moisture on the underside of the roof and shorten the life of the shingles.

Houses with finished attic spaces and roof insulation invariably have a *closed deck* of full sheathing. Installing wood roof shingles on this unventilated surface also invites deterioration because the shingles cannot breathe. Get the shingles "off the roof" by nailing them to 1 × 4 nailers or sleepers attached to the roof deck. This allows for air circulation under the roof and across the shingles, similar to that of an open-deck system. Many roofers use pressure-treated lumber for nailer stock, sometimes leaving a small gap between butting boards to increase ventilation and allow any condensation to run out. Roofing felt should be applied to the deck before the nailers are installed so that it does not come in contact with shingles. As an alternative to roofing felt, some recommend housewrap, a nickname for spun-bonded olefin (popular brand

gles as they come from the bundle (which may be quite damp if stored uncovered) and then space accordingly. The typical keyway for today's shingles (even less stable than those cut from old-growth timber) varies from 1/8 inch to 3/8 inch—often the width of a pencil or 20d nail.

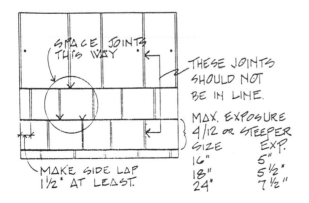

SPACE JOINTS THIS WAY

THESE JOINTS SHOULD NOT BE IN LINE.

MAKE SIDE LAP 1½" AT LEAST.

MAX. EXPOSURE 4/12 OR STEEPER

SIZE	EXP.
16"	5"
18"	5½"
24"	7½"

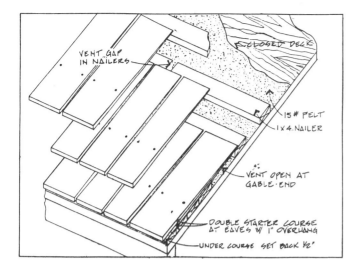

VENT GAP IN NAILERS

CLOSED DECK

15 # FELT

1 X 4 NAILER

VENT OPEN AT GABLE-END

DOUBLE STARTER COURSE AT EAVES W/ 1" OVERHANG

UNDER COURSE SET BACK ½"

names are Tyvek and Typar). Housewrap reduces air infiltration while allowing moisture to escape.

To keep insects out of the vent space at gable ends, run a strip of quality metal screen under and over the nailer ends before shingling.

Sheet Metal Roofing

Expansion and contraction of the metal sheets often strains the joints so that they open and break. Even though you can resolder them, odds are they'll open up again unless expansion joints are installed that allow for movement in the roof—no small task!

Since you can't replace a damaged sheet in a metal roof that has interlocking joints, patching is the only option. Soldered patches are best. If soldering is beyond you, make a "cold" patch using a commercial sealing product.

WOOD-SHINGLE ROOF CARE

Assaulted constantly by moisture and sunlight, which break down wood fibers, and by wood-eating organisms, wood-shingle roofs require constant care. Without regular attention, a wood roof may last only ten or fifteen years.

Keep all roof surfaces clear of leaves, pine needles, and other debris as they prevent the roof from shedding water effectively and trap decay-promoting moisture near the shingles after rain or snow. Valleys should be cleared with a broom regularly, but the same is true of the keyways between shingles, which may need cleaning with a stiff brush. Trim back overhanging branches to reduce the amount of shade on the roof and increase air circulation and drying.

You may also want to treat the roof with a chemical cleaner or another treatment that inhibits or prevents plant growth; traditionally, linseed oil in one form or another was a favorite. (Test any of these treatments first in an inconspicuous spot before proceeding with an entire roof.)

Cleaning with chemical cleaners (primarily bleaches) improves the appearance of old or neglected roofs and can remove many difficult stains and discolorations. They are also effective for restoring natural wood tone to cedar shingles and for killing mildew and algae. Apply bleach solutions to a clean roof either manually (for localized cleaning) or with corrosion-proof garden sprayers having plastic or stainless-steel parts. (*Note:* After spraying, clean all equipment with two tablespoons of household ammonia in a gallon of water to prevent corrosion.)

Generally, solutions do not have to be scrubbed once they are applied, but they should be allowed to stand for fifteen to thirty minutes before being rinsed off with a garden hose or pressure washer. Do not allow bleaches to remain on the wood much longer than thirty minutes, however, or apply them in direct sunlight. Chlorine solutions can corrode metal roof parts and burn shrubs or other plants that surround a house, and these items should be rinsed thoroughly if exposed to cleaners.

Power washing with high-pressure rigs also has come into its own (especially on the West Coast) as an effective mechanical method for occasional cleaning of wood-shingle roofs. Here, the water stream loosens and washes the top fiber layer away from the shingles, taking weathered or discolored wood and growth (such as moss or lichen) with it. The process is time-consuming (and can erode shingles or drive water under the roof if not done correctly), but on some roofs it is the best method for removing the heavy buildup of dirt or plant growth. Cold, clear water alone is used, usually at moderate pressures of 1,000 to 1,500 psi (pounds per square inch) and a flow rate of 4 to 6 gpm (gallons per minute). You can rent power-washing equipment, widely used to clean boats and cars, by the day from tool-rental companies.

Growth-control treatments and preservative treatments will kill and inhibit plant growth on a wood-shingle roof. These contain copper or zinc mixed with water and can be sprayed onto wood-shingle roofs to kill moss, lichen, and other plant growth. Also, certain types of garden products intended for controlling moss on the ground have proven useful for arresting it on roofs. If dry, water moss and similar large growths before spraying to maximize the absorption of the treatment.

Many of these chemicals are corrosive and/or harmful to plants, animals, and humans, and should be handled with care. Some zinc compounds, in particular, can corrode copper roof parts and should be used only near galvanized metals. (The reverse is generally true for copper compounds.) Follow manufacturers' directions and use proper safety precautions when applying. Choose a calm day to spray, and stand upwind. To minimize runoff, apply only when rain is unlikely. Keep spills, contact with metals, and accidental sprayings to a minimum, and rinse liberally when they occur.

Finally, though not a cleaner or preservative, here is an often-requested treatment for giving new cedar shingles an aged ash-gray color after making repairs: Dissolve 1 pound baking soda in 1 gallon of water and spray on. Shingles will gray in sunlight in several hours.

You can also make a temporary patch with sheet metal and flashing cement. Clean the metal with a wire brush or steel wool. Cut a sheet metal patch that overlaps the hole at least 3 inches on all sides. Coat the back of the patch with flashing cement. Press the patch firmly into place— just hard enough so the cement doesn't ooze onto the roof. Paint the patch to match the rest of the roof.

Metal shingles of galvanized or terne-coated steel will

	ACTIVE INGREDIENTS	COMMON OR TRADE NAME/SOURCE	APPLICATION	ADVANTAGES	DISADVANTAGES
BLEACHES	Sodium Hypochlorite	Laundry bleach (Clorox, Purex, etc.)	Mix liquid laundry bleach (5% sol.) 1:1 with water; use commercial bleach (12–15% sol.) diluted	Inexpensive, easy to use	Temporary cleaning and growth kill; corrosive
	Calcium Hypochlorite	Dry pool chlorine (HTH, etc.)	Mix 4–8 oz. per gallon of water	Same as above	Same as above
	Oxalic Acid	Wood bleach (available at paint stores)	Mix 4 oz. per gallon of water	Same as above	Poisonous—should be used sparingly
	Sodium Hydroxide	Flake caustic soda	Mix 1–2 lbs. per 5 gallons of water	Same as above	Strong caustic (use safety precautions); may darken wood
GROWTH-CONTROL TREATMENTS	Zinc Sulfate (monohydrate)	Available at garden or farm supply, hardware store	Mix 3 lbs. powder in 5–10 gallons of water	Inexpensive	Toxic; corrodes copper (use with galvanized roof metal)
	Copper Sulfate	"Blue stone"; available as above	Mix 1/4–1/2 oz. per 10 gallons of water	Same as above	Toxic; corrodes zinc (use with copper roof metal)
	Zinc Chloride	Available as above	Mix 1 pint in 3 gallons of water	Same as above	Toxic; corrodes copper (use with galvanized roof metal)
	Potassium Salts of Fatty Acids	Available at garden supply stores	Follow manufacturer's directions (These products work by breaking down cell walls)	Non-toxic; biodegradable, non-corrosive	Avoid contact with plants; rinse over spray
PRESERVATIVE TREATMENTS	Copper Napthenate	Widely available	Most effective when contains at least 1–2% copper. Follow directions for coverage	Effective (up to 5 years protection with some products)	Has green color in pure form; tinting may be desired
	Zinc Napthenate	Widely available	2–3% solutions best for 3-year protection; higher (i.e., 4%) may yield longer protection	Good color match for silver weathered roof	Less effective than copper solutions; frequent renewal possible

WOOD-SHINGLE TREATMENT SUPPLIERS

For further reading on wood-shingle-preservation treatments, contact the manufacturers listed or Oregon State University, Publications Orders, Agricultural Communications, Dept. OHJ, Administrative Services Bldg. 422, Corvallis, OR 97331-2119. Ask for publication EC 1271; cost and mailing: $1.
Contact each manufacturer for a list of distributors.

American Building Restoration Chemicals, Inc. 9720 South 60th Street, Dept. OHJ Franklin, WI 53132 (800) 346-7532 Natural Seal Clear X-100, Cedar-tone 101 oil-based preservatives (specify "roof grade")

AMTECO, Inc. 815 Cass Avenue, Dept. OHJ St. Louis, MO 61306 (800) 969-4811 TWP roof and deck sealant, oil-based preservative available in clear and cedar-tone formulas

Chapman Chemical Company P.O. Box 9158, Dept. OHJ Memphis, TN 38109 (901) 396-5151 Cunapsol 1 ("Wood Green"), pigmented water-based copper napthenate preservative

Safer Chemical Company 189 Wells Avenue, Dept. OHJ Newton, MA 02159 (617) 964-2990 Environmentally safe moss and algae killers

last indefinitely if kept painted. Don't put off painting until rust spots appear. If there are rusted areas, wire-brush and apply an iron oxide metal primer before applying the finish coat.

To solder a metal roof:

1. Remove any paint from the metal surrounding the patch with paint stripper. Also remove roofing tar by scraping, followed by scrubbing with kerosene, gasoline, or mineral spirits. Caution: These solvents are very flammable.

2. Clean both the roof and the patch piece by scouring with a wire brush or steel wool.

3. *For soldering copper:* Apply muriatic acid for sixty seconds to dissolve any oxides. Wash and wipe dry. Paint on liquid soldering flux (zinc chloride). Apply flux *only* where you want solder to go. Pre-tin the area by heating with a soldering copper and applying a thin coating of solder. Apply patch and hold in place with heavy weight, or fasten it mechanically with two copper rivets or nails. Follow directions for soldering in step 4.

For soldering galvanized steel: Apply muriatic acid as in step 3. The muriatic acid will also serve as the flux, so after sixty seconds leave acid in place, apply patch, and solder as indicated in step 4.

For soldering lead-coated copper, terne, and tin plate: Apply liquid flux (zinc chloride). Apply patch and hold in place with weight or nails. If you use nails, be sure they are the same metal as the roof; otherwise, you risk galvanic corrosion. Solder as indicated in step 4.

4. Use bar solder that's 50 percent tin and 50 percent lead. For roofing work, you'll need a large soldering copper (1 to 1 1/2 pounds or bigger). A home workbench

soldering iron won't transmit enough heat to the roof to get solder to flow under the patch.

5. A well-tinned copper is a must! You want to heat the metal as well as the solder so the solder flows into the seam. Since most of the heat is in the base of the tip, hold your soldering copper as shown. If you held the patch with nails, be sure solder covers the nailheads.

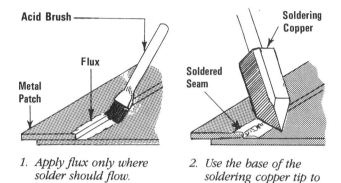

1. *Apply flux only where solder should flow.*

2. *Use the base of the soldering copper tip to heat the entire seam.*

6. When soldering is complete, rinse off all excess flux with water and wipe dry. If patch is galvanized, terne, or tinplate, paint to match rest of roof.

Note: For safety's sake, beware using flame tools for soldering on the roof. The danger of setting the roof on fire is always present.

GUTTERS

Without clean, properly functioning gutters, water can't properly drain off and away from the house. Regular inspection and cleaning not only prevents block-

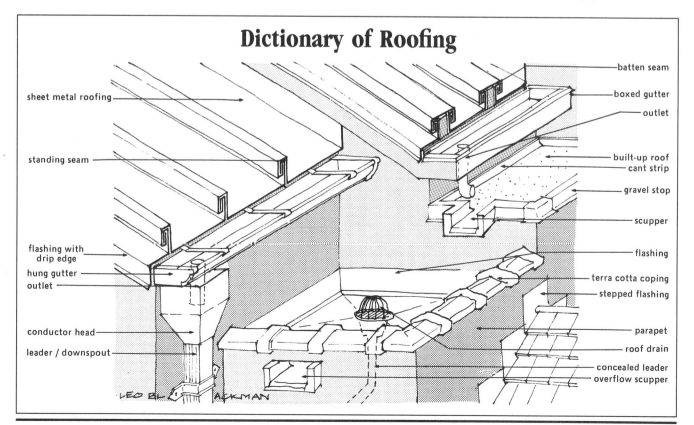

Dictionary of Roofing

sheet metal roofing
standing seam
flashing with drip edge
hung gutter
outlet
conductor head
leader / downspout

batten seam
boxed gutter
outlet
built-up roof
cant strip
gravel stop
scupper
flashing
terra cotta coping
stepped flashing
parapet
roof drain
concealed leader
overflow scupper

LEO BLAST ACKMAN

age (and subsequent water backup), but it also extends the gutter's life, whether wood or metal. The accumulations of leaves and organic debris from overhanging trees, as well as loose minerals from man-made roofing, traps moisture in the gutter trough, preventing it from drying completely. This constant moisture promotes decay of wood fibers and rusting of ferrous metals.

As with any maintenance chores, annual inspections are good practice, but buildings with a lot of overhanging trees frequently need attention twice a year. Old gloves and a small child's rake are favorite tools for cleaning gutters. Some folks also gather up leaves and muck with a large rubber pastry spatula. Wire strainers that fit in the trough drain have been used for years to keep sticks, baseballs, and other large objects away from the downspout. The value of wire or plastic screens that cover the entire gutter is questionable. On some houses, these screens collect leaves rapidly, which form a partial "roof" over the gutter. This allows rainwater to run right off the eaves, and shades the trough from sunlight. Drying then becomes difficult or impossible, and the water and fine debris that do pass through the screen create an ever-moist sludge.

Paint the outside of wood gutters to protect the wood; copper and galvanized gutters generally do not require an exterior coat, but you might want to paint them to match exterior trim.

Depending on their construction, you may want to paint the inside or trough of the gutter. Do not coat any gutter with roofing tar, asphalt products, or elastomeric compounds. These materials eventually break, trapping water between the coating and gutter, and wood or metal starts to deteriorate.

For wood gutters of any type, painting the trough is not recommended. Wood gutters must "breathe" through the trough surface to dry out when not conducting water. Paint in the trough will only lead to rot. Painting wooden gutters with used engine or gear oil is also a bad idea. Not only can these oils cause paint-adhesion problems once they saturate the wood, but they also carry acids and combustion waste products in suspension—no better for wood than for engines.

What is recommended seems to fall into the category of

A new redwood gutter makes its way to the eaves. While you may want to paint the outside of the gutter, painting the inside is not recommended.

a highly breathable coating or none at all. In the northeast, Douglas-fir gutters are usually maintained with a treatment that resists liquid water but is permeable to water vapor. This can be a commercial (toxic) wood preservative (Cuprinol Clear or Woodlife, for example) or raw linseed oil thinned between 1:1 and 3:1 with mineral spirits or turpentine. (Some people thin linseed oil with a preservative.) Apply the treatments annually when the wood is thoroughly dry; multiple coats may be required. This treatment also works for cypress and redwood gutters (although one West Coast manufacturer reported redwood needs only to be kept clean and allowed to dry).

Galvanized steel gutters, on the other hand, benefit from trough coating with a good quality metal primer or metal roof paint. Popular products are Tin-O-Lin Red Iron Oxide Linseed Oil paint, MAB Check-Rust primer, and Rust-Oleum primer. Coatings should be touched-up or renewed every year. *New* gutters, though, should not be painted until after their first or second season. The galvanizing process produces a smooth and oily, "toothless" finish on the new gutter, which will cause paint to flake off shortly after it's applied. Once the gutter has been exposed to the elements, however, its surface becomes slightly etched, so that after a full cleaning and wash with a mild acid (vinegar works well) the paint can grab the metal.

Copper gutters, essentially maintenance free, should not be trough-painted. While the metal takes paint well (better than galvanized steel), painting is not required for longevity. In fact, one of the beauties of naked copper is that it shows its flaws. On bare metal, small leaks leave watermarks or trails where they have originated; when painted, problems are harder to detect. Repairs, too, are much simpler on an unpainted gutter. The natural *verdigris* oxidation (that also helps preserve the metal) is easily cleaned with flux after light sandpapering. Most punctures or broken seams can then be soldered shut again by a competent craftsman. A painted surface, however, complicates cleaning and makes repairs more difficult and less secure.

If you need to caulk joints in wood gutters, use a butyl rubber caulk. It has good adhesion, water resistance, and a life of five to ten years. Polyurethane caulks cost more but last longer (fifteen to twenty years) and are preferred by some people. Both products clean up with paint thinner.

If your gutters always seem to have standing water in them, check their pitch. Ice, fallen limbs, or settling of the house may have shifted the gutter so that it does not drain quickly or completely. Strictly speaking, ideal pitch is a function of gutter size, roof area, and average rainfall, but many builders and gutter tradesmen use a rough rule-of-thumb for minimum pitch (1 inch drop per 10 feet of length, for instance). Adjustments often have to be made to this guideline if the gutter is very long or the eave is not level. To check the operation of a gutter system, get up on a ladder and run a hose in the gutter or do a "bucket test" to see how water flows.

Run a hose or pour a bucket of water into a new gutter to be sure it's properly installed.

Check the location and number of drains and downspouts as well. Older buildings (particularly Victorians) are often under-spec'd in this regard, and adding outlets may improve drainage or spillover problems. For example, gutters over thirty-five feet long may be better served by downspouts at each end rather than a single outlet. The gutter is rehung with the high point at the center and a drop toward either downspout—also making steeper pitch more feasible for long gutter runs.

FLASHINGS

Chimneys, dormers, and other protrusions through the roof need flashings around them to prevent water leakage. The flashing system is the weakest link in many roofing systems. If the existing flashing shows signs of repeated patching, then it may be at the end of its life and replacement may be in order.

Replacing flashings often requires lifting and relaying a substantial portion of the roof, depending on the number of valleys and dormers. Thus, if the roofing material itself is in marginal condition, you may have to replace everything. If you see deterioration resulting from design errors in the flashing, gutter, and leader systems, don't waste time and money simply replacing materials. This calls for changes in the flashing design.

Flashing is made up of thin sheets of waterproof material, lapped in such a way that water can't penetrate or back up under a roof. Flashing is usually made of thin metal such as copper, aluminum, or galvanized steel.

You'll also find flashing where vertical walls intersect roofs, such as at dormers and porches. At these points the siding should be at least 2 inches above roofing with flashing protecting the joints. On vertical joints, two pieces of flashing are normally used: *base flashing* that extends at least 4 inches under the roofing; and *cap flashing* or *counterflashing* that laps the base flashing at least 4 inches. The

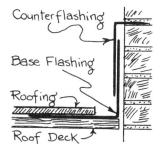

counterflashing keeps water from leaking behind the base flashing. The junction between the house wall and porch roof, too, should be protected by a metal flashing.

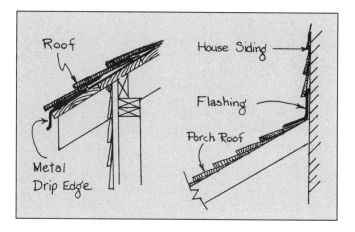

Although roof coverings should extend at least 1 inch beyond any wood at the eave and rake edges, metal flashing—called a "drip edge"—at the edge of the eaves diverts water away from the cornice or rafter ends. If flashing wasn't installed when your house was built, add it by slipping a strip of noncorrosive metal (bent off the edge of the roof) under the shingles. Fasten it to the edge of the roof decking with noncorroding nails.

To repair flashing temporarily, cut a piece of sheet metal about 1 inch bigger on all sides than the hole being patched. (The patch should be the same metal as the flashing.) Coat the back of the patch with a thin coat of roofing cement and press into place. In general, avoid daubing roofing cement over anything but asphalt roofing.

One of the most common flashing problems occurs around a chimney. To repair chimney flashing follow these steps:

1. *Layout:* Determine what measurements you'll need. If you have an existing chimney flashing (that was done correctly!) save the old pieces and use them for patterns. You might also have a cricket, a water-diverting ridge in the roof right behind the chimney. If so, follow the old flashing as a pattern.

The base flashing must extend over the shingles a minimum of 4 inches, and also up the chimney a minimum of 4 inches. Counterflashing must overlap the base a minimum of 4 inches. Go around corners 2 inches for double overlap.

2. *Materials:* A professional roofer would probably use cold-rolled copper (a stiff material, difficult to bend). However, easier-to-work, 16-ounce, soft-tempered copper may suit the job. Copper isn't much more expensive than other metals, and if you're doing all the work, there's no reason not to use the best material. If you're worried about green stains from the copper, use lead-coated copper.

Lay roofing felt on the roof decking beneath the base flashing if none exists. Use only copper nails with copper flashing. Size the nails so you get at least 1-inch penetration into roof deck.

3. *Cutting and Bending:* Mark all bends, cuts, notches. If you have to cut and bend pieces yourself, regular metal cutting shears can cut 16-ounce copper.

If you have the measurements or old flashing as a pattern, you may be able to get the shop where you buy the copper to cut and bend it for you.

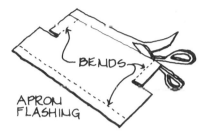

To form pieces without having to buy bending breaks, tongs, and so on, clamp a 2 × 4 over the flashing piece, with the bending line at the edge of the work table. Use an additional piece of 2 × 4 as a block to place against flashing. Bend by striking with a hammer. This will give a 90-degree bend. Where necessary to create a hem, unclamp and continue hammering against a 2 × 4 to bend metal edge over.

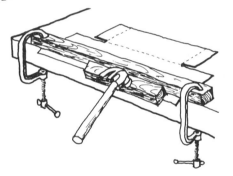

4. *Reglet:* The reglet is the slot cut in the chimney to hold the cap flashing. The reglet goes straight across the front, is stepped along the two sides, and goes straight across the back (assuming there's no cricket, a tentlike piece of flashing between the roof and chimney on the uphill side). Use a diamond blade with a water-spray attachment in a hand-

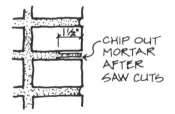

held circular saw, or a portable grinder with a masonry blade. A circular saw with a carbide masonry blade will work, but not as fast as a grinder. In many cases, a cold chisel is really all you need.

Make two passes in the mortar joint with the blade set at 1 1/2 inches. Then use the cold chisel to knock out mortar between cuts.

5. *Base Flashing—Apron:* Remove shingles on three sides of chimney. Remove to next full shingle beyond the 4-inch minimum. Don't remove any shingles on the down side.

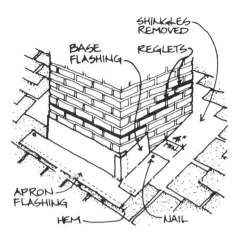

Install apron flashing over shingles on lower slope. There should be a hem at the bottom edge. Place one nail at each top corner where it will be covered by the first piece of side base flashing.

6. *Stepped Base Flashing:* Install base flashing on sloped sides. Note the placement of a single nail in the flashing and two nails in the covering shingle. The first piece of side base flashing comes around the corner to overlap the apron, so there's double coverage at each corner.

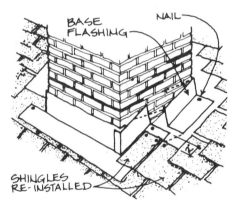

Allow 2 inches of base flashing to extend above the top of the covering shingle. The flashing should be 1/2 inch above where the butt end (bottom) of the covering shingle will be.

Continue to interweave the base flashing, then shingle. Be sure that the shingle covers the nail in the base flashing, and the next piece of flashing covers the nails in previous shingle. Note the dimensions of the overlap. The

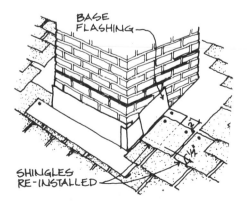

length of each piece of base flashing is determined by the length and headlap of the shingles. Relay shingles with the same lap they had previously. Continue up the slope on each side of the chimney.

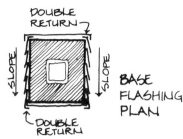

Then install a continuous strip of base flashing on the up-slope side of the chimney, much like the apron flashing at the bottom, except that this piece goes *under* the shingles that were removed earlier. Create a return at each corner of this flashing to overlap the base flashing. Replace the shingles on the up-slope side of the chimney.

7. *Counterflashing Apron:* All base flashing is counterflashed with cap pieces let into the reglet. All cap pieces have a 1/2-inch lip on the edge inside the reglet. A hem at the bottom of the cap flashing will stiffen the edge, but if it's too difficult to bend, it's not necessary. Note how the apron counterflashing returns around corners. The apron counterflashing can extend all the way down the vertical surface.

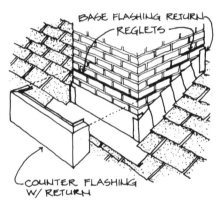

Use rolled metal wedges (either lead or copper) no more than 12 inches apart to hold cap flashing in the reglet.

8. *Stepped Counterflashing:* Install each piece of

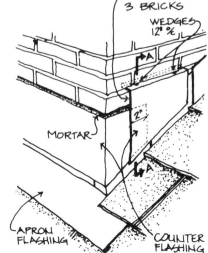

stepped counterflashing according to the drawings. Maximum step-up between pieces is 3 bricks. If slope is very steep, cut more (and narrower) pieces to compensate.

Place metal wedges every 12 inches in reglet, a minimum of two for each piece of stepped flashing. Capflashing must overlap base flashing at least 4 inches, but it can come all the way down the vertical wall if desired. Each piece of stepped flashing overlaps the previous one 2 inches on the vertical seam.

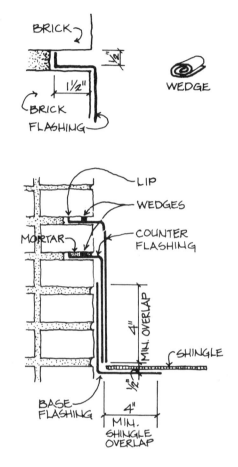

9. *Remortaring:* Repoint the reglet with a mortar that matches the original in composition, color, and shape of joint. Alternately, use caulk, but this will require annual inspection and maintenance.

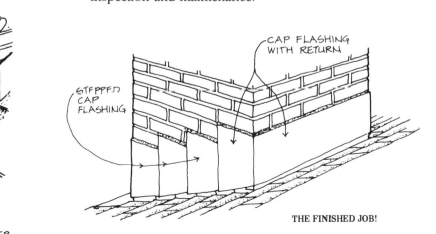

THE FINISHED JOB!

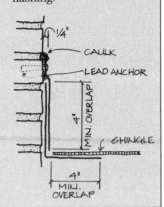
CHINNEYS

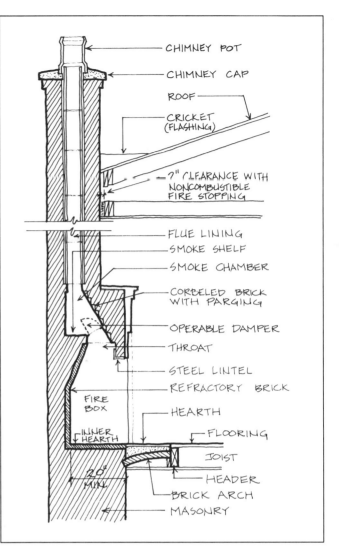

O f course there's more to caring for a chimney than what you see on the roof. You should make annual inspections of a working chimney, and make a thorough inspection of an old chimney before using it. A leaning chimney more often results from a buildup of the by-products of burning various fuels than wind, though your problem may simply be deteriorating mortar and brick, which is affected by wind. Use the inspection guidelines here before doing any work on your chimney.

Chimneys need a thorough going over from the inside out. Are there cracks and settling at the foundation? Do you see any crack evidence that indicates the chimney is moving away from the house? Inspect the rack (the widening of the chimney where it becomes the fireplace) for weathering. Protect racks with a course of paving brick or wide, flat stone (the most durable method), or with mortar wash. Mortar wash should fill each step of brick (but not bridge over each course, or horizontal layer); you may have to remortar eroded parts.

Determine whether the chimney is lined. While a flue liner is required by code (and for safety), most nineteenth-century chimneys were built before they were common practice. Clay-tile liners, used since about 1910, can crack and come apart, sometimes as a result of a chimney fire. Byproducts of new, high-efficiency coal burners and gas appliances also affect them. Cement and metal liners are newer, but should also be checked. Unlined chimneys may suffer from mortar deterioration inside and need a liner. Check the condition of the interior mortar joints. Look up the hearth with a mirror or through the stovepipe thimble. Corrosive action of burning byproducts literally erodes a chimney from inside out, leaving half-empty mortar joints on the flue side. Chimneys not attended to will eventually be destroyed. If the chimney has a liner and you discover bad mortar joints, have the chimney re-lined by a contractor.

You should also note and remove any obstructions. You may find electric wires, pipes, television cables, and the like in an old, nonworking chimney. If the chimney is straight, sighting up or down the flue will tell you whether it is clear. You can locate obstructions by tying a rope to a weight (window sash weight is ideal) and lowering it down the flue until the rope goes slack. Measure the amount of rope let out to tell you where the obstruction is. Sometimes drawing the weight up a few feet and dropping it on the obstruction breaks it up. Persistent blockages (such as a cluster of fallen bricks) may require breaking through the chimney wall.

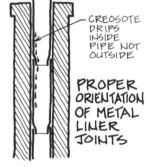

PROPER ORIENTATION OF METAL LINER JOINTS

For chimneys with bends, do a smoke test. First, close all known openings, including the top. Then put a small, smoky fire or a smokebomb (made for the heating trade and available at supply houses) in the fireplace. You'll quickly identify leaks where plumes of smoke come through the mortar. Repair any cracks with heat-resistant (refractory) mortar marketed for chimney repair.

Also check mortar joints for creosote or soot bleeding through them. A faulty liner or the joints themselves are usually to blame and buildup inside the chimney is likely.

Creosote—the dark spots on the chimney—leaking through mortar joints is a sure sign of problems.

You'll also want to repair any poorly patched holes at this point. Breaches may have been repaired with brick pieces and wadded aluminum foil or an unused stovepipe thimble (the portion of a metal stovepipe passing through the wall of a chimney) may be sealed with a metal "pie plate." Poorly patched holes may have been wallpapered over, leaving telltale bulges.

The chimney's cleanout door, at its base and usually in the basement, should also be sound. The cleanout door should be made of ferrous metal, cast cement, or other fireproof material and must create a tight seal when closed. In an unused chimney, check for soot, leaves, twigs, and nesting materials inside the cleanout door. Remove debris before and after repair and cleaning.

Check to be sure the damper operates properly. If you don't find one, install one to make an efficient fireplace. In an old chimney, so much debris may have collected on a closed damper that you won't be able to open it. Dig around the slots in the damper with a long tool and rake out soot and dirt. This is a messy job, but eventually a hole through the debris will develop and the accompanying draft up the flue will draw away dust.

Finally, if the fireplace has an ash pit, empty the ashes and double check that the passage to the fireplace floor is clear. Stovepipe thimbles (and stovepipes too) should never protrude into flue space where they will impede draft. But they should extend fully through the chimney wall and stop flush with the inside surface. Where wood or coal stoves are installed, the connector pipe should continue inside the chimney at least to the beginning of the flue liner. Such installations should *not* be made in chimneys where a cross-sectional area of flue is more than three times the area of the stovepipe.

Inspect your chimney once a year. Most people recom-

mend the spring, as the heating season is over and warm weather will allow you to make repairs. Also, the by-products of burning are still fresh and have had little time to corrode metal and mortar. We recommend chimney cleaning by a professional, particularly if it is very dirty or hasn't been cleaned in a long time. Many chimney-cleaning brushes and devices are on the market, but the basic process remains the same: brushing soot and other by-products off flue walls from top down, then vacuuming the residue from the hearth and smoke shelf.

On the roof, make sure the chimney is at least 3 feet higher than the roof surface where it comes through, and 2 feet higher than any roof surface within 10 feet.

ROOF SAFETY

When working at great heights, a little apprehension will keep you safe, but get someone else to do the job if you're *too* apprehensive. Follow these guidelines—and *always* use a harness, even if it's a small job.

• Wear rubber-soled shoes with a nonslip tread (preferably sneakers with high tops for ankle support). Avoid wearing loose clothing.

• Wear a safety belt or harness and secure it to the chimney (if it's in good shape) or to a window on the opposite side of the house. Leave only enough slack so you can work comfortably in one area, and adjust the slack as you work on other sections of the roof.

• If the roof is especially steep, lay a ladder on the roof and secure it with a safety bracket hooked over the ridge.

• Be sure the roof is clear of debris and water. Avoid stepping on damaged or crumbling roofing materials.

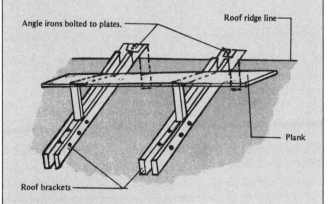

• Use a rack to hold your tools and supplies. Do not stand on it unless it's a scaffold specially designed to support you as well.

You can get roofing brackets from Murray-Black Company, 1837 Columbus Avenue, Dept. OHJ, Springfield, OH 45501; (513)323-3609 and from Qual-Craft, P.O. Box 559, Dept. OHJ, Stoughton, MA 02072-0559; (800)231-5647.

Note: Some racks may not be safe to stand on. Check with the manufacturer.

Shorter chimneys frequently have draft problems; they may spew live sparks on the roof.

Is your chimney leaning excessively? Chimneys lean because of the effects of sulfur dioxide. The sulfur dioxide combines with lime (calcium carbonate) in mortar and converts it to calcium sulfate—a compound that occupies a larger volume than lime alone. The mortar joints on the side of the prevailing wind, which brings wind-driven rain, gradually become thicker than joints on the lee side. The result is a lopsided expansion of the mortar and a leaning chimney. Minor leaning poses more of an appearance problem than a structural one, but if the chimney shows signs of cracking and imbalance, it may have to be dismantled to the roofline and rebuilt.

Check the flashing and the cricket (if there is one) between the chimney and roof on the uphill side. Look for leak evidence on rafters or the underside of the roof. Seal open joints with cartridge caulking or roofing cement, or repair the flashing as described on page 87. Caulks should be a good grade polysulfide, butyl, or silicone rubber sealant, not oil-based. Also check the chimney cap at the top, which keeps water from penetrating masonry.

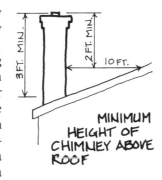

MINIMUM
HEIGHT OF
CHIMNEY ABOVE
ROOF

Open seams in roof flashing or caulking can cause water leaks.

REPAIRING THE CORNICE

Cornices add architectural interest to an old building. Even though they are difficult to get at, inspect yours carefully for water damage, which eventually could damage the building wall and roof. A severely deteriorated wood cornice is dangerous—decorative elements might fall off, and the whole cornice could pull loose.

Cornices are constructed in three ways. The *parapet cornice* is used on both wood and masonry buildings. Built on top of a parapet wall, which extends above the roof of a building, it projects out over the facade and may be partially supported by its decorative brackets. The ele-

REPOINTING

With a hammer and chisel, remove all the loose mortar to a depth of at least 1 inch (although some recommend removing mortar to a depth of two to two-and-one-half times the width of the joint—about 1/2 inch to 3/4 inch). Rake the joint clear to the brick or stone on top and bottom, and square along sides and back. Brush all loose material and dust from the opening, and wet the joint with a rag or coarse brush so the new mortar does not have its own moisture drawn off.

Unless your chimney is pointed with soft mortar (popular until 1870 when portland cement became standard), use a type N, portland-cement lime mortar. Matching mortar is important because some mortars are too rigid for certain types of brickwork. When the bricks expand in hot weather, they'll break on hard mortar; when they contract in cold weather, they'll crack away from the mortar. Modern mortars are much harder than soft mortar, which has a high lime content. A good soft mortar-type formula:

> 1 part portland cement
> 3 parts hydrated lime
> 3 to 5 parts sand to 1 part of the
> cement-lime mixture

Fill joints in layers to limit shrinkage and pack them well. Tool the joint with a jointer just after the mortar sets but while it is still soft. This tempers and shapes the exposed surface of the joint. Tooling should match the rest of the masonry. (Mortar profiles are designed to shed water.) Finally, pointing mortar will develop to maximum strength if allowed to cure slowly. Cover the new work with burlap or old tarps and keep them damp for three consecutive days.

In the combustion chamber and hearth, use fireclay mortar in accordance with ASTM C 105. Fireclay mortar comes in cartridges like caulking compound, which are well-adapted to repointing, as well as in dry mixes commonly used for new work and major repairs. Make combustion-chamber mortar joints as thin as possible—typically 1/16 inch to 3/16 inch; no more than 1/4 inch—to minimize cracks and movement from thermal expansion. With cartridge mortar lay the mortar in with a gun after raking, dusting, and wetting. Finish off flush with the brick with a putty knife or trowel. Follow the manufacturer's directions for curing before lighting a fire. More extensive repairs will probably mean using traditional fireclay mortar. Rule-of-thumb allows thirty days for curing after construction before starting a fire in a new or repaired hearth.

ments extending down over the facade often are attached with spike boards. The *top-of-the-wall cornice* resembles the parapet cornice, but is lighter weight, which allows for deeper paneled decorative surfaces. It usually rests on a masonry wall or facade that stops at or slightly above the roof line. It is not attached to the facade. You'll see the *flush-mount cornice* on facades between floors, or it may be surface-mounted on a parapet. It is often attached to

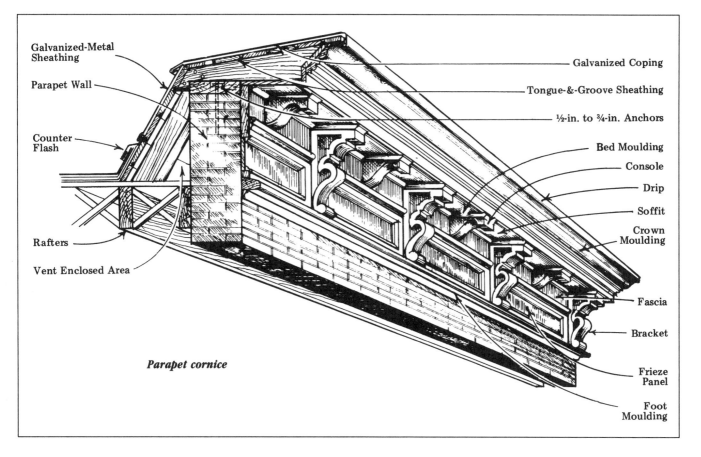

Galvanized-Metal Sheathing
Parapet Wall
Counter Flash
Rafters
Vent Enclosed Area

Galvanized Coping
Tongue-&-Groove Sheathing
½-in. to ¾-in. Anchors
Bed Moulding
Console
Drip
Soffit
Crown Moulding
Fascia
Bracket
Frieze Panel
Foot Moulding

Parapet cornice

the wall through spike boards (surface-mounted or set into the masonry). Sometimes floor joists or other interior supports extend through the facade to support the cornice.

First inspect the cornice from the ground using a pair of binoculars. Look for loose or missing pieces, signs of water damage, overall sagging, and separations between the cornice and the building. If it looks like it needs repair, rent welded-tube scaffolding from a local scaffolding rental company and have them erect it. Ladders are too dangerous and suspended rigging often requires a city license (not to mention experience working on rigging).

Up on the scaffolding, identify any missing, damaged, severely deteriorated, and nonoriginal elements. Examine old photos of the building as a guide, and take some of your own to jog your memory later when you're trying to put all the parts together. Also, photos will be useful for off-site work. It may be easier to take the photos and

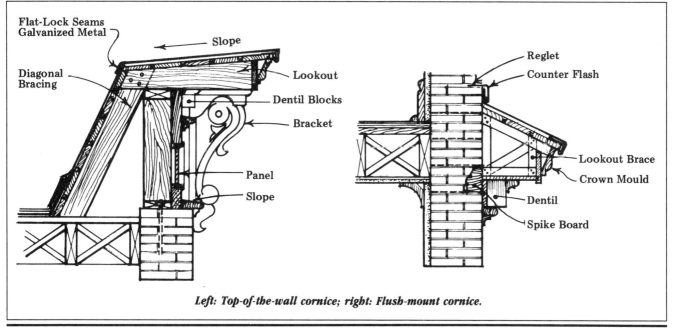

Flat-Lock Seams Galvanized Metal
Diagonal Bracing
Slope
Lookout
Dentil Blocks
Bracket
Panel
Slope

Reglet
Counter Flash
Lookout Brace
Crown Mould
Dentil
Spike Board

Left: Top-of-the-wall cornice; right: Flush-mount cornice.

Note the deflecting bricks in the parapet wall on the left side of the photo. They indicate that the cornice has begun to lean back, creating an unsound structural condition.

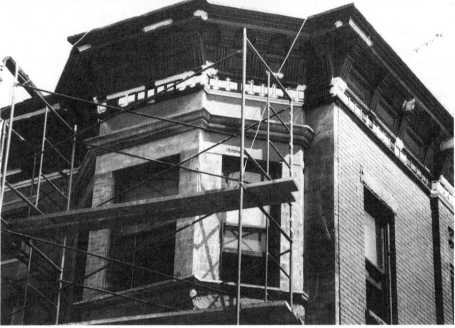

With few horizontal surfaces to trap water, this cornice has held up well. The primed (white) pieces are replacements; duplicates of each replaced element have been set aside, in case any future replacements are needed.

measurements to a millwork shop to duplicate a bracket than to remove and take along a sample bracket.

Most cornice deterioration results from moisture. Sometimes structural weaknesses and deterioration in supporting walls are hidden by the cornice. You may find you have to repair the supporting wall once you remove sections of the cornice. Trace leaks back to their sources and look for weakened, water-damaged structural members. Use an ice pick, awl, or knife to gently probe for deteriorated wood.

Paint failure and subsequent wood decay start at joints where moisture and dirt collect. Some particularly susceptible areas include:

- Horizontal projections (foot mouldings)
- Mitered or butted joints (frieze mouldings)
- Exposed end grain
- Laminations of built-up pieces (brackets or trusses)
- Vertical surfaces washed by rainwater (crown moulding, fascia, frieze panel)
- Areas where flashing was ineffective or has failed

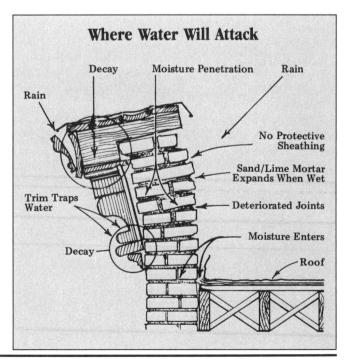

Where Water Will Attack

Decay   Moisture Penetration   Rain

Rain

Rain

No Protective Sheathing

Sand/Lime Mortar Expands When Wet

Deteriorated Joints

Trim Traps Water

Moisture Enters

Decay

Roof

Look twice before you pull, bang, or lean on an old cornice. While they seldom come tumbling down in one piece, on masonry buildings the spike boards may have warped and their fasteners may be rusty. This can cause the cornice to warp and twist away from the building. Support and secure a loose cornice before you work on it.

Repair the supporting wall if necessary. Most well-built cornices on masonry parapet walls have shed roofs (or properly designed coping and flashing) to protect the back of the wall from weather. Woodframe parapet walls are shielded with metal copings, wall pans, flashings, and counterflashings. If the coping and flashing are bad or missing, the wall and even the roof may suffer from water damage. You may have to repoint the wall, or in some cases you may have to dismantle it down to sound bricks or stone and relay it.

Strengthen woodframe parapet walls by removing the exterior sheathing from their backs, and bolting new structural timbers alongside existing ones. For major repairs, seek the advice of a structural engineer.

Note: Stabilizing a cornice that's come loose from its moorings is dangerous work and should be done *only* by experienced professionals.

Cornice Structure

The internal framework of a wooden cornice varies considerably. Small cornices may have no enclosed interior spaces; larger ones may have spaces big enough to crawl into. Cornice frameworks usually consist of 2 × 4s (sometimes 2 × 6s). Most cornices were built in place, so their structural-support systems make removing the cornice in one piece impossible. You'll have to partially disassemble the cornice to reveal the nature and condition of its internal support system.

Try getting to the framework from the top. Carefully remove sections of the roof covering and wood sheathing below and you can look directly down at the structural supports. Avoid removing either decorative trim or facing boards if you can, and make your repairs from the roof.

Use wooden gusset plates, diagonal bracing, and additional framing members to strengthen the existing structural members. (Get specifications for them from an engineer.) Use screws to fasten interior framing members; for stronger joints, use waterproof glue with the screws. Also use treated lumber if wood rot is likely to recur.

To reanchor a cornice that's pulled away from the building, you have to know how it was attached and understand what forces have been pulling it loose. Except for some flush-mounted cornices, most of a cornice's weight rests on top of the facade wall. When the front of a cornice has pulled away from the building, you may be able to pull it back again by installing anchors (either through-wall or expansion bolts). Avoid using masonry anchors or bolts that are shot into the masonry with a powder charge. Installing too many anchors, especially through-wall, can weaken masonry parapet walls, so plan repairs carefully.

If the cornice is beyond repair, you'll have to remove it entirely. Some can be lifted free with a crane and lowered to the ground; others have to be dismantled piece by piece. If possible, you can restore the old cornice in the shop using epoxies or traditional carpentry repairs. You may be able to salvage some of the decorative parts, saving money as well as original materials. Try to exactly duplicate missing or unsalvageable pieces. Plywood used on exposed panels nearly always ends up looking like plywood, so avoid using it.

You may find you have to modify the cornice design slightly if the original design did not weather well. Use the "shingle principle": overlap all joints and fastener holes from above to shed water. The tops of large horizontal

Water has gotten inside this cornice through the deteriorated roofing and flashing. It has weakened the interior supports, causing the cornice to sag—and to pop off pieces onto passersby. A cornice left in this condition is bound to fall off eventually.

projections aren't visible from the street, so flash them. You'll also need to provide an exit for water (both liquid and vapor) that might get inside the cornice.

For closed interior spaces provide adequate ventilation. Moisture buildup leads to peeling paint and wood decay. If your cornice has no boxed-in enclosures, then there's nothing to ventilate, but cornices with enclosed spaces should be vented. If possible, provide plenty of cross-ventilation from the soffit through the cornice and out the back side of the parapet wall or lean-to shed. Screen the vents to keep out rain, snow, birds, and insects. The small, ready-made, circular, painted-aluminum louvered screen vents are easy to install, but admit far too little air. Use them only in the smallest enclosures. For larger areas, use bronze screen wire, which provides better ventilation.

Bronze Screen Wire
Soffit Vent

Decorative Trim

Decorative trim may warp and pull away from the surface. Nails rust off or the wood decays around the fasteners, allowing them to pull out. You can reattach loose trim after cleaning out any debris behind it. After removing the trim, cut the remaining original nails and reposition the piece. Blunt the ends of nails or predrill pilot holes to reduce the chances of splitting. Renail through new holes in sound wood; old holes are probably too large to provide a tight grip.

To reattach loose screws, use high-quality, long-lasting fasteners such as

• Hot-dipped galvanized finishing nails, or brass or stainless steel marine wood screws.

• Self-starting drywall screws—these can rust, so use them only where they can either be countersunk and plugged over, or covered with another element.

• Galvanized screws for use with a screw gun—be sure heads aren't visible from the surface of the cornice.

• Monel "Anchorfast" boat nails—they have the holding strength of similar-size screws (due to their ring-shank design) and won't corrode or rust.

Fashion replacement parts out of the same wood used in the cornice, although some restorations have used parts cast in fiberglass-reinforced plastic or high-density foam. New wood replacement parts should have the grain running in the same direction as the original, ideally with no end grain exposed to the weather. Weldwood phenol resorcinol is an excellent waterproof exterior wood glue for repairing splits or attaching decorative pieces. Availa-

ble at most hardware stores, it comes in two parts that have to be mixed together. (It shrinks on setting, so use it only as a glue, not as a filler.)

Cornice Patches

Though covering problems with a metal patch sounds like a poor shortcut, on cornices you may have no other choice. If your cornice's ugly gaping holes are letting in birds, animals, or water and you can't do a full restoration of the cornice, reversible metal patches may be the answer.

Galvanized steel lasts indefinitely if painted regularly and is the most common patching material. Terne, terne-coated stainless steel, and copper also serve as good patching materials. (Remember, patches that touch metal flashing should be made of the same material to avoid galvanic corrosion.)

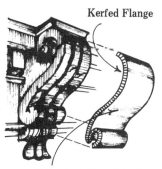
Kerfed Flange
Galvanized Sheet Metal Primed & Painted

Overlap the hole by at least 1 inch, making sure the patch reaches sound wood. Predrill holes in the patch 1/2 inch in from the edge and an inch or less apart—this helps the patch follow the contour of the area being repaired. (Use galvanized nails to refasten a galvanized or terne patch, copper nails for a copper patch.) Prime the back of the patch. Set the patch in a bed of high-quality, paintable, exterior-grade caulk before nailing. Wipe off excess caulk, then prime and paint the front of the patch.

Wood patches, particularly the carpenter's "dutchman," offer long-lasting and attractive repair. Carefully hand-saw or chisel out the damaged area to a prescribed size and shape, and then cut a piece of wood to fit the opening exactly. Glue the patch in place with epoxy or waterproof glue, and secure it with dowels or screws. A dutchman, properly sanded and painted, is a smooth and almost invisible, permanent repair.

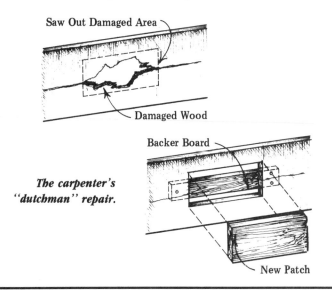
Saw Out Damaged Area
Damaged Wood
Backer Board
The carpenter's "dutchman" repair.
New Patch

Moisture-damaged, rotted, cracked, split, and even missing wood cornice elements can be repaired, filled, and reconstructed using two-part, high-performance epoxies that are specially formulated for this purpose. Epoxies allow you to patch in place; they're quick, easy to apply, easy to tool and finish—but they're not cheap. However, unlike the less-expensive auto-body fillers and latex wood fillers, high-quality epoxies adhere well and stay put.

As a general rule of thumb, if 40 percent or more of a wooden piece has rotted, it's more cost-effective to replace it. Below that percentage, epoxies are an excellent way to retain many original wood pieces that otherwise would have to be removed. (Millworks have never been keen on tooling up to make a 12-inch length of crown moulding, and there's certainly no point in replacing all 30 feet of moulding when only a foot needs repair.) Where many intricate wood replacement pieces would require many hours to produce and install, consider patching with epoxy thickened with compatible fillers (available from the epoxy supplier).

Also use epoxies to consolidate even rotted wood, reducing its tendency to soak up moisture. This is particularly handy for decorative millwork on cornices, which tends to trap moisture and lose paint. For proper adhesion, paint and varnish have to be removed from wood before treating; if it's wet, the wood will have to dry out. Low-viscosity epoxy can be brushed, poured, or injected into rotted wood until it's fully saturated. For best adhesion, prewet deteriorated wood with either low-viscosity or regular epoxy, before you apply the epoxy filler. Filling large areas usually requires several applications. (Epoxy gives off heat as it cures, so you want to apply only a thin layer at a time. *Don't* apply in direct sunlight; watch it, and keep a hose or fire extinguisher nearby.)

The hole in this wooden cornice is being filled with filler epoxy which will be sanded down to the proper contour and smoothness. To ensure the best bond between wood and epoxy, all the surface paint around the area to be filled has been removed.

This decorative cornice has typical crown-moulding decay caused by the failure of the drip flashing and roof. The miter-cut, curved crown moulding (top left) has fallen apart at the saw cuts. The frieze trim at the base of the bracket at right has dropped off because water rusted the nails. The cornice is in such bad repair that a pigeon (center top) has been able to make its home here.

Cornice Roof and Flashing Repair

As with chimney flashing, be sure you use the right material. Good metals for cornice roofs, coping, and flashing are

- Copper (16- to 20-ounce)
- Lead-coated copper (16- to 20-ounce)
- Terne-coated stainless steel (24- to 26-gallon)
- Terne metal (IX 40#)
- Galvanized steel (22- to 24-gallon)
- Hard lead (3-pound) or chemical grade, aminonial, or copper-bearing lead (4- or 6-pound, though 6-pound lasts longest)

On masonry buildings, flashing is often set into a reglet. If the joint packing (mortar or caulk) fails, the flashing may pull out and allow water in. Clean out the joint and reanchor the flashing in the reglet by installing lead wedges then repacking the joint with mortar that matches the original.

Be sure to install an effective drip edge (see

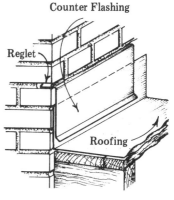

Counter Flashing

Reglet

Roofing

page 87) along the front of the cornice where the crown moulding meets the roof; this forces water to drip free rather than run down the front of the cornice.

Caulk and Putty

Wood putty, fillers, and doughs are misused cure-alls for every type of exterior wood deterioration. Exterior fillers work fine for covering small nail holes, but shouldn't be used to fill joints or seams. They can't expand and contract with the wood, and so larger patches usually fail in short order—wrecking a good paint job, forming a trap for moisture, and opening up the wood to further decay.

Sealants, more commonly known as caulks, come in four common varieties: polysulfides, silicones, acrylics, and butyls. Of these, polysulfides tend to provide the greatest elasticity without breaking away from the seam or joint. They're also sandable—meaning you can fill a seam and sand flush for an imperceptible joint. Their disadvantage is that they're slow to dry (up to ten days); they usually can be painted just after installation, but can't be sanded until dry. Polysulfides work best with two-sided seams; if the sealant is attached to three sides, one side may pull loose. For best adhesion, the seam should be a minimum of 1/8-inch wide and 1/4-inch deep.

Compared to polysulfide, the other sealants dry very quickly, in twenty-four to forty-eight hours. Silicone rubber can't grip nearly as strongly or take as much expansion and contraction as polysulfide can, and although some varieties can be painted, it can't be sanded. Acrylics are less expensive, shorter-lived polymers; limit their use to tight narrow joints. Butyls, the most common and least expensive of sealants, work in applications similar to

This cornice is really for the birds. The missing scrolls on the consoles and brackets are now a sparrow motel. All the missing parts had surfaces that trapped water, dooming them to fail.

acrylics. Though they may be painted when cured to a rubber and stand up well to moisture, they're somewhat stringy to apply and can't be sanded.

Sealants are indispensable for sealing joints and seams on cornices where expansion and contraction movement occur, where dissimilar materials meet, or where two or more objects are joined together. Horizontal seams and joints on cornices are notorious for opening up and trapping all kinds of debris and moisture, so be sure to allow yourself plenty of time to caulk all the open seams you find on the cornice. It's also a good idea to bed elements being reattached to the cornice in sealant, at least around the perimeters. But don't use sealants as fillers or adhesives.

Primer and Paint

Before removing any old paint, look for "ghosts": missing pieces often leave behind a clue to their contour in the form of a paint line, or ghost. You might also want to test for original paint colors before you remove paint down to bare wood.

Keep the following in mind while planning the paint job:

• Prepare the surfaces properly—remove flaking paint, dirt, and the like.

• Use paintable sealants.

• Use primer that is compatible with the topcoat of paint—primer and topcoat from the same manufacturer is best.

• Back-prime all decorative elements before you install them.

• Never leave primed wood exposed to the weather for longer than forty-eight hours before applying the topcoats.

• High-gloss alkyd enamel works well as a topcoat on exterior wood. High-gloss paints are slightly more weather resistant than those with lower sheens. However, you can get good results with a semi-gloss alkyd paint or latex paint.

• Don't use cheap, substandard paint, and don't try to get away with applying only one topcoat—always apply two. (You don't want to have to do this again next year.)

• Don't spray paint a cornice; it has too many sharp angles and recesses to be properly covered by spraying—brush paint carefully, making sure to get every nook and cranny.

At least once a year, you should make a routine inspection of the cornice, and make whatever small repairs and touch-ups are necessary. Make the paint job last longer by washing painted surfaces of the cornice annually. Once the cornice is restored, you may be surprised to find that your efforts have set off a trend of cornice restoration in your area. No one seems to notice the beauty of cornices until one in the neighborhood gets restored.

CHAPTER 7

Exterior Repairs and Painting

J ust as projections through the roof, such as chimneys, will likely spring leaks, attachments and openings in the walls are subject to leaks and decay. Likely candidates include the framing around doors and windows, which may have seams that permit water to reach the end-grain of wooden components. Also carefully inspect small balconies and roofs over bay windows, window sills, bottoms of posts and columns, and ends of railings.

Besides caulking joints in wooden framing, make sure that the elements are shedding water properly. For example, window and door framing is normally protected by flashing or a drip cap. Old window sills may now be incorrectly pitched because of settlement, and may hold rather than shed water.

Of course, if you have more serious problems such as noticeably bowed walls, you should check into the major structural repairs first. And you'll want to check the general condition of the house's siding, particularly in moisture-prone areas such as around the foundation or where plants grow close to the house. (Also see chapter 3, "The Crack Detective," for a discussion of evidence that indicates major structural repairs.) Finally, once you have made all necessary repairs, invest in a good paint or stain that will last, and will help protect the house from the elements.

——BOWED WALLS——

W alls often bend because of the way houses are constructed. Bowing will cause horizontal cracks on the interior where the plaster has been slightly crushed by the compression on the inside of the bend. There will also be horizontal cracks on the exterior where the bowing has opened the joints between clapboards or brick courses. And there will be interior cracks where the outside wall has pulled away from abutting floors and walls.

Bowed wood walls are probably caused by lack of a connection at each floor. This usually occurs only with balloon framing—where the studs on the outside walls are more than one storey high. For problems with other types of framing, see the section on beams in chapter 12.

Ground settlement and a wall that is too thin cause bowing of masonry walls. If the wall is not attached to the floor framing, as with the front wall of a townhouse, check the likelihood that the wall will collapse by measur-

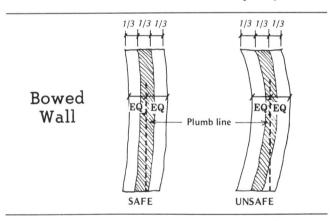

ing the thickness of the wall and the amount of bowing. Then draw a section of the wall to scale. Draw a line from the center at mid-point of the bow, straight down to the bottom of the wall. This line should always fall within the middle third of the wall.

You can apply the same rule to tilted walls. When part or all of the building tilts together, such as a leaning chimney, the center is in the middle of the entire structure. This means that with the same amount of tilt, an unattached leaning wall is more likely to fall down than a leaning chimney or tower. The Tower of Pisa is the most famous example of a leaning structure that follows the one-third rule.

In the case of a leaning or bowing wall that is 12 inches thick, the amount of lean or bow must be less than 2 inches, no matter how tall the wall is. Remember that when the lean reaches this point, the structure is already very dangerous. When the floor joists are resting on the bowing or leaning wall, the amount of displacement that is safe is much less. Also, eroded mortar reduces the effective thickness of the wall, thereby reducing the permissible amount of movement.

Reconstructing Bad Connections

Reconstruct failed connections in the house. Invention and ingenuity play a big part in redesigning and integrating structural connections. The joists-to-girder connection is a common failure. The easiest repair involves using a metal joist hanger. (Since the ones available today aren't sized for yesterday's lumber, you'll have to have one made up by an ironworker or welder. Or you can try wedging between the hanger and the wood joist.) Connections for heavier loads, such as a girder that carries several joists or a bearing wall, should be designed by an engineer. Bolt, don't nail, the hanger.

Also use metal connectors to tie bowed or leaning walls into the rest of the structure. A combination of tie-rods, connecting plates, and even reframing the building may be involved. Your aim should be to make sure the whole house acts as one structure rather than a bunch of individual elements. For example, arrest bowing walls on opposite sides of a house by connecting them with tie-rods running all the way through the house. If the

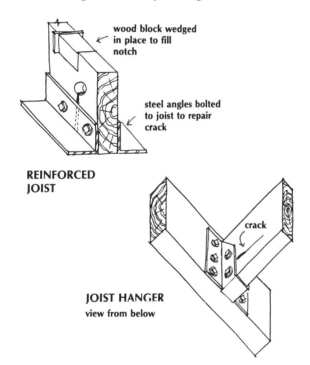

REINFORCED JOIST

wood block wedged in place to fill notch

steel angles bolted to joist to repair crack

crack

JOIST HANGER
view from below

walls were merely tied to the joists nearest them, the wall would just move the joists sideways. In this case a creative architect can be a great help.

In bearing failures, you'll need to spread the weight over a larger area. If the wood beam is being crushed,

sistering the end can double the area bearing on the wall. If the brick in the wall below the beam is being crushed, a metal plate, wider than the beam, will spread the weight over more of the wall. An engineer should calculate the area you need for bearing.

For badly bowed walls, install protection right away and get expert advice. Failing arches and lintels should be shored up inside the window openings. The support should be designed so that the arch is supported all along its length. (On the inside you may find plaster and masonry cracked enough that it may fall. Remove it or shore it up with plywood.)

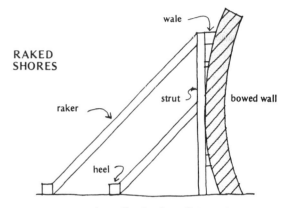

RAKED SHORES

wale

raker

strut

bowed wall

heel

In extreme cases, install raked or flying shores to support the walls. This kind of shoring is like a smaller version of the flying buttresses on Gothic cathedrals. The shoring transfers the horizontal load on the wall down to the ground.

Drive hardwood wedges into horizontal cracks. This procedure will both fill the space and re-establish bearing on the wall below the crack. Be careful: over-driving the wedge may accelerate the movement causing the crack. If the wedges loosen up over time, that probably means the movement is continuing.

Arch Trouble

Masonry walls most often fail around the top of the window and door and openings. This may be caused by beam failure (see chapter 12), or it may be a case of arch failure. As built by the Romans, arches rarely failed because of their semi-circular shape. As square windows and doors became fashionable, though, arch problems appeared more often. The flatter an arch, the more likely it will crack over time. Generally, arches that have less than 1 inch of rise per foot of width will crack unless some additional restraint is added.

The sideways force of an arch pushes the ends of the arch apart. Any small movement of the ends or abutments of the arch causes the center to drop, resulting in a pyramidal cracking pattern above it. The way in which the abutment and the arch

Pyramid cracking

Abutment movement

move will help you identify the correct crack suspect.

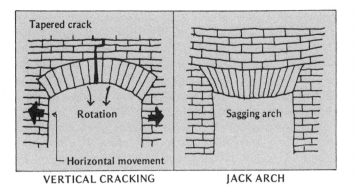

VERTICAL CRACKING **JACK ARCH**

commonly, from walls that are not wide enough on either side of the arch. When there is a row of arches in a wall, they all push against each other; all the stress ends up on the last arch in the row. The center arches may stay in place while the wall at the side of the end arch cracks horizontally at the base of the arch. The push from the arch may also tilt or bow the side wall around the corner from the end of the building.

If one side of the arch falls relative to the other, you'll find movement again at the top of the arch. The underside of the arch will have a jog where one half has dropped lower than the other half. This job may be a clean break or have several steps at different mortar joints. The suspect in this case is one of the settlement types described in chapter 3.

If the abutments move horizontally, the sides of the arch will tilt toward the center, causing a vertical crack that is wider at the bottom. This may also result in a different movement pattern, in which the sides keep their original shape and the center bricks at the top of the arch fall downward. Typically, they will jam in the opening after moving a quarter of an inch or so. If the abutments continue to spread, however, the bricks may fall out completely.

Jack arches are particularly susceptible to this kind of failure. In a jack arch the bottom is flat and the arch is formed by specially shaped bricks that slant toward each

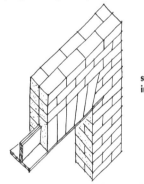

steel angles placed in a jack arch

side. Almost every jack arch ever built sags in the middle. This sag results from horizontal movement of the abutments and insufficient—that is, nonexistent—arch height.

Abutment movement itself occurs when walls don't have enough mass to push back against the ends of the arch. This may result from walls that are too thin or, more

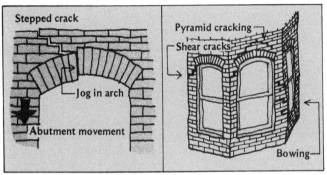

DIFFERENTIAL SETTLEMENT **BAY**

Arch failures are endemic in Victorian bays. The Victorian taste for large windows and narrow corners left most arches with nothing to push against. The cracking pattern commonly found will include pyramidal cracking above the arch, horizontal shear cracks at the base of the arch, and possibly tilting or bowing of the sides of the bay.

In some cases you may see the cracking pattern on the inside of the building, and not the outside. This happens when a wood lintel supports the interior course of bricks and an arch supports the exterior course. When the wood compresses or rots, the plaster on the inside wall will crack while the outside arch remains in place. Similarly, the arch and the brickwork above it may collapse without the inside wall falling down.

Abutment movement also may cause buckling failure

Abutment Movement

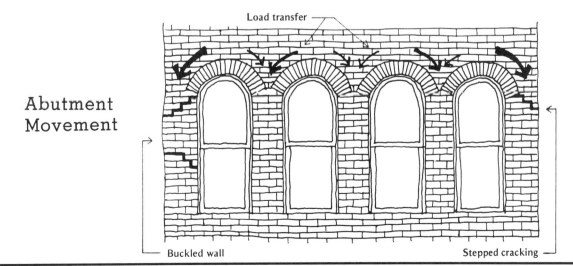

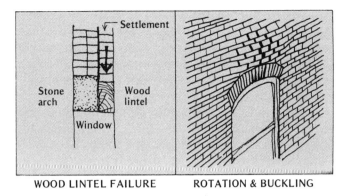

WOOD LINTEL FAILURE   ROTATION & BUCKLING

in an arch. As the arch moves slightly, the bonds between the bricks or stones break at the joints. The weight of the wall above may push sections of the middle of the arch downward and to the front. This may cause the bricks or stone to rotate from their original position, further weakening the arch.

Correcting Bad Arches

To solve arch problems, you need to stop the movement at the ends of the arch. If the movement is a horizontal spreading one, then tie-rods can sometimes be used to relieve the force pushing on the wall. A new tie-rod consists of two steel rods threaded on both ends, a turnbuckle connecting them in the middle, and cast-iron stars or square steel plates on both ends.

Install the tie-rod as close to the bottom of the arch as convenient. For aesthetic reasons on the interior, this will most often mean sticking it in the joist between floors. Place the plates or stars on the outside of the side walls, and tighten the turnbuckle at the center. In most cases you just want to stop further movement—turn the turnbuckle only to hand-tight.

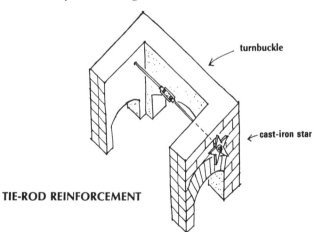

turnbuckle

cast-iron star

TIE-ROD REINFORCEMENT

If ground settlement causes arch failure, deal with it as you would with foundation problems (see chapter 5). You want to stop water and you may have to underpin.

On the interior where the problem is a wood lintel, replace it with a reinforced concrete lintel. You may find a precast concrete lintel at a masonry supply house that will fit. Or, install a steel angle and fill the space where the wood was with brick. As with all difficult jobs of this type, check with an architect or engineer.

Once you have stopped arch movement, you can rebuild the arch. First remove the bricks or stones in the "triangle" above the arch. Old mortar should make this job easy—just lift it out. Temporarily shore up under the arch with pieces of wood and remove the keystone. Watch out: The rest of the pieces will fall onto the shoring.

Replacing the arch may be more difficult. There are few masons around today who can, or will, produce the thin mortar joints often found in an old house. However, it is important that the joints be duplicated, as a bad patch can ruin the appearance of a masonry building forever. It's also very important that the mason build a true arch, not just fill in the space with bricks. Do not replace arches with horizontal brickwork that just rests on the wood frame of the window below; this will cause more cracks in the future. If the original arch was a jack arch, use steel angles for support. Expect to pay a few hundred dollars per arch, plus the cost of scaffolding.

Consider whether the arch really needs to be rebuilt before undertaking all that work. An arch can be quite distorted without actually failing. Once you've arrested its movement, a bit of repointing to keep the water out may be all that's required.

SIDING

Once structural problems are taken care of, carefully inspect the house's siding for damage. If much of it requires repair, you may be tempted to cover the whole mess with a substitute siding. Regular *Old-House Journal* readers are probably familiar with the aesthetic and structural damage aluminum or vinyl "clapboards," plastic "bricks," and asbestos "shingles" can do to an old house. Contrary to what sales people tell you, these sidings are not maintenance free, and synthetic siding will almost certainly destroy the architectural integrity of an old building. It may even contribute to the building's deterioration.

Synthetic siding hides a building's design details and ornaments. In fact, if your old house has synthetic siding now, the details may have been removed when the siding was installed. Synthetic siding even can ruin the proportions of an early twentieth-century frame house. Window casings, drip caps, mouldings, and door trim are often obstructed, destroying the three-dimensional appearance.

Many sidings act as exterior vapor barriers, trapping excess water vapor, which condenses and damages the wood. Rot and insect attack may proceed unnoticed. If installed incorrectly or damaged, runoff water may enter behind the siding and be trapped. Also, artificial sidings offer no structural support, so that if continued deterioration leads to failure, the siding will buckle and separate from the building.

In addition to all these crimes, aluminum siding tends to dent and scratch, and its color coating can peel and fade. Solid vinyl siding punctures and tears; it is sunlight-sensitive, becoming brittle and faded if not treated with an ultra-violet inhibitor. Since the industry frequently

The aluminum siding has covered detailing, and the house has a flat monotonous look.

This house's original clapboard was covered twice, first by wood shingles (front right) and then by asbestos (along the corner of the house).

changes its product lines, replacing a section of damaged siding may be impossible. Successfully painting siding is also difficult.

If you're sold on siding for its fire safety and insulation qualities, think again. Aluminum siding may make it difficult to get at a fire's source, while vinyl siding melts, curls, and sags. The Federal Trade Commission reports that synthetic sidings have little or no insulation value. If siding seems like a bargain because you won't have to paint every few years, consider that the manufacturer's guarantee (usually twenty years, some up to forty years) is prorated: The manufacturer's liability is limited to a decreasing percentage of labor and materials costs as the warranty period progresses.

Aesthetic value, of course, is not quantifiable. Yet it may be an economic consideration because a property will retain greater value with properly maintained original materials. While siding may enhance the short-term resale value, authentic materials and style increasingly command a premium. Real-estate appraisers and potential buyers may also wonder what problems the siding may be hiding.

If there's a last word in siding, it's *beware*.

What Is Clapboard?

Traditional New England *clapboard* is plain-beveled lap siding, a near isosceles triangle, thinner at one edge than the other when viewed from the end grain. It has no shiplap edging or milled matching. Clapboard is often—but not always—installed over wall sheathing.

Other types of horizontal siding, both beveled and nonbeveled, include *weatherboards* and *drop siding* (also called *novelty*). Weatherboards appear most often in the Southeast, are lapped like clapboard, and are usually rectangular on their end. Drop siding is nonbeveled and nonlapped. It is edge-matched with a shiplap or tongue-and-groove so that it installs flat on wall framing without sheathing. It is also milled on the exposed face in a tremendous variety of patterns. Efficient and economical, drop siding most often appears on outbuildings, barns, and garages.

Clapboards are made in three different ways. From the Colonial era until the early 1800s, New England clapboards were hand rived from logs rarely longer than four feet. Each board is pried radially out of a log by working with the grain, something like cutting sections from a grapefruit. Rived clapboard is exceptionally stable as the board follows the tree's natural structure; the grain runs perfectly parallel to its length and perfectly tangent across its edge. After they dry, the boards are handplaned for a smooth surface and regular dimensions.

Machine-made clapboards, which did not appear before the first true band saw around 1830 and were common by 1890, are made by resawing rough lumber at a bias with a band saw to create beveled siding. The best product is *quartersawn-resawn*. These boards are resawn so

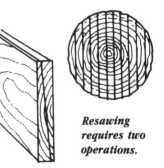

Resawing requires two operations.

they approximate the grain orientation of rived boards. The least desirable is *flatsawn-resawn*. With these boards, the grain can run in any direction, creating a board prone to warping. The pattern used to initially saw a log determines the proportion of near quartersawn to almost flat-sawn lumber it can yield and thus much of the clapboard quality. After sawing, clapboards are edged and surface planed on one face in a power planer. Resawing is the fastest and most common way to make clapboards by machine.

Riftsawing duplicates hand riving. First appearing during the 1820s, riftsawing reached its heyday during the late 1800s when clapboarding was most popular. (Of course, it's no coincidence that the great pine forests were fast disappearing about the same time.)

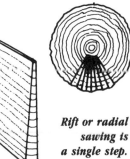

Rift or radial sawing is a single step.

Though labor intensive, riftsawing produced more siding from a log than any other process.

Suspending logs by spindles in a carriage *over* the circular saw blade (rather than beside it as in a standard mill) meant the logs could be rotated and beveled clapboards cut complete in one operation by working radially around its circumference. Some early mills cut only with logs divided into quarters, but later designs could suspend an entire log. Once cut, individual clapboards were pried off the log core, dried, and then planed and edged like the resawn product.

Though riftsawing was slower than resawing and required large, prime timber, it had many advantages. It made excellent use of the tree, turning out more siding and less sawdust. It also reduced waste from knots. Riftsawing also produced a superior quality clapboard that was always truly quartersawn. This meant boards were highly stable and showed a minimum of shrinkage and

After turning, the dowel is hoisted over to the carriage. With the overhead carriage, individual clapboards 8 feet long are cut from the log one at a time. After each cut, the log is rotated and a new board is started. Then, a small spade-like tool called a slick *is used to pry freshly cut clapboards off the log.*

warping. In addition, a quartersawn face took paint well and was highly durable when exposed to the weather because a minimum of soft summerwood—the harder, less porous part of an annual ring that develops late in the growing season—was subjected to the elements (important with a species like pine). Quartersawing exposes a minimum of rings.

The best New England clapboards were made from #1 Eastern White Pine, a wood still in service on houses over two hundred years old. When good pine was not available, hemlock or spruce were also used (hemlock's a little better), but this type of clapboard eroded between annular rings or "washboard" and wore out more quickly than pine. Northeastern cedar, although good for shingles, was a little knotty, had "sloped" grain, and tended to powder and flake as it aged.

Other regions developed siding from different tree species. Poplar had limited use in New England, but was common in Southern states where it stood up well and was readily accessible. Cypress, back when it was plentiful, was also common in warmer states. When railroads reached the big timber forests of the Northwest around 1900, West Coast products such as California Pine and Western Red Cedar spread out across the country to compete with local materials. The huge trees made very wide siding that was both appealing and economical. Although not the traditional stock for clapboards, these woods were highly popular during the building booms of this century.

Laying Up Clapboard

Clapboard is either installed from the bottom up, as in shingling, or from the top down. Working from the bottom up is the most popular method. Start the initial board at the watertable or foundation line of the house, and lap each succeeding board over the one that preceded it. You can use any nailing method when working from the bottom up; it is the only technique that allows you to use blind nailing.

Working from the top down sounds awkward to the non-carpenter, but it may have originated as the easiest way to lay up longer courses of machine-made clapboards, which were eventually far longer than the hand-rived version. Those who recommend this method swear

Horizontal lapped siding can often be rectangular rather than beveled.

SIDING GLOSSARY

Bevel Siding

Rived clapboard: Handsplit and handplaned.

Riftsawn clapboard: True quartersawn grain; shaped like an isosceles triangle with a fine feather edge when viewed on end.

Resawn clapboard: Quarter- to flatsawn grain; forms a near-right triangle.

Bungalow: A thicker and wider variety of resawn bevel siding, known as "Colonial" in some areas.

Rustic Siding

Each rustic siding is milled so that its actual thickness is less than its appearance. This approach saves lumber and allows the use of extra nails on wide patterns to prevent warping.

Log Cabin: A log look-alike with shiplapped joints.

Dolly Varden: Rabbeted-edge bevel siding.

Anzac: Bevel siding shaped on the back to lie flat on studding.

Weatherboards

Wide, sawn, lapped siding laid parallel to the ground. Nonbeveled weatherboards (also called "Colonial" in some areas) are rectangular on the end and often incorporate a bead. Other types have a gradual taper less than true beveled siding.

"Colonial," or lapped, siding on a house in Port Royal, Virginia, built about 1750.

Drop Siding

Lies flat on wall studding, is usually 3/4-inch thick, and can be used without sheathing. It has matched edges, either shiplapped or tongue-and-groove, to make tighter joints than bevel siding. By some standards, drop siding is only tongue-and-groove and in many areas all patterns are called novelty siding. The ubiquitous "cove" pattern, also called "novelty," was popular by 1880, and may have been patented fifteen years earlier.

This type of drop siding, sometimes nicknamed "waterfall," appears in Shohola, Pennsylvania, and was built about 1907.

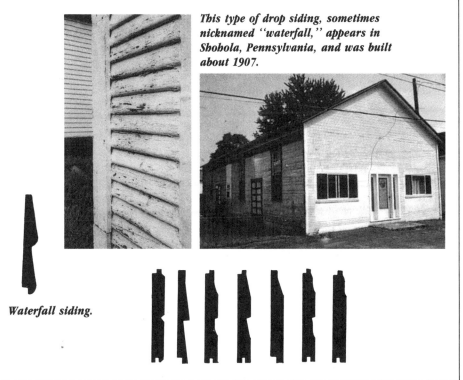

Waterfall siding.

to three advantages: 1) It simplifies fitting the top course in a weatherproof joint at the eave (usually in a rabbet, a groove cut along the edge of the clapboard, under a piece of trim); 2) each new board is slid under the previous course, and will be cinched in position for nailing (which speeds installation and allows a person to work alone); 3) "wedging" the courses together in this fashion produces tight lapping.

A unique advantage of clapboard and other simple lapped sidings is the flexibility in course spacing. Edge-matched siding (like drop) must be the same width in every course, which means boards will be notched somewhere in a wall when going around obstacles. You can adjust clapboard spacing, on the other hand, to neatly fit in whole boards around windows and doors.

Systems for determining spacing vary, but many carpenters start by dividing the height of a window into equal units that produce a likely weatherface exposure for the clapboards (for example, 4 1/2 inches). This dimension, used as the basic spacing for the area above and below the windows, can be adjusted where necessary to make the courses finish evenly on the wall. Many carpenters calculate these measurements on a *storey pole*, a piece

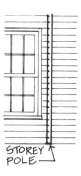

The clapboards are lap jointed, their ends tapering and overlapping rather than merely butting.

of light lumber the height of a wall used as a gauge to standardize spacing on the walls. Hold the storey pole vertically up snug to the frieze board (or other eave trim) and transfer the spacings to the wall. Then snap off the course lines with a chalkline.

The technique for *joining the clapboards* in courses depends on the clapboard. Where rived clapboards had to meet each other they were *skived* instead of butt-jointed. In skiving, the clapboard ends are shaved with a swipe of a drawknife to produce a featheredge that laps with the next board. The skived area was roughly four times the thickness of the butt (the thick edge), and could be cut at an angle to the board end as well as parallel to it. Skiving not only produced very weathertight joints efficiently, but it also eliminated the problem of fitting handplaned boards of irregular thickness so that they looked uniform. It also meant a joint could be made with one nail instead of two—a serious saving in the days when everything was handmade.

With machine-made clapboards, avoid joints in corners

as much as possible by careful planning and using long lumber for stretches under windows. Where joints are necessary, however, use a butt joint with ends cut at a slight bevel to improve the fit. You may paint ends with prime or preservative, but use of caulks or sealants is not recommended. In the best quality work, plan joints so they land on a wall stud. This way, the ends of both clapboards are nailed to framing and the joint is less likely to shift open.

The only rule that applies to determining the *weatherface exposure* on clapboards is "wide enough to do the job." Two factors guide builders: the maximum width of the board and the intended visual effect of the completed siding. The latter varies by region and architectural period.

Traditional clapboards and most bevel siding have to be lapped by 1 to 1 1/2 inches to be weathertight, and this has a big influence on the exposure. Hand-rived boards could be split to a maximum width of about 4 1/2 inches, so the resulting exposure was typically 3 inches. Machine manufacturing of clapboards in the 1800s made 5- and 6-inch riftsawn clapboards possible, along with larger sizes for resawn versions. These products allowed exposures of 4 1/2 inches and greater. When the broad West Coast woods grew popular in this century, siding with an exposure as large as 9 inches became both feasible and fashionable.

Even when clapboard that permitted exposures of 3, 4 1/2, or 9 inches was available, it was not always used to its full capacity. Course widths were often varied to side evenly around windows and doors. They were also compressed in hard weather areas to make a thicker, more weather-resistant cladding for the house. Also, there is strong evidence that exposure was governed by "look." On the Maine coast, some solidly massed Adam houses have very narrow clapboard exposure, undoubtedly intended to make a visual statement with a great number of shadow lines. Buildings of the same style and vintage with substantially different exposures are not hard to find, either. Exposures can even differ on a single building facade and be graduated up the height of the wall (once again, like shingles) to achieve a foreshortening effect. In the eighteenth century, this kind of spacing might be used only on the front face of the house—the side where an aesthetic statement would have most impact.

Clapboard Detailing

Dealing with corners and ending clapboards at eaves and foundations both require special treatment. The two classic treatments for outside corners are mitering and cornerboards. In mitering, the boards in the same course are simply cut at 45 degrees where they meet, and then nailed to the cornerpost of the framing. Manufactured corner caps provide an alternative to plain mitered corners (which can open up as they age and let water in). Historically, mitering probably offered an economical way to finish a corner because it didn't require additional hand-cut lumber.

Look to cornerboards for the preferred corner treatment, both for appearance and weathertight integrity. Here, nail appropriate trim to the cornerpost first (usually two lapped boards of different widths), then butt clapboards to this lumber. Cornerboards can be designed to appear the same width on both walls, or substantially wider on the main facade to have a pilaster effect. The pinnacle of cornerboard treatments perhaps was in the Georgian and Greek Revival eras, when corners were detailed into full-blown pilasters and wood quoins.

Wooden "quoins" mock stone corners.

Though never as involved as outside corners, cornerboards also appear on interior corners. Nail a single square stick (often 3/4 × 3/4-inch but dependent on the thickness of the siding) in the corner first. Then fit clapboards so they finish at the board.

As far as ending clapboards at eaves and foundations, tuck clapboards into a rabbet under a frieze board or other trim at the eaves. (This is also the best way to install clapboards under windows.) The treatment for gables is a matter of taste: Hide the clapboards behind the gable end boards, or rake boards, or just end them at the rake.

Last, foundation treatments also vary according to taste and building style. Early Colonial houses were sometimes clapboarded right down to the soil line, a straightforward method that promoted wood rot. Where masonry foundations were used, the first clapboard might instead begin at the sill with just a starter strip to support it. A better arrangement was some form of trim designed to throw rainwater running down the wall away from the foundation—a watertable. These treatments ranged from a simple drip cap to a widely flared skirt. In addition to deflecting water, the foundation detailing also anchors a house to its site in an attractive finish.

Clapboard Repair

In most cases, you won't have to worry about replacing the clapboard on an entire building. Most wood siding can be salvaged, even if some boards are warped, cracked, rotting, or half missing. Don't put off these repairs: Bad siding admits moisture, cold air, and even little critters.

For boards with cracks and splits, gently open them a little bit, clean out any debris, and evenly coat both edges with a two-part phenol resorcinol waterproof wood glue such as Weldwood or U.S. Plywood. Use an artist's pallet knife to spread the glue. Now squeeze the split closed snugly using a little wood block and one or two nails to hold it until dry. Be careful not to split the siding with the nails. The resorcinol doesn't work well as a filler, so wipe off the excess.

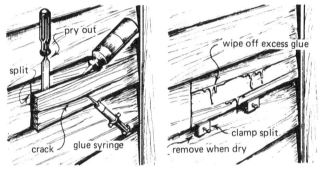

Scrape and prime salvageable boards. After the primer is dry, fill small imperfections with exterior wood filler. Apply fillers sparingly, and *never* use them to span large holes or gaps. Moisture that gets behind a thick filler will pop it off and ruin your paint job later. As soon as the filler dries, sand it down and prime the patch before it gets wet.

To repair larger gouges and holes, drill them out and insert plugs. Buy a plug-cutter bit for your electric drill and cut the plugs from scrap siding. The grain of the wood in the plug should go in the same direction as the siding. The plugs, if they get wet, can expand and split the siding, so prime and paint them soon after installation.

Repair a large surface split or missing sliver in a board with a dutchman, or wood splice (see example on page 108). Use a saw or chisel to tidy up the hole, then cut a new piece of wood to fit.

When you need to replace sections of siding, take a section of the original along with you to the lumberyard. Most lumberyards carry beveled, drop, and other novelty siding, but it may not match the original exactly. To save money, adapt ready-made siding when possible rather than have a custom millworks run an exact match for you. Do any planing, reshaping, and sanding on the back of the boards. If you must get new siding milled, be sure to shop around. Find a shop that already has cutter blades that are the right size and shape, otherwise you'll pay for those along with your siding.

When choosing ready-made siding, be picky. Ask to hand-pick the boards to avoid getting warped, bowed, cupped, split, or knot-hole-infested boards. Saw off minor splits at the ends of boards. Siding boards damage easily during handling and installation, so be careful. Stack them carefully during construction to keep them dry and to prevent warping.

You don't always have to replace the entire board if only part of it is damaged. Simply saw through and remove the damaged section. Make all joints over studs, unless sheathing is present. Use a backsaw and carefully angle it to avoid cutting the siding below. We don't recommend electric saws as they can damage adjacent siding.

Once you've made the vertical cut, split and remove the board with a hammer and chisel. If you try to remove it by pulling out on the bottom, you may bend and split the board above and end up replacing more siding than you bargained for.

The top inch or so of the damaged siding board will usually remain lodged up under the siding above. If nails hold it in place, try to pull them out from the surface. If that doesn't work, gently work small wooden wedges or thin pry bars up under the siding, just enough to allow you to cut and remove the nails. Stanley's mini hacksaw is a good tool for this.

Cut and test fit the new piece into place. Try for a close joint between the old siding and the new, but avoid filling the joint with rigid adhesives as the board will expand and contract with changes in the weather. Dip-soak the ends in waterproofer and prime the wood before installing it to offer the best protection for the exposed end grain of these joints. Once in place, seal the joints with a quality elastic caulk you can paint.

Back-prime new clapboards with primer or stain, depending on whether the top coats will be paint or stain. Seal any knots with a commercial knot sealer formulated for outdoor use—don't use shellac. In high-moisture areas, consider presoaking or brushing the siding boards with a waterproofer before you prime.

Your patched-in boards should match the exposure of

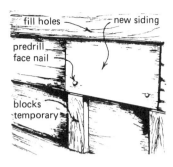

the existing siding. Use simple spacing blocks fashioned from 1 × 4s and cut to the existing exposure. A person at each end of the siding board holds a block in place with one hand and hammers nails into the siding with the other.

When replacing several adjacent courses of siding, stagger the joints. Vertical joints that line up make the patch more obvious and are prone to leak.

Predrill holes in the siding to reduce the chances of splitting when nailing. Nail shiplap siding that's 4 or 6 inches wide with one nail per stud. Boards 8 inches wide or wider are attached with two nails per stud. Use 8- or 10-penny nails for 1-inch thick siding, and 6- to 8-penny nails for thinner material. Nails should be long enough to penetrate at least one and one half inches into sheathing and studs. Generally, drive nailheads in flush with the surface without attempting to countersink or putty their heads.

Before the Industrial Revolution, builders used 3-penny square or rose-headed nails. Today, choose a weatherproof, thin-shanked, 3- to 5-penny wire box nail. Hot-dipped galvanized, aluminum, copper, monel (an alloy of nickel and copper), bronze, and stainless steel nails last the longest and don't stain the wood. Siding reacts to heat, cold, moisture, and wind and tends to tug at the nails. For this reason, nails with ring or spiral-threaded shanks hold best; blunt or diamond-pointed nails reduce the chances of splitting the siding. A large head is useful. Special splitless siding nails are thinner than regular nails and are the best choice.

Where corner or window-facing boards cover both ends of the siding, you usually have to remove only one of the two boards in order to remove and replace the siding. Occasionally, each end of the siding has to be sawn through to get it out, and the new piece may be sprung into place.

Prime and paint all new boards with two top coats of a high-quality exterior house paint. Plan to wash the siding with a mild detergent or plain water at least once a year to remove built-up dirt. Keeping the siding clean lengthens the paint life. And while you're hosing down the house, inspect siding for signs of damage and weathering. Making small repairs early often means the difference between salvaging existing siding and having to replace it entirely.

USING EPOXY TO REPAIR
ROTTED WOOD

Modern high-tech epoxy materials are great for exterior wood repairs on historic houses. Restore and strengthen porous decayed wood by soaking it with liq-

NAILING CLAPBOARD

There are three different ways to nail beveled-up siding, and each has its own application.

Two-course nailing illustrates the traditional method for hand-rived clapboards. Space nails 1/2 inch to 3/4 inches above the butt of the clapboard so that they also anchor the top of the board in the course below. Rived clapboards on buildings over two hundred years old have survived without cracking or splitting using this method (undoubtedly because of the limited expansion and contraction of this kind of clapboard). Two-course nailing appears on houses with rift-sawn clapboard for the same reason, and is also seen on buildings with resawn siding. Most modern producers of rift-sawn clapboards recommend this style of nailing, as do carpentry references dated before 1915.

Single-course nailing is recommended by much beveled-siding literature today. With this method, place nails a sufficient distance up from the board butt to miss

the top of the underlying course entirely. This nailing practice does not hold the width of the board "captive" in the event of expansion, and may have become popular with the widespread use in this century of nontraditional siding stock such as Western Red Cedar. (Some argue this method increases the chances a board will split or cup.) Single nailing also appears on lapped, rectangular, weatherboard-type siding with wide and fairly thick boards.

Blind nailing has been noted on some buildings with rived siding no wider than 4 1/2 inches, and is of more interest as a historical technique than a practical method. Nails are driven 10 to 12 inches apart only at the top of each board, much like shingles. The butt edge is left unattached so that no nails are left exposed in the finished job and nailheads are protected from weathering. In many cases, though, the butts wound up being spot-nailed years later anyway to close gaps.

uid epoxy, which will then solidify within the wood. Fill gaps and holes with an epoxy-based paste that hardens with similar characteristics to wood.

However, not every wood repair calls for epoxies. Handled improperly during application, epoxies pose a serious health and safety hazard. And they are not a miracle cure for all decay problems. When applied without regard

to a few basic principles, epoxies can actually promote decay.

The advantages of using epoxy are that they hold up well against the weather. They are waterproof, don't decay, and hold paint or stain very well. With them, it may not be necessary to remove affected parts from the building. Also, epoxy repair saves much of the original material.

Don't confuse these epoxy materials with epoxies formulated for other uses, such as five-minute adhesives, bar-top coatings, paints, or structural-repair epoxy.

Generally, the more special a part, the more it makes sense to use epoxy. We recommend using epoxies on fancy parts like mouldings, turnings, and carvings. You can repair flat, straight boards and other plain parts less expensively by replacing them or using a wood dutchman. Use epoxy only where long life is a goal of the

The decayed and broken cap atop the pedestal was not worth saving as it was built up of ordinary 2 × 8 lumber in a recent repair.

It was economical and historically correct to replace the raised cap with a solid 3-inch piece of pine, shaped to match nearby originals. The pedestal top, however, was better treated in place with epoxy.

So that epoxy consolidant will penetrate, 3/16-inch holes are drilled to just short of the underside.

project. Use other, less costly materials if you know you will be working on the area again within five or ten years.

Glossing over problem areas with epoxies only leads to more problems in the future. You must find the root cause of the decay. Complete treatments often involve taking the problem area apart entirely for access to hidden parts and surfaces.

After the decayed top and broken piece have been saturated with consolidant, the piece is glued into place with a mixture of consolidant and paste filler.

The top is now much more weather-resistant. Note that epoxy was not used in the railing joints, as this could make future repairs more difficult.

The methods described here are good for repairs to most trim and other nonstructural wood parts of a building. This includes railings, mouldings, doors, and windows. *Don't use these epoxies on parts that must carry a structural load.* For example, you wouldn't use these epoxies in the base of a hollow wood column. If it has an interior column to support the load, these materials are fine. But if there is no interior column, then these epoxies may be too soft. They may creep and change shape under the load. Harder structural epoxies are formulated especially for structural use.

When a baluster or railing cap decays, the loss of wood is progressive. At first, the mass of the wood diminishes but it still retains its original size and shape. As decay continues, the wood shrinks and then begins to crumble.

Epoxy consolidants replace the lost mass, restoring strength to the wood. Holes and gaps can be filled and built up with *epoxy paste fillers.*

Wood repair materials must be at least as flexible as the wood around the repair to be most effective. Auto-body fillers such as Bondo are far too rigid to adjust to the movement of wood. Bondo, as well as common wood putties and "spackles," are not adhesive enough to stick to exterior wood if the paint fails. While epoxy formulated for wood repairs is flexible and extremely adhesive, you may encounter adhesion problems on dusty or greasy surfaces.

If not applied carefully and effectively, epoxy consolidant actually traps moisture, causing further decay. The decayed wood must be completely dry to its full depth, or the epoxy will form an impervious shell that traps moisture in the wood beneath.

Protect parts to be treated in place by covering loosely with poly sheeting. You might have to remove the decayed parts and set them aside for several days or weeks in a cool, ventilated area.

Mixing and Using Epoxies

Both consolidant and adhesive paste-filler epoxies come as two-part systems that you mix together. The mixture gels, or begins to harden, after several minutes to

Treatment of this gable-end return cornice moulding will be easier if it's removed.

Even with careful removal, the fragile end fell to pieces.

The porous, decayed wood at the end of the moulding was tacked to a piece of plywood covered with poly sheeting to hold pieces in place as they were soaked with consolidant and then glued. The final repair is a sturdy original moulding ready to nail in place without cutting or fitting.

several hours. The length of time depends on the original formulation and on the surrounding temperature.

The mixture hardens due to a chemical reaction from within, which generates heat. When large amounts are mixed or thick sections are treated, heat builds up causing faster setting and even more heat buildup. This cumulative cycle of heat can make it set sooner than you want, or even cause a fire, if you're not careful.

After several days the epoxy reaches its final strength and hardness. Depending on the original formulation, the epoxy will be more or less flexible, to match the characteristics of the surrounding wood.

Consolidants are syrupy liquids formulated especially to soak into fibrous materials such as decayed wood. Generally, a consolidant that is thinner in consistency and takes longer to gel will penetrate further than a thick, quick-setting one.

Adhesive *paste filler* is made of a two-part liquid epoxy very similar to consolidants. Powdery thickeners are blended in to make a paste that ranges from the consistency of mayonnaise to stiff mashed potatoes. Other fillers give the cured paste the strength and flexibility characteristics of wood.

While you can formulate your own paste of epoxy consolidant with sawdust and a little cornstarch, the commercially prepared materials are much more reliable.

When mixing and using epoxies, housekeeping and cleanliness are essential. Try to keep all of the epoxy in containers or in the wood you're working on. Wipe up even small drips with a small rag and toss it in a trash container. Using rags only once may seem wasteful, but it is important to keep these hazardous materials out of your eyes and off your bare skin until they have cured.

Keep your work area organized. You are often working against the gel time of the epoxy, which always seems too short. You need to have all of your parts and materials at hand without tripping over a lot of clutter.

It may help to keep your storage and mixing equipment lined up with A-parts on the left and B-parts on the right to avoid mixing errors. Label caps and lids. If they get on the wrong container they will be glued there forever.

Have all preparatory work complete before starting with the epoxies.

Retard setting of consolidant by mixing small amounts, working in the shade or during cool weather.

Be careful not to inadvertently glue parts together. Even experts have been known to embarrass themselves by gluing a sliding sash into its frame when they installed it before the epoxy was set.

Mixing requires some care. Proportions aren't supercritical, but you must follow these guidelines. Use clean mixing equipment to avoid contamination. Don't use the same container again right away. Remnants of the old batch will accelerate the new batch, causing it to set much too quickly. Thorough mixing is necessary for the reaction to be complete.

Containers can be disposable or flexible so that hardened epoxy can be broken out once it has cured.

WORKING SAFELY WITH EPOXY

Epoxies are toxic chemicals. Read product safety warnings and directions before starting.

Avoid contact with eyes and skin. Use goggles, gloves, long sleeves, and a heavy work apron.

Avoid breathing fumes. Work outside or in a well-ventilated area. When sanding epoxy patches, wear a high-quality dust mask. For maximum protection, wear a vapor respirator with proper cartridge when mixing or applying epoxies.

Watch out for spills and drips. Mask off areas next to the repair. Clean up spills promptly with cloth rags. Avoid vapor hazard by placing all cleanup and mixing materials in a trash can outside the house.

Use soap or detergent—not epoxy solvents—to wash epoxy off your skin.

Use disposable stir sticks and gloves. Launder soiled clothing separately.

Epoxies are flammable. Store in a cool location. Don't smoke or use an open flame. Heat can build up when large amounts are mixed. Keep an eye on mixed batches, feel the container for excessive heat. Have a CO_2 extinguisher on hand.

Mix only as much epoxy as you will use before it begins to gel. If working alone, you probably won't need to mix more than a cupful at a time. Working with small batches also helps avoid heat buildup.

Mix small amounts of consolidant by squeezing the correct amount from the part-A and part-B bottles into a clean application bottle. Stir the mixture for four full minutes by hand with a thin stick or for two minutes with a bent coat hanger chucked in an electric drill.

Mix two-part paste fillers on a flat board. Use heavy sticks to scoop equal parts of the paste out of each container. Mark the sticks "A" and "B" so you don't contaminate one supply with the other. With a 1 1/2-inch putty knife spread the paste out and then scrape it up into one lump, again and again until the mass is smooth and thoroughly mixed. It usually takes about five minutes.

When you've finished mixing leave the paste spread out thin across the board. This helps prevent heat buildup until the paste is applied.

Consolidating

Maximum penetration is the key requirement for effective consolidation of decayed wood. Often, a thin layer of sound wood forms a shell over deep decay. Drilling holes in a honeycomb pattern speeds and increases penetration. Don't drill all the way through the part or the consolidant will just drain out the back before it soaks in.

Use plasticene oil clay—an oil-based clay found at any art supply store—to dam up cracks and holes where the consolidant will leak out. Allow time for epoxy to soak in by moving from one area of treatment to the next. Finally, come back to the first area, which will be ready for more consolidant.

Check for complete penetration of consolidant into decayed wood by drilling a hole or cutting out a small section of treated wood. Then you can see if any decayed wood has not been saturated with consolidant. Check before the consolidant begins to harden, so more can soak in if needed. This is a messy business. But it is the only way to be certain the treatment is complete and effective.

EPOXY TOOLS

This epoxy tool kit consists of two parts. A "ready kit" is a small tool tray you can move easily around a job site. It has everything ready to go. Use the "backup kit" to refill supplies in the ready kit. Everything fits into a 15 × 20-inch crate with the ready kit nestled on top.

Ready Kit

- Two 10-fluid-ounce cans with snap-on lids, each labeled and filled with A- and B-parts of adhesive paste filler
- Two 8-fluid-ounce bottles, each labeled and filled with A- and B-parts of consolidant
- A few empty bottles for mixing and application
- Rags—a dozen large and small, stuffed into an old sock
- Gloves—several thin disposable pairs, and one heavy-duty pair
- Goggles and respirator
- Oil clay (from a hobby store)
- Putty knives
- Mixing boards—several of 1/8 × 8 × 12-inch Masonite for mixing paste filler

Backup Kit

- Epoxy materials—a gallon each of A- and B-parts of both consolidant and adhesive paste
- Two dozen application bottles
- Rags torn to size: tear up rags ahead of time and stuff them into old socks for easy handling—small ones for one-time use wiping off spouts and caps; large for cleanup
- Mixing sticks—a bundle of thin wood sticks 8 inches long for scooping out paste and stirring consolidant
- Gloves—one box disposable vinyl; extra pair medium-duty nitril rubber
- A package of oil clay (for stopping consolidant from leaking out of cracks)
- Bottle cleaning tools: It's a toss-up whether it is worth cleaning out application bottles. Cleaning them takes three to five minutes—barely worth it economically, but it is less wasteful.
- Channel-lock pliers to open stuck caps
- Allen wrench to clean out cap hole
- Needlenose pliers to pull out hardened epoxy

EPOXY SUPPLIERS

Suppliers for epoxy materials are becoming more common. Check with your local marine suppliers or use the following manufacturers who make direct sales:

Conservation Services
8 Lakeside Trail, Dept. OHJ
Kinnelon, NJ 07405
(201)838-6412

These products cure more slowly than Abatron's (below). This makes them especially good for repairs to thick parts left in place for treatment such as window sills. The cured epoxy is also more flexible.

Con Serv (t) Flexible Consolidant 100
Slow cure allows five to seven hours application time for deep penetration, cures to a rubberbandlike hardness in three to six days; especially good for thick sections or when application is from only one side of the part.

Con Serv (t) Flexible Patch 200
Puttylike filler, comes in four parts; mixing in small amounts is more difficult than WoodEpox (below) but gives you more control of consistency and hardness; expands and contracts with wood when cured.

Nitril rubber gloves
Heavier than disposable gloves, but thin enough so you can feel what you're doing.

Abatron
33 Center Drive
Gilberts, IL 60136
(708)426-2200

These products cure somewhat faster and harder than Con Serv—good for projects such as a window sash where there is a lot of repetitive work and deep penetration is not needed because the parts are small.

LiquidWood-1 (consolidant)
Quick gel time allows one to two hours application time for higher production rate but less penetration.

WoodEpox-2 (adhesive paste)
Adhesive paste filler comes as two pastes you mix in equal parts which simplifies mixing; final hardness adjustable by varying the ratio. Can be thinned with LiquidWood but this makes it less flexible.

Your local drugstore

Application bottles
8-fluid-ounce hair-dye bottles for mixing and applying consolidant. They are inexpensive, have a liquid-proof screw-top seal, and measurement markings on the side that help in mixing. (ROUX Color Applicator, by Roux Laboratories, Jacksonville, FL, is especially good if you're cleaning and reusing bottles.)

Disposable gloves
Close-fitting vinyl gloves are good for light work.

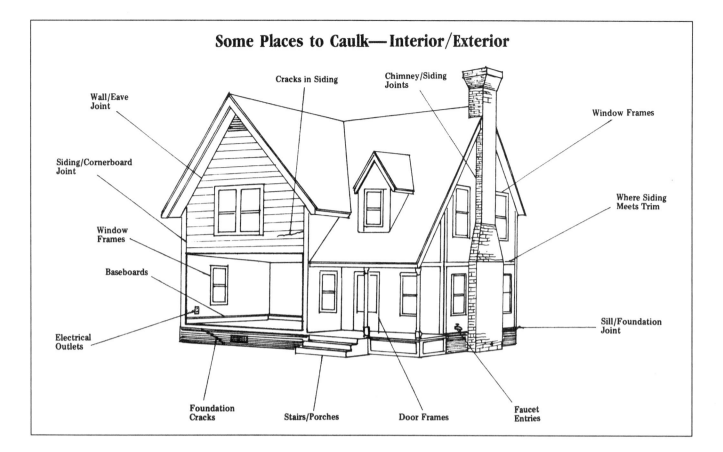

Some Places to Caulk—Interior/Exterior

Wall/Eave Joint

Cracks in Siding

Chimney/Siding Joints

Window Frames

Siding/Cornerboard Joint

Window Frames

Baseboards

Where Siding Meets Trim

Electrical Outlets

Sill/Foundation Joint

Foundation Cracks

Stairs/Porches

Door Frames

Faucet Entries

Filling and Gluing

Once the decayed wood is consolidated, fill in missing wood with adhesive paste filler. If you are filling wood not already treated with consolidant, apply some consolidant as a primer. Fill large voids in layers up to an inch thick at a time, letting each layer harden before applying the next. More than an inch might cause excessive heat buildup.

After the filler is cured you can work it with ordinary woodworking tools and methods. It can be carved, drilled, rasped, and sanded. A hand plane will make shavings that look just like wood, except for the color. The epoxy will hold screws and nails; it's usually wise to predrill a pilot hole.

Use a mixture of consolidant and paste to make an excellent gap-filling, weatherproof glue.

An epoxy surface planed or sanded smooth will hold oil-base paint without any problems. When making future repairs, new epoxy will adhere well to the old.

CAULKING THE EXTERIOR

Provided you have repaired or arrested major structural failures and replaced damaged siding, you may want to consider filling any remaining gaps with caulk. Caulking stops up cracks and crevices, eliminates air flow through tiny spaces, and keeps rainwater out. (Just because the house is old, don't resign yourself to occasional drafts and high fuel bills. Weatherizing an old house is described in more detail in chapter 11.) If the area of all

the cracks in a typical old house were combined into a single opening, it could total nine square feet or more. Caulk can save you fuel bills, considering that about 50 percent of the average fuel bill goes to make up losses caused by air infiltration.

Much attention has been given to the need to caulk a house's exterior. This can lead to serious problems: As you make the outer skin of the house more vapor-tight, there is less opportunity for water vapor from inside the house to escape. Trapped water vapor can lead to condensation inside the walls of wood frame houses during freezing weather. Condensation leads to peeling paint and possibly rotten wood.

More emphasis should be placed on the need to caulk inside the house. Caulk around electrical boxes, baseboards, and door and window frames. Use acrylic caulk to seal around the baseboards and door and window frames. Around electrical boxes, use rope caulk, tape, or acrylic caulk. For electrical boxes flush with the wall, you may seal them with foam gasketing that fits under the plate cover. The idea is to make the inside

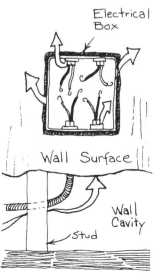

Electrical Box

Wall Surface

Wall Cavity

Stud

walls of the house more vapor-tight than the exterior walls.

For interior nonweathering joints, acrylic latex caulks do the trick. They clean up easily with water. The operative word is "acrylic" latex. Don't be fooled by the other types of latex caulks on the market—of lower quality—that don't contain the acrylic material.

Outside, don't get carried away. For example, you won't need to caulk underneath window sills or under each clapboard. Rain can't penetrate here, and the air infiltration helps carry off any water vapor that gets inside the wall. To decide where to caulk, visualize a sheet of water running down the side of the building. Caulk anywhere water could penetrate: Primary areas include construction joints and joints between dissimilar materials, such as where wood siding abuts a masonry chimney.

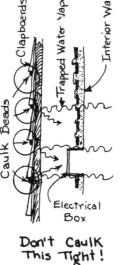

Don't Caulk This Tight!

For those hard to reach places such as cornices, invest in a high-performance sealant that will last fifteen to twenty years. You may need to replace cheaper oil-based caulks within two years. Caulk comes in bulk containers, but these are too inconvenient for all but the professionals. Stick to the standard caulking gun-and-cartridge system. Approximately one cartridge of caulk will seal a fifty-foot crevice, two door frames, or two window frames. To find high-performance sealants like polyurethane, you'll probably have to find a dealer that sells to contractors. Look in the Yellow Pages under "Water-proofing Materials." If the dealer insists that you buy in bulk, you'll have to share your case of twenty-four cartridges with a neighbor.

The first choice for all-around exterior caulking is a urethane sealant, such as Vulkem. Urethane bonds to just about any surface without priming. It works easily, has little shrinkage, weathers superbly, and can be painted. It's the preferred caulk of the pros. As a second choice, buy a good-quality butyl.

Caulking Technique

Caulking looks easy when a professional runs a smooth bead in a couple of seconds. However, proper caulking requires even pressure in the cartridge as you run it along the seam at an even, smooth rate. Practice on some inconspicuous cellar windows until you get the hang of it. Before you reach the end of the crevice, you must begin to relieve the pressure in the cartridge. Disengage the plunger rod on the gun. If you don't, caulk will continue to squirt out. As you practice this pressure-relieving maneuver, carry a rag with you to wipe any excess caulk from the nozzle.

Prepare the surface before you caulk. Caulk will not bond to dirty surfaces. Scrape off all loose paint, old sealant, and dirt. A putty knife and an old screwdriver may come in handy for scraping and digging out debris. Clean greasy surfaces with mineral spirits. In fact, the best time to caulk is during painting, just after the priming coat has dried thoroughly.

When you are ready to start, cut the plastic nozzle of the cartridge at a 45-degree angle. The closer to the tip you cut, the narrower the bead you'll make. Start with a thin bead, and recut the nozzle as needed until you find the right size bead for the crack.

A bead should fill the crack to a depth equal to the width of the crack. For gaps wider than 3/8 inch and

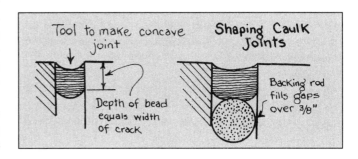

Tool to make concave joint — Depth of bead equals width of crack

Shaping Caulk Joints — Backing rod fills gaps over 3/8"

CAULKS OF CHOICE

	RECOMMENDED SEALANT	LIFE EXPECTANCY	CLEANUP SOLVENT	TYPICAL BRAND NAME
EXTERIOR	Polyurethane	15–20 years	paint thinner	Vulkem Sikaflex
	Butyl	7–10 years	paint thinner	DAP Butyl Flex Tiger Grip Butyl Rubber Caulk
INTERIOR	Acrylic Latex	5–10 years	Water	UGL Acrylic Latex Caulk DAP Acrylic Latex Caulk

deeper than 1/2 inch, fill the crack first with a backing material such as oakum (a tar-impregnated rope) or a plastic foam backing rod such as Ethafoam. Oakum may leave a greasy film on the surface, which can interfere with the caulk bond and with paint adhesion. You'll find plastic foam backing rods at weatherproofing supply stores. Buy a size just a bit bigger than the crack; friction holds it in place. In a pinch, stuff large cracks with scrap fiberglass insulation, then form the sealant bead over that.

Force the caulk into the joint to the proper depth. If you don't get sufficient penetration with the gun alone, "tool" the joint by running your finger over the bead, or use the bowl of an old spoon. If the caulk sticks to the tool, keep it moist by dipping it in the proper solvent or soapy water.

PAINTING

A good paint job depends on careful preparation. Unless the surface beneath the paint is dull, clean, firm, sealed, and primed, the time and effort you spend painting will be wasted. First thoroughly inspect the building and repair any sources of water damage. Bushes near the house hold moisture. Cut them back from the house, and reglaze all loose windows. Also make sure you have made all necessary repairs to siding.

Repaint only when the old paint no longer protects the wood. You don't want too many paint layers. A dingy house may only need laundering. Diagnose any problems with the existing paint job, too. In addition to alligatoring, peeling, wrinkling, and surface cracking (see box on page 116), you may encounter the following:

Blisters. Cut open blisters to determine their cause. If you find bare wood, blame moisture. Fix the problem and let the wood dry completely before priming. If you find paint, solvent probably was trapped beneath paint film that dried too quickly. This occurs when the surface is painted in direct hot sun. Scrape or sand the area.

Stubborn dirt or discoloration. Mildew most often causes stubborn stains. If a few drops of chlorine bleach on the area blanches, you've got mildew. To kill the fungus, scrub hard with a solution of 3 quarts hot water, 1 quart chlorine laundry bleach, 2/3 cup detergent (Spic'n'Span, Soilax, or Tide), and 1/2 cup TSP or borax (optional). Rinse this off thoroughly with a hose. Prime the area once it is thoroughly dry. Use a mildew-resistant primer and finish paint.

Chalking or streaking. While some exterior paints chalk a bit to keep the surface clean, others chalk because of poor quality, inadequate priming, or a badly weathered surface. Bare or weathered wood absorbs the binder from paint, leaving the pigment (solids) to chalk. (Do not use "self-cleaning" paint on such locations.) Streaks on bricks are best left to wear off gradually. Before repainting, wash chalking surfaces with 1/2 cup detergent per gallon of water. Go over the surface quickly with a bristle brush,

Excessive chalking of the paint from the clapboards caused this streaking on the bricks.

then hose off the siding and let it dry before priming with an oil-alkyd primer.

Before Painting

Noting where paint peels will lead you to the source of water problems. Near the ground, check the foundation, grading, and other drainage details. Paint peeling on masonry is usually caused by moisture. Salts are dissolved out of the mortar or plaster when water frequently contacts the masonry. Bricks are especially porous and act as moisture wicks. The water that's absorbed, with leached salts in solution, migrates toward the sun-warmed surface. The water evaporates and deposits the salts. This efflorescence is harmless, if unsightly, when the masonry is unpainted. When it's painted, however, staining and peeling result. (See chapter 9 for more on painting masonry.)

If possible, hose off the entire house. Pay special attention to "protected" areas that are not weathered by sunlight and rain such as soffits. Wash protected areas with a mild detergent solution and bristle brushes, then carefully scrape and sand.

Remove any paint that is not tightly bonded to the substrate. If the paint bond anywhere in the paint layer sandwich is weak, applying new paint will cause paint failure. New paint shrinks while curing, and the old paint underneath loses elasticity over time. This can cause intercoat peeling, alligatoring, and cracking.

Weathered wood must be sanded before priming or it

PAINT FAILURES

Assuming you haven't used a low-quality paint, common paint problems often are caused by improper penetration, application mistakes, or problems with the building itself. While four of the most typical conditions are discussed here, the cause of your problem may be different. Call in a paint specialist if you're unsure.

Cracking and Crazing

Generally caused by paint that has aged to an excessively hard finish, the paint film no longer expands and contracts with the wood. Hairline cracks allow water to enter and seep down to the wood. As the wood swells, it widens the breaks to form more cracks. Cracks form mostly parallel to the grain.

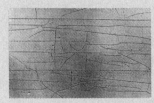

If you discover cracking before it becomes severe, wire brushing and repainting should solve the problem. Choose a paint brand different from the one that is cracking. When cracking occurs all the way down to the wood, completely remove the paint. After removal, prime with an oil-alkyd primer, followed by either an oil-base or latex topcoat.

Wrinkling

When the top film dries before the underlying paint cures, the dry film moves as the underlying paint dries, thus creating wrinkles. Wrinkling is caused by applying a second coat before the first is dry, applying too much paint, inadequate brushing out, painting in hot sun or over a too-cold surface, or applying a hard finish over a softer coat without priming.

Remove wrinkled layers by sanding or scraping. Prime with an oil-alkyd primer and follow with an oil-base or latex topcoat. To avoid wrinkling, brush out each coat thoroughly and allow it to dry completely. Don't paint in direct hot sun, or when the temperature is below 40 degrees Fahrenheit (50 degrees Fahrenheit if using latex).

Peeling

The most common paint failure, peeling results from one of three causes: painting under adverse conditions, inadequate surface preparation, or moisture.

Heat blisters form when the surface is painted in direct sun. This often occurs with dark colors, since dark colors will absorb heat more readily than light colors.

Inadequate surface preparation may leave a grimy greasy surface to which new paint won't stick. This often shows up on soffits and other protected areas.

Peeling also occurs when water reaches the wood behind a paint film. The wood swells, causing the paint to crack and peel. The moisture comes from many sources including:

- Cracks and seams in siding and trimwork
- Areas inside the house, especially bathrooms, laundries, and kitchens—this problem can be aggravated by condensation on sidewall insulation that isn't protected by a vapor barrier
- Leaks into the wall partition caused by clogged gutters, ice dams, leaking roofs, and the like
- Vegetation growing too close to the house

Get rid of the moisture before you deal with the paint. After eliminating the source of the moisture, allow the wood to dry thoroughly. Scrape off all loose paint, prime with an oil-alkyd primer, then finish with an oil-base or latex finish coat.

If there's a coat of sound paint beneath the peeling, remove all loose material by scraping and wire brushing. Light sanding will remove surface dirt from the sound paint and any additional paint that may be loosely adhering. After thorough brushing to remove sanding dust, coat with an oil-alkyd primer, followed by an oil-base topcoat.

Alligatoring

An advanced case of cracking and crazing, when it extends all the way down to bare wood, usually signals an old thick paint film that has lost its flexibility.

Alligatoring of a topcoat also occurs when it's unable to bond tightly to a glossy paint coat beneath it.

To cure alligatoring, remove all the paint down to the bare wood. Coat with an oil-alkyd primer and an oil-base or latex topcoat.

If only the topcoat alligators, try removing as much of the alligatored film as possible by scraping and sanding. Sand any underlying glossy paint to a dull finish. Prime with an oil-alkyd primer, followed by an oil-base finish coat.

will not hold the paint. Hand-sand with a sanding block and medium-coarse paper, or use a small belt sander if the area is large and flat. Treat weathered wood (and new bare wood) before priming to keep the wood from drawing all the binder out of the paint. Use two parts boiled linseed oil and one part turpentine. For greater protection and resistance to insects and rot, use a water-repellent preservative instead. Let the treatment cure for twenty-four hours, then spot-prime with an oil-alkyd primer that doesn't contain zinc oxide, which is hydrophilic.

Every good paint job requires at least spot-priming. If the old topcoat isn't chalking or peeling, and is tight, you can probably skip all-over priming. An alkyd—rather than a latex—primer should be used if you don't know the formulation of the last paint layer, if the substrate is dirty, if the wood is new or weathered, or if you're changing paint systems (i.e., switching to a latex topcoat when the house has always been painted with oil-base paint).

Practically every old house will be better off with alkyd primer. Spot-prime the edge and both sides of new clapboards, shingles, and trim before installation. Spot-prime any scraped and sanded areas, and wherever the wood was treated with a preservative or linseed oil. Prime mildly dirty areas that you couldn't wash and rinse. As you discover protruding nailheads, set them below the surface, fill with putty, and spot-prime.

To seal knots that bleed through paint, varnish them and wait until the next day before roughing up the varnish with steel wool or sandpaper before priming. Pigmented shellac is good for sealing knots, but not outdoors where it's likely to come in contact with water.

Paintbrushes

Before you contemplate the finish coat, make sure you have the right tools. Professional tools cost more than consumer grades (you'll find them at larger paint suppliers rather than hardware stores), but pay for themselves through superior performance. A good paint job depends as much on quality paint and brushes as it does on preparation of the surface. A good brush will have

• Long, flexible bristles of varying lengths.
• Flagged bristles. Flagging (splitting) at the ends of the bristles makes for fewer brush marks. In synthetic brushes, look for both flagged and tapered filaments.

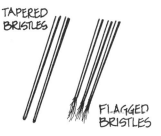

• Treated wood or aluminum spacer plug at the ferrule. The spacer plug holds the bristles in place and creates a void that allows the brush to hold more paint. To find it, spread the bristles at the ferrule. Cheaper brushes will have cardboard plugs.
• Wooden handle shaped to fit the hand. Varnished handles may cause blisters.
• A sturdy, corrosion-resistant ferrule (nickel-plated,

stainless steel, copper, or brass) securely fastened to the handle.
• Bristles set securely in vulcanized rubber, epoxy, or chemically inert cements. Work the brush back and forth across your hand to see if it loses bristles. A good brush will lose some bristles or filaments, a cheaper brush will lose more.
• A "cupped chisel" design (a filament-setting method) in which the filaments are set into a wooden handle at varying lengths to create the chisel shape rather than cut. Check the manufacturer's catalog for this information.
• Bristles or filament with a resilient spring to them. When brushed against your hand, the bristle should feel smooth and silky and should spring back into shape.
• Balance.
• A slight taper from the heel to the edge. Good brushes have a "square edge" (for holding more paint and painting large, flat surfaces) or a "chisel edge" (for broader filament contact, more even application, and precise cutting in). Use a chisel-edged brush for inside corners and edges.

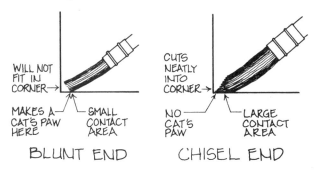

Whether you use natural bristle or synthetic filament, be sure to buy high-quality brushes. "Bristle" has become synonymous with "filament" (natural or synthetic). Bristle actually refers only to the hair of hogs. Hog bristle makes a good brush filament because of its natural flagging. Hog bristles are slightly oval and grow naturally to a taper. This gives them spring and elasticity and helps them maintain their shape.

China bristle is the most common natural bristle, and is best suited for non-water-soluble finishes (alkyds, oil enamels, oil-base stains, varnish, polyurethane, shellac, lacquer, and the like). Untreated natural bristles in a water-based finish become limp as they absorb water.

Stay away from China or ox-hair blends. A blend may contain as little as 1 percent China or ox-hair bristles. A good brush will be labeled with the percentage of bristle used.

Nylon and polyester are the two most commonly used synthetic bristles. Nylon (such as Dupont Tynex) is used in low- to medium-priced brushes. Use it for oils, alkyds, latex paints, oil stains, varnish, and polyurethane. Nylon cannot be used for creosote, methyl- or ethyl-alcohol-based shellacs, or finishes containing ketones (like two-part epoxy finishes). Don't buy imported nylon as some become limp in water.

Medium- to high-priced synthetic brushes are generally made of polyester or a nylon/polyester blend. Dupont Orel is one brand name. The longest wearing synthetic brushes are 100 percent polyester. It has higher solvent and temperature resistance than nylon, and better bend recovery. Polyester is also more resilient than nylon and can be used with any finish. Look for brushes with an even mixture of flagged and tapered filaments.

Avoid brushes made of styrene, unless they are for a single, crude job, and you plan to throw them away. Polystyrene is a tough filament used mostly in wallpaper brushes. Stay away from synthetic brushes with coarse filaments. If the filaments stay bent when you pinch them with a fingernail, they're hollow, not as durable, and likely to lose shape sooner.

Paintbrush Sizes and Shapes

Match the brush to the job. The proper size and shape can make the difference between a neat, fast job, and a sloppy, slow one.

Common Brushes

Wall brushes (3 to 5 inches). If you don't have to worry about cutting in, the general rule of thumb is, the bigger, the better. Keep in mind that if you're handling a full-bodied brush more than 4 inches wide, your arm will start to ache after a couple of hours. If painting clapboards, match the width of the brush to the width of the clapboard.

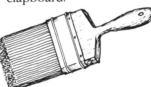

Flat sash and trim brushes (1 to 4 inches). Chisel-edge trim brushes in this size range make easy work of window and door surrounds, baseboards, wall corners, and so on. Brush width depends on the size of the trim you want to paint.

Angle sash brushes (1 to 3 inches). The long end of an angle sash brush helps you reach into inside corners on window sash. Don't allow the angle alone to convince you this is the right brush; a fine tapered edge is the most critical element of a sash brush.

Semi-oval varnish and enamel brushes (1 to 4 inches). These tools have wider centers, longer filaments, and rounded edges. They carry a lot of paint, apply it smoothly, and make it easier to paint sharp edges. They usually have round handles.

Round or oval sash brushes (even numbers 2 to 20). Not very common, but they're excellent for fine work. Their dense bristles and thick profiles allow them to hold a lot of paint. They're compact and have a well chiseled edge, making cutting in easy. They are especially appropriate for spindle work because they won't "splay out" as easily as flat brushes.

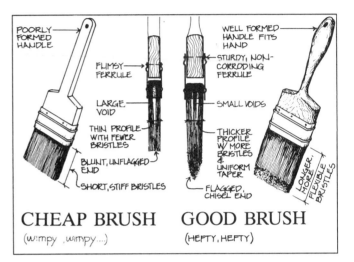

CHEAP BRUSH (wimpy, wimpy....)   **GOOD BRUSH** (HEFTY, HEFTY)

Specialty Brushes

Flowing brush. Use anytime the finish must be smooth and free of brush marks (as on a broad, flat surface with a gloss finish). The most commonly used bristles are white hog, badger, and fitch (skunk). These bristles are combined in a multitude of different grades and blends. The thinner the finish, the softer the flowing brush should be. If you're applying alkyd or oil paint, use a slightly stiffer flowing brush.

Whitewash brushes. Use with whitewash—a water-based lime paint, essentially liquid plaster. Made of white tampico (cactus fiber) or horsehair and bristle blends (more resistant to the lime base than other bristles), the brush attaches to a wooden handle—and looks like a push broom.

Calcimine brushes (or block brushes). Available in natural and synthetic bristles and blends. Use on rough surfaces and with whitewash. The plant-fiber bristles resist lime.

Masonry brushes. These carry a lot of paint, making them excellent for rough surfaces. They resemble calcimine brushes, but have horsehair or tampico filaments.

Radiator brushes. These brushes come in two varieties. One has a long handle to reach between the fins of a radiator. The other has an offset handle for those hard-to-reach places behind the radiator.

Rough rider. This is actually the brand name of a common shingle-siding painting tool. Great for painting the rough, uneven surfaces and edges of shingles.

Cleaning Up

Clean brushes immediately after use. Once clean, hang the brushes by their handles in a clean, dry place. After they dry, fold some kraft paper around them (or, if you can find them, use the protective envelopes they came in) to keep the bristles in shape. Never store a brush so it rests on its bristles.

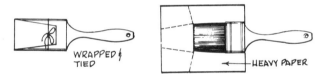

WRAPPED & TIED — HEAVY PAPER

For *latex cleanup* you need only water. Run warm, not hot, water on the face of the bristles only, not between the bristles with the brush upside down. Don't bend the bristles down hard against the sink. Pat the brush sharply against the palm of your hand to bring the watered-down paint to the surface, and keep rinsing. Rinse until there's no hint of pigment. Be sure to work all the paint out of the heel of the brush.

A little mild soap (such as Ivory Liquid) helps remove the paint and serves as a good gauge to judge when the brush is thoroughly rinsed—when the soapy water lathers up easily, the brush is clean. Rinse the soap completely from the brush.

To expel excess water, twirl the brush rapidly back and forth between the palms of your hands. If it's a good sash brush, just shake the water out; that way, you'll be less likely to cause permanent spreading of the bristles.

For *oil/alkyd cleanup,* rinse with the solvent you used to thin the paint (check the label). For most oil-base paints and varnishes, you'll need mineral spirits (paint thinner); some will call for turpentine. (For lacquer, use lacquer thinner; for shellac, denatured alcohol.)

Work the brush dry on kraft paper, newspapers, or paper towels. Don't distort the brush in the effort; just brush as you normally would until no more paint comes out. Fill a coffee can about half full with solvent, and work the brush up and down in the solvent for a few minutes. Save the solvent to use as a first rinse for all your brushes.

After the first rinse, pour fresh solvent in another coffee can. Use only as much as needed to rinse the brush. Add the spent solvent to your "first-rinse" can. Three to five rinsings in fresh solvent is typical, although you may have to do more. Flex the brush gently against the bottom of the can to help squeeze out thinned paint. Be careful not to bend the bristles too far, and flex evenly—one side, then the other. Seal the used solvent tightly. In a couple of days, the pigments will settle to the bottom, and you can reuse the solvent for another brush.

If you plan to use the brush for oil-base paint in the future, simply squeeze out the excess solvent and store. If you want to use it for latex, rinse the solvent out of the brush with warm, soapy water.

The Finish Coat

Independent paint researchers recommend exterior latex paint for outdoor use over an alkyd primer. Buy the same brand topcoat as primer.

Use a 4-inch quality brush for clapboards, shingles, and other large flat surfaces. (A 5-inch brush holds more paint, but is very heavy. Use your judgment.) Beyond that, a 3-inch trim brush and a 1 1/2- to 2-inch sash brush with tapered bristles should do the job.

Paint the body first, then the trim. Let the body color lap over the trim where they meet. This makes it easier to paint the trim neatly, and also assures that every square inch is protected with paint.

Those who mask their window glass with tape haven't learned to paint. The bead of paint that comes over onto the glass, covering the glazing putty, helps keep water out. When you razor-blade the connection of wood and glass, water can penetrate into the crevice.

A tapered sash brush helps push a bead of paint out in front of the brush, depositing it at the edge of the glass. Paint all around the glass first, then go back and fill in the sash, then the frame. It will be slow at first, but you'll eventually learn how much paint to leave in the brush and how quickly to draw the brush. Slight variations outdoors won't be noticed anyway.

The experts disagree as to the number of finish coats. A single topcoat over a well-prepared and primed surface is sufficient in many cases. In high-abrasion areas, such as window sills and other horizontal surfaces, we recommend a primer coat plus two topcoats. On a solid dry substrate, just good preparation and a single topcoat may do. However, you'll have to weigh the cost of labor and the problem of too many paint layers (now or in the future) against the longevity of a two- or three-coat job.

Stripping Paint

Unless your house paint suffers from a catastrophic paint problem such as those discussed on page 116, you

areas such as clapboards; use a heat gun for detail work, such as posts and balusters; a high-intensity lamp is less effective for exterior work.

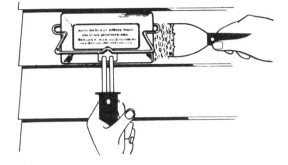

Chemical paint removers. These come in two broad categories—organic removers containing methylene chloride (such as Zip-Strip and Strip-Eze), and alkaline strippers. Always test strip with a chemical stripper before starting a job. Alkaline paint removers will raise the grain of some woods. The drawback to methylene chloride removers is expense and volatility. They dry out before they have softened, and you often have to recoat the surface. Also

Chemical paint stripping is best done by an experienced company.

probably won't have to resort to paint stripping. If you do, there are a wide variety of stripping methods to choose from. We recommend that you stay away from flame tools, such as blowtorches that soften paint so it can be scraped off, sandblasting, and high-pressure water blasting. Flame-producing tools can start a fire in a wood house. The spark may smoulder for hours undetected. Sandblasting raises the grain of woodwork so that it winds up looking like driftwood. While low-pressure water washers (under 400 psi) may safely remove loose paint and wash off salts and dirt, high-pressure water-blasters (up to 2,000 psi) can be as abrasive as sandblasters. Also, at such high pressure a tremendous amount of water is pumped into the house, with possible adverse consequences for interior finishes.

Better tools for stripping include the following:

Rotary tools. Buy drill attachments for stripping paint. While metal discs and rotary sanding discs remove paint quickly, they don't work fast enough and leave circular marks on the wood. Whirling wires tear into wood; other tools have flat metal leaves that are gentler, but they only remove flaking paint. Use only for small sanding jobs.

Heat tools. Electric heat plates, heat guns, and high-intensity "torch" lamps will ignite paint if left in one spot too long. However, risk of fire is less with heat tools than with flame-producing tools. Use a heat plate for stripping flat

STRIPPING PAINT SAFELY

Eye Damage

Always wear safety goggles with sanders, chemical removers, or wire-type rotary strippers. If you use a high-intensity lamp, you should wear dark glasses to protect eyes from the bulb's glare.

Chemical Hazards

Make sure there's plenty of ventilation, and always wear rubber gloves and goggles. Many of these materials are highly toxic—keep them away from your skin.

Lead Poisoning

Dust from sanding or scraping an old house may be toxic if the old paint contains lead. Wear a dust mask, wash thoroughly after sanding, and launder your work clothes immediately. A blowtorch or other flame tool will vaporize lead compounds, creating very toxic fumes.

Fire Hazard

Keep a fire extinguisher on hand if you use a flame-producing tool or any heat tools. Heat tools—electric heat plates, hot-air guns, and high-intensity lamps—will catch paint on fire if left in one place too long.

Heat Tool Hazards

Wear goggles and clothing to protect your skin from hot, falling paint. Again, keep a fire extinguisher nearby and use heavy-duty outdoor extension cords that have 3-prong grounding plugs that connect only to grounded receptacles that accept 3-prong plugs. Don't use in damp surroundings or in the rain. Never leave a plugged-in unit unattended.

consider what the runoff may do to vegetation with both types of chemical strippers. While chemical advocates say that the runoff will not damage shrubbery if the ground is soaked thoroughly beforehand, residue may damage some plants.

Color Selection and Placement

Old-house purists choose colors to fit the style and period of their buildings. Between 1820 and 1920 preservationists identify four major color phases: late Federal through Neoclassical (c. 1820–1840); Gothic and Italianate Revival, or early Victorian (c. 1840–1870); late Victorian (c. 1870–1890); and Colonial Revival (1890–1920). While this grossly oversimplifies American architectural history, these four periods have fairly definable color palettes ranging from a dominant white trimmed with green, through pale earth tones, to the dark, rich—if somewhat "muddy"—colors that most people associate with late Victorian buildings, to a gradual return to white and light pastels.

In addition to the protection it offers, paint is a cosmetic. As any beautician will explain, the application of cosmetics is a subtle skill; the trick is to enhance the best features without calling attention to the effort. If you want to aim for historical accuracy consult the color guide on pages 123–25. *Century of Color: Exterior Decoration for American Buildings, 1820–1920* by Roger Moss (American Life Foundation, 1981) also provides an excellent source for identifying accurate colors for old-house styles.

Of course, color selection depends on personal preference. No matter how "correct" a color may be, if you don't like it you won't want to use it. Fortunately, there is a wide enough range of historically acceptable colors that you

In this example of the historical approach, a refined scheme in three colors—peachy tan, rust, and burgundy-brown—accentuate the house's detailing.

can express your individuality and be fair to the history of your house.

First select a body color, then choose trim colors that will match the body color. After selecting colors, be sure to place them properly. Nearly all houses built in America before World War I were intended to be defined by the trimming color. Houses are outlined by certain architectural elements such as cornerboards, cornices, the watertable, and the belt course. All of these elements are usually painted in the major trim color. Then the main vertical and horizontal elements of the porches are outlined in the same fashion. Finally, the window and door openings are outlined. Keep in mind that a large house can be made to appear smaller by selecting a trim color that is darker than the main body color.

You can introduce additional colors after the house has been fully outlined. The simpler the house, the fewer the colors. Some recommend reversing the body color within major areas painted in the trim color rather than introducing a third major color. Cornice brackets and porch balusters, for example, usually look better painted in the body color against the trim. Those with a more modern approach might choose another accent color.

One area that causes many people problems is the brackets on Italianate roof and porch cornices. Usually these are painted out with the cornice. The exception to this rule is when the brackets are fabricated from three or more boards so there is a recessed face or recessed scroll on the sides. In those cases the recesses are usually picked out in the body color for contrast.

Sashes and shutters, however, will probably carry two different colors. For historical accuracy, these elements generally will be the darkest parts of the house. Especially for houses erected between 1840 and 1900, the sash is darker than the trim. This gives the effect of the windows receding into the facade rather than projecting, which is exactly the effect that was intended.

Many historical old-house paint schemes lose their impact at the last moment by painting the movable sash white, the light body color, or, even more unhappily, by installing white storm windows. Shutters, too, were usually darker. Paint them in the trim color with recessed panels picked out in the body color, or in an even darker shade of the body-trim combination. If you paint your shutters in the trim color, be sure to paint the backs of them in the body color (with the recessed panels picked out in the trim color) so when they are closed there will be definition between the window frames and the shutter rails. Little tricks such as this enliven a facade and show that you really understand how the nineteenth century used paint.

American color schemes throughout the nineteenth century were relatively simple. Only in the late Victorian period, and especially on the Queen Anne house, did multicolor schemes arise to enhance the architectural detail. In houses of this period stack dark to light shades of the same color with the darkest shade on the first floor, medium on the second, and the lightest on the third.

WORKING ON YOUR PAINT SCHEME

Make an elevation drawing of your house and get copies made to work on in choosing colors for your old house. Since the front facade often shows all of the design elements in the house, you may need a drawing only of the front (or of the front and one side). Feel free to do all sides, if you want. If you're no artist, take black and-white photos of each side and get 8 × 10 or larger prints made, then trace them. Making the drawings will give you a real familiarity with the building. You'll get a feel for the different areas, the size and distribution of trim, and how the detailing is layered and arranged.

Looking at your drawings, separate out the main areas: body, trim, windows, gables, repeating details, and so on. Notice what stands out and your favorite parts. Don't color your drawings—there are about thirty colors at the art store and 1,600 colors at the paint store. Combining just the right shades is what makes a paint scheme great or only fair. Your house will never look like your drawing. Instead, shade the drawings in black-and-white with a lead pencil. Laying out your building in terms of value will give you a better feel for the balance and how to handle the details. (Value refers to the light-to-dark scale of colors such as black, dark gray, medium gray, light gray, and so on, while hue refers to the specific color used. Choose your palette so there is a relationship of both hue and value running through all the colors.)

Now photograph your house with a 35mm camera using color print film. Take some distance photos as well as close-ups of window areas, entryway and front doors, ornamental details, and under-surfaces such as soffits. Shoot an entire roll. Develop the film into 3 × 5 glossy-finish prints.

Collect color booklets and color chips. Buy or borrow

Shade drawings of your building in black and white to lay out the paint scheme in terms of value *(not hue), and to develop a sense of the details.*

a paint fan-deck, which contains all the colors the company makes. Cover a table with white paper. When possible, work in natural light. Place your photos in front of you and have a list of "givens" for your building: its interesting—and awkward—features; its surroundings; the colors of its roof, stone, tile, landing, or stained glass; and its exposure and orientation.

Lay the chips on the white paper and see which colors appeal to you. Arrange the chips into groups according to preference. Select color(s) for the body and then the trim. Choose your accent colors last.

Moving into the twentieth century, American domestic architecture began to return to simpler lines. With this Colonial revival, paint colors also changed. Body colors returned to pastels and white became the most popular trim color, even on sash. Still, the cornice, cornerboards, and belt courses were defined against the body color— even when the body was light yellow and the trim an ivory white.

Only the introduction of bungalows and later tract housing weaned us away from multicolor paint schemes. Fortunately, Americans have rediscovered the importance of exterior decoration of their homes, and will no longer accept the chromatic monotony of the past half century.

Orchestrating Color

You can take the historic approach to selecting colors, or you can take a more contemporary approach. You may elect to glean the best techniques from the past and combine them with imaginative solutions, such as exterior stencilling, trompe l'oeil, and faux finishing. You can select a palette that primarily reflects your own personal

color preferences. The following are some guidelines to orchestrating the color:

- Color **intensity** increases as the volume and scale of the color increases. Select the gray and muted hues. Exterior light greatly amplifies the intensity of color. What may look dull on a paint chip will become very lively on a large expanse.

- To achieve **balance,** distribute color evenly over the building from top (or hat), to its middle (belt), and to its base (shoes). For example, a building with a light-colored base and a dark-colored peak may look top-heavy and ungrounded. A well-balanced color arrangement will have visual unity.

- **Rhythm,** keeping the same colors touching and interacting, is just as important. Repetition of color juxtaposition creates a pleasing visual rhythm.

- Select colors for major surfaces that are **durable** and neutral. The sun will fade pure bright tones quickly.

- Choose strong **accent colors** only in small expanses so they will fade gracefully. Use accents on undersurfaces, such as soffits, to add an element of surprise and create

A HISTORICAL GUIDE TO COLOR SELECTION

Choosing colors initially intended for your house's style will show it in its best light. Paint even a house built years after its style was at its peak (a Greek Revival built in 1870, for example) in the colors suitable for that style.

Paint colors, like house styles, did not conveniently go out of fashion as soon as a new color combination appeared. It's best to study the details on your house (shape, mass, type of roof, windows, porches) and determine which style it most closely resembles. Many houses possess elements of two or more styles. In the guide that follows, odds are you won't find a house that is exactly like yours. But you should be able to find a style—or combination of styles—that approximates it, and the suitable color ranges.

Saltbox (1600s–present)

Usually left unpainted, the saltbox weathered to a brown-gray color; today you can use stain. Even after paint was introduced, colors were limited.

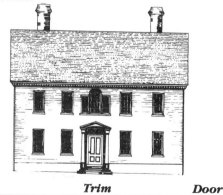

Body	Trim
White	Same
Spanish brown	Same
Indian red	Same
Ochre	Same

Georgian (1700–1800)

Classic formal Georgian houses were most often painted white, with green or black shutters. Earlier, less formal houses were sometimes painted in darker, Colonial colors.

Body	Trim	Door
White	White	Dark brown
Dark brown	Same	Black-green
Barn red	Cream	Dark blue
Dark green	Any of above	Red

Federal Rowhouses (1735–1835)

These urban houses were often painted in light, severe colors with white or cream trim. Doors were dark—black or natural dark wood. Shutters were dark red, green, or brown.

Body	Trim	Door
White	White	Black
Pale yellow	Cream	Natural
Cream	Same	Dark green
Medium blue	Any of above	Dark brown

Classic Farmhouse (1800–present)

Built throughout the nineteenth century, these were painted with whatever colors were popular at the time. Many were painted white, sometimes with red roofs. Often these houses were painted plainly all in one color, with only the doors colored dark brown or red for contrast.

Greek Revival (1820–1865)

Suitable "classical" colors include white or pale yellow, accented with white or cream trim.

Body	Trim	Door
White	Cool white	Dark green
Pale yellow	Dark green	Medium blue
Light gray	Sandstone	Black
Sandstone	Any of above	Any of above

(continued on next page)

Gothic Revival/Carpenter Gothic (1840–1860)

Gothic Revival mansions and Carpenter Gothic cottages alike were painted in light browns and pinks. Trim was painted in the same or similar colors, or painted dark brown. Doors and shutters were dark.

Body	*Trim*	*Door*
Rose beige	Dark brown	Natural
Light brown	Medium brown	Dark red
Dark brown	Light brown	Dark brown
Medium blue	Light gray	Dark green

Vernacular Italianate (1840–1880)

Painted in warm, light colors with contrasting trim and dark doors. Trim was often the same color, but in a different shade— lighter or darker.

Body	*Trim*	*Door*
Warm brown	Beige	Natural
Dark brown	Warm brown	Dark green
Dark gray	Light gray	Dark brown
Light green	Medium gray	Any of above

Second Empire/Mansard (1860–1880)

Details were picked out in dark greens, reds, and browns. Earlier houses continued to be painted in Italianate colors that resembled stone. Trim was generally lighter, with doors and shutters in subtle contrast to the trim.

Body	*Trim*	*Door*
Dark green	Beige	Natural
Dark red	Cream	Dark brown
Brown	Light brown	Green-black
Beige	Yellow	Any of above

Stick Style (1860–1885)

Body and trim were painted in contrasting dark colors to heighten the decorative trim. Doors were often oak or another unpainted hardwood.

Body	*Trim*	*Door*
Medium gray	Dark gray	Oak
Indian red	Dark brown	Unpainted wood
Ochre	Green-black	Either of above
Dark blue	Beige	Either of above

Stick-Eastlake (1870–1900)

Bold, colorful contrasting color schemes earned these West Coast houses the name "painted ladies," even as far back as 1885.

Body	*Trim*	*Door*
White	Cream	Oak
Light yellow	Warm white	Unpainted wood
Tan	Either of above	Either of above
Medium gray	Either of above	Either of above

Colonial Revival (1800–present)

This style witnessed the return to pale colors. These houses were bigger than earlier true Colonial style, often with a big front porch.

Base	*Body*	*Trim*	*Sash*	*Door*	*Cornice*
Pompeian red	Olive	Bronze	Indian red	Oak	Terra-cotta
Indian red	Maroon	Seal	Yellow	Oak	Terra-cotta
Granite	White		Bronze	Oak	Sky blue

Craftsman Bungalow (1900–1930)

Bungalows, like other turn-of-the-century styles (Tudor, Shingle), were unpainted. The natural materials were untreated except for an occasional stain to darken the wood.

Queen Anne (1875–1915)

The darkest, most vivid colors were popular during this period. As a result, these houses were painted several dark colors to highlight all the detail. Some elements of Queen Anne were part of the early stages of the Colonial Revival style, which reached its heyday about twenty years afterward. Colonial Revival harkened back to early styles including Georgian Revival and Queen Anne, even though most of the early styles evoked were American, not British.

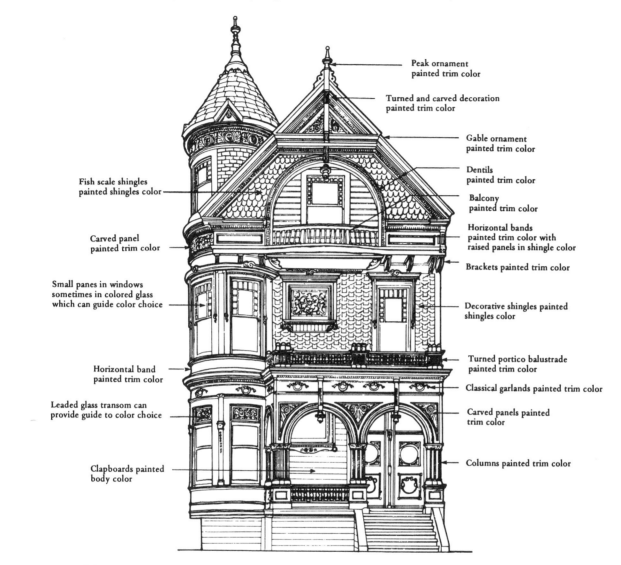

Peak ornament painted trim color

Turned and carved decoration painted trim color

Gable ornament painted trim color

Dentils painted trim color

Balcony painted trim color

Horizontal bands painted trim color with raised panels in shingle color

Brackets painted trim color

Decorative shingles painted shingles color

Turned portico balustrade painted trim color

Classical garlands painted trim color

Carved panels painted trim color

Columns painted trim color

Fish scale shingles painted shingles color

Carved panel painted trim color

Small panes in windows sometimes in colored glass which can guide color choice

Horizontal band painted trim color

Leaded glass transom can provide guide to color choice

Clapboards painted body color

Queen Anne Color Schemes		Shingles				Trim				Sash				Blinds			
		DARK RED	REDDISH BROWN	WARM BROWN	LIGHT GREEN	MAROON	REDDISH ORANGE	BRONZE YELLOW	DARK GREEN	MAROON	DARK RED	DARK GREEN	OLIVE	DARK GREEN	TAN	DARK RED	DARK BLUE
CLAPBOARDS	Buff																
	Olive																
	Dark brown																
	Gray																

surface texture. However, be careful not to overuse accents as this can cause visual chaos.

• Use trim to create a **skeletal structure** for the building. This will define and unify the architectural elements. Create a contrast in value between the body and trim.

• Keep color **interaction** in mind. White drains color from the color it touches. Black accentuates the color it touches. Gray is chameleon color. If gray touches red, it makes the red appear redder and it takes on a reddish cast itself.

Choose colors from paint sample chips of a good brand—better paint will be truer to its chips. Cut a window in a sheet of white paper; use this to isolate colors on the chip.

Pick your colors outside in open shade or under an overcast sky. The glare of sunlight inhibits your ability to see colors well and distinguish their subtleties (and you know what fluorescent lights do to color).

Refer to your "given" colors—stone, brick, roof shingles, and so on. These are the colors your color scheme must be based on to give the house a whole feeling. Most colors can be adjusted to fit. Now, make sure that the combinations of colors you choose go with each other as well. Isolate them together on both a light and dark background, and make adjustments as needed. When you've found the body color(s) you like, try different trim colors until one works. Then do the same for your accent colors. Make sure these colors correspond in value (darkness or lightness) with the black-and-white plans you have made.

When you're happy with the selection you've made, get quarts of sample paint mixed at a paint store. Now find a small but significant section of the building where all of the colors come together and paint it completely. Live with the painted sample for a few days. Look at it in every kind of light. Squint a lot.

If one color seems to be wrong, modify or change it and put the new one up. The addition of white, called tinting, lightens your color. The addition of black, called shading, darkens it. If two adjacent colors don't harmonize, try mixing some of color one into color two. This blending creates an "essence of one another" feeling; the colors become complementary. If you want to experiment with color mixing, take a look at a book on color theory—*Elements of Color* by J. Itten (Van Nostrand Reinhold, 1970), for example—and a color compass or wheel by Grumbacher.

STAINING

Exterior stains come in many different permutations—oil and latex, semitransparent and opaque, preservative and weathering. Stains are gaining popularity in new wood construction because they are cheaper than paint and don't build up to a thick film, and stains weather more gracefully than paint. (Opaque stain doesn't hold up as well as paint on exposed south-facing walls; recoat more often where degradation is apparent.) Stains also make maintenance less troublesome because preparing the surface before recoating is easier. Also, modern tastes accept and even prefer that the wood texture show through the finish. Keep all this in mind if you're adding an outbuilding or a rear wing.

Stain applies less to already painted older houses. Switch to stain only if the paint film has weathered away to virtually nothing, or if you've stripped off all the paint to bare wood. However, the decision to switch will probably be based on your unwillingness to start the whole painting cycle over again. In harsh environments where paint regularly fails (such as on a seacoast), you might try stain instead.

Stick with paint (which has better hiding characteristics and color retention) on clapboards, but switch to a semitransparent stain on new or stripped rails and balustrades. Stain is excellent for use on these high-abrasion surfaces. (It's the only practical choice for a deck.)

Old-house owners might consider a stain finish for new wood-shingle roofs. Nothing can "bring back" already-weathered shingles or shakes. But a new wood roof will look good longer (and maybe last longer) with a semitransparent preservative stain on it. (Don't use paint or opaque stain on a roof; it won't hold up.)

Though there are many different names used by manufacturers, most stains fall into two categories:

1. *Semitransparent,* which allows some of the wood's color, plus its grain and texture, to show through

2. *Solid-color or Opaque,* which has greater opacity, giving a consistent color finish, but allows more texture to show than paint does

Most stains are oil-based. They penetrate the wood rather than forming a surface film. However, *latex opaque stains* are a compromise between paint and stain. They can be used over previously coated wood, especially useful for old buildings.

Some products contain a wood preservative, commonly TBTO (tributyltin oxide), which is effective yet doesn't appear to have the human toxicity associated with bad actors like pentachlorophenol. Most contain a mildewcide such as Folpet (N-trichloromethylthio-phthalimide). Check the label for active ingredients.

Special-use stains include *weathering stain* (for new wood only) and *natural stain*. Weathering stain imparts a soft gray finish on application, then chemically assists weathering to a natural silver gray in six to nine months. (Some companies call them "bleaching stains.") The natural stains keep the wood looking new. They do have pigment in them (the color of raw redwood, cedar, or fir); a truly clear coating would allow ultraviolet light to penetrate and discolor the surface.

What Stain to Use When

Oil-base stains penetrate the wood; latex stains form a thin, flexible film. If there is any paint whatsoever left on the house, you should use a latex opaque stain. Prepare the surface as for painting—get rid of loose paint, rough edges, dirt, mildew, and so on.

Also use latex opaque stain to

• Get a traditional, color-rich finish without using paint.

• Go from a semitransparent or opaque oil finish to a lighter color. (To use a light-color latex stain on dark woods, you may have to prime with an undercoat product from the same manufacturer.)

• Cover over previous stain that contained creosote.

• Get an opaque-stain coating on new, bare Southern yellow pine, maple, and other close-pored, impervious wood species.

• Limit mildew when it is a recurring problem. (Latex stains are more mildew-resistant than oil-based ones.)

• Ease in the application and cleanup (latex is water-soluble).

Most stains are oil-based (penetrating) products. The most effective (and justifiably expensive) of these are chiefly linseed-oil-based sometimes modified with a long-oil alkyd. For a semitransparent finish, use only an oil-based product (not latex).

For weathered wood that already shows signs of deterioration, you can color with an *oil-base,* semitransparent or solid stain, but only after careful preparation. First, clean the wood with a weak oxalic acid/water solution. Then waterblast or wire-brush all weathered wood (use a noniron brush) to remove loose and damaged wood fibers. You'll have to stick to dark colors if any graying or discoloration remains.

Manufacturers of preservative chemicals used to treat new lumber say that pressure-treated wood *can* be stained under certain conditions. For example, stain Wolmanized brand wood with one coat of an oil-base, semi-transparent stain after exposing the wood to full weathering for at least two months. (Be aware that the green tinge in treated wood will affect the color.) Check with the manufacturer's technical literature or personnel.

Use oil-base stains, not latex, on open-pored woods such as redwood, cedar, mahogany, and fir.

Applying Stain

We've all been spoiled by the ease of application of high-quality latex paints, which are almost foolproof. Many inexperienced applicators give up on the idea of semitransparent or bleaching stain because they can't get even coverage.

Applying stain does take a little more care, but it doesn't take any longer than painting. (And the next time, preparing a previously stained surface will be easier than preparing a painted one.) Follow these guidelines when applying stain:

1. Pour the top oils out and stir the pigment-rich contents. Then put the oils back in and stir thoroughly. It's best to pour two or three gallons into a five-gallon pail; stir together for uniform color and pigment dispersion.

2. You do have to box your stain; that is, mix one batch of stain into another to avoid pigment concentration and color differences. Never use the bottom third of a can; stir it into the next batch.

3. Stir the stain often during application.

4. Don't stain in direct sun.

5. To avoid lap marks, always keep a wet edge. On clapboards, take a few courses and apply stain to a natural break such as a window or cornerboard. On vertical siding, start at the top of a few boards and work down.

6. A good brush is the best tool for staining. But if you're using a low-viscosity (very fluid) semitransparent

---

Use this chart as a guide to choosing the correct stain for the material.

		USES							
		Weathered Wood	New Wood	Painted Wood	Freshly Stripped Wood	Bleeder Woods	Horizontal Surfaces	Shake Roofs	Masonry, Stucco, Metals
F I N I S H	Clear or Transparent	Yes	Yes	No	Yes	Maybe*	Yes	Yes	No
	Semitransparent	Yes	Yes	No	Yes	Maybe*	Yes	Yes	No
	Opaque Oil	Finish Coat	Finish Coat	No	Yes	Yes	No	No	No
	Opaque Latex	Finish Coat	Finish Coat	with proper preparation	Finish Coat	No	No	No	Yes
	Paint	Finish Coat	Yes	Yes	Yes	Yes	Maybe*	No	Yes

*See product literature for instructions.

or bleaching stain and it's running all over the place, switch to a foam-pad applicator.

7. Follow directions on the label whenever possible. With latex stain, don't apply when temperature is below 50 degrees (or will go below 50 within twenty-four hours); doing so could affect the cure. (Applying oil-base product below recommended temperatures will affect drying time, but not usually durability.) On hot, dry days, dampen the surface before applying latex stain. (Always apply oil stain to a dry surface.)

8. When possible, remove trim that is to be stained a different color from the body. Cutting-in with stain is almost impossible.

9. On new work, prestain if possible. It's easier to control the finish when the clapboards are lying across sawhorses in the shade.

CHAPTER 8

Porches and Architectural Ironwork

Wood porches and exterior ironwork are major maintenance challenges. Porches are particularly prone to decay because there are many horizontal surfaces to trap water, wood is near or in contact with the ground, and a lot of end grain is exposed. Architectural ironwork presents another problem because it is often neglected, and little information is available when repairs are made. Often repairs fail and even add to the problems.

PORCH HISTORY

The porch originated with the classical portico. The classical portico made an emphatic architectural statement and defined the entrance with an elaborate framing element. Unlike a verandah, the portico is not meant to be used as a living space. Rather, with its columns, pediment, and often a grand stair, the portico is designed to impress and inform the visitor.

Verandahs as living spaces were introduced in the United States by Andrew Jackson Downing, a nursery man, landscape designer, and architect. He seized on the English idea popular in the late eighteenth and early nineteenth centuries of the naturalistic landscape as outlined by men such as Lancelot "Capability" Brown, Humphry Repton, and John Loudon: A house and its gardens should be carefully integrated into nature. Downing's work caused "verandah mania" during the mid-nineteenth century. Old farmhouses were modernized with porches or verandahs and with another of Downing's ideas—the bay window. (The bay window permitted a wider perspective on the landscape.) No new home was complete without its porch, verandah, or piazza.

Today a porch goes by many names, depending on its construction and style:

Gallery. A roofed promenade, especially one projecting from the exterior wall of a building. Synonymous with

This Italianate house with campanile demonstrates that the porch is often the most expressive element, even on a grand house. Its piazza offers paired, turned colonnettes, a fan-motif balustrade, turned newels, and ball finials. Also note the porte cochere to the right.

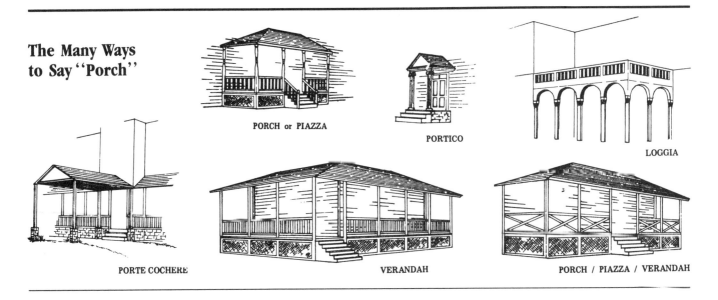

The Many Ways to Say "Porch"

PORCH or PIAZZA

PORTICO

LOGGIA

PORTE COCHERE

VERANDAH

PORCH / PIAZZA / VERANDAH

verandah and piazza, the word is used regionally and for certain architectural styles.

Loggia. A covered gallery or passage, arcaded or colonnaded, open to the air on at least one side. Often the roof of the loggia is formed by the upper storeys of the building. Usually associated with Italianate architecture.

Pavilion porch or gazebo porch. A roofed garden structure such as a gazebo or pavilion, which is incorporated into an attached verandah.

Pergola-porch. A porch with an open roof (usually with exposed rafters or trellises) such as found in a garden pergola. Common on Bungalow-style houses.

Peristyle. A promenade of columns surrounding a building or open court.

Piazza. Originally an Italian term for an open public space surrounded by buildings, it also describes a long, covered gallery with roof supported by columns. During the nineteenth century, with the fascination of all things Italian, the term began to be used interchangeably with "porch" or "verandah."

Porch. The general term used to describe a roofed space outside the main walls of a building. Strictly speaking, the term should be limited to a covered entrance for a building, having a separate roof projecting from the wall. Longer roofed galleries attached to a house and intended as outdoor living spaces are more accurately identified as "verandahs" or "piazzas." The porch can be called a "portico" if it has columns and a pediment making it resemble the front of a Greek or Roman temple.

Porch hood. An abbreviated form of the portico, a hood is a small roof placed over an entryway, supported by brackets or directly attached to the building wall.

Porte cochere. A carriage porch, designed to permit passengers to alight from a carriage and enter a building without being exposed to the elements.

Portico. The roofed space—generally open on three sides—forming the entrance and centerpiece of the facade of a temple, house, or church. It has columns and a pediment. A portico can be further defined by the number of columns; for example, a "tetrastyle portico" has four columns. The terms should be restricted to classical architecture and buildings based on classical models.

Sleeping porch. Popular during the 1800s and through the 1920s, the sleeping porch was usually adjacent to a bedroom (frequently appearing on the second floor).

The porch pavilion was a favorite during the Colonial Revival era.

The band saw inspired carpenters to new heights of expression. The vine motif on the sawn porch posts at the Carpenter Gothic–style Peter Davis House in Noank, Connecticut (c.1855), is a work of art.

A classical portico on a Greek Revival house in Marshall, Michigan.

A sleeping porch could simply be a room left open on two sides.

Used especially on summer nights, it was advocated by "experts" of the period who prescribed fresh-air sleeping nearly year-round.

Stoop. A small porch, platform, or staircase leading to the main entrance of a house or building. Term derives from the Dutch "stoep" for step. Used mainly in northeastern United States.

Umbra or umbrage. From the Latin word meaning "that which offers shade." Victorians occasionally used this term instead of "porch" or "verandah" to show their familiarity with classical Italy.

Verandah. From the Hindi word "varanda," which denotes a roofed, open gallery or balcony extending along the outside of a building, and which is designed for outdoor living in hot weather. The word was transplanted to England, where it was applied most often to an open gallery with a roof carried on light metal supports that ran across the front of a building. With its emphasis on warm-weather leisure, the term "verandah" should be applied to any gallery extending across two or more sides of a building. A gallery extending across one full side can be called a "verandah" or "porch." Any gallery that is less than a full side of a house or building is best called a "porch."

Porch Color and Furnishings

Though balustrades, trim, and columns were painted to match or complement the house, there were two universal customs about porch colors: The floor was almost always painted with battleship gray, while the boards of the ceiling were painted a light blue to enhance the illusion of sitting under the open sky.

To create the feeling of a room, the verandah was outfitted with straw, hemp, or sisal rugs. Wicker, cast iron, bentwood, and wood and canvas all were traditional. (And don't forget the porch swing, historically called a glider.)

Wicker was popular for so long, it went through many evolutions. Early Victorian wicker often had complex cur-

This renovated cottage boasts sawn-wood ornamental fretwork and a spindlework frieze on the porch.

licues and twists of reeding decorating high backs and legs. During the early part of the twentieth century, wicker was more simplified, with reeds woven in and out in a straightforward lattice pattern, known in some areas as the "Bar Harbor Style."

The well-equipped porch also had a canvas awning, used instead of, or in combination with, curtains or blinds made of canvas, wood, or reeding. These awnings and curtains were raised and lowered with an array of ropes and pulleys that required the skill of a sailor to master.

No American porch was complete without a metal holder for the flag staff. On Memorial Day, Fourth of July, and other patriotic holidays, every front porch flew its own Stars and Stripes.

Finally, there were other decorative details such as a variety of plant stands. Traditionally, many house plants were brought to the porch for a summer airing. Ferns, palms, and aspidistras abounded. Planting boxes attached to the railings held annuals. Trellises, too, were popular during the late-Victorian and turn-of-the-century periods. Most supported climbing roses, wisteria, ivy, and morning glories.

RESTORING A PORCH

Examine a porch carefully before you begin restoration. If you need to rebuild the porch entirely, try to recycle the original trim elements and duplicate missing pieces as necessary.

When inspecting a porch, be sure to check the following:

• Foundation and substructure. Posts, underframing, and connections where the porch joins the house are likely to rot—especially if there isn't adequate ventilation under the porch.

• Decking. Floorboards have exposed end-grain and tend to rot from the end in. Pitch of the porch floor may have changed due to settlement so that puddles of water form on the deck.

• Steps. Wooden steps in contact with the ground are invariably the first elements to disintegrate. Treads that aren't properly pitched to shed water won't last long either.

• Decay. Inspect carefully for termites, carpenter ants, and other wood-destroying insects. Look for telltale termite mud tunnels running up piers, foundation, and other likely places, or the little piles of sawdust that are the hallmark of carpenter ants.

If you can, find old photos of your porch before beginning its restoration. You may discover that the porch has been modified beyond recognition. As you demolish the old porch you may discover clues that will help you reconstruct the original porch such as "ghostlines" of the railing or roofline.

Of course, not everyone will need to completely reconstruct their porch. Here you'll find guidelines on restoring your crumbling porch from the roof to the ground, while attempting to retain as much of the original work as possible.

From the Ground Up

Anyone repairing or rebuilding porches should use pressure-treated wood or the fiber-tube forms described later in this chapter for the support columns beneath the porch. Support the pressure-treated wood in a metal stirrup secured to a poured concrete footing beneath it. The metal stirrups drain water away from the end grain at the bottom of the post.

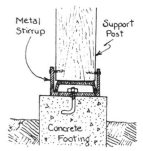

Porch floors generally don't require a subfloor as it may trap moisture and prevent the top flooring from receiving the ventilation from below. Use fir or redwood to replace the floor joists and attach them to the header beam with conventional galvanized metal joist hangers. You may want to apply a panel adhesive to the ends of the joists.

Treat the floorboards with wood preservative or waterproofer. Other elements of the porch—rails, balusters, steps, and the like—will benefit from wood preservative too. Paint on porches often fails at the seams between the porch floorboards because of moisture. One 1899 carpen-

This photo, taken about the turn of the century, shows the old porch with a new roof.

In 1988 this nineteenth-century Federal-style home still retained this full porch—about twice the size of the original.

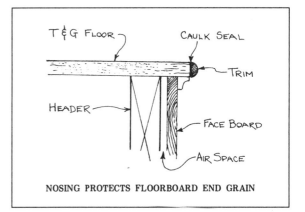

NOSING PROTECTS FLOORBOARD END GRAIN

try manual suggests applying a thick coat of white lead paste along each tongue-and-groove before nailing the boards down. Instead of lead paste, use an oil-based caulk on the joints. Before finishing the floor, remove all excess caulking. Or, apply a thick coat of primer paint in the tongues-and-grooves immediately before fitting the boards together.

The end grain of wood is the first to go on porches. Cover the end grain of all exposed wood—especially the end grain of tongue-and-groove flooring. Use a rounded or square piece of trim on the end grain. Before nailing it in place, run a bead of high-performance caulk (e.g., polyurethane) on the end of the board to seal the joint.

Using a wood preservative or water repellent before priming prolongs the life of the paint on the exposed wood surfaces. We recommend a WR solution (water repellent) as opposed to a WRP solution (water repellent/ preservative). The water repellent in most formulations is the same: a waxy material. The preservative (fungi-killing) material can vary, but the most common is pentachlorophenol, or "penta." Penta is a toxic chemical that can be absorbed through the skin.

You can make your own water repellent developed by the Forest Products Lab in Madison, Wisconsin. The formula is cheap, nontoxic, and works as well as WRP solutions. (However, in warm, humid climates, such as in the southern United States, you may have to add fungi-killing preservative.) To make the formula, mix the following:

Exterior varnish	3 cups
Paraffin Wax	1 ounce
Mineral Spirits, Paint Thinner or Turpentine	Add enough to make 1 gallon

Shave the paraffin block (the grocery story material sold for canning jars) as finely as possible to make dissolving it easier.

Building Porch Piers with Fiber Tube Forms

Using fiber tube forms to pour concrete piers is an economical way to provide stable structural support, and they needn't detract from the historic character of a house. Moreover, settling or winter frost heaving won't shift the porch, opening up joints between wooden parts and al-

Ready-to-use fiber tubes for pouring concrete piers.

lowing water to run in, as sometimes happens with shallow foundations. Over many years, this repeated exposure to water and ice adds up to serious deterioration and expensive maintenance. Piers that stand on a wide

pad and extend well below the frost line will be sturdy and help minimize future maintenance expenses.

Tube forms are large cylinders of spirally plied cardboardlike fiber used to mold round concrete columns. You can find them through building-supply houses in diameters ranging from 6 inches to 24 inches and lengths up to 12 feet. (Industrial versions come even larger.) The forms are designed to be used once and then either stripped off or left in place after the concrete has cured. Most are wax coated on their inner and outer surfaces for weather and moisture protection, and to help release the concrete from the form; as a result, oiling is not required. They can be cut readily with a hand or power saw and trimmed to the desired length, sectioned, or split into half-round, quarter-round, or smaller partial columns.

In addition to their low cost, using fiber tube forms also saves labor because less concrete is required than with other pier-form systems. The forms need only a minimum of external bracing to keep them plumb while the concrete cures, making clamps and ties unnecessary. Cleanup is minimal as the forms are not reused.

To build concrete piers from tube forms you will need the following:

- Fiber tube forms—a sufficient length to build all piers; 8-inch diameter adequate for most projects
- Ready-mix concrete—enough to fill tubes; typical capacity for an 8-inch tube is 50 pounds dry measure per foot of tube, or roughly 60 percent of an 80-pound bag
- Reinforcement bar (rebar)—1/4-inch diameter, as required (available at building- or masonry-supply houses)
- Brick-bat (piece of brick) or 3-inch stone—one per pier
- Shovel—to dig hole
- Cross-cut or saber saw—to cut tubes to length
- Hacksaw or bar cutter—to cut rebar to length
- Siting level, chalkline, etc.—to align tubes

Step 1: Dig the hole. In most cases, site a pier directly under each porch post or column. Sometimes you will need piers under a joint in the sill or to support an especially long stretch of open porch. Hang a plumb bob from the underside of that portion of the porch you wish to support, and mark the position of the bob on the ground. Dig a hole at each pier location, making the hole approximately twice the diameter of the tube. Dig the hole as deep as the frost depth for your area (about 3 feet where winters are moderate) or until you hit hardpan. Center the bottom of the hole on the final position of the pier and make it flat.

Step 2: Pour the pad. To form a pad for the pier, pour some concrete 5 or 6 inches deep into the hole. Be careful not to knock dirt off the side of the hole—dirt mixed with concrete will compromise its strength. Settle or level the concrete roughly. While the concrete is still wet, set a brick-bat or 3-inch keystone in the center of the pad so that half of it sticks up above the surface (see figure 1 on page 134); this stone acts as a key to prevent the pier from

Fig. 1

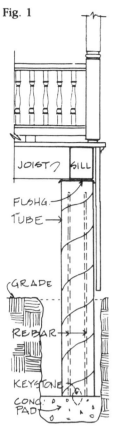

sliding off the pad. Let the pad set up for at least twenty-four hours.

Step 3: Position the tube. Cut a piece of tube equal to the distance from the pad surface up to the final height required for the pier. Brush any dirt off the pad and set the tube on the pad directly over the keystone, then fill in 6 inches of dirt around the outside of the tube. Tamp the dirt to hold the tube in place. Check the tube with a level to be sure it is truly vertical and in the correct position, then continue to shovel in dirt and tamp it until you fill the hole. The compacted dirt holds the tube in the correct position when the concrete is poured. (Piers that extend more than 2 feet above ground may need temporary bracing.)

Step 4: Pour the concrete. Cut pieces of rebar 2 inches shorter than the length of the tube. Prepare a batch of concrete and pour some into the tube until it is about 1 foot deep (see below for what to do if tube access is blocked). Work the lengths of rebar into the concrete, placing them about 1 1/2 inches in from the side of the tube and about every 4 inches around the circumference of the tube. Continue to fill the tube, holding the rebars in the correct position. Settle and compact the concrete by working it with a wooden stick as it is poured into the tube. Check the pier one last time for correct positioning.

If access to the form is blocked, as when you install a pier under an existing porch, you can still fill it easily.

Fig. 2   **Fig. 3**

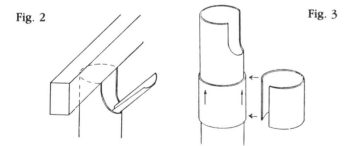

1. With a saber saw, cut a 6-inch-high U-shaped opening in the top of the tube (see figure 2). Do this before you position the tube.

2. Form a simple funnel out of sheet metal. A 2-foot length of 6-inch-diameter stove pipe works well. Leave the seam open and flatten one end of the pipe.

3. Have a friend hold the funnel in place as you shovel in concrete. If you're working alone, rig up a sheet-metal strap fastened to the open end of the funnel and screwed to each side of the sill. Begin filling the form using this funnel.

4. When the concrete nears the bottom of the U-shaped opening, make a door to cover it (see figure 3). Cut a 6-inch length of tube and split it up the side. "Clip" the door around the tube form. If the door doesn't open wide enough without breaking, remove a 1- to 3-inch strip along the split to widen it. Slide the door up as you continue to fill the form. If there is not enough spring in the door to hold it in place, tie it closed with wire or cord, leaving it loose enough to slide.

With practice, you can run the concrete right up against the sheet-metal flashing and sill. If you have trouble with this, just get as close as you can (within an inch) and level the top surface of the concrete when you have finished. When the concrete has set, fill the gap with a short piece of board and tapered wood-shingle shims.

To fill a tube to capacity using a door, slide the door up the tube in stages as you add concrete mix.

Top off the tube when the door is at its maximum height.

Step 5: Remove the tube. Let the concrete cure at least seven days before putting a load on the piers. The tube forms should remain in place during this process, as they assist with the hydration of the concrete (you won't need other curing aids such as wrapping the pier with damp burlap). Once the concrete has cured, strip the form by making two or more vertical cuts with a power saw and pulling the form apart, or by making one 12-inch cut with a linoleum knife and then peeling the form off spirally. Either way, avoid scoring or marking the surface of the column.

Most old porches have a lattice framework to fill the gap between the ground and sill, hiding the piers. If your house is missing such latticework and you're not sure what style is appropriate, check old photos of the building or make note of what is used on porches of similarly styled houses in your neighborhood.

Here are three types of lattice construction that can be handled easily with concrete piers:

Fig. 4

SILL

GRADE

CONC. PIER

Brick pier. Stop the concrete pier just above grade level and continue up to the sill with brick (see figure 4).

Lattice without stile. When your porch calls for a long run of lattice without any breaks, simply remove the tube form and paint the concrete pier black. Once the lattice is up, the pier will recede into the shadows.

This lattice without stile porch apron conceals the poured-concrete pier.

Another porch apron, lattice with stile, will also conceal the porch pier.

Lattice with stile. It was common practice to divide the lattice with vertical stiles. Stylistically, this provides visual support for the column above. Practically, it hides your concrete pier.

Future maintenance of whatever design you choose will be much easier if you build individually framed lattice sections, rather than just nail the lattice to the porch. When you build the lattice, be sure to provide for access under the porch by installing at least one frame that swings out on hinges or removes easily with wood screws.

Failing Railings

Rails and balusters on porches always seem to present a problem. They usually feel their age from years of exposure and being sat on. Often, the whole balustrade is about to fall off.

The point where hand rails (also called cap rails) attach to columns or posts takes much or all of the weight of the rail, and is prone to water penetration and rot. Most rails attach to columns or posts in a butt joint, where the rail end and support surface meet without overlapping. Three suggestions for attachment follow.

Toenailing. This connection, seen on much original work, is still worthwhile if the rail or support wood isn't too weak or chewed up to take a nail. Use galvanized finishing nails (for both weather resistance and grip), and predrill nail holes when possible to minimize the chance of splitting the rail end. Toescrewing is also feasible if there is enough solid wood in the rail to accept the screws, recess the heads, and then plug them. Screws grab wood better than nails can, and will draw members together where gaps are a problem. Using galvanized, bronze, or stainless-steel screws improves weatherability, and the long, slim design of Sheetrock screws (in galvanized or stainless-steel versions) can come in handy.

Kneeplates. Kneeplates are a standard method of anchoring rails to bulkheads on boats and ships. Use them on porch work where toenailing is impractical, as long as the

Shifting of the porch opened these toenailed rail joints, allowing water to enter and weaken the ends.

Kneeplates mount to the porch support first. Then the rail (mortised at the end to accept the plate) is angled on and attached from below.

rail can be maneuvered away from the support to install the plate. Kneeplates need not be elaborate. Use store-bought corner braces or make them on site by fashioning extruded angle metal (such as aluminum) or bar stock to fit. First, mortise the plate into the rail's end grain so it will be hidden when the rail is in place. Then position the plate and screw it to the support. Lower the rail onto it and secure from below.

Rail bolts. These specialty fasteners are designed for joining and anchoring interior staircase rails. They are tricky to use, but will also work outdoors when the porch supports are of solid wood and when there is enough clearance to move the rail onto the mounted bolt. True rail bolts are half wood screw and half machine bolt, quite long (up to 6 inches), and have a special star-shaped nut that can be tightened from the side with a screwdriver. Rail bolts are getting hard to find in hardware stores, but common hanger bolts are almost as long and will usually suffice if notches are ground in the flats of the nut. Rail bolts require two holes in the rail end—one for the shaft of the bolt, and another at a right angle to start and tighten the nut. Bore the shaft hole below the centerline of the rail so that the bolt will support the bulk of the rail when installed and the nut hole is not too deep to be workable.

When reattaching rails, remember that the rail support junction is a likely water trap. Reduce the chances that

A hanger bolt and adapted nut will often double for a true rail bolt.

The nut and machine screw fasten the rail through two holes after the wood screw has been anchored in the support.

Foot rails last longest when constructed to shed water.

water will collect in this joint by fitting the rail end snugly to the contour of the support, particularly when meeting a curved form, such as a turned post or column. Before assembly, seal the end of the rail (and the area it covers on the support) by backpriming with prime coat or thinned topcoat paint. Rail end grain—like all end grain—is more likely to wick up water, which leads to paint loss and decay if left unprotected.

Foot Rails

Without adequate bracing, foot rails (the lower rails) may sag over time, pulling balusters away from the hand rail and opening joints. Add support blocks every 3 or 4 feet of run—typically, a single block halfway down the rail. Popular designs are rectangles, trapezoid shapes, or

uncomplicated turnings that match decoration on the porch. Support blocks last longest when they are small, supporting only key areas, and have minimum contact with the porch floor. You want to cover as little of the porch deck as possible to allow it to breathe. Paint all surfaces before toenailing the blocks in place.

Foot rails also collect snow and rain. Most are milled with a profile that sheds water readily, such as a camber (arch) or gablelike peak. If foot rails rest right on the porch floor, however, they prevent water from running off and trap it between rail and floor. The proper location for a foot rail is 3 to 5 inches off the floor, or roughly the height of the plinth block or base on which it rests at the supporting post or column.

Balusters

Open joints and exposed grain are also the Achilles' heel of the woodwork between the rails, whether turned or sawn. Many balusters are held captive in the top rail by a moulding or a rabbet and toenailed in place at the foot rail (or at both rails). When the old wood is too cracked or brittle for more toenailing, screws can be useful. Toescrewing baluster tops (after predrilling holes) is gentler than the blows of a hammer, and screw heads usually disappear under the hand rail. Where balusters can be rotated in place, dowel screws (which have wood screws at both ends) sometimes work. First, bore pilot holes in the baluster end and rail underside. Then, start the dowel screw in either piece and screw the baluster into place. Dowel screws are less successful for baluster bottoms because of the shape of the rail; securing from below with the use of lag screws often works well.

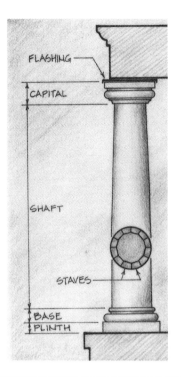

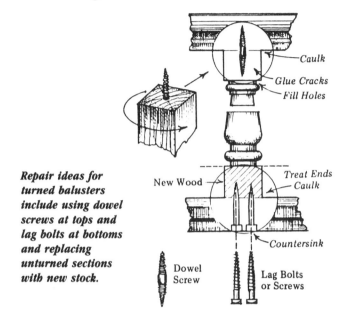

Repair ideas for turned balusters include using dowel screws at tops and lag bolts at bottoms and replacing unturned sections with new stock.

Like other exposed areas of a porch, balusters are prone to rot at their bottoms. When ends are identical (and deterioration is not extensive), balusters can sometimes be inverted in the railing, thereby relocating strong sections to the foot rail and weak sections under the hand rail. Use epoxy consolidants and fillers (see chapter 7) to restore hard-to-duplicate balusters such as turnings or sawn fretwork. You may also need to replace portions of turned balusters with square ends. Here, cut the damaged end from the baluster right where the turned portion begins. Then, dowel and glue a new block of the same size to the baluster, making a nearly invisible repair. When balusters are severely rotted, complete replacement (with stock or custom-made items) is the most practical option. Whatever the choice, backprime and caulk all joints before assembly to give the railing a head start on its next hundred years.

Restoring Columns

Big columns—those over 18 inches in diameter or 20 feet tall—are complex wooden structures requiring special attention. Repairs make good economic sense, as complete replacement costs are high.

Movement and moisture cause columns to fail. Moisture penetrates in several ways: deteriorated flashing at the capital, or the deck of a second-floor balcony may drain into the columns. Failing paint on column exteriors lets rainwater saturate the wood. Backsplash from the

Paint failure tells its own story: Peeling down to bare wood indicates excessive moisture.

Alligatoring and cracking indicates the paint film is too thick. The remedy is to strip and repaint.

roof often attacks column bases from above; rising damp from masonry foundations invades them from below.

Movement, either at the entablature or the foundation, can break columns apart. Sometimes, stresses build up over many years and release suddenly with dramatic, serious consequences (say, the crushing of a base). More

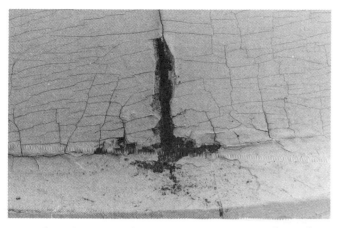

Vertical cracks indicate loose and open wood joints beneath the paint—movement is the culprit here.

Look for cracks in the foundation that indicate movement, possibly breaking up base parts between the joints.

often, column parts just move slightly, adjusting to new positions.

To successfully evaluate columns, look for the underlying causes of problems before jumping to conclusions about what should be done.

Often a thin shell of sound wood covers a seriously decayed area. Tap the suspect area with your knuckle or a screwdriver handle and listen for a hollow sound that differs from the surrounding area. (If the shell is thick, though, the sound won't give you a clue; you'll have to use more invasive methods to find the extent of the decay.)

The National Park Service recommends that you "probe with an ice pick to find soft, decayed wood. Jab the pick into a wood surface at an angle and pry up a small section of the wood. Sound wood will separate in long fibrous splinters, but decayed wood will lift up in short, irregular pieces due to the breakdown of fiber strength."

Drill a hole with an auger bit and brace. Damp chips indicate the obvious, while dry, dark wood may have been very wet at one time. Look for more decayed wood nearby.

To check the alignment of columns, sight down the row of plinths or along the edge of the porch decking, or

stretch a chalkline. Look for sections that are higher or lower than the rest.

Do the same for the capitals above, but be careful on ladders. Sometimes a good view is available from the upstairs of a neighboring house.

Look for cracks in the foundation that indicate movement, possibly breaking up base parts between the joints.

Of all column problems, decay in bases and plinths, loose or open stave joints, and woodpecker holes are the most common.

Decay in bases and plinths. Moisture may rise up through masonry due to hygroscopic action, or drip down from above. Either way, eliminate the source. A moving foundation may be breaking up base parts, leaving gaps at the joints that let water run in. Stabilize the foundation before proceeding with column repairs. Add ventilation to the columns to help keep them dry inside.

Loose or open stave joints. These are almost always caused by movement. Correct poor foundation and structural conditions. The glue in the stave joints may have failed due to moisture, so stabilize by regluing or doweling.

Woodpecker holes. Why did the birds make the holes in the first place? Usually, they were after insects, and the insects were probably there because the wood was very moist. Resolve all moisture and insect problems before you fill the holes. Woodpecker holes are likely to be 1 1/2 inches in diameter or larger.

Wood Plug Repair

Repair small holes (1 inch or less) with epoxy fillers. For those greater than three-quarters the width of a stave, you need to replace a whole section of the stave. Use round wood plugs, though, to fill holes between these two sizes, say, those made by woodpeckers, or any up to 2 1/2 or 3 inches in diameter.

To prepare the column for a wood plug, even-up the hole to a slightly larger diameter with an electric drill and hole saw. Make the hole fairly smooth with straight sides (not undercut).

Next, using a saber saw or band saw, make a plug out of wood the same species and thickness as the column shaft. To match the expansion and contraction of the surrounding wood, the grain of the plug must go in the same direction as the area of the column it's set into. Turn the plug blank to a very slightly tapered shape on the screw-point chuck of a lathe (dressing the sides on a sander works too). Use a sample hole as a guide, and taper the plug so it will stand slightly higher than the surrounding surface when fit snugly in the hole.

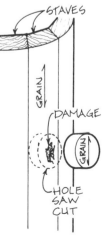

Closeness of the final fit depends on the type of glue you use. With gap-filling glue (like epoxy) a close fit is not critical. A non-gap-filling glue (like formaldehyde-resorcinol) requires a close fit. Glue the plug in its hole with weatherproof glue, checking grain direction. After the glue is set, trim the face of the plug flush with the surface of the shaft.

Replacing Stave Sections

Repairing woodpecker holes near the top of the shaft, or decay at the base, often means replacing stave sections. First determine where decayed wood ends and sound wood begins by using the auger-bit technique. Then saw across the grain of the stave with a keyhole saw or saber saw until your cut meets the stave joint on each side. Make the cut at a slight angle.

Next, prepare the joints of the adjacent staves. Clean off old paint and putty to expose fresh wood without changing the angle of the surface. Existing splines or tongues in the staves may also have to be trimmed even, to mate with the new repair piece.

When making replacement stave sections, use wood stock that matches the column in species and end-grain orientation. Measure the angle of the adjacent stave joint surfaces with a tool comprised of two pieces of sheet metal and a C-clamp. Then transfer the angle to both ends of the stock. Plane the stock down to form a new stave

with a cross section that corresponds to the transferred angles, leaving just enough wood so the block is slightly too large to fit. Next, cut off both ends to the correct length with the same slight angle used to cut out the decayed section. Again, make the stock just a little oversize.

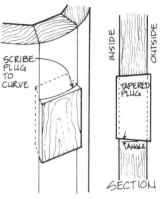

The result should be a block of wood beveled on all four sides. Test fit the block into its opening and trim the sides until the face of the block seats nearly flush with the highest outer surface of the column.

While the block is still in place, scribe both ends with a pencil to match the curve of the shaft surface. After scribing, take the block out again and plane the face to match the curve of the shaft surface. Leave the surface a little proud of the end grain-scribe marks.

An angle copier—improvised from two straightedges and a clamp—is a big help when replacing stave sections. Maneuver the straightedges so they mate with the angle of the "walls" in the opening.

The next step is to remove the copier and transfer the measurement to the new stock. (Be careful not to move the straightedges while working.)

Clamp the block in place.

Now that the glue is set, finish-trim with a hand plane.

Once the block is shaped, clamp it in place with weatherproof glue. After the glue is set, finish-trim the face of this new stave section with a hand plane so that it is level with the surface of the shaft.

Stabilizing Decay with Epoxy

Treating decayed wood in big columns often can be a tricky assignment because the subjects of repair must remain in place. This complicates finding ongoing decay in hidden interior areas, and means you have to repair the columns without the luxury of moving them to a convenient workspace.

Consolidating decayed wood with epoxies is a technique well adapted to working on stationary columns. (See the section of repairing rotted wood with epoxy in chapter 7.) If not applied carefully and effectively, however, consolidants can actually *trap* moisture, causing further decay. The decayed wood must be completely dry to its full depth when consolidating or the epoxy will merely form an impervious shell.

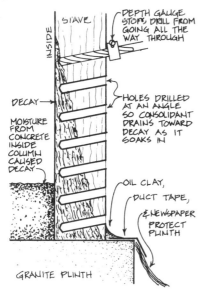

To work successfully, consolidants have to penetrate the fiber of the wood. Specific applications vary from job to job, but often run along the following lines:

1. Drill holes (between 1/8 inch and 3/8 inches in diameter) in the decayed wood to expose the end grain—the best avenue for the wood to absorb consolidant. Spacing holes close together (perhaps as close as their own diameter) ensures complete saturation.

This column shaft is ready for the application of consolidant. The newspapers (and a seal made from duct tape and artist's oil-clay) protect the granite plinth from seeping epoxy.

2. Keep holes filled with liquid epoxy consolidant, fed from hair-dye bottles, saturating the wood until no more is soaked up.

3. Check for complete penetration of the consolidant by drilling a hole into the treated wood (or cutting out a small section) before the epoxy hardens. Examine the wood to see whether or not it has been saturated.

4. Mix epoxy filler in small batches with a putty knife and use to finish the repair. A plastic funnel and wooden

Use a plastic funnel and a wooden dowel like a syringe to fill the holes with epoxy.

dowel used like a syringe work well for applying the mix to fill the holes. Considerable pressure can be developed with this method to force the filler into the honeycomb-like spaces of the decayed wood.

Replacing Missing Capitals

Wooden porch columns topped with terra-cotta capitals are typical of many turn-of-the-century houses. Over time, the capitals may crack and eventually disintegrate as a result of the freeze-thaw cycle of water seeping into the cracks.

Replacing damaged capitals can be difficult. Even if you find them in the correct size, they might not match if the originals have been painted many times. Rather than hunting for new capitals, mold one of the existing capitals in silicone rubber, then cast new capitals in fiberglass-reinforced polyester—exactly duplicating the originals in their present condition.

Choose a model in good condition and one that is accessible. Next make a mold from one-half of this capital, and cast two fiberglass halves from this mold to form one new capital. If the original capitals were fabricated as single units and installed, they can't be removed to make the mold. You'll have to do all mold work in place on a stepladder.

Building and Installing Wooden Forms

First, build a *base platform* on the column to support the weight of the mold and serve as a stage for the other parts. You will also need *parting blocks, wedge slides,* and a *top form* to create mounting surfaces on the mold for the boards that eventually will produce flanges on the fiberglass half-capital. Last, make a set of *taper pins* to reposition the plaster case mold after removal during the casting steps.

First, construct a base platform from 3/4-inch plywood,

large enough to extend 3 inches beyond each of the three scrolls or *volutes* of the capital and 1 1/2 inches beyond its centerline. Square off corners at 45 degrees for accessibility. Screw shelf brackets (8-inch and 10-inch) on the center lines to support it on the column.

Next, cut an L-shaped top form from 1/2-inch plywood designed to fit the porch beam. It should be 2 to 4 inches larger than the corners of the capital. Fashion parting blocks; redwood 2 × 8 scraps would do the trick. Fit cardboard patterns to the capital volutes, and then transfer these profiles to the redwood for cutting with a saber saw.

Movable wedge slides establish the surface of the column in the plaster case mold. In this case, the volutes extend below where the capital meets the column. These devices have to be triangular to fit between the volutes (one per capital "quadrant"). Build them up from 3/8-inch plywood and "screen mould" lumber (1 inch × 1 5/8 inches in actual dimension) set on edge. This provides a total height of exactly 2 inches above the base platform and brings the top surface of the edge slide even with the junction of the capital and the column.

The four locating pins function as keys for holding the plaster case mold in the correct position once it is moved. Each is 3 inches long and 1/2 inch in diameter, with a 4-degree taper at each side. Make them from aluminum or hardwood dowels.

If the column has a turned wood ring or *astragal* just below the capital, which is larger in diameter than the column, eliminate the need to make the wedge slides fit this half-round surface by installing a cylindrical band. Cut the band 2 inches wide from .060-inch high-impact styrene sheet plastic. Pack clay in the void below the astragal to support the band in a vertical position. Seal all wooden forms with shellac and lightly coat with petroleum jelly as a releasing agent. Label each piece. Fasten the forms together and to the column and porch beam with drywall screws of several lengths so they can be assembled and disassembled readily with a screwgun (see photo 1).

Use soft wax (used by graphic artists as an adhesive) to fill in space between the forms and the capital. Choosing a silicone rubber with low viscosity will leak out of the smallest cracks. Also use this wax to repair missing details on the capital, and form it to make a subtle, V-shaped wedge under the flat, horizontal areas of the volutes. Take this precaution so that air will not be trapped by the silicone rubber when the mold is poured.

Making the Clay Spacer

Make a spacer of gray-green Plasteline oil clay (which never hardens) to stand in for the silicone rubber mold while the plaster case mold is created. First, form the clay into slabs by rolling it with a large dowel between two strips of 1/2-inch plywood (see photo 2).

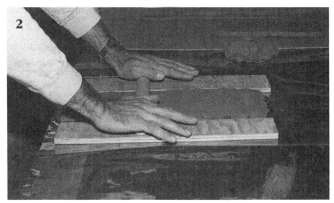

Completely cover the capital with the clay and then smooth it out to increase in thickness gradually from bottom to top (see photo 3). You'll have to remove the plaster case mold from the capital by maneuvering it down and away from the column; this extra buildup at the top keeps plaster off the top surfaces of the volute—which would lock the case mold in place (see drawing). Leave a 1/2-inch space for plaster between the clay under the volutes and the base platform.

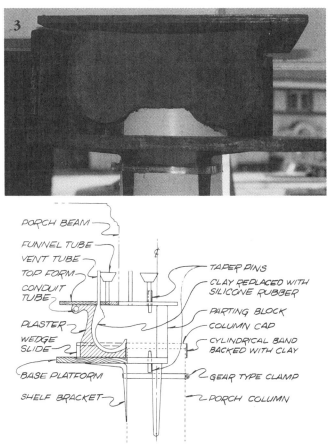

Creating the Reinforced Plaster Case Mold

You'll also need a case mold for casting the silicone rubber mold of the capital surface, as well as to support this mold when the fiberglass capital halves are cast. U.S. Gypsum White Hydrocal plaster reinforced with hemp strands should do the job.

Use a clean polyethylene bucket for mixing the plaster. Leftover plaster causes premature setting of new batches, and a container like this can be flexed for quick removal of scraps. First, pour cool, clean water in the bucket to a depth of several inches. Then, sift plaster evenly around the bucket and into the water by shaking it over the edge of a dry cup (a medium-size strainer also works). Continue to sift (for what may seem like a very long time) until dry islands of plaster appear above the water. Gently mix the batch with a gloved hand, breaking up all lumps, and then leave undisturbed for several minutes to slake (hydrate).

To make the plaster case mold, first brush the clay spacer with a coat of plaster to help prevent air bubbles (see photo 4). Then, coat the taper pins with petroleum jelly and set in place; position the wedge slides. Next, dip loose hemp strands in plaster and apply them to the clay. If these materials tend to slide down the clay, a thick mix of plaster and additional hands may be needed to hold them in place until the plaster sets. Along with additional coats of hemp and plaster, incorporate a piece of thin-wall electrical conduit bent at 90 degrees to act as reinforcement along the top of the case mold. Build up plaster until the mold is about 1 inch thick (see photo 5).

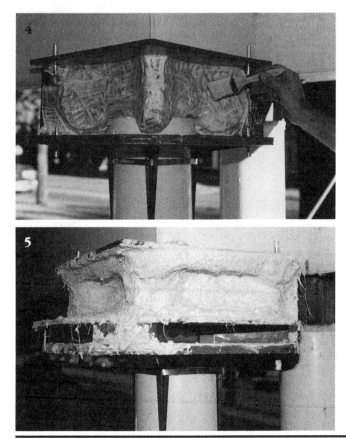

Removing the Clay Spacer and Replacing the Plaster

Once the plaster sets (after about twenty minutes), pull the taper pins and remove the base platform and wedge slides (see photo 6). Lift off the case mold and extract the clay from it to be shaped, stacked, and measured so the cubic inches of silicone rubber required to fill the mold can be calculated (see photo 7). To fill any voids, melt beeswax candle stubs in a double boiler and paint the wax into the plaster mold.

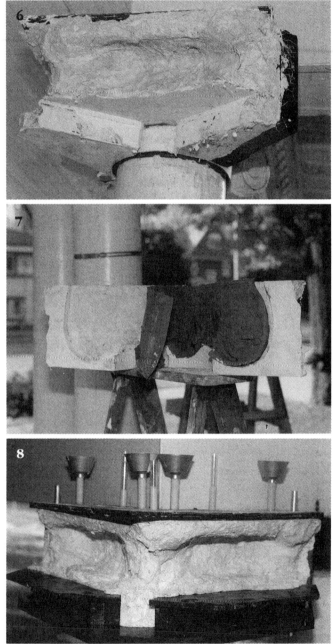

When the plaster is dry and cured, align the top form to it and mark the space occupied by the clay. Drill holes in the top form and install four funnel-fill tubes along with three air-vent tubes (see photo 8). You can then reassemble this completed mold with the wooden forms using the taper pins.

Pouring the Silicone Rubber Mold

Measure the spacer clay to determine how much silicone rubber you'll need to make the master mold. In this case, five one-pound units were needed. Dow Chemical's #3110 RTV product has a low viscosity that will fill the mold without trapping air. Another advantage is that it requires no release agent for polyester fiberglass.

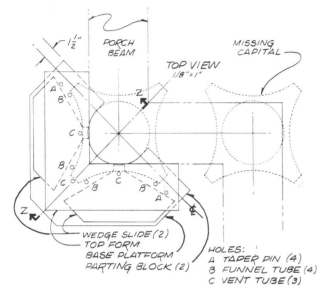

Add the catalyst to the silicone rubber and mix thoroughly. Take care not to trap air into the liquid rubber, which could form craters in the cured mold. Continue mixing as the rubber is poured into the four funnel tubes. When the rubber level is visible in all tubes, the mold is full and it is ready to be left in place for complete curing. If the weather turns cool, erect an insulating tent around the column (see photo 9) with a drop light for warmth. This mold cured in place for two days.

When the mold is fully cured, disassemble the wood forms, remove the plaster case mold, and peel the silicone mold off the capital (see photo 10). Now take both the rubber and plaster molds to the shop for the next phase of casting.

Making the Wooden Forms for Flanges

Cut flange boards to create small fiberglass flanges in the final casting from MDO sign board, a type of 1/2-inch plywood with a smooth phenolic surface. The top flange is roughly 2 inches wide, the bottom flange about 1 inch wide, and the sides from 1/2 inch to 3/4 inches wide. Shellac all flange boards. When they dry, give them a light coat of paste wax and buff (see photo 11). Now fasten the boards to the case mold with 1/4 × 20 bolts and wing nuts.

The initial step in casting an actual capital is to brush on the *gel coat* which becomes the finished surface. Gel coat is polyester resin that contains opaque pigment—white, in this case. This process is not only easier and more durable than painting the capital after casting, but it also bears a close resemblance to the baked-on glaze of the original terra-cotta capitals.

Catalyze the gel coat resin with 1 to 1 1/2 percent MEK peroxide hardener and thoroughly mix, then brush into the mold with china-bristle brushes (see photo 12). Be sure to cover all the inside corners so that the finished surface has no defects (some gel coat resins require a second coat).

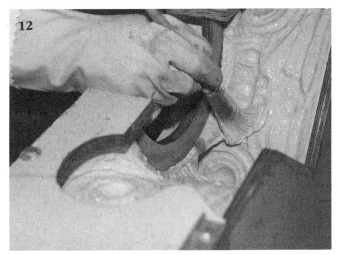

Once the gel coat is on the way to curing, begin lay-up of the main casting. First, cut 1 1/2-ounce fiberglass mat and tear into small pieces; saturate with catalyzed resin (ready-chopped fiberglass can also be used). Next, place these pieces in the mold on the gel coat and tamp and groom them with a brush and paint-stick and additional resin to get intimate contact with the gel coat (see photo 13), and to eliminate any air bubbles. Inside corners require extra care as the glass strands do not take readily to curved surfaces. Continue the process of adding and tamping saturated mat until several layers of fiberglass are built up. As a final touch, you may also smooth a layer of dry, lightweight fiberglass-cloth squares over the saturated glass to absorb excess resin, iron out the inside surface, and give the casting additional strength.

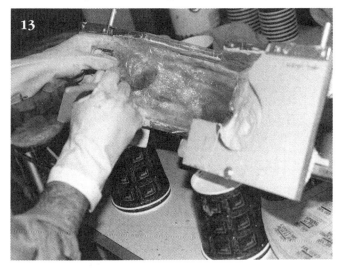

When the fiberglass is at the "green" stage (stiff, but not hard), trim the excess from the mold with a sharp knife. This trick eliminates the nasty job of filing or grinding waste off the casting. When the fiberglass is fully hardened, remove the flange boards; the fiberglass/silicone mold sandwich will part from the plaster base mold (see photo 14). After this, carefully peel the silicone mold off the fiberglass capital, and repeat the process.

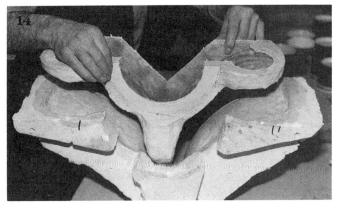

In this case, when the first two fiberglass halves were measured they were 1/4 inch too large to fit between the column and the beam. This difference may have been due to a shifting or compression of the wood beams. To compensate, the mold size was altered by adding 1/4-inch plywood to the top flange board, a change which had little effect on final appearance.

Installing the Reproduction Capitals

Clean up minor imperfections on the fiberglass halves with a small burr tool in a flex shaft driver (see photo 15). Air bubbles on the surface of the silicone rubber mold appear as small spheres on the cast fiberglass, and can be easily removed. Fit the capital halves to the columns and each other with some chiseling and sawing, and then bolt them together. Connect the halves through the volutes

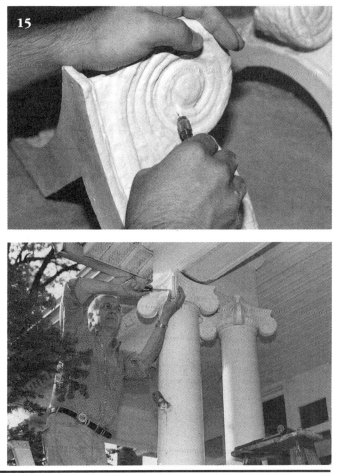

WORKING WITH PLASTER AND FIBERGLASS

Plaster is only workable for a short time before it gets hard, and two factors are an important influence on the setting speed: Water temperature (the warmer, the faster) and the rate of agitation during mixing (more agitation means faster setting). To obtain the desired amount of time for fashioning the case mold, keep close tabs on the water temperature and the amount of agitation. (*Note:* To avoid accidental blockages, do not dispose of plaster or plaster water in household plumbing.)

Casting with polyester resin requires timing too. It cures through a chemical reaction started by the addition of a catalyst. It is important to follow the manufacturer's directions to ensure proper curing. Rate of cure can also be influenced by the temperature of the materials. Working on a hot day (above 65 degrees Fahrenheit) or in direct sunlight can greatly accelerate curing. Conversely, the pot life of catalyzed resin can be extended by keeping it cool in a container of ice or cold water.

Use proper health and safety precautions when working with both plaster and polyester fiberglass materials. Plaster is alkaline, and can burn eyes and dry skin. Wearing gloves and eye protection is a good practice. Polyester resin is flammable, the catalyst is a strong oxidizer, and glass fibers are a skin and lung irritant. Work in a well-ventilated area. Wearing a respirator, gloves, and clothing suitable for fiberglass insulation work—loose-fitting but covering all extremities—is also recommended.

CAPITAL MATERIALS AND SUPPLIERS

Art Supplies

#1 Gray-Green Plasteline
  soft clay
Chavant, Inc.
42 West Street
Red Bank, NJ 07701
(800)CHAVANT[242-8268]

Daige Prostik Adhesive Wax
Makielski Art Shop
117 N. Main Street
South Bend, IN 46601
(219)233-2409

Plaster

U.S. Gypsum White Hydrocal
  plaster
USG Corporation
101 So. Wacker Drive, Dept. OHJ
Chicago, IL 60606
(312)606-4523
(call for nearest distributor)

Silicone Rubber

Dow #3110 RTV silicone
  rubber, Catalyst #1
GLS Fiberglass Co.
1750 N. Kingsbury Street
Chicago, IL 60614
(312)664-3500
(call for nearest distributor)

Casting Materials

Polyester Gel Coat, white
  Polyester Resin and
  Catalyst Fiberglass Mat
  (1 1/2 oz.)
Defender Industries, Inc.
255 Main Street
P.O. Box 820, Dept. OHJ
New Rochelle, NY
  10802-0820
(914)632-3001

using slotted, round-head, 1/4 × 20 bolts and prongless T-nuts (see photo 16). Place the bolts in the centers of the volutes where they will be least noticeable.

Using white gel coat on the fiberglass eliminates the need for paint, but use white, exterior, paintable caulk to seal all seams and cracks. Small mounds of caulk will conceal the bolts. While the caulking gun is handy, take the time to caulk the existing capitals.

EXTERIOR IRONWORK

Corroded cast iron lines residential streets, encloses yards, and decorates buildings. Attempts to repair these exterior decorative elements often create problems. A lack of printed information and professional advice has contributed to the sad conditions. But metalworking expertise isn't required for stabilizing these elements, or for the scraping, priming, and painting operation. *Time* is the essential ingredient.

Cast iron presents repair problems not applicable to wrought iron. First, cast pieces are often bolted together to form balusters, newels, and the like, and these pieces eventually begin to come apart. If not tightened and caulked, the tension and compression that hold the piece upright are lost; also, water gets in and parts may oxidize (rust) from the inside out.

The second problem is lack of available replacement parts. A foundry in full production could turn out quantities of cast-iron pieces of every style. But large iron foundries no longer exist; to have a modern metalworker make a special sand mould, cast a replacement piece, and ready it for painting is necessarily expensive. Try to fix problems before they destroy the iron, and salvage whatever pieces are still around. This is where ad-hoc mending techniques come in.

The maintenance principles for cast iron can be summarized as follows:

A. Prevent Rust and Corrosion

  1. Plug holes
  2. Paint

B. Maintain Structural Soundness

    1. Keep it together with metal plates and bolts, welding, etc.

    2. Brace loose elements by resetting

C. Recreate Missing Pieces

    1. Sheet metal

    2. Casting replacement parts: iron, aluminum, fiberglass, or epoxy

    3. Wooden replacements

Scrape, Prime, Paint

Even the smallest chip in the paint allows rust to spread underneath. Check cast iron periodically for rust and peeling paint. Wire-brush peeling areas, then spot-prime and paint.

If the iron has been neglected, the whole piece should get the scrape/prime/paint treatment. You may want to strip off all of the old paint layers to bring out the details of the casting.

The severity of peeling and rusting conditions will clue you in on what tools to use. For mechanical rust and paint removal use the following:

• Wire brush. Start with this. It removes rust and flaking metal, as well as loosened paint.

• Scrapers. These help you get under the paint and into crevices. Don't chip or bang the paint off cast pieces—you might fracture the iron. (Wrought iron is more resilient.)

• Roto-stripper (or the like). Rotating wires that you chuck into an electric drill, and which flap abrasively against the iron, removing paint very successfully. Wear eye protection!

• Sandpaper. Useful for smaller jobs or final feathering of high paint edges and corners.

You may want to use naval jelly on badly rusted areas. However, naval jelly has its drawbacks. It is phosphoric acid in a gel, so it has certain safety limitations: The run-off during rinsing may kill garden plants. And it must be flushed away with copious amounts of water—the enemy of naked iron. After wetting down iron, it's a good idea to dry it with a heat gun.

Really extensive jobs may warrant sandblasting. Its success rate is directly related to the skill of the operators; they must be able to judge pressure and grit of abrasive, and be diligent about masking all other surfaces. You can rent sandblasting machines; with care and dexterity a first-timer could do a respectable job. Sandblasting has compelling advantages: It means fast and complete paint removal. A major disadvantage is that highly pressurized abrading pits the iron to some extent, increasing its surface area.

Prime immediately after removing paint. You can't wait until the next day, so start early or scrape only as much iron as you'll have time to prime before nightfall. Prime everything you intend to paint. Priming assures bonding of the new paint to the old surface.

Metal primer pigments are usually zinc oxide or iron oxide, which have rust-inhibiting properties. (Zinc chromate, until recently found in popular paint brands, has been named as a known carcinogen.) Red lead has a reputation for being the best iron primer, and it does have unsurpassed qualities; however, it has very definite disadvantages, and recent studies show that iron oxide was probably used even more often than lead in the nineteenth century. Lead paints are now illegal.

Don't prime or paint when the temperature is below 50 degrees Fahrenheit, when it will drop to below freezing at night, in wet weather, or in direct sunlight.

Dependable oil-base paint has a long track record, but it may soon be banned in some states. Oil paint, with its longer drying time, more thoroughly wets the surface and creates a better bond. Generally speaking, latex paint presents a problem when the new paint improperly bonds to the old surface. Meticulous preparation and the use of a compatible primer mitigates the bonding problem.

The primer should be left to cure according to the specifications on the label—usually from three days to over a week. Apply the finish paint to a clean, dust-free surface in two thin (not thinned) coats, allowing proper drying time in between. Exterior enamel—glossy—offers the most resistance to dirt and abrasion. Some people prefer flat-finish paint for aesthetic reasons; it will probably need touching up and repainting sooner than a glossy surface.

The most popular color for ornamental ironwork has always been black. In some instances and locales, cast iron may have been brown or dark bottle-green. For some styles in some regions, more fanciful colors were used. In front of brownstones, the massive cast-iron balustrades were often painted with brown sand paint in imitation of carved stone.

Cracking paint reveals many years' worth of paint buildup.

Minor Repairs

Chances are that old ornamental ironwork is going to need more than paint. Mostly you'll find cracks, holes, and separations between pieces. Even though some of the conditions look quite distressing, we'll call them minor because repairs can be done by an interested homeowner.

An understanding of the on-site assembly of cast-iron elements helps when you have to put it all back together. A balustrade consists of hollow cast balusters, each pinned to a masonry slab by a small protrusion inside, and a two-part cast rail. The bottom piece of the rail is bolted to threaded tabs inside the balusters, and then the top rail is bolted to the bottom rail.

A cast-iron newel is usually four cast sides with a cap or cap and finial. It is put together hollow with minimal bolting and little interior structure. It is held to the ground by a simple bracing system that consists mainly of a central threaded rod the height of the piece, which is set into the masonry and packed in lead.

Years of expansion and contraction cause the pieces to separate from one another. These cracks especially must

A segment of hollow rail has been displaced. The solution is realignment, a bolt through the top and bottom of the rail, and caulk between segments.

be filled with an elastomeric compound that will move with the iron and still keep water out. Choose a high-quality exterior caulk, such as architectural-grade silicone rubber sealant. (You'll find it with builders' suppliers, not in hardware stores.) Paint won't stick to silicone for very long, but this caulk comes in black and sandstone colors. A butyl caulk—which is paintable—is the second choice,

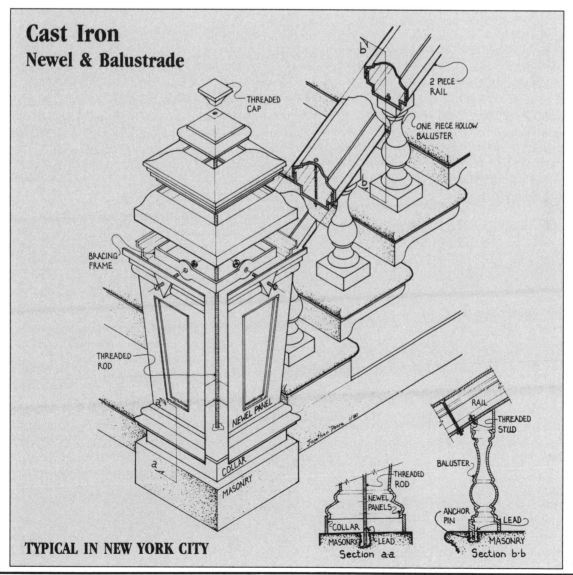

Cast Iron
Newel & Balustrade

THREADED CAP

2 PIECE RAIL

ONE PIECE HOLLOW BALUSTER

BRACING FRAME

THREADED ROD

NEWEL PANEL

COLLAR

MASONRY

TYPICAL IN NEW YORK CITY

RAIL

THREADED STUD

BALUSTER

THREADED ROD

NEWEL PANELS

COLLAR

MASONRY

LEAD

Section a·a

ANCHOR PIN

LEAD

MASONRY

Section b·b

although for large joints in extreme climates, flexibility might not be adequate.

Well-maintained cast iron. All repairs were done by the owners as soon as problems appeared.

In using all of these products, read the labels and follow the directions. If the caulk label says to apply to a clean, matte surface in certain weather conditions, take their word for it. And always be sure to allow sufficient time for curing of sealants and primers.

Small holes can be filled with plumbing epoxy such as Smooth-On, Kwik-Metal "Cold Solder," or Plumber-Seal. Auto-body putty, which is easily found, not hard to use, moldable and sandable, and which has a compatible expansion/contraction factor, is useful for do-it-yourself filling. *Wear gloves when working with epoxies.*

No one knows who started the practice of pouring concrete into hollow cast iron, but in some places it's so common that people (mistakenly?) believe it's original to the construction. It is unacceptable. Concrete absorbs water, encouraging the iron to rust from the inside out. The pieces will eventually buckle outward, which looks ugly, besides admitting water and debris. And moisture that does get into the parts has no chance to evaporate.

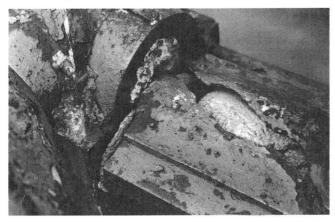

An example of exfoliated iron expanded by rust due to filling with concrete.

Major Repairs

Major repairs mean structural problems that require disassembly or resetting of a cast-iron element, welding, or extensive mending and rebuilding.

A wobbly newel calls for a professional ironworker. Usually it can be repaired on site: In addition to resetting the center rod in the base, he or she will weld "little feet" to the newel at the bottom. Holes are drilled in the masonry step or walk to correspond with these feet. In the best jobs, molten lead is poured into the holes and the newel is reset. Joints are caulked.

The small tabs at the base of the newel are welded to the iron and set into holes in the masonry for stability. This is a shortcut job—the tabs should have been welded on the inside, where they'd be less conspicuous.

Optimally, any iron that is set in concrete or stone should be packed in lead. This creates a barrier to prevent water from rusting the iron; also, lead is soft enough to allow some movement. Nevertheless, it's more common now to skip the lead-packing step. When the piece is set very tightly into the stone, this won't cause any problems for years. If water does get to the metal, there will be future trouble because metal expanded by rust will rupture the masonry into which it is set. Iron that goes into masonry should be scraped, primed, and painted.

Binding and Bolts

Judicious use of steel mending plates and bolts can prevent a balustrade from falling apart. A hidden metal binder will span open spaces and allow more movement than welding would permit.

Where metal is missing because of corrosion, sheet-metal patches are an acceptable answer. The metal should be compatible with iron—steel, for instance, or aluminum or terne metal. Both sides of the patch should be primed, and the underside painted, before installation. Seams can be caulked.

Detail of an owner-repaired rail. The sheet-metal patch, held by screws and caulk, are nearly forty years old.

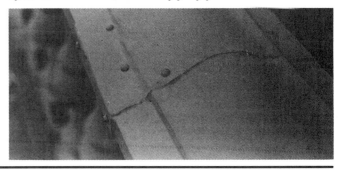

Welding is often an expedient solution for cracks in the iron. This is better than resorting to unattractive mending methods. However, avoid *extensive* welding of cracked pieces, or of one piece to another. Welding an entire fence back together makes a radical change in the original bolted assembly: Pieces can no longer move with the expansion/contraction cycles caused by seasonal weather changes. This produces internal stress which may eventually lead to major structural breaks at the weakest points.

If this is a do-it-yourself job, resist the impulse to call in an ironworker to do all repairs, major and minor—this kind of specialized on-site work is going to be expensive. Best to look to professionals for welding or for major disassembly and bracing. You can make an arrangement with a foundry, sometimes through the ironworker, for casting of replacement pieces. Be aware of the cost before work begins.

Re-creating Lost Pieces

There's a limit to what can be replaced by auto-body filler and sheet metal. Occasionally, an entire cast element, such as a finial, will be missing, or cast newel panels may be deteriorated beyond repair. In these instances,

you'll have to replace a piece. There are two basic choices: a cast replacement or a wooden replacement.

Consider both cost and aesthetic appropriateness; much depends on the piece that's missing and the services available in the region. The very best answer, of course, is a cast-iron replacement. This is usually the most expensive choice, but it is the most correct; you can avoid future problems by choosing such a compatible replacement.

Much ironwork is still available. Cast-iron newels, alas, are not. Some foundries still offer iron casting in a custom-made sand mould. More often, foundries use the lost-wax process, in which a wax model of the piece to be recast is used. From this model an investment mould is made (using a kind of dental plaster or colloidal silica). Next, the wax is electrically burned out of the mould by an induction furnace. Molten iron is then poured into the plaster mould.

Before considering epoxy casting or wooden replacements, check out the availability of iron casting in your area. Check with ironworkers, foundries, and even art schools. Often the shops that offer such a service are not foundries, but sculpture studios.

STEEL FENCES

If a wrought-iron or steel fence has parts over an inch thick, better consult an ironworker. When the metal is lighter, careful unbending with simple tools often works.

Black iron pipe (used for gas lines) is useful for straightening "spikes." Get a 2- to 3-foot length with a 1 1/4- or 1 1/2-inch interior diameter. Slip the pipe over the bent spike and use leverage to gently bend it back where it belongs.

If the bottom of a picket is bent, try a length of straight-grained 2 × 3 with a notch in one end. Hold the notch against the picket and strike the end of the 2 × 3 with blows from a heavy hammer until the picket is nudged back in line (see photo 1). For mid-span bends, start above the center of the picket, then move toward the middle as you work. This way you'll get less spring as you hammer.

Black pipe is also handy for bent scrollwork. Slip the

pipe through the scroll so that one end rests on a concrete-block fulcrum at about the same height as the bent iron (see photo 2). Lift on the free end of the pipe to lever the iron back in place.

For a lot of bent parts, you may want to invest in a *come-along*—a hand-operated winch with a steel cable and hook. Anchor the come-along to a secure base (say, a chain around a tree) and attach the hook to the bent picket. Work the handle until the cable is taut, then ease it a little at a time to make sure that the winch is powerful enough (see photo 3). (Most come-alongs, rated in pounds of force, have handles that will bend if overloaded. Read the manufacturer's directions.) To straighten welded pickets without breaking the welds, tie blocks of wood at top and bottom of the bent picket. These blocks will transfer force to the next picket and protect the welds.

It's usually cheaper to have the piece recast in aluminum. There should be no problem with compatibility of materials, or with reattaching an aluminum replacement. Aluminum has a much higher expansion coefficient than iron has. Compression strength is sacrificed. Backprime all before assembly.

Modern Casting

Replacement casting with modern materials is another option. It's a time-consuming process, and the results are not the same as metal replacement. Nevertheless, it may be a rewarding solution if you're facing an exorbitant bill from a far-away foundry.

The process is relatively simple. A clean model (such as an iron piece identical to the one that's missing) is used to create a rubber mould. Then a casting material (for instance, polyester resin fortified with fiberglass) is poured into the mould. When cured, the new piece is a tough, detail-accurate copy of the original. With proper installation and paint, it does the job.

Different materials are used for the mould, among them latex, polysulfides, silicone, and urethane. In the same way, different epoxy-compound systems are used as the casting material. Some products are not available in all parts of the country; you can't use every casting material with every moulding material; safety requirements differ according to the chemical. It's best to get information about using these compounds from your supplier. The supplier might be a plastics distributor or a large art-supply store that caters to sculptors.

Once you've chosen a moulding/casting system, doing the job isn't complicated. Just be sure to think ahead through the steps, right through to reinstalling the new pieces. (Though the job is different, see pages 140–145 for an example of the necessary steps in a moulding/casting system.) For instance, you might want to cast protruding steel rods into the piece, which later will be twisted around a center rod, or welded or bolted.

When the pieces are in place, seal the gaps with a high-quality caulk. Prime and paint the new parts like iron.

Wooden Replacements?

If you can't find anybody who does casting, you may know someone who could duplicate the missing piece in wood. Generally, this is only acceptable for "free" pieces such as finials, caps, balls, and so on. It's not a good idea to splice wood into an existing iron piece (such as a baluster or newel panel). The expansion/contraction coefficients of wood and metal are very different, causing recurring gaps and sacrificing structural strength.

If a replacement part is turned or carved from wood, give it two coats of paint-compatible water repellent. Then prime and paint the piece. Wood will absorb moisture, leading to rust deterioration in nearby iron. Seal the wood completely with paint and caulk.

Many of these ideas could translate into temporary solutions to maintain the structural and visual unity of your cast iron. Ad-hoc measures can always be replaced again in the future, when the budget allows.

CHAPTER 9

Exterior Masonry

Maintaining your brick or masonry home may not take the same effort it might with stripping and painting a wood house, but it does require attention. Exactly what shape is your masonry or brick house in? Does the brick need to be repointed? Is that paint job revealing water problems? Has your old house suffered the horrors of sandblasting? Here we'll examine brick, masonry, and stucco. Masonry and brick work can be time-consuming and expensive. Make sure you fully assess your masonry using the checklist on page 157 before starting work. Some problems may be caused by seasonal change and may take a few years to appear.

REPOINTING

Repointing is the process of repairing deteriorated mortar joints in brick or stone walls. You'll know your joints need repointing if they show mortar eroded back more than 1/4 inch from the face of the masonry; cracks (hairline and larger) running vertically or horizontally through the mortar; mortar bonds broken or pulled away from the masonry; or joints from which the mortar has literally fallen out, most often horizontal joints. (Sometimes a few vertical joints were deliberately left open to permit water to "weep" out of the wall.)

Failure to keep mortar joints in good repair permits water to penetrate masonry, which can result in severe damage to both the interior and exterior of a building. This damage is often the first-noted evidence that repointing is required.

Typical exterior damage includes open joints, efflorescence (a white "bloom" of salt crystals), spalling, and loosened masonry units. In severe cases, enough water penetrates into the wall to corrode inset metal elements, such as shelf angles above windows. The metal then exfoliates, separating into its multiple layers and expanding

up to ten times larger in cross-section. This expansion causes the masonry around the metal element to "jack" and torque out of place, eventually breaking free from the building.

Even mortar joints that don't appear badly deteriorated may permit large volumes of water to enter the wall, which can trigger interior damage such as failing plaster and stained wallpaper; monitor for water damage in rooms and attics through which a chimney stack passes. Large open joints in the foundation can contribute to efflorescence in the basement and, in severe cases, basement flooding. Openings may also permit entry to foraging mice and insects.

There are five major reasons for mortar joint failures:

• Weathering action. Weathering is inevitable. Masonry mortar, particularly that used in older walls, is purposely soft to allow the wall to flex with expansion and contraction caused by temperature changes. Wind, rain,

Weathering action has taken its toll on this wall. Someone has randomly "repointed" the deepest joints.

and pollution eat away at this soft mortar. On highly exposed areas, mortar joints can weather away to a depth of several inches. Only regular repointing maintenance can prevent severe erosion.

• Settling. Both mortar and masonry can crack due to uneven settling of a building's foundation.

• Temperature cycle. Moisture entering at a bad mortar joint may freeze and expand, causing a section of the joint and perhaps a portion of the surrounding masonry to pop off. This is called spalling. The seasonal cycle of hot and cold, too, causes masonry and mortar to expand and contract, often at different ratios. This eventually breaks the masonry's bond to the mortar.

• Poor original design and materials. The ability of a mortar joint to shed water and preclude penetration is largely the result of its profile. Concave joints provide superior protection from water entry; raked joints, popular because their top-to-bottom inward slant makes for dramatic shadows, are susceptible to premature failure. If the original mortar was too hard, it will have shrunk excessively, resulting in numerous hairline cracks. If it was too soft, it will have yielded quickly to weathering action.

Open joints in the foundation admit water to the basement. The damage this causes can threaten a house's structural stability.

Differential expansion and contraction rates have this portland-rich mortar popping out—and damaging bricks in the process.

• Lack of exterior maintenance. Water sitting in a joint or flowing across it speeds joint erosion. Poorly functioning gutters, downspouts, or flashings contribute to excessive mortar failure. This deterioration is logarithmic in nature. Ignoring a problem speeds up the rate of deterioration.

Foundations and inconspicuous areas can easily be successfully repointed, though it can be a tedious, exacting chore. Hire a contractor for more complicated jobs like chimneys and rebuilding window lintels, or where masonry is loose or missing and the work must be done on scaffolds or extension ladders. You will also need a contractor if the original mortar joints were "beaded," that is, tooled with a raised, round-profiled joint that projects out from the wall.

How to Repoint

When done correctly, repointing will keep your old house weathertight while maintaining the historical accuracy of your brickwork. The effects of misguided repointing, however, can be costly or impossible to correct, and may cause irreparable damage both to the building's appearance and to its physical structure. Armed with just a bag of redi-mix, a case of beer, and just enough knowhow to get into serious trouble, a do-it-yourself repointer can inflict more damage in one weekend than mother nature had in the last one hundred years.

Yet be not discouraged! Pointing, repointing, and pressure grouting all mean the same thing: replacing old, deteriorated, or missing mortar with new mortar. Close inspection will reveal the degree to which the mortar has receded, from little to no weathering under the soffits and overhangs to perhaps a quarter of an inch erosion (or more!) where the exposed brickwork takes the brunt of the weather. Old mortar joints are constantly in a state of recession; water is the chief culprit, although wind, pollution, and seasonal and diurnal temperature changes add to the erosion. If damaged gutters or leaking soffits allow excess water to run across your masonry, fix them before repointing.

Knocking the old mortar out manually is your best bet. It's time consuming, but you're less likely to damage the brick.

Poor preparation leads to poor adhesion of the mortar to the masonry. Don't skimp here! You may elect to have the building chemically cleaned. Cleaning will alter the color of the mortar by removing decades of dirt and grime. Cleaning is best done before removing the old mortar, to deter the chemical cleaner from penetrating the soft sides of newly exposed bricks.

First remove the old mortar, which takes 40 to 50 percent of the total time spent repointing. To remove mortar, take the mortar back to a depth of about 3/4 inch from the brickface with a small mason's chisel (no wider than half the width of the joint) or a cheap, expendable screwdriver and a hammer. A 1/2-inch depth is usually sufficient if the mortar joint is only 1/4-inch wide or less. Some experts advocate raking back a depth of about two and a half times the width of the joint. Remove all obviously deteriorated mortar.

The joints between these stones have been chipped out to a depth of 3 inches and are ready to receive new mortar.

Take your time and be especially careful not to chip or damage the surrounding bricks. Pieces of brick do sometimes fall off; if they're large enough they can simply be glued back with any good ceramic glue. Pulverized brick mixed with glue can also be used to fill small holes left by lead anchors, nails, and the like.

It's not unusual to find that you are not the first person to repoint sections of your house. Your predecessors' distinctive styles and materials are often quite noticeable; sometimes that old mortar proves stubborn. If you're finding it hard going, stop here and scrutinize your work. Is the stuff you're trying to remove as hard as nails? Are you taking off chunks of the surrounding bricks along with the mortar? Does it appear, then, that earlier repointing was executed solely with portland cement? If so, this is the time to weigh a major decision; perhaps you should consider laying aside your hammer and chisel to reach for a power grinder.

Many historical architects and restoration purists decry the use of machinery to remove mortar; but if done carefully, mortar joints of 1/2 inch or larger can be raked out with little risk using power grinders. If you're adept with

power tools and are of sound mind and steady nerve, a tuckpoint grinder with a 4 × 1/4-inch abrasive blade will do the chisel's job considerably faster, eliminating many hours of vexatious, and sometimes destructive, hand work. Don't use an electric saw with a masonry blade—they're much too awkward to handle accurately.

Rake the bed joints (horizontal) with the grinder, then go over them thoroughly with a screwdriver to clean right up to the edges of the brick. Chisel the head joints (vertical) by hand to minimize the risk of nicking the brick.

Working with a grinder takes a lot of concentration; one mental lapse can lead to unsightly gouges in the bricks. Again, power grinding mortar joints of under 1/2 inch are best left to professionals. But don't let the power grinder overshadow the value of hand work, however. Nine times out of ten the old hammer and chisel method works just great, and generally leads to fewer accidents.

If you use a power grinder, use it on horizontal joints only. You're sure to damage the brick if you try it on the vertical ones.

If you are unsure whether certain portions of mortar are deteriorated or not, go ahead and clean them out. Repointing a long joint is easier than filling in small spots, and makes for a neater, more uniform appearance than new mortar interspersed with old, regardless of how closely you match the mortar.

Remove Loose Bricks and Grit

If some bricks need to be taken out and replaced, now is the time to do it. You can safely remove sections of six to eight bricks without jeopardizing the structure. A Sawzall (a reciprocating saw) with a 6-inch carbide-impregnated blade works well. It zips right through soft old mortar. Harder mortar may have to be hand-chiseled.

Finally, clean the joints of all dust and dirt. The joint may be vacuumed, blown clean with compressed air, or flushed with water. If the joints to be pointed have weathered severely, there will probably be a crust of carbon or dirt clinging to the masonry. Mortar won't adhere to this. It may be necessary to scrub the joint with stiff brushes and a detergent (not soap, which leaves behind a residue).

This extensive preparation stage may have taught you something: You'd rather call a professional and go bowling instead. Don't despair if you get cold feet at this point; you can still hire someone to formulate your repointing mortar and press it in. If you're still game, though, press on!

Very thin joints—sometimes called butter joints—take longer. Here, each mason holds a cold chisel perpendicular to the joint, then strikes the chisel to break the bond between the mortar and masonry. The crumbled mortar is raked out with an old screwdriver. This method lessens the likelihood of chipping off corners of the brick.

To regrout butter joints, use a narrow caulking trowel. New mortar in buttered joints should be recessed and tooled with a narrow jointer (either beaded or concave).

Match Old Mortar's Consistency

To produce the most pleasing results, your repointing mixture should match as closely as possible the appearance of the original mortar. Generally speaking, the texture and, to a certain degree, the color of the mortar is determined by the type of sand or aggregate used in the mortar mixture. To isolate the aggregate for identification and duplication, take a small amount of the old mortar and crush it in your fingers (if you can), then place it in a glass of water. (Old, high-lime mortar will crumble easily and dissolve in water. Modern portland cement will break, not crumble, and will not dissolve in water.) Use muriatic acid instead of water, if you have some. Examine closely the pieces of sand or shell that settle out.

Old mortar materials—even sand granules of a certain size—may not be readily available today. Go to a sand and gravel yard with your sample and see what they have. Talk with some old-time masons: What do they remember of local materials and methods? A little detective work here will give you a big jump on achieving accuracy with your final formula. If precisely matching your sample proves unfeasible, get as close as possible.

Now that you've gathered the proper type of sand or aggregate, you're ready to start putting it together into a mixture compatible with the old bricks and their original mortar. The basic ingredients involved are type I or type II gray or white portland cement, hydrated lime, and your sand. Don't confuse portland cement with masonry cement—the latter comes premixed with lime. If you live out West or in the Northeast, hydrated lime is sold at just about any building supply house. In certain parts of the East, though, lime is scarce. If you have trouble acquiring materials, call United States Gypsum—they'll give you the nearest location where you can buy their products. Lime usually comes in fifty-pound bags, portland cement in ninety-four-pound bags; get one of each.

Concoct your mortar with a base mixture of portland and lime. Because you're going to experiment to achieve the proper color and consistency, you may want to limit the amount of material you begin with. If you're matching a weathered-looking mortar joint that hasn't been chemically cleaned, use gray portland. If the building has been chemically cleaned and its mortar is stark white, use white portland cement.

Contrary to many formulas, you can use as much as six parts lime by volume to one part portland. You may go to a five-to-one mix if you need something a little grayer or harder. A mix stronger than four-to-one on a pre-1920 house sets too hard. A small wheelbarrow makes a handy mixing bin; use a garden hoe or square-ended shovel to mingle the ingredients. The lime/portland mix should resemble gray cake flour at this point: light and fluffy.

This mix is now ready to have the aggregate added. If you can see lots of exposed sand on the surface of the original mortar, start by mixing two parts of sand with one part of the cement material. If the original mortar's sand seems to be pretty well hidden within the matrix, start with a ratio of two parts sand to one-and-one-half parts portland-and-lime mixture (4:3). Mix it all up—still dry. Remember, though, these are not hard-and-fast propor-

Finding the right aggregate is the only tough part in preparing the new mortar. Actually mixing it takes only minutes.

tions. They can be altered to fit your particular situation. Experimentation is the only way to get it just right.

Matching Color

Now look again at the existing mortar. What color is it? Is it off-white, gray, beige, red, black? Sometimes sun and weather will bleach portions of a wall, so a single wall may boast half a dozen different shades of mortar. If this is the case, match the color that predominates in the most noticeable areas. Because the colors of lime and cement are white and gray, a mixture of just these two materials can vary in hue from pure white to dark gray. You can also alter your mortar's overall color by increasing the proportion of sand to cementitious material, thereby emphasizing the color of the aggregate.

Others in the know declare that there is no way to match colors exactly; to a certain extent that may be true. Yet at least one expert claims to mix mortar formulas that in the majority of cases are indistinguishable from the original, even after fifteen years. Perhaps some time in the next century some persnickety soul will be able to spot the difference; in the meantime, no one will be the wiser if you mix your colors right. Here's the secret: Take a garden hose and soak a portion of the old brickwork. Notice how the color of the wetted mortar gets darker. Your new mixture, when you add water to it, should be the same color as that section that you hosed down. Such a mortar mix will dry exactly the same color as the old mortar.

To match an off-white mortar, use about 1/8 to 1/4 cup of dark buff dye to five gallons of dry mix (sand and cement and lime). You may have to intermix some cement colors to match your particular mortar; sometimes you may have to use a walnut brown in combination with black and red to match complex burgundies. Off-white and beige mortars are probably the easiest to match; black too is quite simple. Reds and burgundies present the most problems. Add your dye to the mixture dry and stir the compound thoroughly; that way, the final color blend will come out more uniform. Limit your dye to less than 10 percent of the volume of your cement (you'll probably require far less than that).

When you're ready to add water to your final mixture, add only enough to make it damp. You should be able to shape it into a firm ball, but it should not be gushy. At this somewhat dry consistency the mortar mixture will be much easier to pack into the wall and it will not be as likely to smear onto adjacent bricks. With the mixture in a wheelbarrow, use your garden hoe in short, chopping strokes to get the mixture evenly damp.

Some experts advise prehydrating your mortar; that is, stir up the mix with very little water, let it rest for one or two hours, then bring it up to proper consistency with a bit more water.

Now, press a little of your mortar into the wall next to the original. Does it look like the original that you had wetted down? Great! If it doesn't you may add or subtract minor amounts of ingredients to your mix. More likely,

you should throw out your trial batch and start again. Keep a record of your proportions so when you get it right you can duplicate the result.

Pressing in the New Mortar

Once your mix passes the eyeball-on-the-wall test, you're ready to fill the joints. To ensure a good bond, wet the cleaned joints with water before applying the mortar. If you're working inside, a spray bottle plant-mister works great. Allow any puddled water to soak into the wall; the joints should not be visibly wet.

Press the new mortar firmly into place to fill the joint completely without creating voids or air pockets.

Grab up a ball of mortar in one hand (wear rubber gloves) while wielding a trowel in the other. The trowel should be just slightly narrower than your joint (sometimes called a caulking trowel). Begin by packing the mortar, using the narrow trowel, into the deepest voids. Then fill the back of the entire joint with a 1/4-inch layer of mortar. Press the mortar mix into the joints firmly and, in a succession of 1/4-inch deep layers dried to thumbprint hardness, bring your work up to the same depth as the original. Use long, smooth strokes, and do the vertical joints before the horizontal ones.

Some people load some of the mortar onto a mason's hawk—a flat square plate with a perpendicular handle—or onto the bottom side of a regular mason's trowel, and push the mortar off the hawk or trowel into the joint with their caulking trowel.

A tool sometimes marketed as a "tuck-pointing trowel," shaped like a small-scale mason's trowel, is not, despite its name, much good here; don't waste your money.

When your mortar is almost flush with the wall, tool it to match the original surface profile or to mimic the surviving pointing work. If in doubt about your tooling profile, a smooth, slightly concave surface is a standard shape, and has excellent water-shedding capabilities. Don't overfill the joint so that it overlaps onto the brick, though—the joint will appear too wide, and the bricks may spall.

Let your repointing job set up for half an hour or so, then brush it with a wet whitewash brush to feather in the edges to the original. If you need to match a particular style of tooling, do it soon after you put in the mortar; retool if necessary after you brush with water.

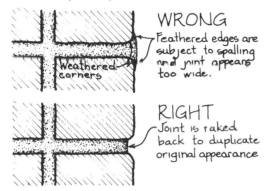

WRONG
Feathered edges are subject to spalling and joint appears too wide.
Weathered corners

RIGHT
Joint is raked back to duplicate original appearance

Matching Mortar Texture

Getting that slightly weathered look can be accomplished with a fine mist from a garden hose. Another texturing technique, called stippling, is performed with the end of a whisk broom or whitewash brush. If you're working on a particularly hot day, you may need to mist your surface periodically to keep your work from drying out too fast. Don't be afraid to experiment here; if you don't like what you've done you can always wash it out with the hose and start again.

Replacement bricks can be laid as you're pointing, using the same mortar mixture. Simply spread a bed of mortar onto the bricks below and point the replacements into place. You will, of course, use replacement bricks that match the old as closely as possible in appearance and characteristics. Remember, old bricks are generally much softer, and more elastic, than new ones. An unyielding patch of new bricks in an old wall will lead to mortar cracking and brick spalling.

Let your work dry for a minimum of a week, then come back with a mild solution of muriatic acid (one part acid to five parts water) or an organic brick cleaner. With a stiff nylon brush, remove any mortar smudges or film that you left on the masonry. Be sure to thoroughly flood the wall with water when you're finished to remove any traces of acid.

If you worked carefully, following these suggestions, your repointed walls should keep you and your family snug until well into the next century.

SALVAGING SANDBLASTED
————WALLS————

Despite the warnings by the National Park Service, the *Old House Journal,* and other preservation-minded groups, sandblasting still occurs, perpetrated on unsuspecting homeowners by callous contractors. If you find yourself the owner of a sandblasted house, all may not be lost. There are measures you can take to help mitigate the negative effects on sandblasted brick.

Sandblasting is by nature an abrasive process by which dirt, stains, and paint are removed from the surface of bricks. Unfortunately, so is much of the outer layer of brick. This is particularly troublesome for older brick because the "skin," or outer layer, is much harder than the softer core. The skin protects the brick from water penetration and pollutants. When it is sandblasted away, the brick becomes more permeable and susceptible to these hazards. Sandblasting also erodes mortar joints, one of the most vulnerable areas in which problems arise.

The pitted surface of sandblasted brick and mortar allows a freer penetration of water from precipitation, run-off, and even moisture in the air. Because brick is so porous, moisture can normally evaporate out; the problems arise from what is left behind. Water-soluble salts and other pollutants (such as sulfates, nitrates, acids, and the like) are deposited as solids inside the brick surface when the water evaporates. For example, salt deposits crystallize and cause spalling. The problem may also be manifested as crumbling, powdering brick and mortar, or as efflorescence.

Increased water penetration can also result in chronic dampness that does damage to interior walls and rots adjacent wooden members. In northern climates, moisture in brick walls can freeze, also a cause of spalling.

What to do then with sandblasted brick? The first solution is to do nothing. Well, not exactly nothing, but before running out to buy some miracle "cure," take stock of the damage—if it's not causing any immediate problems, leave the masonry alone. Your strategy should be to give a thorough and periodic inspection of the sandblasted surfaces, once a year at a minimum. Look for the following danger signs:

- Spalling brick ("sheets" of brick that have detached from the surface).
- Crumbling, powdering, or "rotting" brick and mortar.
- Cracks in the brick and, especially, between the bricks and mortar joints. You'll be looking for a pattern of cracks caused by deterioration, not by structural problems.
- Efflorescence, that white deposit on brick caused by soluble salts leaching to the surface.

Sandblasting was the first crime perpetrated on these bricks. They were then repointed with a hard mortar, speeding erosion.

ASSESSING THE CONDITION
OF MASONRY

Use the following scale to determine the degree of deterioration of your brick by assessing its hardness (or softness). To use this simple method, you will need only a mason's hammer, a cold chisel (1/2 to 1 1/2 inches), and a sturdy slotted screwdriver. Because the method is destructive, use it sparingly and only for areas you suspect are deteriorating.

There is a separate scale for both mortar and brick. Both scales go from 0 to 10, with 0 being the most deteriorated and 10 being the hardest. When you scratch brick, always scratch both vertically and horizontally. When you strike mortar joints, always strike them along their center lines.

Brick Classification

Use this scale to document the condition of your brickwork (sandblasted or otherwise). If your bricks rate a 4 or below, they are for all intents and purposes unsalvageable. In that case, an engineer should be consulted to determine the structural integrity of the building. If your bricks rate somewhere between 5 and 7, you might consider some remedial steps such as sealing or painting.

A brick building typically (especially if it's been sandblasted) has some masonry units that are deteriorated, while others are sound. In that case, you can use this scale to decide which units should be selectively replaced, which side of the building would benefit most from sealing, and so on.

Bricks have totally disintegrated. _____

Bricks have spalled to 1/4 to 3 inches within the wall plane. _____

Bricks have a fairly intact face, but rounded, eroded corners. Surface can be loosened by rubbing with the hand, or powdered by scraping with a fingernail. _____

Bricks are spalling in scaly layers that can be pulled apart by hand. Their component crystalline, jagged fragments are better bonded, and do not powder. _____

Bricks cannot be scratched 1/4 inch with a fingernail nor crumbled by hand, but can be broken apart with poking and jabbing of the screwdriver. Crystalline pieces can be semihard, or can be weathered and resemble compacted clay. _____

The screwdriver carves into the surface of the brick approximately 1/4 inch by hand, but bricks won't crumble after a dozen jabs. This is the first classification of stable, structurally sound brick. _____

The screwdriver must be driven in with the hammer to make the 1/4-inch indent. In doing so, it causes enough cracking to dislodge coarse, jagged pieces. _____

The screwdriver no longer penetrates, but does make a weak impression when hit with the hammer. A slight ring and bounce attest to the solidity of the brick. _____

The chisel makes no indentation or impression, but shears brick cleanly. Strong vitrification of face. Crisp edges and corners. _____

A new brick, with absolute crispness of corners, and a clear ringing sound when struck by a chisel. _____

Mortar Evaluations

This scale is used for comparison. If mortar rates between 1 and 4, repointing is in order. If it rates 9 or 10, and the bricks are fairly soft, the mortar is too hard. In that case, it may be wise to have the rock-hard mortar ground out and replaced with softer mortar. Overly hard mortar will damage the brick with seasonal and daily thermal expansion and contraction.

There is no mortar present within at least 1 1/2 inches of the face of the wall. Mortar has leached or weathered away. _____

Mortar can be scraped away freely with a screwdriver or poked out with a finger. It crumbles freely and has an irregular surface. Joint treatment is unrecognizable and mortar appears sandlike. _____

Mortar can be raked out easily with the screwdriver, but the face of the joint is still intact, with few surface irregularities. _____

When scoring the joint along its center line with the screwdriver, it is easy to collapse it and break its adhesion with the brick. The mortar disengages freely and cleanly. _____

When the mortar joint is scored and tapped with the screwdriver and the mortar prodded out, there is slight spalling at the edges and corners of the brick. _____

The mortar doesn't loosen with a screwdriver. Scored with a chisel, it pops free from the brick without damaging it. _____

When the mortar is lightly scored with a chisel, it disengages. The edges and corners of the brick are marred slightly because of the mortar's adhesion to brick. _____

Successive blows of the hammer and chisel are necessary to crack the joint, but when the mortar disengages, there is still little damage to the brick. _____

Several blows with hammer and chisel are necessary to crack the mortar into short pieces, as in previous step. The bricks are noticeably marred in the process. _____

The mortar is tougher than the bricks, cracking the bricks after successive blows with the hammer and chisel. Rich mortar color, well-defined tooling marks. Solid adhesion apparent throughout brick-mortar interface. _____

The mortar has high content of portland cement, approaching the strength of concrete. When removed with hammer and chisel, the adjoining brickwork is pulverized. _____

- Constant dampness in the brick walls, evidenced by staining on interior walls, peeling paint or wallpaper, presence of mildew, mosses, and so on.

Preventing Damage

You must ensure that water penetration in the future be kept to a minimum. The following preventive maintenance practices are advisable for any brick buildings but are particularly crucial for sandblasted masonry:

- Make sure all the gutters, downspouts, and other water run-off systems are in good repair and clear of debris. Leaky or clogged gutters can cause rain run-off to be diverted down the brick walls—deluging them with water-borne pollutants.
- Ensure that the mortar joints are sound. Check for erosion and cracks and repoint if necessary. As much as 20 percent of a brick wall's surface area may be represented by mortar joints—they're a prime source of water entry. Be sure to consider the special needs of repointing old brick with a fairly "soft" mortar mix.
- Correct conditions of rising damp, splashback, and foundation wetness.
- Caulk all joints between brick and other materials (wooden window frames, doors, eaves, etc.).
- Remove water-entrapping vegetation from or near the brick walls.
- Replace or repair missing and deteriorated pieces of coping on parapet walls; repair all flashing around chimneys and openings; repair all rotted sections of eaves, cornices, roof, etc.
- Don't use salt to melt snow anywhere near masonry walls.

If you follow these recommendations and continue regular inspections, you can greatly reduce the potential for problems associated with sandblasting. But if problems still persist despite your remedial efforts and there is serious spalling, dampness, or brick rotting, you may want to consider painting or water repellents—two "last resort" approaches.

Water Repellents

Like paint, water repellents are unnecessary for sound masonry; they can be expensive, need to be reapplied periodically, and can sometimes cause more problems than they cure. But for deteriorating sandblasted brickwork, they can be helpful because they prevent the penetration of water in liquid form, yet allow water vapor to "breathe" out.

Water repellents (also known as "sealers") differ from paint because they are colorless and are not just surface coatings but solutions that can penetrate up to a depth of 1/8 to 1/2 inches. Transparent sealers work by changing the capillary angles of the pores in the face of the brick wall from positive (suction) to negative (repellency). Their initial cost can be tolerable (15 to 25 cents per square foot) but they will probably need to be renewed every three to seven years.

There are problems with sealers: They might trap crystalline deposits of salt in the brick and thus contribute to spalling. Sealers can also change the color of the brickwork, even though they are transparent. They can make future pointing and removal of efflorescence more difficult; therefore, these procedures should be done before applying sealers. In fact, all the preparations for painting apply for sealers as well.

There are numerous, colorless water-repellent products on the market, including silicones, stearates, waxes, resins, acrylics, rosins, polymers, silanes, and siloxanes. But in general, these products come in two types of solution: water-based and solvent-based. Usually, better penetration is achieved from solvent-based solutions, although they are more expensive.

All manufacturers of water repellents will claim that their product is better than the others. Read the product literature carefully. The Brick Institute of America recommends the following checklist when using a sealer:

- Choose a sealer made by an established, reputable manufacturer with a proven track record. Nationally known brand names are the best.
- Use solvent-based sealers—their molecular structure is smaller, permitting better penetration.
- Apply sealer only to a clean surface that's properly caulked, pointed, and free from all loose mortar and brick.
- Choose a sealer with no less than 5 percent solids, preferably more than 7 percent. The label should also indicate the effectiveness of the sealer, expressed as a percentage figure of repellency and a percentage figure of "breathability."
- Try a test panel in an inconspicuous spot; let it cure for several months and check for satisfactory performance in regard to color change, water permeability, etc.
- Apply the sealer in two flood coats with a 12-inch rundown, or at the application rate recommended on the product label.
- If you hire a contractor, ask to see samples of his work. If possible, get a written warranty from the contractor. Also check the manufacturer's warranty.

Remember, we recommend using water-repellent sealers only to alleviate problems of damaging water penetration that cannot be solved in more conventional ways.

If the sandblasted masonry has seriously deteriorated to a point where it has lost much of its integrity and is visually objectionable, you may want to consider opaque "waterproofers" such as bituminous-based coatings or stucco. These are really last-ditch remedies, though; they will drastically alter the appearance of your house. In some parts of the country, however, brick and stone buildings were traditionally stuccoed, thereby making this solution more acceptable. This is a major project and will require the services of an experienced contractor.

Failed and deteriorated brick units can also be selectively replaced with similar brick. This too is a job for a professional mason and can run into a lot of money. But usually only certain isolated sections of brickwork that are highly vulnerable to weather will require this remedy.

STUCCO

In the early 1920s, right about the time of the Bungalow Boom, the portland cement industry made a big effort to sell architects, home builders, and home buyers on the "charm, beauty, and permanence" of stucco. This campaign was quite successful; many of the houses built during this period were clad in stucco, and many older houses were remodeled with the material. Before 1900, most stucco houses were finished with lime-based stucco, which is particularly susceptible to water damage. There are still a lot of lime-based stucco houses standing, though, and maintaining your exterior will depend on knowing which kind of stucco you're dealing with.

Getting off old stucco isn't easy. Quite often, it's applied directly over a masonry base, with no lath in between—it's probably impossible to successfully undo this kind of stucco job. The specifications for installing stucco over brick in those days called for raking out the mortar joints and gouging the brick to provide a better bond for the stucco. So that isn't pretty brick under the stucco waiting for its natural beauty to be restored; it's a mess, one that's best left alone.

Many stucco remodelings were done for a good reason—to stop water penetration that occurred because of bad original design. Similar problems beset stucco-remodeled frame houses. Furring strips, stop beads, nail holes, and general woodbutchery are what's hiding under the stucco.

If your old house is a victim of a stucco remodeling or remuddling, it's almost always best to let it be—unless you're willing to reface the house after you see what was hidden beneath the stucco. However, you still need to keep the stucco you've got in good shape.

Stucco Problems

Water causes most stucco failure. Improper mixing of mortar, poor installation, building settlement, and just plain exposure to the elements account for other stucco problems. Water-damaged stucco usually bulges or falls away from the building because water causes the coats of stucco to delaminate, and the lath or lath fasteners to fail. (Wood lath can warp, metal lath and nails can rust.) Cracks caused by building settlement or movement of framing members (stress cracks) usually are "clean" cracks, with no surrounding bulging or decayed stucco. Water can, of course, enter a stress crack; then you have both problems at once.

Stress cracks should be repaired only after you've determined what caused them, and whether or not the cracks are still moving. (For help with assessing cracks, see chapters 3 and 5.) Similarly, loose or crumbling water-damaged stucco shouldn't be repaired until after you've found and eliminated the offending water source.

Water damage to stucco usually comes from the following sources:

- Rain
- Migration of water vapor from the interior of the building
- Capillary action from the ground
- Leaky plumbing

Prevent water damage by doing the following:

- Ensuring the proper use and maintenance of flashing, drip edges, and drainage systems on the building exterior
- Using vapor barriers between the building interior and the stucco
- Installing the proper treatment of the termination of the stucco at ground level
- Repairing leaky plumbing

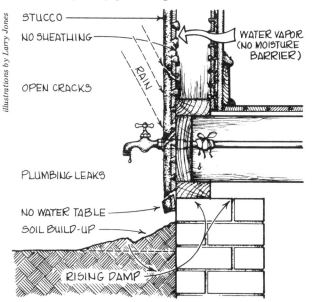

Sources of Water Damage

The best materials for flashing are copper, lead-coated copper, terne metal (which must be painted), and a relatively new and very long-lasting material, terne-coated stainless steel (TCS). Galvanized steel is acceptable flashing, but these other metals are better and cost only pennies more. Aluminum, the favorite of many contractors, is questionable; it's flimsy and it tarnishes. It also takes paint poorly, and won't take lead/tin solder at all, which makes it just about un-repairable.

Drip edges are changes in the plane of materials under horizontal projections, such

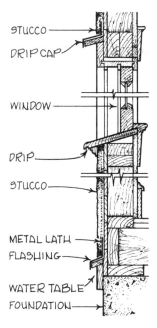

as door and window sills. They interrupt capillary action, causing rainwater to drip away from the walls of the building. Some drip edges are formed out of flashing; others are integral parts of the house trim, such as window sills. Drip edges are often overlooked as sources of water damage, but they can be major culprits if successive coats of paint or stucco have built up on them and rendered them useless.

Gutters must take rainwater away from the house without overflowing or leaking along the way. Rusty gutters with tar patches won't do the job; neither will gutters with broken joints, nor gutters that have settled to the point where they no longer drain to the downspouts. Flimsy aluminum gutters with caulked joints won't do anything well for long. Copper, TCS, or galvanized gutters with soldered joints are best. Accept no substitutes.

The migration of water vapor through the walls of a house causes fewer problems than does rainwater, but it can damage stucco (or exterior paint), especially on masonry buildings. (Frame structures normally have a layer of waterproof felt between the wood sheathing and the stucco, which prevents vapor penetration.)

The areas most susceptible to damage from water-vapor migration are the walls outside kitchens, bathrooms, and chimney flues. If you have damaged stucco near these walls, and can't blame it on stress cracking or rainwater penetration, then vapor migration might be the cause. Make interior walls relatively tighter than exterior walls, by applying vapor-barrier paint on the interior walls, and caulking joints along the interior window trim and baseboards. Vent the bathrooms or kitchens with a sufficiently large exhaust fan. If stucco on a chimney is damaged, line the flue with a nonporous liner (stainless steel is good).

Improper termination of stucco at ground level often results in water-damaged stucco. Most specifications call for stucco to terminate at least 4 inches from the ground. But many old houses aren't built that way; on them, the stucco goes right into the ground. In such a case, you should do everything possible to keep the area dry: Repair and maintain gutters and drains; make sure the ground slopes away from the stucco wall. Only then should you patch the stucco.

Stucco often fails at 90-degree joints such as those between parapet walls and roofs. Deteriorated or improperly installed flashing is usually the culprit. In such cases, you must remove enough stucco to allow you to remove the old flashing and install new material. Consult an experienced contractor before tackling an extensive flashing-replacement job; it might be easier (and cheaper) to restucco the whole house, rather than just restucco over a lot of new flashing.

Patching Stucco

After you've found and corrected any source(s) of damage to your walls, the next step is to determine what type of mortar was used to stucco your house. Whatever it was, you'll want to use the same type of mortar for repairs. Generally, twentieth-century houses are stuccoed with portland cement, whereas earlier houses are likely to have been built with lime mortar. This isn't a hard-and-fast rule; some avant-garde masons used portland cement in the mid-nineteenth century, and some conservative masons used lime mortars well into the early twentieth century.

To test for mortar type, take a chip of the mortar in question, place it in a container of dilute muriatic acid (available at hardware stores), seal the container tightly, and shake it vigorously. If the mortar dissolves, it's lime. If it doesn't, it's portland cement.

Remove damaged stucco before you start patching. There are two schools of thought on this subject. Rationale 1: Remove the smallest amount of stucco possible. Don't make extra work; you can tackle a small job yourself. Rationale 2: Hire a mason to apply new material all the way to a logical break in the building surface—for instance, restucco a whole wall or chimney. The patch will be less noticeable, and a mason probably won't charge much more to restucco a whole wall than to make a patch. Both ideas are reasonable.

To determine the extent of the damage, check for spongy areas by pushing against the stucco with your hand. Any areas that move back and forth while making a squishy sound will have to go. Then, tap the stucco with a hammer handle and listen for the sound of loose stucco—a succession of sounds, like a tap dance. When you reach an area that doesn't move, and that makes only one solid sound, you've found the good stucco.

Don't just start peeling off the loose stucco. If you do, you could destucco the whole house before you realize that you're breaking off sound keys along with the bad ones. Make cuts through the stucco around the damaged area, either with a cold chisel or by drilling a series of holes with a masonry bit. Cut to the lath. Then pry off the old stucco with a broad, flat tool such as a nail puller. Cut back the coats of old mortar in square layers, as shown in

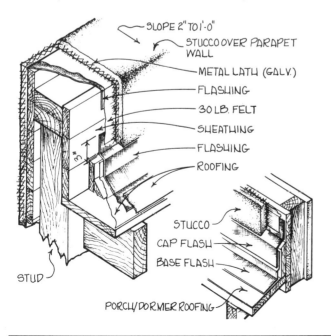

SLOPE 2" TO 1'-0"
STUCCO OVER PARAPET WALL
METAL LATH (GALV.)
FLASHING
30 LB. FELT
SHEATHING
FLASHING
ROOFING
3"
STUCCO
CAP FLASH
BASE FLASH
STUD
PORCH/DORMER ROOFING

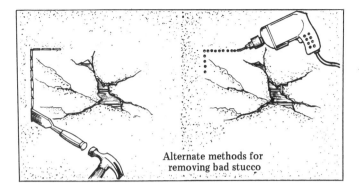

Alternate methods for removing bad stucco

the illustration. Once the old stucco is removed, clean out all the dust, dirt, and loose material with a wire brush. If there's loose wood or metal lath under the old stucco, be sure to nail it back to the sheathing tightly.

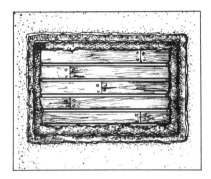

Lath Options

There is continuing debate over whether or not one should apply stucco over old wood lath. People who are particularly disturbed by the idea of using "inappropriate" materials in old-house repair can't bear the thought of metal lath imbedded in a wall that originally had wood lath. If you feel this way, be sure to wet wood lath thoroughly with water containing a little photographer's wetting agent (e.g., Kodak Photo-Flo) before applying the new stucco. Professional plasterers nail metal lath over old wood lath (so they know the stucco will stick) and get on with it.

No one should use metal lath when patching an old building that has lime stucco over a masonry base; metal here causes more problems than it solves. The old lime mortars, when deteriorated, simply fall off the building, exposing the masonry underneath. These bricks or stones can withstand weather reasonably well, and the wall can be patched whenever weather and the repair-person's schedule permit. But if you patch the wall with new mortar over metal lath, you've created two new problems: damage caused by the nails used to fasten the lath; and, should water penetration recur, the patch

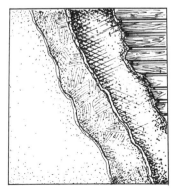

will cling tightly enough to hold in the water, thus causing a further deterioration of the masonry wall.

Applying the Mortar

Application methods are similar for lime or portland cement mortar. The following reminders apply to all stucco work:

• Keep the curing mortar out of the hot sun and away from harsh winds since either of these conditions can cause new mortar to fail. If you must apply mortar on a very sunny or windy day, set up a lean-to or tarpaulin to provide some shelter for the mortar.

• Don't expose curing mortar to freezing temperatures.

• Cross-hatch the scratch, or first, coat of mortar to provide good keys for the leveling, or second, coat. Finish the leveling coat with a screed (a wood float that has a small nail driven through it—only the nail tip protrudes) to provide keys for the finish coat.

• Don't make more mortar than you (or your crew) can use in about one hour.

• Throw away partially set mortar. Do *not* try to apply partially set mortar to the wall.

Trowel on the scratch coat of new mortar to the same depth as the scratch coat of old mortar. Use your screed to straighten the mortar, and then cross-hatch it. Keep the mortar damp (not wet) by misting it, and apply the second coat eighteen to twenty-four hours later. If your repair is three-coat work, you must repeat the above process for the leveling coat. When the base coats have cured, trowel on

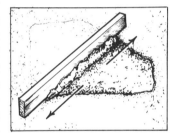

the finish coat. Level it with a screed that rides on the old finish coat (as in the illustration).

If your stucco has a textured or colored finish, or exposed aggregate, you should at least consult with an experienced local mason before you try to match such a finish. Your State Historic Preservation Office (SHPO) is a good place to ask about local masons with preservation experience.

Mortar Formulas

Eye of newt, tongue of frog . . . lime, cement, sand, and water. The recipes for mortar are as arcane as those for witches' brew; it seems every mason has a "secret" formula. And the older the mortar, the more opinions there are on how to duplicate it. The following mortar formulas can be used as starting points for duplicating typical stucco mortar:

—HIGH-LIME MORTAR—

1 bag of hydrated lime
1 shovelful of white portland cement

3 cubic feet of sand (matched to original)
coarse aggregate matched to original (not to exceed 15 percent of total volume of hydrated lime)
Hair or fiber (for scratch coat) matched to original if possible, about 1 pound of hair per 100-pound bag of hydrated lime*

—LIME/PORTLAND CEMENT MORTAR—

1 to 1 1/2 bags of hydrated lime
1 bag of white portland cement
5 to 6 1/2 cubic feet of sand
coarse aggregate, hair, and fiber as above

The lime/portland mix is a good mortar to use in highly exposed areas such as parapet walls. This mortar may well have been used during the transitional period between soft lime and hard portland mortars.

Relatively more lime makes the mixture more "plastic," but it will also be more likely to crack because of shrinkage. Relatively more sand or aggregate makes the mixture harder to trowel smooth, and weakens the mortar. Each grain of cement should be in contact with a grain of sand.

If the mortar was a twentieth-century mortar high in portland cement, start with this formula:

> 1 bag of white portland cement
> 1/2 bag of hydrated lime
> 6 cubic feet of sand
> coarse aggregate, hair, and
>   fiber as above

The process for hand-mixing all three mortars is essentially the same: Place half the sand required for one bag of cement in one end of the mortar box, spread the cement (portland or lime) over the sand, then lay the balance of the sand over the cement. Place the amount of coarse aggregate or hair required for a bag of cement over the top of the sand. Repeat as necessary until all the required material is in the box. Now, with a hoe (a mortar hoe with two holes in the blade is best), start at one end of the box and pull the hoe toward you in short choppy strokes until you've thoroughly mixed all the material. Move all the material to one end of the box.

Now pour water into the other end of the box, and pull the dry material into the water with short choppy strokes. Make sure the hoe cuts to the bottom of the box. Continue to add water, but only as needed to bring the mix to a soft, plastic mass. Keep chopping with the hoe, moving further and further through the wet material. Make your strokes progressively longer, until all the dry material has been wetted and pulled to the end of the box. Then, to ensure a thorough mixing, change direction and pull the mortar to the opposite end of the box. When the materials have been thoroughly combined, the mortar color will be uniform. Don't overmix—this just hastens the setting of the mortar.

*Hair should be clean and free from extraneous materials. Cow hair is best and is available from the Brooklyn Animal Hair Manufacturing Company, 175–185 Beard Street, Brooklyn, NY 11231; (718)852-3592.

It is impossible to duplicate some old mortars precisely; some materials used in the past just aren't available today. (Try to find unpolluted river sand.) The Portland Cement Association provides a service (for a fee) in which they specify modern materials that will match an old mortar in color and density. For further information, contact the Portland Cement Association, 5420 Old Orchard Road, Dept. OHJ, Skokie, IL 60077; (312)966-6200.

PAINTING

Normally, painting brick is not necessary—it's an added maintenance problem and offers little extra protection to sound brick. But to deteriorating sandblasted brick, already seriously compromised, a paint job can add a measure of protection. Properly done, paint can prevent liquid water from penetrating, while allowing vapor water to escape from the bricks underneath. Some paints can seal the surface, preventing evaporation and

A brick house can be sensitively painted. This building has been successfully painted in a Georgian color scheme.

Painting brick can also cause an eyesore.

actually compounding the problem. Stay away from oil- or epoxy-based paints and other nonporous coatings.

As with all painting tasks, preparation is critical. If the brick is already sandblasted, you shouldn't have to remove any old paint, but you may have to attend to these chores:

• Remove all loose and crumbling mortar and brick with a wire brush, screwdriver, or chisel to provide a sound surface.

• Remove any efflorescence by dry brushing at first, followed by clear water and a stiff brush if necessary.

• Remove moss and other organic growth with an ordinary weed killer. Wet the wall with clear water first, so the weed killer is not drawn into the brick. Rinse and scrub the wall well afterward to remove all traces of the chemicals.

• Remove mildew and surface dirt. Try the following homemade cleaner:

   3 ounces trisodium phosphate (TSP)
   1 ounce detergent (Tide, All, etc.)
   1 quart 5-percent sodium hypochlorite (bleach)
   3 quarts warm water

Scrub the brick surface with the solution using a medium-soft brush and rinse with clear water.

• Complete all repointing and caulking before painting.

• Check the label on the paint you'll be using for the acceptable moisture and temperature conditions during application.

What kind of paint should you use? Generally a water-thinned emulsion paint (latex) is best—either acrylic latex or vinyl latex. These paints allow the brick to "breathe" while offering protection from water penetration. Additionally, they are usually mildew- and alkali-resistant (alkali resistance is important when you apply paint over lime mortar). They're also easy to apply, clean up quickly, and are readily available.

Most major paint manufacturers make a latex paint suitable for masonry, and the label should list brick as an acceptable surface. To ensure proper adhesion, most manufacturers will strongly recommend using a specially formulated undercoat before using their latex as a finish coat. Be sure to use the specific undercoat made for the latex you're using—don't mix brands. For example, use Sherwin-Williams Masonry Conditioner (A5V2) as a base beneath their latex top coats, or Wonder Bond (16100) if you use one of Devoe's latex paints. Most of these undercoats should be thinned, as directed, to prevent glazing.

If the sandblasting has caused extensive pitting or cracking, you might consider another type of paint. Cement-based paints, which don't need an undercoat or primer, are capable of filling in heavily marred areas, and they do allow water vapor to escape from the brick. These paints come in powdered form and begin to hydrate when mixed with water, so they must be used immediately.

Although masonry paints can be applied by roller or spraying, brush application is preferable to ensure adequate coverage over coarse-textured brick walls. You can expect a well-prepared job on masonry to last three to eight years. As you can see, painting brick is a major and regular commitment.

What colors should you use? Traditionally, brick was often painted—you guessed it—brick red. This can reduce the visual impact of painting brick that had previously been unpainted. Other colors run the gamut from pinkish salmon to dark reds and browns. Choose a color appropriate for the style and era of the house. White or pale yellow might be suitable for a Colonial Revival house, earth colors such as gray or beige for a Gothic Revival, for example.

When considering color placement, think of the brick walls as the "body" of the house. The body color should be complemented with appropriate trim colors in the same manner as a frame house. Beware of dark body colors, though, as they may make the building look too heavy and foreboding.

STRIPPING EXTERIOR
———— MASONRY ————

One day, the phone rings and it's a reader asking how to get the clinging, flaking remnants of old white paint off his red brick. There's no easy answer. Another phone call, another day, and this time somebody wants to know how to get the romantic, old-fashioned look of clinging, flaking remnants of white paint onto red brick, without waiting a hundred years for paint to weather. There's no easy answer.

The first caller should let time do the job. While one can understand love of the pristine, the need to "finish" the job, one can also sympathize with the second caller and his love of the imperfection of old things. Also it's downright practical to do nothing if you can get away with it. Making things new again is expensive, and awful mistakes are made in the name of restoration.

It's a good thing the owner intended to repaint anyway—stripping revealed patches, bad pointing repairs, and wood trim.

To get back to exterior stripping. Only you can decide whether you have to or really want to. You may want to review the following methods before you plunge in.

To Strip or Not to Strip

Not stripping masonry is cheaper, easier, and less risky than stripping it. There are plenty of reasons not to strip. First of all, maybe the building was meant to be painted. Painted brick was quite popular in the nineteenth century, sometimes for a polychrome paint scheme, and sometimes to follow a European tradition of dark red paint with mortar joints "penciled" in white.

Often buildings were painted—at the time of construction or soon after—for more practical reasons. Cheaper, less attractive, more permeable bricks may have been used by the mason on a budget who expected the building to be painted. Early in the life of the building, water penetration may have been solved with paint, which acts as a less permeable barrier for the brick. Or maybe the paint is later still, masking additions to the building. In short, stripping may reveal ugly bricks, mismatched repairs or additions, or architectural detail that turns out to be sandpainted wood, and not masonry at all.

On the other hand, there are some good reasons to strip masonry. The building may not have been painted until late in life, and then for a poor reason: It was dirty. Also, natural brick is, especially to our eyes, almost always prettier than a flat coat of paint. And once the paint is off, the long-term maintenance of the building is simplified: You no longer have to paint every few years.

Before you strip a masonry building for the sake of aesthetics, strip sample patches all around the building. Be sure of what's under the paint before you spend the money.

There is no sure way to tell if your building was originally painted. Besides relying on historical research and local custom, try looking under the first layer of paint. If the building is clean, it may have been painted early on. If there is clearly dirt under the paint, it stood for some time without paint. That doesn't rule out the possibility that the building was painted for good cause, though: Paint may have been used later on to mask a patch or stop water penetration.

You must strip failed paint from masonry before you can repaint. Depending on the degree of failure, you may have to completely strip the masonry. (There's no need to get every last bit off if you intend to repaint.) For practical rather than aesthetic reasons, you should strip masonry in these two instances:

1. The paint is badly chalking, flaking, or loose. Find the cause! Flaking is most often due to moisture penetration and retention.

2. The masonry has been "sealed" with an extra-heavy buildup of paint layers, or by gloss oil-based paint or aluminum/oil paint. In such a case, the masonry can't give up moisture and salts that accumulate in it. Pressure will build up under the paint layers, and when the paint flakes, it will take some masonry with it. Look for signs of this happening.

The masonry should be stripped with a commercial paint stripper, washed, repointed where necessary, and repainted with a high-quality latex masonry paint. *Note:* Paint will not stick to a powdering surface.

D-I-Y?

When a building must be stripped, most owners hire a contractor. Exterior masonry stripping is difficult and hazardous. Besides needing specialized knowledge, the applicator works with strong chemicals, sometimes several storeys up. Professionals have experience and skill, a source of materials, and expensive extras such as scaffolding. The right masonry-stripping contractor should also know all about collecting and disposing of the effluent that comes off the building.

The first task, whether by you or the contractor bidding the job, is to find out what the job is. The masonry has to be identified, not just in one test patch at ground level, but all over the building. Is the cornice really stone, or is it wood or metal?

Once you've made the decision to strip, the contractor should do a test patch. This will settle the unique specifications for the job, as well as establish a "control" by which the rest of the job will be judged. Determine the following:

- The type of stripper to be used
- The concentration of the stripper to be used
- The dwell time, or optimum time for the chemicals to sit on the masonry
- The optimum pressure/volume of rinse water

An important caution: A higher concentration of the active chemical will speed the job, but high concentrations may etch minerals in certain types of stone, thereby changing their reflectivity and apparent color. If you're going back to the "original masonry," you certainly don't want to change its appearance in the process.

Several types of strippers may be necessary on a single job, depending on the materials to be stripped, especially where there is graffiti to be removed.

The water rinse will introduce water into the masonry. You don't want to introduce it into the house, however, so be sure to inspect the pointing. If you are worried about water entry, at least do a temporary joint-filling job with caulk or soft mortar. It need not be a finished pointing job. In general, it's better to repoint after the stripping operation. You will be able to better match the mortar color, and the rinsing will have dislodged any loose mortar for you.

The season for stripping is important. Do it in late spring or summer only. Be sure to finish up at least a month before the first potential frost. You don't want water freezing inside the masonry!

One more preparation detail: To remove vines and other green things growing up the building, cut them at ground level several months in advance and leave them to die. Now the weakened stems can be removed without damaging the masonry. Don't attempt to remove clinging tendrils and pads.

Chemical Stripping

Chemical technology for strippers is not as diverse or complex as that for masonry cleaners. Generally, masonry strippers are alkaline formulations, some quite basic, others close to pH neutral. In virtually none of the commercial preparations is sodium hydroxide (lye) used, as it often causes efflorescence later. The formulas may contain wetting agents to help the chemical penetrate, modifiers to keep the preparation wet long enough to soften paint, and neutralizers that check alkalinity.

Some chemicals manufacturers recommend a dilute acid afterwash to neutralize the caustic (containing lye) stripping chemicals. This is done after the sludge has been rinsed away, and is followed again by a clear-water rinse. Other solvent-based strippers don't need the neutralizing afterwash, especially if the masonry is not to be repainted. However, if you do intend to repaint, you must neutralize and rinse thoroughly, or the paint will not stay on. Do not repaint until the masonry is completely dry. If you have any doubts, hold off on painting for six months or a year, to allow the masonry to rid itself of residues (efflorescence can be simply brushed off the surface).

Keep in mind that a severe blast of rinse water at high volumes and 2000 psi of pressure can seriously damage the masonry, regardless of how gentle and expensive the chosen chemicals were.

The proprietary chemical strippers are much more expensive than lye-based strippers, but they are worth it in lowering the risk to the building. With lye, removing residue becomes all the more critical. And neutralizing with strong acid would probably damage the mortar. It virtually cannot be neutralized enough to allow repainting. Proprietary strippers contain additives which increase surface activity (where the paint is) while avoiding deep penetration into the masonry.

Is there anything magical about the proprietary formulas? Not at all, yet they are closely guarded secrets. That's because on the one hand, formulas are the carefully balanced result of experimentation and experience with different kinds of masonry. Yet on the other hand, the ingredients are readily available and the recipes easily reproduced. So when you choose a proprietary formulation, you are buying a company's experience, avoiding the labor and hazard of mixing your own ingredients, and lowering risk for your building.

The most well-known stripping products are from the Sure-Klean line, manufactured by ProSoCo. ProSoCo prefers to sell direct to the contractor; the company guarantees its chemicals and wants to know who is using them. They maintain four regional offices, not only for sales but also to answer technical queries. A technician will even visit the site if a problem crops up. For product information or a list of qualified contractors near you, contact ProSoCo at P.O. Box 171677, Dept. OHJ, Kansas City, KS 66117; (913)281-2700.

For the whole job contracted out, expect to pay about $1 to $1.50 per square foot for chemically stripping paint from brick, more if there is a lot of masking or an extra-heavy buildup of paint.

Disposing of Chemical Strippers

Be sure you know what to do with the run-off. What's coming off after stripping is a chemical strong enough to strip paint, mixed with the softened paint itself. The paint sludge that comes off old houses contains lead (among other things) and is classified as a toxic waste. Flushing sludge into the soil will contaminate the ground around the house for many years to come. Sludge will also contaminate well water. Flushing it down the sewers may contaminate ground water and is illegal.

Legally, it's the responsibility of the owner or architect

to specify waste disposal procedures as part of the contract. Most contractors are not up front about the disposal details, so press it: Make the final payment contingent upon your receiving a copy of the hazardous waste manifest. That way, you'll be heeding EPA regulations—and besides, it's the right thing to do.

Catching the effluent is no big deal. Generally, it's contained in weighted tarps covered with absorbent straw. Then it's put in 55-gallon drums and a waste hauler is paid to dispose of it properly. The cost to the customer is about $125 per drum—a proportionately small cost, as a residential-size job may generate only one drum.

PART THREE

RESTORING THE INTERIOR

CHAPTER 10

Plumbing and Electrical Systems

Sometimes old houses earn their charm and character from the mechanical systems that make them inhabitable for their owners. For all the charm of old-house idiosyncracies like groaning pipes, they may signal big trouble ahead. As difficult and messy as the jobs may be, no interior renovation should be tackled without first inspecting the condition of your house's mechanical systems. You don't want to finish your bathroom or kitchen only to find that you need to replace pipes. Discovering bad wiring late in the game spells disaster for that newly plastered living room wall.

If you're like a lot of people, you'll leave the plumbing and wiring to professionals. But there are some repairs you can take care of yourself, and it can't hurt to know something about what might be wrong so you can get the most out of the plumber or electrician you call in for help.

──────PLUMBING──────

Plumbing inevitably develops leaks. It's one thing that doesn't get better as it gets older. From the moment they are put into use, pipes, seals, and fixtures begin to deteriorate. Throw in a remodeling or two, and it's easy to imagine that the integrity of a sixty-year-old-plus system may be less than perfect.

Serious hazards lurk in plumbing that was installed or adapted improperly. Leaks and noise are minor irritations compared to the contamination of supply water or the escape of dangerous gases into a building.

Ironically, real problems are often subtle and long ignored, while the more mundane, such as leaks, appear as minor disasters. Armed with a little knowledge of plumbing basics, however, you should be able to determine which problems are minor and which mean real trouble.

Often the piping networks—the key part of the system—were made of best-quality materials and installed

with expertise. Good old piping invites renovation rather than replacement. It may be tempting for a contractor to "simplify things" by starting fresh. But repair and renovation (instead of wholesale replacement) may offer cost savings as well as higher quality. So be sure your existing system is carefully assessed. Cast-iron waste pipe and copper or brass water lines, common in old houses, are still regarded as the premier materials of the industry. Even galvanized pipe, today regarded as inferior and banned in some cities for new construction, tends to have a thicker, more resistant coating in old installations.

On the other hand, inevitable repairs over the years probably haven't matched the system design, materials, or quality of the original features. And it's not only age that puts old-house plumbing into a special category. Many practices and materials of the past are now seen as inferior. Plumbing technology was in development until well into the twentieth century. A post-Victorian house undoubtedly still contains some or most of the early plumbing. In even older homes, indoor plumbing was a later addition: Initial compromises must have been necessary just to make things fit.

All this is to say that old-house plumbing can have hidden blessings or be an expensive curse. Some flaws *do* require piping replacement—and it's important for the house owner to accept that fact in such cases. But other problems can be remedied by maintenance or selective pipe repairs.

COMMON WATER SUPPLY ──────PROBLEMS──────

Besides routine maintenance of faucets, the most prevalent water supply troubles result from the deterioration of piping. Corrosion is most pronounced with galvanized iron pipe. As the iron corrodes, iron oxide literally grows from the pipe wall. Inside the pipe, the area intended for water flow becomes restricted. The same volume flow of water must pass through at higher speeds and greater pressure losses, resulting in increased noise (or "water hammer") and lower pressure at the fixtures. Eventually the pipe may become completely plugged, eliminating the noise, but also eliminating the carrying capacity of the pipe! If you suspect blockage, the piping must be opened and inspected at a convenient location. Replace pipe as needed. Cleaning is rarely an effective, long-term solution.

Pressure-loss problems are also caused by plumbing additions over the years for which the original service or piping was not intended. If pressure drops below the minimum, flow may become erratic, causing temperature fluctuation and poor water service at the faucet.

Noise in the system can also be caused by piping that is not properly secured. When water flow stops abruptly, as it does when a faucet is shut off, a dangling pipe will bang and rattle. Adding some more pipe hangers allevi-

ates this problem. Another solution to water hammer—regardless of its cause—is to install an air chamber along the supply line near the fixture. There are several different kinds of air chambers, but they all work as a simple cushion, absorbing the shock of the abrupt flow stoppage. Some old fixtures may have capped air chambers that are no longer effective at relieving the shock. If it seems necessary, your plumber can install rechargeable air chambers on the hot and cold branch water lines, or add special shock absorbers to the system.

Copper or brass piping does not corrode as aggressively as galvanized, but problems can develop where these pipes connect to fixtures, valves, or other piping of a different metal. Contact between dissimilar metals sets up conditions for electrochemical reactions called galvanic actions, which corrodes metal.

The result is a restriction of flow area in the pipe, higher velocities, and pressure drops, just as with internal rusting. The difference is that galvanic corrosion is both

Troubleshooting Water Supply

PROBLEM	CAUSE	CURE	COMMENT
Leaky valves and faucets	Normal wear	Replace washers.	Low cost. Routine maintenance by owner.
Leaky pipes and tanks	General corrosion	Replace pipes, fittings, or tanks.	High cost. Contractor repair.
	Dissimilar metals	Replace damaged material. Isolate different pipe materials with dielectric unions.	Moderate cost. May be owner repair. Examine piping for general corrosion.
No water	Dead water supply	Contact water utility or remedy well problem.	
	Plugged pipe	Backflush lines and/or replace piping.	Contractor repair likely. May indicate more extensive problems. Flush lines thoroughly prior to continued use.
	Frozen pipe	Thaw, then insulate, bury, or trace with heat tape.	Moderate cost. Owner repair unless pipe is damaged.
Low water pressure	Corrosion or improper line size	Replace piping with adequate size and quality.	High cost. Contractor repair.
	Low supply pressure	Contact water utility or adjust well pump discharge pressure.	Booster pump is a last resort for this problem—cost about $250.
Noise	Dangling pipes	Install additional pipe straps.	Low cost. Homeowner repair.
	High water velocities	Replace piping with adequate size and quality.	High cost. Contractor repair.
	Water hammer	Install shock suppressor.	Moderate cost. Contractor repair.
Dirty water	Water source (dirt & sediment)	Contact water utility or remedy well problem.	Bad omen: indicates possible contamination of water supply. Well may require investigation by municipal or private experts.
	Corrosion (rust)	Replace pipe or fittings.	May indicate significant problems in supply piping. Investigation appropriate.

more rapid and more confined, generally occurring in the immediate area of contact.

Lead Piping

The use of lead piping was a popular water-supply practice as late as 1940. It has since been recognized as a health hazard. Once so characteristic of water/waste systems that it lent its name to the activity ("plumbing" is derived from the Latin "plumbum," which means lead), lead is now known to contaminate the water supply. The contamination is a potential source of lead poisoning, a cumulative ailment that becomes harmful to people who use a lead system for many years.

Lead is identified by its gray color—silver when scratched—and its relative softness. It should be replaced if present. Because of its flexibility, lead was especially popular for the main service connection at the water meter. It's hard to determine whether an individual service is lead without digging it up, but water utilities will often provide the information. At least they can confirm the date of installation and give you an idea of the materials that might have been used at that time.

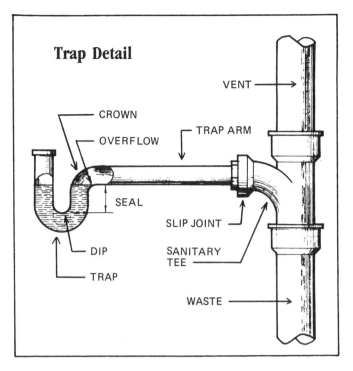

Trap Detail

VENT
CROWN
OVERFLOW
TRAP ARM
SEAL
SLIP JOINT
SANITARY TEE
DIP
TRAP
WASTE

COMMON WASTE PROBLEMS

The waste system piping is subject to the same corrosion as supply lines. Although the conditions in each system are fundamentally different, the result is similar: Piping must be replaced after corrosion has reached an unacceptable level. Corrosion in waste pipes shows up as leaks or slow drainage. Extensive corrosion is visible at joints and fittings. Likewise, if you don't see apparent corrosion at joints and fittings, replacement of piping is probably unnecessary.

Horizontal drain lines must be installed with a minimum of pitch toward the sewer. This statement seems obvious, as liquid does not ordinarily flow uphill. But in old houses, where settlement has occurred, it is often necessary to realign the waste piping to assure that all parts of the system pitch to the drain point with a minimum slope of one-quarter inch per foot.

Much less apparent is inadequacy in the trap and vent system. Your drain piping is connected to a sewage disposal system that has the capacity to generate unfriendly vapors (a fiendish mixture of methane, an explosive gas, with other gases, acids, and caustics). The vapors move throughout the waste plumbing system and, if unchecked, will enter the house. Traps hold the last of a waste discharge to form a seal against entry of these sewer gases. The gases can then migrate to the atmosphere through the vent system. At least that's the way today's accepted plumbing systems work.

Vents also protect the traps from being siphoned dry. Older plumbing usually incorporates some kind of trap, but vents were once considered optional. Consequently, the traps were not always functional. As a volume of water runs down a waste pipe, it creates a higher air pressure on the downstream side and a lower pressure upstream; in other words, it compresses air ahead of itself and creates a vacuum behind, as would any solid body moving through a fluid. Without adequate venting, that vacuum allows atmospheric pressure to push the trap liquid into the waste system, thereby destroying the water seal and leaving open a channel for sewer gas migration into the house.

Such siphoning might occur only under some situations, such as the emptying of a big plug of water all at once. How to resolve a sewer gas problem, therefore, can be quite a mystery. Old houses are vulnerable for two reasons: Either the plumbing may have been originally installed without proper vents, or plumbing additions may have compromised the integrity of the vent system. A similar problem occurs with seldom-used fixtures, such as floor drains. Trap liquids evaporate over a period of several months; if they're not replenished, loss of seal may occur. A trap primer (essentially a constant trickle of water) is often installed to eliminate the possibility of evaporation. If odor problems plague your old house, a careful review of each fixture's trap and vent is in order. You'll have to open the wall and see whether the fixture is vented.

CROSS CONNECTIONS

Contamination of potable water is the most serious potential hazard in plumbing. A review of old-house plumbing afflictions is not complete without an explanation of cross connections. Because it's likely that much of their plumbing was done before cross-connection potential was fully understood, old houses are particularly susceptible. It most commonly occurs through siphoning.

Troubleshooting Waste Piping

PROBLEM	CAUSE	CURE	COMMENT
Clogged drain or slow drain	Blockage	Plumber's helper or drain cleaner.	Follow instructions carefully. Stronger measures may well be necessary. Low cost unless plumber is required.
	Inadequate drain grade	Re-align waste pipe to a minimum 1/4-in. pitch per foot of run.	Low cost if owner repair. Moderate to high cost if contractor repair.
	Inadequate waste or vent	Replace or install piping to suit requirements.	High cost. Contractor repair.
Odors	Poor venting	Replace or install piping to suit requirements.	High cost. Contractor repair.
	Trap evaporation	Use trap regularly or install trap primer.	Trap primer cost $50–100, depending on layout.
Noise	Normal operation	Insulate pipes or replace with cast iron.	Plastic or copper waste pipe conducts noise very well. Insulation helps but cast iron pipe is the most thorough solution.

For example, during a 1920s remodeling, a bathtub was installed without an overflow drain. Furthermore, the faucet was installed in such a place that it's possible to fill the tub so the water level covers the faucet. If, while the tub is being filled and the water is already up over the faucet, there's a pressure drop due to routine demand from another fixture, the tub water could be siphoned into the supply lines.

Primary sources for concern are leaky underground pipes, hose connections, and underground lawn sprinkler systems. In short, any time there is no break between supply water and nonpotable water, the potential exists for cross contamination. Backflow preventers or vacuum breakers can be installed where you suspect cross-connection potential.

REPAIRING
LEAKY FAUCETS

Scores of different faucet designs have found their way into houses since the time indoor plumbing was first introduced. Early, simple types, such as the *ground key* and *Fuller ball,* are now largely obsolete and exist only in very old systems or out-of-the-way locations. The faucet types currently in production, chief among them the *disc, ball,* and *cartridge,* are modern, sophisticated devices developed over the last fifty years and not original equipment in most old houses. The long-standing workhorse of the plumbing industry is the *stem* faucet (also known as the *compression* faucet), which was common by the turn of the century and is still in wide use today.

Stem faucets are straightforward mechanisms that employ a threaded *stem* to bring a *washer* in contact with a *seat,* thereby restricting or interrupting the flow of water. This arrangement is also widely used in *globe*-type valves located in-line throughout a plumbing system, and is therefore almost always the most well represented shutoff in any house. Stem faucets can wear and start to leak, as will any working house part that receives hard service. Every faucet is a little different, but fortunately, their simple construction and time-tested design make problems simple to diagnose and cure. The next time a stem faucet needs a checkup—or major surgery—take the following steps.

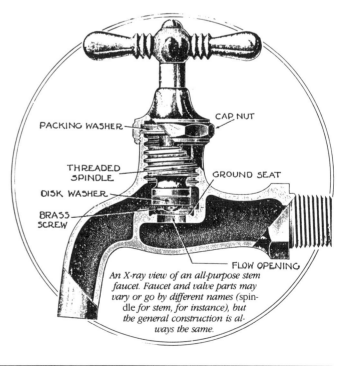

An X-ray view of an all-purpose stem faucet. Faucet and valve parts may vary or go by different names (spindle *for stem, for instance), but the general construction is always the same.*

Washers

Washer replacement is a routine maintenance procedure. Replace washers that are split, eaten away, or no longer pliable. Continued use of leaky washers wastes water and erodes channels in the faucet seat. Keep assorted washer sizes on hand for on-the-spot repairs.

Replacement washers should always be the correct size and shape for the faucet. Flat washers are designed for seats with crowns or ridges, tapered or rounded washers are for tapered seats. Washers that "almost fit" seldom work for long, and some faucet problems stem from just using the wrong washer. Choice of washer composition is a matter of preference. Flat, neoprene rubber washers make up the majority sold today, but Teflon and synthetic fiber washers are also available.

To disassemble the faucet and gain access to the washer you should:

1. Shut off the water supply to the faucet.

2. Remove the faucet handle, normally secured to the stem with a screw hidden under a decorative cap. Difficult handles may require a faucet-handle puller (similar to a miniature gear puller). Faucets with long stems may not need their handles removed at all if there is room to swing a wrench on the cap nut.

3. Back off the cap nut with a parallel-jawed wrench, such as a monkey wrench or adjustable (Crescent) wrench. To avoid marring the finish, first wrap the nut in electrical tape or cushion it with a rag; never use toothed-jaw tools such as water-pump pliers.

4. Replace the faucet handle temporarily and open the faucet to back the stem out of the faucet body.

Use care when removing brass washer retaining screws; old screws may be brittle or have worn heads. A drop of kerosene or penetrating oil may help loosen difficult screws. Also remove any mineral deposits from the stem base or screw area before installing a washer and new screw. For long-term service, change the screw as well as the washer.

When investigating leaks in mixing faucets, which incorporate both hot- and cold-water inlets (such as on bathtubs), start by checking hot-water washers. These invariably fail first due to the temperature and slightly caustic effect of heated water.

Faucet leaks may not be the fault of washers alone. If washer replacement stops a leak only for a short while (or not at all), suspect a nicked or worn seat.

Seats

Inspect seats visually by looking inside the faucet body with a flashlight. Healthy seats look smooth; those with defects show cracks, fissures, or pits. Damaged seats can be replaced (if removable) or dressed (if part of the faucet body).

Removable seats are unthreaded and reinstalled with a valve seat wrench, a straight or L-shaped bar ground at the ends to

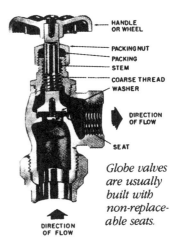

HANDLE OR WHEEL
PACKING NUT
PACKING
STEM
COARSE THREAD WASHER
DIRECTION OF FLOW
SEAT
DIRECTION OF FLOW

Globe valves are usually built with non-replaceable seats.

fit into either a square or hexagonal hole in the seat center. If not badly worn, removable seats can be restored by carefully dressing the face flat again with a fine file or wet-or-dry sandpaper.

Nonremovable seats may be dressed with a seat-dressing tool that acts as a rotary file. Individual tools vary in design and operation, but all fit into the faucet body, replacing the stem so that the cutter can be rotated on the seat with a wheel handle (much like a faucet handle) until the seat face is smooth. Use the proper-size cutter for the seat, work with moderate pressure (seats are brass and soft), and flush all cuttings from the body before reassembling the faucet. Seat dressers are not always successful, but they're worth the investment (under $15) if they save the cost of buying a new faucet.

A typical seat dresser (above) and seat wrench (below).

Stems

Stems last a long time under normal wear conditions, but if they are allowed to close repeatedly on severely deteriorated seats or washers, they, too, may become damaged and require replacement. Worn or bent stems also may cause damage so that the entire faucet must be replaced.

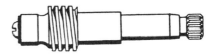

The dimensions of faucet and valve stems are critical and the variety of replacements is bewildering. Always take the damaged stem along when securing replacements, and compare every aspect to make sure the fit is correct. Good hardware stores and plumbing-supply houses carry common stem varieties; specialty plumbing suppliers or salvage yards may be the only source for very old or odd-size stems.

When installing a replacement stem, replace or dress the seat as well (if possible) to avoid premature wear. Coat the thread lightly with petroleum jelly for smooth action.

Leaks where the stem passes through the cap nut can be caused by either a loose cap nut or compressed or worn-out packing. Loose caps can be tightened just enough to stop the leak. (Over-tightening will cause excessive wear in the packing.) Compressed packing can be improved by wrapping a turn or two of braid packing (sold at most hardware stores) around the stem in the direction in which the stem moves when the faucet closes. If a leak persists, the packing will have to be replaced.

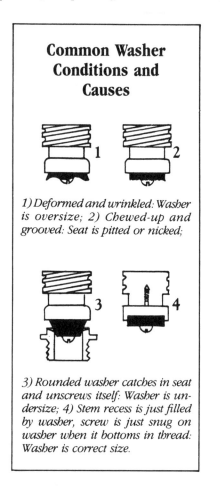

Common Washer Conditions and Causes

1) Deformed and wrinkled: Washer is oversize; 2) Chewed-up and grooved: Seat is pitted or nicked;

3) Rounded washer catches in seat and unscrews itself: Washer is undersize; 4) Stem recess is just filled by washer, screw is just snug on washer when it bottoms in thread: Washer is correct size.

ELECTRICITY

Compared to water and gas, electricity is the youngest service, and the one that truly makes the modern house possible. In its short hundred years, domestic electric wiring has undergone a technical metamorphosis every two decades or so, and has grown from a temperamental novelty to a highly reliable resource. For owners of houses wired with an old system—and most pre-1940 houses are—the big question is: Where do I stand?

The answer is not always simple and has at least two sides: legality and safety. The legality of existing wiring has to be determined case by case. The National Electrical Code (begun in 1897) is a set of model electrical safety requirements published for building and insurance inspectors and electrical contractors, and has no legal power of its own. Most cities and towns adopt the code as their standard, but they are also free to interpret and enforce it according to their needs. The result is that many an obsolete system that would not be permitted in new work is allowed to remain in service if deemed to be in safe condition. A pass or fail depends on the local codes and the judgment of the inspector.

The safety of old wiring, then, is the most important issue. The best remedy for any questionable circuit is, of course, disconnecting the system and installing new materials. In fact, electric wiring of any age has a finite life and might have to be replaced in the future.

While old wiring is in service, its safety can be improved by understanding what the system is and inspecting it with an eye for its known problem areas. Old houses are frequently wired with combinations of systems (for instance, cleats *and* knob and tube *and* BX cable). Understanding the age and specific shortcomings of each type is important in determining whether it is workable, in need of repair, or completely obsolete. In addition, much old wiring falls short of the modern standards for insulation, current-carrying capacity, and grounding. Applying some basic practices, though, can keep these systems operating within their designed limits and help them run safely.

PRE-1940 WIRING
SYSTEMS

Electricity had no purpose in houses until it became a means to light them. The change came in 1879, when Thomas Edison built upon the experiments of many others to produce a practical incandescent light bulb. By 1882 Edison was operating the first plant specifically designed to supply electricity on demand to any consumer: the Pearl Street Station in New York City.

The power was DC (direct current), a cumbersome first choice for domestic electricity. Direct current is not transmitted easily over long distances, and buildings had to be wired in the "tree" fashion to feed early power-hungry bulbs. That is, the wire diameter was gauged down from the bottom to the top of the house by load. *Exposed* systems became the popular choice for finished buildings. The wires were stretched between cleats or knobs spaced about four feet apart, and run in open view on walls and up staircases to reach the next floor.

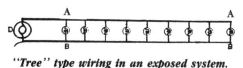

"Tree" type wiring in an exposed system.

Wooden cleats supporting an exposed system, the earliest (and cheapest) wiring method, had disadvantages that were recognized early on. First, the exposed wires were easily abraded and broken. Second, the wood could become an electrical conductor when it got damp and might short-circuit the lines if splinters on the cleats cut into the primitive insulation. They were obsolete by 1900.

Porcelain cleats were intended to make a safer exposed system than wood and started to appear in the 1880s. Single or tandem wires could be carried by mating ceramic halves that were superior to wood as insulators and eliminated the threat from splinters. Porcelain cleats were well adapted to high-voltage and industrial installations: They could be changed readily for repairs and alterations, they were run high on walls and ceilings (out of harm's way), which improved their safety, and they were inexpensive. Always ugly, they saw less use in houses, and were usually restricted to hidden areas such as basements and attics. In addition, they were considered unfit for wiring in damp places or outdoors as early as 1911.

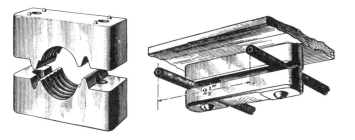

Two kinds of porcelain cleats.

Porcelain and glass knobs were also used in exposed wiring, though the latter versions were more breakable and never as popular. Spacing was, again, required to be no more than 4 or 4 1/2 feet to make sure that parallel lines didn't sag and touch. The National Electrical Code now allows exposed wiring on porcelain cleats or knobs only in industrial and agricultural installations, subject to local requirements.

A glass knob used in exposed wiring.

Direct current systems survived into the twentieth century in pockets around the country, but the seductive advantages of alternating current—with which you didn't need a generating station every three blocks or so—made it the preferred power after 1890. Much of the equipment designed for DC could also be used for AC, but as electricity became more popular, there was a demand for better-looking (and, secondarily, safer) wiring.

Knob-and-Tube Wiring

Knob-and-tube wiring was a concealed (hidden in walls and under floors) version of the exposed knob system. Porcelain knobs carried individual lines along open runs, such as the length of a floor joist, while tubes of the same material were inserted through the wood as

protectors when making runs perpendicular to framing. Knob spacing was still a maximum of 4 1/2 feet, and wires had to be located at least 1 inch off the carrying surface and 5 inches from other wires. Where wires had to cross each other in close proximity, tubes were also employed as protective sheathing by taping them in place on the wire. Loom (made of woven fabric) was usually slipped over wire ends where they connected with switches, outlets, fuse boxes, or other terminations.

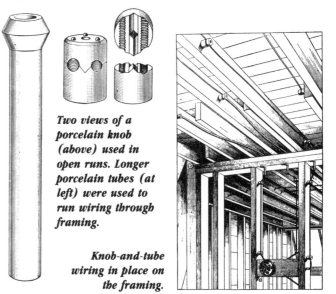

Two views of a porcelain knob (above) used in open runs. Longer porcelain tubes (at left) were used to run wiring through framing.

Knob-and-tube wiring in place on the framing.

Knob and tube could be installed cost-effectively in both new and existing construction, and thus was highly popular, despite its flaws, from the 1890s until after 1920. The considerable in-air isolation of the wires was the system's biggest attribute, making accidental bridging of the lines (with a misplaced drill bit or nail, for instance) unlikely. The system was plagued by most of the drawbacks of exposed cleat or knob work, though, and kept these problems hidden in an environment of wood and sawdust where fires start easily. Completely unprotected from mechanical injury, the copper conductors were essentially naked except for the electrical insulation. Rubber or other insulating material was easily removed by rodents (or nicked by humans while doing alterations), producing a great potential for disaster. Poorly soldered connections on tap lines could heat up to the combustion point, a threat recognized before the turn of the century. Dampness, too, was still an enemy, particularly when parallel knob runs were laid out—contrary to most regulations—on the same rafter or floor joist. Although it saw later use in rural areas, there was a strong call for the outlawing of knob and tube by 1921.

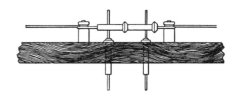

Porcelain tubes taped in place where wires cross.

Wiring Within Moulding

Wood and metal surface moulding were a solution to the aesthetic problems of exposed wiring systems. Retrofitting existing houses with the new power was a big chunk of the early electrical business, but a concealed system was prohibitively expensive for some customers. Mouldings, however, made it possible to wire a building with a nonconcealed system that didn't look like railroad tracks, at about 50 percent of the cost of concealed.

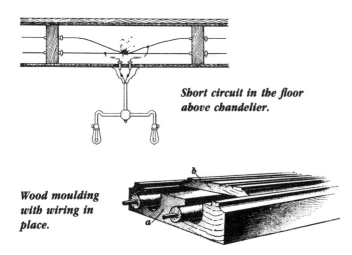

Short circuit in the floor above chandelier.

Wood moulding with wiring in place.

Wood mouldings were decorative, inexpensive, easy to use, and a big hit early on. They were assembled from two weatherproof-painted pieces: a base strip channeled to accept either two or three wires, and a cap that was usually beaded with some ornamental design. Layouts could be planned so that they harmonized with a room by following its lines (much like interior trim) and still service lights and other electrical apparatus.

Convenient as this system was, it had safety drawbacks. Wood moulding offered the wiring it carried little protection from impact, and could even attract trouble by being mistaken for solid wood and having nails driven into it. The wood was so close to the wiring, it ignited readily if there were overload problems, and like wooden cleats, could short the lines if it became wet. Money-saving installation shortcuts often made this system even more dangerous. Mouldings were intended to be made of hardwoods, but softwoods could be substituted at half the price—with even more vulnerability to water. Another economy was eliminating the base strip and just using a grooved version of the cap. This practice didn't guard the wiring, it just hid the problems. By 1911, use of wooden moulding in damp locations was not permitted, and it was not recommended for any application in most communities by the 1930s.

Two types of wood moulding ready for wiring.

Metal mouldings appeared shortly after 1900, and were outselling wood by the 1920s. Also a base-and-cap design, they were made from galvanized sheet metal and were usually large enough to hold four #14 wires. Metal moulding was slim and took paint well, and thus was relatively inconspicuous. As a safety measure, all mouldings had to be grounded at at least two points.

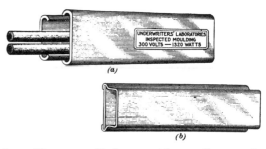

Metal mouldings, usually less conspicuous than wood mouldings, could not be used where moisture might penetrate.

Despite its many advantages, metal moulding had limitations. It could not be used where dampness was a threat, and the National Electrical Code restricted its use to surface wiring. Early types had no galvanizing along the cut edges of the metal, which opened the possibility of either sharp edges or rust compromising the wiring insulation and causing shorts. Improved versions of metal mouldings are still on the market today, and are approved for most dry, surface installations.

Concealing with Plaster

Embedding wiring in plaster or masonry was, both figuratively and literally, a short-lived technique. Even in 1897, the Edison Illuminating Company noted it was "peculiar to modern fireproof building construction, and is rather more popular than its merits deserve."

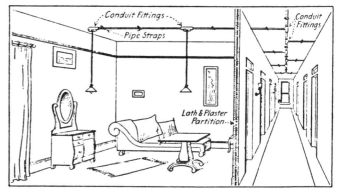

An exposed conduit installation.

Wiring in plaster was supposed to produce a high-quality concealed job. The method was straightforward: Insulated wires were simply mortared over while running cornices, repairing or finishing walls, or laying brickwork. Besides making faults nearly impossible to locate and messy to repair, this kind of wiring was doomed technically. The lime in either plaster or brick mortar decomposed the insulation, rendering the system highly dangerous. The National Electrical Code stopped recommending wiring in plaster by 1901.

Rigid conduit.

Conduit Wiring

Conduit and pipe, always considered the best wiring methods money could buy, had a limited appeal for houses because they took, roughly, twice the money to buy.

Rigid conduit, made from nonmetallic fiber for a brief, early period, was primarily iron or steel piping. The plumbing of gaslight systems undoubtedly spawned the idea of protecting electric wiring with pipe and, indeed, wires were snaked through defunct gas pipes in countless retrofits. In time, the same gauge pipe and fittings, galvanized or enameled on their interiors, were also used for new work.

Rigid conduit provided excellent mechanical protection for the wiring, but it could develop electrical faults. Plumbing that once served as gas lines might retain moisture that would rust the interior of the pipe. This in turn would deteriorate the electrical insulation of the wiring (rubber with a double fabric braid), and the bare copper conductor would come in contact with the metal pipe. If the pipe was resting on damp wood, a short was likely and fire possible. For this reason, all conduit systems were required to be grounded at two locations. Coating the interior of pipes to inhibit rust was a step toward improving this safety problem, but highly reliable conduit wiring had to wait for the introduction of vinyl insulation after 1940. The acceptability of early rigid conduit systems for use today is dependent upon local codes.

Flexible steel conduit, also known as *Greenfield* after the inventor of one model, was manufactured from galvanized steel strips assembled in a manner that allowed the finished "pipe" to be readily articulated in almost any direction. In use, it was first run through walls and voids, secured at bends, and then snaked with wiring to complete the installation.

Flexible conduit appeared at the turn of the century, and seemed to be an ideal means to wire a finished building. It provided good mechanical protection for the wiring, it was well adapted to retrofit installations, and it was easy to work with. Like rigid conduit, though, there was a potential for problems if the wiring insulation failed and sought a ground through the steel. The multiple flexible sections did not provide an unbroken electrical path (as a continuous wire or pipe might), and rust or poor connections along the way could become high-resistance "hot spots" that might heat to the point of combustion. Modern versions of flexible conduit are extensively used, subject to local code requirements.

Armored Cable

Similar in concept to flexible conduit, armored cable came prefabricated with the wiring in place and protected by a continuous spiral galvanized-metal strip. Cable was made practical by (and relied upon) improved insulation compounds that stayed intact when bent in tight turns. The popular versions were known as BX and BXL (which had an interior lead sheath for damp applications).

Cross-section of armored cable. The wiring is already in place.

Rust, again, is early armored cable's worst enemy. The sheet-metal armor was ungalvanized along its edges after cutting (much like metal moulding), and rusted over time. Like flexible conduit, hot spots and sparks were found to develop along the spiral if it should accidentally become a ground path. Years later, the problem was compounded in many installations by hooking up the armor as a working, "third wire" ground—a job it was never intended to perform. The dangers of this practice led to code restrictions for BX in the past. Today, armored cable is manufactured with continuous ground conductors and rust-inhibiting armor, and is approved by the National Electrical Code for dry, residential applications.

Insulation

Electrical insulation, always the Achilles' heel of early wiring, is no less of a problem as these systems age. Mr. Edison resorted to cloth strips soaked in linseed oil, asphalt, and wax after laying bare wires in wood tracks (underground) failed miserably. Prepared papers and varnished cloths in the 1800s had a fair tolerance to heat (about 150 degrees), but succumbed to moisture. Natural rubber compounds stood up to water, but melted in heat and oxidized (dried out and cracked) in air. Care and caution can improve the safety of old insulation still in use.

Flexible steel conduit.

Installing armored cable beneath a floor.

No old insulation can withstand the effects of moisture. Old wiring in damp locations should be replaced.

Rubber insulation (the standard before 1930) seems to have a life of about twenty-five years, so any such system still in use is operating beyond its expectancy. In this light, disturbing old wiring is very risky, as it can crack or break off insulation that is no longer supple, exposing bare copper wire. Extreme care should be taken when altering or even inspecting old lines.

Rubber insulation deteriorates more rapidly in open air than when confined in a conduit or armored cable assembly. Therefore, most of the insulation on open wiring systems (like knob and tube) is frequently very brittle and a potential hazard. Confined wiring, on the other hand, may only be cracking where it leaves its enclosure to make connections at switches and outlets. These leads can be improved by wrapping with vinyl electrical tape or covering with heat-shrink tubing. In the case of armored cable, it is often possible to cut back to fresher insulation if there is enough slack in the cable. (Power must be disconnected before performing either of these operations.)

Current-Carrying Capacity

Old wiring has limited amperage or current-carrying capacity. Most pre-1940 systems were only intended to power lights and the odd radio, refrigerator, waffle or curling iron. Their branch lines are commonly #14 AWG wire, which is rated to carry no more than 15 amperes of load. (In contrast, the general service wiring of contemporary houses is frequently #12—a size larger.) To avoid a fire hazard, it is important to make sure that old wiring isn't overloaded by today's complement of air conditioners and microwave ovens.

The combined wattage of all the lights and appliances on a branch circuit should not exceed the wattage rating of the fuse (or circuit breaker) protecting that circuit. For example: watts = amperes × volts; therefore, a 15-ampere fuse (multiplied by 115 volts, the usual figure) should not have to handle more than 1,725 watts.

The fuse protecting any circuit should be appropriate for the gauge of the wiring. Oversize fuses (installed in an attempt to get more capacity from the circuit) allow a line

to carry more current than it is designed for, with overheating and fire as a potential result. To determine the correct fuse size for old wiring, first disconnect the power, then measure the diameter of the copper conductor with a wire gauge and apply the table below:

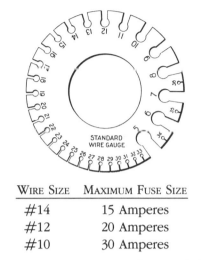

Wire Size	Maximum Fuse Size
#14	15 Amperes
#12	20 Amperes
#10	30 Amperes

The current-carrying capacity of concealed knob-and-tube systems depends on the circulation of free air around the wiring; it should not be surrounded with weatherproofing materials. When wall and attic spaces containing knob and tube are packed with rolled or blown-in insulation, the wiring is forced to conduct at a higher temperature that can break down old electrical insulation and start fires.

Grounding

A ground-continuity test is valuable for determining whether the safety leg on three-pin outlets actually is connected to ground. Since the 1950s, the National Electrical Code has required that new domestic wiring be three-wire grounded, but many three-pin outlets have also been retrofitted to old BX and conduit systems using armor or pipe as the ground conductor. To make sure the electrical path is not interrupted by breaks or loose connections, the ground can be checked either by an electrician or by using simple circuit testers, available at hardware and electronics stores.

CALCULATING ELECTRICAL CAPACITY

Most older houses needed a capacity of only 15 or 20 amperes. As electrical appliances became household necessities in the 1930s and 1940s, 40- and 60-amp service became necessary. In the 1950s, this grew to 150- and 200-ampere service. To estimate the electrical service needs of your house, we recommend the second of the two methods specified by the National Electrical Code (1981). The Code is accepted everywhere in the United States, though some jurisdictions (such as New York City) have stricter requirements. Consult your local building officials to determine if variations from the Code are required in your area.

If your home has circuit breakers, the master switch box (if there is one) or the main circuit breaker box will probably list the capacity in amps. The master switch or master circuit breaker toggle switch may have the amperage printed on the tip.

If you have 230-volt service, you'll probably find that you have two master circuit breaker switches. If you don't have 230-volt service, then your electrical service is probably inadequate. You cannot add an electrical clothes dryer, an electric range, or efficient air-conditioning. This may not be important to you now, but it may be important to a potential buyer of your home. If any doubt lingers as to whether you have 230-volt service, just count the electric wires entering your home. If there are three, you've got 230-volt service.

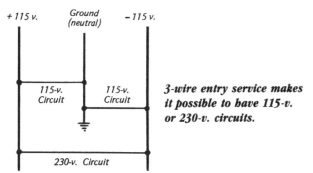

3-wire entry service makes it possible to have 115-v. or 230-v. circuits.

If you have a fuse box, there should be a large black rectangle with a handle labeled MAIN. This contains the two main fuses, and if the fuse box door doesn't tell you the box amperage, you can shut off the power and read the amps from the fuse cartridges. *Be sure* that the power is off before touching the fuse cartridges!

Use the Worksheet on page 180 to calculate the electrical service your house will need. You'll need to figure in the watts used by heating and air-conditioning, lighting, and small and large appliances. Start by entering your current electrical service—found in the fuse box—on the Worksheet on line 6.

Heating and Air-Conditioning Load

This is the most complex item in calculating service needs. Briefly put, the Code requires that the larger of the two loads, heating or air-conditioning, be used in the calculation, since you will not be heating and air-conditioning simultaneously. You must determine the size and/or amperage rating of all permanently wired motors (e.g., water pumps, oil burners, air conditioners) and enter them on the Worksheet. You may not be able to determine furnace motor amperage. Use 10 amps for a hot air furnace blower and 7 amps for the oil burner motor. Figure 10 amps for a well pump. Air-conditioner amperages are listed on the nameplate of the machine.

Now you're ready for the heating/cooling comparison. Use the appropriate section of the Worksheet. If you have central air-conditioning, *add* the furnace blower motor wattage to the air-conditioning side to obtain the total air-conditioning load. Enter the higher of the two wattages on the Worksheet on line 1.

Lighting Load

Next, you'll have to calculate the square footage of the living area of your house. This is calculated from the *outside* dimensions and does *not* include porches, garages, and spaces not adaptable to future living areas. These excluded spaces can include basements, attics, sheds, and so on. However, if your plans call for finishing a basement or attic eventually, you should include it in your calculation.

Multiply the square footage by 3 watts and place this figure in the Lighting Load section on the Worksheet. This figure may seem large to you, but it includes the demands for all lamps, radios, TVs, vacuum cleaners, hair dryers, and the like.

Small Appliances and Laundry Circuits

Allow for two 1,500-watt circuits for small kitchen appliances (to the Code, a refrigerator is a small appliance). The Code requires these two circuits for new construction, and you'll need them if you ever remodel your kitchen. Add a special laundry circuit of 1,500 watts. These have already been placed on the appropriate lines of the Worksheet.

Any appliance served by a separate circuit that serves no other load is called a special appliance. Examples include ranges, separate ovens and cooktops, water heaters, disposals, clothes dryers, and water pumps. Each must be entered at its nameplate wattage. If you do not now have such an appliance but are going to add one, use the Table of Wattages.

WATTAGES OF TYPICAL ELECTRICAL APPLIANCES

Electric ranges	12,000–16,000
Range top	4,000–8,000
Oven	4,000–8,000
Waste disposal	1,000
Dishwasher	1,200–1,500
Clothes dryer	5,000–8,000
Water pump	1,200
Furnace blower	1,200
Oil burner	800
Electric Motors	
1/6 horsepower	450
1/4 horsepower	700
1/3 horsepower	850
1/2 horsepower	1,000
3/4 horsepower	1,350
1 horsepower	1,500
Over 1 h.p.—per h.p. or fraction	1,200

Now total the "Lighting and Other Load" column. The first 10,000 watts of this total are entered on line 2 at full value. The remainder of this "Other Load" total is multiplied by 0.4 (since it's unlikely that you'd use all of it at the same time) and the resulting figure is entered on the Worksheet on line 3.

Add lines 1, 2, and 3 (put total on line 4) and divide the total by 230. (Divide by 115 if you have 115-volt service.) The result on line 5 is the service demand (in amps) or capacity needed for your home.

WORKSHEET FOR ESTIMATING ELECTRICAL SERVICE REQUIREMENTS

HEATING LOAD	Amps	× Volts	=	Watts
Blower	_____	× _____	=	_____
Oil burner	_____	× _____	=	_____
Hot water pump	_____	× _____	=	_____
TOTAL HEATING LOAD				_____

COOLING LOAD	Amps	× Volts	=	Watts
AC No. 1	_____	× _____	=	_____
AC No. 2	_____	× _____	=	_____
AC No. 3	_____	× _____	=	_____
TOTAL COOLING LOAD				_____

HEATING OR COOLING LOAD _____ (1)
(whichever is higher)

LIGHTING AND OTHER LOAD	Watts
_____ sq. ft. × 3 watts/sq. ft.	_____
Two kitchen appliance circuits	3,000
Laundry circuit	1,500
Electric ovens + cooktops	_____
Water heater	_____
Dishwasher	_____
Disposal	_____
Electric clothes dryer	_____
Well water pump	_____
Other	_____
Other	_____
TOTAL LIGHTING AND OTHER LOAD	_____

First 10,000 watts of Lighting and Other
    Load at 100% _____ (2)
Remainder at 40% (_____ × 0.40) _____ (3)
TOTAL OF LINES 1, 2, AND 3 _____ (4)
SERVICE REQUIREMENT IN AMPS
Line 4/House Voltage = _____ _____ (5)
MY CURRENT ELECTRICAL SERVICE IS _____ (6)

WHAT'S A WATT?

For those who are confused by electrical terminology, the "water analogy" can be helpful. Consider the flow of electricity as similar to the flow of water.

Volts are analogous to water pressure. The water at the bottom of a lake behind a 230-foot dam is under twice as much pressure as the water behind a 115-foot dam. The greater the pressure, the greater the amount of work a given volume of water can do. For example, a gallon of water from a 230-foot dam will do twice as much work turning a water wheel as will a gallon of water from a 115-foot dam.

Amperes or *Amps* measure the amount of electricity flowing. It's analogous to gallons of water. The greater the pressure (voltage) behind a given number of amps, the more work (watts) the amps can do.

Watts, wattage is the amount of work or power available in a circuit, or the amount of power an appliance draws while it is doing its work. The amount of work available in a circuit is the total volume of electricity (amps) times the pressure (volts). If you have conductors (wires) that can safely handle a flow of 15 amps, you'll get twice as much work out of the circuit if you have 230 volts available rather than 115 volts. This becomes important when you want to install high-wattage machines like air conditioners or electric ranges.

A *fuse* or *circuit breaker* can be thought of as a safety valve. Your wires (conductors) are rated to carry a certain number of amps safely (usually 15 or 20). If there's an unusually heavy load placed on one of your circuits, and more than the rated number of amps starts to flow through the conductor, the safety valve trips, shutting off the flow of electricity entirely.

AVOIDING ELECTRICAL FIRES

Like a person, wiring develops infirmities as it grows older. Principal diseases suffered by aged wiring include deteriorated insulation, brittle metal, loosened connections, and corrosion, especially in damp conditions. Even if your house was neatly rewired, you may be at risk of electrical fire if the old wiring remains inside the walls. Most electrical fires result from *arcing* between a "hot" wire and ground. Arcing has two primary causes: deteriorated insulation and poor connections. Symptoms of arcing include appliances that flicker on and off and sparks or sizzling as you plug into an outlet.

Here's how defective wiring starts fires:

1. When there's a broken wire or loose connection, external vibration causes the wire to make and break contact intermittently.

2. Each time contact is made, a small electric spark is created. Usually this arcing is harmless, but if there is dust, rodent debris, or other flammable material in the box . . .

3. The spark from the loose connection can ignite the adjacent combustible material and start a fire inside the wall.

Another way defective wiring can start a fire is by a high-resistance short circuit:

1. A high-resistance short occurs when there is an insulation breakdown in the presence of a poor conductor such as dust. Insulation on old wiring can become brittle and fall away. If the bare wire is in contact with high-resistance material like dust in the box, small amounts of current can start leaking from the "hot" wire to ground.

2. The small current flow generates some heat. If there is a current surge (as in an electrical storm), there can be a buildup of heat—or even arcing—inside the combustible material.

3. If the heat builds up to the ignition point of the flammable material, a fire will start in the electrical box.

If you suspect arcing, make the following inspection: Get power *in* all of the house wiring, but don't use any of it. In other words, go through the house and switch on every light, chandelier, and fixture. Then disconnect the load by unscrewing all the bulbs. Don't forget wall sconces, closet lights, outside lights, clocks, and other easy-to-overlook appliances. Unplug the refrigerator and any other timer-controlled device that might switch on.

Your electric water heater may not have an "off" switch, and thus might start drawing power during your test. Disconnect the heater by pulling the fuse or opening the breaker.

Checklist for Old Wiring

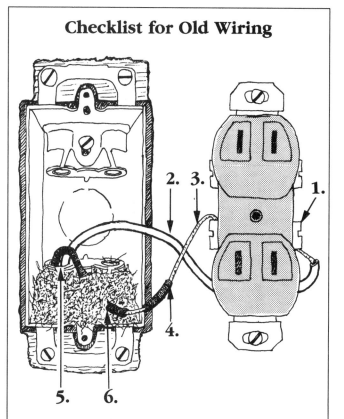

1. Look for loose connections and signs of arcing at the terminals, such as blackening, pitting, or melting.
2. Check for broken wires inside the insulation. Check connections for soundness.
3. Check for insulation that's crumbling or fallen away. Look for signs of arcing. Wiggle the wires to look for loose connections. Also wiggle the wires to be sure they aren't broken inside the insulation. Should you find a break, the remaining wire may be long enough to reach the terminal. If so, strip it back about 5/8 inch, being careful not to nick the wire (this is one of the primary causes of fatigue breaks). If the remaining wire is too short to permit a full wrap under the terminal screw, *don't* attempt to splice a piece onto it. Get an electrician to make the repair. (As a general rule, a splice must be made within a UL-approved box that is located so as to be permanently accessible. In some cases, the splice can be within the box that the switch or outlet occupies. It's best to hire an electrician for this, or you may void your fire insurance.)
4. Wrap bare wire and crumbling insulation in electrical tape.
5. Vacuum dust and debris from box.
6. Make sure that sharp end of the metal armor on the BX cable hasn't cut through insulation on the electrical wires.

MAPPING YOUR ELECTRICAL SYSTEM

Most old houses have raggle-taggle electrical systems that have been added onto over the years. Mapping your electrical system will tell you which circuit breaker to pull when you need to turn off power to a fixture, what other outlets and fixtures will be affected when you need to kill power to do some electrical work, and when a fuse blows, you'll know immediately which fuse or circuit breaker to check.

To make your map, make a floor plan of each room in the house in a three-ring binder, one room per page. On each floor plan show the position of each outlet, light fixture, and appliance.

Now determine by trial and error which fuse or circuit breaker controls each outlet or device. With an assistant shouting down to the cellar to tell you whether the parlor chandelier goes out when you throw breaker #5, you should have the entire house mapped in no time. If you're working alone, plug a radio into the various outlets and listen for it to go off as you pull fuses. For ceiling lights and wall sconces, you can use a screw-in socket/plug adapter and plug your radio-assistant into the various light sockets.

New circuit breaker panels should have numbers on them already. With an old fuse box, you may have to assign numbers to the fuses. Note on your map the number of the fuse or circuit breaker that controls it.

The floor plans show your electrical system room by room. Now create a cross-referenced list of the system, circuit by circuit. Assign a separate notebook page to each circuit breaker or fuse. Then, going through your room maps, list each outlet and fixture that is controlled by that breaker. A further refinement: List the wattage of each appliance on each circuit. Add the total wattage on each circuit and divide by the nominal voltage (120). This gives the total amperage load on the circuit. In the example, circuit #9 has a potential load of 20.63 amps. Since this is a 20-amp circuit breaker, the circuit would be overloaded if all appliances were used at once.

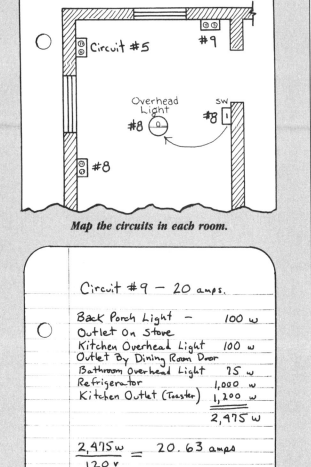

Map the circuits in each room.

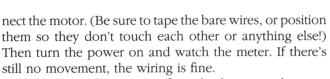

List the loads on each circuit.

Now go watch your electric meter for at least a minute. (The perforated aluminum disc turning under the meter's glass indicates current consumption. The more electricity you use, the faster the rotor turns. Most rotor discs are graduated into 100 divisions around the rim.) If the rotor doesn't move even one small division, you know that all the energized wires are secure. If any fixtures are operated by multiple switches, such as a hall light operated from two locations, flip each switch individually, checking the meter each time.

To check out your water-heater circuit, turn the thermostat down, or wait until the water comes up to the set temperature. In either case, you want to be sure the heater isn't drawing current. Then check your meter for rotor movement.

To check the wiring on remote-switched devices, such as an attic fan with its on/off switch in the kitchen, turn off the power at the breaker panel. Then, go up and discon-

nect the motor. (Be sure to tape the bare wires, or position them so they don't touch each other or anything else!) Then turn the power on and watch the meter. If there's still no movement, the wiring is fine.

If the rotor does move, first check to see that you haven't forgotten to unplug something, like a freezer in the cellar, or a closet light. Now isolate the circuits that are drawing power.

First, remove all line fuses or open all circuit breakers. This disconnects all circuits. If the meter still moves, the leakage is in the breaker panel, main switch, or related wiring. The best bet here is to call in an electrician.

But if the rotor is stationary after disconnecting all the circuits, connect one circuit at a time and watch for rotor movement. As soon as you find a circuit that makes the rotor move, mark it and disconnect it again. Even if you isolate one leaking circuit, continue the checking process. You may find additional circuits with problems.

Repairing faulty wiring is relatively simple. Suppose your bad line serves three outlets and two wall switches, and that the two switches operate a chandelier and a porch light. Turn the power off, and inspect the switches, outlets, and light fixtures. Usually, the bad insulation will be in the last few inches of wire attached to the terminal.

Remove the covers from the outlets and switches, and pull the outlet or switch well out of the box so you can see the wires.

Curing Crumbling Insulation

Sometimes crumbling insulation can be repaired simply by wrapping the bared wires with electrical tape. Often, however, the crumbling continues back into the cable connector where you can't see it—or tape it. While an electrician might advise you to totally replace the old wiring—doubtless the best solution, but also quite expensive—a less expensive solution can add years to the life of your present wiring. Depending on local codes, you may have to leave these procedures to a licensed electrician. But if your electrical code permits, you can complete these simple repairs.

The insulation inside the casing of BX (metal armored) cable is invariably in better shape than the insulation that's been exposed to the air for many years. So to get wire with good insulation, it's usually possible to make use of cable already in the wall.

There should be slack in the BX cable leading to the electrical box. You can cut off the deteriorated segment and reconnect the newly exposed wire to the box. Here's how:

1. Turn off the power at the fuse box.

2. Chip away any plaster overlapping the edges of the electrical box.

3. Remove the fasteners that hold the box in place and pull the box and cable away from the wall.

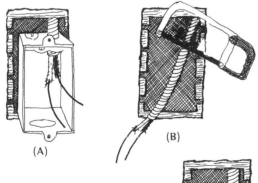
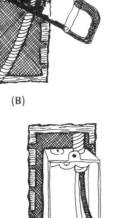

(a) *Step 3. Pull the box and cable away from the wall.*
(b) *Step 5. Cut off the BX armor with a hacksaw.* (c) *Step 7. Push freshly exposed wire back into the box and tighten the clamp.*

4. Remove the end of the cable from the box by loosening the screw on the cable clamp.

5. Pull slack cable out of the wall and cut 12 inches off the BX armor with a hacksaw. Be careful not to cut into the insulation in the wires!

6. Insert red anti-short collar between end of the armor and the wires. You can probably reuse the old collar.

7. Snip off the deteriorated wire. Insert freshly exposed wire back into the box and tighten the cable clamp.

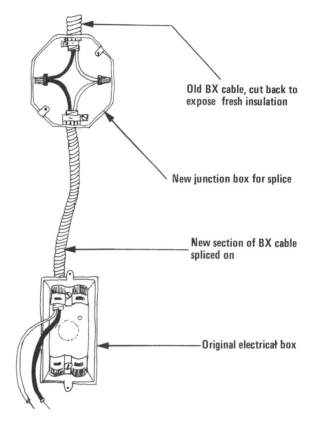

Old BX cable, cut back to expose fresh insulation

New junction box for splice

New section of BX cable spliced on

Original electrical box

8. Fasten box back in place and patch plaster as necessary.

If you don't have enough slack cable, you can disconnect the existing electrical box and cut back the BX cable as described above. Then install a junction box and splice in a short piece of new BX cable as shown.

Another way to fix the problem if you don't have enough slack is to use the existing old cable to guide and pull an entirely new section of cable through the wall. To carry out this procedure, you have to first find which box holds the other end of the cable. It assumes, too, that the old cable isn't being held someplace along its length with staples or plaster that would prevent its being pulled smoothly through the wall.

ROUTING WIRING

You and your electrician should decide how many circuits you need, where switchboxes should be located, and on other wiring issues. But whether you run the cable yourself or coach your electrician, a little planning and preparation will save you a lot of time and headaches.

Ideally, your house will contain unobstructed voids running from the basement to each floor above. Take the time to find these spaces now. Check for the following:

• Pipe chases. Check plumbing to bathrooms, kitchens, and radiators. Waste pipes are vented to the roof, so they run the entire height of the building.

• Abandoned air ducts. Houses once heated with hot air will have unused ducts running through the walls. In city row houses, these can usually be found in the brick common walls.

• Dumbwaiters. Reopening a dumbwaiter will provide a beeline to the floor on which you're working.

• Ventilation shafts. Though most shafts don't run all the way to the basement, they are helpful for running wiring between upper floors.

• Voids next to chimneys. The framing around interior chimneys frequently has ample space to run wiring.

Planning the Route

You'll route wiring either parallel to the studs or joists, or perpendicular to them. You must also be able to cross from a wall to a ceiling. Consider the type of framing the building has. If the house has balloon framing, vertical runs through walls will have fewer interruptions; a house with platform framing has plates and sills that impede vertical runs at each ceiling and floor. Find out which way the joists run, and if they change direction anywhere.

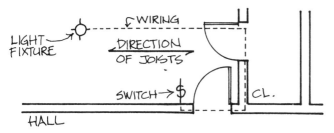

Run wiring parallel or perpendicular to the joists.

Now consider what is above, below, and behind the area being wired. If there is a cellar, attic, or other unfinished space above or below, *that* is where to make your horizontal runs. If there are closet interiors, garages, or other unfinished spaces adjacent to the area being wired, take advantage of them for vertical runs. Neat patching is not critical in unfinished spaces. Also look for mouldings that could be used to conceal wiring. Baseboards, window aprons, and other mouldings can be easily removed to route electrical cable behind them. When the mould-

TIPS ON FISHING

• Fish have a pronounced curve in them because they are stored rolled up. You can use this to your advantage. If the fish gets stuck on an obstacle, just withdraw it a bit, turn it over, and press on. The end of the fish will now rest against the opposite surface and bypass the obstruction.

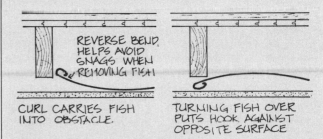

• Helpers are perhaps your most useful resource when fishing wire. It's definitely a two-person job, especially when you're going between floors.

• Sometimes, try as you may, you won't be able to get the fish around an obstacle. After you've spent a reasonable amount of time struggling with the fish, open a small hole in the plaster at the point where the fish is hung up. There's no point in getting frustrated and angry for two hours, just to save an hour's worth of plaster repair.

• When you're notching studs or joists, you should try to avoid breaking any lath. Careful work with a key-hole saw and chisel will allow you to remove two half-sections of lath, allowing plenty of room to pass the cable while maintaining the integrity of the lath framework.

ings are reinstalled, they conceal the wire without the need for plaster patching.

Running Parallel to Studs

Neatly cut a hole in plaster where you plan to locate your switch, outlet, box, or fixture; cut a second hole where the power source is located. Attach the wire to the loop on the end of the fish, and pull the fish back through. A reverse bend on the end of the loop will keep the fish from getting snagged while being withdrawn.

To run wire from one floor to another, start by removing the baseboard on the upper floor. Use a bit extender and spade bit to bore a hole through the top plate in the partition wall of the floor below. Then, neatly cut a hole in the plaster wall about 6 inches from the ceiling of the lower floor, or at the firestop, if one exists. Insert your fish through the hole in the plate, and pass it to the hole in the wall of the floor below. Attach the wire to the fish and pull up to the floor above. Cut a hole at the bottom of the top wall so you can continue to run the cable up. Now notch the floor plate on the upper floor and staple the wire into the notch. The reinstalled baseboard will conceal most of the damage.

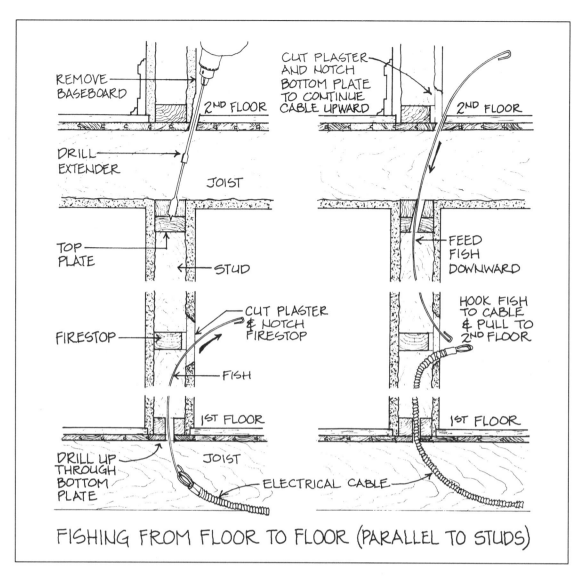

FISHING FROM FLOOR TO FLOOR (PARALLEL TO STUDS)

Running Perpendicular to Studs

Occasionally, you'll have to run wire across the framing members within a wall or ceiling. On walls this can be done behind the baseboard. You can bring the wire down to the baseboard with a simple vertical run, carve a channel in the plaster behind the baseboard, notch the studs, string the wire across, and run the wire back up with another simple vertical run. When you're finished, most of the mess is covered by the baseboard.

If you can't run wire horizontally behind the baseboard or other concealing moulding, or if you're running wire across the joists in a ceiling, cut a small hole in the plaster at each stud. Notch the studs or joists, and fish the cable one section at a time across the wall or ceiling. This also applies when you encounter solid blocking or firestops while running parallel with studs or joists.

While running horizontally across a wall, you may encounter a door, window, or other obstacle. If you hit a door, you can remove the casing and run the wire between the jamb and framing studs. Spacer blocks between the jamb and stud may have to be notched. With win-

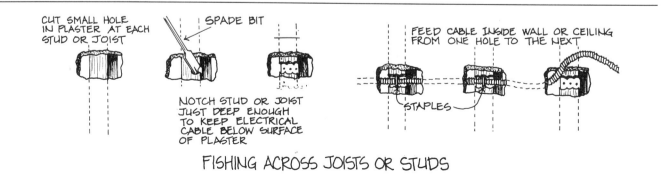

FISHING ACROSS JOISTS OR STUDS

dows, you can remove the interior casing, run the wire down under the apron, and back up the other side. If the original plasterer did a meticulous job, you may have to cut channels in the plaster under the wood trim.

Wall-to-Ceiling Connection

If you're running wire from a wall switch to a ceiling fixture, there are two ways to round the corner at the ceiling wall connection. If there is no ornamental plaster work to go around, you can simply cut a hole in the wall and ceiling at the corner. Pull the wire through, cut a notch in the plate and staple the wire in place, and patch the plaster.

If you have to avoid cutting holes at the corners because of an ornamental plaster cornice, you can use the two-fish method to round the corner. It takes time and patience but not as much as repairing ornate plasterwork. The procedure is as follows:

1. Cut holes in the plaster on the flat parts of the wall and ceiling.

2. Remove the base-board on the floor above the ceiling and drill through the plate with a spade bit on an extender.

3. Push a long fish down through the hole in the plate and work through the hole in the plaster wall.

4. Insert a second fish through the hole in the ceiling and push it through until it contacts the first fish.

5. Work the second fish back and forth until it snags the first fish. This step will require some patience.

6. Withdraw the ceiling fish until the wall fish appears at the ceiling opening.

7. Attach the wire to the fish and pull it through as usual.

MOUNTING A CEILING MEDALLION; HANGING A CHANDELIER

Not many electricians can delicately run wire past ornate plaster. Here are three typical situations and their solutions for installing a new ceiling medallion or replacing one that was ripped out in a previous remuddling.

New Plaster Medallion; Existing Electrical Box

Check the local code, but you probably won't need an electrician to hook up the chandelier wires to the electrical box. Most codes specify that the face of the box be flush with the medallion. A sleeve extender on the existing electrical box can accomplish this. As plaster is not combustible (foam polymer medallions *are*), face-mounting the box is not necessary for safety's sake.

To mount the new plaster medallion do the following:

1. The center hole in the medallion must be larger than a 4-inch round box. To enlarge the hole, drill small holes in the required circle, and cut out with a saber saw.

2. Locate and mark ceiling joists. Practice-fit the medallion, marking points where it will sit under the joists.

3. Predrill and coun-

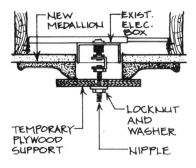

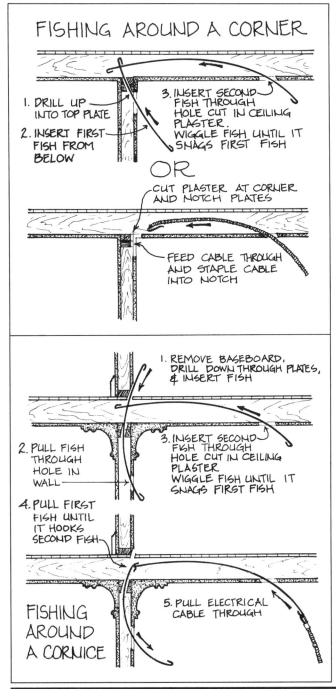

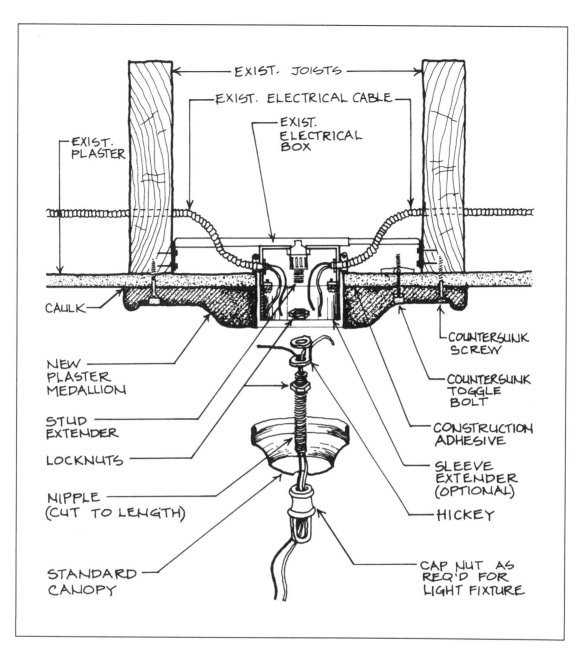

EXIST. JOISTS

EXIST. ELECTRICAL CABLE

EXIST. ELECTRICAL BOX

EXIST. PLASTER

CAULK

NEW PLASTER MEDALLION

STUD EXTENDER

LOCKNUTS

NIPPLE (CUT TO LENGTH)

STANDARD CANOPY

COUNTERSUNK SCREW

COUNTERSUNK TOGGLE BOLT

CONSTRUCTION ADHESIVE

SLEEVE EXTENDER (OPTIONAL)

HICKEY

CAP NUT AS REQ'D FOR LIGHT FIXTURE

tersink holes in the medallion so screws will hit the joists. For extra support for large medallions, also drill for toggle bolts that will hang on the ceiling plaster.

4. If the ceiling is painted, sand it to provide a firm base for the glue. (Sand it to bare plaster if the paint is thick and cracking or it's flaking.)

5. Apply construction adhesive to the back of the medallion.

6. Use a brace suspended from the box to hold the medallion as the screws are being set, or use a T-brace set on the floor.

7. Drive the screws into the joist snugly, but not so tight that the plaster cracks.

8. Use acrylic caulk to seal the edges of medallion; spackle the screw holes.

9. Fixtures over 10 pounds must hang from a stud in the bottom of box. Hook it up as shown.

Existing Medallion; Existing Gas Pipe

When an old gas pipe protrudes through the center of the medallion, hang the fixture from the gas pipe. First be sure the gas pipe is secure enough to bear the weight. Use the following procedure in this situation:

1. Disconnect the gas to the gas pipe. (You may need a licensed plumber for this step.)

2. If there's a cap on the end of the pipe, remove it.

3. Run any required electrical cable to the medallion. If necessary, widen the hole around the gas pipe to pull the cable through.

4. Connect the cable to a shallow box (1/2 inch deep) and slide the box onto the gas pipe.

5. Hold the box firmly against the medallion with a collar adapted from an EMT (electrical metallic tubing)

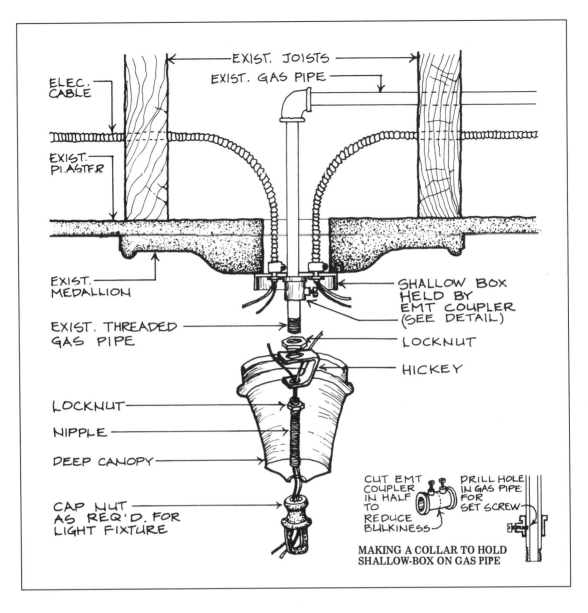

EXIST. JOISTS

EXIST. GAS PIPE

ELEC. CABLE

EXIST. PLASTER

EXIST. MEDALLION

EXIST. THREADED GAS PIPE

SHALLOW BOX HELD BY EMT COUPLER (SEE DETAIL)

LOCKNUT

HICKEY

LOCKNUT

NIPPLE

DEEP CANOPY

CAP NUT AS REQ'D. FOR LIGHT FIXTURE

CUT EMT COUPLER IN HALF TO REDUCE BULKINESS

DRILL HOLE IN GAS PIPE FOR SET SCREW

MAKING A COLLAR TO HOLD SHALLOW-BOX ON GAS PIPE

MINIMIZING LOSS OF ORNATE PLASTER

When installing a new electrical box in an ornate plaster ceiling you'll have to demolish some of the plaster. Here's how to minimize plaster loss:

1. Cut a 4-inch round hole in the ceiling with a key-hole saw. That's just big enough so that with a long screwdriver you can screw a 4-hole fixture stud to the underside of the *floor* above.

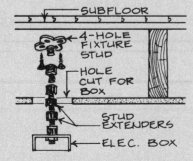

SUBFLOOR

4-HOLE FIXTURE STUD

HOLE CUT FOR BOX

STUD EXTENDERS

ELEC. BOX

2. Attach the stud extender nipples to the fixture stud until you can mount a 4-hole round box flush with the ceiling plaster.

coupler. If the hole in the medallion is so big that the box slides up the pipe into the ceiling, provide backing by attaching another EMT collar *above* the box.

6. Attach a hickey that fits the threads on the gas pipe.

7. Hang the fixture from the gas pipe as illustrated. Use a 5-inch-deep canopy to cover the box, pipe, and electrical connections.

New Polymer Medallion; New Electrical Box

Foam polymer medallions are combustible, so be sure to have the electrical box come out to the face of the medallion. That way, all electrical connections are safely enclosed in metal. Here's how to hang a polymer medallion and a chandelier:

1. Open the ceiling to install a hanger bar.

2. With stud extender nipples and/or a box sleeve, extend a 4-inch round box so it will be level with the surface of the medallion.

3. Connect the cables to the box; patch the ceiling.

4. Cut a 4-inch diameter hole in the center of the medallion.

5. Tack the medallion in place with finish nails or screws driven into the joists. (Polymer is lighter than plaster; no adhesive is necessary.)

6. Spackle the screw holes; seal the edge of the medallion with acrylic caulk.

7. Hang chandelier as shown.

PERIOD LIGHTING FIXTURES: 1880–1930

When electricity began to be used in homes for lighting, designers no longer had to deal with fuel pipes, fuel wells, and other accoutrements of gas, oil, and kerosene fixtures; they were free to create lighting in virtually any shape or material that struck their fancy. Electricity sparked what has been called the single most creative period in the annals of domestic lighting—an incredibly inventive period that produced lights that were extraordinarily imaginative, if at times bizarre.

If you're looking for lighting fixtures for your turn-of-the-century house, there are three things to keep in mind. The most important is the year your house was built. A house constructed circa 1900 originally would have had fixtures that look a lot different from those in a house constructed in the 1920s, or even 1910. A second consideration is the style of your house. Although homeowners were far from pedantic about putting only, say, Arts and Crafts fixtures in their Craftsman house, you certainly can't go wrong by letting house style guide your choice of fixtures. And turn-of-the-century Americans were most fussy about fixtures for their living rooms and dining rooms. For kitchens, bathrooms, and basements, they made do with more functional lights.

The earliest electric lights looked a lot like gaslights, and for good reason. In its infancy, from the early 1880s until about 1910, electricity was not the most reliable energy source, and gas companies lost no time telling homeowners it was only prudent to have both gas and electric fixtures. Fixture manufacturers began supplying lights that made use of both energy sources.

Like typical late nineteenth-century gas fixtures, the

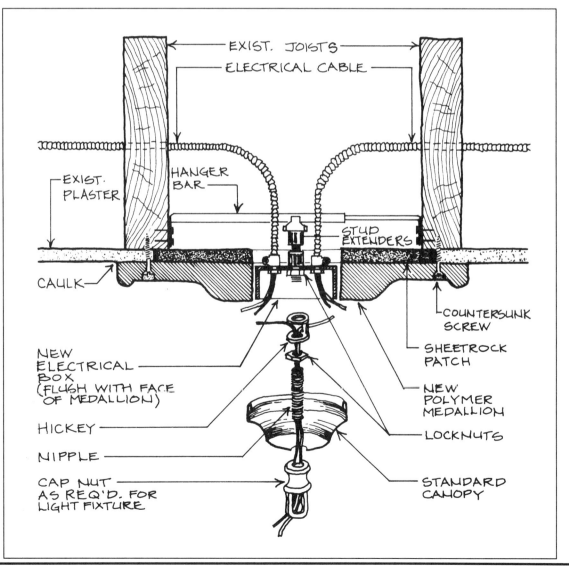

combination fixtures, called *gasolier-electroliers* when they hung from the ceiling, consisted of metal fuel pipes and fuel wells and decorative glass bowls to diffuse the light. The one concession to the Electric Age was a redesigned bell-shaped glass shade more in keeping with the contours of the electric light bulb. While the larger gas globes faced up, the bell-shaped shades were angled down.

As the gas component of the fixture became little more than an emergency feature, gas "candles" began replacing the large gas bowls. Reflecting the eclectic tastes in interior decorating, the combination gas/electric fixtures were available in a plethora of period styles, from Greek to Empire to Colonial.

From the beginning, some intrepid souls were willing to risk all-electric fixtures in their houses. A favorite fixture was a bare bulb, either screwed into a plain socket or dangling from a wire attached to the ceiling. This quintessential, functional fixture continued to be standard in many interiors well into the 1920s, especially in kitchens, bathrooms, and other utilitarian rooms. After 1910, when the intensely bright tungsten-filament bulb became available, these fixtures often had frosted bowls or globes to soften the light.

Since hanging light fixtures were impractical in the low-ceilinged interiors of many early twentieth-century houses, manufacturers came up with truncated fixtures, including *pan lights*. Pan lights, flush-mounted ceiling fixtures with bare bulbs, were popular in bedrooms and less formal family rooms from about 1910 to 1930.

If your house was built after 1910, it should be restored with lighting fixtures intended exclusively for electricity, unless there's solid evidence that electricity was not yet available; in most areas, however, it was. In fact, as early as 1900, electricity had become so dependable and so widespread that all-electric fixtures, or *electroliers,* began replacing the gas-electric styles. But manufacturers were reluctant to design anything too drastic, so early electroliers looked virtually the same as their gas-electric counterparts, with "gas" pipes, fuel wells, and all.

About 1905, manufacturers began to venture from the rigid, pipe-style suspension of the old gaslights. Flexible chain suspension became the rage, and so did *shower fixtures*—fixtures consisting of a number of electric lights hanging by chains from a plate attached to the ceiling.

But it was the tungsten-filament bulb that really revolutionized electric lighting. Glare was always a bit of a problem with the downward-facing bulbs of most electroliers. "Eye strain!" became the battle cry of champions of the "indirect" lighting fixtures that appeared around 1908 and worked by reflecting light off the ceiling. There was a brief flurry of true indirect fixtures circa 1910–1915, opaque bowls suspended from chains. But most "indirect" fixtures in the 1910s and the 1920s were really semi-indirect. The translucent bowls used in these fixtures reflected light off the ceiling and also cast it directly downward. There were also hybrid bowl-and-shower fixtures and bowl-and-chandelier designs.

Art Nouveau

The flexibility of electric wiring and the development of new materials like Louis Comfort Tiffany's handmade opalescent glass for lamp shades coincided with turn-of-the-century design movements, resulting in some exquisite lighting fixtures—*and* some real howlers.

Art Nouveau, a style inspired by nature, particularly the plant world, was the first design movement to sweep the lighting industry off its feet. Art Nouveau's most prominent practitioner was Louis Comfort Tiffany, whose lamps, with spectacular leaded-glass shades, were first offered to the public in 1895. His most famous masterpieces, including the wisteria lamp, were created by 1900.

Suddenly, mass-produced fixtures in the form of lilies, morning glories, and tulips were in virtually every American parlor. The light bulb was the flower bud, shades and sockets were the leaves and petals, and other parts of the fixture functioned as vines, stems, and trunks. One hybrid table lamp was comprised of a female form sprouting leaves and blossoms. This came to be called the *femme-fleur.*

The most common mass-produced Art Nouveau lighting fixture between 1900 and 1920 was the *husk,* a stem-like socket for an exposed light bulb "bud." In more elaborate variations on the theme, multiple husks, clutching their light bulbs, dangled from the chains of shower fixtures.

Art Nouveau aesthetics, once popularized, then resulted in "art glass" table lamps and ceiling fixtures, but these weren't as painstakingly designed and detailed as their high-style Tiffany prototypes. Many were edged with deep, beaded fringe.

Art-glass fixtures were *de rigueur* from about 1900 to 1915. By 1913, Elsie de Wolfe, decorator for the rich and famous, was turning up her nose at this "vulgar fashion of having a huge mass of colored glass and beads suspended from near-brass chains in the dining rooms of certain [read "middle class"] apartments and houses."

Arts and Crafts

While *femme-fleurs* and those "dreadful domes," as Elsie de Wolfe called art-glass ceiling fixtures, were appearing in dining rooms and living rooms across the country, Arts and Crafts designers were trying, in Gustav Stickley's words, "to place within the reach of the middle class purchaser, articles of practical use, which are at the same time, works of art." The sparsely ornamented geometric outlines of Arts and Crafts furnishings were a stark contrast to Art Nouveau's wavy lines and stylized ornament in floral and female forms.

Stickley believed that lighting was of utmost importance in the Craftsman interior, and his fixtures, made mostly of hammered copper (though iron, brass, and fumed oak were also used), were rough-finished to avoid a highly polished, machine-made look. The metalwork designs were rarely very intricate, since Stickley urged his readers to make the fixtures themselves at home. The

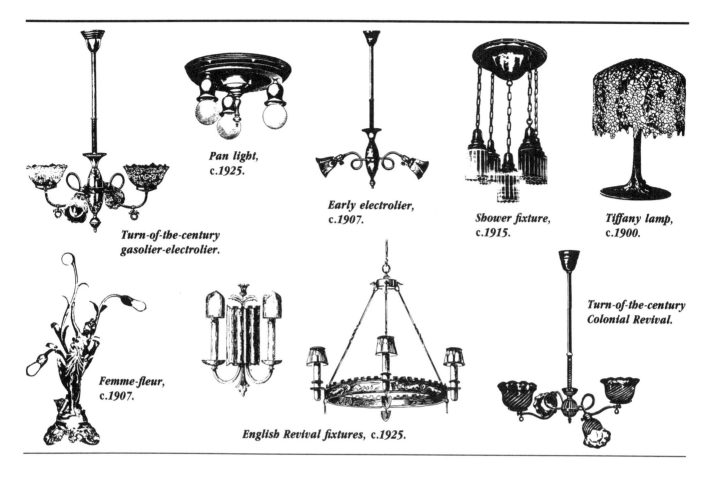

Pan light,
c.1925.

Early electrolier,
c.1907.

Shower fixture,
c.1915.

Tiffany lamp,
c.1900.

Turn-of-the-century
gasolier-electrolier.

Femme-fleur,
c.1907.

Turn-of-the-century
Colonial Revival.

English Revival fixtures, c.1925.

shades on Craftsman and other Arts and Crafts lighting fixtures were made of mica, colored glass, or woven willow.

A favorite Craftsman method of lighting a room was to hang lanterns from exposed ceiling beams, with sconces on each side of the recessed windowseat. Table lamps were designed to burn oil, but Stickley, California-based Dirk Van Erp, and other Arts and Crafts designers also made electrified table lamps. A favorite Craftsman way to light the dining room was to use a row of lanterns hanging from the beam above the dining table.

English Revival

Like Arts and Crafts interiors, the English Revival interiors of the Tudor Revivals, English Cottages, and English Country Houses so popular in America between about 1900 and 1930 were based on simplicity. "There is no pretense about the English House," wrote Curtis and Companies in their 1920 mail-order catalog. "Its charm lies in its informality and its simplicity. It is built for comfort, not for show."

Timbered ceilings were a hallmark of English Revival interiors. Large, circular, wrought-iron or bronze chandeliers, recalling those found in the medieval English houses that were the prototypes of this revival style, were hung from the exposed beams or rafters. However, these medieval-looking chandeliers usually held round electric light bulbs, not candles.

Candlestick-style sconces, also electrified, often il-

luminated the paneled rooms that were another common feature of the Tudor Revival house. The Tudor sconce and "Early English" ceiling fixture were designed by M. Luckiesh, director of General Electric's Lighting Research Laboratory. He added parchment shades to both fixtures to minimize glare from their electric bulbs.

Colonial Revival

By the turn of the century, there was afoot a great patriotic feeling that America should have her own house style. Most historians trace this change of heart back to the New England log-house kitchen, complete with spinning wheel and candlesticks, that was exhibited at the 1876 Centennial Exhibition in Philadelphia. The Georgian style became the symbolic house of America—no matter that it was imported wholesale from England; by the 1890s, it had been here long enough to be considered native.

Early Colonial Revival houses often had Victorian massing, with a few Colonial details grafted on. The average interior probably had neo-Georgian woodwork, painted white, with perhaps a reproduction Windsor chair and a spinning wheel in the midst of Victorian clutter. The Colonial Revival gas-electric fixtures in these houses were also essentially Victorian, with a veneer of Early America in their scrolled arms and garland motifs. Some wealthy Americans, however, were doing painstaking restorations and using antique eighteenth-century lighting fixtures or faithful reproductions.

Colonial Revival houses of the 1920s and 1930s in-

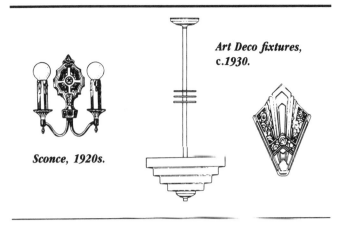

Art Deco fixtures, c.1930.

Sconce, 1920s.

cluded their own, all-electric versions of eighteenth-century lighting fixtures. Colonial-looking "chandeliers" with electric light bulbs, not candles, were favorite dining room fixtures. Electrified candlesticks and sconces were also extremely popular. So were "Colonialized" generic fixtures such as hanging bowls and showers.

Art Deco

By the mid-1920s, Art Deco, America's first industrial design vocabulary, was catching on. During Deco's heyday, objects in the streamlined style could be found in every room, closet, and cabinet—and hanging from the ceiling or wall.

Art Deco kitchens and bathrooms were particularly slick, sleek showcases of the style. Deco baths were often clad in gleaming Vitrolite in patterns of different color. Bullet-shaped faucet handles, angular shower heads, and futuristic lighting fixtures added to the Deco look.

Light Switches and Bulbs

Early wall, ceiling, and table fixtures were operated by a *key-type switch* built into the fixture (similar to lamp sockets today). In the 1880s, builders began encasing the wires in specially designed wood or metal mouldings attached to the wall. A few of these disguised circuits used porcelain-covered knife switches on the wall. Then the surface-mounted *rotary-snap switch* made its debut.

As the 1890s approached, the *push-button switch* was introduced. This switch was soon the most heavily promoted of all residential switches (those used in 110-volt circuits), and remained the most popular switch for the next forty or fifty years.

Most electrical systems in use at the time utilized DC. Direct current has the effect of "holding onto" something once it comes in contact. That made it necessary to design spring-loaded switches so that a certain amount of tension could build up before causing the blades to "snap" away from the contacts quickly enough to avoid drawing out a long and potentially dangerous arc. This resulted in the distinctive click or "snapping" sound—a sound some find as nostalgic as the slam of a screen door.

The trade catalogs of 1898 showed a selection of tumble switches, the great-granddads of today's toggle switch. They apparently did not gain the popularity of the push-button switch until after AC became the standard. It would seem that breaking the hold of DC was more easily accomplished by pushing than by lifting with the side of a finger. But, sometime before World War II, the industry decided that the elaborate mechanisms were becoming too costly and unnecessary. For whatever reasons, the tumble switch was the one chosen to be redesigned and made practical and compatible with the new wiring codes. Except for farm and some industrial applications, DC was all but superseded as the war began. In the mid-1950s, Leviton Electrical Co. produced the last of their push-buttons.

The restoration boom of the 1970s created a new interest in the push-button switch. In 1985, Peter Brevoort of Michigan began manufacturing new push-button switches that he and an electrical engineer had redesigned to meet all modern codes. The new switches retain the same outward appearance—and the mandatory *snap* of the originals.

You can order push-button switches and compatible switch plates from Classic Accents, P.O. Box 1181, Dept. OHJ, Southgate, MI 48195; (313)282-5525.

The incandescent light bulb evolved in stages too. At first, glass envelopes were hand-blown, and even after machine manufacturing took over, they remained "tipped" (with a small point at the head of the bulb, rather than rounded), and unfrosted until the 1920s. The light changed as well, growing whiter and brighter as better filaments were invented.

Edison's bulb was typical of most light bulbs up to the turn of the century. Its carbon filament gave off yellow-orange light at roughly the intensity of today's 25-watt bulb.

GEM lamps (for General Electric Metalized) appeared in 1905, with an improved filament that burned about 30 percent brighter than carbon alone, and didn't blacken the envelope as it aged. These were sold for twenty-five years at 25 cents per bulb.

Tungsten filament bulbs were widely available by 1911, and had more than double the light output of the GEM lamps. They were produced with clear envelopes (both tipped and untipped) and characteristic zigzag filaments into the 1930s.

Early electric fixtures were often designed specifically for the bulbs of the era, and so become overly bright with modern bulbs. To simulate the old-bulb look, you can use low-wattage ornamental or special-purpose bulbs that are unfrosted. You can also reduce the light output of lamps or chandeliers with a dimmer.

Reproduction period light bulbs with carbon and tungsten filaments are available from Bradford Consultants, P.O. Box 4020, Dept. OHJ, Alameda, CA 94501; (415)523-1968.

Energy

Y ou don't have to resign yourself to high fuel bills and some measure of discomfort if you suffer from a love of old houses. Often you can significantly reduce your fuel bill and increase your comfort level simply by spending a modest amount of cash and a lot of time on weatherizing.

Though "weatherization" is a relatively new word, coined in the 1970s, the concept is one that the folks who built old houses were well aware of. After the early years of settlement, firewood was a scarce and expensive commodity. Houses were designed and built to use a minimum of it. Hence the compact, center-chimney saltboxes of New England with no north-facing windows, or the urban row housing of Boston or New York, with thick masonry party walls.

Conversely, in warmer climates, homes were built to minimize solar gain from the summer sun. Exterior balconies, porches and wide roof overhangs, awnings, and shade trees were typical features of early Southern housing. Second floor living spaces to catch breezes and escape the radiant heat of the ground were also incorporated. Early Northern structures tended to have dark-hued exteriors to absorb the winter sun; those of the South were painted in light colors to reflect the summer sun. Old-house owners should understand these inherent energy-saving qualities and take advantage of them.

Here we'll review some of the ways to make your old house more comfortable and less expensive to heat and cool.

GET AN ENERGY AUDIT

T o evaluate the energy efficiency of your old house, arrange for an "energy audit." Many utilities offer this service at little or no cost. Utility audits are no substitute, however, for your own detailed inspection. Audits are geared toward newer housing and emphasize heating systems, window replacements, and capital investments rather than the nitty-gritty sorts of things that are far more cost-effective.

Heat is lost through two processes: infiltration and conduction. Infiltration is air movement through cracks and joints (drafts). Conduction is heat transfer through materials. The greatest heat loss through conduction occurs via window glass. Weatherstripping and caulking limits infiltration; insulating and installing storm windows slows conduction.

LIMITING INFILTRATION

A nti-infiltration work is the heart and soul of weatherization. It's very time-consuming, picky work, and it requires a thorough knowledge of how your house is put together (it's a great way to learn). It has the best payback of any measure you can take. Caulking is the number one priority for stopping infiltration, both interior and exterior. Plan on using a couple of cases, maybe more, to do a thorough job. Buying by the case reduces the cost too. (See chapter 7 for instructions on how to caulk.)

Exterior caulking will prevent more water than air infiltration, though it certainly cuts down on drafts. It's part of the preparation for painting, and worth rechecking now unless you've painted very recently. Caulk around all window and door frames (but not under them), where clapboards or shingles meet edge trim, construction joints, and between dissimilar materials, such as brick and wood. Never caulk the spaces under clapboards or shingles; they allow the house to breathe and water vapor to escape from the walls.

While we're outside, a word about the importance of pointing up foundations is in order: An enormous amount of air—not to mention water—infiltrates through

THE ENERGY-EFFICIENT OLD HOUSE

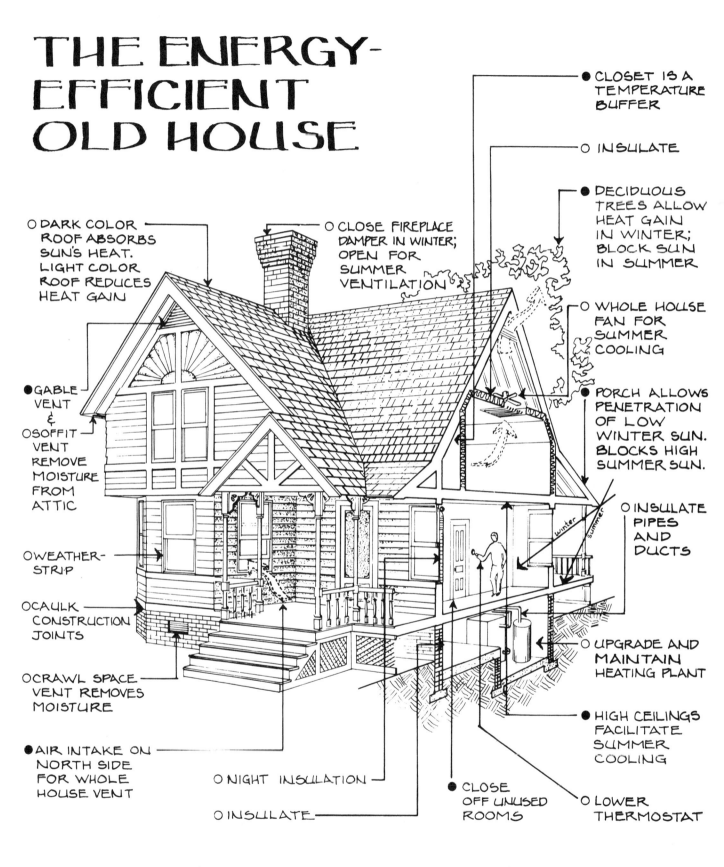

O DARK COLOR ROOF ABSORBS SUN'S HEAT. LIGHT COLOR ROOF REDUCES HEAT GAIN

O CLOSE FIREPLACE DAMPER IN WINTER; OPEN FOR SUMMER VENTILATION

● CLOSET IS A TEMPERATURE BUFFER

O INSULATE

● DECIDUOUS TREES ALLOW HEAT GAIN IN WINTER; BLOCK SUN IN SUMMER

O WHOLE HOUSE FAN FOR SUMMER COOLING

● GABLE VENT & O SOFFIT VENT REMOVE MOISTURE FROM ATTIC

● PORCH ALLOWS PENETRATION OF LOW WINTER SUN. BLOCKS HIGH SUMMER SUN.

O INSULATE PIPES AND DUCTS

O WEATHER-STRIP

winter   summer

O CAULK CONSTRUCTION JOINTS

O UPGRADE AND MAINTAIN HEATING PLANT

O CRAWL SPACE VENT REMOVES MOISTURE

● HIGH CEILINGS FACILITATE SUMMER COOLING

● AIR INTAKE ON NORTH SIDE FOR WHOLE HOUSE VENT

O NIGHT INSULATION

● CLOSE OFF UNUSED ROOMS

O LOWER THERMOSTAT

O INSULATE

THE DETACHED FRAME HOUSE

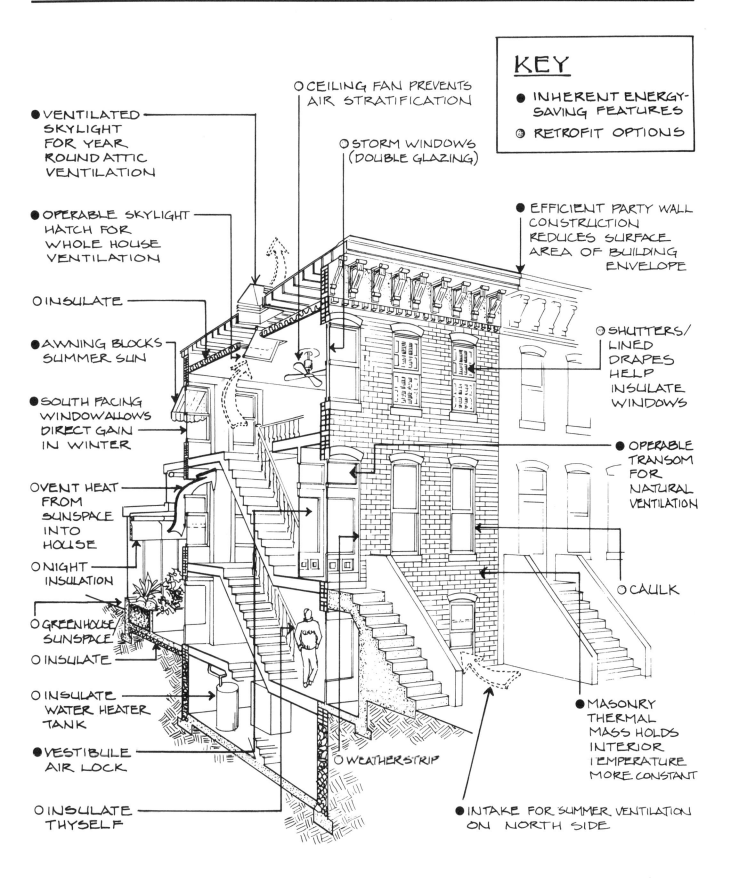

O CEILING FAN PREVENTS
AIR STRATIFICATION

O STORM WINDOWS
(DOUBLE GLAZING)

● VENTILATED
SKYLIGHT
FOR YEAR
ROUND ATTIC
VENTILATION

● OPERABLE SKYLIGHT
HATCH FOR
WHOLE HOUSE
VENTILATION

O INSULATE

● AWNING BLOCKS
SUMMER SUN

● SOUTH FACING
WINDOW ALLOWS
DIRECT GAIN
IN WINTER

O VENT HEAT
FROM
SUNSPACE
INTO
HOUSE

O NIGHT
INSULATION

O GREENHOUSE/
SUNSPACE

O INSULATE

O INSULATE
WATER HEATER
TANK

● VESTIBULE
AIR LOCK

O INSULATE
THYSELF

● EFFICIENT PARTY WALL
CONSTRUCTION
REDUCES SURFACE
AREA OF BUILDING
ENVELOPE

⊙ SHUTTERS/
LINED
DRAPES
HELP
INSULATE
WINDOWS

● OPERABLE
TRANSOM
FOR
NATURAL
VENTILATION

O CAULK

● MASONRY
THERMAL
MASS HOLDS
INTERIOR
TEMPERATURE
MORE CONSTANT

O WEATHERSTRIP

● INTAKE FOR SUMMER VENTILATION
ON NORTH SIDE

THE MASONRY PARTY WALL HOUSE

Limit air (and water) infiltration by pointing up the foundation and repairing damaged siding.

dry stone foundations (common during the nineteenth century) into basements and crawl spaces. A few hours spent with a trowel closing up these holes can make a big difference in comfort and fuel bills.

Now for the inside. Thorough caulking on the interior is often overlooked, yet it is the most effective way to stop air infiltration. (It also helps reduce moisture migration into the walls.) The best time to go sleuthing for drafts is in cold weather, preferably on a windy day. Take along a pad and pencil to note trouble spots and go over all surfaces at close range. No two houses will have exactly the same infiltration spots, but, in general, the following joints should be caulked on the indoor side of all exterior walls:

- Between window and door casings and walls, including tops and under sills
- Joints in window jambs and casings, and the joint between window stop and jamb
- Upper window sash, if stationary
- Joints of baseboards and base mouldings
- Corner joints and joints of boxed beams in post-and-beam construction
- Ceiling-to-wall junctions, including crown moulding joints
- Wall paneling joints, such as where wainscotting meets plaster
- Around ceiling fixtures and penetrations (vent pipes, etc.) on the top floor
- Insides of closets, cupboards, and the like—these spots are often neglected and leak badly

For areas that will not be painted over, use a clear, silicone-based caulk. The results will be virtually invisible if you run a neat bead. For areas you plan to paint, use a high-quality, acrylic-latex caulk. Bargain-grade caulks are no bargain; they'll crack and shrink, and they won't last very long.

Next, seal around electrical boxes. Turn off the circuit and remove the cover plate. If the box is tight to the wall, caulk around it and use a foam gasket under the cover plate. If there's a large gap, use spray foam to seal around the outside of the box.

Sealing Doors

Much of the air leakage in older homes occurs around and through doors and windows that have seen better days. Often weathered, and usually out of square, they give an old house much of its character. Forget all the hype about shiny new, triple-glazed, vinyl-track, super energy-efficient replacement units. The payback on these new doors and windows runs to several generations, and what they take away from the house may never be returned. With some time and care, you can preserve your old doors and windows and make them tight.

Old doors require a lot of work to make them airtight, but it's worth the effort. First of all, the door itself must be in good shape. Getting it that way may involve removing the door, regluing and/or repinning loose joints, adjusting hardware, moving the stops, and, finally, trimming the door to fit so that it latches snugly yet easily (see chapter 13).

Integral-metal and spring metal weatherstrip last the longest, but the materials are rather expensive. A good quality vinyl tube or flap weatherstrip sometimes works just as well. It's available set in either wood or metal.

However, you want to avoid cheap "hardware-store variety" vinyl or vinyl-and-aluminum weatherstrip on doors. Cheap vinyl is usually self-stick, and doesn't adhere well to old, rough woodwork. Inexpensive vinyl-bead weatherstrip that's set in a strip of soft aluminum is just as ineffective. The aluminum is so flexible and the vinyl so rigid that you can't fasten it in enough places to even make contact.

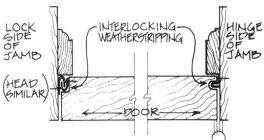

There are two major categories of weatherstripping: interlocking and resilient. Once installed, interlocking weatherstrip becomes an integral part of the door (even visually). It also allows the door to close and latch completely unimpeded. The disadvantage is that it requires carpentry skills to install. The edge of the door must be rabbeted  with a router to receive the weatherstrip, and the two pieces (on the door and jamb) must mate accurately. It could be argued that interlocking weatherstrip does not seal as well as resilient because it doesn't provide continuous contact. The longevity and ease of operation of interlocking weatherstrip outweighs the disadvantage, though.

Resilient weatherstripping (as its name implies) flexes, bends, or compresses somehow as contact is made, thereby sealing the joint. The contact part of the strip must "give" enough to allow the door to shut, yet must be durable. There are six materials to choose from: silicone, EPDM rubber, neoprene, vinyl, wood pile (or synthetic pile), and spring metal.

Silicone and EPDM have the best "memory." They don't permanently compress; they will always return to their original shape. Silicone and EPDM also remain flexible at low temperature.

Neoprene has similar characteristics but is less expensive and less durable. Vinyl is less durable, ages sooner, and becomes less flexible when cold.

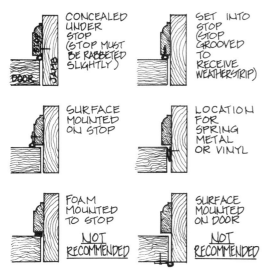

Wool or synthetic pile weatherstrips are better suited for door sweeps than for the jambs because they can span a large gap. For less money, you can buy wool or synthetic *felt*—less resilient than pile.

Spring metal is very durable but can create friction, making the door a little harder to close.

Many products are available for sealing the bottom of the door, but for older houses a quality neoprene sweep that attaches to a mortise in the door can be adjusted to

the slope of the threshold. Particularly useful are the sweeps that operate with a bushing and spring, closing down when the door is shut, and springing up when the door is open. This allows the sweep to clear a carpet or, heaven forbid, a sloping floor.

All bottom seals or sweeps should close against a threshold so they don't have to drag across the floor. There are three basic types of door bottom seals or sweeps: interlocking, resilient, and automatic (drop down).

Interlocking is always a good choice. It does, however, necessitate installing a compatible threshold to receive the hook on the door. Thresholds and hooks are available in bronze or aluminum so they will match your existing door hardware.

Resilient sweeps are available in all of the same materials as resilient head/jamb weatherstrips. (See the illustration for types of resilient door sweeps.) Many different design variations exist; these are most typical.

Automatic door bottoms are the high-tech solution to weatherstripping. They are the most expensive and most difficult to keep properly adjusted. When they are correctly installed and adjusted, they work very nicely. But if they're maladjusted, they can make the door bind or fail to form a good seal. As you shut the door, a button hits the hinge side of the jamb, causing the seal to drop down snugly against the threshold.

Set the sweep so that it just touches the threshold with the door closed. Try the door several times to make sure it closes easily and the weatherstrip contacts all points. Make minor adjustments, resetting the weatherstrip as necessary. When the fit is just right, set the nails, and caulk the joints between the jamb and the stop and the stop and the weatherstrip.

Don't forget the door to the basement, doors into unheated rooms, and the door or hatchway into the attic. Making a new attic hatch and adding a stop may be necessary to get a good seal. Don't neglect this: Heat rises in a chimney effect, and lots of it is lost through loose hatches.

Sealing Windows

Original windows are one of the prime sources of energy loss, because they lose heat by both conduction through glass and infiltration around edges and through joints.

Take the following measures to reduce heat loss through windows:

- Weatherstrip the sash.
- Install storm windows.
- Caulk all joints between fixed parts.
- Install pulley seals.

Caulk all joints to ensure a weathertight seal inside the house.

Pulley slots are a serious source of air leakage. Anderson Pulley Seal remedies the problem. Made of flexible plastic with a self-sealing surface, the pulley seal is unobtrusive, installs easily, and doesn't interfere with operation of the window.

Storm windows are a necessity from a preservation standpoint. (See box.)

INSULATION

Attic or ceiling insulation is a must. Fiberglass batts install easily if the attic is unfloored. Lay the batts, vapor barrier down, between the joists. Butt them tightly together. If the joist spacing is uneven or other than 16 inches or 24 inches on center, try using blown or poured insulation. It will provide more effective coverage than

Rigid insulation partially covered by sheetrock.

First, your windows must be in good shape and properly glazed (see chapter 13). If your windows are in bad enough shape to warrant removal and repair, you might consider installing spring metal or integral weatherstrip. Otherwise, it's not a cost- or time-effective measure. The materials are rather expensive, and rope clay (Mortite, for example) will accomplish the same thing at a fraction of the cost and time spent. If your house is pre-1840, then the upper sash is probably stationary and can be caulked in place.

STORM WINDOWS

Traditionally, storm windows have been installed on the outside of a house to protect the prime window from winter weather—rain, snow, wind, and sleet. Their energy-saving value is chiefly related to conduction. They create a dead air space that slows heat loss through the main window. They are not meant to be completely airtight; in fact, they have weep holes at the bottom to allow moisture to escape.

The old-fashioned wood storm is more efficient than modern aluminum triple tacks—wood is a much better insulator than metal. Wood storms are less convenient, though; they have to be put up and taken down every year, they are inoperable, and they don't have screens. While many preservation purists prefer wood storms, aluminum storms will protect your windows and are perfectly acceptable for old houses according to the Secretary of the Interior's Preservation Guidelines. (They come anodized or enameled in several colors now, so avoid the raw aluminum look.)

Even if you already have storms on the outside, you may want to consider interior storms to maximize energy efficiency. They consist of a rigid aluminum frame, called Bailey or "C" sash, with pile weatherstripping, and either glass or .100 acrylic (a better insulator) in the gasketed frame. Corners can be mitered or square with plastic corners that press in. They're easy to make and can be

Heat-shrunk plastic sheet, or "poor man's storm."

mounted either on top of the window casing or recessed against the stop within the jamb.

When properly installed, interior storms are completely airtight. They eliminate condensation, the primary cause of window deterioration, and they're easily removable, so you can take them down during warm-weather months.

pieced-together batts. Dam around chimneys and electrical boxes (allow a 3-inch clearance).

Attic ventilation—to allow water vapor to escape before it condenses—is usually provided for at gable ends. Metal vents are readily available in a variety of shapes and sizes. But for a period house, it's much more sensitive to fashion a wooden-slat vent (screened on the inside to keep bugs out) that matches the existing trim.

Metal soffit vents, ridge vents, and roof vents are easy to find, though avoid using the latter on an old house, as they will alter the exterior appearance somewhat. Adequate attic ventilation is a must, however, even if it means installing metal vents. Depending on conditions, requirements vary from 150 to 300 square feet of attic space per square foot of vent. Check this out locally.

Wall Insulation

Few weatherization issues cause as much debate as whether or not to blow insulation into the walls of a house without a vapor barrier. While there is no pat answer to this question (with success or failure depending on the construction of the house, the climate, how well the job is done, and other variables), on the whole it seems to reduce fuel bills dramatically with relatively few problems.

In cold climates, wall insulation is a cost-effective weatherization measure. If your house has a wet basement or crawl space, unvented bathroom or kitchen, a clothes dryer vented indoors, or exterior moisture problems caused by plants too close to the house, broken gutters, and so on, *don't insulate.* Remedy all moisture problems *before* blowing the insulation in. After correcting these problems, paint interior surfaces (after caulking) with a vapor barrier paint followed by an oil-base primer or finish coat.

Several kinds of blown-in insulation are available; fiberglass, rock wool, and cellulose are the most common. Cellulose is the most popular because of its lower cost, superior packing properties, and fire resistance. It

Though installing blown-in insulation from the interior side of the wall is not normal practice, it may be an option if there's a lot of plaster damage to be repaired. Here insulation was blown-in from the inside.

will retain moisture and lose some of its insulating value as a result, but if you've remedied all moisture problems, this will be a negligible factor. Foamed-in-place plastics are *not* recommended. All of them have prevalent installation difficulties because the individual contractor has to mix it up on site—so the manufacturing process isn't completed under quality-controlled conditions. There is no way to regulate the mixing of the material, or to know whether the contractor has put in the required amount.

Blowing insulation is not a do-it-yourself project, even though you can rent blowing machines, buy bags of insulation, and attempt the job yourself. You're much better off hiring a reliable contractor, after getting several bids and checking out references, preferably on houses of similar age and framing construction as your own. Understanding framing makes for a good insulation job.

Standard practice calls for drilling holes (1 to 2 inches in diameter) in each wall cavity every 40 inches vertically. Insulation is blown into the holes, the holes are plugged, filled, and primed. If properly done, the work will be nearly invisible.

A better method on clapboard or shingle-sided homes is to carefully remove courses of siding and replace them after blowing. This enables the contractor to probe for hidden obstructions (knee braces, firestops, and the like), and makes for a better looking job. It also gives you an opportunity to check the work for voids and proper pack. Cellulose should be densely compacted in the wall so that there will be little settlement. If properly executed, the insulation will not fall out even if you remove the siding.

RETROFITTING

So far we've assumed that you are dealing with the original walls, ceilings, and exterior siding which, alas, is not always the case where neglected old houses are concerned. While wishing to preserve original material, it's often necessary to remove deteriorated plaster and lath or to replace hopelessly deteriorated siding. This makes it easy to insulate with fiberglass.

If the stud spacing is irregular, use unfaced fiberglass, tightly fitted (it's okay to compress it a bit) and install a polyethylene (plastic) vapor barrier over it, taping all seams, including floor and ceiling, and electrical boxes with duct tape. Then install Sheetrock or rock lath.

If you have narrow stud cavities (many pre-1840 houses have less than 3 inches), or plank walls with no cavities, consider installing rigid foil-faced insulation, such as Thermax or Energy Shield, beneath the inside walls. If you have a narrow wall cavity, fill it with fiberglass batts first, then fasten the rigid insulation to the face of the studs with 2-inch roofing nails. If you're installing it over plank walls, fit it 1 inch away from the wall to provide an air space. One caution: Rigid insulation releases toxic fumes when burned. Local codes may require it be covered with 5/8-inch Sheetrock.

Rigid insulation comes in several thicknesses from 1/2 inch to 2 inches. With the seams properly taped, it forms a very effective vapor barrier, making plastic unnecessary. It has an R value of about 8 per inch, so it's ideal where space is limited. The R value measures the effectiveness of a layer of insulation: the higher the R value, the better the insulation. Assume that existing insulation has an R value of approximately 3 per inch. Thus, 3 inches of existing insulation has an R value of approximately 9. Although you may have to deepen your window jambs, it's worth the extra work in comfort and fuel savings. Do not, however, use it as exterior sheathing. It's a great vapor barrier and will trap moisture in your walls. If you're going to re-side, wrap the exterior in Tyvek, a tough, moisture-permeable sheeting that reduces air infiltration. Siding is simply nailed on top of it.

THE HEATING PLANT

Last, but far from least, we come to the furnace itself. All your efforts to properly insulate your house will come to nothing without an efficient heating system. This is an area for a specialist, of course, but there are a few things you can do to help the system run more efficiently.

DON'T FORGET THE CELLAR

Spending the day in the dingy confines of the cellar bumping your head on pipes and walking into cobwebs is no joy, but it is important. Cellars are often left neglected and can be real trouble spots of efficiency.

First, seal air leaks. Caulk, spray-foam, or point cracks in the foundation, between sill and foundation, and where pipes, wires, and other devices enter the house. Do this on a chilly day so you can use your hand to feel for drafts. If you turn the lights off for a moment, you'll be able to spot minuscule cracks with daylight shining through them. Check windows for proper glazing and weatherstripping.

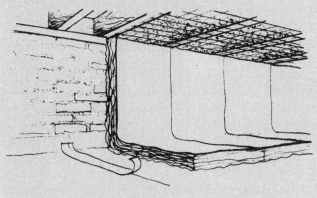

Insulate all around the perimeter with 6-inch faced fiberglass, paper face showing. This will diminish infiltration—it's difficult to seal a cellar by caulking alone. Insulating between the joists with the vapor

barrier up—toward the first floor—will keep your feet warm as you walk around the house. If you have an exterior door or hatchway, make sure it, too, is tight.

Insulating your water heater (if it's more than five years old) and domestic water pipes is a good idea. Rather than buy one of those expensive water-heater jackets, wrap the heater with 3 1/2-inch fiberglass and hold it on with wire. Don't wrap the top or bottom section where the pilot, controls, and vent outlet are. A fire or carbon monoxide poisoning could result.

The best pipe insulation is the extruded-foam kind that comes in 3-foot lengths with a slit down the middle. Duct tape all seams for a tight seal. Insulating cold-water pipes won't save energy, but will prevent sweating in warm weather, if that's a problem for you.

Annual cleaning and tuning of your furnace or boiler saves fuel and headaches down the pike. When you have this done, request an efficiency test and have the technician explain the results to you. You may find the old monster worth replacing. If it's less than 75 percent efficient, investing in a new burner (a Beckett, for example) could raise the efficiency to the 80 to 85 percent range, and pay for itself quickly in a large old house. If your furnace is on its last legs, you should look into the new generation of super-efficient (90 to 95 percent) heating plants that waste so little heat that they require only plastic (PVC) stacks (but check local codes about this). They're more expensive than conventional units but worth investigating.

In oil-fired furnaces, if you have taken any or several of the measures already discussed since your furnace was last tested, you may be able to have the nozzle size on your burner reduced. Nozzles are rated in gallons per hour consumed, and a reduction in nozzle size of 1/2 gph after weatherization is common. If you do down-size the burner nozzle, be sure that all filters on the fuel line are changed at least once a year. The smaller the nozzle, the more easily it is clogged by sediment from the oil tank.

You should also check the flue pipe, the top of the furnace, and the heat-transfer surfaces inside your oil-burning furnace for burnable soot. An accumulation of

unburned carbon indicates incomplete combustion—and is a sure sign that fuel is being wasted.

Some old houses are heated by an old coal stove converted to burn oil. You may have to have the oil burner replaced, de-rate (or down-size) it, and put in a smaller nozzle so you burn less oil. By pumping less oil into the combustion chamber there will be more time for complete combustion to take place. Also, when you burn oil at a lower rate, you supply a lesser volume of air to the furnace. This means that the hot combustion gases will flow through the heat exchanger at a lower velocity—making it possible to extract more usable heat.

When installing a smaller nozzle, you'll have to allow for a too-large combustion chamber. A zero-cost solution is to use some large pieces of firebrick as an inner lining in the existing combustion chamber. Reach through the furnace door (formerly used to feed coal) and lean the pieces of firebrick against the side and back of the combustion chamber.

The extra firebrick continues to glow red for a long time, thus acting as a "thermal flywheel." When the burner starts up again, it doesn't have to heat a cold system.

Your oil-burner technician may warn you that down-sizing the fuel nozzle will cause the burner to "short cycle"; that is, to fire continuously on cold days in an attempt to keep up with the demand of the thermostat. We've found that in most cases the burner will cycle on and off normally, even on days when it's 15 degrees below zero outside.

STEAM-HEATING SYSTEMS

Steam-heating systems present different problems. Steam heating is the oldest form of central heat, dating back to the 1830s. Water is heated in a boiler until it boils. The steam from the boiling water rises through pipes and travels to radiators throughout the building. The cooler metal of a radiator causes the steam to condense back into water, thereby giving off heat. The water returns to the boiler and is there heated once again. (It travels back either via a second pipe or through the same pipe it rose in, depending on the type of steam-heating system that was installed.)

The boiler has several basic attachments: a glass sight gauge, a steam gauge, and a safety valve. Automatic systems will also have a high-pressure limit switch, a blow-off valve, and a low-water-level cut-off switch.

Check the glass sight gauge once a week to make sure that its valves are not clogging. Usually it will have a drain cock at the lower fitting for draining the dirty water in the tube. If the water can't be drained, then the valve is clogged and the unit requires cleaning. (The glass sight gauge is the vertical glass tube located between two valves; it shows the level of water inside the boiler. When cold, the water level should be one-half to two-thirds the

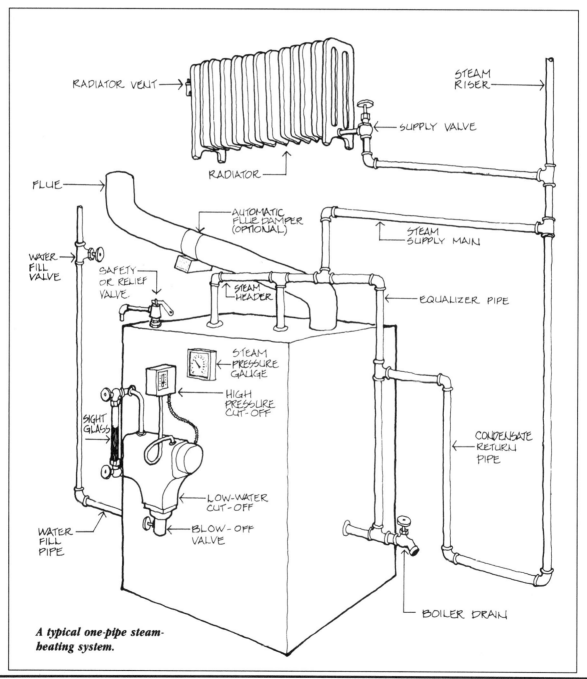

A typical one-pipe steam-heating system.

height of the tube; when hot, the level should be one-third to one-half the height. If there's no water, the boiler is empty or clogged. If empty, shut off the boiler and let it cool for an hour or two, then add water until the gauge shows the proper level.)

To clean the glass sight gauge, empty the boiler. Close the valves above and below the glass. Loosen both brass nuts at top and bottom and remove the sight glass *carefully* (it can break easily) and clean it with ammonia and a round brush. If necessary, take it to a plumbing supply house and have a new one cut (take the brass nuts and get new gaskets as well). Then replace the sight glass and gaskets, making certain that you open the valves and refill the boiler.

The *steam gauge* is the meter with a little arrow. In units of pounds per square inch it measures the steam pressure in the top of the boiler. (Some gauges will have a negative reading scale to indicate a vacuum at the top.) The larger the boiler, the higher its normal reading will be. Average residential service is usually from 0 to 5 psi; about 12 psi is marked as the danger zone.

The boiler is guaranteed safe to 15 psi (and it is likely to withstand at least twice that pressure). If the pressure should reach 10 psi, then the high-pressure limit switch will safely shut down the system. There are two easy ways to make sure that the switch is working properly. One test is to remove the cover while the boiler is operating. You'll see a pivoted lever inside the switch; pressing it upward against the switch should immediately cut off the boiler.

Another way to test this control is to set your thermostat for about 85 degrees and observe the pressure gauge. The boiler should shut off when the gauge reaches the cut-off pressure setting on the switch. If the boiler shuts off before the gauge goes above 10 psi, then it is safe. Do not continue the test if the gauge goes above 10 psi. You should turn the thermostat down and have a repair person check your boiler; it may be unsafe to operate.

The *safety,* or *relief, valve* is preset to open if the pressure should reach 15 psi. It then remains completely open until a predetermined lower pressure is reached, after which it closes once again. To test the safety valve, put on a heavy pair of gloves, stand well clear of the outlet from which the steam is emitted, and pull up on the lever at its back. If it's working it should release steam. (Be *extremely careful* when checking the valve. Released steam can cause severe scalding.) Don't try this test if the valve looks old or dirty. In that case, it's time to replace it.

To replace a safety valve, be sure the boiler is cold and the thermostat is turned down. Loosen and remove the valve with an adjustable wrench. (Get new valves at a plumbing supply house.) Coat the threads with pipe compound and install the new valve, making sure to tighten it firmly.

The *blow-off valve* and low-water-level cut-off switch are one unified system. They allow corrosion products to be drained (blown) off and provide protection from damage that could occur if too little water is present in the boiler. (Accumulation of rust can also interfere with the proper operation of the low-water-level cut-off switch.) The blow-off valve should be opened once a month during the heating season and run until the water coming out is clear. One word of caution: Do not attempt this procedure if you've added to the water a corrosion inhibitor designed for no blow-off use.

Opening the blow-off valve while the boiler is on can be a good test of the low-water-level cut-off switch. (If your system has an internal, self-cleaning blow-off valve, then you cannot check the low-water-level cut-off switch.) Place a large metal bucket below the blow-off valve. Run the water until clear, or until it is the same color as the water in the glass sight gauge was before you started. At some point in the process the boiler should shut off. If it does not, then call a service person before using the boiler again—and check the water level daily until it is repaired.

Corrosion is a boiler's number-one enemy. It is caused by the oxygen and mineral deposits that are present in fresh water. You can minimize corrosion damage by draining and refilling the boiler twice a year, and adding a corrosion inhibitor each time.

First, get rid of the floating corrosion and sediment in the low-water-level cut-off mechanism using the procedure previously described. Then, after the boiler has cooled, remove the safety valve. Draw off a bucket of sediment and water from the spigot of the boiler drain.

The boiler drain is usually found near the floor, often interconnected via a water pipe with the water fill valve. It is usually threaded so that a garden hose can be attached in order to drain the boiler. You'll need either a floor drain or a sump pump to get rid of the water from the boiler. If you don't have either of those, then you'll have to lead the hose to a place outside lower than the boiler chamber bottom (about one or two feet off the ground). If this procedure is not feasible, then remove the water by bucket brigade.

After completely draining the boiler, close the spigot, partially fill the boiler, and drain it again. Do this until the water runs clear. When you refill the boiler add a chemical corrosion inhibitor through the safety-valve hole. Then replace the valve after coating the threads with pipe compound.

CHECKING RADIATORS

If your boiler has been producing steam on and off for a while, inspect your radiator valves for leakage. Steam pipes rarely develop leaks at the joints, but the stem packing of most radiator inlet valves deteriorates over the years. You can often hear the steam leaking out or see water condensing on the stem; rust stains on floors or nearby furniture should also give you a clue. Note which valves leak and then turn the thermostat way down (or use the emergency cut-off switch); the system will cool off and, after a while, you'll be able to work at it comfortably.

You'll need a screwdriver, a knife, an adjustable wrench, and a supply of Teflon valve-stem packing. Un-

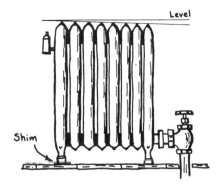

A radiator that slopes the wrong way (away from the valve) will trap water inside itself and the steam bubbling through this water can be noisy. To fix the slope of the radiator, insert wooden shims under the two feet farthest from the valve. Use a level to make sure the radiator is now tipping toward the valve.

screw the valve handle and remove it. Loosen and remove the packing nut; then use the knife to remove the remaining packing from the nut. Wind some fresh packing

around the stem in the same direction in which the packing nut tightens. Then replace the nut, tightening it firmly. To complete the job, just replace the handle. (New handles of insulating plastic are available—they're good, inexpensive replacements for cracked or broken handles.)

Radiator valves function as on-off switches for the radiator. Particularly in one-pipe systems (where steam flows to and from the boiler in a single loop) the valve should be fully on or fully off—*never* in between. If the valve is set partially open, then the steam pressure will keep water from flowing back down the single pipe. Water will then flow out of the valve and soak the area adjacent to it.

Vents are the control mechanisms of the individual radiators. They, not the valves, control the rate at which steam enters the radiator, shutting off the flow of steam when it has filled. The vents have a simple mechanism that allows air, but not steam, to pass in and out. When enough steam has entered the radiator and reaches the vent, the vent closes until all the steam has condensed into water; it then opens again to allow more steam to enter.

The only variable in vents is the size of the hole through which air escapes. The larger the hole, the faster the air escapes and the faster the radiator heats. Thus, fixed vents are rated from "very slow" to "very fast." Variable vents are also available.

If your radiator never heats up, or if steam issues from the vent, then you need to replace the vent. First allow the system to cool, then unscrew the vent, using either a tool or your hand. Replace it with the vent of your choice. Whichever kind you select, you should wrap the threads of the vent with Teflon tape. The tape will make the joint

steam-proof and will also make it easier for you to hand-tighten the vent.

Many old houses suffer from an imbalance in heat: Some rooms are too hot while others never quite get warm enough. You can solve this problem by using a different vent in each room. Vents come in four speeds: very slow, slow, fast, and very fast. If a room is overly hot, use a slower vent; too cold, a faster one. You can also balance the system by using a variable vent in the room where the thermostat is. The temperature of that room regulates the thermostat, and the thermostat regulates the temperature of the house. With a variable vent you can regulate the temperature of the room.

THE HEAT PUMP

The heat pump functions like a reversible air-conditioner. It pumps heat out of the house during the summer and into the house during the winter. Its great advantage is that it produces more heat than the amount of energy it takes to run the motor. While conventional heating systems are between 50 to 90 percent efficient, a standard heat pump is 200 percent efficient. With low-cost electricity, it provides the cheapest heating.

The heat pump does have some disadvantages for an old house. Because it can't generate high temperatures, the heat pump is used only for hot air heating (air-to-air heat pump). This means removing the hot water (or steam) radiators and installing large air ducts, which can be aesthetically traumatic for your house. On the other hand, you can use the same ducts for the air-conditioning, which is part of the heat-pump system.

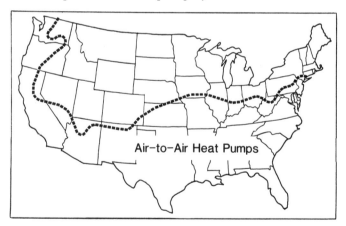

Air-to-Air Heat Pumps

One product that avoids large ducts is the Space-pak heat-pump system manufactured by Dunham-Bush. It uses high-velocity air, circulating in small six-inch diameter ducts, which can be threaded through closets and joist spaces. It seems ideal for use in old houses.

Another type of heat pump is the self-contained through-the-wall type. Generally, it is about the size of a large air conditioner and is mounted through a hole in an outside wall of the house. It supplies hot or cold air directly into the room where it is located. Its advantages are that it avoids ductwork and can be individually controlled. The disadvantages are that the grilles mar the outside of the house, and it is as noisy as a window air conditioner.

Another problem with heat pumps is that they become less efficient as the outside air gets colder. At low temperatures, it becomes cheaper to heat by some other method. In northern parts of the country, a hybrid heat pump—where oil or gas heating cuts in at low temperatures—is more economical than an all-electric system. The dotted line on the map shows approximately where it becomes necessary to use a hybrid heat pump. Some southern areas at high elevation may also require hybrids.

SOLAR

Retrofitting old buildings for solar space heating still, for the most part, means passive solar techniques. They are generally more cost-effective than active systems, less expensive to begin with, easier to integrate, reliable, and simpler in idea.

Passive solar techniques will usually not meet your total heating requirements. But using the sun can decrease your dependence on purchased energy, and at the same time add pleasant, usable space to your house. Solar techniques must complement a total program of energy conservation. Cut down on your overall use of purchased energy first. Solar heating will only contribute significantly if your house is already energy-efficient.

The money spent on energy conservation measures and solar retrofitting should be proportionate to the scale of the heating problem. Energy conservation becomes crucial in areas of 3,000-degree days and over. Larger investments—such as the addition of a sunspace—are worth investigating in these areas.

Passive solar methods can be as simple as making better use of existing windows. When the south-facing wall of a building is not prominent, it may be effective to add more windows. (Be aware of aesthetic and structural considerations.) Clerestory windows and skylights, when they are inconspicuous and well-fitted, can add light and warmth. Opportunities even include big projects such as a Trombe wall that turns a masonry wall into a solar collector.

For most old-house owners, however, sunspaces hold the most promise for increasing solar gain. Attached sunspaces exceed other passive solar techniques in terms of special amenities. Increased south glazing almost always adds natural daylighting, view to the outside, and the perception of a larger, more open space; the attached sunspace, in addition, adds room for sitting, dining, even growing plants and vegetables. Because of this latter use, sunspaces are often called greenhouses.

A sunspace is a separate space from the rooms that it helps to heat. While the rooms of a house seldom have temperature fluctuations in excess of 10 degrees Fahrenheit, a sunspace can fluctuate more than 35 degrees. Its principal features are the following:

Glazing. Place the glass to maximize winter solar gain and minimize summer gain. Invariably, the ideal surface is a south-facing vertical glass wall or clerestory window.

Storage. To prevent all heat gained from going directly into the air in the sunspace, masonry, earth, and/or water in the sunspace provide heat storage.

Heat transfer. Heat transfer into the rest of the house can be by natural convection or aided by a fan. If by natural convection, back-draft dampers are mounted at the top and bottom of the wall between the sunspace and adjacent room. The bottom damper permits a flow of air into the sunspace; at the top, the warmed air exits. Dampers should close to prohibit the reverse flow at night when the space cools down. A fan would require a heat sensor in the top of the sunspace to activate its use. Hot air is drawn off and blown down to spaces or storage. Again, cooler room air returns at the bottom of the sunspace.

Movable insulation. Although not always critical to the functioning of a sunspace, movable insulation is desirable: It both lowers temperature fluctuation and insulates the sunspace against the cold, dark night. Movable insulation simply refers to any material that is cut to fit an area and blocks sun during the day or keeps heat in at night. Window shades and curtains are one type, or you can make insulation panels by wrapping laminated corrugated cardboard in aluminum foil or sandwiching fiberglass insulation between wood veneer panels cut to the right size.

Creating a Sunspace

There are four major ways for you to create a sunspace, some more advantageous than others: You can adapt an existing space, such as a south-facing porch or extension room; select and install a purchased prefab or kit-type greenhouse; design and construct a ground-level, attached sunspace; or design and construct a rooftop sunspace.

Option 1: Adapt

Porches are ideal because they can readily be fitted with removable framed glass panels. In the summer, you can remove and store the glass, or replace it with screens. If properly detailed, the framed glass can be unobtrusive and designed for the architecture. On the other hand, we've all seen converted porches that are a visual mess.

The issue of thermal storage poses more of a problem for an existing house. If the wall between the sunspace and room to be heated is masonry and the sun strikes it, the problem is solved. But if storage must be added, it's likely that existing wood floors will have to be partially or fully removed and rebuilt to make way for footings, foundations, and masonry structural systems. (Thermal mass is heavy.) If direct solar gain is rather low and adding storage is costly (which might be the case in an old house), you may do better to avoid storage. Any heat flowing into the house during sunny days could be utilized for auxiliary space heat, but nothing would remain for evenings and cloudy days. Savings would therefore result only if

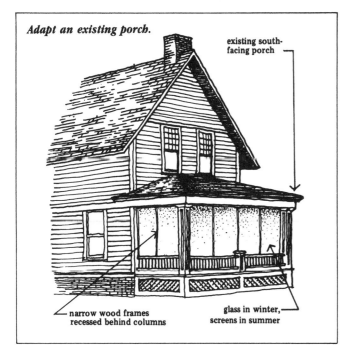

Adapt an existing porch.

existing south-facing porch

narrow wood frames recessed behind columns

glass in winter, screens in summer

the heating system responded to complement the solar gain.

Option 2: Prefab

Greenhouses have been used for many years to extend the plant growing season year-round, but their use for space heating is recent and highly problematic. A well-designed sunspace places glass to maximize winter gain and minimize summer gain. Most greenhouses have glass walls and roof with little or no provision for summer shading. In the winter, the wall readily collects the sun's

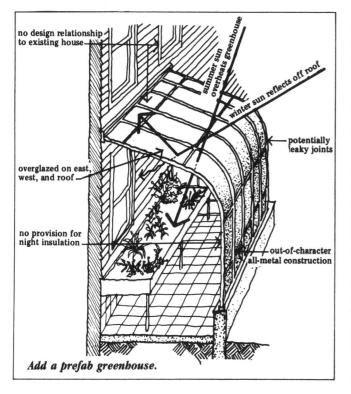

no design relationship to existing house

summer sun overheats greenhouse

winter sun reflects off roof

potentially leaky joints

overglazed on east, west, and roof

no provision for night insulation

out-of-character all-metal construction

Add a prefab greenhouse.

energy. The roof, however, is not nearly as efficient, as the sun's rays strike it at an acute angle, causing much of the heat to reflect away. In the summer, the inverse is true. With the sun high overhead, excessive gain is admitted through the roof.

Other problems result from usual construction practices and detailing. While most old houses are either wood or masonry with wood construction, prefab greenhouses are normally aluminum with glass or plastic. A basic problem is one of aesthetics. The old house and greenhouse have vastly different materials, proportions, and detailing, and are difficult to integrate into a cohesive design.

Functional problems also result. Most greenhouses are entirely glass with minimal framing. Most also are only single-glazed and often not well sealed. While the glass wall is collecting heat, the heat may be lost through infiltration and conduction losses. Add to this the difficulty of providing movable insulation on so many surfaces. Obviously, one should closely scrutinize this method before adopting it as a passive solar strategy.

Option 3: Ground-Level

One of the most difficult but effective answers is the new design of an attached sunspace. Architectural style is established by the existing house. Shape, proportion, mass, and detailing must be as carefully considered as energy issues. The sunspace design illustrated is an attempt to satisfy all these criteria.

Glazing is located on vertical south and, to a lesser extent, east and west walls. These surfaces provide good solar collection in winter. The overhangs (which echo the existing deep eaves) also shade the south glass. As the masonry floor and wall inside heat up, they transfer heat to the air within the sunspace. When a significant temperature difference occurs between the rooms in the house and the sunspace, air is convected into the space via dampers. The system is self-regulating if equipped with back-draft dampers. The only intervention required is the opening and closing of thermal shades morning and evening.

Option 4: Rooftop

The rooftop sunspace is an ideal solution for flat-roofed buildings, such as city row houses. It can often be added with minimal disturbance to the existing building, and it can be made to work regardless of the building's orientation to the sun. Because little or none of it is visible from the street, it can be optimally designed for solar gain, no matter what the house's style.

The shape of the urban sunspace illustrated reflects an optimal solar shape. Most of the glass is on the south surface, and tilted to be roughly perpendicular to the winter sun. Its roof and north walls are shaped to cut down on surface area. This roof structure is of metal, noncombustible construction (often required by code).

When the temperature of the heated air exceeds 85 degrees, a sensor at the top of the sunspace activates a fan

When attaching a sunspace, consider the house's existing design as well as energy issues.

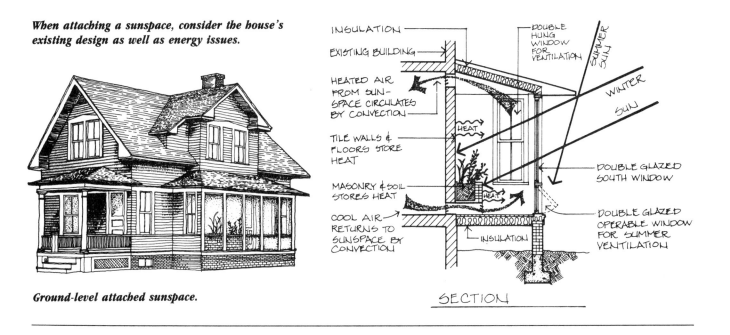

Ground-level attached sunspace.

SECTION

that draws air from the sunspace and ducts it down to rooms below. When the sunspace cools, the fan stops and a back-draft damper prevents air from convecting back to the sunspace. Return air complements the system by opening and closing a second vent to permit recirculation.

A back-up heating system adjusts to maintain constant room temperature. Storage is not provided because its weight would necessitate expensive rebuilding to bring the load all the way down to ground level. On cold evenings, removable insulated panels placed over glass surfaces minimize night-time loss.

These are just a few suggestions for adding solar capacity to your old house. Whenever possible, seek competent, professional help. If the solar method you choose is simple, a few hours of consultation will probably be sufficient. And if the method is complex, that is all the more reason to seek full-scaled architectural or engineering services. Fees will add 10 to 25 percent to the cost, but it's money well spent. A well-meaning but improperly installed solar retrofit can cause structural damage to your house or a neighboring building, or simply add great cost to the house with little or no positive reduction in energy costs.

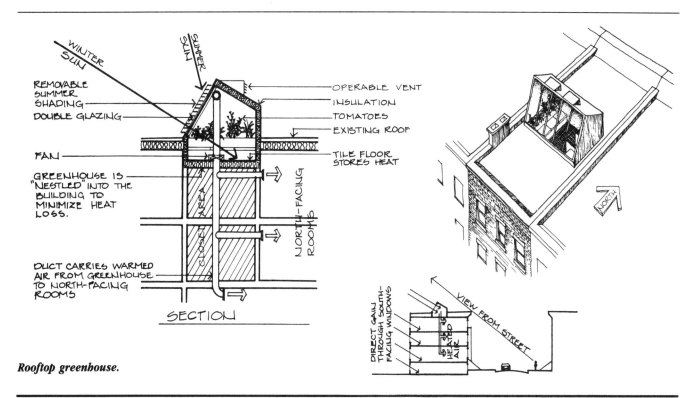

Rooftop greenhouse.

CHAPTER 12

Wet Basements and Structural Work

Some people are under the mistaken assumption that a damp basement in an old house is normal. It is understood that if the cellar fills like a swimming pool every time it rains, the furnace may turn off or the electric appliances may short out. Maybe you don't want a pool table down there because you want to use it to store the old toys that can get a little rusty. In reality, however, a chronically damp basement has within its humid environment the potential to nurture degenerative conditions ruinous to the structure of your house.

In chapter 5 we discussed external solutions to wet basements as well as major structural repair of the sills and foundation. In this chapter we'll examine some interior solutions to wet basements as well as other major structural work such as beam repair, subflooring repair, and repairs to staircases.

THE BASEMENT

A damp, humid basement is not a harmless inconvenience over the long term. It is the optimum environment for the propagation of mold, fungus, and wood-boring insects. The control of these infestations mandates removing the moisture from their habitat.

Adverse water conditions may vary from mere basement humidity, to damp walls or floors, to water flowing through fissures in masonry and flooding floors. Inspect the crawl space or basement for the presence of actual moisture or the telltale conditions that indicate a chronically damp environment. Look for dark irregular stains (often edged in white) on sill beams, the base of posts, and on window casings or bulk heads; fungal fruiting bodies or punkiness of wooden members; high water marks on walls; puddles on the floor; musty odors or mold on leather, cloth, or paper goods; difficulty closing doors or windows to the basement; small piles of fine

powdery sawdust, flight holes, or insect casings; masonry which is spalling or discolored by efflorescence; and bowed or cracked walls.

Note evidence like this on a floor plan of the inspected area, and date observations by month and year, in order to assist diagnosis, as many of these problems may be seasonal.

Before you decide to install a new drainage system inside the house, identify what type of moisture problem you have: leaks, seepage, condensation, or a combination

MOLD AND MILDEW

A damp basement or crawl space provides a good environment for mold and mildew, fungus, and wood-boring insects. Mold and mildew cause relatively minor problems. They create a musty odor, their spores can irritate allergic individuals, and they consume wallpaper, leather, cotton, and paper goods. Besides that, they can stain painted and plastered surfaces and woodwork.

Remove stain damage by washing color-fast surfaces with this solution:

- 3 ounces (2/3 cup) trisodium phosphate (TSP) cleaner
- 1 ounce (1/3 cup) powdered detergent
- 1 quart 5 percent sodium hypochlorite bleach (laundry bleach)
- 3 quarts warm water

This formulation combines the best mold-killing and stain-removing properties in a relatively gentle solution. If TSP is unavailable, just add more bleach.

Wear rubber gloves and safety glasses. Apply the solution to the affected area with a medium-hard brush, using a scrubbing motion. Keep the surface wet until the stain is bleached, then hose or flood with clean water. Allow the surface to dry thoroughly before repainting.

of these. However, keep in mind that the American Society of Home Inspectors notes that most basement foundations will let in water under the right circumstances. Also, many stone foundations laid with mud mortar (no cement or lime) were designed just to support the house, not to keep out water. Basements that have never leaked before may leak after long heavy rains, thorough yard watering, or flash flooding. Other causes of leaks and seepage include altering the contour of the site and landscaping, and gutters that need repair or alterations. New leaks may signal serious structural movement (perhaps the weight of a car parked too close to the house moved the foundation out of plumb).

To reduce moisture from condensation and humidity install good ventilation and use dehumidifiers and/or vapor barriers. The interior drainage systems covered in this chapter will help, though they won't be effective against floor leaks. Drying out walls that have been wet for years may cause you added trouble in the form of settling. Plastic drains can be damaged or unseated by hard pumping. Drains alone will seldom solve all moisture problems, but they can reduce humidity and keep the floor dry.

Water: Identifying the Source

Regardless of its source, liquid water in a basement or crawl spaces will evaporate and humidify the interior atmosphere. When air saturated with moisture is suddenly cooled by a colder object or air mass, the dew point is reached, and the water vapor condenses out of the air in the form of little water droplets.

In the summer, warm humid air from outdoors enters the cooler foundation cavities and condenses. In the winter, exhaust from clothes dryers or damp air from washing machines or a bathroom condenses on cold wall or floor surfaces, on sills, or on joists.

Several approaches will remedy these relatively minor seasonal problems. Remove moisture from the air with a dehumidifier, properly vent dryers, and equip laundry or bathrooms with fans. Insulate cold surfaces from the humid environment by covering cold-water pipes with insulated plastic foam sleeves to stop them from "sweating." You may need to frame the interior faces of outside walls with studs, placing insulation, a vapor barrier, and paneling or plasterboard over them.

For condensation conditions that arise only during the summer when the subterranean spaces are much cooler than the outside air, simply provide adequate air circulation. Place screened foundation vents in the walls or crawl spaces and basements. Leave them open in warm weather, unobstructed by vegetation or banked earth, to allow an easy exchange of air. Air must especially reach the corners of crawl spaces where wood sills meeting walls are not too far from damp soil, because it is here that the most destructive conditions are apt to occur. Use fans to accelerate this air movement and ensure that the timber in these areas is kept at below 20 percent moisture content in order to discourage the various infestations. Porta-

ble moisture meters measure the moisture content of wood. They work like light meters—simply place the electrodes against the wood and measure the moisture content. Moisture meters are available from PRG, 5619 Southampton Drive, Dept. OHJ, Springfield, VA 22151; (703)823-1407. They range in price from $95 to $310.

Plumbing is another source of moisture in the walls or basement of your house. Carefully inspect the plumbing, as leaks in the system may be sources of water in the basement. New plumbing connections may be faulty; more likely, cast-iron or lead-soil pipes or iron water pipes may be rusted or corroded. Leaks from old bath fixtures or commodes often drip down from floors above between partitions and end up as puddles in the cellar. Old supply pipes entering the foundation cavity from seldom used wells or pump houses may leak or siphon water into the house.

One other possible source of water intrusion may be the chimney. Lack of flue tiles, deteriorating mortar, poor flashing, or lack of a chimney cap may encourage the conduction of water into the basement. Check for dampness around the chimney base, and water stains around the clean-out door or the lower mortar joints. (See chapter 6 for chimney repairs.)

Stopping Leaks

No miracle coating exists to stop leaks on the inside face of a sievelike masonry wall. Many techniques and products recommended for this very purpose show limited effectiveness.

Parging (applying a thick layer of cement or mortar to a masonry wall) can retard leakage, but in severe wet-basement conditions your best bet is to attack the source of the problem. However, if you elect to parge, trowel two 3/8-inch coats onto the interior face of the wall, filling voids and surface inequities to create a smooth finish. You can then apply a dry, premixed, cement-based coating to which you add water or water and an acrylic bonder. Such coatings claim to cure all wet basement problems by sealing pores, filling voids, and stopping leaks. Apply them with a stiff brush to a thickness of 1/8 inch or, with silica sand added, trowel them onto the wall. Keep in mind that many of these products are overpriced and overrated.

As another solution, various paint manufacturers offer oil-based and latex waterproofing paint containing cement and moisture inhibitors. These thick slurries, brushed on directly from the can, supposedly create an impervious water barrier on the surface of the walls. Their prices seem reasonable, until you discover that one gallon covers only 50 to 100 square feet. Also, the limitations on the label often make the product's usefulness and effectiveness questionable.

Finally, the clear waterproofing sealers are supposed to be effective on any porous material, including wood, fabric, concrete, and masonry. These solutions of polymerized solids soak into the pores, and when the solvent evaporates, harden and plug up the tiny water passages.

Effective for some uses, they are often sold by ill-informed sales people as solutions to the wet basement problem. But they will not stop water from flowing in through a masonry wall. If you have a severe moisture problem in the basement, consider exterior work (see chapter 5) or install an effective drainage and pump system in the house.

Bailing Out of Wet Basements: Perimeter Drains

Several commercially installed basement water-control systems—available only through waterproofing contractors—deal with water coming through the walls. Steel or PVC troughs are fastened with an adhesive to the basement floor, next to the wall. Water entering through the foundation is collected in these channels, and conducted to the lowest end of the basement, where it may be collected in a sump pit.

The concept of the perimeter drainage system—letting the water leak through the foundation and collect in an interior gutter system—isn't new. Today, manufacturers offer premade baseboards for drainage within the house that can be installed by the do-it-yourselfer. The Channel Drain and Beaver Water Control systems are enclosed baseboard gutters that are glued to the floor along the bottom of the basement wall. They trap incoming water and channel it away to a drain or sump pump. As good as these systems are, however, they still treat the symptoms rather than dealing with the cause.

The Channel Drain system consists of 4-foot white plastic channels that are sealed to the floor and wall with #2 G.E. silicone caulk and then mechanically anchored to the floor and wall, or simply to the floor. This system has several potential drawbacks. The wall and floor must be reasonably smooth to anchor and seal the channel to them. Surfaces to be caulked must be dry for the sealant to adhere properly. The channel appears to be designed

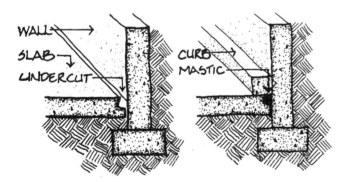

To stop water seeping in the joint between the concrete floor and foundation wall, chisel a narrow groove at the joint 1/2 to 3/4 inches wide, extending down through the slab. The slot should undercut the floor slightly in a modified dovetail. Brush and vacuum the joint and fill the groove with hydraulic cement, packing the cement into the joint. Build it up in thin layers until it's flush with the surface. Now pour a concrete curb measuring about 4 × 4 inches in place over the joint. Add a bonding agent to the concrete mix to improve adhesion.

to trap only the water that enters at the juncture of the floor and wall (and perhaps several inches up the wall). If the wall leaks higher than that, you're out of luck; the company suggests you paint those areas with a moisture barrier paint, which is not often effective. Apparently, you can attach the channel to the floor only, leaving the top unattached and 1/2 inch out from the wall (to catch water from above), but such an arrangement looks flimsy.

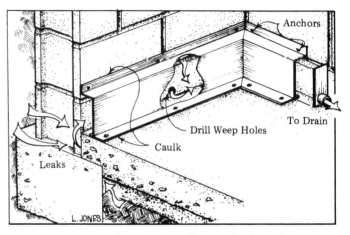

The commercially available Channel Drain system.

Drilling all those anchor holes and the suggested weep holes (for concrete blocks) could be quite a job. It also leaves you with a lot of holes should you decide to remove the system later. Installing the anchors can be messy, considering you have to drill through the channel and wet caulking. With anchors every 12 inches, there's little chance of shifting, but overdriving them could cause distortion in the channels and possible sealant failures. Also, think ahead before you drill holes in your foundation. You don't want to create more leaks in the long run.

The Beaver Water Control system consists of 5-foot long, fully enclosed baseboard units made from PVC, with small openings along the back to admit water. The baseboard is glued into place with a special two-part adhesive that sets up even on damp surfaces. (But play it safe and dry out the surface with heat lamps or a heat gun

The Beaver Water Control system.

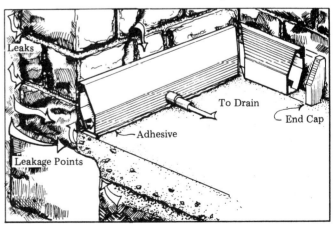

prior to gluing.) It's necessary to glue down the base-board unit only to the floor, although it can be attached to the wall as well. The contour of the baseboard unit is such that it will catch and funnel away moisture that enters the wall from above.

This unique feature also allows a plastic moisture barrier to be applied to the wall surface and tucked in behind the baseboard. Such a vapor barrier directs all wall moisture down into the baseboard, reducing evaporation and the resulting humidity. A waterproof (also with a vapor barrier) stud wall could then be built over it. Beaver system baseboards have a vinyl, hinged front section that can be opened for inspection and cleaning once the unit is in place. Baseboard units can be painted and used with smooth or irregular concrete, concrete block, brick, or stone walls. Should the system have to be removed, you'd have to cut away the guttering, and sand or grind the adhesive off the concrete floor.

Both systems have a relatively neat appearance when installed. The Beaver system has premitered inside and outside corners and joint connectors. Both systems will discharge water into 1 1/2-inch PVC or ABS couplers and can be drained by 3/4-inch plastic pipe.

In some cases you may have to install your own perimeter drain system around the interior of the foundation walls. Consider perimeter drainage if basement slabs were not poured on a permeable substrate, or if the exterior foundation drains are nonexistent or overburdened. It's easiest to install them in earth floors, as trenches must be dug along the inside of the walls.

The system can consist of drains at the base of two, three, or four walls. Measuring 8 inches wide, and extending 8 inches into the soil below the floor, the trench must slope 1 inch every 20 feet to the lowest end. Place perforated plastic pipe or clay drain tile in the trench and cover sides and top with clean-washed gravel. Cap it with concrete if part of a floor slab. The pipes can meet in a sump pit so the water can be pumped out, or the pipes can run under the foundation wall for gravity drainage outside. Note that

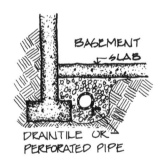

BASEMENT SLAB

DRAINTILE OR PERFORATED PIPE

while the perforated pipes can drain about 8 to 10 feet of area on either side of them, they should be within 3 feet of the base of the foundation walls, if possible.

Finally, as a stop-gap measure, which only controls moisture, place a vapor barrier on a damp earth or concrete floor. Just unroll 4-milliliter plastic sheets on the floors to minimize evaporation of moisture into the cellar air.

Water Through the Floor

Cutting up a concrete floor to hide the drain pipe is definitely not worth the trouble. But cutting a hole in the floor near the wall with the greatest leakage, and placing

a good quality sump pump there, can be helpful. The baseboards can be drained into the sump, and such an installation may even help reduce the moisture beneath the floor slab. You'll need a pipe for the pump to carry water to a suitable drain. Consider an outdoor dry well to handle the drain water.

Hydraulic pressure from water flowing under foundation walls can heave and crack floor slabs, forcing water into the basement. Providing an escape path for the water reduces both the uplift pressure and the potential for seepage through the floor. You may be able to use some of the gravel used under some concrete floors as a filter material. Gravel forms a highly permeable path for the ground water acting against the bottom of the slab.

Penetrate the slab at its lowest point and install a sump pit. This concrete-lined chamber extends below the floor into the ground and will collect the drainage water. Its size depends on the volume of water apt to flow into the sump. Place an automatic submersible pump in the

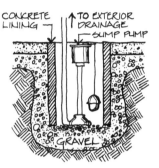

CONCRETE LINING — TO EXTERIOR DRAINAGE — SUMP PUMP

GRAVEL

pit to pump the accumulated water out of the foundation cavity for disposal in a storm sewer, or other drain. A sump pump requires little maintenance, but you must be careful to keep it free from debris that could clog it.

Drainage Out

Building codes in certain areas don't allow basement drain water to be discharged into the sanitary water system, so consult your local codes. It's often fairly easy to tie the drain pipe into a clothes-washer drain or an existing floor drain. Water flows by gravity, so see that the drain is lower than points of collection.

Be sensitive to the old house. You can drill holes through the foundation so pipes can drain outside, but this should be a last resort. Weep holes drilled into foundation walls are also useful only in hollow cavity (cinder block) walls to relieve water pressure. Try several test weep holes to see if they're necessary at all.

Once you have secured the basement from moisture, you can begin major repairs to the rest of the house.

INSECTS

Wood's number one enemy is moisture—especially because wood-inhabiting insects prefer it. Thus insect infestation is usually associated with attack by rot-causing fungi. So if all else fails, keep wood dry!

There are many types of insects that will attack wood. The three most common types are termites, carpenter ants, and wood-boring beetles.

Termites

Most damage done to wood houses is caused by subterranean termites. There are thirteen species of termites

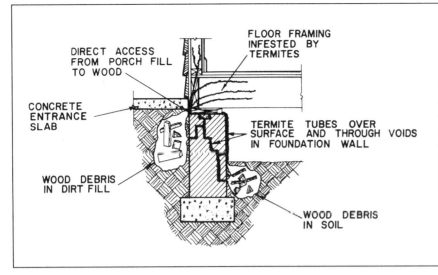

DIRECT ACCESS
FROM PORCH FILL
TO WOOD

FLOOR FRAMING
INFESTED BY
TERMITES

CONCRETE
ENTRANCE
SLAB

TERMITE TUBES OVER
SURFACE AND THROUGH VOIDS
IN FOUNDATION WALL

WOOD DEBRIS
IN DIRT FILL

WOOD DEBRIS
IN SOIL

Termites can find their way through cracks in the foundation—and many other ways so that their shelter tubes are invisible. Buried wood around the house causes trouble because it attracts termites to the vicinity; once they are there it won't be long before they find their way into the structure.

in the United States that cause damage to houses. These species can be sorted into three basic groups: subterranean termites, drywood termites, and dampwood termites. Although termites tend to shun the colder climates of the northernmost states, for all practical purposes consider that every old house presents a potential meal for one or more species of termite.

Subterranean termites obtain their moisture from the soil and must maintain contact with the soil to survive. When subterranean termites invade the wood of a house that is separated from the soil by a masonry foundation or

Cross-section of a network of termites' shelter tubes in a brick wall.

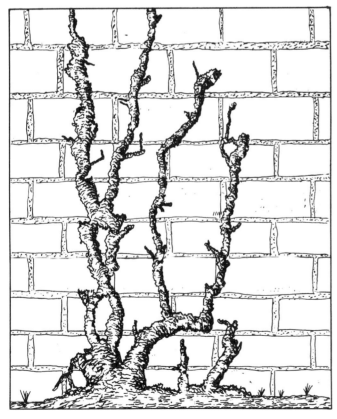

other impervious material, they construct shelter tubes over the intervening surface to get to the wood. Periodically they return to their moist galleries in the soil to replenish the water lost from their bodies.

Because they are so dependent on moisture, subterranean termites will never expose themselves directly to fresh air. If you poke a hole in one of their shelter tubes, they will repair the breach immediately. These termites will enter your house by tunneling into wood that is in direct contact with the soil, building shelter tubes over foundation walls, piers, and chimneys, and by finding cracks or joints in masonry floors and foundations.

Often the first sign of subterranean termites in a house is the presence of swarmers. All termites spread by swarming. Winged adults take to the air from mature colonies to seek greener pastures. In most cases it requires three to four years for a colony to grow big enough to throw off swarmers. Swarming season for most of the country is spring and early summer. Most of the subterranean termite species swarm during the day. If you're not present when the swarm occurs, you may see evidence of the swarm in the form of discarded wings—usually on window sills.

Wood will appear to be quite sound from the outside—until it collapses. Externally, in addition to shelter tubes, you may see soil in cracks and crevices, plus dark or blisterlike areas on flooring, trim, or framing. Infested wood in advanced stages of attack is easily penetrated with a knife or screwdriver. Internal damage can sometimes be located by probing the surface with a hard object, such as a small hammer, to detect sound differences that indicate hollow spaces.

The most distinctive feature of termite-infested wood is the appearance of the gallery walls that they hollow out. They have a pale spotted appearance, like dried oatmeal. This is because termites plaster soft fecal material on the walls of their galleries.

Dampwood termites build their colonies in damp, sometimes decaying wood. There is little external evidence of the presence of dampwood termites other than

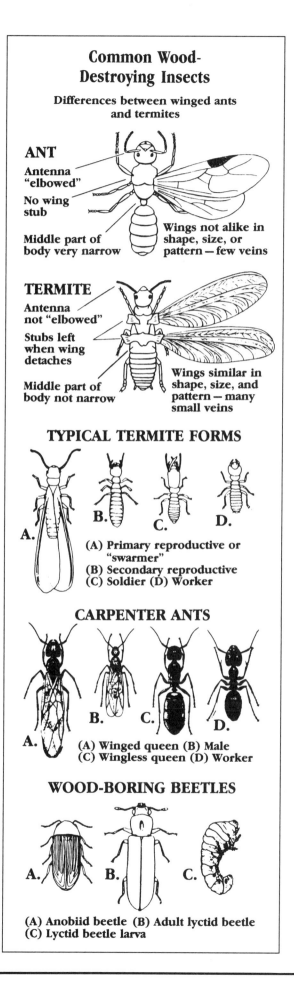

Common Wood-Destroying Insects

Differences between winged ants and termites

ANT

Antenna "elbowed"

No wing stub

Middle part of body very narrow

Wings not alike in shape, size, or pattern — few veins

TERMITE

Antenna not "elbowed"

Stubs left when wing detaches

Middle part of body not narrow

Wings similar in shape, size, and pattern — many small veins

TYPICAL TERMITE FORMS

A. B. C. D.

(A) Primary reproductive or "swarmer"
(B) Secondary reproductive
(C) Soldier (D) Worker

CARPENTER ANTS

A. B. C. D.

(A) Winged queen (B) Male
(C) Wingless queen (D) Worker

WOOD-BORING BEETLES

A. B. C.

(A) Anobiid beetle (B) Adult lyctid beetle
(C) Lyctid beetle larva

---

swarmers or shed wings. Because dampwood termites must maintain contact with damp wood, the primary control measure is simply eliminating moist wood from the structure.

Drywood termites require no contact with the soil or other external sources of moisture; they get the water they need from the wood they inhabit. Drywood termites are most common in southern California, southern Arizona, and southern Florida. The first sign of drywood termite infestation is usually piles of fecal pellets, which are hard, less than 1/25 of an inch in length, with six flattened or depressed sides. The pellets vary in color from light gray to very dark brown—depending on the wood being consumed. The pellets, eliminated from galleries in the wood through round "kick holes," accumulate on surfaces or in spider webs below the kick holes.

Carpenter Ants

Carpenter ants burrow into wood to make nests, and do not feed upon the wood the way termites do. Normally, they don't cause extensive structural damage in houses. Most species start their nests in moist wood that has begun to decay. The most obvious sign of infestation is the ants themselves: large reddish-brown to black ants, 1/4 to 1/2 inch long.

Damage occurs in the interior of the wood. There may be piles of scattered bits of wood powder (frass) that are very fibrous and sawdust-like. The frass is expelled from cracks in the wood or slit-like openings made by the ants. Most often carpenter ants will be found in basements, dark closets, attics, under porches, and in crawl spaces.

Beetles

Wood-boring beetles, known as *lyctid beetles* and sometimes called powder-post beetles, will attack only the sapwood of hardwoods with large pores, such as oak, hickory, ash, walnut, pecan, and many tropical hardwoods. The adult beetles reinfest the wood with their eggs in a continuing cycle until the wood disintegrates. Lyctids range from 1/8 to 1/4 inch in length and are reddish brown to black.

The presence of small piles of fine, flourlike frass on or under the wood is the most obvious sign of infestation. There are no pellets. Exit holes from which the adult beetles emerge are round and vary from 1/32 to 1/16 of an inch in diameter. Most of the larva tunnels are about 1/16 of an inch in diameter and loosely packed with powder. Infestations usually occur in hardwood paneling, trim, furniture, and flooring.

Anobiid beetles are often also called powder-post beetles. Unlike lyctids, anobiids will infest both hardwoods and softwoods. Signs of beetle infestation in structural members of a house are usually caused by anobiids. Attacks often start in poorly heated or ventilated crawl spaces and spread to other parts of the house. Adult beetles emerging from their flight holes will usually reinfest the wood with their eggs.

The most obvious sign of infestation is the accumula-

INSECT	TYPICAL CONTROL TREATMENT
Subterranean Termites	Treat the localized area of infestation and nearby soil with an insecticide, such as chlorpyrifos (sold under various brand names, including Dursban) or pyrethrum (available as Demon). Nematodes are a nonchemical approach.
Dampwood Termites	Eliminate any source of damp wood. Soil treatment as for subterranean termites can be used as a secondary measure.
Drywood Termites	*Isolated infestation:* Locate all nests and apply appropriate treatment, such as a dessicant (silica aerogel in spray or dust form), to these and surrounding areas. Boric acid is also used on occasion. *Extensive infestation:* Fumigating the entire structure with chemicals, such as vicane or methyl bromide, may be an option where other methods fail.
Carpenter Ants	Eliminate any source of damp wood. Use appropriate treatment aimed at killing the queen.
Wood-Boring Beetles	*Limited infestation:* Replace infected wood, or remove wood and fumigate. *General infestation:* In some cases it is possible to interrupt the infestation cycle by maintaining low humidity conditions (or applying extreme cold or heat) in the infected area. Consider fumigation where other options fail.
CAUTIONS	(1) The insecticides listed above are extremely toxic and should be used only by a qualified professional exterminator. (2) Environmental regulations on the use of insecticides change frequently. Be sure to deal only with a reputable pest control company that is familiar with the latest safety and toxicity data.

tion of powdery frass and tiny pellets underneath infested wood, or streaming from exit holes. The holes are round and vary from 1/16 to 1/8 inch in diameter. If there are a large number of holes and the powder is light-colored like freshly sawed wood, the infestation is both well established and active. If all the frass is yellowed and partially caked on the surface where it lies, the infestation has been controlled or has died out naturally.

Humidity and temperature of the air surrounding the wood are key factors in whether or not adult beetles lay eggs in the wood and thus continue the infestation. The drier the air, the less likely that infestation will continue.

Unfortunately, once wood-inhabiting insects are established in your home, the only effective way to control or eliminate them is with heavy-duty chemicals (see chart). These chemicals are quite toxic, and their sale and use is strictly regulated. As a result, insect control is *not* a do-it-yourself job. You'll have to call in the professionals.

BEAM REPAIR

The repairs you undertake to secure the structure will depend on the crack evidence on walls, around doors and windows, and badly bowed walls. All houses shift as they settle with use and age. Cracks will tell you where the stresses are concentrated. (See also "The Crack Detective" in chapter 3 for a guide to reading cracks.) For example, a sheer crack leading up and away from the corner may indicate that a stress concentration has occurred when weight was transferred from one material to another. Since most houses are built of many materials, cracks appear where there is a change in the structural system. A plaster ceiling supported on wood joists will

crack where it meets plaster on a brick wall. Cracks tend to form around a stone window sill surrounded by brickwork. The cracks between a wood lintel and the brick wall it is supporting will show up in the plaster in the house.

Cracks can also result from denser patches within the

MAKING AN EXPANSION JOINT

The best way to deal with expanding thermal cracks is to fill them with a flexible sealant. The caulking can't harden up or it will crack as the building moves again. The sealant keeps moisture and debris out. Try butyl rubber caulk for the interior, and a one-part polyurethane (e.g., Vulkem #116) for the exterior. Polysulfides also have good elastic properties, but won't bond in the presence of moisture.

Fill the joint with enough sealant to absorb continued movement. A sealant can move about 25 percent of its width: If the crack is going to move 1/8 inch, then the joint must be at least 1/2 inch wide. If it's necessary to widen the crack, use a carborundum blade in a circular saw to cut a slot.

The minimum effective size is 1/4 × 1/4 inch, but a 1/2-inch width is better. The depth of the sealant must be at least 50 percent of the joint width. For joints 3/8 inch or wider, use a closed-cell polyurethane backer rod (available at builder's supply houses or concrete materials suppliers). Push the backer rod into the joint to fill up the space behind the sealant; then the sealant is applied with a caulking gun until it is flush with the surface.

material itself. A stone baked into a brick may create a crack on the brick's surface. Repointing with a hard portland cement mortar may also cause cracking of the brickwork.

Cracks also may occur as wood naturally expands and contracts as it gains and loses moisture. When expanded, it is tight against other parts of the house. As it dries out, cracks form between the pieces. A clapboard house may have cracks over the entire exterior in the dry season. They may also appear on the interior as joists, beams, and wall studs shrink. In severe cases, the plaster may crack, but more often the cracks appear in corners and at the edges of the ceiling. These cracks will open and close depending on the weather.

Thermal expansion cracks appear where a part of the structure abutting the outside wall is a different temperature. Interior partition walls will nearly always crack in the corner where they join the exterior wall. Thermal expansion cracks may also be caused by heat in a chimney breast. The high temperatures from the fireplace or furnace will often cause vertical cracks in the plaster above the mantel.

Identifying Beam Problems

Until recently there was no way to calculate the amount of weight a beam or joist could hold. In the old country, things were tested by building them and waiting to see if they fell down. Typically, the owners of a house were more concerned about the bounce of the floor than whether it would collapse. In most cases this was a safe way to judge a floor. Usually floor beams in an old house are bigger than they need to be, rather than too small.

Connection Failures

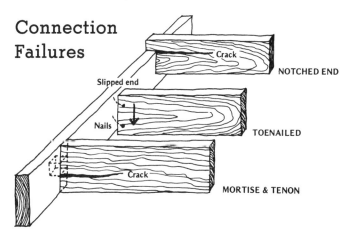

Cracks often appear when connections between beams weaken or fail. In old houses these connections are made with wood. The mortise and tenon joint consisted of a square peg at the end of one beam inserted into a square hole in the supporting beam. The weight concentrated at the end of the beam can split it just below the bottom of the peg.

You'll find this kind of failure at stair openings where the weight of several joists is gathered onto one beam. Look for very localized crack patterns as evidence of a connection failure. This type of failure can be dangerous

if the connection suddenly collapses—so don't just wait for the outcome. If you can't see the beam end, cut a hole in the ceiling below, and stick your head in for a look.

In later houses, nails sometimes substituted for wooden connections. A few toenailed spikes in the end of a joist are not enough to keep it from dropping in the long run. Nails are fine for holding lumber in position where the forces are pushing the wood together, such as in a stud wall. However, when the loads are trying to pull the pieces of lumber apart, nails are not a very reliable connector.

Beams may fail, creating a fracture when they have too much weight on an end to support the area. In a window with a stone lintel and a small amount of bearing on the wall below, a shear crack will run down from the end of the lintel in to the edge of the window. Similarly, a beam carrying several joists may crush the brick below its bearing pocket in the wall. In this situation, the beam can be crushed along with the brickwork.

Bearing Failure

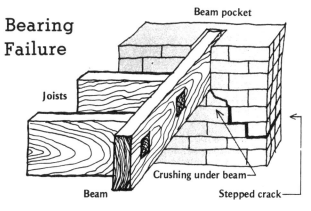

Beams that carry many joists and bearing walls can crack dramatically. The crack will nearly always be exactly in the middle of the beam, where the bending stress is greatest. Stone lintels also act as beams and crack in the center. If the ends stay in place, the bending crack will be wide at the bottom and closed at the top. Since bending failure can have fatal results, excessive floor and beam deflection should be investigated by a professional.

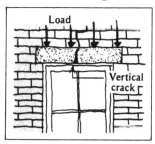

Bending will cause the floor failure from what is really a connection problem. As a joist or beam bends, the number of inches supported on the wall becomes smaller and smaller. Eventually the ends can slip off the wall or out of their pockets and come tumbling down. Start worrying if less than two inches of the joists are resting on the wall.

Undersized columns can also cause structural prob-

Bending Failure

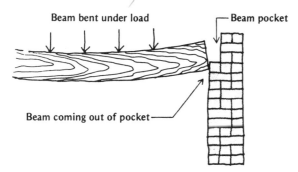

Beam bent under load

Beam pocket

Beam coming out of pocket

lems. If there is too much weight for the size of the column, it will bend to one side or be crushed at one end. The bowing of wood columns is usually easy to see. Brick columns will bow by cracking along the horizontal joints. Look for tapered cracks, all of which are wider on one face of the column. Any significant bowing of a column should be investigated by a professional.

Short columns tend to fail by crushing of the material rather than bending. In wood columns, look for crushed fibers; in cast-iron and stone columns, look for shear cracks near the ends of the column.

Be careful of central-axis beam cracking too. This occurs when there is a series of square holes in a supporting beam. Although the center of the beam is the best place to connect the joists, sometimes so much wood is removed that the beam cracks horizontally along its center line. (More often than not, this can be caused by shoddy plumbing and electrical work. People hired to install new mechanical systems in an old house generally don't spend much time figuring tight tolerances for hole cutting.) The separation in the beam means that there are really two little beams instead of one large one, and more important, only the bottom half is doing any work to hold up the house.

Central-Axis Beam Cracking

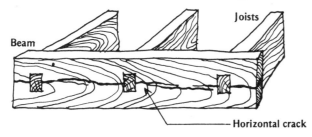

Joists

Beam

Horizontal crack

Replacing and Repairing Beams

In this section, we'll discuss the repair and replacement of spanning, load-bearing members—rafters, headers, girders, joists (not sills, plates, or studs). Throughout we use the generic term beam to refer to the members, even though a rafter is not technically a beam. However, the repair solutions that we suggest for beams also apply to rafters.

If any framing member larger than a single (2-inch) joist

or rafter is damaged, hire an architect or structural engineer to specify methods and materials for repair. You can get into major trouble making "educated guesses" about how to repair a beam that holds up the central bearing wall of a house. You would probably be overcautious, though, to call in a consultant over one bad 2-inch joist. Anyone with moderate carpentry skills should be able to repair a single damaged framing member.

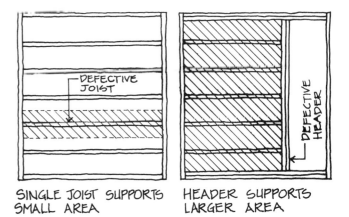

DEFECTIVE JOIST

DEFECTIVE HEADER

SINGLE JOIST SUPPORTS SMALL AREA

HEADER SUPPORTS LARGER AREA

The repair of some doubled framing members is well within the capabilities of an experienced carpenter, but the repairperson must understand how a member is loaded before starting repairs. The load borne by a doubled floor joist under an empty bathtub is not much more than the load borne by any other floor joist (of course, you wouldn't work on the area with a full bathtub). This is not the case, though, with doubled members used as a header in stairwell or hearth framing. In this case, the structural integrity of all of the members tied to the header is dependent on the header.

Before you begin repairs on a damaged structural member, try to determine what caused the member to fail. Usually, the cause is obvious—bugs, rot, or unskilled workers. Sometimes, though, the causes are more esoteric. Floor joists have been done in by the grand pianos and waterbeds of former owners, rafters by long-forgotten fallen tree limbs. If the cause of the damage is not obvious, and if more than one isolated member is damaged, the problem could be a case of bad original design. If you suspect this, call in an architect or engineer.

When repairing a damaged beam, your two easiest choices are either to replace the beam or to "sister" the beam.

If the condition of the wood is bad, replace it with new lumber. (A contractor might use an epoxy and fiberglass to repair it. However, this is not for do-it-yourselfers.) New lumber often is smaller and weaker than the original in your house. However, a new smaller beam, even if adequate, may be more flexible than the old one. This will result in new cracks as the house settles. A smaller beam also will not have as much bearing area where it rests on the wall. Consult an engineer or an architect to size the lumber.

Sometimes, replacing a beam is not as difficult as it

might seem. First, install temporary supports. Use temporary jacks or braces to keep other members in their proper place during repairs (see "Using Jack Posts," page 223). Remove all the blocking around the beam, then use a demolition saw (a Sawzall or equivalent) to cut through the old beam and the old nails. Taking the old beam out sometimes requires the removal of a few bricks in a basement wall, but generally, getting an old beam out is easy.

The difficulty lies in getting a new, full-size beam in. Immovable objects in the house that weren't there when the original beam was installed—things like furnaces, ducts, and water pipes—will get in your way. And where there aren't obstacles, there are impediments, like tiny little attic access doors, or mazes of doors leading to the basement. So before you undertake a beam replacement, make sure you have enough room to get the new beam in place. If you don't have enough room to get a whole new beam in place, you'll have to either make room or sister the beam.

When you replace a beam because it has rotted from moisture, consider using preservative-treated wood. Wolmanized, "Outdoor Wood," or Osmose all sell preservative-treated wood, which is made by a pressure-injected chemical process.

If you need to use wedges to get the new beam to fit, use solid hardwood wedges to fill gaps between new members and bearing surfaces. (Do *not* use wood shingles for shims in this case—they will crush and splinter.) Be careful—you can easily overdrive a wedge and lift a small section of your house. Check for tightness after every hammer stroke and remember that the object is to get the wedge in tight, not to drive the whole wedge in.

Sistering

In many cases, it is often easier to splice a new member next to the old rather than do extensive demolition to replace an entire beam or stud. To repair the ends of beams or joists, "sister" a new member next to the existing one. The overlap must be at least six times the depth of the beam, longer if possible. The sistered beams must be glued and bolted (*not* nailed) together with the bolts alternating between the top and bottom of the beam. A professional should design the spacing, size, and number of bolts. Where twisting is likely, new lumber should be sistered on both sides of the damaged end of the existing wood.

In a masonry building, it may be difficult to install new joists in existing beam pockets. Instead, install two new joists that are sistered together. Each joist will be at a slight angle to the originals, but their combined thickness will provide plenty of nailing surface in the right place. Be sure to fire-cut the ends of the new joists at a 15-degree angle. Resist the impulse to fill in that beam pocket around the new wood in a brick or stone wall. Mortar—which attracts and holds moisture—in contact with the sides of the wood will rapidly rot.

Use sisters to replace the end of a beam; patch anywhere along the run of the beam or to prevent further deflection of a sagging beam. The beauty of the sister solution is that you're always adding—never removing—material, so you don't run the risk of compounding damage already done.

Stagger the location and size of the bolt holes when sistering. Staggering avoids weakening the existing beam along a straight line; the sisters should be just big enough to accommodate 3/8-inch or 1/2-inch bolts. Also beware of fungus-damaged wood when sistering. Remove any you see to prevent the spread of rot to new wood, and brush a liberal coat of Cuprinol preservative onto all wood that surrounds fungus-damaged wood.

Modes of Sistering

There are several ways to sister a beam. The simplest method involves gluing and bolting 3/4-inch plywood

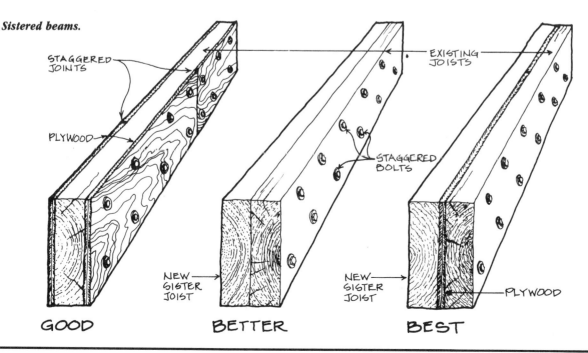

Sistered beams.

STAGGERED JOINTS

PLYWOOD

GOOD

NEW SISTER JOIST

BETTER

EXISTING JOISTS

STAGGERED BOLTS

NEW SISTER JOIST

PLYWOOD

BEST

(which is very strong in this configuration) to the sides of the beam. The individual pieces of plywood are light and easy to handle in a confined space.

Make a somewhat stronger repair by doubling the weakened member with a new piece of lumber the same size. Again, glue and bolt the new wood into place.

The strongest sister repair is a composite of the first two options. Glue and spike plywood to the old beam, and then glue and bolt a full-dimensional sister behind the plywood.

If an existing beam is severely weakened or damaged, or if the beam was underdesigned or underbuilt originally, use a metal flitch plate to stiffen the damaged member. Flitch plates must be installed according to an architect's or engineer's specifications.

Installing New Beams

When installing new beams, keep the following things in mind:

- Sight down the edge of the new beam and look for the high side, or "crown." Install the new beam with the crown up; the idea is that the weight of the load on the beam will cause it to deflect back to straight.
- New beams installed in row buildings that have party walls should be "fire-cut"; this allows a burning beam to fall without taking the masonry party wall with it. Beam pockets in masonry walls often deteriorate due to dampness and the weight of the beam on the masonry units in the pockets. When installing a new beam in such a wall, it is a good idea to use a 1/2-inch metal plate or wood blocking as a bearing surface for the new beam.
- When installing a sister along the entire run of an old beam, it is relatively easy to get the sister in place if you bevel the top of one end of the sister, and notch the bottom of the other end. You put the beveled end in place first, then rotate the notched end into place and shim any gaps.

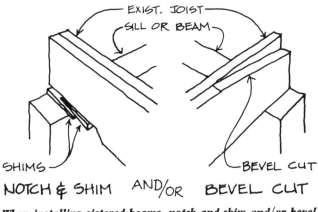

When installing sistered beams, notch and shim and/or bevel cut.

If you must drill or cut holes in framing members, here are some things you should know:

- Try your best to go around the framing member. If you're plumbing, that's what elbows are for.

- If you must drill a hole in a rafter or joist, drill the hole in the center axis of the member (i.e., 6 inches from the bottom of a 2 × 12).
- Try to plan your run so all your holes are near supporting members, away from the center span of the member.

By the way, if you're using a hole saw, drill all the way through the beam first with a long bit the same diameter as the hole saw's pilot bit. This saves you the headache of aligning the holes on opposite sides of the beam. (Most hole saws won't cut all the way through a beam in one pass.)

Splice Joints for Timber-Frame Construction

In the case of timber-frame construction, where a number of hand-fitted members are pegged into long beams, beam replacement or sistering would be impractical or aesthetically inappropriate. In such cases, or in the case of a historic house where the fabric of the building is unique and irreplaceable, use the splice joints described below to repair damaged members.

These splice joints should be employed only in these special cases. The type of joint, glue type, and bolt sizes should be specified by an architect or engineer.

The *splayed lap joint* is slightly easier to execute and can be cut over a shorter run of the beam than the 9:1 scarf joint. The two "extra" bolts (one on either side of the joint) counteract the tendency of the beam to split along its center line due to the force of the wedges formed by the edges of the joint.

Use a *9:1 scarf joint* along the run of a rafter or joist. The slope of the joint distributes the tension and compression forces over a considerable length of the beam; the d/5 shoulders help keep the beam from buckling and prevent slippage of the joint.

Columns and Bearing Walls

Beams will support more weight if they're made shorter between bearing points. This can be done by putting a column between the two ends (not necessarily in the middle). Similarly, joists can be effectively shortened by installing a beam or bearing wall perpendicular to them. Overloaded columns can be relieved by installing additional columns to take over some of the load.

A new column might be right next to the existing one or someplace else along a main girder. The easiest type to install are the adjustable pipe columns sold at lumberyards. A telescoping jacking post doesn't hold as much weight as a solid pipe column with an adjustable screw jack at the head. In either case, be sure to buy a column that will support the new load you want to put on it. Columns can also be made of a 4 × 4 or larger (no 2 × 4s, please) with a house jack on top, or you can use a wood column wedged in place, or a solid masonry pier (8 inches × 8 inches or larger).

When installing columns above the basement level, be

Specialized Splice Joints

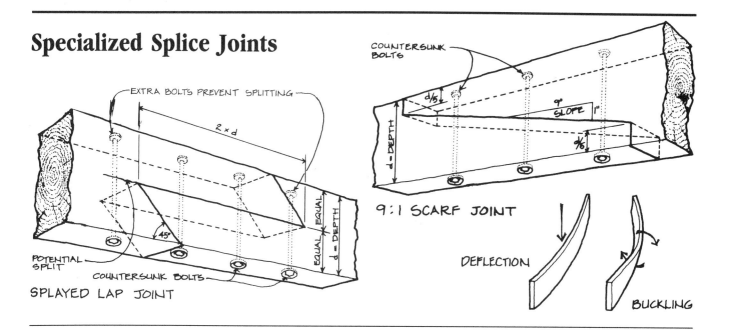

SPLAYED LAP JOINT

- EXTRA BOLTS PREVENT SPLITTING
- 2 × d
- EQUAL / EQUAL
- d = DEPTH
- 45°
- POTENTIAL SPLIT
- COUNTERSUNK BOLTS

9:1 SCARF JOINT

- COUNTERSUNK BOLTS
- d/5
- 9° SLOPE
- 1"
- d = DEPTH

DEFLECTION

BUCKLING

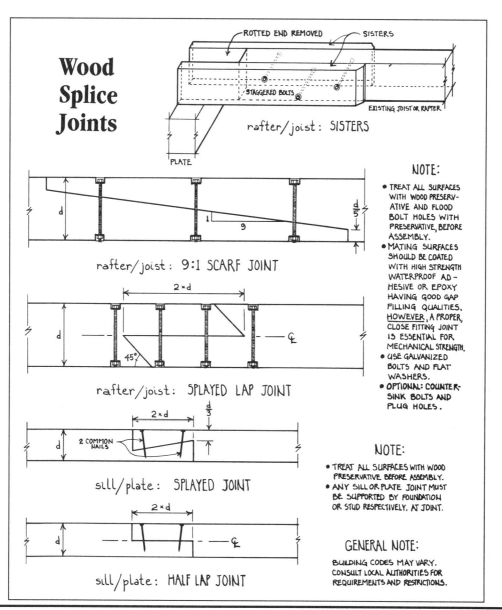

Wood Splice Joints

rafter/joist: SISTERS

- ROTTED END REMOVED
- SISTERS
- STAGGERED BOLTS
- EXISTING JOIST OR RAFTER
- PLATE

rafter/joist: 9:1 SCARF JOINT

- d
- d/5
- 1 / 9

rafter/joist: SPLAYED LAP JOINT

- 2 × d
- d
- 45°
- ℄

sill/plate: SPLAYED JOINT

- 2 × d
- d/3
- d
- 2 COMMON NAILS

sill/plate: HALF LAP JOINT

- 2 × d
- d
- ℄

NOTE:

- TREAT ALL SURFACES WITH WOOD PRESERVATIVE AND FLOOD BOLT HOLES WITH PRESERVATIVE, BEFORE ASSEMBLY.
- MATING SURFACES SHOULD BE COATED WITH HIGH STRENGTH WATERPROOF ADHESIVE OR EPOXY HAVING GOOD GAP FILLING QUALITIES. HOWEVER, A PROPER, CLOSE FITTING JOINT IS ESSENTIAL FOR MECHANICAL STRENGTH.
- USE GALVANIZED BOLTS AND FLAT WASHERS.
- OPTIONAL: COUNTERSINK BOLTS AND PLUG HOLES.

NOTE:

- TREAT ALL SURFACES WITH WOOD PRESERVATIVE BEFORE ASSEMBLY.
- ANY SILL OR PLATE JOINT MUST BE SUPPORTED BY FOUNDATION OR STUD RESPECTIVELY, AT JOINT.

GENERAL NOTE:

BUILDING CODES MAY VARY. CONSULT LOCAL AUTHORITIES FOR REQUIREMENTS AND RESTRICTIONS.

sure they have solid support all the way to the ground. For example, a new column on the second floor has to have support under it at both the first floor and basement levels. If the load isn't transferred to the ground, you'll have new cracks and worse. Likewise, provide support for the under-floor spaces; that is, solid blocking will probably be required in the joist space between the floor and the ceiling below.

Where a bearing wall has been removed or weight has been increased, a combination of beams and columns may be required to bring the load down to the ground. In most cases this will require installing new beams below the original ceiling level. The columns can often be hidden inside existing walls. Use wood beams for short spans and lighter loads, steel beams for longer spans and heavier loads. Since prefabricated pipe columns are relatively short, they will be used mostly in the basement level of older homes. Wood columns will suffice for most loads in residential situations. Both beams and columns must be custom-designed for the particular situation in your house. Consult an architect or engineer for help.

SUBFLOORING

Some floors have no substructure at all, while others have a rough subfloor spanning the joists and supporting the load. In early American construction, a single layer of heavy boards was laid perpendicular to the joists. These were left rough underneath, but planed smooth on top. By the early nineteenth century, builders laid a subfloor of rough boards, with a thinner finish-floor at right angles (90 degrees) to the subfloor, and parallel to the joists. Around 1920, diagonal (45-degree) subflooring was introduced, making it possible for the finish-floor to be laid either perpendicular or parallel to the joists.

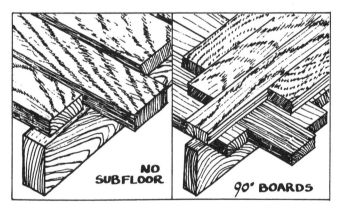

Thick planks of pine and other softwoods continued to be used as flooring long after 1800, of course, and there were other anachronisms. Even if your house was built in the mid-Victorian period, for instance, you might find only subflooring laid in some rooms. Occasionally, wall-to-wall carpeting was put down right over the subfloor. Attempts to refinish rough subflooring as a finish-floor are usually unsuccessful. Save your socks from splinters and put down a hardwood covering, parquet, carpeting, or a modern material.

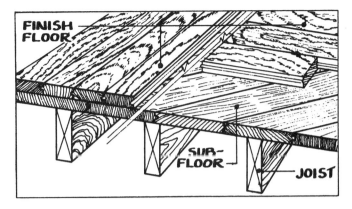

In a late-nineteenth-century house, you might even find a floor with softwood in the middle, and finished hardwood around the edges. This generally means the center of the room was intended to be covered by a large carpet—and the original owner was economizing on expensive hardwood.

Subflooring Repair

All old houses have floors that creak, sag, or slope. Fortunately, few of these conditions mean you have to undertake major structural work. The floors settle along with the rest of the house, and an old wood floor will develop some springiness and squeaks. In an old house, floor problems may be caused by age, which means they won't get worse while you live there.

However, check the supporting elements underneath the floor. If the floor is buckled and the joists are falling out of their pockets in the bearing walls you may have foundation failure. If you have S-shaped walls and window frames so out-of-square that the sashes are all frozen in place, your sagging floor probably indicates gross structural failure.

Getting into the under-floor structure and taking a peek makes it easier to fix problems on the first floor level—over a basement or crawl space—than on upper levels. This will work for you if you plan to replace the ceiling under the affected floor anyway. Tear the plaster down so you can see what the real trouble is in the floor above. If you don't have to replace the ceiling, and you suspect structural damage, you'll have to lift some floorboards.

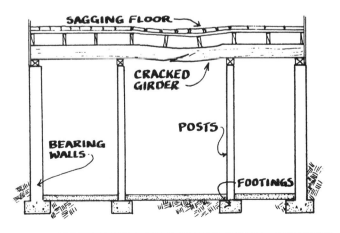

Your subfloor may also need repair if it has gotten very dry or very wet over the years. If the floors were built with a rough subfloor under the finish floor, you'll have to be sure this subfloor is sound before getting around to visible repairs on top of the floor.

If the cause of creaks is a subfloor that has dried and shrunk and no longer rests on the supporting joists, drive a wedge between them. If much of the floor creaks, brace the subfloor by nailing a length of 2 × 6 or 2 × 4 to the sides of the joists, up tight against the subflooring boards.

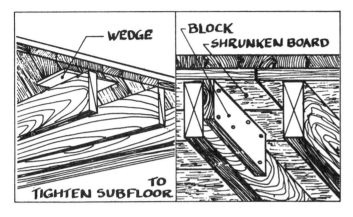

WEDGE · BLOCK · SHRUNKEN BOARD · TO TIGHTEN SUBFLOOR

Check for rotting around toilets, bathtubs, and the kitchen sink. If the finish floor shows signs of discoloring, buckling of the surface, and a spongy texture underfoot, you may well have to remedy a wet subfloor. Also check the subfloor from underneath, looking for water stains, dampness, and existing rot in both the subfloor and nearby joists.

Removing the finish floor is tricky, especially if you plan to save and relay it later. When lifting softwood boards, snip off all the nailheads when possible, before prying up the boards. When boards are tongue-and-grooved, you'll have to sacrifice the first board you remove.

When replacing a limited section of the subfloor, try to get the same thickness as the old boards. New boards may have to be ripped to appropriate thickness because lumber dimensions have changed over the years. Or you can use wood shims, nailed to the tops of the joists, to bring new undersized boards up to the level of the existing floor.

Cut off damaged subfloor boards near a joist. This way you can attach a piece of 2 × 4 to the edge of the joist to act as a support for the end of the spliced-in board.

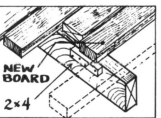

NEW BOARD 2×4

If you lay a whole new subfloor, or major sections of one, use plywood. Plywood is strong and dimensionally stable, it is squeak-resistant, and using it saves you labor. Use 1-inch thick construction-grade plywood sheathing. Always put a layer of building paper down between the subfloor and the finish floor.

If you have a single layer of flooring and want to cover

it with a resilient covering (linoleum, asphalt tile), carpeting, or ceramic tiles, you should first put down an additional underlayment of 5/8-inch plywood, or 3/8-inch hardboard, before installing the finish-floor material. Rough spots, low spots, and cracks will show through and eventually damage resilient coverings and carpeting. A single layer of boards is apt to give a little, so cemented or grouted coverings will soon work loose.

Be sure the existing subfloor is sound—not cracked or rotted. Walk over it, and wherever it squeaks or deflects under your weight, drive extra flooring nails through to the joists. Plane down high spots, and shim low spots with thin pieces of wood or several layers of building paper. Then nail the plywood or hardboard over that, countersinking every nailhead. Now the final finish layer can be put down (see chapter 15).

Generally, a sloping (tilting) floor reflects the settlement of the foundation and/or the interior or exterior load-bearing walls. A sagging floor (with a low area) reflects a problem with the supporting joists or girder. Floor problems on the first floor are the most common, easiest to diagnose, and often the most fixable.

You may find that the joists have shrunk or settled with old age. In this case you'll see a gap between the top of the joists and the subfloor. If the gap is small, insert thin wooden shims between the joist and subfloor. If the gap is larger and the joist is sound, nail a 2 × 4 to the joist, snug up against the floorboards. The shims should eliminate any bounce in the floor, and the 2 × 4 should silence any creaks.

Your floor problem may be the result of termites or wood rot. If you are not up to replacing the entire floor structure, you can arrange a new supporting system by adding a girder, made from two 2 × 10s bolted together and supported by posts. In this case the joists are no longer resting on the foundation. Of course, posts will take up extra room in the cellar. Depending on the severity of the wood rot, this may only be a temporary measure

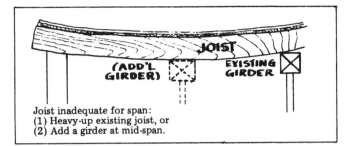

Joist inadequate for span:
(1) Heavy-up existing joist, or
(2) Add a girder at mid-span.

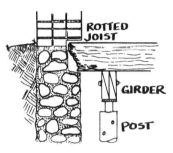

tions. Get help sizing the girder from an architect or engineer. You can make a girder by bolting two 2 × 10s together. The girder is temporarily held in place by timbers, then metal jacking posts are installed every 6 to 8 feet. Be sure you have adequate footings for the posts. To support an existing shrunken girder, drive wood shims in the gaps between the girder and joists, and/or between the girder and the posts.

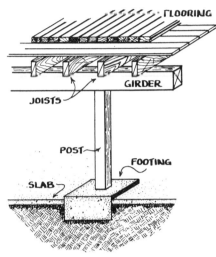

and you'll eventually have to replace the bad wood. If the problem is severe, replace the wood rather than choose a stop-gap method. The best solution, of course, is to get rid of the problem, whether it's insects, moisture, or both.

If the foundation has crumbled where ends of joists or girders rest, prop up beams temporarily with timbers or metal jacking posts while the damaged foundation is repaired. If a joist sags because of notching (perhaps weakened by plumbers hacking away to make room for pipes), jack or push it into place and bridge the notch over with 2 × 4s, or support the notched joist with permanent posts.

If the floor bounces and vibrates excessively, it may suffer from undersized or inadequately bridged joists. Bridging stiffens a floor by transmitting loads to adjacent joists. It's tricky to install crossed wooden bridging once the floor is in place, but you can toenail 2 × 6s between the joists and get the same stiffening effect. If the joists are not large enough for the distance they span, they are also subject to deflection. In this case the floor might be safe enough (if you don't want a grand piano in the room), but you may want to heavy-up the joists. Bolt additional joists of similar sizes to the existing joists. (Push them up against the subfloor to reduce sag in the floor above.) Sometimes you can just add 2 × 4 stiffeners to the bottom of existing joists. Cross-bridging or solid-bridging will also reduce deflection, torsion, and other movement from walking on the floor.

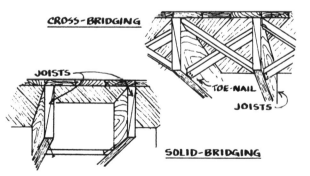

You've got a serious problem if the joists themselves are not adequately supported. Although adding a girder is usually a major job best left for a contractor, a competent do-it-yourselfer can handle it if there are no complica-

On upper floors you can install columns and camouflage them with bookshelves, storage units, or partitions. Be sure the load transfers to a load-bearing surface, usually the foundation footings in the cellar, or the central girder beneath the ground floor. Line up columns vertically with the intervening joists. The joists will transmit the load from one column to those below, and through to the footing.

DIFFERENTIAL SHRINKAGE

A masonry house with a woodframed prop wall (an interior load-bearing wall) will often develop a special inward slope. While the exterior bearing walls made of masonry remain stable, the interior wall shrinks and settles down. Telltale signs of this might be a large gap between the walls and the floor on the top storey, and a slant toward the interior that gets more pronounced the higher you go in the house.

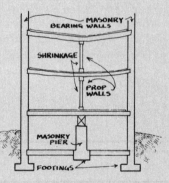

If a slope becomes more apparent on upper stories, this probably indicates benign internal settlement. If the slant is most noticeable on the first floor, it's due to inadequate support by girders or footings. Check that the interior bearing wall is properly supported throughout the house and down to the ground. Wood posts in the basement may have deteriorated, or sit on improper footings. If a previous owner removed a bearing wall on the second storey, the middle of the third storey no longer bears on anything.

USING JACK POSTS

Assuming you don't need to correct a structural problem, you can use jack posts to level a sagging floor. (Using jacks for the wrong problem could mean you lift the whole floor—sag and all—upward and right off the sill, aggravating an already big problem.) Jacks also provide temporary support as you work on repairing beams. The main thing to remember when using jacks is this: Don't overjack. You don't want to lift, you want to provide support to keep things from falling. When using temporary jacks, jack just enough to allow a new member to squeeze in. Don't automatically jack beams until they are level. In an old house, if you jack or otherwise force a framing member to level or plumb, you'll probably break plaster, or at least move window and door trim into undesirable configurations.

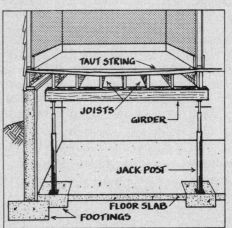

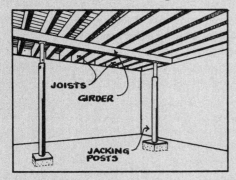

To determine where to place the post, check the underside of the sagging joist or girder with a spirit level, or stretch a string tightly across the floor of the room above and measure the distance from the string to the lowest point of the sag. Occasionally you can use only one post strategically placed under the sag's midpoint. Usually, however, you'll need two posts and a piece of heavy timber as a brace for all the joists under the sagging area. (You can use two 2 × 10s bolted together.)

Have enough support under the post. If the basement floor is at least 4 inches thick and not cracked or crumbling, it will probably support the weight. Otherwise, pour a footing for the post. Break a 2-foot-square and 12-inch-deep hole in the cellar floor. Mix your own concrete from 1 part portland cement, 2 parts coarse sand, and 4 parts gravel. (Get gravel mix if you buy ready-mix concrete.) Let the new footing cure for a week before installing the post.

When ready to install the jack post, position the base plate first. Attach the plate to the concrete with lead expansion anchors or as the directions recommend. Set up the steel tubes, raise the post to the approximate height, and insert the pin or pins in the proper holes to lock the post in position. Attach the adjustable screw jack on top. Be sure the screw jack is fully lowered with the top plate almost touching the beam.

Slowly raise the adjusting screw only until the top plate is in firm contact with the timber. Check to see that the post is perfectly vertical. Give the screw one more half turn, then stop.

Three or four days later, give it another one-quarter turn. Proceed gradually as this tremendous pressure could damage other areas of the house. Continue turning the screw no more than one-quarter turn every three or four days until the floor is level. Faster jacking could crack plaster walls, damage other structural beams, and even rupture masonry or plumbing.

Though you can leave the steel jack post there permanently (some cities require that you weld the screw jack in position, or that you box it in), you may want to replace it later with a wood post or metal lally column. In this case, jack the floor a bit off midpoint of the sag to allow for proper placement of the permanent post. Use hardwood shims to bring the permanent post to the precise level of the jack post(s).

STAIR REPAIR

Even when a staircase is undeniably in bad shape, most of us put off making repairs. Stairs have a mysterious hidden structure, and we're sure the work will be very disruptive. The trick in fixing a staircase is knowing the hidden mysteries of construction. Once you understand what's behind a loose rail or a squeaky tread, most repairs require only simple carpentry. Others may require starting from scratch and routing new stringers. See the drawing on page 224 to understand how a typical staircase is put together.

Before the days of uniform production parts, a stair builder came in as one of the construction crew, and built a stair to fit the new house. Leveling an old staircase presents problems of geometry and materials. For stairs to be safe, more than the treads (steps) may need repair or replacement. If your staircase sags and creaks, take into account the rise between the treads and the run of the entire staircase.

If your staircase sags, this indicates an overall structural problem. In masonry buildings, your staircase may suffer from differential settlement—the interior wood frame may shrink and settle, while the outer masonry walls remain stable. When the interior suffers from differential settlement, either the wall string is pulled away from the wall, or the stair gets pulled apart, with steps coming out of the wall-string housing. The result in either case is an out-of-level stair. This calls for stair rehabilitation.

Whenever the stringers, which house the treads and risers, the newel post, or the support structure underneath need repair, you've got a big job on your hands. Shaky handrails caused by broken or missing balusters (spindles) are minor repairs that any reasonably skilled carpenter can handle.

In the old days, the stair builder would lay out the rise and run of the stairs according to the size of the opening, and would do much of the fabrication and assembly on site. Today, builders put up a house around production parts. Consequently, there are few stair builders capable of handling the geometry and skills that were once a standard part of the trade.

Stair Geometry

A staircase creates the hypotenuse of a triangle from floor to floor in your old house. The overall run runs the length of the floor from the end of the stringer to the point where the upper floor edge overhangs the floor below. A stringer accommodates a measured number of treads al-

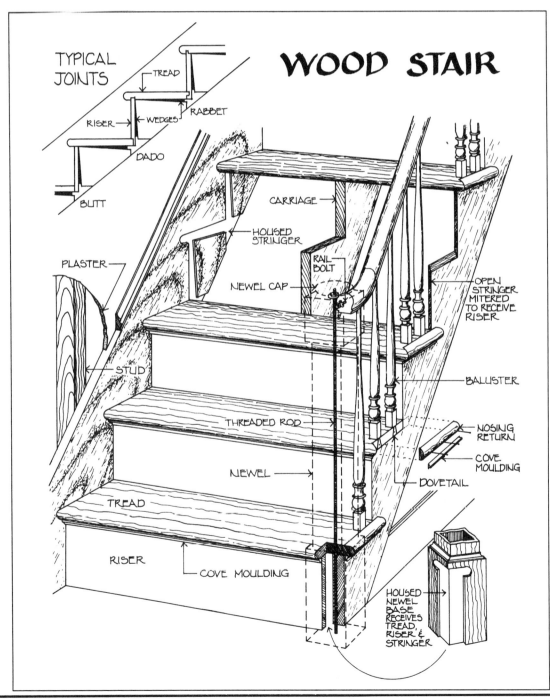

lowing head room above (at least 7 feet) and a comfortable (and safe) rise between treads.

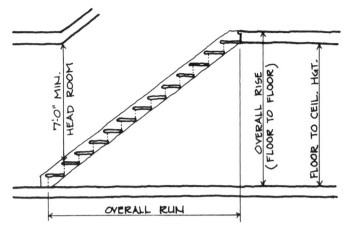

Measure the *overall rise* of the staircase by determining how many treads you should have when the standard rise between them is 6 5/8 to 7 3/4 inches. Determine the *run* by subdividing the available horizontal length of space into a run that fits the amount of space you have. Keep in mind that standard tread sizes are 9 1/2 to 12 inches deep, with 1 to 1 1/2 inches nosing.

If we think of the simplest, straight-run cellar staircase, the stair builder will have to shorten the stair run to provide more headroom. Find the run for each step by dividing the overall run by the number of treads. When determining step runs you can round to the nearest 1/4 inch. The measurements for the individual risers, of course, are fixed and unchangeable. If the floor above or below slopes, measure the floor-to-floor height at the bottom of the stair to get the critical dimension.

Once you have these measurements, you can make a *story rod* to check your riser dimensions. Cut a piece of 1 1/2-inch × 1 1/2-inch dressed stock slightly longer than the floor-to-floor height. Stand the rod up in the well so that it's plumb and mark the floor-to-floor height on the rod. Then divide the rod into equal parts corresponding to the number of risers (for example, 14 equal parts for 14 risers). Use a pair of dividers to help with the mathematics. Figure it to the fraction of the inch, then use dividers to make the divisions exactly even. You won't need the overall run dimension unless the stair must fit into a confined, preexisting space.

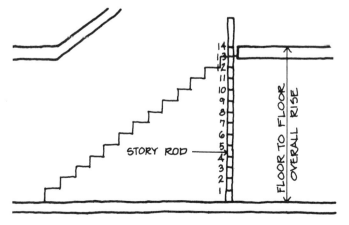

If the stairs are more than 2 feet 8 inches wide, provide a center carriage to support the steps. House treads in the stringers, and fasten them with cleats.

Repairing Stairs at the *Old-House Journal*

We repaired a staircase in our old *Old-House Journal* offices. The stairs were severely out of level (3/4 inch per foot or more), and the treads pulled out of their housings on the wall string. This was caused by differential settlement—the interior wood frame had shrunk and settled, while the outer masonry wall remained stable. On our stairs, the wall string was attached to the masonry party wall, but the outside string rested on the sloping floor.

Even if your stair isn't like ours, the following techniques apply to almost any traditional wood stair.

In general, stair problems (separate from handrail problems) stem from three sources: differential building settlement, wood shrinkage, and occasionally poor detailing and workmanship. Look at the

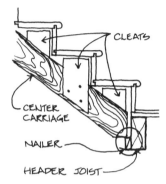

underside to see if poor structural detail contributes to the pronounced sag, which creates a potentially hazardous condition.

Assuming the structure is sound and you can't level the floors, you need to level the stairs. Stairs must maintain a consistent rise (height) for each step. Otherwise, walking rhythm is broken and people trip. If we leveled our stair completely, the height of the riser at the top step would be reduced by over 1 1/2 inches, meaning a level stair would meet an out-of-level landing. As

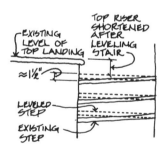

a compromise, we jacked up the stair only until it was comfortable to walk on, yet maintained a relatively consistent rise. Then it could be made secure.

Demolishing and Bracing

Remove any plaster under the stair to get to the entire substructure. (Measure and record any decorative plaster mouldings first so you can replace them later. You'll probably have to run a new cornice moulding in place or duplicate the moulding with stock wood mouldings.) Underneath, we found poor original detailing. The carriages had merely been toenailed to a little nailing strip attached to the header joist at the bottom of the flight. Now the center and outer carriages were perched on the very edge of the nailing strip.

Before lifting and pushing the staircase back into place, remove any items that obstruct the movement of the stair

REPLACING TREADS AND RISERS

Follow the original construction of the staircase. Get underneath it—if it's an old stair, be prepared to replace some plaster in the stair soffit under the stairs. These instructions are for one of the most difficult repairs—a closed-string staircase with a center carriage underneath. (Working on an open-string stair is easier because treads and risers go in from above—though gluing and wedging must be done from underneath—and there is no center carriage in the way.)

When you can get underneath the stairs, it's simple to replace treads and risers following these steps:

1. Remove plaster behind bad treads and risers and keep the edges clean with a utility knife for plaster patching, if necessary.

2. Remove glue blocks by tapping them smartly with a hammer or a chisel.

3. Knock the wedges out by hammering against an old screwdriver behind each wedge.

4. From above, cut the treads and remove them to get to the risers.

5. Cut the new tread a bit shorter than the old one to fit it into the housing. Cut one housing slightly deeper than the other so you can insert the tread into the deeper housing, drop it into place, then slide it into the opposite housing. Minimum bearing in the housing should be about 1/4 inch. (It wouldn't be wise to build an entire stair this way, but it's adequate for a few replacement steps.)

Make one housing 1/4-inch deep and the opposite

housing 1/2-inch deep with a chisel. With later stairs, you may have to shim a housing up to 1/4-inch deep instead. The shim, a strip of wood set into the housing, acts as a stop to keep the new tread from moving and dropping off its bearing on the string. Obviously, cut the new tread or riser 1/2-inch longer than the distance between the strings, giving 1/4-inch bearing on each side.

6. Insert risers before treads. The tongue on the back of a milled stair tread will interfere with its installation from the top. In the unlikely case that your center carriage is stepped, or cut to shape, you'll have to plane the tongue off and fill the groove in the riser with a strip of wood. Force such a tread *back* against the riser for a tight fit.

If the center carriage is a nailing strip with individual cleats, leave the tongue on, and simply remove that cleat that bears against the riser above. Also, remove the wedges from that riser. Swing the riser back so you can insert the tread. Now swing the tread all the way *forward* in the housing. (Put some glue on the joints between treads and risers.)

7. Temporarily wedge the treads (without glue). Now rewedge all the risers. Then go back and glue the tread wedges, driving them home.

8. Attach two or three glue blocks under each step, using a rubbed glue joint and a couple of small nails in each. Glue blocks prevent squeaking later, so definitely use them. Make all new glue blocks and wedges; the old ones are not reusable because of the old glue in the pores. Any good cabinet glue, white or yellow, is fine.

9. Back-nail each step, using 6d common nails toed in opposition every 6 inches through the back of the riser into the tread.

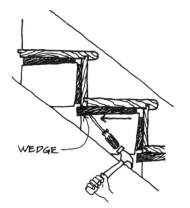

WEDGE

as a single unit. Take out wedges and misguided repairs from the past. Reposition misaligned treads and remove any badly warped treads. To brace the staircase you want to push the stair back toward the wall, jack it up some, and then refasten the carriages to the header joist.

Place a plank against the partition wall opposite the stair to distribute the load, and to protect the plaster. Place another plank against the stairs. Place two more planks, cut slightly longer than the space between the

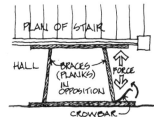

PLAN OF STAIR

HALL — BRACES (PLANKS) IN OPPOSITION — FORCE

CROWBAR

stair and the wall, in opposition. By wedging the planks in tighter and tighter with a crowbar, you can force the stair back into its housing against the masonry wall.

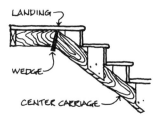

LANDING

WEDGE

CENTER CARRIAGE

At the same time, place braces under the carriages at the top and bottom of the flight to push the stair back up to a more level position. To hold the stair in this braced-up position, drive a wedge in between the upper end of each carriage and the joists under the landing.

Use joist hangers ("Teco clamps") to secure the carriages to the header joist. Once the carriages are secure, remove the braces under the stairs. Leave the wall-to-stair brace until all of the substructure repairs are completed, including rewedging the treads and risers.

Throughout this process keep an eye on stress points, and be ready to open a joint in the string to relieve stress. Otherwise, the string itself may crack. In our staircase, we had to keep the cylinder, a weak point, from moving too much.

Wedging

Replace all the wedges to be sure they are tight. Cut new ones from 3/4-inch pine. Cut them in an alternating

Replacing Treads and Risers
in a housed, closed-string stair with center carriage

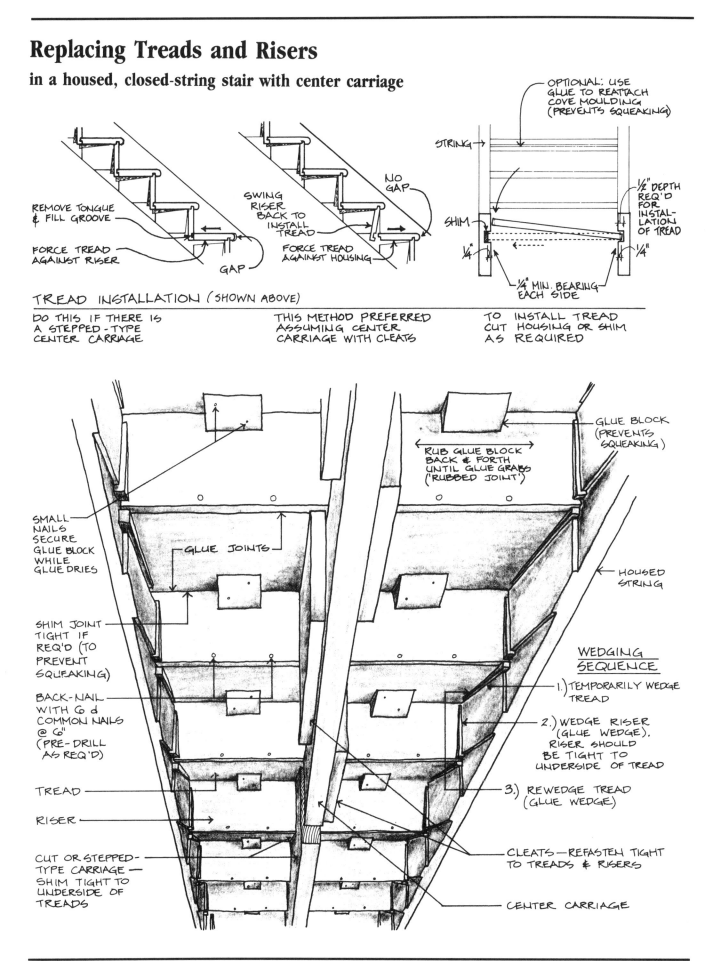

OPTIONAL: USE GLUE TO REATTACH COVE MOULDING (PREVENTS SQUEAKING)

STRING

SHIM

½" DEPTH REQ'D FOR INSTALLATION OF TREAD

¼"

¼"

¼" MIN. BEARING EACH SIDE

REMOVE TONGUE & FILL GROOVE

FORCE TREAD AGAINST RISER

GAP

SWING RISER BACK TO INSTALL TREAD

FORCE TREAD AGAINST HOUSING

NO GAP

TREAD INSTALLATION (SHOWN ABOVE)

DO THIS IF THERE IS A STEPPED-TYPE CENTER CARRIAGE

THIS METHOD PREFERRED ASSUMING CENTER CARRIAGE WITH CLEATS

TO INSTALL TREAD CUT HOUSING OR SHIM AS REQUIRED

GLUE BLOCK (PREVENTS SQUEAKING)

RUB GLUE BLOCK BACK & FORTH UNTIL GLUE GRABS ('RUBBED JOINT')

SMALL NAILS SECURE GLUE BLOCK WHILE GLUE DRIES

GLUE JOINTS

HOUSED STRING

SHIM JOINT TIGHT IF REQ'D (TO PREVENT SQUEAKING)

BACK-NAIL WITH 6d COMMON NAILS @ 6" (PRE-DRILL AS REQ'D)

TREAD

RISER

CUT OR STEPPED-TYPE CARRIAGE — SHIM TIGHT TO UNDERSIDE OF TREADS

WEDGING SEQUENCE

1.) TEMPORARILY WEDGE TREAD

2.) WEDGE RISER (GLUE WEDGE). RISER SHOULD BE TIGHT TO UNDERSIDE OF TREAD

3.) REWEDGE TREAD (GLUE WEDGE)

CLEATS—REFASTEN TIGHT TO TREADS & RISERS

CENTER CARRIAGE

Retired master stair builder Harry Waldemar checks the level of the stair at the old Old-House Journal offices. It had dropped 1 1/2 inches over a 2-foot run, due partly to interior building settlement.

Note the treads pulling out of their housings in the wall string. "Wainscot" is just grained plaster.

The staircase is literally being pulled apart.

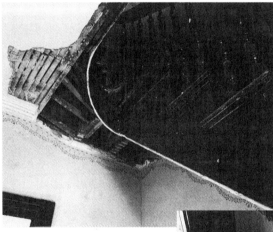

Plaster and wood lath were removed along the entire soffit under the stair, revealing the cylinder braces. Ours is a typical row-house cylinder stair, or well stair.

The stair is braced against the partition wall opposite it. This operation pushes the steps back into their housings.

To solve the problem of the slipped carriages, the stair is jacked up a bit. A piece of lumber is wedged between the carriages and another plank laid on the steps below.

After driving in the wedges to hold the carriages in place, Harry installs a metal joist hanger on each of the outside carriages. They make the carriages secure to the header joist.

Driving new wedges in the wall string housings.

After gluing the wedge in place, drive a nail through the wedge and tread and into the string. The wedges under each tread and behind each riser secure the steps in the string housings. Note the wood cleat nailed to the center carriage (at right). The cleats prevent deflection of steps.

The white pieces of wood are new glue blocks. The photo shows the front (outer) carriage and string, where glue blocks are doubled.

The old newel is removed and the opening is squared up. The newel base is fitted into the floor and against the bottom step by trial and error. (Harry had to chisel "a little bit more" off the newel base before installing it.) If it's fitted accurately, the newel should stand sturdy even before nailing.

Apply glue only near the miter joint on a return nosing. Flat decorative brackets, return nosings, and cove mouldings (covering the joint between the return nosing and bracket) are installed step-by-step, from the top of the flight to the bottom. Assembly order depends on each return nosing being installed after the bracket on the riser above it. The cove moulding goes on last because it hides the joint.

Nailing the return nosing in place.

pattern to maximize long grain. You can set up a jig on a table saw to maintain the critical dimension of the wedges. This way, variation in length doesn't matter, because all wedges will be driven in to the same extent, and then excess can be trimmed off.

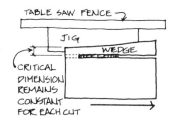

Glue each wedge in place. As a time-saver, make a "bouquet of wedges." Put carpenter's glue in a wide-mouth container and keep a handful of wedges skinny-end-down in the jar. When you need a wedge, take one out and spread the glue with a scrap of wood or another wedge.

Insert the wedges from the top of the flight to the bottom, with the tread always wedged before the riser below it. The wedge must make even contact on both the surface of the step and the string. If it doesn't, the wedge won't effectively secure the step and you may split the string while driving the wedge. Hammer the wedge in until it's snug, but be careful not to apply too much force. Last, drive a nail through the wedge and tread into the string to help keep the wedge in place.

Cleats

Cleats, or stepped wood blocking, on the center carriage take the springiness out of each step and deaden the hollow sound of footsteps. If the cleats don't meet the underside of the treads after the carriages are braced up, pry off the existing cleats and renail them snugly against the back side of each riser and the underside of each tread. Toe one nail into the tread, another into the riser. (Be careful to angle the nails so they don't go through riser or tread.) Install the cleats alternating from one side of the carriage to the other. That way the carriage won't tend to twist when load is applied to the stair.

Glue Blocks

Whether or not a stair has existing glue blocks, install new ones at this point. These are attached to the underside of the stair where the tread and riser come together. Install them with a rubbed glue joint (put a glue-smeared block in position and rub it back and forth until the glue grabs or resists the rubbing motion). This creates quite a strong joint. Drive two finish nails into each block to keep it in position while the glue dries.

Glue blocks prevent the stair from squeaking by increasing the surface area of the tread-to-riser joint. They also provide additional strength at the joints. You may be able to put the new glue blocks in next to the old. We used two per step between carriages, and two more where the steps were joined to the front string.

Nails

Back-nail each step (we used 6d common nails). Place a nail every 6 inches along the back side of the riser. Toe the nails slightly to add some strength. If a tread has

sagged or warped, don't force it upward for back-nailing; there's a chance the pressure of the warp will split the riser at the nail.

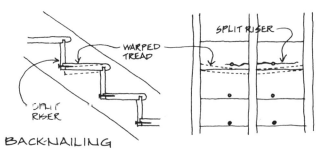

Generally, all of the fastening done on a stair is underneath and hidden from view. Face-nailing can provide additional strength, but it never looks great, so avoid it if possible. If you must

face-nail the treads, try using two #8 finish nails in the top of each tread, down to the riser.

To complete the substructure repairs, drive some #10 finish nails through the front string, into the front carriage. This helps make the flight less springy.

While the structure is now more secure, the balustrade and newel still need finishing.

The Balustrade and Newel

The balustrade—the assembly of the handrail and the balusters that hold it up—and the newel need to be repaired once you have checked out the structural problems with an out-of-level staircase. If the baluster is wobbly and out of plumb, you need to straighten it. To plumb the balustrade, remove the newels and disconnect the rail bracket. Use a plumb bob between the balusters to level the balustrade—a level won't work as there may be no flat surfaces to rest it on.

With the newels removed, you can push the balustrade into a plumb (vertical) position. If it resists, you may have to loosen or remove some of the balusters. Nail a temporary brace in place to support the balustrade, and work on replacing the newels.

Square up the existing cutouts in the steps and floor before fitting the new newel. Then cut the newel to fit the opening. Once the newel is fitted into the proper position at the correct height, trace the profile of the level rail onto the newel. Then mortise out the newel for the rail. If your stair rail does not have an easement, which allows you to make the intersection between the rail and newel perpendicular, merely butt the rail against the newel.

Cut the rail mortise out with a chisel. An *incannel gouge* will help square up the curved profile of the mortise. An incannel gouge will cut perpendicular sides on a mortise (a standard gouge cuts sloping sideways). After

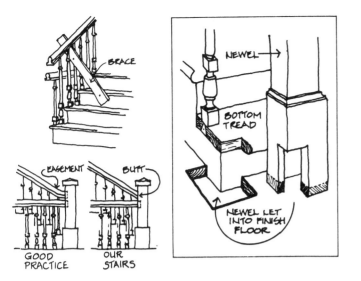

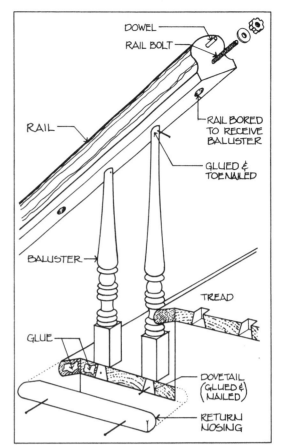

cutting the mortise, brace the newel into a vertical position using a block of wood wedged between the wall and the newel to hold it solidly in position for toenailing. If there's no wall to brace against, brace the newel with blocks of wood resting on the floor. Drive finish nails through the subflooring, the bottom riser, and the front string. Likewise, toe finish nails through the handrail into the newel.

Install the second newel as you did the first. With both newels nailed in place, you can remove the temporary brace from the rail along with the newel brace. Replace all the return nosings and brackets. To make it easier to adjust the fit where existing joints and surfaces have become uneven, you may want to cut the replacement parts as separate pieces. Our master stair builder Harry Waldemar cut the new brackets—short pieces of 1/4 × 2-inch lattice—slightly oversize to be cut to fit later.

Nail old and new balusters in place with #6 or #8 common nails through the dovetail into the tread before installing brackets and return nosings. To avoid splitting the wood, nip off the end of each nail so it crushes rather than splits the wood fibers as it is driven. You can tighten overly loose dovetail joints with wood shims before nailing. Toenail the top of each baluster with a #6 or #8 finish nail. You probably won't need to glue the balusters when installing or tightening them.

In an open-string staircase, the outer string is cut to reveal the stepping of treads and risers. At the bottom, the balusters are dovetailed into the treads. At the top, they fit into a bored hole in the underside of the rail.

Closed-string stairs often have balusters let into grooves in both the handrail and the outer string. Spacers, or pieces of finished wood that cap the groove between balusters, help hold the assembly rigid.

Balusters

If a dovetailed baluster is loose, it's best to remove it so it can be cleanly reglued and nailed. Carefully pry off the return nosing to expose the dovetails. Take out any nails you see and remove the baluster. Clean all connections of old glue and varnish. If there is no longer a tight fit be-

A dovetailed or open-string staircase. After the dovetails are repaired, the return nosing is glued back into place.

A closed-string stair.

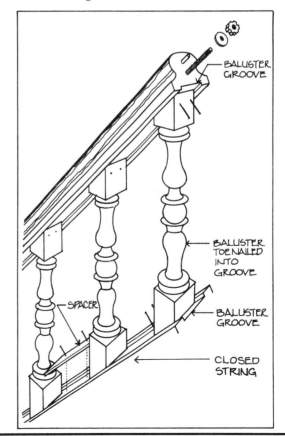

tween baluster and rail, or between baluster and tread, use wood shims rather than driving a lot of random nails. After the loose connections are shimmed and glued, one finishing nail driven into each dovetail is quite enough. Toenail at the connection between baluster and rail.

When you drive a nail into dry old hardwood, there's always a chance of the wood splitting. Where there is the greatest likelihood of splitting, such as at the top of a slender baluster, predrill a hole before nailing. Otherwise, nip the end off each nail before driving it. This way the blunt end will crush rather than split the wood fibers.

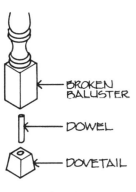

BROKEN BALUSTER

DOWEL

DOVETAIL

If the dovetail is broken off or split, fabricate and attach a new one by doweling. Now refasten the return nosing. Glue at the miter and just adjacent to it, then nail it in place. Gluing along the full length of the nosing could cause the tread to split. Gluing at the miter only will keep the miter joint closed, while allowing for expansion and contraction of the tread.

In a closed-string stair, the balusters are let into grooves top and bottom, and anchored with nails. If these balusters are loose, carefully toenail them in place.

Handrails

A wobbly handrail can make a staircase as dangerous as loose steps. Handrails don't often come apart at the seams, but if yours has, it should be tackled before you reglue all the balusters. Sections of rail are connected by rail bolts, wood dowels, and glue. It is possible to reglue and tighten a loose joint in the rail without removing the whole handrail. Disassembly involves unplugging the access hole to get at the special star nut that clamps the two sections together. Loosen the nut by tapping a screwdriver or nailset against the edge of the nut. Pull the joint apart just far enough to insert a chisel; scrape away old glue and varnish, then reglue. Work the glue into the dowel joint well, since this is where the strength of the connection really is.

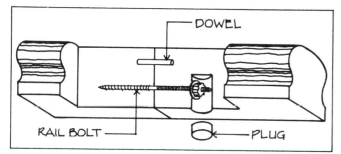

DOWEL

RAIL BOLT

PLUG

In fact, there are several kinds of rail bolts. The most practical and widely used is the one just discussed. It has wood-screw threads on one end, and machine-screw threads and a star nut on the other end. But there's also a twin-nut rail bolt with machine-screw threads along its entire length; this is less practical because it necessitates

two access holes, one for each nut. The third type, a simple double-ended screw, often strips out and should be replaced with a rail bolt if this should happen.

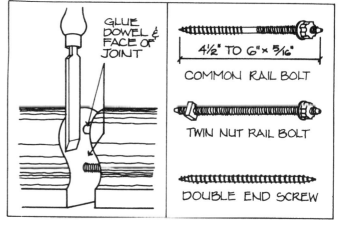

GLUE DOWEL & FACE OF JOINT

4½" TO 6" x 5/16"

COMMON RAIL BOLT

TWIN NUT RAIL BOLT

DOUBLE END SCREW

A rail bolt is much like a hanger bolt, but with a point on the machine-screw end. (The point makes it easier to slip the star nut on in a tight place.) Hanger bolts are available at most hardware stores, and a common hex nut can be ground into a star nut configuration. But stair-rail bolts—*with* pointed ends and star nuts—are still sometimes available at older hardware stores and stair-parts suppliers.

If the wood-screw threads work loose on an existing rail bolt, try screwing the rail bolt deeper into the wood. This also remedies stripped-out machine-screw threads on the other end, since now the nut is in a new position.

Installing a new rail bolt where there was a double-ended screw before requires boring an access hole that intersects the bolt hole. You'll need to scrape a flat spot *inside* the access hole for the washer to rest upon. Don't change the shape of the hole at the surface, or the plug you make for it won't fit neatly.

Newels

The newel connection to the bottom step is a vulnerable joint. Because of its height, the newel acts as a lever when something bumps against the top of it. This weakens the connections of the newel to the bottom step and to the floor.

Newels come in many sizes and styles, but there are really only two main construction types: solid and hollow (box). Solid newels can be made from a solid piece of wood or they can be glued up. This type is often turned on a lathe. In most cases the wood joint at the base of the newel is housed, or cut to let in the step. The newel is fastened through its face to the string and/or riser and to the floor. Alternately, it might be bored through the bottom step.

The box newel is built from several pieces of wood and can be anything from a simple four-sided hollow post, to a grand nineteenth-century newel with recessed panels and mouldings. Again, the newel is housed to receive the bottom step. The newel is probably toenailed to the step and the floor, but its stability most often comes from a threaded center rod that is tied in to the top of the newel,

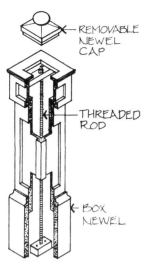

REMOVABLE NEWEL CAP

THREADED ROD

BOX NEWEL

and then attached to the floor. Since its purpose is to support the handrail, you'll find a newel at the bottom and top of open-string stairs, as well as wherever the handrail abruptly changes pitch or direction along the run.

If you need to repair the newel, you'll have to disconnect the handrail. With a box newel, take off the cap (usually nailed in box construction). The wood-thread end of the rail bolt will be screwed into the rail with the nut inside the hollow newel.

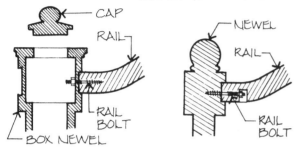

CAP
RAIL
RAIL BOLT
BOX NEWEL

NEWEL
RAIL
RAIL BOLT

In a solid newel with an easement in the rail just above the newel, the nut is in the rail and the wood-screw threads are in the newel. (The rail is also mortised into the newel on expert jobs.) With a straight rail, the rail is just butted and toenailed to the newel. When the rail ends in a volute, the newel is bored into the rail's underside, glued, and toenailed. Of course, if you have a loose rail-bolt connection, it'll have to be tightened.

Nailing

If a glued-and-bored or a nailed joint loosens up, a few well-placed nails may do the trick. Take the time to understand the construction of the

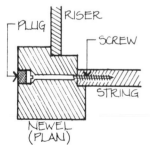

PLUG
RISER
SCREW
STRING
NEWEL (PLAN)

joint, because a lot of random nails can actually weaken or split the joint. No need to worry about splitting a solid newel, but as always, drill a pilot hole or nip off the end of the nail if you're going into a thin piece of hardwood.

Without taking apart the stair, you won't know for sure if the riser and tread were cut away to let in the housed newel. If nails won't hold,

screw through the newel base into the front of the riser or the open string. Counter-bore any screws and plug the holes. Screwing into the string will always strengthen the newel connection; the disadvantage, of course, is the plugged hole left in the face of the newel.

If a newel is very loose, you might as well remove it to examine the actual connections, rather than taking pot luck with random nails. First, disconnect the handrail. Pull the newel loose from the floor; it's probably toenailed, but if the newel was loose to begin with, removal should be easy. Take out all the old nails, and start over on the assembly. Don't use glue except on a bored connection into the rail or tread. Drive nails at an angle to the grain; nailing directly into end grain makes for a weak connection.

To tighten the connection between the box newel and the floor, take off the cap and see if there's a center rod. If there is, tighten the nut to pull the newel against the floor. If the rod is no longer connected to the floor, remove the newel and secure the rod to the floor. If there is no rod, install a threaded rod the height of the newel.

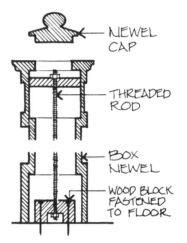

NEWEL CAP

THREADED ROD

BOX NEWEL

WOOD BLOCK FASTENED TO FLOOR

If you have swell-step construction, the least sophisticated of all stair joinery, the newel is merely bored into the bottom tread. In somewhat better construction, the bottom "pin" is carried through the rib, and also wedged just under the tread.

If you have access from under the stairs, you can see if the connection was wedged. When it does eventually loosen up, drive the wedge tight again from beneath. Of course, you can always create such a connection if the bottom of the newel is long enough to be mortised out and wedged. If the newel wasn't extended down far enough to be wedged, or if you don't have access from below, you'll have to work from above. Reglue and toenail the newel connection into the tread.

CHAPTER 13

Windows and Doors

Windows get into bad shape because they're subject to exterior weathering and because they have moving parts. Old windows are easy to fix because they're very simple—just two counterweighted sashes running in a slot—and because they're made of wood, the easiest building material to renew.

As long as you have someone to do the simple carpentry and painting, window rehabilitation is often less expensive, less disruptive, and keeps the house more in character than replacing windows entirely.

Doors can get into trouble as a result of settlement and faulty or worn hardware. An endemic old-house problem, doors may also suffer from too many layers of paint. As with windows, you can usually rehabilitate doors rather than replace them entirely.

HOW WINDOWS WORK

You'll find two kinds of mechanical systems in old-house windows: the sash-weight system and the tape-balance system. Sash-weight construction consists of a pulley and weight balancing act. Tape-balance systems are spring-loaded, with the spring and steel tape assembled in a housing in the window. Before getting to work on your windows, you should understand how both systems work.

Sash-Weight Windows

Sash windows first appeared in Europe as unglazed oak frames (the word "sash" comes from the French "chassis") which slid horizontally or vertically in crude tracks. By the late seventeenth century, glazed sashes counterbalanced with clumsy weights and pulleys had made their way from Holland to England; eventually they reached colonial America. Sash windows resisted the harsh new-world climate far better than swinging case-

ment types, and soon evolved into the modern double-hung window.

While sash windows are still a very popular and important part of house construction, the balance hardware of the past has not fared as well. Balances perform two roles: holding the window in position once it's opened, and minimizing the effort needed for opening by counterbalancing the weight of the sash and glass. New window construction favors the tube, block-and-tackle, or channel-spring balances—which have a limited weight capacity—or friction mechanisms that steady the sash but don't make it any easier to lift.

With the advent of new window mechanisms the advantages of weights and pulleys (or its competitor, the tape balance) were largely forgotten. So, too, were many of the technical details and specifications that made these systems work efficiently.

Pulleys

Pulleys, the critical part of the system, were manufactured in many grades and a variety of designs. Economy pulleys made from rough cast iron (today they appear as "built-up" stamped-steel halves) turn on a simple wire or pin axle. These pulleys suffice for light sashes, but heavy sashes with large lights (windowpanes)—especially those hung by chain—require steel, gun-metal, or brass axles; ball or roller bearings; and a cold-rolled steel wheel. The best units incorporate brass or bronze lathe-turned wheels.

Pulley diameters range from 1 3/4 to 3 inches and are determined by the thickness of pulley stile and the clearance needed for the weight to travel in the weight box. (Multiplying the thickness of the stile by 2.25 is one way to calculate pulley size.) Diameters over 2 inches are preferred, as they give the cord or chain a comfortable arc over which to travel, and extend its life. In the past, some manufacturers also offered special overhead pulleys for installation on top of the window frame rather than in the pulley stile. These models came with single or double wheels and saved space to accommodate twin windows: All weights could be at one side of the sash.

Today, the range of available pulleys is severely limited. Some hardware stores carry light-duty stamped-metal units, but few supply the rugged, long-life pulleys of the past. In fact, many restoration millwork companies go for salvage when they need sash pulleys, recycling them either from discarded frames or from the ones they're replacing. Here are some tips on reusing sash pulleys:

Take extra care when removing pulleys that are not obviously mounted with two wood screws countersunk in the face. Some novel designs were friction-fit or used hidden spurs to anchor the pulley. Don't pry the pulley out by wedging a screwdriver between the wheel and case, as this can break cast parts.

Strip old paint by machine buffing or soaking in a solution of lye (such as household drain opener or oven cleaner) or TSP. Consider replating for a like-new appearance with bronze and other fancy finishes.

As low-rpm devices, sash pulleys fail more from abuse than from wear. In most cases, a quick lubrication helps them run more smoothly and quietly before pressing them back into service. To get at the wheel-and-axle surface use "pinpoint" oilers, such as aerosol cans with extension tubes or disposable glue syringes (available from craft and woodworking supply houses). Using motorcycle-chain lube and powdered graphite in similar applicators may also do the trick.

Weights

Weights—far simpler in operation than pulleys—consist of round bars of rough cast iron, but may also be square or made of lead in limited weight-box space. Installing them involves little more than attaching them to the sash cord with an appropriate knot or hooking on a chain with a cup.

Weights usually range from 3 to 20 pounds each. Matching the weight of the sash is important for the balance to work effectively. Remove sashes from the frame and weigh them on a scale, or leave the sash in place and estimate its weight. To estimate sash weight do the following calculation: *add* 1 pound for every square foot of single-thickness glass, or 1 1/3 pounds for double thickness to the height in feet plus the width in feet of the wood sash multiplied by one of the following: 2.1 for 2 1/4-inch sash, 1.67 for 1 3/4-inch sash, or 1.33 for 1 3/8-inch sash. For example, for 4 square feet of double-thickness glass, and a height and width of 1 3/4-inch sash of approximately 2 1/4 and 2 feet, respectively, the calculation would look like this: $(4 \times 1 1/3) + 1.67 (2 1/4 + 2) = 12.43$, or just under 12 1/2 pounds. Some old references recommend that the weights for upper sash be 1/2 pound heavier than the sash, and lower weights 1/2 pound lighter.

Sash-weight manufacturing peaked years ago, with the result that today hardly any window-parts suppliers carry them in stock. Sash weights have value as scrap iron; you can sometimes find them at metal-recycling yards (as well as house wreckers) for around ten cents a pound. Salvage is inevitably cheaper than new castings, which might run a dollar or more per pound and usually involve shipping costs as well.

A second, more experimental route is making weights from PVC pipe. Select a tube as close as possible to 1 1/2 inches in diameter and cut it to length. Cap off the ends and fill it to the desired weight with sand or lead shot. Add an eyebolt to one end to complete the project.

If you need a large number of weights in specific sizes, you may want to order new ones. A few foundries dealing in short-run and specialty items still make weights (see suppliers list on page 236). If they don't already have one in stock, the foundry will need to work from a pattern or sample of the desired weight.

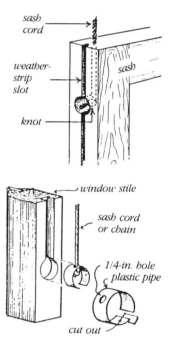

sash cord

weather-strip slot

knot

sash

window stile

sash cord or chain

1/4-in. hole plastic pipe

cut out

Weights hang from the sash on cord or chain—cord for lightweight windows, chain for heavy ones. Cord, made of braided cotton (modern versions have a nylon core), should be the correct size for the weight of the sash (see illustration). Domestic windows commonly take cord size #7 or #8. Chain, too, comes in several sizes, with the lightest designed for sashes 40 to 75 pounds and the heaviest for sashes over 150 pounds. You can still buy both at a serious hardware store or window-parts supplier.

Methods for attaching the cord or chain to the sash depend on the design of the sash:

• Most make use of a large hole bored in each sash stile, which will accept sash cord tied in an overhand knot (sometimes anchored with a wood screw). Chain installed with just wood screws was usually intended for a circular cup or ring.

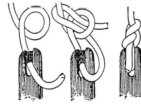

Attachment of sash cord to a sash weight.

• When these cups are missing or unavailable, small split rings sold by hardware or shoe-repair stores might substitute. Or you can resort to cutting cross sections of plastic pipe and fashioning them like expandable clips.

Tape Balances

Unlike their spring-loaded counterparts, only tape balances have a considerable history in old houses. Fortunately, they are still available today. Many patented spring-loaded balance designs appeared during the nineteenth century, intended to simplify the construction of twin and triple windows by eliminating the weight box. Most have gone the way of the buffalo. Today's two most popular spring devices appeared relatively recently: tube balances in the late 1930s and the block-and-tackle in the 1960s.

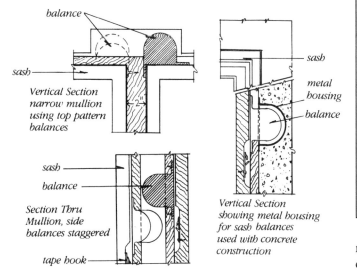

balance

sash

Vertical Section
narrow mullion
using top pattern
balances

sash
metal
housing
balance

sash
balance

Section Thru
Mullion, side
balances staggered

tape hook

Vertical Section
showing metal housing
for sash balances
used with concrete
construction

The tape balance—in use for about one hundred years—consists of a long spiral spring enclosed in a drum, onto which a steel tape is wound. The whole assembly is housed in a case similar to (and installed like) a sash pulley. The window sash is suspended by the tapes, which terminate in a small bail that catches a hook mounted on the sash stile. In many installations, this arrangement allows for disconnecting the tape and changing the balance without removing stops or sash from the window frame.

Manufacturers point out that tape balances are more versatile than a weights-and-pulleys system. They conserve space on either side of the window frame—especially when they are staggered—and make narrow mullions possible in twin- and triple-window construction. As with pulleys, overhead models are made for installations where the pulley stile has no room for hardware.

Of course, tape balances also have certain drawbacks. Sash weight is critical: Sash frames and glass have to be weighed—not estimated—for proper mating with balances, which are manufactured in many different sizes and spring tensions (and are often made-to-order). Most stock balances have a maximum limit of about 45 pounds when used in pairs; some special-order, heavy-duty units can counterbalance 100-pound sash.

It pays to "over-spec" the tape-balance size if there's any question about the right unit for a sash. Undersize or marginal balances tend to fail prematurely. You'll achieve

maximum balance life when the mechanism performs a certain percentage *under* its capacity.

Tape balances can break too. They are not user-serviceable and fixing them is usually more expensive than repairs on pulley systems. There are only two options for repair: complete replacement with a new unit, or rebuilding by the manufacturer. (Not all manufacturers offer this service and not all models can be rebuilt.)

Nonetheless, in recent years tape balances have experienced something of a revival. They allow energy-conscious house owners to fill the empty weight cavity with insulation. (Caulking the weight pocket and the exterior window casing, however, usually saves as much energy.) Also, tape balances offer a usable alternative to weights and pulleys for retrofits in historic buildings where hardware for the original system is either unavailable or impractical. Although not identical, tape balances are far closer in appearance to sash cord and pulleys than are contemporary spring balances, and they don't require remilling the sash stiles or other extensive changes to original design.

REPAIRING OLD WINDOWS

Before undertaking major window repair, take the time to watch the problem window in action. If the lower sash sticks a little, you may be able to fix it by just moving the stop moulding out a bit. If the sash is loose, simply reposition the stop closer. (Pry off the stop moulding carefully. If it splits, purchase similar stock at a lumberyard.) Above all, don't jump to conclusions and plane the

TAKING APART A DOUBLE-HUNG WINDOW

Study the diagram to help you disassemble your window. Remove the stops; lift the bottom sash out; unscrew the sash cords from the window. Tie a knot in the cord to keep it from falling into the weight well. With a sash chain, drive a small finishing nail through one link to hold it in position. To remove the parting bead, carefully pry it out, starting at the sill and working your way up to the bottom of the upper sash. Then lower the upper sash and pry from the top down. Lift out the upper sash, and secure the cords as you did with the lower ones. (See chapter 16 for tips on removing trim without damaging it.)

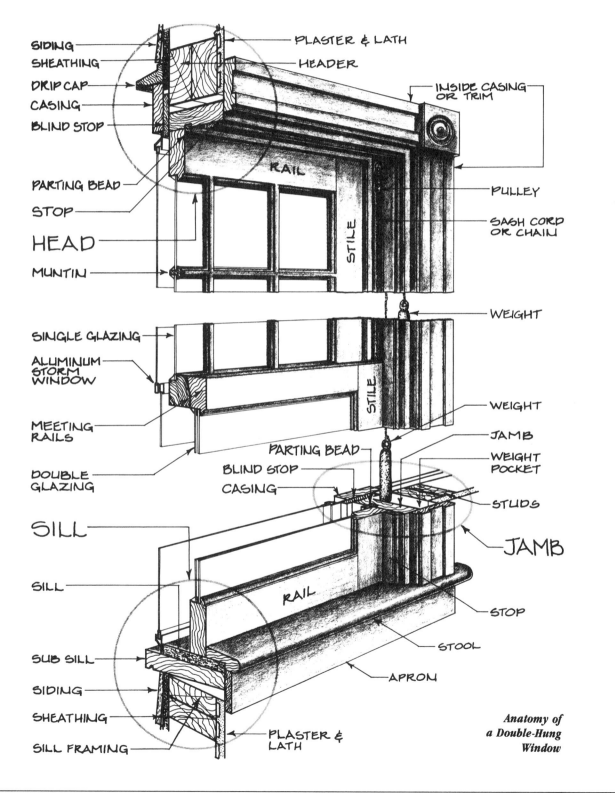

Anatomy of a Double-Hung Window

sash to keep it from binding. Planing madly before understanding the problem may leave you with a loose sash that still binds. Look first for easy-to-fix troubles like loose hardware, paint-encrusted sash chains, misplaced stops, or improperly installed weatherstripping.

Stuck Windows

Excessive paint layers between the sash and the parting bead or stop often cause window sashes to bind up or get stuck. At best, you'll have to carefully remove and reposition the window stop. At worst, you'll have to remove some of the paint buildup.

Following are the steps to take if the window is:

Painted shut. Using a screwdriver to break the paint film will permanently damage the wood. Use the *right* tools—and a little patience.

Use a razor knife to cut the paint film between the sash and jamb. Then gently work a wide-blade putty knife between the stops and sash all the way around the window. To deal with paint buildup between the sash and stops, insert the putty knife between one end of the sash and the sill. Work a flat prybar under the putty knife, and place a scrap of wood under the prybar to protect the window frame. Pry (apply leverage to) one side of the window at a time until it's free. If it resists, work the putty knife around the window and try again.

Swollen or warped. If all the paint has rubbed off an isolated part of the sash, you probably have a case of warping. Check the surface for trueness with a straightedge. Plane the bowed areas of the sash after you've removed the paint. However, severe warping means replacing the sash.

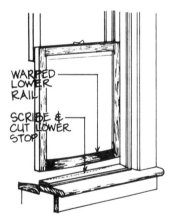

Though you can plane a swollen sash so it runs smoothly, even a well-maintained window swells up in humid weather. In very humid weather expect some minor resistance. If the window was improperly (or not recently) painted, the sash may have patches of swollen bare wood from recent exposure to rainwater. Allow the wood to dry and shrink back to its natural size before planing.

Sticking or binding. Lubricate windows that resist opening and closing. Scrape excess paint off the inside of the stop, off both sides of the parting bead, and off the stiles. After you repaint, wax the mating surfaces with a bar of paraffin, then reinstall the sash.

Loose or Broken Glass

Windows with loose, cracked, or broken glass ought to be repaired or replaced. First, remove the old putty—you can usually pick it out with your fingers. If the putty still

After cutting away paint between the sash and jamb with a razor, apply a little more pressure to work the window free.

Work the window loose with a prybar and putty knife. Be sure to place a scrap of wood under the prybar to avoid damaging the window frame.

has good bond, soften it with paint stripper. Use a thick, methylene-chloride-based stripper; this softens the putty without dripping all over the rest of the window. In windows with missing glass, use a heat gun or a soldering iron to soften hard-glazing compound. (*Beware:* Heat guns tend to break glass.)

Once the putty is gone, pull out the glazing points (the thin pieces of metal that hold the glass in place) and remove the pane of glass. Wear heavy-duty work gloves and goggles when handling glass. Thoroughly clean debris out of the groove. While the glass is out, prime any bare wood on the muntins or sash with a mixture of linseed oil and turpentine to improve the bond between the wood and new glazing compound.

Practice cutting replacement panes with an unusable

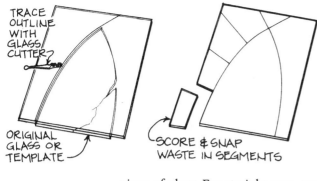

TRACE OUTLINE WITH GLASS CUTTER

ORIGINAL GLASS OR TEMPLATE

SCORE & SNAP WASTE IN SEGMENTS

ALIGN PUTTY WITH INSIDE OF SASH

GLAZING POINT FULLY CONCEALED IN PUTTY

piece of glass. For straight cuts, use a straightedge as a guide and score the piece with one firm, even stroke of a sharp glass cutter dipped in oil. Then tap along the line to break it off or break it off with a quick, downward snap with plastic glass-cutter's pliers. Cut the piece ever-so-slightly smaller than the window opening.

Curved pieces present more of a problem. Make a template out of Masonite or cardboard. Break off gradual curves in one piece, but remove one small section at a time for extreme curves.

Place the new pane in the window and secure it with several glazing points. Roll some glazing putty between your hands to form a bead; press it in place along the edge of the glass. Smooth into a triangular shape with a flexible putty knife. Try to run an even bead that clears the glazing points.

Counterweights and Cords

If the sash doesn't run smoothly after removing excess paint, check the counterweights and sash cords. Get to the weight pocket through the access panel at the bottom of the jamb. For windows without access panels, carefully remove the inside window trim. First check that the weights move freely through the pocket. You may have to remove badly placed nails or screws from the casing.

Counterweights are easily accessed through a panel in the jamb.

Frozen pulleys like this one can be fixed by removing excess paint.

Pulley problems. Frozen pulleys present the most common problem with sash cords. Tie off the sash cord and remove the pulley—it's usually held with two finishing nails or small screws. Dip the pulley in chemical paint stripper to remove all traces of paint. Straighten dents in the pulley with a pair of pliers. Apply some oil to the pulley before reinstalling to ensure free spinning.

Paint-encrusted sash chains. On windows with an access panel to the weight pocket at the bottom of the jamb, unscrew the chain from the sash and tie a string to the end. Remove the access plate and let the weight drop to the bottom of the pocket. Disconnect the chain from the weight and pull it out from the top. Bathe the chain in water-rinseable paint stripper until the paint softens. Rinse thoroughly, dry, and apply a little WD-40 or other nonstaining lubricant.

SOLUTIONS TO COMMON WINDOW PROBLEMS

Use this chart in conjunction with the more detailed instructions in this chapter to quickly identify the probable solution to your window problem.

Problem	Solution
Sticking sash	Remove accumulated paint; lubricate with soap or paraffin; plane wood only if absolutely necessary.
Air infiltration	Caulk and weatherstrip.
Broken sash cord	Replace cord or chain.
Broken glass	Reglaze; while sash is out, do other reconditioning.
Loose and missing putty	Remove loose putty; reputty; paint.
Peeling paint on frame	Eliminate unusual moisture sources; strip or scrape loose paint; caulk; prime and paint.
Loose or rotten bottom rail on lower sash	Brace existing rail connection with flat angle, or splice in new bottom rail.
Broken or missing muntin	Repair with epoxy if possible, or make or buy new muntin.
Rotted sash	Consolidate existing sash, or replace sash.
Rotted sill	Consolidate existing sill, or replace sill.

Broken sash cords. Fix rope cords in much the same manner. Tie a small weight to one end of the replacement cord and feed it down to the weight. Temporarily attach the other end of the cord to the sash, and test the window before cutting to final length. When the lower sash is all the way open, the weight should be close to the bottom of the pocket without "bottoming out"—there should always be tension on the cord.

Wood Rot

Fortunately, wood can be patched, filled, consolidated, and selectively replaced using simple, relatively inexpensive techniques. (By contrast, if one element of a new vinyl-clad aluminum window fails, it's very difficult to fix without replacing the entire assembly.)

A broken sash cord.

Before replacing or repairing rotted wood, stop the source of the moisture. If the sill pitches in toward the window, for instance, it's trapping water against the lower sash. Unflashed openings above the window allow water in, as does missing or deteriorated glazing putty.

Patching techniques. Standard wood fillers are good for very small areas and nail holes, but less effective on large areas. Auto-body fillers won't last because the filler won't expand and contract with the wood.

Epoxy consolidants and fillers patch rotted areas of exterior wood most effectively (see chapter 7 for instructions on working with epoxies). Consolidants are low-viscosity liquids that penetrate deteriorated wood fibers. When dry, the consolidant strengthens the wood and prevents further decay. Epoxy fillers replace "rotted-out" sections after consolidating the surrounding wood.

Chisel out unsound wood around the area to be patched. Wherever possible, undercut the hole you've created. Before mixing any filler, be certain the area is free of any paint, dirt, or loose splinters—such debris interferes with proper bonding. Mix the patching material according to manufacturer's directions and work it thoroughly into the hole; don't leave any voids or air pockets. As the filler begins to harden, scrape off excess with a sharp putty knife. Leave the patch to dry, raised slightly above the surrounding area. After the patch is thoroughly dry, sand it flush and smooth. (Be sure to wear a dust mask when sanding fillers.)

Patch larger areas (a section of the window sill, for example) using a carpenter's dutchman. Carefully saw out unsound wood. Square off the area to be patched, and cut a new piece of wood to the exact dimensions of the hole. Use the same kind of wood in the window and make sure the grain runs in the same direction. Glue or screw the patch in place, fill the joints after the glue has dried, and sand the patch smooth.

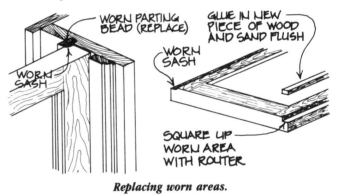

Replacing worn areas.

Separated joints. An old window frequently starts to separate at glued joints. Worse, delicate pieces such as muntins may be nearly or completely rotted through. Several low-tech, inexpensive measures will stabilize the window and arrest further decay without complete disassembly and rebuilding of the affected window.

The joints of the stiles and meeting rail in the upper sash usually separate first. (Nobody ever paints the meeting rail, and a lot of condensation runs down the upper window panes.) If the window isn't a focal point at eye level, simply reattach the separated stiles and rails with a metal mending plate—from the street, no one will notice your time-saving trick. If you're really fussy, chisel out a small mortise for the plate: Once you've screwed it in place, the plate will be flush with the rest of the window and nearly invisible after it's painted.

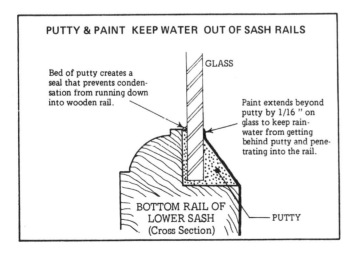

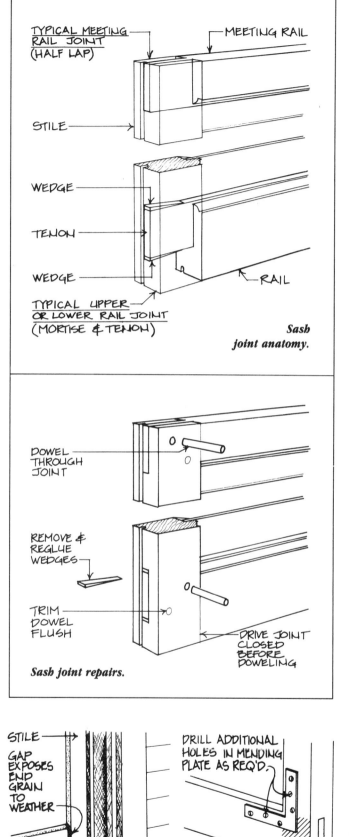

Sash joint anatomy.

Sash joint repairs.

Left: The problem; Right: The mending plate solution.

If the window is a real attention-grabber, reattach the loose pieces using more traditional woodworking practices. Reglue mortise-and-tenon joints and drive a small wedge next to the tenon. Secure half-lap joints by drilling a hole through both pieces and inserting a glued dowel. Clamp the joint together while it dries.

Draftiness

If windows run smoothly but snugly in their channels, if they close all the way and have no gaping holes or broken glass, then they're already pretty tight. But you can improve the energy efficiency and reduce air infiltration even of windows with storm sash (see also chapter 11).

Caulking. Seal around the window casing with a paintable caulk to reduce air flow. Caulk around the visible points where the trim meets plaster for appearance. Also check above the top of the window casing, and below the apron. (See chapter 7 for caulking instructions.)

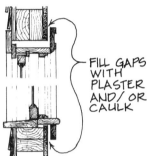

FILL GAPS WITH PLASTER AND/OR CAULK

Sash locks. Sash locks greatly reduce infiltration by pulling the meeting rails together and holding the window tightly closed. Install new locks if necessary, or strip paint off the existing locks and adjust them so they close completely and snugly.

Weatherstripping. Countless varieties of weatherstripping materials—adhesive-backed plastic springs, metal-backed felt, adhesive-backed strips of felt, tubular gaskets . . . the list goes on—do have suitable applications in an old house. However, generally they prove too conspicuous (ugly), wear out too fast, or do not form a complete seal. For a double-hung window, we recommend either spring-metal or integral-metal weatherstripping.

Spring-metal weatherstripping: Install this type in the sash runs, between meeting rails and along the head and sill. Spring-metal requires no complex carpentry to install—just nail it in place. It works as well as integral weatherstrip, but won't hold up as long.

Integral-metal weatherstripping: Integral-metal weatherstrip is perhaps the most common—and the best. (Integral-metal weatherstripping is often called carpenter-installed weatherstrip—you can often find carpenters who are old hands at this.) Use the following procedure if you want to install it:

1. Remove the lower sash and cut a slot (usually 7/16-inch deep) down the length of the lower rail and both stiles. (Read the instructions included with the weatherstrip before you begin.) Rout the sash with a radial arm saw, table saw, or router. Channel the upper sash through the top rail and both stiles.

2. Install the metal strips in the jamb, head, and sash. Cut the strips to leave a gap at the pulleys. Test fit the metal strips by attaching with just a nail or two with the

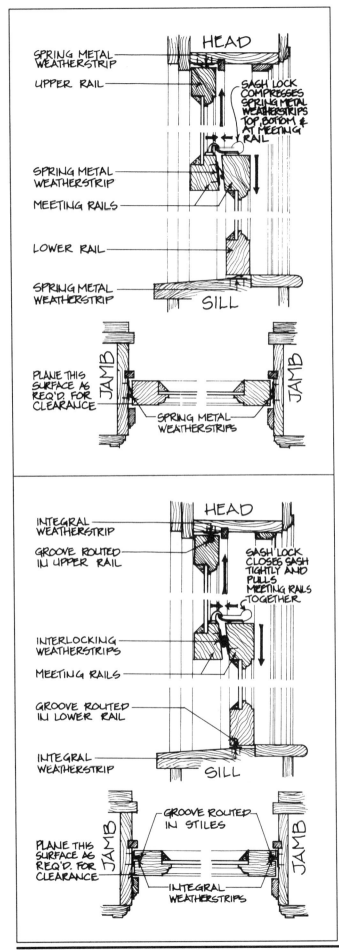

SPRING METAL WEATHERSTRIP

UPPER RAIL

SASH LOCK COMPRESSES SPRING METAL WEATHERSTRIPS TOP, BOTTOM & AT MEETING RAIL

HEAD

SPRING METAL WEATHERSTRIP

MEETING RAILS

LOWER RAIL

SPRING METAL WEATHERSTRIP

SILL

PLANE THIS SURFACE AS REQ'D. FOR CLEARANCE

JAMB

JAMB

SPRING METAL WEATHERSTRIPS

INTEGRAL WEATHERSTRIP

GROOVE ROUTED IN UPPER RAIL

SASH LOCK CLOSES SASH TIGHTLY AND PULLS MEETING RAILS TOGETHER

HEAD

INTERLOCKING WEATHERSTRIPS

MEETING RAILS

GROOVE ROUTED IN LOWER RAIL

INTEGRAL WEATHERSTRIP

SILL

GROOVE ROUTED IN STILES

PLANE THIS SURFACE AS REQ'D. FOR CLEARANCE

JAMB

JAMB

INTEGRAL WEATHERSTRIPS

window reinstalled; make any minor adjustments before securing them.

3. Attach interlocking weatherstripping to the meeting rails, reinstall the sash, and test for fit. Work the sash up and down to be sure they run smoothly. Make certain they close all the way, and that the weatherstrip at the meeting rails locks snugly.

Other options: If you use the window only for ventilation in warmer months, weatherseal with a little Mortite or other temporary roll-type caulking shoved between the moving parts of your window. If the window never gets used, you can even caulk it shut permanently with an acrylic latex caulk (of course, this makes for additional work the next time you have to clean or paint the window). Some people caulk only the upper sash, to leave the lower sash operable.

Painting Windows

Had they been properly maintained, your windows wouldn't have been such a mess. Keep them correctly painted inside and out to protect them from the elements.

A trick to save the new paint job on even severely weathered wood: Seal it with linseed oil before priming. Mix boiled linseed oil and paint thinner 50/50, and liberally brush it onto the wood. Allow it to dry for twenty-four hours, then repeat the process. Badly weathered wood requires a third application. Allow three days for the oil to dry before sanding and priming.

Paint all the parts with an alkyd primer. Cover every surface, especially where bare wood is exposed. Follow with two coats of a high-quality latex or oil/alkyd finish paint, preferably from the same manufacturer as the primer. To paint windows correctly do the following:

1. Remove all hardware from the window, including curtain hardware, sash locks, and handles.

2. Scrape the windows with a single-edge razor blade before painting to remove previous painting errors. Reverse the sash, and begin by painting the lower half of the upper sash. As you paint the rails, stiles, and muntins, run the paint slightly up onto the glass. Slopping paint all over everything and scraping the glass later will break the paint seal where the glass meets wood.

3. Close the windows and finish painting the sash. If you put the paint on so heavily that it drips between the sash and jamb, you'll cause paint buildup again. Work from the sash to the jamb to the casing to the apron. Don't paint the sash cords or chains. Pull them out of your way and paint behind them.

4. When the paint is almost dry, but still slightly tacky, open and close the window to break the paint seal.

FIXING OLD DOORS

Doors fall victim to house settlement, insensitive repairs, warping, paint buildup, or a combination of these. Often do-it-yourselfers resort to planing to make the door shut. However, building settlement usually causes bad alignment. Take care of all structural work—

STRIPPING WINDOWS

If you want to "start fresh" and remove years' worth of unnecessary paint layers, there are some things you should know about stripping windows:

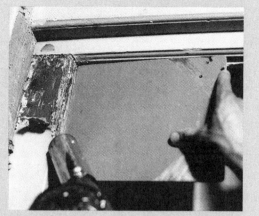

When using a heat gun to strip windows, protect the glass—a better solution would be to remove it.

Use heat on the sill, runs, stops, parting beads, and casing. *Remove the glass* before using a heat gun on the window sash.

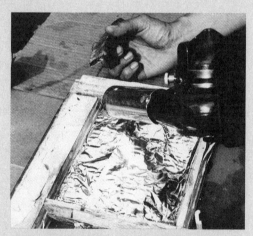

This do-it-yourselfer uses foil-covered corrugated cardboard to protect the glass.

Advantages: Fast and efficient. Dry cleanup. No materials cost. Minimized health threat from lead dust or solvents.

Disadvantages: High risk of glass damage. Leaves thin ribbon of paint next to glass that you'll need to strip with a chemical or razor.

Use chemicals. A thick, methylene-chloride-based product is best (Zip-Strip, Bix Tuff Job, and Rock Miracle are typical brand names). Apply a heavy coat of stripper and wait twenty to thirty minutes before scraping. When using solvent-based strippers, choose a semipaste product and, if working vertically, thicken it further with cornstarch. Paint on stripper a section at a time and cover it with Saran wrap or aluminum foil to reduce evaporation. Scrape the loosened paint off with a putty knife or other small tools such as a table knife ground to the muntin profile. Clean up with more stripper and steel wool or brass brushes. Once the paint is removed, use mineral spirits and steel wool to remove any sticky residue.

Advantages: Low risk of damaging glass. Will remove all paint with enough applications.

Disadvantages: Messy to work with vertically, particularly cleanup.

Dip-stripping is an option if you have many windows to strip. However, it will soften old putty and can loosen sash joints. We generally don't recommend this method. If you must use it, remove the glass before taking windows to the strip shop.

Advantages: Very few.

Disadvantages: Alkaline strippers (caustics) raise wood grain. Can soften glazing putty and loosen joints in sash. Often leaves a residue that keeps paint from adhering, especially on exterior surfaces. Caustics like lye will raise the grain, loosen glued joints, and, if not properly neutralized, will cause failure of your new paint job.

Allow the wood to dry thoroughly before priming (this may take a couple of weeks). Seal bare wood with linseed oil or an alkyd primer as described on page 242.

---

foundation work, joist or subfloor repairs, any jacking—before tackling the doors.

Understanding how a door and jamb are constructed will change your ideas about indiscriminate planing. First, observe the door. Open and close it a few times, noting where it rubs against and where it clears the jamb. A door should never have to slam to close completely. Ideally, there should be a consistent gap of 1/16 to 1/8 inch between the door and jamb on all sides. A door should swing silently and effortlessly on its hinges and latch crisply. A closed door shouldn't rattle around between the latch and stops.

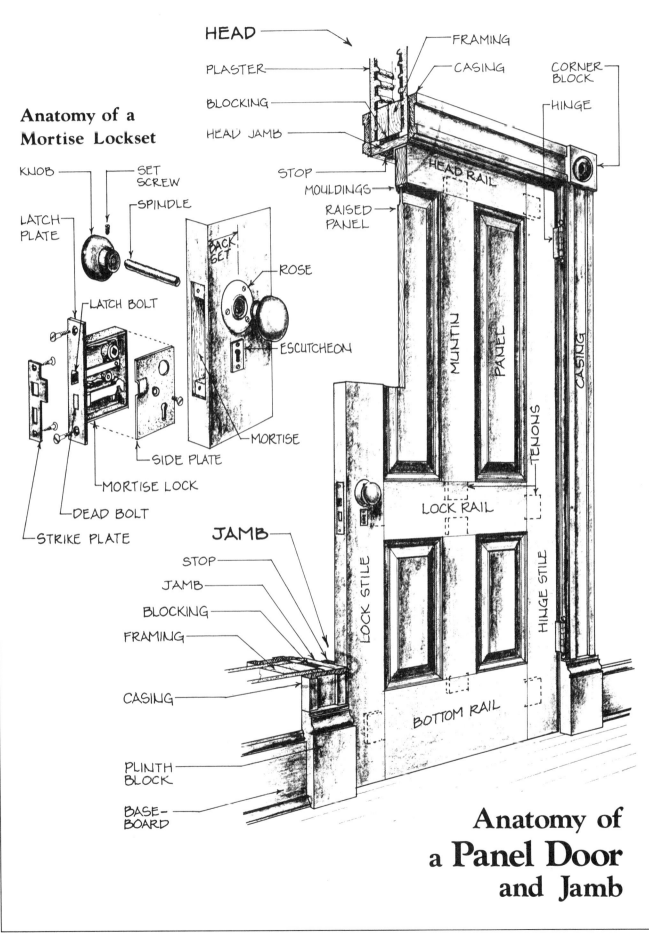

HEAD

FRAMING

PLASTER

CASING

BLOCKING

CORNER BLOCK

HEAD JAMB

HINGE

STOP

HEAD RAIL

MOULDINGS

RAISED PANEL

Anatomy of a Mortise Lockset

KNOB

SET SCREW

SPINDLE

LATCH PLATE

BACK SET

ROSE

LATCH BOLT

MUNTIN

PANEL

CASING

ESCUTCHEON

TENONS

MORTISE

SIDE PLATE

LOCK RAIL

MORTISE LOCK

DEAD BOLT

LOCK STILE

HINGE STILE

STRIKE PLATE

JAMB

STOP

JAMB

BLOCKING

FRAMING

BOTTOM RAIL

CASING

PLINTH BLOCK

BASE-BOARD

Anatomy of a Panel Door and Jamb

Common Door Problems

Here you'll find some solutions to door problems that all do-it-yourselfers can fix.

Binds Evenly Along Latch Side and Head

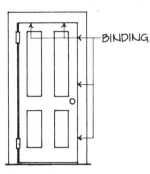

Paint buildup. Remove excess paint with heat or chemical removers. If the paint flakes off, simply pull a sharp paint scraper along the length of the mating surfaces. Be careful not to gouge or otherwise damage the door or jamb, especially if stripping and refinishing seem worthwhile.

Seasonal expansion. This will cause the door to swell during humid periods, making it difficult or impossible to close. Plane the door during the peak of the humid season.

Binds Along Top of Latch Side and/or on Floor

Loose upper hinge. Open the door part way and push the top in toward the jamb, while lifting up on the doorknob. If the hinge moves, it may be loose enough to allow the door to sag away and bind against the jamb or drag on the floor.

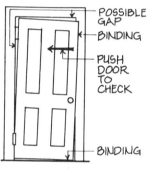

If the hinge leaves move within their mortises, tighten the screws. For stripped screw holes, resecure the leaf that contacts the door to the stile with longer screws. Longer screws won't work to secure the leaf mortised into the jamb because the jamb is only about 3/4-inch thick. If the gap is small, a screw may catch the stud. Otherwise, drill out the screw holes in the jamb, plug them with (glue-coated) dowels, and redrill pilot holes for new screws.

When driving the new screws, make sure they go in straight so the flat heads sit flush with the face of the hinge. (Don't use a screw that's too big.) A protruding screw head will undo the repair by acting as a fulcrum, causing the hinge to pull out of its mortise.

Loose lower hinge. This may be the problem if the hinges have an unusually wide throw—like those installed on an entry door to clear the deep trim profile. Lift and pull the bottom of the door away from the jamb to see if the lower hinge is loose. A loose bottom hinge causes trouble most when the door is being swung open or shut, and cannot

rest against the jamb for support. The door may drag on the floor. Repair following the same procedures as for a loose upper hinge. Remember: An entry door is usually very heavy and wide-throw hinges provide a lot of leverage for the weight of the door to pull them loose. Be sure to make a strong, sound repair.

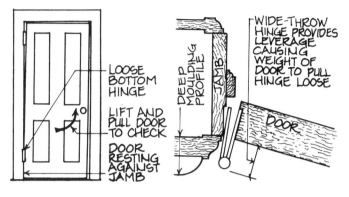

Worn hinge pin. This problem will become evident if the hinge leaves in their mortises do not move when you lift and push the door and the knuckle moves or is misaligned. Tap the hinge pin down into position if it is not set all the way into the hinge. Often, unworn areas of the pin will tighten the sloppy fit. If the pin won't move, take it out and straighten it. If necessary, remove the hinge to straighten bent knuckles.

If the knuckles are still loose and misaligned, replace the pin or the whole hinge. When made of malleable material such as brass or wrought iron, you may be able to tighten the knuckles slightly by disassembling the hinge and squeezing the knuckles in a vise.

Open joint between upper rail and stile. This joint usually opens because of the weight of the door. Less frequently, it's the result of warping of the stile or rail. In either case, fix the joint rather than trim the door.

First, remove the door. Then remove paint, filler, and caulk from the joint. If the door has a through tenon with a wedge (the rail tenon extends all the way through the stile), remove the old wedges, tug gently at the joint, and push it closed a few times. Inject carpenter's glue into all exposed areas of the joint. Work as much glue as possible onto the broad sides of the tenon (these are the only effective gluing surfaces). Clamp the joint tight. Make new wedges slightly longer than necessary, glue them, and drive them in snugly. Wipe up all excess glue. When the joint dries, chisel wedges flush with the edge of the door.

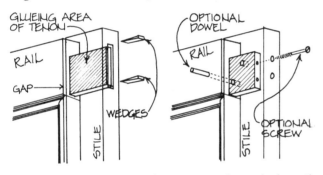

If the tenon reaches only part way through the stile, simply reglue. If the joint opens again, add a dowel or two through the stile and tenon. If the door has or will get a clear finish and you don't mind seeing the pegs on the face of the door, screw the joint closed from the edge. Reglue the joint and clamp tight. Then continue to countersink two long screws through the stile into the rail. Fill the holes with tinted filler or plug with wood and sand smooth.

Springy Resistance to Closing; Hinges Work Loose

Paint buildup on hinge side.
This is the culprit if you feel a slight springy resistance and the hinges seem to rock in their mortises as the door reaches its closed position. Selectively or completely strip paint. Make sure the screw heads are flush with the face of the hinge.

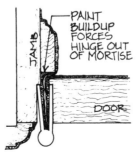

Hinge mortise(s) are too deep. If in a previous repair more material was removed from the mortise than necessary, this may be the problem. Shim the hinge out flush with the jamb. Use a thin scrap of wood cut to the exact dimensions of the mortise. Or, use thin, plastic or metal prefabricated shims (available at most hardware stores). Avoid cardboard and wood shingle shims.

If the door is a little tight in the opening, plane the hinge side enough to bring the hinges out flush with the edge of the door.

Hinges Creak and Grind

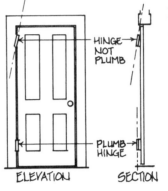

Lubricate hinges. This will keep them quiet.

Hinges are not plumb. If they continue to creak loudly, there is slight resistance. Nonplumb hinges create friction on the knuckles, causing the hinge to wear out prematurely. Shim and/ or remortise the hinges.

Door Drags on Floor and Gap on Latch Side of Head

Building settlement. This is most often the cause of a dragging door. A gap between the top of the door and the head differentiates this problem from a simple loose hinge problem. Check the squareness of the door opening by putting a level on the head and along both sides of the jamb. An old building usually settles downward with only secondary lateral movement (leaning); usually the head is furthest out of alignment.

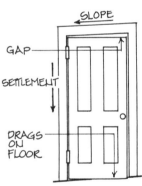

If the gap at the top of the door is small enough that the door still meets the stop on the jamb head, plane the bottom of the door. If you can look right through the gap into the next room with the door closed, reframe the door.

Reframing a door involves removing the side jambs and head jamb and starting from scratch. You can buy stock door frames from a mill or have them cut to fit. To install the door frame, use a wedge-and-shingle system between the rough-opening studs and the new jamb to set the jamb plumb and square. Be sure the wedges are tight and nail the jambs through the wedges and shingles with eightpenny finishing nails. You may use five or more sets of wedges and shingles to hold the door plumb. Saw the shingles flush with the wall. When installing the door casings, nail them to both the framing studs and the jambs, again using eightpenny finishing or casing nails.

Binds on Latch Side of Head and Gap at Floor

As with a door with a gap at the top, plane or reframe. The top rail of a door is usually narrower than the bottom and is more of a focal point. Planing it to follow the slope of the head may leave it very unsightly and distorted. If you have to remove a lot of material, you may even expose the tenon and weaken the door.

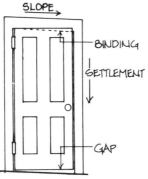

Door Binds Along Some Sections of Jamb and Leaves Gaps Elsewhere

Bad or unnecessary planing. You should notice unevenness, gouges, and torn wood grain along the edge of the door. Check the edge of the door by holding a straightedge against it.

If the door is not straight (with a consistent bevel), swing the door against the edge of the jamb and mark the high spots. Plane them down even with the rest of the door.

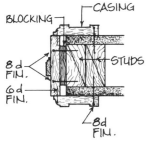

Jamb is not straight. Place a straightedge against the jamb to see if it bows or undulates. First secure the jamb. Try pushing and twisting the jamb. Pull high spots where the jamb is loose back into line and secure with finishing nails. Use 8d finish nails through the jamb into the framing, and 6d finish nails through the trim into the jamb.

If you cannot force the jamb back into position, remove the casing on the least conspicuous side. (Use a wide-blade putty knife to protect adjacent surfaces from the prybar.) On the opposite (most conspicuous) side, loosen the casing just enough to get a hacksaw blade behind it. Cut the nails that hold the casing to the jamb. This way you free the jamb without completely removing the casings from both sides.

Now shim out the low spots in the jamb while cutting down the high ones until the jamb is plumb and correctly spaced from the door. To do this, drive some wedges

SOME TIPS ON PLANING

- **Remove paint from the surface.**
- **Set the blade for shallow cut** for maximum control and minimum tear-out.
- **Keep your tools sharp.** A dull plane will make the work more difficult and will damage the door. A sharp plane removes uniform ribbons of wood; a dull plane catches and slips, tearing out chunks of wood and rippling the surface.
- **Bevel the edge of the stile** to avoid producing a large gap when the door is closed. Remove more material from the side of the stile that passes the jamb first, and leave more material on the side that lines up with the jamb only when the door is completely closed.

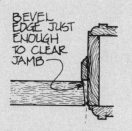

- **Start at the corner on end grain** (top and bottom of stile). Running the plane off the end grain of the stile will splinter the wood.
- **To avoid knocking off corners,** bear down on the nose of the plane at the beginning of the cut; bear down on the back at the end of the cut. This is especially important when you're using a power plane; it can round off a corner in just one pass.

PLANE IN "UPHILL" DIRECTION

- **Plane sections in alternate directions** if the grain is wavy and the plane tears out wood in some places. If you're always planing "uphill," the plane can't dig in.
- **After planing, deepen hinge and lockset mortises** as required to ensure hardware is flush with the edge of the door. Make sure spindle is centered in rose.

between the jamb and blocking to shim out the low spots in the jamb. (Use solid wood blocking, not wood shingles.) Chisel out existing blocking behind high spots and replace with smaller pieces of wood. (Sometimes there are small shims between the blocking and jamb. In that case, simply remove the shims and renail.)

Secure any new blocking with 8d finish nails driven through jamb, blocking, and stud. If you are working with fine woodwork with a clear finish, hide the finish nails by removing the stop before driving the nails. The nailheads will be concealed when the stop is resecured. After the jamb is plumb and straight, reinstall the casing.

Lockset Binds and Latch Doesn't Spring Back

If the doorknob resists turning and doesn't spring back to position when you release it, put a few drops of oil into the latch. If that doesn't do the trick, look for the following:

Paint-filled lockset (when paint or dirt gum up the mechanism). Remove the knobs and spindle. Unscrew the lockset and remove it from its mortise. If it resists, remove the excess paint. Unscrew the side plate from the lockset to expose the mechanism. Scrape dirt and paint from the latch and its opening; replace any broken parts. Be sure the return spring is intact and in the correct position. Oil all moving parts before reassembling.

Spindle is not centered in the rose. The rose is the metal plate that covers the hole under the knob. If the knob binds on the rose and prevents the latch from returning, the spindle is not centered, probably because the door was planed and the lockset mortise was deepened.

SPINDLE NOT CENTERED IN ROSE

Be sure the lockset is set all the way into its mortise so that it's flush with the edge of the door. Unscrew the rose or trimplate and shift its position so that the spindle will be centered when inserted. Rotate the rose a few degrees and redrill new holes so the screws don't split the wood alongside the abandoned screw holes. Remove any paint buildup from the mating surfaces between the knob and rose.

When you reinstall the spindle and knobs, tighten them and leave only enough play so they don't bind against the rose. Tighten the set screws firmly against a flat surface in the spindle. If the screw doesn't bear squarely on the flat of the spindle, the screw will eventually loosen and the knob will fall off.

Lockset Functions Properly, but Door Doesn't Latch

Paint buildup on stop and door. Thick paint on the latch side will prevent the latch from reaching the strike plate. Remove paint as necessary.

Latch is misaligned with mortise in the strike plate. Look into the joint between the door and jamb to see that the latch and mortise line up vertically. If the joint is too small for you to see (it ought to be), look for wear marks on the strike plate. Or, close the door and make a scratch on the outside of the strike at the top of the latch. Then open the door to see if the mark lines up with the mortise.

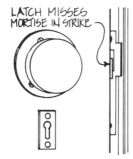

LATCH MISSES MORTISE IN STRIKE

If the mortise in the strike is just a bit high or low, remove the strike plate and file it to accommodate the latch. If the misalignment exceeds about 1/16 inch, move the strike (assuming all other door repairs are complete). Extend the mortise for the strike with a chisel as required. Plug the old screw holes and refasten the strike in its new position. On extremely fine millwork, fill the exposed section of mortise with a thin piece of matching wood.

Door is warped. This is the problem if the latch lines up with the mortise, there's no paint buildup, and the door still refuses to latch. Sight across the face of the door or put a straightedge diagonally across the face to see if the door is twisted. Check along the face of the latch stile to see if it's warped. It's impossible to unwarp a stile, and hard to take a twist out of a door. It's easy enough to remove the stops and reset them so they conform. Renail stops with the door closed, so they can be bent slightly to follow the warp. There should be just enough space between the door and stops so the door closes easily without rattling.

Door Rattles Between Latch and Stops

Stops are too far from door. Remove them and renail closer to the door as previously described.

Latch is worn. See if the latch is loose within the face plate of the lockset. If it is, replace the lockset.

FIXING SLIDING
──────DOORS──────

Sliding doors almost always need some work. At best, the old doors will shimmy and grind; at worst, your delight at discovering them behind a Sheetrock partition could turn to horror when you see that all the hardware is missing. Earlier doors rolled along a floor track on recessed rollers, while later sliding doors were top hung. Both types will need attention to keep them running smoothly. It doesn't take much for them to get out of alignment, and there isn't much leeway in the small wall pockets into which they recede.

Of course, you should take care of the cause of bad alignment—building settlement—before repairing any door. But fix sliding doors *before* finish plastering or decorating, since you may have to break through plaster to get at repairs in the pocket.

Floor-Track Pocket Doors _____

These doors move along a metal track into their hidden pockets. Read through all the symptoms and solutions here before ripping apart walls to repair your doors. The problem may result from a combination of things. Similar symptoms can point to very different problems.

Door Stuck in Pocket

Unused doors may be nailed into their pockets. Look for toenails through door edges or a stop piece nailed across the top.

Warped doors. Attach a temporary handle if the hardware is missing by threading some heavy wire between two screw eyes set a foot apart into the edge of the door. Pull gently, rocking the door. You may have to use force, though it may damage the door. If you still can't get it out, break through the plaster, then wedge studs apart to free

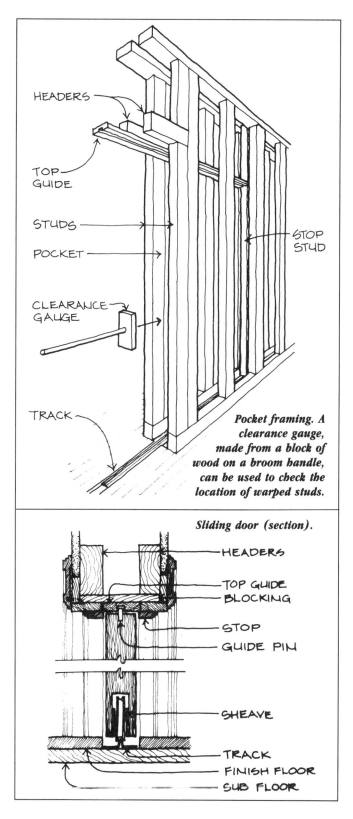

HEADERS

TOP GUIDE

STUDS

POCKET

STOP STUD

CLEARANCE GAUGE

TRACK

Pocket framing. A clearance gauge, made from a block of wood on a broom handle, can be used to check the location of warped studs.

Sliding door (section).

HEADERS

TOP GUIDE
BLOCKING

STOP

GUIDE PIN

SHEAVE

TRACK

FINISH FLOOR

SUB FLOOR

Debris in the track. Lift upward on the door, rocking it and pulling the door forward inch by inch. While a helper lifts up on the door, insert a metal rule underneath to scrape away debris.

Door has jumped the floor track. Lift and rock the door to get it back on track.

Door has left the top guide inside the pocket. Wiggle the door around to get it back on center. Poke a rule in along the side to guide the door out. Force it if you dare.

Doors Roll Out Beyond Center— Rear of Doors Are Visible; Top of Door No Longer in Grooved Track

Missing metal stop piece. For tongue-in-groove doors, get a steel mending angle, cut down one of its legs so it just meets the top of the door, and screw it into the center top track. If the doors have rounded edges, use an appropriate size piece of pipe, cut in half and welded to a metal plate.

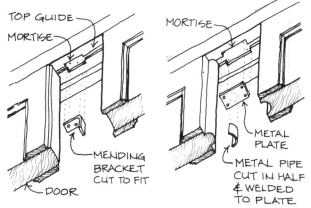

TOP GUIDE

MORTISE

MENDING BRACKET CUT TO FIT

DOOR

MORTISE

METAL PLATE

METAL PIPE CUT IN HALF & WELDED TO PLATE

Making a center door stop for the top rack.

Door runs below the level of the top groove. This means that the building has settled. The stop mouldings may be missing in this case. Be careful as the door could flop out of the opening from the top. Add to the depth of the stop mouldings that form the top track.

If the top of the door has guide pins, increase their length using wood dowels. Sometimes you can shim the bottom track to alleviate settlement. Shim too much, however, and people will trip on the bottom track.

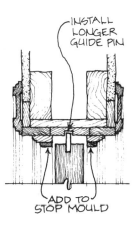

INSTALL LONGER GUIDE PIN

ADD TO STOP MOULD

Top track has warped inside the pockets. In this case, the door leaves the top guide inside the pocket and binds. Move the door out of the way and pull down on the top board that forms the upper guide. Fasten the board where you want it by screwing it through a small hole in the wall plaster, through a stud, and into the board.

the door. Afterward, if doors are salvageable, shave down the studs to provide clearance.

Warped studs in the pockets. If the closest set of studs binds the door, push one back by inserting a wedge-shaped piece of wood between the stud and the door. For rear studs, break through the wall. Shave warped studs with a drum rasp attached to a drill.

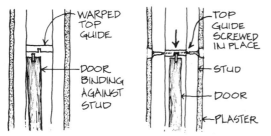

Doors affected by settlement will never run like new. Concentrate on getting them to run smoothly and meet flush in the center of the opening.

Doors Don't Slide All the Way Back Into Pockets

Debris in the track, a badly warped door (shave down the studs to provide clearance), or **warped studs.**

Door may be chronically off the track. Clean the track, see if it was mislaid or not screwed down inside the pockets. You might also have trouble with the top guide (see previous solution).

Doors Bind on Track, Get Balky, Make Noise

Debris on the track.

Recessed rollers in the door bottom may be rusty or dirty, out of alignment, or broken. To remove the door, have a helper push up on the door while you swing it out at the bottom. Sometimes you'll have to remove the stop mouldings. Clean and oil rusty or dirty rollers.

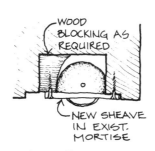

Severe floor settlement or sags and bumps.

A Space, Wider at the Bottom, Between Double Doors

Sag in the floor. These doors are out of plumb. Shim a little here, a little there. Try taking up the center floor track and shimming beneath it. Again, shim the track too much and you'll have guests stumbling over them.

If the problem is with a single pocket door, or if double doors are only slightly out of plumb, try inserting a shim between the roller case flange and the bottom of the door. Shim only the roller closer to the center. Use different size shims on each side of flange to bring the sheave parallel to the existing angle of the floor

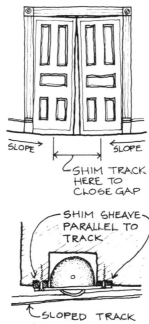

track. Shim too much, though, and you'll create a visible gap under the door.

A Space, Wider at the Top, Between Doors

Settlement sag. If this floor buckling isn't caused by a serious structural problem, try shimming out toward the pockets. Also shim between the roller sheave and the mortise in the door, this time on the roller closer to the pocket.

Doors Slope in Same Direction

Differential settlement. These out-of-plumb doors are caused by differential settlement between the outside of the building and the interior walls. You can alleviate this situation but not really fix it.

Check the top guide along its entire length. Add to the depth of stop mouldings if necessary. Shim out or replace the center stop if it doesn't keep the uphill door from sliding past center. Restore or install a new latch to hold the doors together.

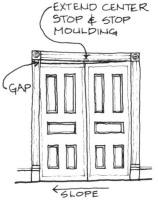

When the doors are open, the uphill door will always roll into the opening. When the doors are closed, the downhill door will always roll back into its pocket. Here you'll have to treat it as an endearing characteristic of your old house. Make a finely finished hardwood wedge to match the doors—use it with panache.

Floor Track Missing or Unsalvageable

Make an ad hoc track. You may not be able to find new track to fit the rollers if they work. Drill holes down the center of flat stock (mild steel). Using a steel rod that matches the diameter of the groove in the rollers, tack-weld the rod onto the flat plate from behind, through the holes. Drill countersunk screw holes into the edges for installation on the floor.

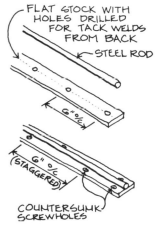

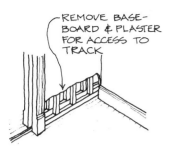

REMOVE BASE-BOARD & PLASTER FOR ACCESS TO TRACK

Buy a new track and matching rollers. To get at the floor track inside the pockets, you'll have to break through the plaster and lath near the floor. Remove the baseboard and carefully cut a V in the plaster with a utility knife or a chisel. Demolish the lower plaster with a wrecking tool and pull off the lath. You only need enough clearance to use a screwdriver in the space.

Door Goes Too Far into Pocket

Stop block attached to the back of the door may be missing. Some doors have stop studs in the center back of the pocket. Pull the door all the way out of the pocket by removing the metal stop piece at the center of the top guide. Replace the stop block.

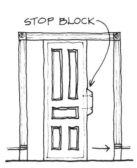

STOP BLOCK

Other doors stop in the pocket by a cross brace that goes across the pocket from stud to stud. If that's missing, open the wall to replace it.

Top-Hung Pocket Doors

Top-hung doors come in two varieties. Some have side-by-side rollers, front and back, which roll along matching wood tracks. Others have single rollers (front and back) on a single metal track. Just shine a flashlight up into the track opening above the doors to see which kind you have.

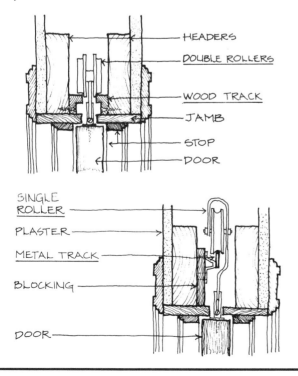

HEADERS
DOUBLE ROLLERS
WOOD TRACK
JAMB
STOP
DOOR

SINGLE ROLLER
PLASTER
METAL TRACK
BLOCKING
DOOR

Here you'll find solutions to problems that deal with top-hanger hardware and mounting top-hung doors. You can use the solutions outlined in the section on floor-track pocket doors for settlement, warping, and alignment problems with top-hung doors.

Making Adjustments

Oil the rollers with an aerosol lubricant with a plastic extension nozzle (WD-40 or Tri-Flo) to alleviate balkiness and unpleasant noises. Release the rear stop on the door to roll the door all the way out into the opening so you can reach the back rollers.

Top-hung doors stop from rolling out too far by a retractable metal or wood finger mounted on the rear edge of each door. The finger catches on the jamb when the door rolls out into the opening. To release the door, retract the finger by pulling the door out as far as it will go, then slipping a screwdriver or a piece of stiff cardboard in to flip it up.

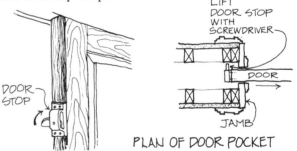

DOOR STOP

LIFT DOOR STOP WITH SCREWDRIVER

DOOR

JAMB

PLAN OF DOOR POCKET

Doors often bind along the floor or along the track above because of settlement or vibration. Roller height is adjustable. If the door scrapes the floor, turn the adjustment screw to pull the door upward. First, tap shims under the door to temporarily hold it about 1/4 inch off the floor. After turning the screw and removing the shims, the door should hang at least 3/16 inch from the floor. If the door binds on the track above, again adjust the vertical position

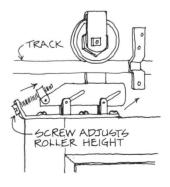

TRACK

SCREW ADJUSTS ROLLER HEIGHT

of the doors with the screw on the hanger: Turn it so it lowers the door.

If the stop mouldings that guide the door along the side jambs or along the top track are loose or warped, remove the stops and renail them in the correct alignment. Sometimes the door itself has warped, causing it to bind along the stops. You can't correct a warped door, so try moving the stop mouldings out of the way.

Removing the Doors

If you can't fix a door by simply oiling it or by vertical adjustment, you'll have to remove it to trim it at the bottom. If the doors need repair, extensive refinishing, or replacement, or if the track or rollers are disconnected, broken, missing, or loose, get the doors out of the way.

If you have side-by-side roller doors hung on wood tracks, look for an access panel at the top. (Part of the upper track is removable in this case.) Remove the panel and reach in above the door to unscrew the flange that attaches the roller assembly to the top of the door. Pull the roller out through the access panel. Now move the door into a position where you can reach the other roller through the access panel.

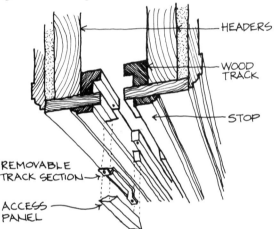

For wood-track doors without an access panel, first remove the stop, jamb, and wood track on one side. If that doesn't provide enough clearance to unscrew the roller from the door (or to pull the roller assembly out), then remove the other side of the upper track too.

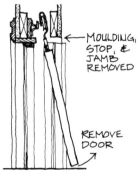

No access panel usually means the doors run on a metal track. This will be attached to only one side of the overhead framing. Remove the casement moulding, stop, and jamb only on the side opposite the track mounting. Now slip the door out with the roller assembly still attached to the door. The track will still be in place above. Of course, if there is not enough clearance, you'll have to unscrew the roller assembly from the top of the door.

Going Through Plaster

Major work on the overhead track means you'll have to remove plaster along one side of the track, enough to expose the entire track assembly. (First remove the trim, stop, and jamb on that side.) If you're just repairing the existing track or replacing it with a similar one, remove a 4- or 6-inch swath of plaster. If you're replacing the track mechanism with modern hardware, remove more plaster.

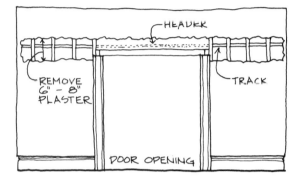

The least expensive option requires the least demolition: Repair the existing hardware if possible or find salvaged hardware. Anyone with modest carpentry skills can duplicate wood tracks. If the hardware is missing, or if it's too far gone, change over to a modern sliding assembly.

Installing New Hardware

Mounting modern ball-bearing hardware is a little different from the old-style trolleys. Install blocking between the door framing above to provide a nailing surface for attaching new track. (Side-mounted hardware is harder to install.)

Follow manufacturer's specifications for installing new hardware and adjusting the height of the doors. First you'll screw in the new track assembly overhead, with rollers already popped in place. Then screw the new flanges to the top of the door. These will mate with the roller-and-track assembly you've installed above. Now install the door and adjust the height according to instructions.

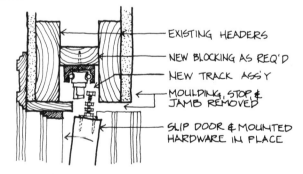

Some of the new top-hanger hardware comes with a floor track too, for guiding the door along. These are meant for use with bypass doors: those not guided by pocket framing, such as closet doors. If you have well-adjusted old pocket doors that never had a floor track before, you don't need one now.

CHAPTER 14

Plaster and Drywall

Plaster in old houses inevitably cracks. After you've completed major structural work and taken care of the mechanical and electrical systems in your old house, your next step will probably be taking care of those cracking, falling-down walls. Assuming the plaster wasn't poorly formulated or damaged by water, patching is much cheaper than wholesale demolition and replacement with drywall. (See the plastering glossary later in this chapter to clear up plaster and drywall vocabulary that confuses all of us.) While big jobs require a lot of practice working with the materials and may better be left to the professionals, often the do-it-yourselfer can salvage plaster with a few relatively simple, inexpensive techniques.

However, if you find your plaster ceiling or walls are unsalvageable, you have three basic options for replacement: real three-coat plaster, drywall, or veneer plaster. Most contractors recommend easy, economical drywall, but drywall in an eighteenth-century house looks anachronistic. On the other hand, real plaster has aesthetic appeal as well as the best insulating and sound-deadening characteristics. Don't dismiss the concept of replacing plaster with plaster until you get prices. If you live in a place (usually urban) where you can find a plasterer, plaster may be quite competitive with drywall.

Veneer plaster is an in-between choice. Here, a real troweled finish coat of plaster is applied to a prefabricated gypsumboard base. (Sometimes a base coat and finish coat are applied over the gypsum base.) Get prices locally before you decide which way to go.

WHAT IS PLASTER?

In old houses, plaster is most often a three-coat system of lime- or gypsum-based, trowelable mortar applied wet over wood lath strips. The first two coats contain sand (and perhaps animal hair); the finish coat is thinner and contains no aggregate or binder. The base coat of plaster has a mechanical and adhesive bond to the lath: mechanical through keys, or hardened slumps of plaster that went through the spaces between lathing strips; adhesive by virtue of suction created between the wood lath and wet plaster.

WHY PLASTER FAILS

Plaster fails because of imperfections in the material itself or because of stresses in or failure of the structural system that supports it (house framing, studs, lath). Chapter 3 provides an overview of the kinds of cracks that appear and why, and if your cracking indicates major structural repair ahead.

Hairline cracks are no threat to the integrity of the wall or ceiling, but you'll want to patch them before painting. Open the crack with the point of a can opener or a putty knife, and fill it with spackling compound. However, for cyclical cracks—those that open and close with the seasons as humidity causes the lath to swell and shrink—it's best not to spackle them with rigid plaster. Instead, bed fiberglass tape in joint compound and feather over with more compound.

Alligatored paint layers indicate an unsound substrate. You can fill the "alligator skin" with joint compound, but it will only last about six months. For alligatoring, you have only two choices: Strip the paint down to bare plaster, or, if the paint layers are well stuck, canvas the walls or ceiling.

Structural cracks or large cracks usually happen early in the building's life and often are stable. Of course, if the crack moves over time, check with an architect or structural engineer. Simply tape straight cracks, but dig out long spidery cracks, undercutting slightly to provide a key for the patch plaster. Vacuum out all debris. Patch with

Settlement cracks should be patch-plastered and taped.

Paint and plaster failure from water penetration.

the appropriate patching plaster, finish with a layer of compound, sand or sponge, and prime.

Crumbling or wet plaster will never "re-cure." If the plaster lost its integrity (becoming bowed and crumbly), it probably is unsalvageable. Remove damaged plaster only, back to sound material at a stud or joist. Secure surrounding sound plaster with washers if necessary; make a drywall patch.

Plaster badly damaged by water effloresces. The dry powdery bubbles are salts in the plaster brought to the surface by the water. If it's minor—merely a stain caused by a short-term water leak—brush away the efflorescence and seal the plaster with shellac before painting. Shellac will keep the stain from bleeding through the paint. More often, efflorescence is not a good sign. Water-damaged plaster will not hold paint and, worse, it will eventually fall.

Buckling or delamination of the finish coat of plaster is another common problem in old houses. It occurs because of a bad original bond between the brown coat and the finish coat. Problems in the manufacture of the raw materials, or with the on-site mixing, application, or humidity interfered with the chemical reaction that causes the plaster to cure.

If finish-coat failure is limited to small areas, use joint compound (the restorer's best friend). Just be sure to remove all areas of loose finish coat, because it will fail. If delamination is extensive, it makes more sense to replaster the finish coat; call in a plasterer unless you're willing to invest some time in learning the skill yourself.

PLASTER REPAIRS

Depending on the problem, plaster repair may lead you to plaster washers, drywall patch, plaster patch, or canvas. *Plaster washers,* also called repair discs or ceiling buttons, are an old-fashioned fix for pulling sound plaster back up to lath (when the keys have broken), or for pulling plaster and lath back to the studs or joists. Use them in conjunction with flat-head wood screws or drywall screws, and cover with joint compound. They're useful for securing areas of sound plaster before you remove damaged plaster nearby.

Even bowed plaster can be saved by anchoring it with plaster washers. The plaster itself must have integrity—it can't be crumbly or soft due to water damage. If the plaster-and-lath assembly together has separated from the structure, drive long wood screws through the lath and into studs or joists.

Plaster washers may be hard to find. We know of two companies that will ship them to you via mail-order: Charles St. Supply Co., 54 Charles Street, Dept. OHJ, Boston, MA 02114; (617)367-9046; and Fastenation, P.O. Box 1364, Dept. OHJ, Marblehead, MA 01945; (617)846-6444.

Use a *drywall patch* when the hole is more than 4 inches in diameter, or when you have to cut the plaster back to the studs or joists. This method is usually easier for nonplasterers—you don't have to buy and mix and trowel traditional plastering materials. Remove the areas with bad plaster. Then square up the hole and cut a neat patch from drywall to fit the hole. Cutting the plaster back

Washers secure the remaining old plaster around a hole that has been patched.

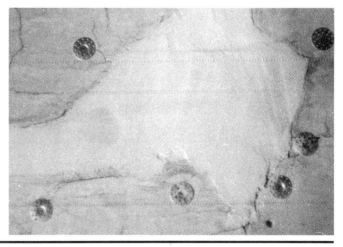

to studs or joists gives you something to which to screw the drywall.

You may have to shim the drywall to bring it up to the surface of the surrounding plaster. The gap between patch and plaster is treated just like a Sheetrock seam: taped and finished with joint compound. (Joint tape also can be used to mend cracks. Taping allows some movement without the crack reopening.) You can skim the entire patch with compound, too, if it's necessary to level it or impart a troweled finish texture. All patches, taped cracks, and skimmed areas *must* be primed before painting. (See the detailed instructions in "Making a Drywall Patch" on this page.)

Patch plastering is the alternative to drywall patching. For holes less than 4 inches in diameter, fill to not-quite-level with patching plaster (such as Structo-lite) and finish (skim) with joint compound. Larger holes down to the lath will probably require three coats. For the scratch and brown coats, use Structo-lite Regular (USG's perlited gypsum plaster) or the equivalent. The top or finish coat is finish lime mixed with gauging plaster. (See the detailed instructions in "Three-Coat Plaster Patching" on page 260.)

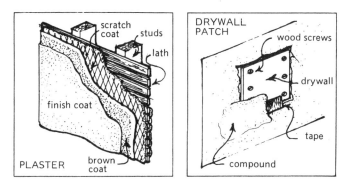

Remove damaged plaster very carefully. You can't just bang it out—unless you were intending to remove the whole wall and whatever is on the other side of it. Cut it with a chisel and gently pull it away with your hands, using a prybar. Anchor salvageable surrounding plaster with washers as described previously. Resecure loose lath to the studs or joists, predrilling to avoid splitting lath. Vacuum out all debris. We suggest installing metal lath over the wood lath before patching with plaster; this makes the patch less likely to fail.

Wall *canvas* or modern substitutes line plaster walls before they are painted or papered. The canvas is primed, making it ideal for painting. (Order it through wallpaper stores. Don't confuse it with lining *paper,* which is not primed.) Decorative painters in the past used to canvas walls before stencilling to protect the fancy painting from hairline cracks. You can use it over patched walls or ceilings, as long as the plaster is basically sound. It's a good way to resurface if you've got less-than-perfect patches, a lot of hairline cracks, uneven paint layers, or other minor imperfections. Canvas can't bridge holes or disguise badly uneven patches, however, so do your stabilizing, taping, and patching first.

SECRET OF THE SCREW GUN

A screw gun comes in handy for installing both plaster washers and drywall patches. By the time you bang nails into the drywall, the surrounding plaster will have cracked and crumbled further. And debris caught behind the patch will keep it from laying flat. A screw gun is an electric screwdriver with a retractable sleeve that controls the screw depth. It's fast, and the depth adjustment allows every screw to be countersunk just below the surface of the drywall without breaking the paper face. But its greatest advantage in patch plastering is that it avoids the hammer impact that would damage fragile plaster.

Making a Drywall Patch

Earlier we described the procedure for making a drywall patch: Remove the bad plaster down to the lath, square up the hole, and screw drywall into the lath. Sounds simple enough, but to make the perfect, seamless drywall patch without destroying surrounding plaster requires the right tools combined with the right technique. Follow these step-by-step instructions to make your perfect patch.

Making the Patch

1. Remove crumbling plaster around the area to be patched. Cut the opening to a regular shape (to make cutting the drywall patch easy) and cut to the nearest stud. Exposing studs enables you to nail the Sheetrock patch directly to the studs.

2. Secure the plaster edges with wood screws. Use plaster washers if the plaster is sound but its keys are broken.

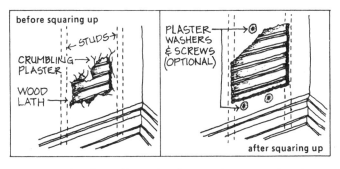

3. Cut the drywall patch. The gap between the Sheetrock and plaster should be minimal so the tape will span the joint and avoid the possibility of future cracks. Shim the patch to bring it flush with the surface of the adjacent plaster.

4. Nail or screw the drywall in place. Set nailheads and screw heads slightly below the surface of the drywall (dimpled), but without breaking the paper. If the hole is small and misses nearby studs, screw the patch into the wood lath (nails won't hold).

PLASTERING GLOSSARY

The terms used in plastering vary regionally and have been altered by changes in technology and the passage of time. The result is that some definitions have become as plastic as the materials themselves!

Aggregate: A mass of granulated particles, such as sand and crushed rock. In plastering, aggregates are important to ensure that the applied plaster shrinks uniformly as it hardens, and without excesses that would cause cracking; to form channels for the crystallization of calcium; as fillers for economical purposes. Lightweight aggregates, such as *vermiculite* and *perlite,* are increasingly popular because of the improved resiliency, fire resistance, sound deadening, and weight reduction they offer over traditional materials such as sand.

Autoclave finish lime: Double-hydrated lime requiring *no* soaking before use; it can be mixed on site and used immediately. Some plasterers feel that Type S (single-hydrated) lime has better workability. Plaster prepared with autoclave lime may be less resistant to environmental moisture (water leaks).

Base: Any continuous surface to which plaster is applied. A base might be a continuous masonry wall or *lath* over structural framing.

Base beads (base screeds): Metal strips, attached to the lath before plastering, that provide a division to work against when troweling plaster that will end at the top edges of base boards.

Brown coat: The rough base coat of plaster used with rock-lath systems. With metal- or wood-lath systems, it is the second application of wet, base-coat plaster.

Browning brush: Fine-bristled, water-carrying brush used to moisten base coat while working.

Casing bead: Metal casing beads are sometimes used around door and window openings. Like a wood *ground,* they indicate the proper thickness for the plaster.

Cat faces: Finish-coat surface imperfections that show up as hollows after *floating.*

Ceiling buttons: See *plaster washers.*

Corner beads: Wire mesh with a rigid metal spine used on outside corners. Be sure to install a corner bead plumb.

Cornerite: Wire mesh used on inside corners of adjoining walls and ceilings to keep corners from cracking.

CORNERITE

Darby: A *float* with two handles and an extra-long blade, used for further leveling and straightening any of the plaster coats.

Devil's float: A wood *float* with one or two nails protruding 1/8 inch from the sole, used for surfacing the *brown coat* after it has dried twenty-four hours. Scratches left by the nails provide tooth for adhesion of the *finish coat.*

Dots: Small plaster spots placed as depth guides during work on walls and ceilings. They are plumbed and leveled like *screeds* to aid in *rodding* the surface.

Drywall (wallboard, plasterboard, Sheetrock, gypboard, gyp-rock): Rigid, insulating board of plasterlike material (usually gypsum), covered on both sides with heavy paper. Also, the system of wall surfacing using this material.

Drywall nail: Short, heavy nail with large head designed for installing *drywall,* often ribbed and/or coated for maximum grip into framing.

Drywall screw: Phillips-type screw fastener designed for power-tool installation of drywall.

Featheredge: Leveling tool similar to *rod* except that blade tapers to a sharp edge for cutting in corners and sharp, straight lines.

Finish coat: Pure lime, mixed with a little *gauging material* (in ratios ranging from 5:1 to 2:1), used for the very thin finish surface of a plaster wall. Fine sand can be added for a sanded finish coat.

Finish plaster: Fine, white plaster made from lime putty and gauging plaster.

Finishing board: A 5-foot × 5-foot *mortarboard* on which finish-coat lime plaster is hand-mixed.

Float: Surfacing tool consisting of a flat, short board with a large handle, that is glided over the surface of plaster to fill voids and hollows or impart texture. Also, the plastering operation involving this tool.

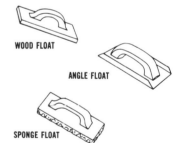

WOOD FLOAT

ANGLE FLOAT

SPONGE FLOAT

Gauging material (gauging): A plaster additive intended to produce early strength and to counteract shrinkage tendencies. For interior work, common gauging materials are *gypsum gauging plaster* and *Keene's cement;* for outdoor work, *portland cement.*

Ground: Metal or wood strips around the edges of doors and windows and at the bottom of walls. These grounds help keep the plaster the same thickness and provide an edge for it to stop against.

Gypsum: A naturally occurring sedimentary rock, originally mined from large quarries near Paris. In its natural form, gypsum is calcium sulphate. When heated in the calcining process, water molecules are driven off, leaving a hemihydrate of calcium sulphate—the material commonly known as plaster of paris. When mixed with water again for use as plaster, the process reverses and the gypsum recrystallizes or "sets" into rocklike calcium sulphate. The plaster cures by a chemical process, not by drying, giving it strength and integrity. Until 1910, not enough was understood about the set of gypsum plaster. At around that time, plasterers found that a lime/gypsum combination gave them the best of both worlds: the workability of lime with the quicker cure of gypsum.

Gypsum bond plaster: Calcined gypsum mixed with 2 to 5 percent lime by weight, designed to bond to properly prepared concrete bases.

Gypsum gauging plaster: A special material made from gypsum carefully processed so that it sets in a definite time interval. On the job, it is added to slaked lime to provide initial surface hardness in mortars like finishing plaster.

Gypsum neat plaster: Gypsum plaster without *aggregate* intended for mixing with aggregate and water on the job.

Gypsum ready-mixed plaster: Gypsum plaster and ordinary mineral aggregate, requiring only the addition of water for use.

Gypsum wood-fibered plaster: Plaster composed of calcined gypsum and finely shredded wood fibers, used to produce base coats of superior strength and hardness. Wood-fibered plaster has great fire resistance, insulating, and sound-deadening qualities. It is also able to withstand vibration due to its flexibility, and weighs about two-thirds as much as sanded cement plaster. Wood-fibered plaster is slightly more expensive than a sand mixture, but its other advantages make it the recommended *scratch coat* for all kinds of lath.

Hair: Animal hair (usually from cattle) once included in scratch-coat mixtures as a mechanical binder.

Hardwall plaster: Gauging plaster mixed with *perlite* aggregate to form a lightweight base-coat plaster. Sold under trade names such as Structo-lite.

Hawk: A square, lightweight, sheet-metal platform with a vertical central handle, from which plaster or mortar is applied to the wall with a trowel.

HAWK

Hydrated lime: Lime prepared at the factory by adding controlled amounts of water to *quicklime*. Two basic grades are available: mason's hydrated (for construction) and finishing lime (for plastering). Finishing limes are used in the final plaster coats, and are the modern, quick-to-prepare versions of quicklime. They can be categorized into three general types by the amount of *slaking* they require:

Autoclave: Can be used immediately after mixing with water.

Type S: Requires less than sixteen hours slaking.

Type N: Requires sixteen to twenty-four hours slaking.

Joint compound (wallboard compound, drywall compound, "mud"): A ready-mixed preparation used for finishing joints and seams in *drywall* construction. Because it is ready-mixed and easy to apply, trowel, and sand, it is widely used for patching and resurfacing plaster.

Keene's cement: A fine, high-density plaster that produces a very hard, fine-textured finish coat. It is produced by heating crushed gypsum rock until nearly all the water of crystallization is driven off, and then adding alum as an accelerator. In decades past, Keene's cement had many uses especially in moulded and cast work. Today it is a specialty product (and somewhat altered in composition) that seldom plays a role in house plastering and patching.

Key: Plaster that has penetrated through the narrow openings in *lath* hardens to form keys that create a mechanical bond.

Lath: Any of several types of perforated *bases* secured to structural framing. For years, thin wooden strips called wooden lath were used, but these have been superseded by gypsum and metal products. Gypsum lath and rock lath are boards with gypsum cores sandwiched between two sheets of absorbent paper, and used mostly in new construction. Metal laths are popular for both new and repair work, and have been manufactured in many (generally interchangeable) forms, such as rib lath (expanded metal screen with ribbing), sheet-metal lath (sheet metal with perforations), and wire lath.

Lime: Found in limestone formations or shell mounds, naturally occurring lime is calcium carbonate. When heated, it becomes calcium oxide *(quicklime),* and after water is added it becomes calcium hydroxide. This calcium hydroxide reacts with carbon dioxide in the air to recreate calcium carbonate.

Mortarboard: Mixed plaster is initially transferred from the mixing box or mixing pan to the mortarboard, often a large version of a *hawk.* The mortarboard is usually a large, flat piece of smooth, clear plywood.

Perlite: Volcanic glass which, when flash-roasted, expands to produce frothy particles of irregular shape. Perlite is a lightweight aggregate often used with calcined gypsum. It is roughly three times as effective an insulator as sand, and is much lighter.

Plaster: Any pasty construction material of mortarlike consistency, which is applied in a plastic condition and hardens in place after being applied. As a surfacing for the walls and ceilings of buildings, plaster denotes an interior covering, while *stucco* denotes an exterior one.

Plaster of paris: See *gypsum.*

Plaster washers (ceiling buttons): Discs of stamped sheet metal, perforated, with a central screw hole, designed for repair work on plaster walls and ceilings.

(continued on next page)

In use, plaster washers help stabilize areas where broken *keys* have caused the surface to come away from the *lath*.

Plasterboard: See *drywall*.

Portland cement: An extremely strong hydraulic cement, produced by burning silica, lime, and alumina (an aluminum oxide) in a kiln in proper proportions. Portland cement plaster is used where an extra hard or highly water-resistant surface is required, such as in walk-in refrigerators and cold storage spaces, toilets, showers, and basement spaces. It should, however, never be applied over gypsum products, such as gypsum lath. Portland cement plaster is also widely used in exterior applications.

Pumice: A naturally formed volcanic glass aggregate, similar to but heavier than perlite. Pumice can double for perlite in most applications but is less popular because of its greater cost (which is the result of its greater weight).

Quicklime: Limestone that is processed but not hydrated. Chemically, it is calcium and magnesium oxides formed by firing limestone over 1700 degrees Fahrenheit. To make plaster, quicklime must be slaked with water in an operation that sets off a violent, boiling reaction. This hazard was made avoidable by the introduction of *hydrated lime*. The principal use of slaked quicklime today is in masonry mortars.

Rod (straightedge): Wood or lightweight metal blade with slotted handle, often 6 inches wide by 4 to 8 feet long. This is the first tool used in leveling and straightening applied plaster between grounds. See also *slicker*.

RODDING BETWEEN SCREEDS

Sand: An aggregate traditionally used in plasterwork. Sand improves the strength and workability of plasters. It must be of high quality—clean, sharp, without harmful chemicals or organic impurities, and screened to a uniform size—or it can cause defects.

Scarifier: A rakelike tool for adding furrows in *scratch coats* that will improve the bond between the scratch coat and the *brown coat*.

Scratch coat: The first base coat put on metal or wood *lath*. The wet plaster is "scratched" with a broom or the point of a trowel to provide a rough surface so the next layer of base coat will stick to it.

Screed: Plaster screeds are ribbons of mortar, leveled, plumbed, or otherwise trued on walls or ceilings, which serve as guidelines for a straightedge to run on

when *rodding* the surface. They are usually the depth of two coats of plaster, and ensure that the new work is spread at a uniform thickness. Metal screeds, like *grounds*, provide a guide for plasterwork.

Sheetrock: U.S. Gypsum's trade name for a *drywall* product, now used generically like Kleenex and Band-Aids.

Slaking: The process of adding water to lime to hydrate it in preparation for mixing it to form a *putty*.

Slicker: A flexible straightedge used for leveling wet plaster.

Slip: The richness, plasticity, and workability of mixed plaster. Slip is a hard-to-define characteristic but is determined in large part by the quality of the plaster used. Plasters with slip mix easily, go on quickly, and spread far, resulting in maximum coverage with minimum effort. Slip is also the thinned plaster used as an adhesive between, say, a cast-plaster ornament and the ceiling.

Spackle: Muralo Co.'s trade name, often used generically, for a plasterlike preparation used in cosmetic repair work, or as a *joint compound* in new *drywall* work. Spackle is available as a dry powder or a ready-mixed, moist compound.

Structo-lite: Trade name for a dry-mixed, under-finish-coat plaster preparation, often used for patch repairs. See also *hardwall plaster*.

Stucco: The term applied to plaster whenever it is used as an exterior covering on walls and buildings. Stucco plaster is made with masonry cement (particularly portland cement), sand, and water. Once cured, it is hard, strong, fire resistant, and weather resistant. See also *plaster*.

Tape: In *drywall* construction, paper or fiberglass strips applied in conjunction with *joint compound* to reinforce joints and seams. Tape is usually 2 inches wide, and can be purchased perforated or nonperforated.

Trowel: A hand-held, bladed tool used to apply, spread, and smooth plaster. Trowel sizes and shapes vary widely, and are determined by the purpose for which the tool is used.

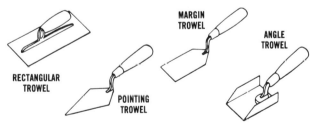

RECTANGULAR TROWEL   MARGIN TROWEL   ANGLE TROWEL   POINTING TROWEL

Vermiculite: A soft, light, mineral aggregate made from the layered mineral mica, added to gypsum plaster as a substitute for sand. Vermiculite has gained popularity not only on the merit of its light weight but because it imparts substantial insulating qualities to plasters that allow them to be used as fireproofing in steel construction.

Taping

To properly complete the patch, you will need a 6-inch flexible taping knife, a 12-inch flexible taping knife, a hawk, sanding sponge, and, of course, drywall and joint compound, nails or screws, and paper or fiberglass-mesh tape. (You could use a float instead of a taping knife, but novices will find this awkward.)

1. Brush out loose plaster and prepare the area to be taped. You may want to dampen the raw edge of the plaster with a mister so it doesn't draw the moisture out of the compound.

2. With a small amount of joint compound on the hawk, begin filling the joint between the drywall and plaster using a 6-inch knife. Work the compound into the joint to ensure that there will be no voids under the tape.

3. Now apply a fairly smooth, heavy coat of compound over the joint. Put it on a little wider than the tape itself.

4. Center the joint tape over the length of the joint. Holding the 6-inch knife at about a 45-degree angle, press the tape into the compound. Make sure there are no air pockets or voids under the tape. Then apply a thin, smooth layer of compound over the tape.

5. Apply a first coat of compound to nails or screws at this time also. Keep compound flush with the surface of the drywall. Do not leave blobs or thick edges that will need sanding later.

Second Coat

1. As the first coat dries, there will usually be some shrinkage and cracking in the compound. Invariably, there will also be ridges and pimples. These should be knocked off, using the taping knife as a scraper. Applying more compound over bumps and ridges will only make the surface more irregular.

2. Apply the second coat with the 6-inch knife, feathering it out 6 to 8 inches. "Feathering" means that the thickness of the compound should taper down to nothing at the edge. To achieve this, apply a generous coat of compound 6 to 8 inches wide. Then scrape the knife clean against the side of the hawk. Now smooth and feather the joint with the knife in long continuous strokes the entire length of the joint.

3. While you smooth and feather the joint, much of the compound you just applied is taken away. But the point is to apply it in a generous coat and smooth to a thin, even coat. Try not to leave any voids or irregularities. If you make a mistake, simply reapply and resmooth right away.

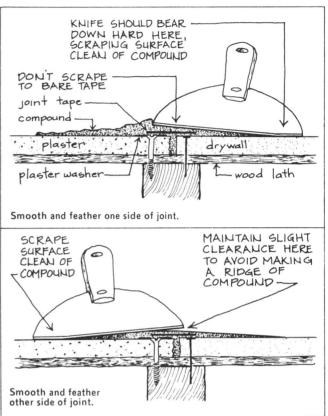

Smooth and feather one side of joint.

Smooth and feather other side of joint.

Third Coat

The third coat is a repeat of the second coat, only wider. You can tell when a coat is dry by the color. Wet compound is dark gray; dry, it is a gray-white. Compound in a nailhead dimple can be dry in half an hour, but a bedded tape joint may have to dry overnight before the next coat is applied.

1. Once the second coat is dry, use the 6-inch knife to scrape off any ridges or bumps. Then apply the third coat of compound. But this time use the 12-inch taping knife and feather the joint out 12 to 14 inches. When smoothing and feathering, start with the knife scraped clean of compound, or, if necessary, with just a little bit of compound at the center of the knife. Excess compound at the edges of the knife will leave ridges. Smooth and feather in long, continuous strokes.

2. After the third coat is dry, touch up low spots with additional compound, or high spots by light sanding with a *wet* sanding sponge (block sponges with black sandpaper bonded to them, available at any hardware store). Use a medium-fine grit and rinse it out as necessary.

Wet sanding keeps down dust. Once you get good at smoothing and feathering the compound, touch-up will be minor.

Three-Coat Plaster Patching

Making a good three-coat plaster patch requires different skills than those required for making a drywall patch. You probably won't become a master plasterer following these guidelines, but you can learn to make minor repairs. Those areas that have failed all the way to the lath require a three-coat repair. The scratch (first) coat stiffens the lath and provides a consistent base for the brown (second) coat. The brown coat is applied over the scratch coat and is built up to about 1/8 to 1/16 inch below the finished wall surface, providing a smooth, level base for the finish (third) coat. Common areas where complete failure of plaster occurs include around doors and windows, on stair soffits, and, in a restoration project, wherever plumbers or electricians have worked.

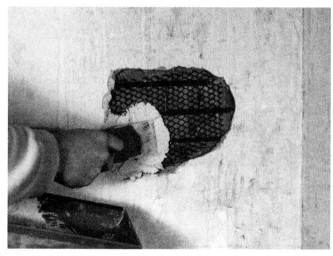

Applying plaster to a new section of metal lath.

First collect the appropriate tools, then begin removing the bad plaster. If it's just the top coat, you can use a putty knife. If water damage caused the finish coat to fail, you may find the underlying coats of plaster firmly keyed but crumbly and soft. Remove all the plaster in this case. Test the plaster by poking the corner of the putty knife into the brown coat. If it cuts through easily, the existing coat will not be able to hold new finish plaster.

When removing bad plaster, don't just start banging away with a hammer and chisel—this will loosen sound plaster and expand the damaged area. Pull loose plaster from the walls with your hands. If the bad plaster is hard to pull away, use a flat prybar to bring it down. Be certain you have removed or resecured all loose plaster. (As described earlier, use plaster washers to resecure weakly keyed areas.)

If you have to remove sound plaster to add an electrical outlet or get to plumbing, drill holes in the line of your cut with a carbide drill bit, then carefully cut directly from hole to hole with a cold chisel. Hold the chisel at a low angle when cutting into the wall or ceiling. Then cut the resulting plaster "island" free from the lath by chipping the keys from the side (again holding the chisel at a low angle).

COLD CHISEL

Once wood lath is exposed, you'll probably find that some of it has pulled away from the studs. If necessary, cut the plaster back to the stud, and resecure the lath with drywall nails. Predrilling the old lath will lessen the chances of splitting it. If there are a few broken lath between the studs, don't worry. You'll be bridging over them with metal lath anyway. Knock back any plaster that's stuck between the lath into the wall cavity. Vacuum all dust, loose plaster, and other debris from the hole with a shop-vac or sweep it out with an old paintbrush.

Lathing Up

Install metal lath over the wood lath. Metal lath provides better keying than wood lath and lessens the likelihood of cracking caused by the old wood lath drawing too much moisture out of the new plaster.

Drive a finishing nail into an exposed stud or drill a hole in the lath and push a finishing nail in place. Hang a piece of lath slightly bigger than the hole on the nail. This gives you a "third hand" to hold the lath in place while you cut it to conform to the hole. Cut the lath to shape with tin snips. For small holes, snip the ribs in the lath one at a time rather than using the tin snips like scissors—it's easier and you'll cut a more precise pattern.

Secure the metal lath over the wood lath with tie wire. Always install the metal lath horizontally—it holds the wet plaster better this way. Bend a 6-inch long piece of wire into an elongated U and pull it around the old wood lath. Twist it tight with needlenose pliers and snip off the excess. Space the tie wires every 6 inches. To secure the lath at studs, drive 1-inch drywall screws between the lath into the stud.

Mixing the Mud

Keeping your tools clean when working with plaster makes the job much easier. Keep a bucket of water handy just to rinse your tools. Mix each type of plaster in a separate bucket and don't use the same scoop for different materials. Put waterproof dropcloths under the areas where you mix and apply plaster. When you finish a work session, clean and dry your tools immediately.

For the scratch and brown coats, use a regular "instant" plaster—you just add it to water. The biggest trick is deciding how much to mix up. If you mix up more than you can use before it starts to stiffen—about one hour—you'll waste some. A novice working steadily might use about half a five-gallon bucket in an hour; a professional probably could use about twice that amount. It depends on the type of plaster failure you have. You'll spend more time (and less material) repairing many little patches than you will filling a large area of failed plaster.

To mix half a bucketful, pour about two quarts of cold, drinkable water into the bucket, then dump in about a third of a bucketful of plaster. Professionals normally mix plaster in a mortar pan with a hoe, but you can mix in the bucket using a mixer attachment on an electric drill. Then fine-tune the mix by adding a little more water or plaster until the consistency is right. The ideal mix will be fairly

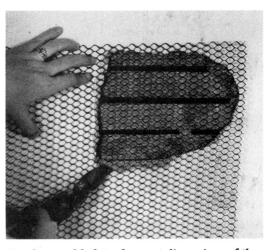

Cut the metal lath to the exact dimensions of the hole.

Use tie wires to secure the new metal lath to the old wood lath.

stiff. To make sure the plaster cures properly, keep the room above 55 degrees Fahrenheit until the plaster sets. Provide plenty of ventilation while the plaster cures.

Applying the Scratch Coat

Moisten the old wood lath using a spray bottle so it won't draw moisture out of the wet plaster. Holding the hawk slanted about 45 degrees toward your body, cut into the plaster with the plasterer's trowel thumb side down. Bring the plaster directly to the wall with the trowel. Apply it to the wall in an arcing motion (left to right for righthanders), making sure to work it well between the lath. Keep the hawk close to the wall under the trowel to catch falling plaster (and be sure to cover the floor with dropcloths). Use a margin trowel to work the plaster into edges and corners. It's sometimes easier to throw plaster off the end of the margin trowel into the patch than pack it into hard-to-reach areas.

Don't build the scratch coat up any thicker than the old scratch coat (about 1/8 to 1/4 inch). As it starts to set, score shallow, random scratches in it diagonally about every inch or so to give the next coat something to grab. Let the scratch coat set for forty-eight hours.

Cut plaster from the hawk and . . .

. . . apply it to the lath.

Applying the Brown Coat

Use the same plaster for the brown coat that you used for the scratch coat. Mix it the same way and apply it in a similar manner. This time, however, you want to make it smooth and level so that it will provide a solid, level

Smoothing the brown coat with a slicker.

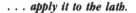

base for the finish coat. To do this, run a slicker over the entire patch after you apply the coat. You can use a 2-foot-long straightedge/paint guard or a length of beveled siding.

Keep the brown coat below the level of the surrounding finish coat by about 1/8 inch. When you're done "dressing" the brown coat, sponge or scrape the wet plaster off the surrounding finish coat. As the brown coat starts to set, knock off any high spots that you missed during your touch-ups. Plasterers use an angle plane (a specialized trowel with several sharp blades set at various angles) for this, but any sharp edge works well. Let the brown coat set for forty-eight hours before applying the finish coat.

Mixing the Finish Coat

The trick to the finish coat is making the proper mix and working quickly. If it takes you twenty minutes to mix the plaster, it will be nearly set before you can get it on your hawk. Practice the steps outlined below on the smallest patches before mixing up a large batch to do a big area.

If you're applying finish coat over an old brown coat, moisten the brown coat well before applying the finish coat. This step is not necessary on a new brown coat. The old plaster will absorb water faster, causing cracks in the finish coat as it starts to dry.

Lime is very caustic. Always wear goggles, a dust mask (better yet, a respirator), and latex gloves when mixing lime. Store it away from children and pets.

Place about two quarts of cold, drinkable water in a five-gallon plastic bucket, then scoop in autoclave finish lime until it starts to float, rather than sink into the water. (If you're using a single-hydrated lime, you'll have to sift the lime into water the day before, and let it slake overnight before mixing.) Mix thoroughly with a mixer attachment on an electric drill or by hand with a pointing trowel. Then, just as with gypsum plaster, fine-tune the mix by adding small amounts of water or lime as necessary, working for a mix in which all the lime is wet and in which there are no lumps or standing water. This mixture is called lime putty and should be about the consistency of joint compound.

Toss some lime putty onto a smooth mortarboard. Use your margin trowel to form it into a ring. Now fill the center of the ring about two-thirds full with cold, clear water. Slowly sprinkle in gauging plaster until the water can't take up anymore. You want about one part gauging plaster to three parts lime putty. Mix the water and the plaster in the middle of the ring together—it should be a bit stiffer than the lime putty. Then fold in the lime putty and mix until all of the ingredients are well acquainted. This is the finish plaster—get to work since it sets up pretty quickly.

Applying the Finish Coat

Using your plasterer's trowel, pull the plaster onto your hawk. Then, using the same motions described for applying the scratch and brown coats, trowel it into the patch. It's not difficult to work the finish coat smooth. The finish plaster will stiffen as you level and smooth it; as it does, you can add little dabs of plaster to fill in hollows, and you can smooth out ridges. To get the finish coat really slick, spray a fine mist of water onto the plaster and make a few final passes with your trowel. Straighten edges or corners with your margin trowel.

Once the finish plaster starts to set, discard any that you haven't used—don't try to "retemper" it by adding water. Retempering will not slow the chemical reaction; it will only weaken the resulting plaster. You'll know the plaster has "gone off" if it becomes stiff and unworkable. You'll soon learn how much you can use before it starts to set; then you can adjust the sizes of your batches accordingly.

Let the finish coat cure for about a week, then check for shrinkage. You may find a few spots where the new finish coat has shrunken away from the old one. Tape the cracks with cloth mesh tape and joint compound as you would tape any minor plaster cracks. Chip out and replaster large cracks.

LINING MATERIALS

Some people elect to cover walls and ceilings in need of repair with lining materials, commonly called lining canvas. Consider linings for walls with cracks that keep coming back, cinder-block walls, and for covering that tacky artificial wood paneling. Most lining materials are polyester or fiberglass coated with latex, usually an acrylic, which is pigmented white. This coating bodies the base fabric and acts as a primer. You can paint or wallpaper most wall linings, depending on their weight.

Use the heavier linings—about 18 to 20 mils thick—on cinder block, cement block, and brick. The fabrics are thick and stiff enough to bridge open areas, including mortar joints. They show a surface texture, so are more frequently finished with wallcoverings to hide their texture rather than finished with paint.

Use lightweight fabrics for relatively smooth walls that have suffered minor damage such as flaking paint, cracking plaster, efflorescence due to past water damage, or less-than-perfect previous patching. You can apply paint or wallcoverings over these liners.

Hanging Wall Liners

The type of lining you choose and how you install it depends on the kind of wall—concrete or wood, painted or unpainted. Here are instructions for most types of wall you will encounter:

Masonry (concrete, cinder block, cement block, brick). Smooth bumps and protuberances on these rough surfaces by knocking or sanding them off. While the liner will bridge pits and mortar joints, you should fill in crevices and joints when covering cinder block. (Also use a latex block-filler for a smoother surface on cinder block.)

Whether or not you use block-filler, size the wall. Use a 50/50 mix of water and ready-mixed vinyl adhesive.

Allow to dry at least two hours. If the wall was painted, replace the vinyl-adhesive size with an acrylic-emulsion primer (Roman's R-35, Zinsser's Shieldz, Insl-X's Aqualock, or any other product specifically designed to go under wallcovering).

Cut each strip of the lining material 2 to 3 inches longer than the height of the wall. For the first strip measure from the corner approximately 1/2 inch less than the width of the material, so you can cover the corner. Paste the back of the strip, giving special attention to the edges. When you carry the strip to the wall, fold it over loosely, paste side to paste side.

Hang each strip vertically, from the top down. Use a plumb line to make sure the hanging is exactly vertical. Smooth with a sponge or smoothing brush, one foot at a time. (Don't use too much pressure, or you'll force the lining into the joints and cracks.) Work from the center of the strip out to eliminate air bubbles. Butt the seams—do not overlap. Trim the top and bottom with a razor blade.

Allow at least four to five days drying time—more if the area is poorly ventilated or in humid weather. When dry, prime the lining with an acrylic-emulsion primer and let it dry for several hours. These materials may then be painted or wallcovered. When hanging a wallcovering, make sure its seams don't coincide with the seams of the liner.

Paneling (wood, composition board, plastic, and the like). Apply heavier lining materials to bridge grooves, seams, and other irregularities. First roughen the surfaces with a coarse sandpaper (80 D production paper). You should also wash these surfaces thoroughly, as they've frequently been waxed or oiled. If you can stand the odor, ammonia makes a good wash; otherwise, use a heavy-duty cleaner such as Ajax. Rinse it off completely when you're finished.

The paneling should then be primed with an acrylic-emulsion primer. Allow two or three hours drying time. Use a ready-mixed vinyl adhesive and hang the lining material horizontally. (This will give you the smoothest results.) If you find it easier, hang the material vertically, but be careful that the seams don't line up with the grooves in the paneling.

Painted walls. Lining materials are most frequently used on walls that have been repeatedly painted over the years. It can create a new wall by removing all sorts of problems: peeling from water damage; cracks in the paint film (which sometimes extend to the plaster underneath); badly done spackling or other repair work. The liners for these jobs are usually smoother in finish and more lightweight than those used on masonry. But heavier material may be best for badly damaged walls.

Prepare the wall by sanding off all bumps and protrusions. Flaking and peeling paint must be rigorously scraped off. Fill wide cracks and depressions deeper than 1/4 inch with a paste spackling. Don't bother filling fine cracks.

The smoother the surface when you start, the smoother

PRO-DUCT NAME	MAKER	BASIC USES	COMPO-SITION	THICK-NESS	TEX-TURE	ROLL SIZE	COST (per sq. ft.)
Wall Cover No. 9962	Imperial Wall-coverings, a division of Collins & Aikmen	As a lining over cinder block, concrete block, and other irregular surfaces. Recommended particularly for use under flexible wallcoverings, but may also be painted. Heavier and stiffer than most liners.	25% cellulose 38% synthetic fibers 37% acrylic latex saturant	20 mils	slight surface texture	28 in. W × 15 ft. L; packed three single rolls per bolt, approx. 105 sq.ft. per bolt	29¢
						42 in. W × 150 linear yards, total 1,575 sq. ft.	27¢
Wall-Over No. 20950	Columbus Coated Fabric, a division of Borden Chemical	A heavy, somewhat stiff lining fabric for use over masonry, painted surfaces, and drywall. It will bridge grooves and other deep imperfections, and result in a slightly textured surface that may be painted or wallcovered.	65% polyester 35% natural cellulose acrylic primed	18 mils	slight surface texture	27 in. W × 15 ft. L; approx. 34 sq. ft. per roll	30¢
No. 30950						54 in. W × 150 ft. L; approx. 675 sq.ft. per bolt	24¢
Wall-Tex Lining Canvas No. 20990	Columbus Coated Fabric, a division of Borden Chemical	Lightweight, primed canvas for repair and restoration of damaged walls. Creates a new, smooth wall surface for painting or for hanging wallcovering. Not heavy enough to bridge deep or wide grooves & cracks unless filled.	80% cotton 20% polyester acrylic primed	12 to 14 mils	very slight texture	27 in. W × 15 ft. L; packed in double rolls, approx. 68 sq.ft. per double roll	30¢
No. 30990						54 in W. × 36 ft. L per bolt, approx. 162 sq.ft. per bolt. Also 54 in. W × 48 yards L (144 linear ft.) = 648 sq. ft.	25¢
Glid-Wall No. 70127	Glidden Coatings & Resins, a division of SCM Corporation	Repairs cracked and damaged walls, ceilings, and woodwork. Can also be used on rough masonry and cement block. Creates a new, permanent surface that strengthens and smooths the substrate. Must be primed with Insul-Aid Primer Sealer.	Johns Manville Fiber Glass not primed*	22 mils	smooth mat	48 in. W × 300 ft. L; 1,200 sq.ft. per roll	10¢*
No. 72659				30 mils	smooth mat		13¢*
No. 70884				22 mils	burlap finish	40 in. W × 300 ft. L; 1,000 sq.ft. per roll	14¢*

*Additional cost of primer is approx. 15¢ per sq.ft.

the final result. Apply an acrylic-emulsion wallcovering primer before hanging the liner. Then hang the fabric vertically using a ready-mixed vinyl adhesive.

Regardless of the type of wall underneath, liners of synthetic fabrics are always butted at the seams; liners of cotton canvas can be overlapped and double-cut at the seams because cotton is subject to shrinkage. Remove air bubbles under the liner by slicing them open with a razor blade and pressing the material back into place.

Allow at least four to five days drying time before painting. Liners are usually factory-primed, so primer is unnecessary under a flat finish. For semigloss and high-gloss enamels, however, either an alkyd or latex enamel undercoater should be applied. If you're going to hang wallcovering over the liner, always prime with an acrylic-emulsion wallcovering primer.

TEXTURED PLASTER FINISHES

Textured finishes are so widespread, and the techniques for producing them so diverse, that it is almost impossible to pin down exactly which wall finishes are appropriate for which houses. Victorian-era texture finishes were created simply by tooling the finish coat of plaster. (A plasterer has to work fast and add lots of retarder to the mix.) But these decorative finishes were rare during the Victorian period. They became fashionable during the early years of the twentieth century and remained popular until about 1935. Textured finishes often appeared in the Bungalows, Cottages, Foursquares, and English and Colonial Revival houses of the period.

Not all of the textured finishes from this period were done in the finish coat of plaster. "Plastic paints" appeared during the 1920s to produce these effects. Similar products are available today; they are generically called "wall texture," "texture paint," or even (rather humbly) joint compound. One of these products, Textone, manufactured by U.S. Gypsum, was sold as a plastic paint in the 1920s, and is still sold today. Early Textone came in powder form, and had to be site-mixed with water and/or sand. The modern product comes premixed in four different formulations: a smooth texture, a sand texture, and two coarser textures. The Muralo company markets a dry powder product, Mural-Tex, that must be mixed with warm water to form texture paint. Several other paint companies currently make texture-paint products; these products vary from one region to another.

To fix a textured wall, first patch any holes. The textured finish can be worked into a coat of finish plaster or a coat (or two) of texture paint, but either of these materials must be applied over a sound substrate. The wall should be properly patched with patching plaster or joint compound, sanded smooth, and sealed with shellac or latex paint.

You can use either site-mix plaster or a premixed texture paint. If the area to be repaired is large, plaster will be less costly but more hassle (dust, leftover plaster to dis-

card). If the damaged area is small, the cost (and hassle) differential is negligible. Either material should produce satisfactory results.

Once the wall is ready for texturing, practice making the desired texture pattern on a piece of gypsum wallboard before you work on the wall. When you have the hang of it, try it on a section of the damaged wall. If the texture looks wrong, don't let it dry—scrape the unsuccessful texture off the wall with a putty knife and start again.

We've selected a few finishes popular between 1915 and 1930 to illustrate the tools and methods traditionally employed to produce textured wall finishes. Once you're familiar with them you should be able to match the wall finish in your old house.

Holland plaster. Named after the historic textures in old Dutch houses, this finish is suitable for formal or informal rooms. Generally, in a smaller room, the effect would be understated; in a larger room, exaggerated.

The plaster (or texture paint) is applied with a trowel but the raised and rough edges left by the trowel are retained, giving the appearance of torn edges of paper. One popular treatment: Tint the texture material a cream color, then apply a medium-dark stain overglaze, and lightly sand the high spots to reveal streaks of the base color.

Early colonial plaster. This is a sand finish, most easily produced with a commercial sand-texture paint.

Brush the paint on in a "thick and thin" manner, then go over the partially set material in all directions with a bricklayer's small pointing trowel. Then immediately stipple the surface with a whisk broom, and smooth up the high points again with the trowel.

Italian plaster finish. Use plaster or texture paint to produce this finish. Brush the material on with a large paintbrush, then randomly stipple with a stippling brush. After the plaster or paint becomes tacky, brush in random semicircles with a short-bristled paintbrush. As soon as the material has set enough to hold its shape, lightly skim the surface with a plasterer's steel trowel. Glaze topcoats were often used with this finish.

Imitation brick/stone/tile. These finishes are usually done in plaster. Brick finishes are done with colored plaster; stone finishes often have colors brushed into the wet plaster to simulate natural grain. Brick textures are simulated by wire brushing; rough stone textures are produced by laying on plaster in crude, irregular gobs, then brushing out the roughest spots with a coarse brush. Imitation tile or smooth stone is worked into smooth plaster.

Achieve a "mortar joint" effect by applying the finish plaster coat over a dry coat of contrasting-color plaster, and then cutting the "joints" with an old screwdriver, using a level as a guide. Lightly brush out the sharp edges produced by the cutter.

Brush finishes. To create brush finishes apply a thick coat of texture paint then brush the material in tight semicircles with a short-bristled brush. After the material has set enough to hold its shape, press a plasterer's trowel into the paint, pull it out a little, then shift to one side to drag the material.

To achieve another kind of finish, roughen a thick coat of texture paint with a stipple brush, then pull the material up into points with a plasterer's trowel, pushing it in and quickly pulling it out. Then randomly smooth down any rough edges with the trowel.

It is also possible to create a very rough brushed texture suitable only for large rooms. With a stippling brush, stipple a thick coat of texture paint, then whisk-broom into large semicircles. At the end of each semicircular stroke, pull the whisk broom away sharply. After the material dries, use sandpaper to knock off the sharp points.

Stippled finishes. Stippling brushes, wadded paper, or sponges can be used to create many subtle and striking effects. You can produce a finish by daubing a texture paint with a stippling brush or by stippling texture paint with a sponge.

Hand finishes. A wall finish can be produced by hand-daubing plaster into place or by pressing hands into texture paint, then pulling them straight back. You can also cover a wall with fingerprints.

Removing Unwanted Texture Finish

In some parts of the country, the textured wall finish became such a craze that splendid Victorian homes were slathered in a wall-to-wall coat of rough-textured finish—decorative woodwork, ornamental plaster, and all. Worse, some homeowners were assured that a coat of texture finish would cure (hide) plaster failure, but the extra weight only accelerated deterioration. Alas, if not professionally applied to a well-prepared surface, texture finish eventually fails. So even if you want to reapply a texture finish, it may be necessary to remove some or all of the existing finish.

Before you can figure out how to take it off, it helps to know what it is. Victorian-era texture finishes were created simply by tooling the finish coat of plaster. This is tough to remove. And even if you do remove it, you'll have to apply a new finish coat because only the brown coat will remain. Occasionally, a lime-based product like Plastint, a colored finishing plaster designed to create a rough, tinted finish, was added over an existing finish coat. In that case, it will surely be weakly bonded, and may be removed using the steam method described below.

During the 1920s, "plastic paints" became popular. Essentially precursors to joint compound, they provided longer working time than finish plasters. In the years that followed, several companies introduced their own "plastic paint" products, such as U.S. Gypsum's Textone. *Caution:* Many of these products contained asbestos. Send a sample of your texture finish to a laboratory for an asbestos test. Any building inspector can tell you where to send a sample for testing in your area. Asbestos removal requires special procedures and precautions.

"Sand paints" had abrasive ingredients added to produce a stippled effect when applied with a brush or roller. Because they are in fact paints, they can be removed using standard paint removal procedures.

You'll have to experiment if you don't know what finish graces your walls. If you think you know what the finish is, select one of the methods described here. If that doesn't work and experimenting with other methods leads nowhere, you may choose to hide the problem rather than destroy all the plaster. Try skim-coating the finish with joint compound, laminating with gypsum board, or applying metal lath and replastering.

Steaming

Most lime-based and "plastic paint" texture coatings will succumb to steam. Albeit time-consuming, hot and sweaty, the procedure is uncomplicated. The trick is to work carefully so you don't damage the underlying plaster, and so that you get the majority of the texture finish off in the first pass.

Wall steamers—available through rental services and hardware stores—are most often used for removing wallpaper. The steam flows through a perforated metal pan where some of the steam condenses and collects, so keep

Spending the day with a wall steamer and putty knife is no joy, but these simple tools will remove most texture finishes effectively.

a bucket handy to pour the condensate into—even if you've thoroughly masked the floor.

Wear heavy, gauntlet-type gloves when using the steamer. Hold the pan tight to the wall until the finish is saturated. Move the pan down a couple of inches and scrape the loose finish above the pan away with a putty knife. (Round the corners of the putty knife with a file to reduce risk of gouging the underlying plaster.) Keep the steamer pan against the next patch of the wall while you're scraping; there's no point wasting time and electricity.

Use a "combat chisel" on the remaining finish.

Continue scraping the wall from the top down. The finish will become easier to remove as you near the bottom of the wall. The condensed steam running down the wall softens the texture finish below. Be thorough—it's easier to remove the stuff now, while it's soft, than after the steamer is shut off.

After steaming, go back over areas where texture finish remains with a "combat chisel" (a chisel that's been retired from your fine woodworking tool box but still has a reasonably sharp edge). Hold the chisel at a flat angle to avoid digging into the wall. Most of the remaining finish should pop off the wall fairly easily. Sand off pimples and high spots—wet sanding will avoid creating a lot of dust. Don't attempt a mirror-smooth surface; you're going to have to apply a skim coat of joint compound anyway. Just give the wall a quick once-over to remove the little bits of debris that are stuck to the wall. Rinse the wall thoroughly

Wear a dust mask when sanding.

Use a taper's sanding stick for greater reach.

with plenty of clean water and a sponge to remove any chalky residue. Powdery traces of the old finish will interfere with the bond of joint compound or paint.

Finally, apply a couple of thin coats of joint compound over the wall with a 10- or 12-inch taping knife. Joint compound fills in nicks and covers over any remaining slight protrusions. If the wall didn't come as clean as you'd hoped, you may need several coats of compound. Tape cracks in the plaster with cloth mesh joint tape.

Removing Sand Paint

Remove sand paint from plaster using the same techniques to remove any thick paint film from plaster. Heat stripping works well because sand paint is applied in one or more thick coats. Make sure to file the sharp edges off your putty knife, and scrape gently. After using the heat plate on plaster, chemical cleanup is usually not required. Any residual bits of melted paint can be easily knocked off the plaster with a putty knife or chisel.

Stripping Mouldings

Mouldings present the most difficult chore. Cast plaster—those elements that have sculptural detail, such as dentils, egg-and-dart moulding, medallions, and the like—are the biggest headache. Take the mouldings off the wall or ceiling if you dare—there is always the danger of damaging the mouldings during disassembly. We recommend stripping them in place.

For lime-based and "plastic paint" finishes, use a wall steamer. Disconnect the pan from the hose so you can point the steam from the hose directly where you need it. As the finish starts to soften, remove it carefully as described below.

For sand-paint-encrusted mouldings, use chemical paint remover. Even when you buy paste-type removers, additional thickening is desirable. A good thickener is Cab-O-Sil, a fumed silica made by Cabot Corporation of Boston. (It's available at some art supply dealers and through epoxy distributors.) Fumed silica is extremely irritating to the respiratory tract. Be sure to use caution, work in a well-ventilated area if possible, and wear a fine-particle mask when handling it. Less effective alternatives to Cab-O-Sil include cornstarch and whiting. Add thickener until the stripper is nearly the consistency of Jell-O.

Cover the moulding with polyethylene sheeting after applying the stripper. This allows the stripper to work longer, permitting it to soften the sand paint even in the deepest grooves.

Once the paint is soft, getting it off is the hard part. Experiment with small chisels, awls, sculptor's tools, dentil picks, and the like to gently dig the slime out of the moulding's recesses. Soft bristle and polypropylene brushes also work well.

Covering Up Unwanted Finish

Sometimes nothing works when trying to remove a textured finish. If you don't want to demolish the wall and replaster there are several ways to cover a texture finish. The least labor-intensive method is to laminate the walls with gypsum board (Sheetrock). Knock off the highest spots on the walls and screw the gypsum board into the studs right through the existing plaster. This method changes the moulding profiles a bit and eliminates the hand-worked, wavy appearance of plaster. Both of these negative effects can be minimized by using 1/4-inch Sheetrock; this thickness will flex enough to follow the undulations of the plaster somewhat. If necessary, you can remove and reset baseboards, cap mouldings, and casings. It may be necessary to deepen window and door jambs to accommodate the extra wall thickness.

Replastering over the finish with joint compound is a better and less expensive, though more labor-intensive, way to cover most texture finishes. Skim coating itself goes fast, but preparing the surface to accept and hold the joint compound is especially time-consuming. Scrape clean all poorly bonded texture finish with a combat chisel. Also thoroughly wash the entire wall to remove any chalky residue or dirt prior to skim coating.

Fill in all the nicks and scratches first, using a 6-inch taping knife. Let joint compound dry completely before applying another coat. Apply the first skim coat horizontally working from the top of the wall down. Put pressure on the dry side of the knife (the lower edge) as you move across the wall. That way, the knife won't create ridges in the wet compound. Small overlap marks will be all that remains. Apply the second coat vertically, again bearing down on only one side of the knife. By putting each successive coat on perpendicular to the previous one, you'll eliminate the overlap marks, and make the wall flatter.

Joint compound can cover even high-relief finishes because you can build it out to a thickness of about 1/4 inch. But you can only apply joint compound to a thickness of about 1/16 inch at a time—any thicker and it will shrink and crack. As an alternative, screw wire lath directly over the texture finish and replaster on top of it. However, plastering over the existing surface will add

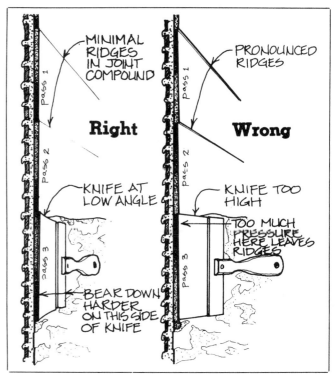

How to skim.

quite a bit of thickness to the walls and drastically change moulding profiles. The only expense saved with this method is the cost of demolishing the existing plaster, which is relatively inexpensive, so you're better off starting from scratch.

Saving Plaster with Injected Adhesive Bonding

Bulging plaster beneath decorative surfaces presents a difficult repair problem—especially when you want to preserve the decorative finish. Keys often break, especially on ceilings where the original work was poorly done. If the wood lath strips were placed too close together, or the lath was nailed directly over planks, the keys do not form properly, and the plaster may eventually sag away from the lath.

When broken keys cause plaster to come loose from the lath, the typical solution is to tear down the loose plaster, and patch the resulting hole, which destroys the irreplaceable finish on the plaster. Even if the plaster doesn't have a decorative finish, it may be less expensive to resecure the loose plaster than to remove and replace it, using a technique called "injected adhesive bonding."

Morgan Phillips and Andrew Ladygo developed this method for reattaching loose plaster for the Society for the Preservation of New England Antiquities (SPNEA). They inject specially mixed acrylic adhesives into the space between lath and plaster through holes drilled in the face of the plaster (or through the lath from behind, when accessible). The plaster is then pressed back into place, usually with a sheet of plywood, until the adhesive sets. After removing the plywood, they fill the injection holes.

All loose texture finish has been removed and the wall has been rinsed; now the first coat of joint compound can be applied.

When executed properly, this method provides a continuous bond between lath and plaster, limiting the stress on any given area of the plaster; the bond is stronger than the bond with the original mechanical keys. It's an especially valuable method with heavy ceiling plaster. Because the stress is spread over the maximum surface area, the relative flexibility of the adhesives isn't a problem; in fact, it may be a benefit, as it allows for the differential expansion and contraction of the substrate, plaster, and adhesive.

However, the special adhesives used by SPNEA are expensive, and they must be mixed with fillers and modifiers such as fluid coke, lime, Microballoons (tiny, hollow glass spheres), and other thickeners. We have adapted the techniques and materials for resecuring loose plaster so that the technology can be "brought home," and attempted by the more casual restorer. (See "Materials" box on page 271.)

Identifying Problem Areas

First mark out the areas of loose plaster with chalk. To test the surface, press it gently with the palm of your hand or with a T-brace made from 2 x 4s. If the plaster seems to move in relation to the studs and lath beneath, then the keys are broken. Be careful not to punch a hole in the loose plaster. With greater pressure you may find a similar movement, indicating that the plaster is well keyed to the lath, but the lath is loose from the studs. (This condition requires further investigation for decay and structural damage.) Thumping with your finger makes a solid, snappy sound on good plaster; a hollow and dull sound on loose plaster.

Treat an entire loose area at once to reduce the stress on the plaster when it is pressed back into place. On ceilings with access from above, begin by vacuuming up

Use a drill stop on your bit to keep from drilling through the face of the plaster.

debris. Leave loose and broken keys in place to channel the adhesive later. Then drill 1/4-inch injection holes through the lath. Use a drill stop on your bit to keep from drilling into the plaster. If there is no access to the back (as on most walls), drill directly through the face of the plaster, and fill the holes later after removing the plywood. Of course, walls don't need as many holes as do ceilings. Position the holes 3 to 6 inches apart and at the center of the lath. If possible, place the holes in inconspicuous areas of the wall.

Cleaning, Consolidating, and Priming

Cleaning the space between the lath and plaster is the key to success with this technique. Use a bent wire tool and a vacuum to loosen and suck dust out through the injection holes. On walls, break open the plaster at the bottom of the loose area where chunks of broken keys

have collected and clean out the debris. (Unfortunately, you may have to lose some of that irreplaceable finish.) The debris prevents the loose plaster from moving back into place.

Next, prepare the adhesive. Most come in standard caulking-gun cartridges. Trim the tip so it just fits in the wood-lath holes; when injecting through plaster, trim the tip just slightly larger to make a tighter seal with the plaster.

If the adhesive is water-based and has no primer, it's a good idea to prewet both the plaster surface and the substrate with adhesive thinned way down with water and a little denatured alcohol added as a wetting agent.

Adhesives won't stick to crumbly, water-damaged plaster. Remove the water-damaged areas, and patch with new plaster. If the plaster has an irreplaceable finish that must be saved, stabilize crumbly plaster with Acryloyd B-67, an acrylic resin that comes in dry beads manufactured by Rohm & Haas. Dissolve the beads in mineral spirits to a 20 percent solution and brush or spray it onto the water-damaged areas. As the solvent evaporates, the resin hardens, consolidating the plaster.

Injecting Adhesives

Because you'll be gunning the adhesive "blind" into each hole, it's difficult to gauge the flow of adhesive when injecting. Judge the amount that comes out with each squeeze of the handle by testing beforehand. While injecting, give the adhesive enough time to flow into the space between plaster and lath, but move quickly between holes. Stop applying adhesive if you feel back pressure on the trigger of the caulking gun—excessive adhesive will make it difficult to press the plaster back into place, and may over-stress the plaster.

Injecting the construction adhesive through the face of the plaster.

Next, set 1/2-inch plywood as big as the patch area in place with 1 × 2 wood braces. Thick plaster that will not move back into place completely will need to have the force of the ply spread out with a layer of 1/2-inch foam carpet pad between the ply and the plaster. Protect the ply

T-braces are wedged against the plaster to press it into place. Note the excess adhesive squeezing out.

Additional braces are required to apply pressure to a large area of loose plaster.

or pad it with wax paper and hold it in place against the patch area initially with a T-brace. Spring additional braces into place to press the plaster back against the lath. If braces are impractical, draw the plaster against the lath with screws driven through washers and wood shingles.

As the plaster is pressed back into place, excess adhesive will squeeze out through the injection holes and between the laths, thereby binding to an even greater surface area. When the adhesive has set, remove the ply. If the ply is stuck to the plaster, twist it sideways (in the same plane as the plaster surface) to break the bond.

ORNAMENTAL PLASTER

Ornamental plaster can be divided into two main categories: cast work and run work. *Cast ornament* is formed by pouring wet plaster into a mould. The mould is removed when the plaster sets, and the cast pieces are then applied, singly or in combination with other pieces, to form decorative elements. *Run ornament* involves forming a profile by pushing a template over plaster when it's still wet. This is how cornices and other linear mouldings are formed. There are two methods for making run plaster ornament: bench work, in which the moulding is run on a flat surface and later applied to the ceiling or wall; and cornice work, which is usually run in place in the room.

Moulding plaster is finer than regular or gauging plaster in particle size, and thus produces finer detail in castings and mouldings. An even finer grade of plaster, known as casting plaster, is used to make models for cast sculpture, and also in dental work.

Pure gypsum plaster, while suitable for casting, sets too fast to be used for running large mouldings or troweling in finish-coat work. Lime is added to give the gypsum a longer working time, and to increase the plasticity and trowelability of the mix.

"Plaster" can be used to refer either to plaster of paris alone, or to the plaster-and-lime mix. When plasterers want to refer to pure plaster, as distinct from the plaster-and-lime mix, they use the term *neat plaster.* By contrast, the word *putty* always refers to the lime putty, never to the mixture of lime and plaster, although both are similar in texture and appearance.

Run Ornament: Bench Work

Run ornament, especially in-place cornice work, is perhaps the most advanced and difficult of all plasterwork. It requires a good sense of three-dimensional geometry, a familiarity with the plaster itself, and experience in working with it. You need real skill to apply and run the material, especially when it is overhead. In-place cornice work requires a minimum of two people—one to mix and apply the plaster, and another to push the template, or mould.

To run mouldings, you use a mould with a metal template into which the reverse profile of the moulding has been cut. The template, which is mounted in a wooden

MATERIALS

Water-Based Adhesives

A water-based adhesive like "Big Stick" Construction Adhesive (by DAP) can be thinned down to make a primer for itself that is sure to be compatible. Use this primer formula:

> 4 parts (by volume) tap water
> 2 parts denatured ethyl alcohol
> 1 part water-based adhesive

Mix the adhesive with one of the four parts of water first, then mix in the rest. The alcohol acts as a wetting agent, making the primer spread out and soak into the dry, dusty wood lath and plaster surfaces better than water alone.

Squirt the primer into the injection holes and let it soak in and begin to set for about an hour or until it starts to get tacky. This consolidates and seals the dry, dusty surfaces, so the adhesive will stick better.

Solvent-Based Adhesives

These readily available, solvent-based adhesives for reattaching loose or bowed plaster may not work well with porous plaster or when the space between lath and plaster is extremely dirty (experiment to see if they will work in your situation). Prewetting the surfaces helps, but compatible solvents are too hazardous. They do work with clean, hard plasters that can be moved back into place against the lath. The best types for this use have a thin consistency and long "skin-over" or open time and are "gap filling."

Supplier of Adhesives Used by SPNEA

Acryloyd B-67 and Rhoplex resins are special SPNEA adhesives supplied by Rohm & Haas. To order these products from Conservation Materials, you must first be a member of

American Institute for
Conservation
3545 Williamsburg Lane, NW
Washington, DC 20008
(202)364-1036

There is a $55 membership fee.

Conservation Materials, Ltd.
1165 Marietta Way,
Dept. OHJ
Sparks, NV 89431
(702)331-0582

For More Information

Society for the Preservation of New England Antiquities
185 Lyman Street, Dept. OHJ
Waltham, MA 02154
(617)891-1985

The following societies sponsor plaster workshops:

The Preservation Institute
for the Building Crafts
Main Street
P.O. Box 1777
Windsor, VT 05089
(802)674-6752

Campbell Center for Historic
Preservation Studies
P.O. Box 66, Dept. OHJ
Mount Carroll, IL 61053
(815)244-1173

Eastfield Village
Box 145 R.D.
East Nassau, NY 12062
(518)766-2422

Association for Preservation
Technology
P.O. Box 8178, Dept. OHJ
Fredericksburg, VA 22404
(703)373-1621

SPNEA ON ALTERNATIVE ADHESIVES

The formulations we describe may not be easily accessible to the average consumer. While our formulations are designed for optimum performance, there *is* much room for compromise within this system. However, understanding the *principles* is a necessary prerequisite in attempting to formulate adhesives by using more readily available materials.[1] Although such homemade formulations will sacrifice performance, with reasonable care an acceptable product can be formulated.

The Rhoplex emulsions we use cannot be purchased outright by consumers. But they are the basis for both masonry bonding agents and adhesive caulks. Acryl-60 by Thoroseal[2] is one product that is an acceptable substitute, and it's available at most masonry supply houses. As for adjusting viscosity, remember that it is better to fill a thin material than to dilute a thick one. By reducing filler, the product becomes more expensive (more adhesive) and less apt to fill voids. Using an unfilled version of the adhesive with Cab-O-Sil[3] to adjust viscosity would often provide adequate adhesion. If the

plaster can be pushed up to mate with the lath, the filler becomes less critical to the adhesive's function.

In adapting our procedures, success would be more likely with an aqueous-emulsion adhesive than with a solvent-based system. I'm certain that many other proprietary acrylic or PVA products used in a similar fashion, with a variety of bulking agents, could perform under most circumstances. But I cannot recommend any one product which, by itself, meets all of the necessary criteria.

—Andrew Ladygo
Architectural Conservator, Society for the Preservation of New England Antiquities

---

[1]For a full technical discussion of the principles, see *The Bulletin of the Association for Preservation Technology,* Vol. XII, No. 2. A photostat of the article will be provided by SPNEA to those interested. Write to Society for the Preservation of New England Antiquities, 185 Lyman Street, Dept. OHJ, Boston, MA 02154.
[2]Thoro System Products, 7800 N.W., 38th Street, Dept. OHJ, Miami, FL 33166.
[3]Cabot Stains, 100 Hale Street, Dept. OHJ, Newburyport, MA 01950.

frame, is pushed over the plaster as it hardens, thus forming the finished profile. The metal template and supporting wood frame together are referred to as the mould. The specific shape of a mould varies, depending on the kind of moulding to be produced, but its basic components are always the same. Each of these parts has its own name.

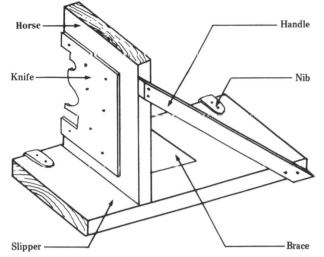

A sample mould, one for running a small moulding on the bench, consists of the metal template, known as the *knife,* which is nailed to a supporting piece of wood, called the *horse.* These together are mounted at right angles to another piece of wood, known as the *slipper,* which serves as the guide for running the moulding. To these are added a handle for pushing and a brace to keep the horse at right angles to the slipper. Any mould designed to run over a plaster surface will have *nibs,* small strips of metal that are nailed to the slipper and the horse. They allow the mould to glide smoothly over the plaster without digging into or cutting it.

The first step in making a mould is to cut the profile in the knife. Use a piece of galvanized sheet metal, at least 26 gauge in thickness, for the knife. The piece must be stiff enough so that any points or tabs of the profile won't bend over when pushing the knife against the plaster.

If you're taking a profile from plans or out of a book, copy the outline onto a piece of tracing paper and lay the paper on top of the metal. With a punch and hammer, transfer the profile to the metal in a series of punch marks. You can also use carbon paper, but the blue marks are sometimes hard to see on the metal and can get smudged while cutting.

There are several methods for duplicating an existing profile:

1. Trace the profile onto a piece of cardboard or posterboard with a pair of dividers or a compass, which means that you first cut the pattern in the cardboard with a sharp mat knife. Then hold the pattern up against the moulding and readjust it a few times until you get an exact fit.

2. Use a profile gauge, consisting of small metal "fingers" held in a row, to transfer the contour onto cardboard or paper.

3. If you're removing all or part of the existing moulding to carry out a repair, square off the end of one piece with a saw and then trace directly onto the paper with a sharp pencil.

4. One of the simplest and cleverest ways is to saw through the moulding on the wall with a backsaw, insert a piece of cardboard into the slot made by the saw, and then trace the outline onto it. The slot can later be refilled with new plaster.

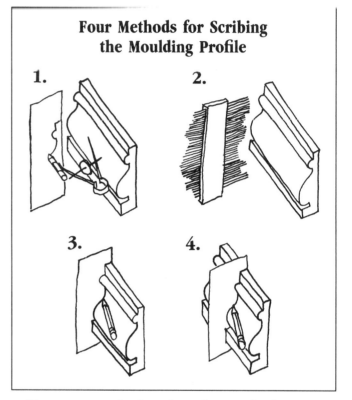

Four Methods for Scribing the Moulding Profile

1.   **2.**

3.   **4.**

Plaster cuts easily: Just draw the saw back to you a couple of times, guiding the blade with the back of your thumb to establish a kerf (just as you would with a piece of wood). Then saw with gentle, steady strokes, so you don't chip or crumble the plaster. Use an old saw, as plaster will dull the teeth of a good saw.

When copying the profile of existing mouldings, make sure accumulations of paint aren't distorting the outline (unless you're going to match it against existing pieces that can't be stripped of paint). Otherwise, they should be thoroughly stripped before you attempt to reproduce them.

Once you have scribed the profile onto the metal, cut out the knife with combination tinsnips. Be careful not to bend the edges of the metal with the tinsnips while you're cutting, especially in any tight corners. Use files to get where the tinsnips can't reach. (Have a selection of small triangular and rattail files on hand for working on corners and tight curves.)

You can't be too careful at this stage. The edge of the metal will actually be forming the moulding, and any jagged edges or lumpy curves will be faithfully reproduced by the obedient plaster. Check the knife against the moulding or the original outline and make sure that it still has the correct contour. Is it smooth and free of rough file marks, gouges, or nicks? Fine tune if necessary. Burnish the edge with a nail or similar smooth round object to remove the last file marks. Round the corners lightly with the same tool to remove any burrs.

Now that the template is perfect, you're ready to construct the mould. In our sample, the mould is a simple one, the kind used for running small mouldings on the bench. (Neat plaster was used for the mouldings in the photos, but we'll tell you what you need to know about mixing plaster. The moulding profile has been cut in the mould twice, so that two pieces may be run at one time. To ensure that the two pieces would be identical, both knives were cut simultaneously by clamping them together.) Construct the mould from 3/4-inch pine, free from large knots. (Plywood may bulge and delaminate when wet.)

To make the horse, trace the outline from the knife onto a piece of wood. Mark a new line about 1/4 inch beyond that one, so that the metal will protrude just past the edge of the wood. Cut this new outline with a coping saw, held at roughly a 45-degree angle. Be sure the saw slopes away from the side to which the metal will be fastened. This bevel you've created will prevent plaster from building up behind the knife and clogging the mould.

Fasten the horse to the slipper, which will guide the mould. In our example, the "fence" or guide which we'll run against is the edge of the bench. Therefore, we've rabbeted the mould so that the edge of the slipper sticks

out beyond the bottom edge of the horse. Then a handle is added for guiding and pushing. (In the sample, because the mould is so small, we've dispensed with the brace.)

Mix the plaster for running mouldings in basically the same way as for finish coat work, except that the ratio of plaster to lime is greater. For finish coat work, approximately 1 part plaster to 3 parts lime is typical; for running mouldings, the ratio is closer to 1:1. This higher proportion of gypsum gives a harder, finer surface and accelerates the setting time, which means retarder must be added unless the moulding is extremely small and simple. Setting time without retarder can vary from about ten to twenty minutes.

For a mixing surface, take a square piece of plywood, about 3 feet on a side, and set it on horses at a comfortable height. The wood has to be smooth; you should be able to run the edge of a trowel over it without catching the trowel or forming splinters. (After mixing a few batches, the board will accumulate a coat of plaster, which should be scraped clean each time.)

Step 1: Make a ring of lime putty with an extra blob in the center. Pour in water plus retarder, then sprinkle in plaster. Mix it with a trowel, making sure water doesn't break out of the ring.

Dump the lime putty onto this board—an amount roughly equal to half the size of the batch you want to make. Using a trowel, form the putty into a ring about 3 inches high around the outside of the board. A small, square-edged trowel with a blade about 5 inches long by 2 inches wide (a margin trowel) is ideal for this and other mixing work. Leave a blob of putty in the center.

Pour enough water into the ring to dissolve an amount of plaster equal to the putty. Before adding the plaster, however, mix retarder into the water and stir carefully until it has thoroughly dissolved. One or two teaspoons of retarder to a batch of plaster is sufficient to allow a working time of 20 to 30 minutes.

Next, slowly sprinkle the plaster into the water. Allow it to soak in until it begins to float on the surface rather than sink in. Let the plaster stand in water for a few minutes, soaking it up, before beginning to mix the plaster and lime putty together.

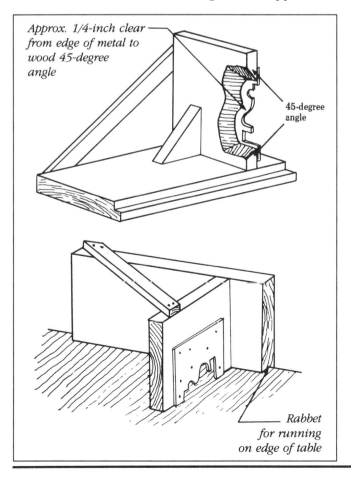

Approx. 1/4-inch clear from edge of metal to wood 45-degree angle

45-degree angle

Rabbet for running on edge of table

Spread the blob of putty through the plaster using your trowel. Then work in the lime from the outer ring, folding it into the center. Be careful not to let the water in the center flow out through a break in the ring. As you mix, the consistency will be soupy at first; it should gradually reach a trowelable state as more and more lime is mixed in. The mix should just cling to the vertical face of the trowel without sliding off. For mouldings run on the bench, the mix can be a little more liquid.

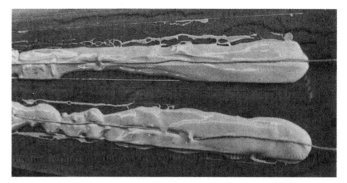

Step 3: Put a cotton string in the plaster to reinforce the moulding and make it easier to handle.

Step 2: Pour a line of plaster at least as wide as the moulding. (Here, two mouldings are being run simultaneously.)

Step 4: Run the mould the full length of the piece, steadily and slowly, without stopping.

Now you are ready to run the mould. Use a flat surface in which both the top and edge are completely straight. Any lumps or curves will transfer to the moulding. To keep the plaster from sticking to the surface, use a parting agent such as stearic acid or a liquid soap such as Ivory. Brush the agent onto the surface and allow to dry. Brush on just enough to allow the piece to break free from the surface once it has set. If you use too much, the plaster won't stick to the surface at all, or might pop off while you're in the middle of running the piece.

Run the mould along the edge of the table to see that it runs smoothly. Make a light pencil mark on the surface where the moulding will be formed. Now you can run the piece. If possible, use only one batch of plaster for each piece to be run. First pour a line of plaster at least as wide as the moulding along the bench. Place a cotton string into the plaster to bury it in the finished moulding. For wider pieces, use several strings or narrow strips of burlap. This reinforces the moulding and makes it easy to handle later.

Now make the first run with the mould. Push it the full length of the piece, steadily and slowly, without stopping. Don't apply any real pressure; just keep the mould flat to the surface and against the edge of the table. After the run,

remove the mould and clean it. Take it back to the beginning, pour more plaster along the line, and run the mould a second time.

Run the mould in exactly the same track each time. Examine it after each run, especially on the slipper and the horse, to make sure plaster isn't building up there and throwing you off course. Clean the horse just behind the knife after each run to prevent plaster from hardening there and clogging the mould. Look out for small pebbles of hardened plaster. The mould can rake them up and drag them across the plaster, forming long gouges.

Continue to build up the moulding, adding more plaster each time; you'll see the profile form right before your eyes. The repeated action of the mould accelerates the setting of the plaster. The moulding starts to set up before the rest of the mix, so you shouldn't run out of plaster. Run the mould over it every few minutes. Plaster swells slightly on setting; if you leave the piece for too long, it may get too big to fit the mould over it.

Once you've formed about 80 percent of the profile, you'll notice gaps or pocks in the surface. Dab plaster directly onto them and run over them with the mould. As the unfilled areas get smaller and smaller, mix up a new, somewhat watery batch. Brush it on the surface to remove the bubbles and irregularities.

Trim the final surface with a very watery mix. Now the knife is scraping up a fine powder as it passes along the moulding; it's actually trimming the surface of the swelling moulding. Keep the surface wet at this stage by splat-

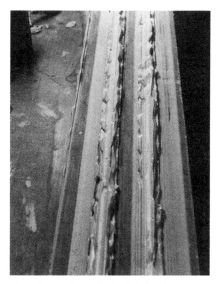

Step 5: Continue to build up the moulding, adding more plaster with each run.

Step 6: Clean away the plaster buildup that gathers behind the knife after every turn.

Step 7: Dab plaster on the gaps in the moulding and run the mould over them.

Step 8: Use a putty knife to scrape away thin plaster left on the surface of the bench after you've finished running the moulding.

tering it with water from a brush. With the water, these scrapings will form a milky film that fills all minute holes in the surface and leaves it with a polished, shiny appearance.

The whole process for a moulding this size takes 10 to 15 minutes. Plaster heats as it cures; let it get hot and cool down again. The piece should take 15 to 30 minutes to dry thoroughly. Then remove it from the bench, using a putty knife to scrape away any thin plaster left on the surface.

To break the moulding free of the table surface, gently pry it up with a thin blade. The moulding won't be at full strength—total curing takes several hours—so don't place too much strain on it. Be careful not to chip or gouge the surface. Saw off ragged ends, cut the piece into convenient lengths, and let them stand overnight to dry thoroughly.

With some variations, plaster mouldings can be used just like wood mouldings. You can glue, nail, miter, and saw them. (For sawing at 45-degree angles, use a small miter box.) They can also be shaped and planed using Stanley's Surform tool or a rasp for auto-body filling work.

Apply mouldings directly to a plaster wall or ceiling by using a slip of pure gypsum plaster mixed to the consistency of glue. You can support a fairly large piece with a slip provided it's held in place while the plaster sets. This can be done with simple finger pressure; it normally takes a minute or two for the plaster to grab. Both the wall surface and moulding should be thoroughly dampened before gluing, or else the plaster will suck out the water from the slip before it sets. Score the back of the moulding to improve the bond of the slip.

To score the piece, lay out a strip of putty narrower than the piece to be run before pouring the plaster. Sprin-

kle sand over the putty, and make the moulding as described above. The sand and putty roughen the back of the piece when it's removed, providing a good key for gluing.

Strip any paint on the surface that will take the moulding—otherwise the bond will be no stronger than the paint film. If you don't strip, toenail the moulding to reinforce the gluing. Always toenail when applying larger pieces, whether the surface is painted or not. Use finish nails of an appropriate size and predrill the moulding to the right hole size, to avoid breaking the piece. Then set the nail and fill the hole with plaster.

Run Ornament: Cornice Work

Cornice work is the most exciting and challenging of all plaster work. Much of it will be beyond the capabilities of the average homeowner, although the fundamental techniques are those we've already described. Constructing an elaborate cornice is a complicated job, but you shouldn't let that scare you away from a small-to-medium-size project. (The hassle of finding qualified people to do the job may force you to attempt it yourself!)

The mould for running a cornice must be designed to run on two surfaces that form a 90-degree angle. A simple approach is to construct a backing box of two long, straight boards that are fastened edge to edge at right angles. If you're running a larger moulding, add an angled piece of wood to the inside corner of the box. It prevents the use of unnecessary amounts of plaster, and reduces the weight of the moulding.

Running a section of cornice on the bench lets you shape almost any contour; even undercuts are possible, because the mould runs out at either end of the piece. You can repair a damaged section of cornice by forming a replacement on the bench. Simply splice it in by cutting back the existing cornice to sound material and then installing the new piece in the missing section. The area behind the cornice itself also needs to be cut back of any material that would interfere with the correct placement of the new piece. Investigate this condition before constructing the backing box for the new piece; the cornice already in the room was most likely formed in a slightly different fashion.

Installing a piece of any size requires more than a simple "gluing" with plaster; you have to nail or screw it to the wall and ceiling. This involves predrilling and careful nailing with finishing nails. Be sure that the nails find wood—wood lath, if that's the foundation material; studs or joists, if the backing is metal lath.

Then fill the inevitable gaps between the new and old sections with plaster. Pure gypsum plaster is fine for small-to-medium-size cracks. Trim away the excess with a *joint rod:* a 1/16-inch piece of steel, about 4 inches wide, with a good straight edge that measures from a few inches

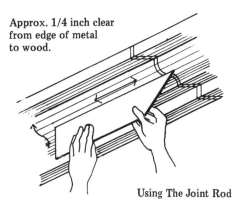

Approx. 1/4 inch clear from edge of metal to wood.

Using The Joint Rod

to 2 feet in length (also called a "miter rod," as it is used to form miters for cornice work). One of the ends is cut at a 45-degree angle, so it can get into tight corners. You can find one at a masonry- or plastering-supply house or you can make your own from a piece of steel. Use a stiff steel that will not bend easily in your hands. (Aluminum or sheet-metal flashing is too soft.) Be sure the edge is perfectly straight.

To use the joint rod, hold the straight edge against the cornice and move it up and down so that the rod follows the contour and trims away the excess plaster. A slight back-and-forth motion helps cut away the wet plaster and leaves a smooth surface.

Of course, bench-made cornice sections can take on even slight twists or rackings in the wood of the backing box; you can't expect all the pieces to meet each other perfectly. The box-formed pieces can also be distorted if they're laid on an unsmooth surface before they've fully dried. And if you could get them perfectly straight, they wouldn't fit any unusual bends in the wall or ceiling.

If you can do bench work, you're ready to try the same process overhead in place. Don't be frustrated if this may seem like a hopeless task the first time you try it. It takes practice. Running a cornice in place is definitely a task for two people. The basic process has only minor variations from the one that's already been explained. There are only two principal difficulties: applying and working the plaster overhead, and timing.

Timing will probably be harder to master than mixing the plaster. The two people on the job must coordinate the work: one mixing and applying the material, the other running and cleaning the mould. You should eventually establish a rhythm in which there's little wasted motion—and equally little rushing.

Unlike the mould described for bench work, this mould is made to be guided along the wall by the edge of the slipper; along the ceiling by the top edge of the horse. Thus, for most cornices, the horse angles out toward you, beyond the outer edge of the slipper. The

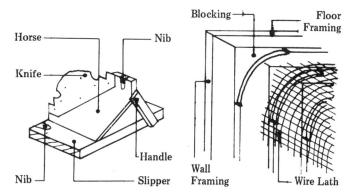

handle is set at a corresponding rake. Note too that this mould includes nibs (which were mentioned but not included in the earlier mould). You'll be running this mould on plaster, and the sheet-metal nibs provide a smooth surface on which the mould can slide.

To reduce unnecessary plaster and weight, the lath behind the cornice should follow the final profile as closely as possible. This is usually done by blocking out between the studs of the wall and the joists above, with pieces cut to the basic contour of the cornice, leaving about 1/2 to 1 inch for lath and plaster. Then nail the lath to these blocks, as shown.

Apply the base coats as you would with flat work, starting with the scratch coat, then a brown coat that serves as the base for the finished work, or "white coat" (which here is the cornice moulding). Be sure to score the scratch coat in a crisscross pattern, let dry, and trowel the brown coat in along the

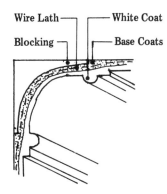

curve of the cornice, leaving just enough room for 1/4 to 1/2 inches of white coat, along with any projections or beads in the final moulding.

The moulding will be run on two surfaces, wall and ceiling; in most cases, they'll correspond to the finished wall and ceiling surfaces. These new surfaces are called *screeds;* the term also refers to any surfaces about 4 to 6 inches wide, which are used to establish a level in plastering. Screeds for cornice work are formed out of the same material as the cornice itself.

Establish the wall screeds first. Determine the level of the finished wall in the corners of the room at a level just below the bottom of the cornice. Apply dots of high-gauge plaster to the wall and trowel smooth. These screeds must be absolutely straight, because they'll determine both the line of the cornice and the surface of the finish walls. Double-check corners for square; compare the level of the ceiling against a level line run around the room. (A water-level or just a length of clear plastic hose filled with water will be quite handy.) Record level marks on all the walls (mix a little food coloring or powdered blue chalk from a chalk-line into the water, to make the level easier to see).

Once the corner dots are set, establish intermediate dots around the room, spacing them so that a straightedge can reach from one dot to the next. Form these intermediate dots by stretching a line between the corner dots and leveling to that line. For greater accuracy, hold the string off the corner dots by wedging a finish nail under it. Use the same size nail as a spacer gauge for intermediate dots.

When all the dots are established, enlarge them by building up material above or below each dot and pressing a *plumb dot,* a dot about 6 inches long, pressed vertically to the other dots. Use a hand level and a piece of paper over each dot to prevent the level from sticking to the plaster. Form screeds to the dots, all the way into the corners, completing a band of white-coat plaster around the room, just at the bottom of the cornice line.

Mark a level line onto this plaster band; use the water level to establish levels in the corners, and then snap lines around the room with a chalk-line. Use this line for the top edge of the batten on which the mould will eventually rest; establish its height by holding the mould itself in place and marking against the bottom edge of the slipper. Hold the water level against the mould to ensure it isn't

crooked. Leave enough space between the top of the mould and the ceiling for the ceiling screed. Take particular care in the corners of the room: The lines marked on each wall must come together exactly, or it'll be impossible to form the miters of the cornice.

Nail good, clear, pine strips, each about 1/2-inch thick by 1 1/2-inches wide, into the screed, keeping the top edge of the strip exactly on the line. Space the nails about 18 inches apart. Do this slowly and carefully: When the ends of the two battens meet, both in the corners and along the wall, one better not be higher than the other! Once you've checked the accuracy of the wood strip, reinforce it with blobs of high-gauge plaster over the batten and against the wall. Space them every 12 inches or so, to keep the batten from moving while the cornice is being run.

Form the ceiling screed in much the same manner as the wall screed. Establish dots around the room on the ceiling, using the mould itself as the gauge. Set the mould with the slipper resting on the cornice strip that's fastened to the wall. Level it with the water level. Use a vertical batten nailed against the horse at right angles to the slipper as a guide for the level.

After the dots set, form a band of plaster, connecting the dots with a straightedge. The ceiling screed must be extremely straight and true, with no pocks or bumps, because the top edge of the mould has only one point of contact with the ceiling (whereas the length of the slipper can compensate for any small irregularities on the wall).

Now, before you go on to run the cornice, check your setup one more time. Make sure you have enough materials (lime putty, plaster, water) on hand. Have a separate supply of water for cleaning tools and a garbage pail for old plaster and other junk. Your mixing board should be at a comfortable height, and located so the mixed plaster can be transferred easily up to the cornice.

Make sure your scaffolding is comfortable and safe—no wobbly planks or precarious perches! Your staging must be wide enough and solid enough for you to walk confidently on it while your attention is on running the

The cornice has been blocked out, and the plasterer, Steve Zychal, can now begin troweling on the white coat.

mould. Just to be sure, first run the mould dry a couple of times. Check that it runs smoothly and straight. Strike a line on the ceiling screed, where the nib of the horse runs; it'll serve as an additional visual check that you're not running off course as you go. Run the mould once just to observe whether or not the top edge of the horse follows the line on the ceiling. If it swerves off, something's wrong with your layout. (If it veers outside the line, shift the cornice strip on which the slipper runs down; if it veers inside, shift the strip up.)

Do the first application with the trowel, directly onto the cornice area. Run the mould over the plaster to cut off any high spots and to start forming the profile. This formation of the rough shape of the cornice is called *blocking out*. As you run the mould, it will remove the large

David Flaharty is seen here with the mould used to run the cornice in the Greek Revival room of New York's Metropolitan Museum of Art. That was a pretty elaborate job, but its basic principles are the ones explained here.

amounts of plaster that stick out beyond the finished profile. The person applying the plaster should stand by with the hawk and trowel, ready to catch these falling pieces; besides saving waste, this will keep the scaffolding from becoming a mess. At the end of the run, you can reapply this material to low spots, and run the mould again.

Once the profile begins to take shape, you can start applying more plaster directly to those areas that need it. Retard the plaster used for blocking sufficiently, so that you can have plenty of working time. As you apply the plaster, be sure to keep it off the cornice strip and screeds, so that the mould isn't thrown off course. Examine those areas after each run and check that they're clean. Also make sure you keep the mould clean of accumulating plaster.

When the cornice is about 80 percent formed, begin "stuffing" (applying plaster directly to) the mould. Use either a trowel or a rubber glove. Push the plaster up against the front edge of the knife while the mould is being run; this will fill out the gaps in the profile and form the fine details of the cornice. To ensure enough working

time, mix a fresh batch of plaster for stuffing. If you are running a long section, you'd do well to set aside half of one batch unmixed.

Repeat the stuffing procedure until the cornice profile takes shape. Remember to clean the mould well between runs, especially on the back of the knife where plaster builds up. Watch out for plaster build-ups on the screeds and the batten too.

The mould will run the cornice up to within a few inches of the corners, but because of its construction it won't complete the corner of the room. Fill in the remaining space with a joint rod—don't let plaster build up in the corners beyond the profile of the cornice.

As the cornice nears completion, touch up any small pocks and voids in the surface with a slightly looser mix. The plaster will swell as it sets, so keep running the mould over the cornice every minute or so, even if you aren't adding more plaster. If you wait too long between runs, the cornice could enlarge beyond the profile of the mould.

Give the cornice its final "polishing" by applying water ahead of the mould with a large brush. The action of the

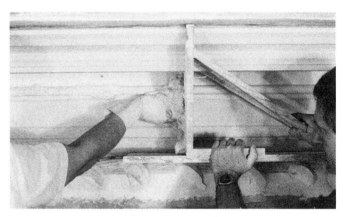

Steve, with the rubber-gloved hand, stuffs the mould while David Flaharty pushes it. The mould is moving from right to left in this photo—note the roughness of some of the cornice on Steve's side.

Running the cornice is just about complete. That gaping section of wire lath visible at the far right is one of the miters that still have to be closed up. What's special about this particular miter is that it's one of the two points where the chimney breast extends out of the wall and not just one of the room's corners.

The running of the cornice is complete and Steve can get to work on the miter. In this photo, the top section of the moulding has already been blocked out; the lower part, right by Steve's hand, hasn't yet been started.

With the completion of the return of this chimney breast, the entire cornice is finished. It's virtually impossible to detect where the mould left off and where the craftsman shaped the plaster himself.

knife and the water on the curing plaster should create a smooth, shiny appearance.

After the cornice has been run around all the walls of the room, use a joint rod to complete the corners, or miters, of the cornice. The rod must cover the size of the miter, which is the distance it must span, plus 6 inches to ensure a bearing on the cornice which can guide you in projecting the members of the cornice into the corner.

Mix the plaster for the corner in the same proportions as the rest of the cornice. Fill in the miter area, roughly blocking it out with a trowel. Bear part of the joint rod's surface against the completed cornice; complete the miter by running it over this surface with a slight back-and-forth motion. This procedure requires a good deal of control to get good results. The straight edge of the rod must bear completely against the surface of the cornice at all times— but don't use too much pressure, especially when you have fresh plaster forming the corner.

Keep alternating from one side of the miter to the other, to ensure that the profiles line up and to create a sharp corner. Be careful when working from one side

Of course, there's always something else to do, even after the job has been completed. In this case, the something extra involves casting sections of plaster ornament and attaching them to the cornice with wet plaster.

with the joint rod that you don't damage the adjacent section. Once the miter has begun to take shape, use the joint rod to remove any high spots. With a smaller margin trowel, daub additional material onto any areas requiring more plaster. Fill small voids in the profile by brushing on a mix of loose plaster. (This avoids damaging the newly shaped sections with a trowel.) Carefully level these small areas with the joint rod.

Do the final shaping of the point where two walls meet by hand with a small sculpting tool shaped like a miniature mason's trowel. You need a good eye and a steady hand to create sharp profiles and a straight corner. The final touch is a clear, crisp joint: It's traditional to scribe a line in the corner exactly where the two profiles meet. Use a trowel guided on a straightedge held at a 45-degree angle away from the wall.

Casting Plaster

Casting is a process for reproducing an original piece of ornament. The original is called the model and may be either a cast element itself (for example, a leaf ornament, or a section of egg-and-dart moulding), or it may be sculpted from clay or carved in wood.

A rubber mould is poured over the model. The rubber is liquid when applied, but when it sets it becomes a flexible reverse image of the original piece. After the model is removed, the mould gets new plaster poured into it. When the plaster has set, it's removed from the mould, and you have an exact copy of the original piece. Any number of castings can be taken from one mould and combined together to form repeating decorative elements.

Among other odds and ends mentioned later, to cast plaster you will need the following:

• Moulding (or casting) plaster—plaster with fine particles that reproduce fine detail. Plaster of paris, or gypsum, can reproduce incredibly fine detail in casting.

• Rubber mould—most commonly used are urethane or polysulfide rubbers, which come in a two-part formulation. They set into flexible rubber when the parts are mixed. Some mould materials are formulated in either a trowelable or brush-on consistency, so you can take moulds of an existing element that's in place on a wall or ceiling.

- Separator or parting agent.

The Greek Revival Style ceiling medallion pictured appears complicated, but it's actually made up of many smaller, repeating elements. These elements are cast separately and then assembled into the completed ornament. The circular pieces at the center form a sort of abstracted seed pod of the flower. Two sizes of leaf also radiate from the center. The design is finalized with a flower or leaf ornament called an *anthemion*, derived from classical Greek ornament, and a small flower that fills the space between these outer pieces, completing the outer ring. To show the steps in casting, we'll concentrate on the larger, outer anthemion. This element has a long, stemlike piece that fits in between the large leaves.

First obtain a model or original piece from a plastering shop. You can compose different ornaments by recombining or slightly modifying these elements. If you already have some pieces from an existing ornament then you're way ahead of the game. If not, shape the model in clay.

Apply parting agent to the model and the background surface. Brush it on with a soft brush, working it up into a lather that reaches all the surfaces and recesses of the model. Once the piece has been thoroughly coated, remove the excess foam and soap with a dry brush. Examine the model to make sure that no bubbles or specks of dirt adhere to it.

Build a wall around the model to hold the liquid rubber until it cures before pouring the rubber. Master ornamental plasterer David Flaharty (pictured in the photos) uses strips of tin held together with small clamps. These handy devices can be expanded, contracted, or bent to any shape, depending on the size of the model; they're reusable too. (Clay or small slats of wood can also be used for the wall.) If you use wood or sheet metal, you must seal the bottom edge of the wall with clay or plaster to keep the rubber from leaking out.

The centerpiece in the Greek Revival room of the Metropolitan Museum of Art in New York City.

Parting agent is thoroughly applied to the model. Note the marble slab—the model must rest on a smooth, level surface. Any warps or twists in the surface can result in an imperfect cast piece, which won't lie flat against the ceiling.

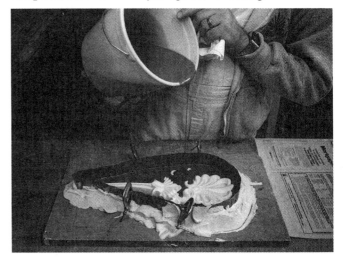

The next step is to pour liquid rubber over the model. The bottom edge of the tin strips has been sealed with plaster to keep the rubber from leaking out.

Mix enough rubber to cover the model completely—about 1/8 inch to 1/4 inch above the model. More than that, and the mould will only become stiffer, making the pieces more difficult to remove. David uses a urethane rubber that's mixed in equal parts by weight, but you should follow the directions for the product you have.

Pour the rubber in a small, steady stream, so that any bubbles formed during the mixing will break on the way down. Applied this way, the rubber will also flow smoothly over the model, without trapping air in any of the crevices.

After the rubber cures (about sixteen hours), remove the retaining wall and the plaster or clay around it. Lift the mould and model off the surface in one piece and flip it over. Then remove the model by gently peeling back the rubber mould.

Now cast as many pieces as you want with the mould—you won't even need to use a parting agent when casting new pieces from fresh plaster. Simply mix the plaster in a small bowl (a flexible plastic bowl is good because old batches of plaster can be left to dry and then just popped out), then pour it into the mould, making sure it reaches all surfaces. Pieces with long narrow parts, such as this one, can be reinforced by placing a small stick of wood in the wet plaster.

After the rubber hardens, you have a flexible mould that is an exact reverse image of the model. The plaster poured into this mould will become an exact duplicate of the original piece.

Before the plaster sets, the back of the cast piece must be leveled, or else it won't lie flat against the ceiling.

To ensure that the plaster completely fills the mould, jiggle it and slap it gently on the tabletop; this also brings any air bubbles up to the surface. Before the plaster dries, level the back surface by scraping off the excess. Scrape small gouges into the surface to provide a key in action when the piece is attached to the ceiling.

Once the plaster has set (after fifteen minutes or so) remove it from the mould just as you did with the model. There's your finished piece, ready to be used in the medallion. Any ornaments in low relief can be made with this process.

For deeper pieces, you may need an additional back-up mould. Use this extra, or "mother," mould around the rubber mould to keep it from bending out of shape when

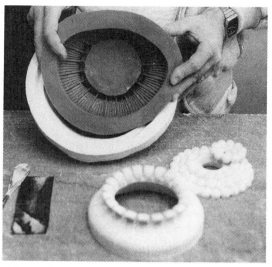

The rubber mould for the center of the medallion.

the plaster is poured into it. The mother mould is usually made of plaster itself.

If you want to try this in your own home, by all means have fun when you do it—exuberant ornament like this should be a joy. But it's also a cultivated taste, and so you should educate your eye by looking around at good examples before you plunge ahead with your own design. And remember our motto: To thine own style be true. Not only period style but also ceiling height, room proportions, and degree of formality all play an important role in the design of ornaments in general.

The centerpiece shown here was made for the Greek Revival Room at the Metropolitan Museum of Art. Thanks to the Museum for allowing us to take pictures of the installation, and to David Flaharty for the pictures in his shop and his generous help.

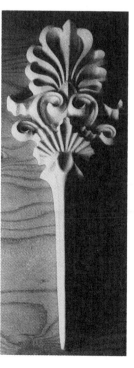

The finished anthemion.

Plaster Casting Materials

The three most commonly used rubber casting materials are polysulfides, polyurethanes, and silicones. Of these, polyurethanes are the most tear-resistant and easiest to use. They come in a two-part formulation, mixed either 2:1 or 1:1 by weight. Working time ranges from twelve to thirty minutes, and the material sets in about sixteen hours.

Some polysulfides are useful when you must work on a model that is in place. Some of these products are formulated to be brushed on, or, with additional thickeners, troweled on.

CHAPTER 15

Floors

Repairs to flooring should be completed after the bulk of the interior finish work on walls and ceilings is complete. Try to finish any work involving water before focusing on floor repair. An accident during roofing or plumbing could cause a leak that would spoil newly laid flooring. Even moisture evaporating out of fresh plaster may cup or swell and buckle new floorboards.

Here you'll find an overview of historic floor construction and styles as well as techniques for repairing and finishing floors. If your floor suffers from more than loose boards and popping up nails, also see the section on subflooring in chapter 12 for a discussion of the structural problems a sloping or sagging floor may indicate.

EARLY FLOORS

Before the Victorian era, most American homes boasted untreated, bare wood floors, undecorated by carpets or rugs. It's little wonder that few unaltered examples have survived. You're most likely to see the real thing in a carefully restored house museum. If they weren't replaced, most early floors were eventually painted, stained, or given some kind of protective finish like varnish, shellac, oil, wax, or polyurethane.

Even the most ardent old-house purist usually opts for floors that are painstakingly "restored" by sanding and finished with an application of some stain-and-varnish combination that brings out the warm richness of the wood's grain and imparts a mellow sheen. While this look

pleases our twentieth-century tastes, it was virtually non-existent in houses that predate 1840. Generally, only the wealthy would have had floors with any kind of decorative treatment. Painted, stenciled, marbleized, and carpeted floors were the exception, not the rule.

The boards of early floors usually were sawn at a local mill. The up-and-down reciprocating action of these water-powered saws left distinctive parallel marks on the wood. Usually, such telling marks still can be seen on the unplaned undersides between the joists in places like the basement ceiling. (Hold a raking light from a flashlight across the face of the board. If you see perpendicular, parallel marks, chances are the boards are circa 1840 or earlier.)

Much rarer are pit-sawn boards (they have angled parallel saw marks) or handhewn boards smoothed with an adze or drawknife. Only vernacular buildings like log houses, barns, and other outbuildings would have had hewn floorboards. Hewn boards whose undersides are left "in the round," sometimes with even the bark still attached, are called *puncheons.*

Pine—plentiful up and down the East Coast and easy to work with—was far and away the favorite wood species used for floorboards. White pine predominated in the Northeast, although Northern yellow pine was used occasionally. From Virginia and Maryland, Southern yellow pine (sometimes known as longleaf pine or heart pine) was nearly ubiquitous. Because it is harder, denser, and more resinous than white pine, yellow pine was, and still is, a superior wood for floors.

Another important factor in a floor's durability was how it was sawn—"quarter-sawn" or "plain-sawn" (flat-sawn). Plain-sawn wood was cut across the entire width

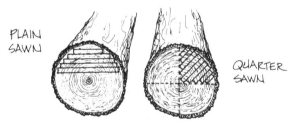

PLAIN SAWN

QUARTER SAWN

of the log, producing boards of varying widths, each containing a spectrum of wide and narrow growth rings (see also chapter 7). Quarter-sawn wood was cut from logs that first were split into four quadrants, making each board narrower, with less variation in growth rings.

In the Northeast, white pine was commonly plain-sawn, resulting in distinctive random-width floorboards. Although today these exceptionally wide boards are much admired, they weren't the best for flooring. Changes in humidity and temperature tended to warp the boards, forcing open the joints. Wide, plain-sawn boards also wore unevenly. The softer middle sections of each board wore away faster, causing an undulating, cupping effect. Why carpenters in the Northeast chose this particular technique is unclear, although using wider boards meant that fewer of them were needed, and so floors could be laid down faster.

In the South, quarter-sawn yellow pine flooring was the norm. Less susceptible to the ravages of temperature and humidity, these reddish-hued floorboards wore more evenly and were more standardized in width. Unfortunately, only about 1 percent of the estimated 100 billion board-feet of yellow pine which once stood in this country remains.

Other woods were also used, especially in areas where an indigenous species was common. Hence, rot-resistant cypress was used in Gulf Coast floors; oak or hemlock was used in mid-Atlantic floors, as was white spruce (which gave off a pleasant aroma). There was scattered use of long-wearing but now extinct chestnut in New England, the mid-Atlantic states, and the upland South.

In most regions of the country butt (also called straight or square) joints were by far the most common. Boards usually were face-nailed directly onto the joists; subflooring was not customary outside of New England. Wrought nails were used before 1800, cut nails thereafter (providing another way to determine the age of old floors). In elaborate homes, the boards were often blind-nailed. Tongue-and-groove and shiplap joints were tighter but required greater skill, and tended to be uncommon.

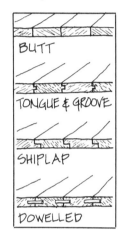

BUTT

TONGUE & GROOVE

SHIPLAP

DOWELLED

Scattered examples of floorboards that were doweled together can be found in the mid-Atlantic. Blind, horizontal dowels connected the abutting edges of the boards, much like tabletop leaves. The "old-time" pegged oak floor so popular today apparently has no early historical precedent. It may have been popularized during the Colonial Revival period, when oak floorboards were screwed down and the countersunk heads of the screws were covered by wooden plugs.

In most cases, once an early floor was laid, it was considered finished. There was, of course, the periodic cleaning. Lye, from wood ash, was a popular cleaning agent that could remove spilled food or drippings from tallow candles. A weekly scrubbing with hot, soapy water would leave the floors with a "silvery whiteness," according to one observer. Another technique was "sanding" the floors clean. Sand was sprinkled over the bare floors to collect dirt and grease, in the manner that dry-cleaning compounds are used in today's automobile repair shops. When the sand was swept up, the week's dirt went along with it. An occasional good scrubbing with sand and water kept floors looking relatively new. And in accordance with an early American naval tradition, floors also were "holy stoned"—that is, a porous, pumice-like stone (sometimes sandstone) was rubbed across a sanded floor to clean it.

A less common, but not rare, practice was to create a "sand carpet." Decorative patterns were created in sand spread across the floor. According to one account, the

Flooring typical of Southern houses in a 1787 North Carolina restoration.

best parlors were "swept and garnished every morning with sand sifted through a 'sand sieve' and sometimes smoothed with a hair broom into quaint circles and fancy wreaths." Herringbone patterns were also documented.

Waxing floors was very rare, although one diary from the early 1800s recommends a formula of two parts boiled linseed oil, two parts turpentine, and one part lemon juice or vinegar as a sort of early "Scotchgard" treatment to resist stains. Don't you try this concoction, however, because it most likely would darken the wood and make for a rather sticky surface.

If you're one of the few restoration purists who decides to live with authentic bare-wood floors, you might take the suggestion of a fellow devotee who recommends a cleaning regimen of regular scrubbing with a tri-sodium-phosphate (TSP) solution. Over time, daily wear and TSP will turn the raw wood a mellow brown. But don't expect perfect floors. You'll have to live with the inevitable scratches and stains.

If the original floor has been removed (check to make sure it's not hidden under a later floor), there are numerous companies that can supply either old, salvaged flooring of hard-to-find woods or new yellow- or white-pine floorboards cut in appropriate widths. Most of these companies remill salvaged floorboards to make them attractive and easy to lay. Purists should be aware, though, that some restoration experts and historians argue that the introduction of old, salvaged flooring into an antique house gives misleading architectural clues that may confuse future historians.

For authenticity's sake, use the wood species that historically was predominant in your area. For durability's sake, remember that quarter-sawn wood is more durable

than plain-sawn wood. If you use face-nailing to put the boards down, the nailheads will be exposed, so consider using reproduction cut nails for early- to mid-nineteenth-century floors and reproduction wrought nails for eighteenth-century examples.

Painted Floors

Not all early floors were bare; painted floors were uncommon but not rare. This tradition seems to have been widespread, if geographically spotty. The best-known examples are in New England, but painted floors have also shown up in Texas and the Midwest, for instance.

Painted floors had their advantages: Paint made the surface more stain resistant. It also made for a more colorful floor and enabled homeowners to tie the floor into an overall decorative scheme. (See page 291 for a discussion of historic colors.)

The painted floors most valued these days are the decorative ones. Examples dating from as early as the mid-1700s have been discovered, and the practice continued well into the mid-nineteenth century. These floors were either done freehand or stenciled, sometimes by the homeowners themselves but more often by itinerant artists. Just as wall stenciling was a relatively inexpensive imitation of wallpaper, the decoratively painted floor was an imitation of the rugs and carpeting that were highly prized but out of the reach of the average homeowner.

Extant examples show a wonderful variety of patterns. Although there were occasional striped floors, painted borders were more common. The middle of the floor was often embellished with geometric diamond patterns, floral motifs, zigzags, and checkerboard designs. Landscapes and animal motifs or flower-petal, heart, or oak-leaf designs were sometimes used. At the very center was often a large design with some correlation to the prevailing popular architectural and decorative styles of the day. During the Federal era, for instance, urns, swags, and garlands were all the rage. Stenciled floors naturally tended toward precise, repeated patterns, while freehand work was more whimsical and random.

Throughout much of the nineteenth century, marbleized floors, though still comparatively rare, were sometimes used. Painted geometric blocks in white, black, or grays were "veined" like marble. Marbleized floors were usually found in entry halls or in the formal parlors of the finest houses. Unfortunately, very few have survived. There still may be evidence of painted floors, however, in hidden places: under built-in pieces of furniture, behind later partition walls and closet additions, under newer floors and carpets, or beneath baseboards subsequently added. Any surviving remnant can serve as a valuable model for a reproduction.

Floorcoverings

Philadelphia was one of early America's most affluent cities. Yet a study of eighteenth-century household inventories indicates that, even there, fewer than 3 percent of households had any kind of floorcovering at all. Floorcoverings, whether carpets, rugs, oilcloths, or mats, were luxury items, status symbols. Before the 1780s, almost all floorcoverings were imported, primarily from England, and therefore extremely expensive. Pre-Victorian floorcoverings came in two varieties: carpets and rugs, and their more modest counterparts, painted floorcloths and grass matting.

Painted floorcloths were the precursors of linoleum. Like both linoleum and painted floors, they were stain-resistant, easy to clean, and decorative. Painted floorcloths were imported from England until after the Revolution, when Americans began making them. They remained popular until the 1850s, when carpeting became more affordable.

Painted floorcloths were made from canvas—cotton, linen, hemp, or wool—painted on both sides to make it impervious. With up to five, even seven, layers of paint on each side, they could be a year in the making; curing could take two years. The decorative patterns on floorcloths were applied freehand, stenciled, or "blocked" on, often using the same bright, intense colors and fanciful motifs as those applied on painted floors. Geometrics—checkerboards, hexagons, diamonds, triangles, and the like—were popular. So were faux tile and marbleized designs, as well as imitations of carpets. One example was described as featuring a "poussy [sic] cat and little spaniel."

Painted floorcloths were not strictly the poor man's carpet; the wealthy also used them. They were most popular in vestibules, hallways, parlors, and dining rooms (particularly under tables). Fortunately for restorers, there is a resurgence in the art of the painted floorcloth.

Matting, another early floorcovering, was imported from England, India, China, or Japan. It was made from grassy or marshy fibers like straw, hemp, jute, rush, or even corn husks. Matting remained popular into the 1800s, even into the Victorian age. It often was used under dining room tables over valuable carpets. (Drugget, a coarse, plain wool floorcovering, was also used over carpets for protection. Today, a large piece of unfinished awning canvas can substitute for drugget.) Matting often replaced carpets during the summer months; according to some experts, it didn't become a year-round floorcovering until the 1830s.

Although matting was relatively inexpensive, it stained easily and didn't wear well. Few examples have survived, but straw matting seems to be making a comeback. You easily can find tatami, a modern matting from Japan. It comes in strips about a yard wide, which must be seamed together to make a room-sized covering. It's also available in tiles with nonslip backs, that can be pieced together.

Carpets and Rugs

In pre-Victorian times, carpets and rugs were the Cadillacs of floorcoverings. (Carpets generally denoted wall-to-wall coverings tacked down in place; rugs were portable pieces used to cover smaller areas.) Until America's own carpet-mill industry was firmly established in the mid-1800s, carpets were seen only in wealthy households, though by about the 1830s they could be found in some middle-class homes. All carpet owners went to great lengths to protect their investments, reserving them for the best rooms, taking them up during the summer months, and partially covering them with protective drugget or matting.

Pre-Victorian rugs and carpets were of two basic types: flatwoven and pile. Flatwoven carpets have no tufts or piles and were woven on two-harness looms, much like a piece of linen cloth. The width of the loom limited the width of the carpet, so strips had to be seamed together to make wall-to-wall coverings.

There were several major types of flatwoven carpets:

Ingrains were easily the most popular carpets throughout the 1800s, accounting for up to 50 percent of all woven floorcoverings at the time. Ingrains were reversible; that is, both sides had the same pattern but with the colors reversed. Because they were routinely turned over, the life of ingrains could be extended—a good thing, since they were not very durable. Ingrains could be colorful and highly patterned.

Venetian carpets were warp-faced carpets, cheaper than ingrains and usually woven into colorful strips that made them popular in hallways and on stairs.

Rag rugs have been homemade for centuries. Woven from strips of cotton rags or fabric, they had a distinctive coarse, informal look. In pre-Victorian days they were used primarily in more private spaces like bedrooms or upstairs halls.

Pile carpets have always been considered the cream of the crop in carpeting. Durable, plush, and colorful, pile carpets had superseded flatwovens as the carpets of choice by the late 1800s, when they were being mass-produced.

The face of the pile carpet was formed by cut or uncut upright loops of yarn. The carpets often featured designs that picked up on the popular styles of the period: Classical and Adam motifs were common during the Federal era, Grecian ones during the American Empire period from the 1820s to the 1840s, and florid rococo designs during the early Victorian era.

There were three principal types of pile carpet:

Brussels were woven carpets with an uncut loop pile. They featured bold, dark colors, elaborate designs, and, often, borders.

Wiltons, similar to Brussels, had a cut pile.

Axminsters historically were the top-of-the-line carpets, with hand-knotted cut piles. Axminsters were English imitations of the Turkish carpet (then, as today, known generically as "Orientals"). Although they were a sought-after luxury during the sixteenth century, Axminsters waned in popularity toward the end of the 1700s. They enjoyed a revival in the late nineteenth century, when a mechanized production process was invented.

You can still find many of the rugs and carpets described here through specialty carpet manufacturers or the ever-increasing number of custom weavers. If you want to learn more about carpets, we recommend past *Old-House Journal* articles on the subject or *Floor Coverings for Historic Buildings* by Gail Caskey Winkler and Helene von Rosenstiel (Preservation Press, 1988).

By the 1840s, American floors began to look dramatically different. Mass-produced floorboards were narrower and standardized in size (from 2 to 5 inches). Tongue-and-groove joints became common. Stains and varnishes could mask imperfections, and as they came into use, the quality of the wood became less important. Hardwood floors were "in." So were parquet floors. The tastemakers of the day, like Charles Eastlake, promoted the area rug, a trend that continued into Colonial Revival times (which partly explains why the oak-floor-with-Oriental-rug look is sometimes misidentified as "Colonial" today). Gone was the era of the bare wood floor. Fancy floors became the fashion.

FIXING FLOORS

Once you've repaired inadequate girders and rotted subflooring (see chapter 12), you can repair any damaged floorboards. First go over the whole floor, resetting nails and looking for loose boards. Secure loose boards that don't need to be replaced using a nailset (a piece of old carpeting or a thick layer of newspaper over

the raised board with a block of wood on top of it). Most of the time, just resetting old nails won't permanently fasten a loose floorboard. Still working from above the floor, you can provide additional holding power with flooring nails or wood screws. See the drawing for five simple nailing techniques.

Special flooring nails, called screw nails or spiral nails, should be used in repairs. When fastening boards to the subfloor, always drive two nails at opposing angles. A sharp-ended nail may split dry old wood, so before driving a new nail, drill a slightly smaller pilot hole into the wood. Alternately, you can nip off the tip of each nail: A blunt end will crush rather than split the wood fibers.

In wide-plank, butt-joined floors, the wrought nail-heads, or plugs over the screws, are part of the finish pattern of the flooring and should not be changed. Drive new nails into the edges of the board at an angle.

Wood screws provide even more security than flooring nails. When repairs must be made from above, counter-bore screws and plug holes with a piece of matched wood. When the under-floor is exposed it's better to screw from below, through the subfloor and into the loose board to pull it into firm contact. You will need the extra grip of screws when refastening a warped board. Saturate a badly cupped board by keeping a damp towel on it for several days; then screw the edges down to the subfloor.

To fix loose boards and squeaks in flooring between joists, nail the floorboard to the subfloor. Whenever possible, drive nails or screws into a joist. If fasteners won't bite securely into the top of a joist, nail a block of wood to the side of the joist to receive the nail or screw. Locating the joists is easier if the underside of the floor is open for inspection. Otherwise, tap across the floor—the floor will sound solid (not hollow) over a joist.

COUNTER-SUNK NAILS   BLIND-NAILED TONGUE & GROOVE   SCREWED & PLUGGED

If the floor has no subfloor, joists will be at right angles to the floorboards; if the floor is pre-1920 and has a subfloor, joists will probably be parallel to the boards. Joists are evenly spaced, most commonly every 16 inches on center, but in an old house it might be 20 inches, 24 inches, or more. On wide boards with visible face-nails or plugs, the nailing pattern will outline the joists.

Mr. B. M. Jackson of Atlanta, Georgia, is an expert on repairing old floors. Mr. Jackson, who is now in his seventies, has worked with wood floors for more than forty-five years, and continues to restore flooring for Flint Hill Construction Company and ByGone Era of Atlanta. He has seen many floors and all kinds of damage in his time, and says the most frequent problems are rotting wood, stains

Diagnosing Your Floor

SYMPTOM	CAUSE	CURE
Floorboards squeak	Friction between boards or loose floorboards	Lubricate edges of rubbing boards with graphite or talc. Refasten loose floorboards.
Sound floor creaks when weight is applied	Sagging, damaged, or inadequate joist	Mend or replace damaged joist. Nail a 2 × 4 to sagging joist up tight against subflooring.
Floor is springy when walked over	(1) Floor not making contact with supporting joist, or (2) Joist weakened or cracked allowing obvious movement of joist when weight applied, or (3) Joist is undersized or inadequately bridged	(1) Nail a 2 × 4 to joist, up tight against subflooring. (2) Reinforce, mend, or replace damaged joist. (3) Add cross or solid bridging to spread load to adjoining joists.
Floor sags or has a low spot	Insufficient support at the point of sag—because joist is damaged, inadequate, or shrunken away from subfloor; or because post support is damaged, missing, or inadequate	(1) Reinforce damaged joist. (2) Add joists or girder. (3) Jack up low spot with additional post support. (4) If shrinkage has stabilized and support is adequate, live with it or drive wedges between joist and subfloor.
Floor slopes toward center of house	(1) Differential settlement: Exterior masonry walls stayed rigid while prop wall shrunk and/or settled, or (2) Insufficient support of prop (interior) wall	(1) Live with it or re-lay a level floor. (2) Check post support of girders. May need replacement, additional support, new footing.
Floor slopes toward exterior bearing walls	(1) Foundation settlement, or (2) Damage to exterior load-bearing walls	Live with a stabilized condition. Have expert check foundation and footings.
Floor buckled upward	(1) Extensive damage to an exterior load-bearing wall or foundation footing, or (2) Too much upward pressure exerted in a jacking operation	(1) Call in the experts. (2) If nothing cracked, let the weight back down very slowly.

1. *A flooring nail driven through to a joist firmly secures loose floorboards.*

2. *When driving nails only into subfloor, drive two at opposing angles.*

3. *When under-floor is open, screw loose boards from below.*

4. *Screwing from above will hold warped boards; counter-bore and plug holes.*

5. *To stop squeaks from slightly warped or shrunken boards, drive finish nails into cracks at an angle.*

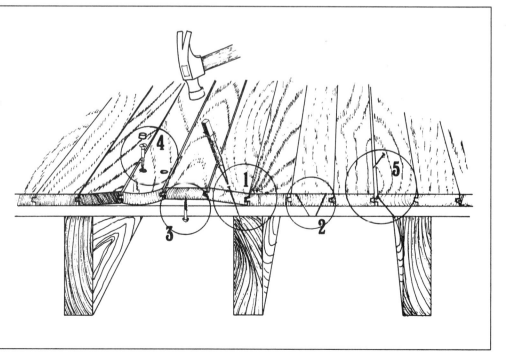

from dog or cat urine, and severe scarring from objects being dragged across the floor. According to Mr. Jackson, repairing a floor involves three basic steps: 1) locating replacement boards, 2) removing the damaged portions without marring the surrounding floor, and 3) installing the new boards in the original floor so the patch is not obvious.

Removing Damaged Sections

Dents and dings, worn spots, variation of color and texture are marks of character, the charm of an old room. Replace only those boards that are inadequate or hazardous, including severely warped and buckled boards, deeply nicked and splintered boards, boards with noticeable and irreversible urine stains, boards or sections with holes, and missing sections of border or inlay.

Before pulling out the damaged boards in a floor, it's good practice to lightly chalk or pencil a cutting line around the area you need to remove. This kind of planning is particularly important in pre-1850 floors because, without a subfloor, all boards must end on a joist for support. For instance, if a portion of a board can be saved, the damaged part must be cut off at a point over a joist so both new and old ends are held up. Pay close attention to the staggering of joints. Side-by-side boards with joints that are in line look awkward and will squeak. In the same way, floors that have a specific stagger pattern, say, every three joists, have to be repaired with the same pattern for a pleasing job. In practice, this usually means replacing whole boards rather than cutting out bad sections.

Repairing Pre–1850 Floors

Repair of wooden floors is a branch of carpentry unto itself, and working with pre-1850 floors is really a specialized area within this branch. One reason for the breakdown is that floors more than 150 years old are built differently from those that came after. Almost without exception, old floors are nailed directly to the supporting floor joists, and not to a subfloor that was laid down first (as in modern homes). Also, old floors were built before there was machinery to make true tongue-and-groove joints, so most consist of large boards with square edges, butted tightly together. (Or at least the boards were tight when the floor was laid.) These differences in construction, as well as the task of matching worn and often scarce lumber, can make repairing and restoring a pre-1850 floor an intimidating project, even for woodworkers.

If it's unnecessary to remove the entire length of a floorboard, the bad section can be isolated by parting the board along the cutting line. Use a hammer and chisel, the latter 18 inches long and "about three fingers wide." Place the chisel along the cutting line, with the bevel side toward the damage, and strike a sharp blow with the hammer. It should start a nice clean cut through the wood, which will have to be repeated across the width of wide boards.

After the board has been cut, or in the process of cutting, you may need to "channel" the waste piece. Move

the chisel about an inch onto the damaged section (with beveled side down) and angle it at close to 30 degrees. Striking the chisel at this angle will peel off pieces from the end of the damaged section, like sharpening a pencil, and help free the board for removal. Work across the full width of the board. Board ends that are nailed can be freed either by channeling clear of the nails, or driving the nails through the board with a set. After both ends of the damaged section have been channeled, it might be loose enough to remove with

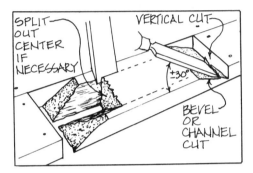

a little delicate prying. If not, you'll have to split the center out for removal. Make cuts with the chisel down the face of the board, so that a middle strip is split out and the board is divided into two pieces. Prying with the chisel after hammer blows helps speed the splitting. Once the center is gone, the other pieces will come out easily. In the same way, once the first board in a damaged area is removed, neighboring boards are much simpler to work on.

Before installing the replacement flooring, it's important to ascertain how the existing floor was nailed down. A quick inspection will tell you whether the boards were *face-nailed* with heads exposed, or *blind-nailed* with the heads hidden between boards. Use the same method for repairs. Looking at the nails will also tell you which way the floor was laid; that is, which side of the room the floor was started on when it was first installed. The angle of the nails will be the key

here, with the heads pointing away from the direction of the first board. Occasional hammer prints where a nail was struck too hard will also be a clue, indicating which way the carpenter faced as he worked, laying the new boards in front of him. The lay of the floor is important because the new work will have to be installed in the same direction—both for looks and integrity. If the lay is still not clear from looking at the nails, check for a fitted, partial-width board on one side of the room. This will be the final piece of flooring put down in the original job (the last board always has to be "fudged" into an odd-size space) and will mean the lay starts on the opposite wall.

After you understand how the old floor went down,

start the new work. Each board in a repair will probably have to be cut, trimmed, and fitted individually into the space it will occupy. Each board may also have to be planed on the top face to blend as closely as possible with the level of the old floor. To match the look of some eighteenth-century floors, it helps to regrind the plane blade in a gentle arc so the repair simulates colonial workmanship.

Attention to the spacing of the boards also helps produce a quality job. Old floors draw up over the years, and the gaps that develop between the boards will be wider than in any new floor. When repairing, a trick is to use spacers like washers or small wooden wedges to set up gaps between the new boards that mimic the old. Keep in mind, too, that while quarter-sawn lumber has no top or bottom, flat-sawn flooring should be placed with its grain rings (viewed from the end of the board) pointing down. This will keep the boards from "cupping" as they age.

There are fine points to nailing too. First, choose the right nails. If the floor is blind-nailed or the look of the nailheads isn't critical, use eight-penny "casing" cut nails (available from Tremont Nail Co. as the N-3 Floor Nail) for pre-1850 floors. Common cut nails can work too, but these tend to split the wood. Both types, though, are preferable to smooth, wire nails for grabbing a joist and holding the floor tight. If reproduction nails are purchased (to blend with a floor full of hand-wrought originals), a little more "distressing" to each head adds individuality. For any type, predrill holes through the flooring if the wood is too hard or thick to nail easily. Also, use a nailset when making the last couple of blows to avoid ugly hammer prints.

When a repair job gets down to putting in the last board, you'll have to coax it into the space any way you can—usually with a prybar and hammer, in both cases protecting the board with pieces of scrap wood. The last board is special also because it can only be face-nailed even if the rest of the floor is not. To hide the nailheads, drive them deep with a set, then cover them with color-matched wood filler. In a repair of only two side-by-side boards, it is usually easiest to face-nail both these boards as well.

Our old-flooring expert recommends working when the humidity is low.

Repairing Tongue-and-Groove Floors

Use a small handsaw (keyhole saw) or a circular saw to remove damaged boards. If you use a circular saw, set the depth of the cut to the thickness of the finish floor, and use a carbide flooring blade that will cut through nails. Finish the cut with a chisel so you don't accidentally cut into the next board.

To start the cut, drill a hole in the damaged board near a joist, and insert a keyhole saw in the hole. Saw across the board to free an end. (Or drill large overlapping holes.) Avoid drilling into the subfloor. When there is no subfloor it's especially important to cut near a joist—the joist or a block nailed to it will give support to the replacement board.

After removing the damaged board, but before inserting a replacement, square up the remaining cut edge of the board. Holding a sharp chisel perpendicular to the board, chisel a shallow groove across the grain to break the wood fibers. Then chisel toward the groove so the wood splinters off at the cut. Continue scoring and chiseling in this fashion until you have cut through the depth of the board.

Measure the new piece of board so it can be dropped into place, turn it over and chisel or plane the bottom shoulder of the groove off. Place shims under the new board if it is thinner than the old boards. Then knock it 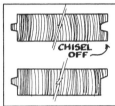 into place using a set and face-nail it into the subfloor. Board ends can be nailed into the joist or into nailing blocks that have been fastened to the joists. Countersink nailheads and fill holes.

Very often several adjacent boards will need replacing. When fitting in sections of tongue-and-groove flooring, remember that only the last board needs to be dropped in and face-nailed. Other boards can be fastened in the usual manner—with a flooring nail driven through the tongue. Also, stagger the joints when replacing a section of flooring. Cutting all boards off at the same joist both weakens the floor and makes the patch obvious.

FILLING CRACKS

Wood floors develop cracks from *compression shrinkage,* or *compression set.* Floorboards swelling beyond their normal range are stopped short by neighboring boards, which also expand. As the moisture

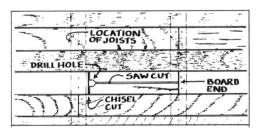

Compression shrinkage takes place when flooring that just meets under normal conditions (1) absorbs additional moisture. Expanding boards press against each other (2), crushing or compressing the wood along board edges, which shows up as cracks (3) when flooring returns to its earlier moisture level.

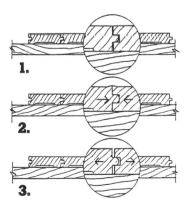

FINDING REPLACEMENT LUMBER

"The most difficult part of the project is getting floorboards to match," says old-flooring expert B. M. Jackson, "something most people don't consider until they've ripped out the damaged boards." In fact, the quality of the match between old flooring and repair lumber occasionally decides whether a floor with large areas of damage is repaired in sections or replaced altogether because additions would stand out. Finding wood of the same species is the first step, but other matching characteristics are just as important: cut, grading, and moisture content.

Flat-cut (flat-grain) boards have annual growth rings that usually run parallel to the face board and a characteristic grain pattern. *Rift-cut* (quarter-sawn, vertical-grain) boards have annual rings that are vertical to the face of the board, and are much more uniform in grain. Look to duplicate the "tightness of the grain" (number of rings per inch) as well as "figures in the grain," the natural grain and color markings, such as "bird's eye" maple (which is cut to reveal a wavy grain with small circular markings). (See chapter 7 for a description of the difference between flat-cut and rift-cut lumber.)

Also match the grade between old and new flooring. Criteria like the size and frequency of knots and other defects play a big part in the look of a floor. Make an educated guess about the grade of your old floor, and keep this in mind when evaluating new lumber, By modern standards, quarter-sawn flooring has two grades: Clear and Select. Flat-sawn flooring has four grades: Clear, Select, No. 1 Common, and No. 2 Common. The Clear grade for both types has almost no surface imperfections, while Select has a few, such as small, tight knots. No. 1 Common has more defects, but must contain material that will make a sound floor without cutting. No. 2 Common has even more imperfections, but still provides a serviceable floor. The percentage of sapwood in the lumber also influences grade and floor appearance, particularly in softwoods like heart pine. Since standards vary widely, the best advice here is to look for as much heartwood as possible when shopping for softwood flooring.

Finally, store new flooring stock in the room where it will be installed for a period to help control moisture content. This ensures that the repair is "in sync" with the moisture cycle of the room. Store the wood for at least five weeks, but the longer, the better. In the same way, when stock is newly cut from a mill (and has a very high moisture content), the minimum seasoning period, where the flooring dries out at the mill, should be six months.

---

in the wood increases, the edges of the flooring are put into compression, compacting the wood fiber. The wood never completely recovers from this injury, and so when its moisture content drops, the floorboard is slightly smaller than its original width. After repeated cycles (perhaps over decades), compacting stops because boards have been shrunk and no longer expand enough to suffer compression again—but they do show cracks when the wood is dry.

Sometimes compression results from poor installation (such as working in a damp building) or when dirt builds up in dry-weather cracks, which takes up the space needed by swelling wood. Plank floors are prone to this because the normal heating-season shrinkage of the wide wood is greater per board than that of strip flooring.

Cracks also appear where high-moisture flooring was installed. It will shrink in a normal house environment and leave cracks that never close. Conversely, keeping a house drier than its typical humidity level may cause the floor to "draw up," especially near forced-air heating sources. Building settlement can cause cracks that never go away. Uneven construction or the gluing effect of finishes can cause some floors to "panelize," so that the combined movement of several boards produces a single large crack.

Most cracks are best left well enough alone. They will close up enough during the humid months. Sometimes you can remedy the crack problem simply by running a humidifier to raise the humidity level in the house. Where excessive moisture is at fault, use a dehumidifier or vapor barrier (such as placing sheet plastic in an under-floor crawl space).

For cracks that need to be filled, you can use a traditional homemade *paste filler,* such as sawdust mixed with varnish, shellac, or white glue as a binder. Another period concoction (with no track record) is this 1909 formula from *American Carpenter and Builder Magazine:* "Make a pulp of paper, tissue paper being the best, though any paper will do, and add to it glue size and calcined magnesia until you have a mass like putty. Press this into the

The cracks in this tongue-and-groove floor are actually dry-weather fissures in compacted dirt, which have opened to catch debris.

cracks with a putty knife, make the surface smooth and level with the floor. The filler may be colored as desired."

Fibrous materials such as cloth strips soaked in linseed oil or glue give and take with the movement of the flooring. Hemp rope strands have also been tried. The strands are packed in the crack like shop caulking, using a large screwdriver or putty knife (or a caulking iron) and applied two layers deep if one does not fill the crack. The hemp can be stained to match the floor either before or after it is installed, and then varnished over if desired. The result is unobtrusive. Felt weatherstripping has also been used in the same way, and although not as stainable, it's resilient and barely noticeable.

Wood strips were cut into this plank floor because the cracks were a menace to high heels. Widening the cracks to highlight the strips was preferred over attempting a subtle repair.

Elastic caulks are silicone products that adhere well to wood; marine caulks may have longer curing times (particularly if they are polysulfide based), but are usually available in several wood tones. With any caulk, carefully mask off the crack to ensure a clean job. Gun or squeeze the caulk into the cracks when they are at mid-cycle, usually in spring or fall. Very wide cracks should first be partially filled with some sort of pliable backing material. This saves caulk and limits its adhesion to the sides of the floorboards, producing a more flexible seal.

A less subtle repair uses *wood fillets* or *cant strips* to fill large gaps between square-edged, wide-plank floorboards. It is difficult to match the look of existing boards, and adding more wood to the floor may only reintroduce compression problems by making the boards touch again in the wet season. However, when the floor shows large cracks that border on dangerous throughout the year, wood strips may be the only choice. Clean the cracks thoroughly by following a screwdriver, putty knife, or

coat hanger with a vacuum cleaner. Then cut and fit the wood as closely as possible; either glue and toenail with brads to one board or (when large enough) facenail to the joists or subfloor below.

FLOOR FINISHES

Deciding what finish—if any—to use on your floor depends on your commitment to historical accuracy and being true to the original finish, as well as on the practical service or level of maintenance you will expect to get from and give to the finish. As we've seen, before the mid-nineteenth century, many homeowners left their floors bare. For those with colonial- and post-colonial-era houses who feel strongly about historical accuracy, no finish would be the way to go. High-traffic areas can be protected with runners, floorcloths, or carpets, which may then be removed when it's time to show off the floor.

Paint

Painted floors date back to the mid-1700s in New England, and tongue-and-groove floors continued to be painted into the twentieth century in the workaday rooms of simple or rural houses. Floors were likely to be painted in shades that hid dirt, such as brick or "Indian" red, gray, brown, or green. Light blue, yellow, ochre, and other light

The practice of decorative floor painting with the use of pattern stencils was a familiar one in the early 1800s, and is stylish again today for many floors.

colors also were surprisingly popular in colonial America. Painting floors in decorative designs continued to be a fashionable, if somewhat "high end," practice well into the mid-1800s. Stenciling was one technique that could be used to decorate just the border or the entire field of the floor. Geometric patterns such as checkerboards, diamonds, and zigzags all had their heyday, as did floral motifs, marbleizing, and designs imitating carpet patterns.

Paint is a durable, low-maintenance finish. Oil-based paints specifically made for floor and deck use still stand up best; apply these in two or more coats. Their moderate gloss either equals or comes close to the look of earlier floor paint.

Wax

Wax wears quickly and offers the wood little protection from abrasion. As hard finishes came into vogue in the latter half of the nineteenth century, wax frequently was applied over shellac and varnish, both to give an added, easily renewable luster to the floor, and to protect the finish itself. Wax also was recommended to be applied over penetrating oils during the 1920s and 1930s, to enhance their look and protect the wood.

In a modern house, wax alone is still a qualified choice for floor finish. Although it has been popular for tongue-and-groove hardwood floors off and on in the last 100 years, there is little indication that it was used in earlier decades on wide-plank floors. Still, it may be a compromise between a hard finish and no finish at all. Though it builds up in low-wear areas and can be slippery under rugs, it does help flooring by repelling potential stains like spilled food long enough for them to be wiped up. Rela-

Wax wears away fast on a floor that's subjected to heavy traffic, but it will add a subtle luster (and limited protection for the wood) for as long as it lasts.

tively hard paste waxes (such as Trewax or Butcher's wax) are used for floors, and can be cut with alum if a reduced shine is desired. Although dirty or built up wax can be dissolved with turpentine or mineral spirits, once applied to bare wood it effectively closes the door to other finishes unless radical measures (such as sanding) are used. In addition, it is not compatible with every hard or oil finish (polyurethanes are often a problem).

Oils

Oils penetrate wood rather than lay on top and harden like paint. At the turn of the century, commercially sold floor oils made from crude petroleum, kerosine, or paraffin wax were available for use over varnished floors. Warmed paraffin or drying oils, such as linseed oil, which polymerize into a film when they react with oxygen, were also applied over bare wood. Penetrating sealers and finishes appeared later and are still popular for strip hardwood and parquet floors.

Oils have their own peculiarities as floor finishes. Generally, they require at least two coats for an adequate finish and sufficient drying time between coats (typically at least a week). Because they are not surface film-forming finishes, oils tend to hold dirt, making it imperative to keep an oiled floor clean. They also wear in traffic areas, with touch-ups usually being a fact of life, and give the wood only marginal protection from spills or abrasion. Most oils also significantly darken as they age. Oils generally are not a reversible finish, but many will accept a traditional varnish over them if you want to change the look later. Still, penetrating oils are a favorite choice for many old floors because they are easy to apply and repair (new oil blends well with old), and, particularly for softwoods, they are an attractive, low-gloss alternative to no finish at all. Penetrating oils are available as generic oils and proprietary products (Watco, Minwax, and Daly's are some national brands).

Shellac

During the Victorian era shellac was widely used—it produced the desired shine and a strong visual impression. Shellac is a *spirit varnish* composed simply of a natural resin (secreted by the lac beetle) dissolved in alcohol. Once the solvent (alcohol) evaporates, it leaves behind a coating of resin. Shellac gained early popularity because it is easy to work with, dries quickly, repairs well (touch-ups are almost invisible) and, when more sophisticated varnishes were still being perfected, it was reliable and fairly durable. Its natural amber color also gave wood a beautiful warm tone.

Shellac has several shortcomings that led to its decline as a floor finish and make it an unlikely choice in modern homes. First, water will spot and mar a shellacked surface by turning it white. Second, alcohol completely lifts the finish, causing it to be easily disfigured by accidents such as a spilled cocktail. Added to this, shellac is relatively brittle and performs better on hardwoods (which are fairly stable) than on softwoods. For those willing to put up with its limitations, shellac can be an attractive and authentic finish for a late-nineteenth-century floor. Sold in either dry (to mix with alcohol) or liquid form, it should be purchased in the original orange (rather than bleached-white) versions. Shellac has a short shelf life, and using the freshest product minimizes drying problems.

Oil Varnishes

Like shellac, oil varnishes, with their incomparable "depth" and shine, came into their own in the latter half of the nineteenth century. Oil varnishes, however, differ from shellac in that they do not form a film simply through the evaporation of a solvent. Instead, these varnishes, which are made by cooking drying oils with hard resins, harden slowly into a film through oxidation. Oil varnishes are manufactured in different oil-to-resin ratios—referred to as long-, medium-, or short-oil—which also affect the drying time and eventual hardness of the finish. Medium-oil varnishes have been a favored floor finish because they remain relatively soft (like oil-based paint) and can flex and adapt to the movements of both hardwoods and softwoods, yet are hard enough to wear well.

Tung-oil varnish on a maple floor provides a moderate gloss.

Although regarded as obsolete by some, oil varnishes are still very viable finishes that protect and beautify floors. Besides being historically appropriate for many houses built in the last one hundred years or so, these finishes bond well to older woods and do not show scratches as readily as some modern synthetic coatings. The common objections—that they require care to apply and twenty-four hours or more between coats to dry—may be overlooked if you regard the application problem as a one-time investment. Very soft, short-oil varnishes, however, are vulnerable to embedded dirt, and none are as durable as their space-age counterparts. In the past, many oil varnishes were domestic versions of marine products (such as spar varnish) and produced a very reflective sheen. Modern versions are sold in a variety of sheens, although a glossy finish still resists dirt and scuffing the best.

"Swedish" Finishes and Polyurethanes

These recently developed, synthetic resin varnishes are not original to any pre-1940 houses, but they are popular for floors. *"Swedish" finishes,* based on urea-formalde-

hyde chemistry, share many traits with polyurethanes. They are easier than oil varnishes to apply and are noted for their scuff resistance. They are temperamental though when it comes to application on old floors, and work best on new or freshly sanded wood. Also, "Swedish" finishes have a very high VOC (volatile organic compound) content which, when coupled with their formaldehyde ingredient, makes them controversial for health and environmental reasons.

Polyurethane floor finishes are tough.

Three classes of *polyurethanes* are commonly sold as floor finishes: moisture-cured, oil-modified, and water-based. Moisture-cured varnishes were among the first polyurethanes on the market and cure through the action of water in the air. Moisture-cured polyurethanes are tough, and are often chosen for industrial and heavy-traffic floors such as gymnasiums. They also contain a high percentage of solvents, making proper ventilation important when they are applied, and currently putting them under VOC restrictions in some areas.

Oil-modified polyurethanes cure through the action of oxygen, much like traditional varnish, largely due to the addition of drying oils. These oils also make it possible to produce them in a variety of sheens, while still retaining the advantages of polyurethane resins.

Water-based polyurethanes (also called *water-borne*) employ water as a major component of the coating and are just starting to become regularly available. Developed in part to meet the increasing regulation of organic solvents in finishes, water-based polyurethanes have the added consumer advantage of water cleanup.

Polyurethanes are a dream finish for many, but they have proved less than ideal for some old-house restorers. First, they have a "plastic" look to some eyes, which clashes with aged or traditional finishes in the same room. Second, polyurethanes are hard, unsupple coatings that have been known to delaminate from softwoods or floors that move a lot. They also do not bond well to poorly prepared floors or those previously coated with wax, shellac, or the stearate compounds that are sometimes found in stains and fillers. They don't even bond well to themselves, which can cause difficulty in making repairs and touch-ups. Third, in some houses, the hardness of polyurethanes also makes them highlight scratches in floors.

Some of these objections may be chalked up to the chemistry of this type of finish, and ruled out upon considering polyurethane's advantages. Self-leveling (for a smooth finish) and quick drying, it is easy to apply. Its legendary toughness also makes it easy to maintain. It can even help hold splinter-prone floors together. Choosing the right product helps too. Moisture-cured polyurethanes were often designed for a thick, "industrial" look, but oil-modified products, already akin in makeup to oil varnishes, are sold in satin and matte sheens. Applying these finishes in thin coats also minimizes the plastic look and improves their flexibility.

CHAPTER 16

Woodwork

Wood trim is perhaps *the* indispensable feature of an old house's interior. It is the kind of old-house detail that, with a little extra attention, can be the humble grace note that brings character and elegance to featureless walls. The knee-jerk response to painted woodwork and old, tired, darkened clear finishes is to strip it all off. Here you'll find easy and inexpensive techniques for restoring clear finishes as well as the pros and cons of paint stripping. People who own an old home wouldn't dream of removing woodwork, unless they have to strip paint, refinish the floors, rebuild the windows, replaster the walls, or install new wiring, plumbing, or insulation. So you'll also find detailed instructions on removing and replacing woodwork sections.

—REVIVING A CLEAR FINISH—

Wood with a clear finish may not have to be stripped at all; a finish reviver may suffice. A finish reviver cleans the surface of the old varnish by dissolving the uppermost layer where most of the dirt is. The household cleanser Top Job is a finish reviver of sorts; it has mild paint-stripping qualities and an aroma to go with it. Various fine commercial brands of finish reviver, such as Hope's, Daly's, and Formby's, are available.

There are four reasons why a clear finish may look dark or worn out. The remedy in each of these cases is quite different:

1. The finish may be covered with layers of dirt, grime, and old wax.

2. The finish itself may contain some coloring agents that were used originally to disguise cheap wood.

3. The finish itself may have darkened. The darkening may be a) concentrated in the top surface of the finish itself, or b) go completely through the finish.

4. The finish may have cracked due to aging.

You'll need to strip only in cases 3 b) and 4. If the finish is dirty, simple cleaning will renew it quickly and economically. Also, if the finish has deteriorated, finish revivers are usually preferred to strippers.

First determine if you have a shellac, lacquer, or varnish finish (see box on page 297). When considering a new finish for your woodwork, a new, "better" product may not be the best choice. Though shellac doesn't have much resistance to alcohol or water and darkens slowly with age, it does have some advantages. It can produce an elegant high gloss without a plastic look and is easily removed with denatured alcohol.

Finish Cleaners

For finishes with a minor accumulation of dirt and grime, simple cleaning with mild soap suds or mineral spirits usually does the trick.

Soap. Whip a tablespoon of Ivory Liquid in a quart of warm water to create a lot of suds. Dip an old wash cloth or piece of terrycloth toweling into the suds—not the water—and rub the test area vigorously. Wipe with a dry towel to absorb any dampness. This should remove grime without damaging the patina. (But it won't remove wax buildup.)

Mineral spirits. If soap doesn't work, brush some mineral spirits (paint thinner) onto the test patch. Allow to soak for three minutes. Then take a pad of fine steel wool (0000) and gently rub the surface in the direction of the grain. (For high-gloss finishes, use a terrycloth rag instead; steel wool will dull the gloss.) On carved detail, scrub out softened wax and dirt with an old toothbrush.

Wipe up excess mineral spirits with a paper towel, then let the test patch dry for an hour. At this point it will look quite dull. Apply a bit of lemon oil or paste wax to the test patch and see if you like the result. *Note:* Never apply

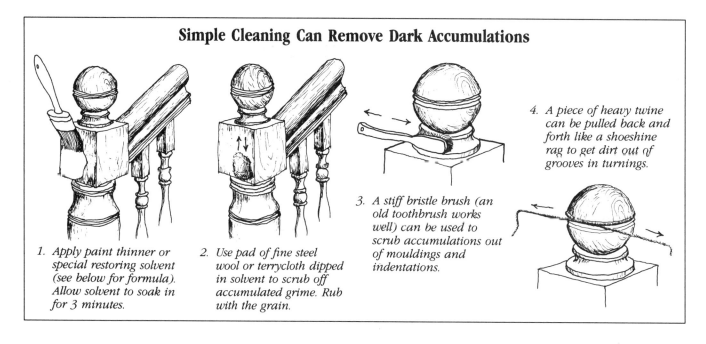

Simple Cleaning Can Remove Dark Accumulations

1. *Apply paint thinner or special restoring solvent (see below for formula). Allow solvent to soak in for 3 minutes.*

2. *Use pad of fine steel wool or terrycloth dipped in solvent to scrub off accumulated grime. Rub with the grain.*

3. *A stiff bristle brush (an old toothbrush works well) can be used to scrub accumulations out of mouldings and indentations.*

4. *A piece of heavy twine can be pulled back and forth like a shoeshine rag to get dirt out of grooves in turnings.*

lemon oil over paste wax, or vice versa. Lemon oil dissolves wax.

Cleaner-restorer. If mineral spirits fail, try an old-time recipe:

> 1 cup boiled linseed oil
> 1 cup white vinegar
> 1 cup turpentine

Shake vigorously to mix the ingredients. Apply to the surface with an old paintbrush, and allow to soak for three minutes. Then dip a pad of fine steel wool (0000) in the restorer and gently scrub off the loosened grime. Again, substitute terrycloth for steel wool on a high-gloss finish.

Wipe off excess restorer with paper towels or rags. (They contain linseed oil, so there's the danger of spontaneous combustion. Get them outside *immediately,* and either burn them or store in a water-filled metal can.)

Let the restored patch dry for twenty-four hours. A little paste wax gives you the final result. If you like the look, repeat the process on the entire surface.

Super-strong cleaners. Fantastik or Spic 'n Span will clean, but they'll also remove some of the finish. Test gingerly on a small area. You can also make your own strong cleaner by dissolving 1 pound of washing soda in 1 gallon of hot water. Wearing rubber gloves, rub down the surface with your cleaner and fine steel wool. Work with the steel wool damp, rather than dripping, and wipe up any water immediately with paper towels to avoid water spotting.

These cleaners will definitely leave the surface dull. Polish with lemon oil or paste wax to get the final effect.

Finish Revivers

If simple cleaning didn't do the job, then you've got to remove some more of the old finish. There are a number of commercial finish revivers (or "refinishers"). A finish reviver is a solvent soup, containing such chemicals as toluene and methyl alcohol. You can also experiment with your own formulas. Start with "A" and work down the list:

A. 15 percent by volume lacquer thinner in mineral spirits
B. 50/50 lacquer thinner and denatured alcohol
C. Pure denatured alcohol
D. Pure lacquer thinner

The procedure for using these finish revivers is the same, whether you're working with a commercial product, or your own concoction:

Put the reviver in a wide-mouth jar, and keep covered. (The solvents are highly volatile and evaporate rapidly.) Dip a small piece of fine steel wool (0000) in the reviver, and squeeze out any excess. Gently rub a small area (about 1 square foot at a time). The pad will start picking up the old finish, so either rinse frequently in your reviver solution, or discard the pad and start fresh. Remove finish until you get a color you like, or until all tackiness disappears.

Allow the test patch to dry, then apply a coat of finish; tung oil is the usual choice. Apply tung oil with your hand or with a lint-free rag. Apply a thin coat, rubbing with the grain, and wipe off all the excess. One coat gives a satin luster; two or more coats give a higher gloss. (Beware of spontaneous combustion in any rags or paper towels containing tung oil!)

If the test patch is satisfactory, go over the whole surface with finish reviver, doing about one square foot at a time. You may have to go over the entire surface a second time with a dampened steel wool pad to remove any lap marks between sections.

But if the test shows the finish is too far gone for reviving, you've no choice but to strip.

Route to the Best Method for Restoring Clear Finishes

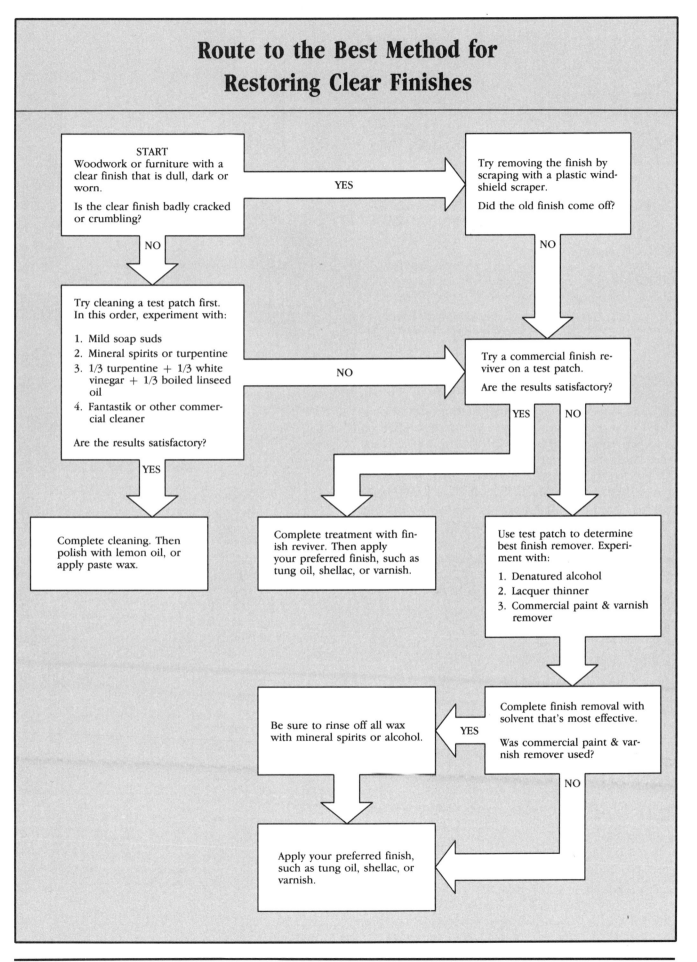

START
Woodwork or furniture with a clear finish that is dull, dark or worn.

Is the clear finish badly cracked or crumbling?

YES →

Try removing the finish by scraping with a plastic windshield scraper.

Did the old finish come off?

NO ↓

Try cleaning a test patch first. In this order, experiment with:

1. Mild soap suds
2. Mineral spirits or turpentine
3. 1/3 turpentine + 1/3 white vinegar + 1/3 boiled linseed oil
4. Fantastik or other commercial cleaner

Are the results satisfactory?

NO →

Try a commercial finish reviver on a test patch.

Are the results satisfactory?

YES / **NO**

YES ↓

Complete cleaning. Then polish with lemon oil, or apply paste wax.

Complete treatment with finish reviver. Then apply your preferred finish, such as tung oil, shellac, or varnish.

Use test patch to determine best finish remover. Experiment with:

1. Denatured alcohol
2. Lacquer thinner
3. Commercial paint & varnish remover

Be sure to rinse off all wax with mineral spirits or alcohol.

YES

Complete finish removal with solvent that's most effective.

Was commercial paint & varnish remover used?

NO

Apply your preferred finish, such as tung oil, shellac, or varnish.

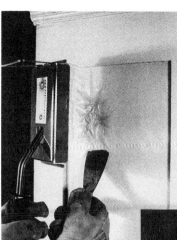

The heat plate in action.

The heat gun pulls all the paint out of fluting.

STRIPPING WOODWORK

There's almost a worship of stripped wood these days. Many people feel compelled to strip any wood detail, regardless of the type of wood or historical accuracy. Often little flecks of original paint stare out from the pores of the wood and it has a dull hazy look, all encased in two coats of shiny polyurethane. Never assume that you have to strip wood. Paint stripping is messy, time-consuming, and hazardous. There are three major reasons for removing paint:

1. To reveal the color and grain of beautiful wood (usually a hardwood), or to reveal a fine material, such as marble, underneath.

2. To remove cracked or peeling layers prior to repainting.

3. To remove excessive layers that obscure architectural detail prior to repainting.

You'll notice that two of the reasons for stripping are for repainting, so you won't have to do a perfect removal job.

Most of the woodwork in homes built in the late eighteenth and early nineteenth centuries was painted. The same was true in most post-Victorian houses, especially in bedrooms. Clearly "going natural" with woodwork is not always the best choice, and for good reasons besides being historically appropriate. First, wood that was originally painted is usually a softwood such as fir or pine and doesn't have a particularly beautiful color or grain. Second, if the wood was painted from day one, the original paint probably soaked into the pores of the wood, which makes removing it nearly impossible. If you sand it out, you end up with damaged profiles and old wood with no patina. If you don't sand, you wind up with paint freckles.

Nonetheless, many projects do require stripping wood-

work. On hardwoods, such as oak, walnut, mahogany, chestnut, and cherry, use heat to get the paint off down to the varnish or shellac layer. For broad areas, use a heat plate, which melts twelve square inches of paint at a time. For moulded areas, including inside corners, fluting, and narrow surfaces, use a heat gun. For big jobs, you'll want both heat tools to get the bulk of the job done fast. Then, go back with a chemical remover to take off the varnish and what little paint residue is left.

For softwoods such as pine, use a heat tool if there are many layers of paint built up. Toward the bottom layers,

Starting out with chemical stripper on thick paint layers creates a sludgy mess.

Architectural Woodwork:
To Strip or Not to Strip?

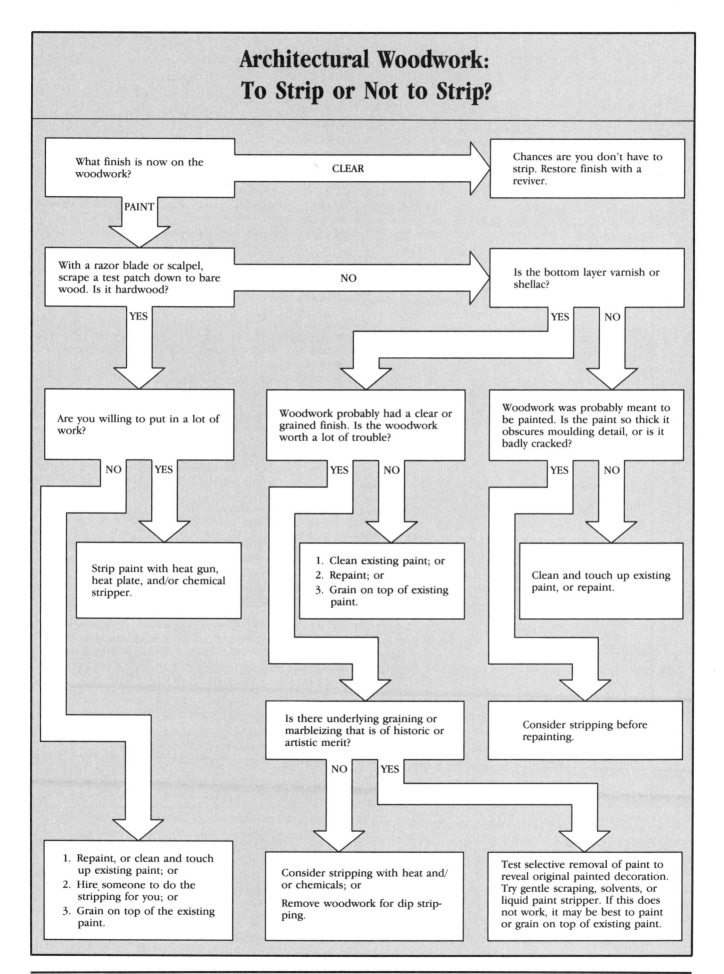

What finish is now on the woodwork?

CLEAR → Chances are you don't have to strip. Restore finish with a reviver.

PAINT ↓

With a razor blade or scalpel, scrape a test patch down to bare wood. Is it hardwood?

NO → Is the bottom layer varnish or shellac?

YES ↓

Are you willing to put in a lot of work?

NO / **YES**

Strip paint with heat gun, heat plate, and/or chemical stripper.

1. Repaint, or clean and touch up existing paint; or
2. Hire someone to do the stripping for you; or
3. Grain on top of the existing paint.

Woodwork probably had a clear or grained finish. Is the woodwork worth a lot of trouble?

YES / **NO**

1. Clean existing paint; or
2. Repaint; or
3. Grain on top of existing paint.

Is there underlying graining or marbleizing that is of historic or artistic merit?

NO / **YES**

Consider stripping with heat and/or chemicals; or

Remove woodwork for dip stripping.

(From "Is the bottom layer varnish or shellac?")

YES / **NO**

Woodwork was probably meant to be painted. Is the paint so thick it obscures moulding detail, or is it badly cracked?

YES / **NO**

Clean and touch up existing paint, or repaint.

Consider stripping before repainting.

Test selective removal of paint to reveal original painted decoration. Try gentle scraping, solvents, or liquid paint stripper. If this does not work, it may be best to paint or grain on top of existing paint.

		CONDITION		
METHOD		**SPLITTING, ALLIGATORED PAINT on Flat Walls & Ceilings**	**PEELING PAINT on Ceilings, Coves, & Mouldings Underlying Calcimine**	**THICK, ENCRUSTED PAINT ON . . .**
				Straight-Run Mouldings	**Moulded Elements: Medallions, Egg & Dart, Acanthus Leaves, etc.**
	ABRASION: Belt Sanders, etc.	Sand off all splitting, cracked paint. Advantages: cheap, relatively fast. Disadvantages: danger of lead poisoning; very dusty; possible scratching of plaster.	Not Applicable	Not Applicable	Not Applicable
	CHEMICAL STRIPPERS	Soften paint with chemicals and scrape off. Advantages: simple. Disadvantages: expensive and messy; labor intensive; scrapings may contain lead.	Chemical removers can strip overlying paint; hot water will then be needed to remove the calcimine. Advantages: It will work. Disadvantages: See left; more effort required than moisture method.	PREFERRED METHOD Thickened stripper is applied, covered, and allowed to soak. The softened paint is lifted off with scrapers. Advantages: It works. Disadvantages: messy; expensive; very time-consuming.	PREFERRED METHOD Same process as at left.
	HEAT GUN/ HEAT PLATE	PREFERRED METHOD Melt paint with Heat Plate & scrape off. Advantages: simple & cheap. Disadvantages: messy & labor intensive; scrapings may contain lead.	Process at left will remove the overlying oil-based and latex paint. Thorough washing with hot water needed to remove residual calcimine. Advantages and disadvantages same as at left.	Heat Gun blows heat into the moulding. Specially shaped scrapers remove melted paint. Advantages: lower cost. Disadvantages: working with heavy heat tools overhead.	Not Applicable
	MOISTURE: Steam, Hot Water	Not Applicable	PREFERRED METHOD Steam can penetrate & loosen calcimine, if overlying paint is thin. If paint is too thick, work from edges of flaked area. Advantages: least effort of all the methods. Disadvantages: may not work.	Not Applicable.	If medallion can be removed from ceiling, soak it for 2 days on damp towels. Remove the loosened paint with scalpels. Advantages: cheapest & easiest way to remove paint. Disadvantages: Medallion may be damaged in dismounting & mounting; damp plaster easily scratches; lengthy process.

things may get gummy, and much will remain in the pores of the wood to be cleaned up with chemical stripper. If there are only one to three coats of paint on softwood, use a chemical stripper to start. Heat is less effective when there wasn't a varnish or shellac layer to separate the paint from its bond with the wood. (Remember, if there is no varnish layer, the wood was painted from day one, so you should really be stripping only to reveal details and sharp outlines concealed by paint, in which case you don't have to do a great job because you'll be repainting anyway.)

In most situations, follow this stripping sequence when removing paint from wood:

1. Scrape off all loose paint.
2. Remove paint with heat (for many layers of paint, otherwise skip to step 3).

3. Remove any remaining paint with chemical stripper.

4. Rinse with alcohol or mineral spirits. While many strippers are water-rinsable, water will raise the grain on some woods.

5. If you plan to apply a clear finish, you may need to pick out paint residue from cracks and carvings with dental picks, pointed dowels, sharpened screwdrivers, and other similar instruments.

6. Fill and sand as needed. (See "Woodwork Repairs," page 310.)

7. Apply paint or clear finish, as appropriate.

If you want to or need to strip away a clear finish, check first to see whether it's varnish or shellac. (Though many clear finishes may be restored using the techniques described in this chapter.) Rub it hard with denatured alcohol; if it's shellac it will come off. Continue with the alcohol and rags, or alcohol and bronze wool if necessary. If it's varnish rather than shellac, the alcohol won't dissolve it. Heat won't remove varnish or shellac very effectively. But even the thickest, darkest layers of varnish will come off quickly when slathered with conventional chemical paint-and-varnish removers.

PAINT STRIPPING TIPS

Paint stripping can be a tedious and difficult task. If your woodwork just won't strip clean, perhaps one of our tried and true paint-stripping tips will help:

Tools

Fit the tool to the job. Your dentist can be a good source of delicate scraping tools. See if the dentist can provide curettes and other "picking" tools for you. A small cake-frosting knife may be handy when stripping layers of old paint from Victorian mouldings with a heat gun or heat plate. The curved tip follows the contours of the moulding. Other around-the-house tools that people use to clean hard-to-reach spots include knitting needles, awls, toothpicks, crochet hooks, straight pins, sculptor's tools, nutpicks, the filed tips of small screwdrivers, wooden dowels sharpened to a pencil point, blunted ice picks, and "church key" can openers.

Buy "shop towels" for cleanup—grocery-store paper towels just aren't strong enough. You can find shop towels at an industrial supply store.

Industrial strength rubber gloves—the sleek, flexible, super-strength, long-wearing type—will outlast any grocery store brand by weeks.

When the Finish Just Won't Come Off . . .

On cedar, use a heat gun to remove as much paint as possible without scorching the wood. Then brush water-soluble stripper on the paneling and leave for twenty minutes. Use a tough scrub brush and wash it off with a solution of 1 cup trisodium phosphate (TSP) for each gallon of boiling water. The hotter the water, the better it will work.

Allow paint stripper to penetrate, then cover the stripper with a generous portion of sawdust. After the sawdust soaks for a while, brush it off by hand with

Here, a heat gun melts multiple layers of paint off a baseboard.

heavy-duty rubber gloves. You can reuse the sawdust several times.

On a shellacked or varnished surface, use a heat gun or electric heating coil until the paint bubbles. (To avoid vaporizing the paint, don't hold the heater too close—it takes a bit of experimenting to get the right combination of distance and timing.) Let the paint reharden, then peel it off with a razor blade or wallpaper scraper. The heat breaks the bond between the paint and the shellac or varnish, so the paint comes off in strips.

When dealing with a difficult-to-remove layer of paint that was rubbed into the pores of the wood and meant to stay, remember that sanding is time consuming and changes the surface of the wood. First try a thick stripper like Zip-Strip. Leave it for half an hour, then apply more and *rub* it with a fine (0000) steel wool.

If this doesn't work, sometimes you can shellac the surface, let it dry, and then strip the shellac with denatured alcohol. The paint in the pores may come with it. As always, try a test patch first.

Sometimes you'll encounter a casein (milk) paint, calcimine, or some old "home brew" paint that resists stripping. Dissolve casein paints by scrubbing with full-strength ammonia. Calcimine can be stripped with a hot TSP solution. With home-brew paints, you'll have to experiment with various solvents.

Calcimine and whitewash on ceilings sometimes can be removed with just wallpaper paste. Apply a coating of old-fashioned wheat paste. The paste shrinks when it dries, and the surface tension may pull the old paint off.

For a Fine Finish . . .

When refinishing furniture, the directions on most cans of varnish recommend applying the finish with a soft, natural-bristle brush. Sometimes you're left with a thick, gummy-looking finish. Try applying the varnish with an old nylon stocking, rubbing it in as if waxing a car. Between coats buff with 0000 steel wool and then wipe all surfaces with a tack cloth. Three coats is usually sufficient.

To get a smooth finish on stripped turned objects (such as baluster), use an emery cloth rather than fine sandpaper. Cut the emery cloth into narrow strips and then pull them back and forth like a shoeshine rag. Because of its fabric backing, emery cloth is more flexible than sandpaper and lasts longer in this application.

COMMERCIAL PAINT STRIPPING

Subcontracting a stripping job can save you lots of stripping headaches. But before you hand over your woodwork to a professional, make sure the contractor does the following:

• Tests the methods and materials on a small patch before beginning the big job. If you approve the test based on a solvent-based stripper, write that into the specifications.

• Write masking techniques into the specifications to protect anything you don't want ruined.

• Is fully licensed and insured and uses safety precautions such as ventilation, goggles, gloves, and containment of effluent.

• Properly disposes of toxic wastes such as those from lead-based paint and methylene chloride. Many architects are writing proper waste handling procedures into the contract. Reputable contractors who take stripping jobs of any size do legally dispose of the sludge as toxic waste through a licensed waste handler. Most say that the Department of Environmental Protection regularly inspects their procedures.

• Specifies the degree of finish. Do you want just paint buildup removed or do you want the contractor to remove paint from wood pores, do stain removal, or sanding?

Contractors may work on a time-and-materials, hourly, or per-square-foot basis. Some give a fixed price for the job, based on one of the above. Consider time costs too. A larger crew will get in and out faster, which may make a difference in scheduling.

A reputable contractor will probably want to come in and test the surface before he quotes a price. The number of finish layers, presence of an original varnish coat, and the type of paint all make a significant difference in the difficulty of the job, and thus the price.

Besides full masking, the operator uses a shield to control overspray during pressure rinse.

A careful contractor can do extensive paint stripping in a finished house if masking is thorough.

Some contractors pressure rinse after stripping, removing water with a wet vac.

Tape, plastic, particleboard, more tape, and newspaper mask carpeting on a staircase.

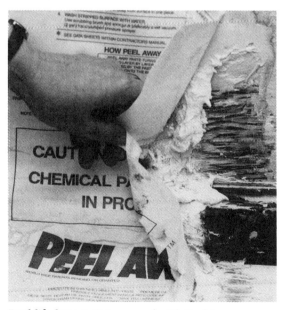

Real-life latex-paint removal with Peel-Away.

Sources of Commercial Stripper

The following companies are major manufacturers of stripping chemicals for commercial jobs. Most sell a full line of products, including restoration cleaners and exterior strippers, but the information below is confined to products recommended for interior use.

American Building Restoration Chemicals, Inc.
9720 S. 60th Street, Dept. OHJ
Franklin, WI 53132
(800)346-7532
Manufacture of stripping chemicals for interior use, including several methylene-chloride-based formulas and a newly developed line of caustics called Grip & Strip. These are alcohol-based products with potassium-hydroxide content of 0 percent to 65 percent (classified as nonhazardous waste). Applied by trowel, they form a skin that contains sludge and facilitates removal. Also manufactures stain removers and other solvent-based refinishing products. Sells through suppliers and direct. Training videos and regional seminars are available. Technical catalog, $1.25. Commercial-scale customers may call for technical assistance: (800)346-7532.

Bix Process Systems, Inc.
P.O. Box 3091, Dept. OHJ
Bethel, CT 06801
(203)743-3263
Sells their own stripping chemicals direct or through extensive network of distributors (for Tuff-Job only) and dealer/applicators (for commercial products). Independent contractors are licensed by Bix and trained at their facility in Bethel. Excellent systems for masking finished surfaces and hazardous-waste containment and disposal. Also sells commercial-scale stripping equipment of their own design.

Diedrich Chemicals-Restoration Technologies, Inc.
7373 S. 6th Street, Dept. OHJ
Oak Creek, WI 53154
(414)764-0058
Manufacturer of both solvent-based and alkaline (caustic) stripping chemicals. Nationwide, 700 distributors sell the products to contractors. (Most of these industrial-strength paint strippers are not recommended for do-it-yourself jobs.) Patent pending on "Rip-Strip," promised as the next generation of the concept introduced by Peel-Away: Rather than employing a paper covering, the material itself forms a film to which paint adheres. Manufacturer claims it is more economical and not as caustic as Peel-Away.

ProSoCo, Inc.
P.O. Box 171677, Dept. OHJ
Kansas City, KS 66117
(913)281-2700
Best known for their strippers and cleaners for exterior masonry, ProSoCo also sells methylene-chloride-based strippers for interior woodwork. They are not standard products, but rather specially manufactured to the architect's or contractor's specifications for the job. (Call for the number of your district or regional manager or sales representative and explain the job you have to see if they can help.) ProSoCo does not generally recommend their caustic formulations for interior use.

QRB Industries
3139 U.S. 31 North, Dept. OHJ
Niles, MI 49120
(616)683-7908
Although this company's Standard Remover (solvent-based but nonmethylene-chloride and noncaustic) is available by the gallon, their expertise is specially formulated strippers for commercial projects. Multisolvent-based, methylene-chloride-based, and combination caustic-plus-solvent-based formulations are available to spec for graffiti removal, dipping or flow-over stripping, water-rinsability, and so on. Custom orders by the 55-gallon drum (a test gallon will be prepared for client approval). Consultation and audio-cassette tapes available.

Contractors

We thank the individuals listed below who provided us with technical tidbits and informed opinions. The list of stripping contractors is, of course, not comprehensive.

Jack Tadych
American Building
  Restoration
9720 S. 60th Street
Franklin, WI 53132
(800)346-7532

Stephen Toth
Montclair Restoration
  Craftsmen
21 Clover Hill Place
Montclair, NJ 07042
(201)783-4519

Randy Berno
Stripping Unlimited
RD 1, Box 870
Moretown, VT 05660
(802)244-5756

Doug Kleeschulte
Warwick Refinishers
P.O. Box 35
Warwick, NY 10990
(914)342-1200

Wayne Towle Inc.
8 Thayer Street
Boston, MA 02118
(617)738-9121

DIP-STRIPPING AND FLOW-ON STRIPPING

It sounds like the easy route—remove the woodwork, cart it away to the dip-stripper, and it comes back paint-free. But dip-stripping can severely damage wood: a valuable oak mantel comes back looking like a gray sponge. On the other hand, many people say dip-stripping beats the mess of hand stripping.

Most commercial strip shops have three dip-stripping tanks:

1. A "cold tank" filled with a paint stripper based on methylene chloride and methanol.

2. A "hot tank" containing a solution of lye or

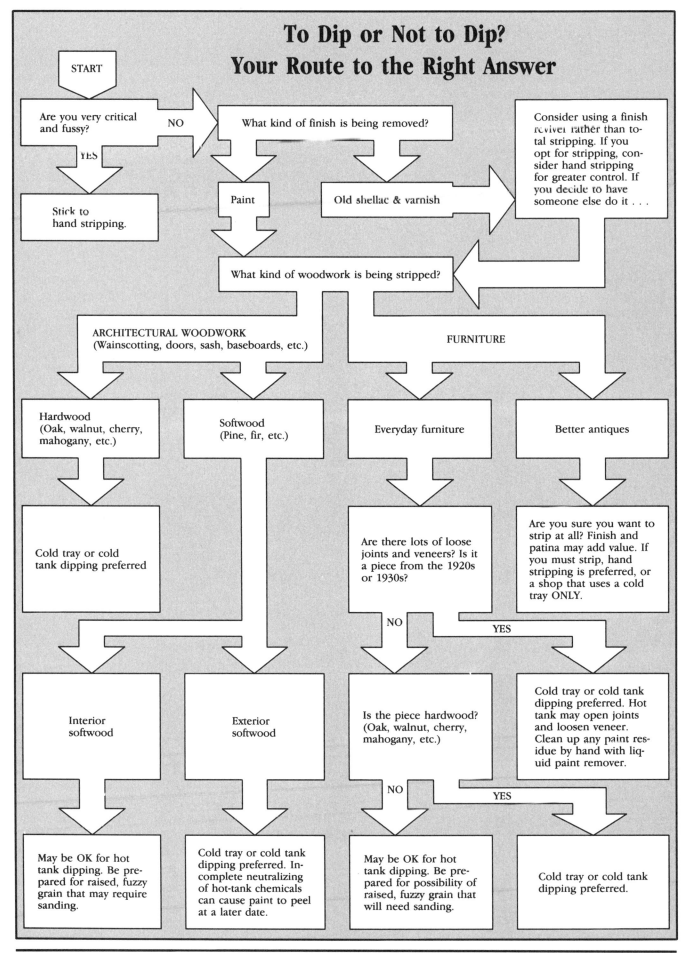

To Dip or Not to Dip?
Your Route to the Right Answer

START

Are you very critical and fussy?

NO

YES

Stick to hand stripping.

What kind of finish is being removed?

Paint

Old shellac & varnish

Consider using a finish reviver rather than total stripping. If you opt for stripping, consider hand stripping for greater control. If you decide to have someone else do it . . .

What kind of woodwork is being stripped?

ARCHITECTURAL WOODWORK
(Wainscotting, doors, sash, baseboards, etc.)

FURNITURE

Hardwood
(Oak, walnut, cherry, mahogany, etc.)

Softwood
(Pine, fir, etc.)

Everyday furniture

Better antiques

Cold tray or cold tank dipping preferred

Are there lots of loose joints and veneers? Is it a piece from the 1920s or 1930s?

Are you sure you want to strip at all? Finish and patina may add value. If you must strip, hand stripping is preferred, or a shop that uses a cold tray ONLY.

NO

YES

Interior softwood

Exterior softwood

Is the piece hardwood? (Oak, walnut, cherry, mahogany, etc.)

Cold tray or cold tank dipping preferred. Hot tank may open joints and loosen veneer. Clean up any paint residue by hand with liquid paint remover.

NO

YES

May be OK for hot tank dipping. Be prepared for raised, fuzzy grain that may require sanding.

Cold tray or cold tank dipping preferred. Incomplete neutralizing of hot-tank chemicals can cause paint to peel at a later date.

May be OK for hot tank dipping. Be prepared for possibility of raised, fuzzy grain that will need sanding.

Cold tray or cold tank dipping preferred.

As soon as you hear, "my own secret formula," head for the door!

Most problems occur in the hot tank. Caustic strippers remove old finishes very effectively. But in the hands of a careless operator, caustic strippers will not only dissolve old glues, but will also attack the surface of the wood itself. And since it is a hot aqueous solution, it's almost impossible not to wind up with some raised grain.

It's important for the customer and the strip-shop operator to understand the difference between fine woodwork and run-of-the-mill architectural woodwork. A run through the hot tank might be fine for paint-encrusted baseboards, but disaster for walnut wainscotting. Caustic stripper sells for much less than methylene chloride stripper, so it's easy to see why an unscrupulous operator might keep a cold tank around for show, and run all the work through a hot tank.

Cold tanks are less harsh than hot tanks. They operate at room temperature; the stripper is a combination of methylene chloride and methanol, similar to the liquid paint stripper available at the hardware store.

The cold tank avoids soaking wood in water; nonetheless, the wood is immersed in a strong chemical. It will absorb some of the chemical depending on how long it soaks. And it's possible to get some swelling and grain raising through the combination of immersion plus water rinsing. Also, it's possible that not all of the methylene chloride will be washed out of the wood.

Some areas require hand-cleaning with a brush.

trisodium phosphate (TSP) in water. These tanks operate from 125 to 180 degrees Fahrenheit.

3. A bleach tank containing oxalic acid. This tank neutralizes the caustic from the hot tank, and bleaches out any darkening of the wood that occurred in previous steps.

Between dippings, dipping chemicals are usually rinsed off in pressure wash booths. One, two, or all three tanks may be used in stripping a piece.

The unhappy recipients of dip-stripped wood report fuzzy grain, loosened joints, bubbling veneers, and drastic color changes. Most unhappy customers probably did not know what chemical was used, which was part of the problem. Some commercial strippers resort to secrecy to hide the fact that they are dipping fine woods in harsh chemicals. They will assure customers that they have their own secret stripper that's guaranteed not to harm wood.

Commercial strip-shops may also have a "cold tray" for flow-on paint stripping. The piece is coated (not immersed) with a methylene-chloride-based stripper. This is the gentlest of all the commercial stripping methods. As the used chemical runs off the wood, it collects at one end of the tray. A coarse screen removes large pieces of stripped paint, and the chemical is recycled back onto the woodwork. When most of the finish is loose, the softened paint or varnish is scraped off with a putty knife. More stripper is pumped back onto the piece to remove the remaining finish. Some especially intricate areas require hand cleanup with picks, small scrapers, or a brass brush.

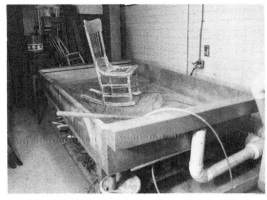
The flow-on tray.

Scraping off the softened paint.

Power rinsing the goop.

The stripped piece is then transferred to a water-rinsing tray to remove the remaining chemical and dissolved paint. A small amount of water is sprayed onto the piece at high pressure to halt the stripping action of the chemical and remove all traces of the old finish.

The water rinse is the step most likely to cause problems. With a minimal amount of water, you shouldn't experience any adverse effects. However, should the operator get carried away and drench the piece under a continuing stream, it may lift the veneer, raise the grain, or cause splitting or warping. There is no substitute for a knowledgeable and conscientious strip-shop operator.

The water-rinse booth.

Flow-on stripping requires less stripper than either hand stripping or dip-stripping. As with hand stripping, the chemicals are applied only where they're needed. Therefore, no chemical soaks into bare wood. Unlike hand stripping, the chemical is reused. A five-gallon bucket of stripper usually does an entire day's stripping.

Less stripper means less waste for the shop and lower cost to you. In many ways, flow-on stripping is less hazardous than other stripping methods. The flow-on trays used by BIX Process Systems, Inc., feature an integral ventilation system. Fumes from the stripping chemicals used are heavier than air and settle within the walls of the tray. Vents along the sides of the tray exhaust outdoors through a powerful fan.

The flow-on method is more ecologically sound than some other stripping methods because less waste is produced. At the end of each day, the sludge is collected and stored. Once a drum has been filled, the solid wastes are disposed of in an approved site according to EPA standards.

Liquid effluent produced in the water-rinsing tray goes through a 300-gallon filtration tank where it passes through three progressively finer filters that remove most of the solids. The water is then forced through an activated charcoal filter to remove the finest solids and much of the suspended solvent. Depending on state and local requirements, it is then introduced into the soil, or contained for disposal in an approved landfill.

REMOVING TRIM

Removing trim isn't a terribly complicated job if it's done with forethought and patience.

The main tool for removing trim is a short, flat prybar. Often used in pairs, it's designed for just this kind of work. You'll also need these tools for your woodwork-removal tool kit:

- Clawhammer
- Nail puller or pliers
- A couple of putty knives
- A pair of sturdy work gloves

If you want to add a screwdriver to this list, don't. It will leave chewed-up edges on the wood.

Cut through paint buildup or wallpaper that overlaps the wood with a knife or scraper before pulling away the trim, so you don't flake paint or rip wallpaper. Repair any splits or defects in the trim itself before it's removed. Mending the wood at this stage is easier than trying to reassemble splintered pieces after the trim is off.

Note the construction of a corner before you work on

it. Generally, outside trim corners are mitered (both pieces cut at 45 degrees); inside corners are coped (one board cut with a coping saw so that it fits the contour of its mate at 90 degrees). The coped board was installed after its mate, so remove it first; then you can cover any evidence of your initial prying when the trim is nailed back into place. Pry each board at the edge or joint exposed by the board you've just removed.

To remove moulding, gently hammer the bent edge of the prybar between the wall and the wood at one end of the trim. Start at the tops or bottoms of windows and doors. Begin at the corners if you're removing baseboards or ceiling mouldings.

Position a wood shingle or a wide-bladed putty knife to protect the wall from the prybar, and lift the end of the prybar carefully, using the wall as a fulcrum. Work the wood away from the wall until you see a nail. Hold open

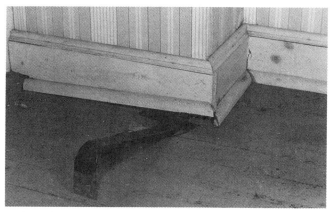

Either of the base shoes used in this mitered outside corner can be removed first.

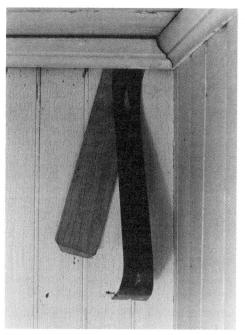

The coped board, which was installed in this interior corner after its mate, is removed first.

Using two prybars in opposite directions is the easiest way to remove the stop moulding of a window.

the space between the wood and the wall with another prybar or a wood shingle, and then pry at the exposed nail until a second nail is visible. Continue prying in this manner down the length of the board, working at the nailed spots only, until the trim is free of the wall. Once the whole board has been pried out and is suspended by a few nails, you can usually tug it away from the wall by hand.

Very soft trim woods can show marks from the prybar even if you're careful. Use two wide putty knives, one to protect the wall and the other to protect the trim. Insert them at the edge of a board and tap them in until a gap is opened. Then slide the prybar between them and continue prying in the normal manner.

Sometimes you have to separate two mouldings from each other; for instance, when you're removing the stop moulding from a window. Use two prybars next to each other and work them in opposite directions. (The handles can face the same way or in opposite directions—whichever works better.) Opposing prybars exert a lot of force, so work carefully. The inside window sill, or stool, is the first board the carpenter installed. You'll have to pry off the casings above it and the apron below it before removing it.

In most cases, the nails holding the woodwork will be small-headed finishing nails. They'll either pull through the trim and remain in the wall, or come away with the

After you've freed the corner, hold the gap open with another prybar and continue prying at the next nail.

the trim and remain in the wall, or come away with the trim. To remove any finishing nails still in the wood, take a nail puller or pliers and pull them out from the back—never hammer them through the front of the board. The nailheads were originally set below the surface and filled with putty; knocking them through the front can dislodge the putty and splinter the wood around it.

If you're unlucky, your trim was secured with large-headed common nails. Pry the moulding about 1/4 inch away from the wall, as described above. Then, with a wood block, tap the moulding back against the wall. The offending nailheads will protrude enough for you to either remove the nails with your prybar, using a wood shingle or putty knife under the prybar to protect the moulding, or cut the heads off the nails with your wire cutters. If the nails are thin enough, use the second method and avoid further prying.

Cut any remaining common nails in the removed wood with heavy wire cutters close to the back of the board. Then file down any protrusions of the nails, so they don't scratch the other pieces when you bundle up all the woodwork.

The best way to remove nails is by pulling them out from the back of the board with pullers or pliers.

For wood that splits easily, such as old redwood casements, you may want to use a hacksaw blade to cut off nails behind the trim. This reduces the strain on the wood. Use a sheet of coke-tin (or a flattened tin can) to protect walls or other nearby woodwork. Stanley and others make a handy handle-gadget for use with hacksaw blades, but in a pinch you can make a handle by wrapping friction-tape around the hacksaw. You'll get the best cutting motion on the pull stroke.

After you remove all the trim, prepare the pieces for temporary storage. Number each one on the backside, and note its location on a map of the room. Carve or stamp the numbers into the wood (pencil or ink marks will disappear with paint remover or light sanding). Then tie the complete set of mouldings for, say, a window and label it.

Reinstalling trim is much like fitting brand-new trim. To do so, you will need:

- Hammer (12-ounce clawhammer preferred)
- Handsaw (backsaw or dovetail saw preferred)
- 12-inch combination square
- Ruler (Rulers are more accurate than tape measures)
- Coping saw
- Nailset
- White or yellow glue, wood putty, and sandpaper for final touch-ups

To reinstall a piece of trim, tack it in place temporarily with two finishing nails partially hammered in. If it fits, nail the board back in place with finishing nails. To avoid putting more holes into the woodwork, nail through the existing nailholes, but at an angle so the nail goes into new wood. (If the trim piece is less than 5/8-inch thick, nail in new positions.) Hammer the nail until it's one or two blows from being flush with the wood, then set the nail about 1/8 inch below the surface with your nailset. Fill the holes with putty, and wipe the patches clean with a rag, or sand them as necessary.

To avoid splitting the wood, never nail closer than 2 inches from any board ends. If you're working with delicate or thin strips, blunt the nails on a hard surface or snip the tips before using them. This causes them to act more like a punch than a wedge when they penetrate the wood. With hardwoods such as oak, prevent splitting by drilling

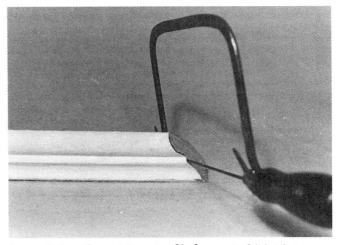

One technique for making a profile for a coped joint is to cut the piece in a miter box. Then saw along the edge, undercutting slightly so the cut will match the contour of the trim.

Another technique is to set a compass to the width of the lumber, butt the boards at a right angle, and draw a compass along the joint so it scribes the profile of the board.

Then you cut along the line, and . . .

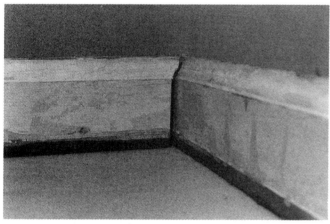

. . . the finished profile is identical to the trim.

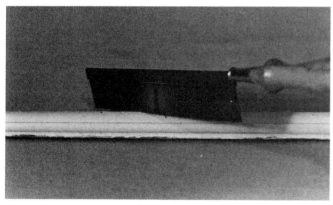

The "Mirror-Saw" Trick: Pivot the saw on the trim until the reflection in the blade is 90 degrees to the board being cut.

pilot holes for the nails. Use a drill bit with a diameter slightly smaller than that of the nails.

Bring mitered corners that have been pulled apart by warping or shrinking wood closer together by undercutting with a saw on the hidden side of the miter on one or both of the mating boards. If the crack is still objectionable, fill it with putty or caulk if the wood will be painted. If you'll be applying a clear finish, use linseed-oil putty tinted with stain or oil colors, or white glue mixed with sawdust.

Replacing Short Moulding Sections

If you don't have all your original moulding, you'll have to install pieces that aren't premeasured and precut. When mitering trim around "picture frame" enclosures such as windows, doors, or raised-panel wall mouldings, make measurements for length to the "short point," or inside edge, of the rectangle; that is, to the points that will be on the short sides of the trim board when the miter is cut. Cuts measured this way produce neat joints and accurate lengths. Measure, cut, and fit one miter at a time. For greater accuracy when cutting trim, mark your boards with a knife rather than a pencil. You can line up your saw more accurately with this sharper line. And, of course, remember to cut on the waste side of the line.

There are two techniques for making a profile for a coped joint. The first, which works best with smaller mouldings, is to initially cut the piece to the correct length in a miter box. The sawn edge along the moulded surface then becomes the profile to be cut with a coping saw. When making this cut, undercut slightly to assure a tight joint.

The second technique, which is usually used on larger lumber such as baseboards, is to scribe the profile. The board to be coped is butted at 90 degrees against the board with which it will mate. A compass or pair of dividers, set to the thickness of the board, is then drawn up along the inside of the corner, so that it draws the profile of one board onto the other. This line is then cut with the coping saw.

Coping is also necessary when ending a window apron or a milled chair rail. In most cases, the trim stops without meeting another board, so it should have the profile returned for a finished look. Cope the ends to make a moulded edge that matches the front. An alternate method is to miter the board and return the profile with another small mitered piece glued on the edge. Both techniques produce nice results.

If you have to make a ceiling moulding, baseboard, or similar long piece of trim from two or more pieces of wood, join them in a scarf joint rather than butt them. This joint is made with two matching 45-degree miters. Position it on a wall stud for good nailing. The scarf joint is much less obtrusive than a butt joint in the finished job, and resists shifting when the house settles.

A clever way to miter a 45-degree angle without the benefit of a square or miter box is the "mirror-saw trick." It works best on small mouldings such as 5/8-inch (or smaller) cove or quarter-round. And it's fine where absolute precision is unnecessary, such as for woodwork that will be filled and painted. (Don't try it on very deep or wide pieces because the saw may wander.)

All you need is a shiny saw blade, so you can see the reflection of the piece being cut. Most people can't "eyeball" a precise 45-degree angle, but almost anyone can recognize an accurate right angle. A right angle is what you see in the saw blade when it's set at 45 degrees. Set the saw at the proper length on the moulding and then pivot it on this point until a right angle is formed by the moulding itself and its reflection in the saw. Then cut. When measured afterward, it turns out the cut is exactly 45 degrees—or certainly close enough. Works every time!

WOODWORK REPAIRS

Old woodwork always needs fixing before you can refinish it successfully. After stripping and before refinishing, check the woodwork for open joints, cracks and checks, warpage, damaged veneer, mismatched or missing pieces, scratches and gouges, and stains. Follow these guidelines for remedying these common woodwork problems.

Open Joints

Each time woodwork is painted, paint fills in the joints. When the wood expands and contracts, the joints open up again. After you strip a panel door or wainscot that had a dozen coats of paint on it, you might find gaps of up to a quarter of an inch between the moulding and the panel. If possible, the best solution involves removing and replacing the moulding. Follow the instructions on pages 306–310 for removing moulding and heat- or chemically-strip or scrape down the backside of the piece with a chisel. To ensure a crisp, tight joint, do not gouge or mar the mating surfaces. Renail as illustrated.

If you can't remove and reinstall the woodwork, you

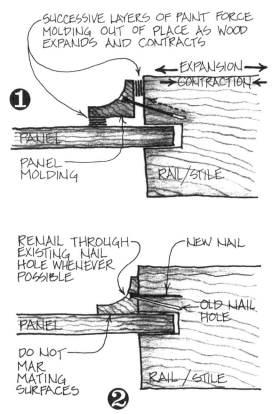

1. *After stripping paint, you may find gaps of up to 1/4 inch between moulding and the panel.*
2. *Renail through old nailholes to close the joint.*

may be able to *fill* the joints and paint them out. This is not the best solution with wood-to-wood joints as matching the color of clear-finished wood is difficult. But this technique may work for woodwork-to-plaster joints.

Occasionally, you may have to leave the hardened paint in a woodwork joint, filling voids with a resilient wood filler. Let's take a section of panel wainscot as an example. There are open joints at the miters in the panel moulding, and open joints between the moulding and the rail or stile. Paint buildup between the moulding and rail or stile causes the moulding to bulge; the miters gap from paint buildup as well. Closing one joint further opens the other.

Instead of discarding and replacing the mouldings, try a combination of closing some joints and filling others. You can't close the joints between the mouldings and rail or stile *and* close the miter joints. Decide which joint would look less noticeable with a matched filler in it. If the moulding-to-rail (or stile) joint is in deep shadow because it's recessed, make this the filled joint. Maybe both joints should be left just slightly open and both slightly filled. At the very least, refasten the mouldings so they're not bulging.

Use resilient wood filler in these joints, matching the color of the filler as closely as possible to the wood. It's better to err on the dark side than on the light side; the joint is in shadow, and a slightly darker color is less noticeable than a lighter color. After filling, use artist's colors to "paint out" whatever traces of old paint remain. Get out all the paint you can, though; it doesn't accommodate expansion and contraction as well as resilient filler.

Cracks and Checks

Cracks and checks from uneven shrinkage occur most often in wide pieces of solid wood (such as panels) or in large, glued-up pieces (such as newel posts). Cracks and splits may also be the result of impact damage or improperly placed fasteners. Repairs can sometimes be made in place; more often the piece must be removed for clamping.

Short, wide, jagged checks are difficult to actually close and repair. It may be easier to clean the paint out of the check and fill it. Use commercially available wood fillers or make up your own of white glue mixed with sawdust from matching wood.

Long cracks resulting from impact or a fastener being driven too close to the end of the piece of wood can be stripped of paint and debris, glued, and clamped closed. Casings and miscellaneous trim can usually be glued in place. But panels should be removed; start by carefully prying off the panel mouldings. Before regluing any splits, make sure the joint can be forced back together, remove any obstructing fasteners, and clean all old glue and paint off the joint. White or yellow carpenter's glue is fine for this repair. Preparing and clamping the joint is more important than what glue you use.

Force the joint apart slightly to get the glue in. Use a glue syringe if necessary. Close and open the joint a few

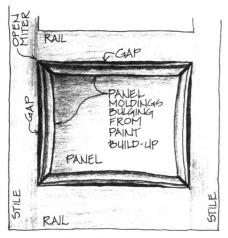

A section of panel wainscot with open joints at the miters in the panel moulding.

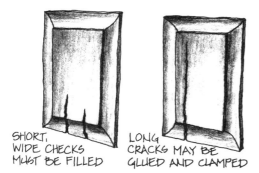

SHORT, WIDE CHECKS MUST BE FILLED

LONG CRACKS MAY BE GLUED AND CLAMPED

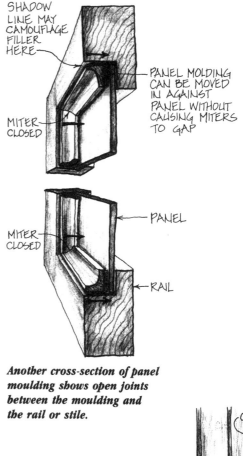

Another cross-section of panel moulding shows open joints between the moulding and the rail or stile.

Repairing a crack with a dutchman. Trim the shim with a chisel and sand it flush when the glue dries.

times to spread the glue around. Clamp the joint closed using as many clamps as required; don't skimp on clamps. Use blocks of wood (cauls) under the clamps to protect the wood from marring, and clean up all excess glue with a damp cloth. Glue left on the face of the wood will show up as whitish stain through the finish. Casing, jambs, rails, and stiles can usually be glued and clamped in place, but a recessed panel should be removed for repair. Because it's a broad, flat area, it's very visible; repair with extra care.

Sometimes it's impossible to clamp a piece of woodwork in place, and it's also impossible to remove it. Wedge, tape, and/or weight the piece in place while the glue dries; the strength of the joint depends on it. Give the glue time to set before removing the clamps, especially if there is a lot of stress on the joint (such as a split or check that took great clamp pressure to close). Overnight is best.

In frame-and-panel construction, the panel "floats" to allow for seasonal swelling and shrinkage of wood. If you make a mistake of gluing or nailing the panel itself in place, it will probably crack with the next change of season. The panel *moulding* holds the panel in place, covering the joints, and still allows it to move freely.

For finer cabinetwork or woodwork, use a wood patch or dutchman when a split can't be closed up. Use wood of the same age, species, and grain orientation. Using only that portion of the tapered shim that fits the split exactly, coat both the shim and the split with a thin layer of glue and press the shim into place. Clean off excess glue with

a damp cloth. Leave the shim a little proud of the surface so that it can be trimmed with a sharp chisel and sanded flush after the glue dries. When done properly, the patch will be nearly invisible.

Warpage

A few well-placed fasteners will usually bring bowed or twisted architectural woodwork back in line. Make sure there is something solid to nail to before driving any fasteners.

Toeing the nails will make them hold better. A large, heavy profile moulding might resist straightening if only nails are used. Use one or two wood screws. Carefully predrill and countersink the screw in a location where you're sure there's good fastening. Plug the hole with a wood plug cut from the same species and grain orientation. A plug cutter is an inexpensive item available from most well-stocked hardware stores.

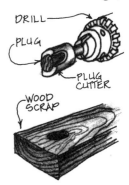

Warped or cupped panels can't be nailed back in place. Remove the panel and place it on a warm radiator, concave side up. Put some damp rags on the panel and leave it for a few days. Weight down edges if necessary. Another solution is to lay the panel cupped side down on damp ground in bright sunlight and weight the center.

Damaged Veneer

Doors and other paneled woodwork are often veneered. Sometimes even door and window casings are veneered. A burled section is usually a clue that a veneer is present. Even the best veneer can blister and delaminate, especially when exposed to moisture. Loose or blistered veneer can be reglued easily; damaged sections can be replaced.

To reglue: Splice open a blister parallel to the grain. Work some white carpenter's glue under the veneer with a flexible knife, press the blister flat, clean up excess glue, and weight or clamp the piece until the glue sets. Be sure to separate your cauls or weights from the veneer with a sheet of wax paper so they don't get glued to the veneer.

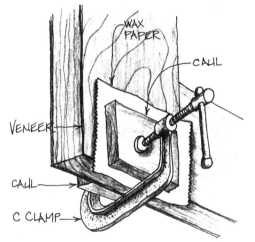

To reglue veneer edges, first pry up the loose part slightly with a putty knife. Check exactly how much is loose and remove all the old glue, along with any paint or finish that might have seeped under the veneer. Reglue the veneer as described above.

To patch: If a section of veneer is badly gouged or missing, cut out the bad section and replace it with new or salvaged veneer. If there are no spare doors or other woodwork with matching veneer, consider taking some veneer off an inconspicuous area such as the back of a closet door. Try to match the color and grain figure. Cut out the new or salvaged piece first. (Try moisture, heat, or a combination to loosen the veneer.) Do not cut out a neat rectangle or other regular shape as this will only accentuate the patch. Instead, cut in an irregular shape that approximately follows the grain figure. Use a straightedge to make a series of short, straight-line cuts. Using the patch piece as a template, trace the shape onto the area to be patched and cut out the damaged area. Cut out the damaged veneer carefully. If you make a neat cut, you'll have no filling to do after patching in the new piece. Glue

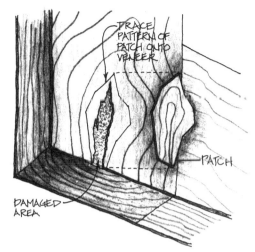

the patch in place as described above. Sand to flush as required.

Scratches, Gouges, and Dents

Tackle these problems after completing the more major repairs described above, and just before putting on the new finish.

Sanding scratches. A scratch is a defect that can be sanded out, whereas a gouge must be filled or the piece it's in replaced. When sanding out a small scratch, be aware that the sanded area will end up looking lighter than the surrounding area because the patina or aged color of the wood is being removed. Selective staining can be done on this spot to blend the color. Also be aware of whether what you're sanding is solid wood or veneer. It doesn't take much to sand right through veneer.

Filling gouges. A gouge may be filled with a number of different products. For such minor imperfections as small gouges and nailholes, linseed putty or glazing compound can be tinted with universal tints or with the sediment from the bottom of a can of stain. For larger areas where a level surface is essential, a sandable filler should be used. There are several categories of sandable fillers.

Water-mix wood putty comes in powder form and is mixed with water, as the name states. It is easiest to tint by mixing powder pigment with the putty when it's still a powder. It has a fair amount of resiliency but poor moisture resistance.

Solvent-based wood fillers (such as Plastic Wood) harden by solvent evaporation. These are a little more difficult to sand than other fillers, and they require solvent instead of water for cleanup. Adhesion and moisture resistance are good, but shrinkage is a problem. You can overcome some of the drawbacks associated with shrinking by building up deep areas in several layers. Solvent-based fillers are not tintable, but they do come in a variety of premixed colors. As with any filling or staining task, test on a scrap piece first.

Acrylic latex wood fillers (such as Elmer's Professional Wood Filler) have been developed recently. This type of filler has better adhesion, moisture resistance, and flexibility than water-mix wood putty. Again, deep voids should be filled with several applications to avoid excessive shrinkage.

Two-part polyester fillers such as Minwax High Performance Filler are similar to auto-body filler. The Minwax filler has excellent adherence, is moisture resistant, exhibits minimal shrinkage, and takes stain well. But because it's a two-part filler, it's a bit more time-consuming to mix.

Lifting dents. Unlike a scratch or gouge, the wood fibers in a dent are not torn or missing; they have just been compressed. More often than not, a dent can be lifted out using a steam iron and a moistened cloth. You'll have more success lifting a dent out of softwood than out of hardwood. The moisture will, of course, lift the grain slightly, but once the wood dries, the area can easily be sanded smooth again.

Stains and Discolorations

Many stains are impossible to remove entirely. But they can be considerably lightened. Water stains are the most common. These are usually dark gray and show up strongly even through the darkest pigmented stain you'd consider applying to wood. Discoloration is commonly found where a partition or other element that had been abutting a piece of woodwork was removed. The wood that had been covered will have aged a little differently, creating a slightly different color patina. This also happens where some portions of the wood have had a finish and others have not. If additional applications of chemical stripper don't lighten a stain, the next step is to bleach the area. There are several different products with which you should experiment when faced with the task of bleaching out discolorations.

Use household bleach to lighten water stains. Make a poultice with paper towels to keep the bleach working on the stain rather than spreading to the surrounding area. Rinse with plenty of clear water, allow to dry, and sand smooth.

Oxalic acid comes in crystal form and is available from most hardware stores and pharmacies. The crystals are dissolved in warm water to form a saturate solution. Keep adding water until there are just a few crystals still undissolved on the bottom of your container. Now you have the strongest possible solution. Rinse with clear water after applying the acid. Oxalic acid will lighten water stains, but it will also take most of the color out of the wood, making it difficult to blend the bleached area back into the surrounding woodwork. Unless you are especially adept at blending and controlling wood stains in small patches, it's advisable to bleach an entire surface and then use stain to bring it to a consistent color.

A & B or two-part wood bleach is normally available at a well-stocked hardware store. This type of bleach is used to achieve a consistent color tone in the wood. The A part is the bleach, the B part is the neutralizer that stops the bleaching action. The longer the bleach is left on, the lighter the wood gets. A & B bleach is suitable for blend-

---

CHOOSING THE RIGHT FILLER

Before finishing, many woods will need to be filled. You'll need a filler for open grain, "large-pored" woods such as oak, mahogany, and ash. Without filling with a paste wood filler, a smooth finish will be difficult to achieve. Generally, filling should not be done if you'll be using an oil finish. Sometimes renewed old wood doesn't need filling the way brand-new, unfinished wood does. Test in an inconspicuous place.

Use *paste wood filler* before varnishing but not with penetrating oil finishes. It packs the small, exposed cell structure of open-grain wood in such a way that finish varnish flows over the surface. Be sure to read the label: Some paste wood fillers are supposed to be applied after the stain; others, prior to staining. Generally, we recommend choosing a product that is used prior to staining, as this avoids the grayness that occurs in certain woods. Paste wood fillers also come in many colors. In making a selection, you should try to approximate the basic color of the wood. This stuff is not intended for use as a crack filler.

Putty is best for filling nailholes, and is used after staining and sealing. Use it last if you're doing an oil finish. Use it after the first coat of varnish but before the last coat. If you use it before the finish is applied, you may stain the wood. There are two basic types of putty:

1. Nonhardening oil-based: This kind is tinted to the final color by the user. It is the same as the putty used for glazing windows. In a pinch, synthetic glazing compounds work as well.
2. Waxy fill sticks: These are crayonlike sticks that come pretinted to the final color.

Plastic wood is a hard-drying cellulose compound used to fill larger voids. While often sold to fill nailholes as well, it is not nearly as good as the softer putties.

---

ing wood with uneven patina as described above. Use the bleach on the selected areas that need lightening. Some stain blending may be required to blend the bleached area with the rest of the wood.

STAINS AND FINISHES

Once you've stripped and repaired woodwork, you may be overwhelmed by the number of sealers, stains, dyes, shellacs, lacquers, waxes, oils, and varnishes. Of course, before finishing open-grain woods, you should use a filler. Woods such as pine, fir, hemlock, and maple (close-grain woods) have a smooth texture and need not be filled. Old, previously finished wood that has been stripped probably won't need prime-sealer either. New wood or heavily sanded old wood should be "sealed" prior to staining or finishing.

The word "sealer" is somewhat misleading. In the context of priming surfaces, these products should not be confused with finishing compounds such as penetrating

Stain Removal & Bleaching Flow Chart

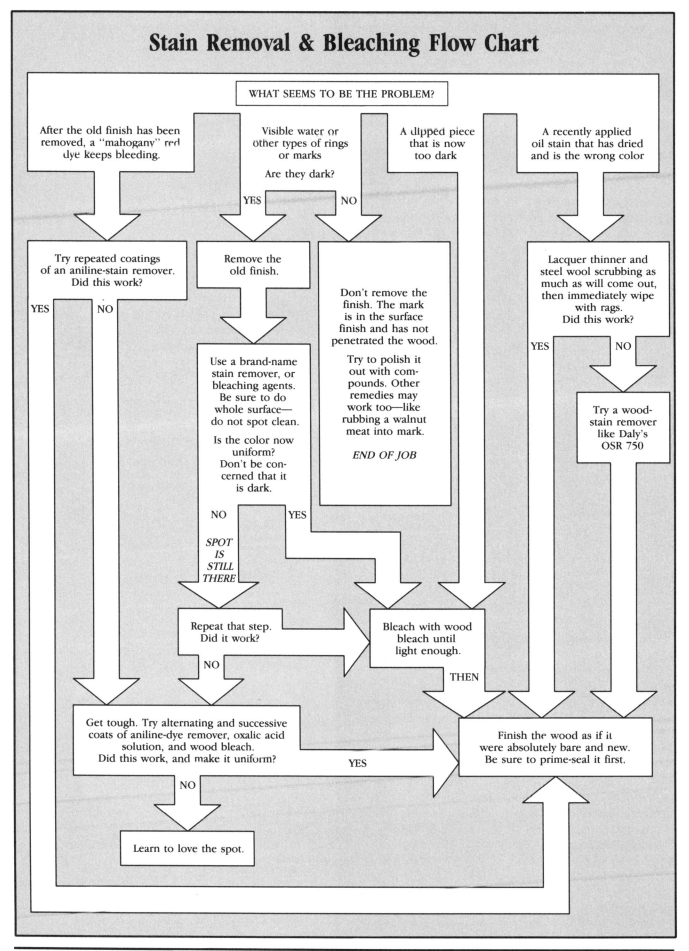

WHAT SEEMS TO BE THE PROBLEM?

After the old finish has been removed, a "mahogany" red dye keeps bleeding.

Visible water or other types of rings or marks

Are they dark?

YES   NO

A dipped piece that is now too dark

A recently applied oil stain that has dried and is the wrong color

Try repeated coatings of an aniline-stain remover. Did this work?

YES   NO

Remove the old finish.

Don't remove the finish. The mark is in the surface finish and has not penetrated the wood.

Try to polish it out with compounds. Other remedies may work too—like rubbing a walnut meat into mark.

END OF JOB

Lacquer thinner and steel wool scrubbing as much as will come out, then immediately wipe with rags. Did this work?

YES   NO

Use a brand-name stain remover, or bleaching agents. Be sure to do whole surface— do not spot clean.

Is the color now uniform? Don't be concerned that it is dark.

NO   YES

SPOT IS STILL THERE

Try a wood-stain remover like Daly's OSR 750

Repeat that step. Did it work?

NO

Bleach with wood bleach until light enough.

THEN

Get tough. Try alternating and successive coats of aniline-dye remover, oxalic acid solution, and wood bleach. Did this work, and make it uniform?

YES

NO

Finish the wood as if it were absolutely bare and new. Be sure to prime-seal it first.

Learn to love the spot.

oil finishes, which actually "seal" the surface with a coating. What these products do instead is set the wood grain prior to the application of stains or finish coats. Without priming, the final result can be rough and uneven (especially when bare or sanded wood is stained). Without the prime-sealer, dark, spotty areas can appear where wild-grain areas absorb more stain or finish than the rest of the wood.

Stains

There are two general types of interior stains: surface and penetrating. Surface types come in either a brushable varnish base, or a spray lacquer. Both surface types are hard to handle when working on fine pieces, so this discussion will center on the penetrating types, which can be applied with a rag.

Penetrating stains are available in two types:

1. Pigment. The major advantage of this type is that it is colorfast and easier to wipe.

2. Dye. This type has excellent color depth and brilliance, but sun-fades badly. Dye stain is available in both a water-soluble (sometimes alcohol) and an oil-soluble base, both of which are non-grain-raising. Because of their depth of color, dye stains are often used in advance of a pigment stain as a precolor and then treated with the pigment type for colorfastness and durability. In most instances, dye stains are best finished with a varnish system.

Finishes

Interior finishes are also divided in two major categories: penetrating and surface. Penetrating finishes are usually dull or satin; surface finishes, gloss or semigloss. Surface finishes include lacquers, shellac, and varnishes.

Penetrating finishes come in two types:

1. Wax. Because waxes remain very light in color over a long period of time, they are excellent for paneling. They're also useful as a final polish to varnished wood. However, waxes tend to waterspot, and so require maintenance. Waxes will also build up if too many thick coats are applied—especially spray waxes. Avoid these; beeswax too, which is quite soft, fingerprints badly, is not necessarily water-resistant, and builds quickly to a sticky surface.

2. Drying oil finishes. Usually tung and linseed oil-based, these finishes are easy to apply. (There are no brush marks or dust to contend with; just rag on and wipe off the excess.) They have excellent wear characteristics and can be renewed easily. They also tone unstained woods. We don't suggest using straight linseed oil, however. It will darken with age and offers no resistance to alcohol, water, or mildew. It's also very slow to dry and tends to be sticky.

Surface finishes are available in three types:

1. Lacquers. The one advantage of lacquer is that it's fast-drying. However, it isn't recommended for amateurs.

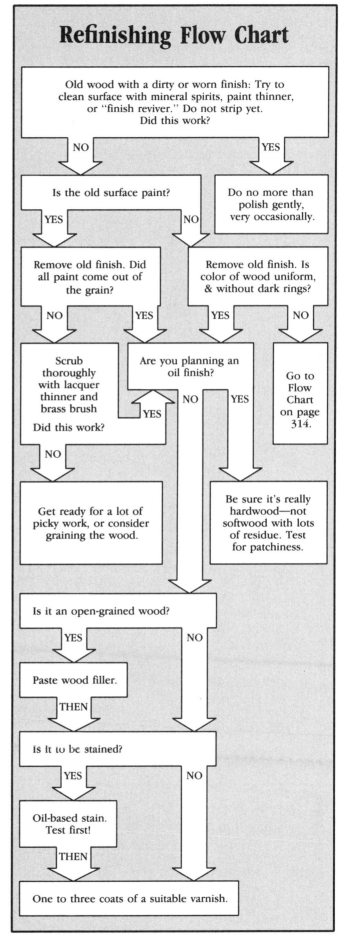

There are some good brushable lacquers that can be successfully applied by a novice, but there are still drawbacks. Most lacquers have poor resistance to water and grease, and tend to be thin and brittle.

2. Shellac—found on very old furniture and some hardwood floors and woodwork—will discolor with age, is quite brittle, has little resistance to water, alcohol, and abrasion, and is very scratch prone. So in areas where you want high wear-resistance, it is not an alternative to slower-drying varnishes. However, shellac is easier to remove than other finishes. And it may be used when you wish to duplicate an older finish for the purpose of color-matching, but then apply a standard oil-based varnish for maximum wear. (Do not use a urethane varnish over shellac; they are not compatible.)

3. Varnishes:

- Plastic varnish—called polyurethane or just urethane. These are very hard and very useful on new interior work such as cabinets and children's furniture. They are fairly fast-drying and harden quickly. But urethanes may not bond well to older surfaces, especially if the older surface was shellacked. If the item has an older shellac job, and you plan to use varnish, then don't use urethane; use a standard oil-based varnish instead.

  Urethanes do not do well on areas exposed to weather, especially direct sunlight. Thus they should never be used on front doors, exterior smooth siding, window trim, railing, or marine surfaces. The proper treatment for varnishing exterior surfaces is to use a standard marine spar. But don't use a spar varnish on interior items because the product is too soft and slow-drying.

- Nonplastic varnishes, although softer and slightly slower to harden than the urethanes, will bond to most surfaces and are available in a wide variety of products to answer almost every need (floors, paneling, etc.). Should you decide not to use a penetrating oil finish, then this type of varnish should be used on antique wood items.

- Water-based varnishes don't harden well enough and tend to feel sticky. They don't level well either, so brush marks show up even more than they do with traditional varnishes. Their best feature is that they hold color well with little yellowing, and so would be good for paneling.

THE HAND-RUBBED FINISH

There's no comparison to the silky smooth, rich luster achieved from basic hand-rubbed finishing techniques. With the right materials and techniques, you can rub out a finish to a dull luster or a super gloss. Hand rubbing is a labor-intensive refinishing method best suited for fine woodwork. It's especially appropriate for pieces that have broad, flat surfaces that exaggerate minor imperfections in the finish.

Rubbing is like sanding in that you create finer and finer scratches going with the wood grain until you've arrived at the finish you want. Each time you rub the finish, you remove ever-finer imperfections. When we speak of gloss, we're talking about smoothness as well as reflectivity. A thick coat of polyurethane hastily applied in a dusty room will reflect a lot of light, but close inspection will reveal bumps, bubbles, bristles and brush marks.

Each coat applied in a hand-rubbed finish is sanded, or "rubbed," until it is smooth and level, eliminating brushmarks, pimples, and debris. The abrasives should be fine enough so that the scratches do not show through the next coat of finish. Successive coats are applied and rubbed down until a sufficient thickness is built-up (three to six coats is typical). The final coat is leveled and then rubbed with pumice or rottenstone and oil to achieve the desired gloss.

Preparing the Surface

Smooth surfaces produce smooth finishes. Paste wood fillers, such as Behlen's Por-O-Lac, help you produce smooth-as-glass finishes on open-pored woods like oak, ash, and mahogany. (Don't confuse fine wood fillers with wood putties and doughs.) Tinted fillers are mixed to the consistency of cream and brushed into the bare wood pores. Burnish off the excess by rubbing across the grain. Then sand smooth with #220 grit or finer abrasive paper. Allow to dry for forty-eight hours before finishing.

Don't make more work for yourself by starting with a coarser grade of paper than necessary. Use a sanding block to avoid creating wavy surfaces and rounded edges. Don't rely too heavily on fillers, stains, and top coats to hide sanding irregularities.

Practically any gloss varnish, lacquer, shellac, or enamel can be rubbed down to get the surface sheen you want. It's best to select a product specifically designed for rubbing. (Behlen's 4 Hour Rubbing Varnish, McClusky's Hour Varnish, and McClusky's Bar Top Varnish are three examples.)

Apply the finish carefully. No matter what material you choose to apply, how fine your brush is, or how well you dust the surface, there's bound to be some imperfections in the finish. Neat work habits and careful application will minimize these nuisances. Don't do this work while any demolition or construction is going on—you want the environment to be as dust-free as possible. As for the remaining imperfections: Rub them out!

You can quickly achieve a relatively smooth finished surface by avoiding between-coats rubbing. Apply a minimum of three coats of varnish and allow each to dry hard (some varnishes may take forty-eight hours or more to dry completely). Then, rub out the top layer only.

Don't use this abbreviated method on an especially fine piece, though. Building up coats with no intermediate rubbing may trap hard, sharp grit in the finish coats. Rubbing the top coat may cause this foreign material to pull out of the finish, imparting deep scratches. If you do use this method (for less-than-outstanding woodwork),

A thick cork block makes an excellent applicator for wood filler. It forces the filler deep into open pores and doesn't pull it out on the backstroke.

A sanding block ensures even rubbing during the initial wet-sanding stage. Here, the refinisher is using mineral spirits and fine wet-or-dry sandpaper. Mineral spirits won't raise the grain and clean the paper better than water. Grocery store baking tins make a convenient container for the lubricant.

keep one thing in mind: The cleaner your equipment and environment, the better the results.

If the quality of the final finish is very important, you may wish to lightly sand out each coat of varnish (after the second one). Be sure each coat is completely dry before applying another. Expert wood finishers use this technique to build one layer on top of another, producing flawlessly smooth finishes. Each sanding removes the dust and other surface irregularities that settle into the varnish as it dries. For the greatest depth and luster, apply four or more coats of varnish and lightly sand before rubbing. Highly visible or heavily used surfaces may need more coats than less noticeable areas.

Sanding the Initial Coats

Most traditional hand-rubbed finishes are initially smoothed out with garnet, silicon carbide, or aluminum oxide wet-or-dry sandpaper and oil to produce a dull matte finish.

Rub lightly with dry #220 or finer sandpaper on the first primer/sealer coat. For subsequent coats, try #280 or #320 with oil. For top coats that are fairly smooth, start with #400 wet-or-dry sandpaper and move up to #600. Dip the sandpaper into oil periodically. Between-coat sanding with oil will leave a residue. Clean up with benzine before applying the next coat. As you would with any toxic substance, wear gloves and a mask when working with benzine.

Sanding grit can't be rubbed out of a varnished surface without damaging the finish, so be careful to remove all the grit before you apply the next coat. Keep the paper clean (if you drop it on the floor, get another piece).

You might try using a newly developed 1200-grit wet-or-dry sandpaper. On smooth surfaces you can produce practically the same quality of rubbed finish as that obtained with pumice. These super-fine sandpapers are available from woodwork supply dealers.

You can use water as the lubricant on varnish, enamel, and lacquer, but water will damage shellac finishes. The process is the same as with oil rubbing. The paper will cut into and remove the finish faster with water, so be careful. Use a damp chamois for cleanup and drying. Don't let water stand on the finish.

Stainless steel or bronze wool are also good for rubbing down finishes, provided you use the right grade. (Regular steel wool may leave splinters that will rust under

THE VARNISH BRUSH

Fine brushes are the best buy; there is no economy in cheap or neglected brushes. For lacquer, varnish, shellac, or enamel, soft hair brushes such as fitch, ox, or badger are best. Don't use your varnish brush for other coatings—dried pieces of paint will contaminate your finish.

Keep your brushes clean. To reduce the chances of getting loose bristles in your work, before you start you should gently tap the brush against the palm of your hand (never hit it against a hard surface—you'll ruin the bristle setting). Twirl the brush rapidly back and forth between your palms, and vigorously run your fingers through it several times. Work clean varnish into the brush by dipping and wiping off a few times.

Break in a varnish brush by using it for undercoats only. Never use your brush sideways or poke and jab with it. If you're doing a lot of varnishing, store the brush, fully submerged, in a container of clean exterior spar varnish. Keep the brush suspended in the varnish (with a wire or rod)—never allow the bristles to touch the bottom of the container. Keep the container tightly sealed.

When your project is complete, clean your brush immediately. Wipe out the excess varnish, then work the bristles while submerged in benzine. Follow with a washing in turpentine. Clean shellac brushes in denatured alcohol, and lacquer brushes in lacquer thinner. Shake or gently squeeze out excess solvent and allow the brush to dry. Fold blotter or brown wrapping paper over the ends of the bristles to maintain shape during storage.

the new finish and discolor the piece.) Grades 2/0 (00) and 3/0 are a good choice for a satin finish; 4/0 will add more sheen. Don't use coarser grades; they'll scratch the wood. Steel wool can be rubbed dry or used with a light mineral oil to soften the cutting action and reduce dust particles. Always rub with the grain. Steel wool pads disintegrate fairly quickly and have to be turned over periodically to expose fresh cutting fibers.

Rubbing with Pumice and Rottenstone

Pumice is produced by grinding volcanic ash into various grades of coarseness. Pumice powder is a white, fine-grain, hard abrasive that resembles flour.

Pumice is ideal for amateur use because it cuts the finish slowly. It can be used alone or with rottenstone, depending on the finish you want. Rottenstone (also known as tripoli powder) is a very fine, ash-gray abrasive that comes in only one grade. Pumice is used first because it's coarser. Think of rottenstone as a final polishing agent

Apply the pumice evenly over the entire surface. Try to put on enough pumice to do the whole area at once. Adding more may produce dull spots in the finish.

Oil and pumice are being rubbed across the finish with a dense felt rubbing block. Blocks like this one make it easy to apply uniform rubbing pressure.

Don't shake, stir, or strain varnish: You'll create air bubbles that will mar the finish. Dip the brush into the varnish about two-thirds of the bristle length. Gently tap off the excess on the inside of the container. With a little practice, you'll develop a feel for loading the brush with just enough varnish to avoid drips.

Flow on the finish slowly and smoothly in the direction of the grain. Avoid flexing the brush. After laying on each brushload, go back and cross-brush it into the surface. Finish off with a final smoothing using only the tips of the bristles. Overlap and repeat this process in the next area.

Complete one section at a time with a uniform coat. Use breaks in the surface, such as seams, edges, and mouldings, as starting and stopping points. Look for drips, sags, and runs as soon as you finish each section. Use raking light to spot "holidays" (skipped places). Carefully brush out "fatty runners" (varnish that collects along edges). Avoid fat edges by applying the finish first at the center and working toward the edges. Before the finish begins to set up, give the entire surface a final brushing with a fairly dry brush using long, light strokes extending past the edges.

to be used where you want super gloss. Both of these abrasives are inexpensive. You can find them at most paint and hardware stores, but don't be surprised if they're on a dusty back shelf, and nobody in the place knows what they're used for. For small projects, one-half pound may be all you'll need.

Although pumice is available in solid bricks, powder is most useful for rubbing finishes. It's available in coarse (1F), medium (2F), fine (3F), and extra fine (4F). For most jobs the 2F to 4F grades are adequate. Some stores sell pumice in medium and fine grades only. Try the fine grade first. Take great care to keep foreign matter out of the powders (sift the abrasives before use).

Lubricants must be used with pumice stone and rottenstone, or else the heat generated by rubbing friction will damage the finish. To repeat, water can be used on varnish, lacquer, and enamel finishes, but will cloud watersensitive shellac. Water and pumice cut a finish down very quickly, so work carefully. Adding a little soap to the water helps slow the cutting action of the pumice, giving you greater control. Unlike oil, water won't leave behind a residue.

Oil is a good lubricant for use on all finishes. It's especially suited for intricate decorations where it's very easy to rub through the finish. Paraffin oil (a clear mineral oil with wax content) is the most commonly used and the easiest to find. It can cause some finishes to cloud or turn white, so test in an inconspicuous location first.

Other good mineral oil lubricants include white neutra oil (the stuff used in lemon-oil furniture polishes) and light sewing-machine oil. Still another option is white

THE RUBBING PAD

For the smoothest finishes and fastest cutting, felt pads are best. (Old cotton rags and the like trap the abrasive in the weave.) You can make your own felt rubbing pad from an old felt hat, but for the smoothest "felting down" of a surface, buy several hard felt blocks from a woodworking supply house. The blocks or pads are made specifically for rubbing finishes. They can be ordered in thicknesses of 1/4 inch to 1/2 inch, in sizes from 3 × 5 inches to 6 × 5 inches. These dense felt blocks make it easier to apply uniform rubbing pressure and improve the cutting action of the abrasive. Cut the pads into smaller pieces for rubbing intricate mouldings and carvings.

While they work great for flat surfaces, felt blocks won't conform to rounded shapes—use a thin scrap of felt instead. For vertical surfaces like this chair spindle, dip the felt into the lubricant, then coat it with a thin layer of pumice. Again, coat with enough pumice to do the whole piece.

A natural-bristle toothbrush is ideal for intricate details.

nonblooming rubbing oil; it too is a high-grade mineral oil, but it doesn't leave behind the white film common with other oils.

Begin by sprinkling pumice and lubricant over flat horizontal surfaces. Prewet the felt pad (see "The Rubbing Pad" on this page) before you start by dipping it into lubricant. Rub back and forth with the grain. It's easier to rub one small area at a time. Overlap your strokes and the areas you work. Don't rub any more than you have to—you may cut through the finish. Check your progress often by wiping away the residue and examining the surface under a strong light.

Be careful when working near edges. The finish is thinnest here, and there's a tendency to apply more pressure. Avoid using felt rubbing pads for rounded surfaces like turnings and chair legs. The pressure of the pad on a small area will cut through the finish. Use small pieces of felt cut from an old hat instead—they're thinner and will conform to the surface.

On really intricate carvings, use a short-bristle brush to

TACK-CLOTHS

A tack-cloth picks up dust, lint, grit, and other foreign matter from whatever surface you're getting ready to finish. To make one, all you need is soft cheesecloth or clean soft linen. Avoid coarse materials, synthetics, and fabrics with hems or stitching, since they may scratch. Shake a few drops of varnish into the rag and work it around until it's completely coated—a little goes a long way. Keep working the rag until it, and your hand, are good and sticky. That's it!

Gently wipe the surface with a tack-cloth after each sanding, before the first coat of finish, and between coats. Add a little more varnish periodically to spruce it up; you'll be surprised at how much dirt it can hold! Store your tack rags in an airtight container to avoid spontaneous combustion. When you do throw them out, soak them in water first, and dispose of them out of the house.

Never use silicone-impregnated dust cloths: Once the silicone gets on a surface, finishes won't adhere.

Wolf Paints and other finish suppliers stock a wide variety of ready-made tack-cloths in every degree of tackiness. They're sold by the amount of resinous material they contain: A 50 percent tack-cloth contains resin that's equal to half the dry weight of the cloth. They're reusable and won't catch on fire. Find them at woodworking supply dealers, paint stores, and automotive paint distributors.

WOOD-FINISHING PRODUCTS AND SUPPLIERS

Epifanes USA
1218 S.W. First Avenue, Dept. OHJ
Fort Lauderdale, FL 33315
(305)467-8325
This company carries professional paintbrushes and high-quality marine finishes. They also sell Italian round, oval, and elliptical black Chinese Boarbristle paintbrushes of unusual quality.

Daly's Wood Finishing Products
3525 Stone Way North, Dept. OHJ
Seattle, WA 98103
(206)633-4200
Daly's manufactures a line of high-quality wood-finishing products including Benite Clear wood sealer for varnishes, Penlac sealer for use with lacquers, Paste Wood Filler, and others. Wood Finishing Class Notes booklet is $2 postage paid; the catalog is free.

Garrett Wade Co.
161 Avenue of the Americas, Dept. OHJ
New York, NY 10013
(212)807-1155
The Garrett Wade catalog is more like an information-packed cabinetmaker's book than a catalog of supplies. They carry all the Behlen finishing products and an excellent book selection.

Mohawk Finishing Products
Rt. 30 North, Dept. OHJ
Amsterdam, NY 12010
(518)843-1380
Behlen's—sold under the Mohawk label to consumers—has long been known as the most complete line of high-quality wood-finishing supplies.

The Woodworkers Store
21801 Industrial Boulevard, Dept. OHJ
Rogers, MN 55374
(612)428-4101
Send for their $2 catalog loaded with wood products, specialty cabinet hardware, finishing supplies, and tool books. They also carry sanding blocks, wood fillers, stains, and shellacs.

---

rub the abrasive. Keep the bristles clean. A natural-bristle toothbrush is great for small places. Dip the brush in lubricant, then into the pumice. Again, watch your progress, especially at the edges.

When all the sanding marks in the finish have been removed, clean up the residue by carefully rubbing clean with soft cloths. Fine abrasive residue will be stuck in the grain, in corners, and carvings. Clean with a stiff, fine bristle brush dampened with benzine. Follow up with a soft, benzine-moistened cloth. Wipe the entire surface to remove any oil that remains on the finish. To clean surfaces rubbed with water, soften the dry pumice residue with a damp sponge. Rub the surface in the direction of the grain with a soft chamois to remove excess water and residue.

If you wish to produce a high gloss or super-polished finish, then there's one final step. Allow the surface to dry for twenty-four hours before polishing with rottenstone. The process is identical to rubbing with pumice. Make sure the surface is clean (dust free), and use a different felt pad than was used for the pumice. When you reach the sheen you want, clean the surface, and you're ready to wax.

Rubbing compounds, developed for automotive finishes, also work well on wood finishes. Compounds come premixed, with abrasives and lubricant combined. Rubbing compound corresponds to pumice; polishing compound, to rottenstone. Both are used in exactly the same manner. Clean rubbing pads often, to prevent dried abrasive from scratching the finish.

The thickness of compounds makes them handy for vertical surfaces, but their residue is sometimes hard to remove. Compounds made specifically for woodworking come in colors that match the wood, making the residue less noticeable.

Protect your fine finish. Waxes protect the finish from wear, enhance the colors of wood, and make dusting easier. A good quality carnauba furniture wax is the only kind to consider. The more carnauba in the wax, the harder it will be, and the better the shine you'll get. Purchase a wax that dries neutral or get one that comes pretinted to match your wood. (S. W. Gibbia's book *Wood Finishing and Refinishing* [Van Nostrand Reinhold, 1981] explains how to make and tint several good paste waxes.) Avoid abrasive polishing waxes; your rubbing has eliminated the need for further polishing.

CHAPTER 17

Kitchens and Bathrooms

The needs of a modern kitchen or bathroom challenge any old-house restorer to balance practicality with historical integrity. In the kitchen, particularly, considering modern appliances, traffic, storage needs, and the need for counter space often present real design problems during restoring.

Preservation fanatics might argue that the modern kitchen or bathroom has no place in an old house. But bad design and construction appear in older work as much as in new work. So consider making changes in your kitchen and bathroom to reflect both the historical accuracy of your home and its modern usefulness.

KITCHENS

Many older kitchens were designed as work spaces for servants, not as an eat-in room for the family. In updating your kitchen, you will have to decide which features are most important to retain, and which you'll have to sacrifice for usefulness. What features are missing in your kitchen? Is there enough counter space? What about the plumbing, wiring, and appliances? You may be able to retain a period feel to your kitchen by finding period fixtures through salvage. Fifteen years ago, the stark, let-it-be-modern approach was in vogue. That was superseded by various "antiquing" approaches: kitchens with "rustic" bare brick, kitchens invaded by High Victorian parlor details. These two extremes—jarringly new vs. inauthentically old—are giving way to gentler, more sophisticated approaches that take cues from the individual house.

Here, we present some answers to the kitchen question. You won't find the gleaming white surfaces that are the current trend, but neither will you find museum-house kitchens, educational and unliveable. In designing your kitchen, remember the two Golden Rules: "Don't destroy good old work" and "To thine own style be true." Beware of fads and ask yourself: Will the kitchen still look right twenty years from now?

The Pre–1840 Kitchen

Smoke drifts out of the massive chimney in a horizontal line as the sun's first rays peek over the hills in the clear cold dawn. Inside the two-room clapboard house, Mis-

This kitchen was designed around its rebuilt chimney.

A kitchen table, rag rugs, and early furnishings recreate a nineteenth-century kitchen.

Behind the chimney, appliances are unobtrusive.

tress Brown stirs the bean porridge in a great iron pot hung from a lug pole of green beech in the cavernous fireplace. The day begins in colonial New England, centered around the hearth, that symbol of warmth and hospitality in early America.

Those of us who are restoring early homes can tastefully capture the flavor of the colonial hearth while incorporating the modern conveniences that have become a part of our lives. Though the kitchen as we know it today did not exist in pre-1840 houses, food preparation was a time-consuming and vital part of everyday life. Hence the area devoted to culinary activities was a prominent feature of most early houses.

The earliest houses throughout North America were one- or two-room affairs without a specific area devoted to food preparation. Chimney location varied widely with region and ethnicity, but we'll use a typical New England house as an example. It had a massive central chimney, on one side of which was the hall, or keeping room, where most activities took place. It was a combination kitchen, dining room, and living room. On the other side of the chimney was the parlor where the master and mistress slept and entertained on special occasions.

As houses got larger, specialized areas for kitchens were added. In New England, a shed was added to the back of the house, and the saltbox house form was created. In warmer climates, a wing or ell usually housed the kitchen. From early on, around the mid-eighteenth century, there were marked differences between urban and rural dwellings. The row houses of Boston, New York, Philadelphia, or Alexandria, Virginia, usually located the kitchen in the cellar or on the ground floor, as the main floor was often set several steps above ground level. In the deep South the kitchen was often a separate building, minimizing heat and the danger of fire.

The fireplace was, of course, the focal point of the kitchen up until about 1840, when cast-iron stoves came into common use, particularly in the Northeast. Cooking fireplaces were massive, with openings as large as five feet square and three deep. Later in the eighteenth century, they became more sophisticated, with bake ovens, iron cranes, trammels, and adjustable pothooks.

Utensils were rudimentary and few in number for the average household. Pots, trenchers, bowls, dishes, and knives and spoons were usually kept in plain view, being prized possessions, meticulously listed in will inventories (our best insight into colonial furnishings).

Furniture was sparse and portable. (Our ancestors were, like ourselves, a surprisingly nomadic lot.) Built-in cupboards were commonly restricted to areas in and around the chimney where dead space existed. Pantries usually had open shelves floor to ceiling. Cupboards, dressers, water benches or dry sinks, trestle tables, spoon racks, knife boxes, and hanging open shelves were typical furnishings of early kitchens. These can serve as the basis for creating a modern kitchen in a pre-1840 house that is both functional and visually appropriate.

There are no hard and fast rules about what the appropriate design approach to restoring a pre-1840 kitchen might be. The aim is *not* to authentically re-create a colonial kitchen (the museum approach), but to use elements of an earlier lifestyle—materials, furnishings, layout—to create the impression of this age. This doesn't mean that everything in your kitchen has to date back to before 1840. Early antiques, turn-of-the-century cupboards, and modern appliances can exist quite harmoniously together, if they're matched properly.

Early kitchens tended to be rather large rooms or spaces. They were the center of day-to-day activity, places to be lived in, the complete opposite of the small, sterile "laboratories" of the 1940s and 1950s. Try to get the space itself as closely as possible back to what it originally was, both in terms of layout and materials—floor, walls, ceiling, doors, and windows—and let this dictate how you will go about designing the kitchen to fit this space.

If you're lucky enough to have an original fireplace (often boarded up or covered over), let it serve as the focal point for the kitchen. A cast-iron wood stove, cooking or otherwise, can serve the same function and is appropriate historically. Stoves came into use in the late eighteenth century (remember Ben Franklin) and were in wide use early in the nineteenth century.

The kitchen needn't be a separate room at all. This was the situation with the early one-room and hall-parlor houses of colonial America.

You may want to use materials that would have been used when the house was built (obviously excluding appliances). This means lots of wood, plaster, and maybe brick, slate or tile, but no linoleum, laminate, or plastic. Somehow over the years the housing industry has managed to convince most folks that wood is an inappro-

priate material to use for kitchen floors and countertops, not to mention walls. Hardwoods—oak, cherry, walnut—are suitable for countertops. They also make excellent floors, but they are expensive. Pine, either white or yellow, was more commonly used for floors and will stand up well with a good finish on it.

Tile, brick, and slate are also ancient building materials, used for chimneys and hearths in the north and for floors in warmer climates where houses were built on the ground. Used with discretion, these materials enhance a kitchen.

Using period furniture rather than a lot of built-in cabinets creates the feel of an early kitchen. Use a combination of antiques, reproductions, and custom-built pieces for specific needs. Two excellent sources for ideas on appropriate furniture are *The Pine Furniture of Early New England* by Russell Haws Kettel (1929), and *Shaker Furniture* by Edward Deming Andrews and Faith Andrews (1987). Both are published by Dover. The former is a wonderful compendium of early country furniture with working plans for many of the pieces, and the latter is one of the best introductions to the work of the Shakers, whose cabinetwork is unsurpassed in elegant simplicity of form and function.

The Victorian Kitchen, 1840–1898

During the Victorian era the kitchen was very much a work space for servants rather than a living space. Sinks were soapstone, the ice box stood in place of the refrigerator, and in some old houses you may still find an annunciator—the bell system used to call servants from the kitchen to the dining room or other areas of the house. The Victorian kitchen had none of the conveniences of today's kitchen—no electricity, a wood burning stove, and a dry sink (see page 330) with no running water. Even so, you can restore some of the feel of this period by installing an old sink with original hardware, refinishing the floor to its original state, and installing window and door trim appropriate to the period and the house.

Choose custom over ready-made cabinetry.

Nothing characterizes modern kitchens so much as the cabinetwork that dominates them: yards and yards of Formica-topped counters with lipped doors and drawers underneath and walls lined with more cabinets, looming down from the ceiling, all the same, be they pseudo-Colonial, French provincial, or Danish modern. This is the first thing to avoid in designing a kitchen for a nineteenth century house. Victorians got along quite nicely without them and so can you with a little imagination.

Some counter space is, of course, necessary. It's the obvious place to locate a sink and the most unobtrusive way to incorporate a modern stove. Eight to ten feet of counter space with sink and stove included is perfectly adequate. Functional counters needn't be designed the way most modern ones are. Counters that reflect the style and period of the rest of the house and that look like eighteenth- or nineteenth-century cabinetwork rather

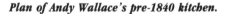

Plan of Andy Wallace's pre-1840 kitchen.

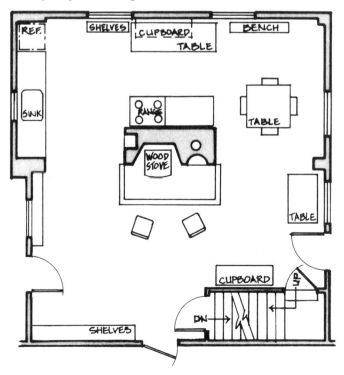

Contemporary beechwood cabinets accommodate modern kitchen needs.

Sometimes the kitchen and dining room were simply separated by a large cupboard that opened to both rooms. Cupboard doors in the dining room might feature small-pane or leaded glass, while the kitchen had plain, solid wood doors free of decorative trim.

"A place for everything and everything in its place" was the motto of the day. Thus the kitchen began to feature large built-in cupboards for household accessories such as dishes, pots, and pans. Built-in ironing boards and dumbwaiters were also installed. A movable cupboard, now commonly called a Hoosier, was introduced about 1900 and was soon popular in many kitchens. In it dispensers were provided for flour (with a built-in sifter) and sugar, in addition to specific storage areas for spices, linens, and other necessities. A narrow, plain wooden table provided additional work space to perform everyday kitchen tasks. By 1910, the table had an enamel top or was zinc-covered. A marble-topped table for making bread was considered essential when space and finances permitted.

Gas stoves with baked-enamel finishes were common by 1900. They were used singly or in combination with a wood- or coal-burning stove. (Gas, being cooler, was used in summer; coal or wood provided additional warmth in winter.) This was common practice in some houses until about 1930. Electric ranges and appliances were available just before 1900, but not used in most households until the late 1920s because electricity was expensive and unreliable. Whichever mode of cooking chosen by the housewife, metal ventilating hoods commonly carried off cooking odors and helped maintain the mandatory "sanitary conditions."

The refrigerator was a necessary appliance for the turn-of-the-century homemaker. Until the 1920s, most homes had insulated, metal-lined, heavy wooden iceboxes. The icebox stood on the back porch or along an exterior wall of the kitchen for outside "icing." By 1930, the coil-top

A gas stove dating from 1920.

than factory-produced, twentieth-century built-ins *can* be built at reasonable cost. In general, avoid the setback for the kickplate at the bottom, bring out the top lip 2 inches or so, and make the drawers and doors flush to the front frame, and you'll be headed in the right direction. Avoid matching wall cabinets overhead. There's no historical precedent for them and there are other more creative ways to provide adequate storage.

Modern appliances appear in a restored kitchen, but blend in with their surroundings, taken for granted. If you want to top off your kitchen with real late-Victorian flavor, install a stamped pattern tin ceiling.

The Modern Kitchen, 1899–1930

At the turn of the century, all but the plainest of house plans featured a kitchen and a dining room, commonly separated by a pantry. The pantry could range from a large butler's pantry to a small closet or walk-through. A butler's pantry was a large room, about half the size of the kitchen, equipped with a sink for washing good glasses and china, and a serving/preparation area. The pantry featured large built-in cupboards and was accessible through swinging doors fitted with kick- and push-plates.

electric refrigerator was a familiar sight in upper-middle-class kitchens.

White glazed ceramic tiles replaced wood wainscotting in the kitchen at the turn of the century. Wall areas not tiled were given a shiny coat of white enameled paint. (Enameled paint stood up to ceaseless scrubbing.) Before 1930, wallpaper, unless glazed, was considered unhygienic for kitchen walls. Any kitchen woodwork was usually made of birch, free of decorative mouldings, and painted with white enamel. The only exception to this was the occasional mahogany-stained door. Another deviation from this pure, white, sanitary-looking environment might be a course of colored tile as trim in the wainscotting, or a patterned linoleum floor. This was especially the case by 1910. Blue and white or black and white were the most common color touches. Ceilings, whether plastered or metal, were painted white as well.

By 1910, kitchen floors were covered in a variety of durable materials including large, red-clay quarry tiles, small white hexagonal ceramic tiles, concrete, and granolith (an artificial stone made of granite cement). The last two types of floor coverings would have been tooled to resemble tiles. Pine and hardwood floors were acceptable only if you couldn't afford one of the other "superior" coverings. Linoleum, which had been introduced in 1863, was still considered the most desirable floorcovering. Solid colors like battleship gray or checkered patterns (usually in black and white) were preferred. Substitutes such as heavy, painted oilcloths were used when cost was a factor. Whatever choice one made for overall flooring, it was suggested that a resilient cork or rubber mat, or carpet runner, be placed in front of the sink, range, and work table for the comfort of the cook's feet.

In addition to windows, light was provided by oil-lamps on metal wall brackets, gas fixtures, or bare electric light bulbs. During the transitional period from oil to electricity, most kitchens had at least two of these means of light. There was always at least one fixture above the stove, and another by the sink. Another essential feature of the working kitchen was a reliable mantel clock on a special clock shelf, or a key-wound eight-day wall hanging clock. A good selection of pots and pans in graniteware, aluminum, tin, or cast iron was considered a necessity. By 1920, plate-rails or shelves were coming into style; one would have been installed in the kitchen if there wasn't a dining room. In some kitchens, especially commercial ones, a hanging rack for utensils and pots would be placed over the work table for easy access.

With clean-burning gas and electric stoves, long-wearing linoleum, and tiled walls, concern over sanitary conditions waned just before 1930. Now the kitchen was an inherently cleaner place. Gas and electric appliances, enclosed in streamlined units, predominated. The sink and work area were also enclosed, often with storage cabinets underneath, eliminating the need for a pantry.

At this time, there was a reaction against the "laboratory kitchen." One reason was that the dining room began to shrink or even disappear from house plans. The

In a 1934 kitchen the cabinets are not yet continuous, the countertops are Monel.

kitchen became a place to gather and eat, not just work. In place of sanitary white, pastel shades (especially beige, light green, and light blue) covered the woodwork and bright primary colors were used to decorate. Washable wallpapers in folksy patterns and prints became popular in the early 1930s and continued in vogue until the 1950s. Cotton-hooked rugs of a vague Colonial design were laid over existing linoleum in front of the sink and under the kitchen table. By this time, furniture was being mass-produced specially for the kitchen; a kitchen set usually included a table (wood or metal) with four matching painted chairs. Painted china spice canisters, iron trivets, salt and pepper shakers, and brass and copper pots were frequently displayed on corner knick-knack shelves and on wall shelving.

Interpretive Restoration: The Modern Kitchen

Some things are unsalvageable. Consider the kitchen that doesn't allow counterspace or an efficient work triangle. The plaster is failing and there's nothing but subfloor under the spongy, curling layers of linoleum. The cabinets are poorly designed, cheaply constructed, and falling apart. You can't make sense of the original design—you've got a small dark warren of rooms (a cramped kitchen, unusable small "maid's room," toilet, and closet filled with broken plaster) containing no original fixtures or furnishings.

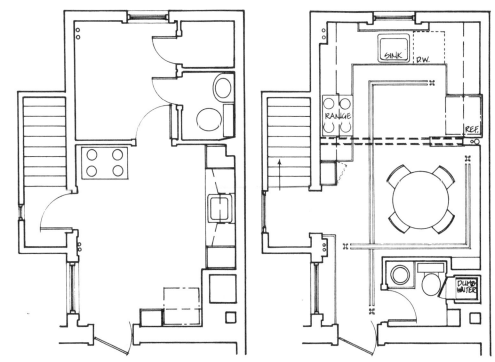

In the original plan (left), each room was too small (8 × 9 and 6 × 7) and too poorly laid out to be useful. The circulation pattern was undesigned and irrational: You walked diagonally through the middle of the kitchen to go to the maid's room or toilet. This, with the lack of uninterrupted wall space and small size, made it impossible to have counter space.

The lavatory was relocated. This created an entry hall to the kitchen (off which the lavatory door opens). The sense of two rooms is retained by a beam structure and, on one side, by a low wall where the old partition wall was.

With cases like these, the only solution is starting over. And rather than attempt a "period" kitchen that would be phony—a lot of effort to create a conjectural room, all of it new, which would undoubtedly be less comfortable than a modern kitchen and might even make the house harder to sell—consider installing a modern kitchen taking cues from the house.

Despite a frankly modern layout and unconcealed appliances, you can still make the kitchen fit in sensitively. Follow these guiding principles:

• Look to original elements of the house for design cues. For example, the muntin detail on the cabinets is adapted from the front windows, and from the French doors in the dining room.

• Use old or authentic or traditional materials whenever it won't compromise quality. (Examples: Salvaged and remilled oak for the woodwork, lending patina; the stove hood is copper; the floor and backsplash are ceramic tile.) You can use modern materials where there is a distinct advantage in practicality, but detail their use in a way that is sympathetic to traditional design. (Example: The plastic-laminate countertop is inlaid and edged with oak.)

With this type of restoration, you can use our advantage of hindsight to look at the best examples of design from the period when the house was built (in the kitchen shown, 1911). In interpretive restoration, we have the opportunity to study the principles and vocabulary of a period. Although this is a builder's house with a modest interior, the "modern" influences of the Prairie school and the Arts and Crafts movement are apparent in the floor

Traditional details keep new materials from creating a jarringly modern context.

plan, stair and mantel details, and (especially) in the dining room with its beamed ceiling and oak plate rail. This is the design cue we worked from.

Detailing. Built-ins were incorporated into the new design. Strongly associated with the period, they are an efficient use of space and tie the room together visually. The shelf pocket in the breakfast nook, the window seat, and the cabinets appear built in because of continuous wood mouldings. Lighting (in the beam and plate-rail sconces), window and door trim, and the room-dividing beam structure all are integrated.

Standard frame-and-panel detail of cabinets was slightly modified to suit the horizontal emphasis in the room: The rails, not the vertical stiles, are continuous and uninterrupted. Vertical stiles and muntins are slender. Muntins were used on solid panel doors as well as glass doors to carry the rhythm throughout.

Drawer fronts stand proud of the cabinet doors, rather than flush. It's a furniture-quality detail that deviates from the standard flush-front cabinets; the change in plane and resulting shadow line add another horizontal.

The floor tile is a moderately priced, standard 2 × 2 tile. A hand-laid border pattern both adds a decorative detail consistent with the period and defines kitchen area, breakfast nook, and entry hall while knitting them together.

The shelf alcove in the breakfast nook has a built-in character.

Lighting. The flexible, appropriate lighting may be the project's strongest design feature. The designer purposefully avoided the two most popular types of modern lighting: Recessed down lights ("cans") cast ghoulish shadows and are both inadequate and inappropriate for a human work space; track lights, best suited for theatrical or spot lighting, are often harsh, shining in your eyes as you move through a room. Indirect lighting was invented during the post-Victorian period, and sconces were popular. Both remain practical, appropriate, and attractive. Sconces in the plate rail and the lights integrated into the beam cast direct light downward and indirect light upward to softly bounce off the ceiling. Additional indirect lighting comes from warm incandescents atop the cabinets. Balance and strong task light come from cool fluorescent tubes under the cabinets, which directly illuminate counters. Each type of light source is on a separate switch. Sconces and beam lighting, as well as the hanging fixture over the table, are on dimmers, so illumination can be made to move from strong work light to a candlelight effect.

There is no sense of shock at finding a modern room as you step through the swinging oak door. As you pass the lavatory, the nook comes into view and there is a great sense of perspective in this average-size room. Horizontal and vertical elements wrap around, tying the spaces together into a unified whole. Materials, finishes, and colors all contribute to the period ambience. Stainless steel, glossy surfaces, high-tech design, and harsh contemporary lighting were avoided.

Countertop Options

Chances are you won't be able to gather many clues about what was originally in your pre-1939 kitchen just by looking at the room. If you're lucky, your kitchen might have some nice old built-in cabinets, or you might have a freestanding Hoosier cabinet. Most likely, you have a kitchen that was remodeled in the 1940s or later, with continuous base cabinets and a drop-in sink. Maybe your counters are fine. On the other hand, you might have scuffed-up mint-green counters, complete with scum caught in the black seams.

What kind of counters would have been original to your kitchen? Did your kitchen originally even have counters? Probably not, since continuous base cabinets and counters popular today were just becoming established in the 1930s. So what do you do? Find out what countertop materials are available, how long they've been around, and decide on something that will be completely functional without turning the kitchen into a time capsule or a space capsule.

Plastic Laminates

Today, Formica is the best-known plastic laminate used for countertops—so well-known that the company has gone to court to keep Formica from becoming a generic term. There are other brands, such as Nevamar, Micarta, and WilsonArt.

Standard laminates are made by impregnating layers of brown kraft paper with phenolic resin, then laminating the sheets, under heat and pressure, between plates of polished steel. The brown kraft paper is visible at the edges of standard laminate; that's what causes the dark line at the edges of a laminate countertop. It's easy enough to cover up the dark line with wood trim.

Formica was first marketed in 1913 as electrical insulation. It was billed as a substitute "for mica"—thus the name. It wasn't sold as a countertop material until the late 1920s, at which time only dark-colored woodgrain and marble patterns were available. Formica didn't really catch on as a kitchen countertop material until the late 1930s, when lighter colors were introduced. The lighter-colored sheets were made (and still are made) by impregnating a more highly refined, light-colored top layer of paper with melamine.

Standard laminates are available in hundreds of colors and patterns. There are Art Deco–inspired geometrics, post-Modern patterns that look like chainlink fence, and, for that late 1970s look, there's always beige or butcher block.

Laminates are virtually indestructible. They'll be here, along with cockroaches and Styrofoam cups, long after we're all gone. You can chop celery (gently) on laminate countertops, put hot pots (up to 275 degrees Fahrenheit)

A 1930s kitchen.

A typical 1920s kitchen with freestanding appliances and worktables.

on them, get water or alcohol on them, and it takes years for them to show any wear. However, laminates will scratch, so don't scrub them with abrasive cleaners. There are scratch-resistant laminates, but even these should not be scrubbed with anything abrasive. For general cleaning, a damp sponge is often adequate. For more thorough cleaning, use Bon Ami, liquid cleanser, or a nylon scouring pad.

Standard laminates are inexpensive, as countertops go. The cost of the laminate itself is less than the cost of the 1-inch plywood base it has to be glued to.

In the early 1980s, Formica introduced Colorcore. It's a sheet product much like standard laminate, except that it's a solid color, and the color goes all the way through the sheet. With Colorcore, the joints don't have that dark line. This product is made with layers of refined (as opposed to kraft) paper, and is impregnated with melamine rather than phenolic resin. Colorcore costs somewhat more than standard laminate.

Ultra-high-gloss textured laminates—with raised ribs, chevrons, dots, and such—are available from Formica, though most distributors don't stock these items. (They're much more popular in Europe than in the United States.) Though they may look very "modern," textured laminates were first marketed in the 1930s. They're harder to clean, however, and are best used as backsplashes.

Plastic Slabs

The first plastic slab, DuPont's Corian, was introduced in the early 1970s. It's an acrylic product that comes in 1/4-inch, 1/2-inch, and 3/4-inch thicknesses. It can be worked with heavy-duty woodworking tools with carbide bits. Installing Corian is tricky, and should be done only by experienced installers. Two special considerations for old-house installation of Corian: The base cabinets have to be level, or at least levelable—unlike plywood and

laminate, Corian does not bend (try to bend it and it cracks). Also, paint stripper will melt Corian.

Because it can be planed, routed, and shaped like wood or marble (which it more closely resembles), Corian lends itself to some interesting detailing: Edges can be shaped into ogees, chamfers—anything that shaper bits can cut. Corian can be routed and inlaid with metal, wood, or ceramic tile.

Minor nicks, scratches, and burns in Corian can be sanded out with fine sandpaper; and, every few years, the whole counter can be "resurfaced" with a vibrating sander. Although there are no Corian counters over twenty years old, it would be reasonable to expect the material to have a very long life.

For general cleaning, treat Corian the same as plastic laminate. Even though the surface can be repaired, there is no reason to scratch it unnecessarily with abrasive cleaning methods. When you do need to make repairs, sanding wet with wet-or-dry paper will prevent the paper from clogging and cut faster. The manufacturer recommends finishing up by polishing the surface with a nylon scouring pad such as a Scotch-Brite pad. Polish in a gentle circular motion until the repaired area blends with the surrounding surface.

Formica recently introduced a product to compete with Corian—it's a polyester slab called 2000X. This product can be mated with Formica's Colorcore laminate, so edges can include such details as pinstriping and wood or metal inlays.

Ceramic Tile

Ceramic tile is a timeless countertop material; it blends well in just about any period kitchen. Costs vary widely—a do-it-yourself job with tiles glued to a plywood deck could cost as little as laminate; a professionally done "mud job" with a complex pattern could cost as much as a car. A tile counter can be strikingly handsome, and possibilities for colors, patterns, and textures are infinite.

Whether you have glazed or unglazed tile, clean with a damp mop or sponge and all-purpose cleaner such as Top Job, Mr. Clean, or other ammonia-based cleaners. For heavy-duty cleaning, use a nonabrasive household scouring agent such as Ajax Liquid, Liquid Comet, or Bon Ami. Scrub stubborn stains with a nylon scouring pad and rinse with clear water.

Linoleum

Linoleum, which was invented in 1863, is probably best known to old-house restorers as the wretched stuff that had to be peeled, piece by tiny piece, from the hardwood floor. But from the 1930s through the 1950s, it was also the most widely used countertop. Linoleum wasn't a bad countertop, but it wasn't a good one either. It was cheap and easy to install, and it was nonporous—until you cut it during the routine act of slicing a vegetable, at which time it "self-healed" until water got in. Then it puckered and self-destructed. Over time, even undamaged linoleum turned brittle, because of the linseed oil used in its manufacture.

Probably the most endearing thing about linoleum is that it came in some great patterns, from prissy florals to psychedelic geometrics. Linoleum counters were typically edged with aluminum trim.

Linoleum fell out of favor as better low-cost materials—laminates and vinyl flooring—caught on. The last large domestic manufacturer ceased production in 1974.

Metal

In the late 1930s, Monel metal (an alloy made largely of nickel and copper) was aggressively advertised as a countertop material. Steel cabinets were very popular in kitchens at the time, and metal countertops seemed just the thing. The International Nickel Company in New York promoted its Monel counters, complete with integral double sinks, in women's magazines. In 1937, Emily Seaber Parcher had this to say about Monel counters in *Better Homes and Gardens:* "It was the man of the house who suggested metal for the cabinets and sink, for working counters and sink basin, too—the kind [Monel] that resists rust, corrosion, and tarnish. You can imagine that the idea wasn't hard to sell to the lady of the house."

Stainless steel enjoyed some popularity as a countertop in the 1960s; it's widely used in industrial kitchens and laboratories today. In upscale houses in the days of servants, copper was used as a countertop. The idea was that the servants would drop some china from time to time, but the soft copper wouldn't break the dishes. When servants fell out of fashion, so did copper—it was too hard to maintain.

Wood

Wood has been used for tables and work surfaces since before the kitchen as we know it came to be. Early twentieth-century kitchen work tables often had painted wood tops. Handsome counters can be fashioned from wood, and every now and then somebody installs an all-wood kitchen countertop.

Upkeep of a wood countertop is difficult. Wood expands and contracts, and it's porous. It's hard to think of a wood finish that can withstand all the abuse that a kitchen counter takes. And, once the finish cracks, fluids soak into the wood. Disinfecting the surface becomes a daily chore.

On noncutting wood surfaces an oil-type finish will stand up better than a varnish- or urethane-type finish. Remove the finish down to bare wood. Heat linseed oil very carefully in a double boiler, as it is extremely flammable. When it's warm to the touch, apply the oil to the surface, then rub down with steel wool. Apply three coats, allowing one day between applications. Clean regularly with lukewarm water and mild soap. Reoil occasionally.

On cutting surfaces, don't use anything toxic. To renew the surface and get rid of old stains, use a cabinet scraper to remove a thin layer of wood as well as built-up layers of grease and food stains. To fill cracks and seal the wood,

A soapstone sink with original hardware surrounded by wood is in keeping with the original 1883 features.

mix 1 part paraffin to 4 parts mineral oil. Melt them together in a double boiler. Apply it to the wood, allow it to harden, then remove any excess with a nonmetallic scraper. Touch up every two or three weeks with a coat of mineral oil. Don't use vegetable oil because it will go rancid; linseed oil will get very hard and dark.

Marble, Slate, and Stone

As long as there have been civilized kitchens, there have been marble counters. A whole kitchen full of marble would be very expensive and not entirely practical (it stains and it's hard to repair), but people who bake sometimes like to have a little marble counter for use in preparing bread. (It stays cool.)

For general cleaning of marble, try a poultice of Tide (or similar) detergent. Make a thick paste by adding water to the detergent and spreading it over the marble. Allow to dry. To slow drying and deliver more cleaning power, cover the poultice with plastic to keep it from drying out too quickly. Then scrape the poultice off with a soft plastic spatula. Rinse and dry.

To polish marble—and get out minor etching and scratches—rub out with powdered tin oxide (slow, but effective). Sprinkle tin oxide on surface of marble and rub vigorously with moistened felt pad or chamois. When surface has been restored to its original luster, rinse and dry thoroughly with soft cloth.

For general polishing, start with wet-or-dry sandpaper of appropriate grit. If the marble is rough, begin with 80 grit, then move through 120, 320, 400. If the marble is dark, continue to 600. Keep the surface wet so the paper will continue to cut without clogging or gouging. Rinse and wipe the surface frequently to remove excess grit, especially when going from one grit paper to another. Follow with a buffing powder, tin oxide, or aluminum oxide. Use water and a rubbing pad or buffing wheel. Marble polish can be used for the final step if no food will be on the surface. Never use oil-base polish or soft waxes such as beeswax, as they may discolor marble.

Granite has the attributes of marble and tile with advantages such as seamlessness and a close grain (no stains!). But the people at DuPont and Formica say granite was popular only in New York and L.A., among people who wanted the most expensive thing.

You may find other stone in your kitchen. It can be maintained much the same way as unglazed tile. If the stone is rough and porous, try a test patch before using any kind of poultice, scouring powder, or other type of cleaning method that could potentially leave a hard-to-remove residue. (White-powder residue on dark stone would be very noticeable.) Lemon oil applied over slate will make it dark and lustrous. You can also use a thin coat of wax on stone to help seal it and bring out the color. Again, test before doing the whole job.

Slate makes a good countertop. Slate quality varies widely; you have to buy slate that's milled for countertops—it's thin, nonporous, and smooth. It's expensive, however, and it's tough to detail and install.

SINKS

Getting hot and cold water from a kitchen or bathroom sink is taken for granted nowadays, yet as little as one hundred years ago it was a pure luxury. As recently as 1930, less than one out of ten rural American homes had running water in a bathroom, and only 16 percent had piped-in water. In the 1920s, water systems were more common in the cities, yet one out of four homes didn't have a sink with running water, and only half had bathrooms as we now know them.

No one restoring or living in an old house, however, would choose to be so "authentic" as to omit sinks, even though they may not be original to the house. Modern kitchen and bathroom sinks are concessions to today's way of life, even in the most meticulous restorations. Yet for those wishing to go an extra step, there are alternative solutions—so-called "period" sinks that can add to the particular flavor of your house.

For thousands of years, water for washing, drinking, and cooking was hauled from a stream, spring, or well. (Occasionally, rainwater was collected in cisterns as a source of soft water, preferred for bathing and washing.) Only rarely did advanced cities, such as ancient Rome, have anything like a running-water system.

In early America, food preparation and dish washing were commonly done in a wooden tub that was usually set on a kitchen table. Water for bathing (an infrequent activity at best) was also put in bowls or small tubs. The whole concept of a bathroom was unheard of until the 1800s—the "great outdoors" served our forebears' needs for personal hygiene just fine.

In this country, it wasn't until the late-eighteenth century that something resembling a bathroom sink came about: It was the washstand. Following English prototypes, washstands were simply small tables on which were placed pitcher-and-bowl sets; sometimes the bowl rested in a hole cut into the tabletop. Washstands reflected the popular furniture styles of the day—Eastlake, Renaissance Revival, Hepplewhite, Chippendale, Empire—but regardless of their style, almost all had a backboard that served as a splashboard; many had shelves or small drawers for soap and other toiletries. During the nineteenth century, washstands became larger and bulkier, often with towel bars along the sides and a cupboard below to store the chamberpot (our first indoor toilets).

From about 1820 to 1900, another piece of furniture—the dry sink—was also commonly used in American homes. This was a low, wooden cabinet with a trough built into the top. This trough was often lined with zinc or lead sheets, and held bowls or buckets of water for use in food preparation or dish washing. Like washstands, dry sinks had back splashboards and shelves or drawers for cleaning supplies. But dry sinks were usually very functional in design and only nominally reflected the prevailing furniture styles.

Thus, the washstand was the precursor of the bathroom sink; the dry sink, the forerunner of the kitchen

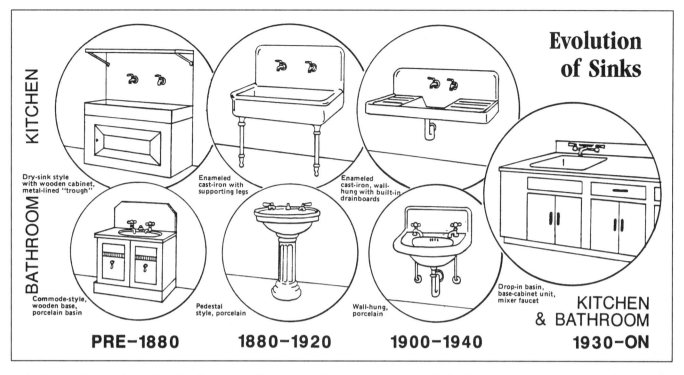

Evolution of Sinks

KITCHEN

Dry-sink style
with wooden cabinet,
metal-lined "trough"

Enameled
cast-iron with
supporting legs

Enameled
cast-iron, wall-
hung with built-in
drainboards

BATHROOM

Commode-style,
wooden base,
porcelain basin

Pedestal
style, porcelain

Wall-hung,
porcelain

Drop-in basin,
base-cabinet unit,
mixer faucet

KITCHEN
& BATHROOM

PRE-1880   **1880-1920**   **1900-1940**   **1930-ON**

sink. So it isn't surprising that, in their quest for authenticity, many house restorers have converted dry sinks and washstands into perfectly usable sinks with running water. By introducing faucets through the splashboard and providing for a watertight basin with a drain, these furniture pieces offer attractive adaptive-reuse options (particularly appropriate for owners of houses that pre-date the last quarter of the nineteenth century). Victorian-era washstands can still be found at reasonable prices in many antique stores. (Converting a washstand or dry sink into a sink with running water will destroy some of its value as an antique, so it's best to stick to the common factory-produced pieces rather than the high-quality formal examples.)

The first municipal water system in America was built in 1802 in Philadelphia. After an initial resistance to buying water, city dwellers accepted the idea, and by 1850, eighty-three American cities had their own systems. At first, they were steam-powered, with the water filtered through charcoal or sand. Early distribution networks consisted of cast-iron or wooden pipes.

During the mid-1800s, the adoption of water and sewer systems, along with such advancements as central heating and balloon-framing techniques, changed the way the typical American house functioned and looked. Interior spaces became more specialized—the living room, library, dressing room, dining room, laundry—and the kitchen became less the all-purpose, live-in "family room" it was in colonial times. (The indoor bathroom was pretty much a new concept altogether.) After the Civil War, the "domestic science" movement, as espoused by Catherine Beecher, her sister, Harriet Beecher Stowe, and others, did much to popularize efficient, labor-saving kitchen and bathroom designs.

During these formative years, sinks became a fixed and

integral part of the house. Not surprisingly, these sinks resembled what they had replaced. In the illustrations of Stowe, Beecher, and A. J. Downing, the kitchen sinks are very similar to dry sinks except for the addition of faucets and drains. The first bathroom sinks (also called "lavatories") initially resembled a washstand; slick ceramic models came later.

Water and sewer systems may not have been available in many rural areas, yet the idea of a permanent sink took hold—often with a hand pump attached to one end. Advancements in pump design and their mass production (which made them relatively inexpensive) brought indoor running water even to remote farmhouses. Hand pumps connected to sinks remained popular and were offered in Sears and Montgomery Ward catalogs well into the twentieth century.

During this time, hot water was generated in a small boiler that was usually connected to the wood- or coal-fired kitchen stove. Later, boilers connected to the furnace supplied hot water throughout the house, including the bathroom sink and tub which eventually came to be seen as necessities.

Major developments in sink designs came later in the nineteenth century, as the "sanitary movement" (as some at the time called it) became popular. Kitchen and bathroom designs were given a great deal of "scientific" thought regarding efficiency, motion study, and sanitation. The elements of the kitchen—such as the stove, icebox, work areas, and sink—were no longer thought of as individual free-standing pieces, but rather as a whole. This was the beginning of the "continuous work surface" concept, in which standardized table, stove, and sink heights, coupled with mass-produced kitchen components, eventually evolved into the modern kitchen.

White, because of its association with sanitation, became the prevalent color for sinks and the other fixtures and surfaces in bathrooms and kitchens. This obsession with sterility led one observer to complain that when cutting up "a fowl in these kitchens one felt quite like a surgeon performing a major operation." White retained its dominance until the 1920s, when there was a return to color in wall coverings, floors, and even ceramic sinks.

The heyday of sink designs (approximately 1890 to 1930) saw a proliferation in materials and styles. The old metal-lined wooden sink gave way to models in cast iron, enamel, porcelain, china, stainless steel, galvanized iron, zinc, tin, soapstone, and even marble. In kitchens, enamel, metal, and soapstone sinks were the most popular because of their durability. China (porcelain) and marble sinks were popular for bathrooms, as they were considered more elegant.

Enameled sinks, often referred to as "enamelware" or "whiteware," were manufactured as early as the 1870s. They were made by casting an iron sink, reheating it to a red-hot state, and then uniformly sprinkling ground glass over it; once cooled, the enamel surface was smooth and shiny. By 1900, enamelware had become the most popular type of kitchen sink.

Soapstone, long used for a variety of items, was also a popular material for sinks. Its advocates praised soapstone because it didn't absorb acids or grease, as marble did; could be cleaned easily; and didn't chip like enamelware. Marble, a more delicate stone, was usually restricted to top-of-the-line bathroom sinks. (In 1855, a marble sink with silver-plated fixtures cost $50, a tidy sum in those days.) One-piece marble sinks were the most expensive, and so the basin and sink top were usually separate pieces. Often a marble top was combined with a porcelain bowl.

Porcelain, particularly popular for bathroom lavatories, was a vitreous material made from cast clay fired in a kiln and then coated with a glass-like glaze during a second-firing. Because it was manufactured by a casting process, porcelain was produced in a wide array of elegant shapes. At the other end of the scale, cast-iron sinks were the

cheapest but required periodic "oiling" to prevent rusting. Galvanized iron, and later stainless steel, eliminated this problem.

Early kitchen sinks had basins of generous proportions, larger than today. Double side-by-side basins were common, especially for cast-iron enamelware. The earliest sinks were freestanding, like furniture, usually resting on cast-iron legs (often painted white to match the enamel or porcelain). The legs imitated table legs with fluting, ball or claw feet, and a variety of details simulating lathe-turning. Later, the back of the sink was hung on the wall, and the front was supported by large cast-iron brackets or a pair of legs. Kitchen sinks sold in early twentieth-century Sears catalogs offered an option of either brackets or legs. For bathroom lavatories, the pedestal type was extremely popular.

Architecturally, kitchen and bathroom sinks reflected the details of the times. In the late-Victorian era, sinks had routed, incised, curved, and turned designs, all imitatively cast into enamel or porcelain models. Scallop-shaped basins, angular bevel-edged tops and splashboards, even wooden Eastlake-styled cabinet bases appeared in bathroom lavatories.

As the nation turned to the Colonial Revival, sinks became less elaborate, with cleaner, more refined lines. Classical elements showed up in the ogee-shaped edges of the splashboard, oval-shaped bowls, and particularly the pedestal bases which often looked like classical-order columns. Throughout the early twentieth century, sink designs became even simpler—almost all architectural detail was dropped and edges were rounded, giving them a unified sculptural look. This trend was in part due to the "sanitary" movement that viewed elaborate designs as providing a multitude of dirt-catching nooks and crannies. Simple lines, rolled rims, and streamlined design was the favored look of the 1920s and beyond.

Continuous countertops with drop-in sink basins, the kind we know today, first appeared during the 1930s. This development was partly due to progressive schools of architecture, such as the Bauhaus, which sought uniform

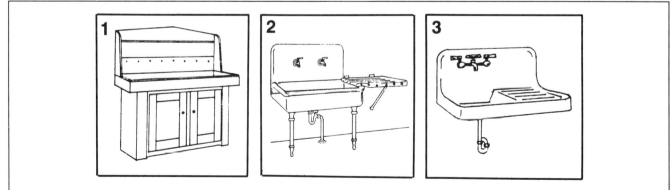

1. *The nineteenth-century dry sink was the precursor of the kitchen sink. With the introduction of hot and cold running water faucets through the backboard and a drain into the zinc-lined trough, the age of the kitchen sink began.*

2. *The earliest kitchen sinks were freestanding, usually on cast-iron legs that were often painted white to match the enamel or porcelain.*

3. *A later development was the wall-mounted sink.*

Three Types of Faucets

1. *A single-pronged "lever" style, with handle and base of porcelain.*

2. *A four-pronged "cross" (or spoke) style, with porcelain handle and chromed base.*

3. *"Cross" with chromed handle and base.*

solutions for house design. Countertops became a standard 36 inches high and 24 to 25 inches deep. Modern materials were used: linoleum and Formica for countertops, stainless steel for basins. Base cabinets, with drop-in sink and stove units, ran around the kitchen perimeter and were usually topped by continuous wall cabinets.

Faucets, Drains, and Other Hardware

The earliest faucets were merely water cocks in which a handle was directly connected to a valve in the water line. These were capable of functioning in only two positions: on and off. Although cocks are still occasionally used (as in line-shut-off valves, for example), by the late 1800s they were largely superseded by compression-valve faucets. In a compression valve, a rubber washer is attached to the end of a metal stem and is seated against the body of the faucet when fully closed. A compression-valve faucet allows for a continuous range of water flow from fully on to fully off.

Initially, there were separate faucets for hot and cold water. They were usually made of iron, often nickel plated. Top-of-the-line faucets were brass or copper, but some were even gold or silver-plated. Chrome plating was introduced after the turn of the century. Faucet handles were also plated, but perhaps most commonly were made of porcelain. Two styles of handles were prevalent: a four-pronged knob or "cross" style and a single-pronged "lever" style, a type still popular in Europe. The words HOT and COLD were usually inscribed directly into the handle, or sometimes on porcelain buttons set into the top of the faucet.

The first spouts were fixed, but by the twentieth century swinging spouts commonly appeared in kitchen sinks. High, goose-neck spouts were an early type that have made a comeback. Spray attachments on flexible hoses showed up as early as 1915 in some kitchens. "Mixers," in which the hot- and cold-water handles were connected to a single central spout, were a welcome development (as anyone who still has separate hot- and cold-water faucets can attest). By 1920, mixers were commonplace.

Kitchen drainboards evolved from simple, fold-back wooden shelves (hinged on the wall next to the sink) to metal shelves flanking the sink and permanently affixed by brackets. Metal drainboards usually had ribs pressed into their surface to direct the water back into the sink. By

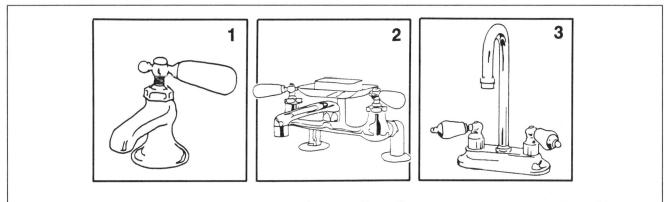

Three Types of Spouts

1. *Spout and faucet in one unit, with "lever" handle.*

2. *"Mixer" with hot- and cold-water handles visibly connecting into a single spout.*

3. *"Mixer" with goose-neck spout and hidden connection.*

the 1920s, most kitchen enamelware sinks had integral drainboards incorporated into either side of a double-basin center.

Other sink-related inventions appeared in the early twentieth century. Automatic dishwashers that connected to the kitchen faucet arrived in the 1920s. In 1929, General Electric introduced the "electric sink," their term for an electric garbage disposal. Countertops adjacent to the kitchen sink, at first made of soapstone, slate, or zinc sheets, eventually were made of new products such as linoleum, asphalt tiles, or Formica, as described earlier in the chapter. The "butcher-block" look, popular for countertops today, actually appeared first about 1917 when one-inch white maple strips were used.

In the bathroom, pedestal-base sinks remained popular. Amenities such as soap receptacles and towel bars were incorporated into sink designs. From 1900 on, mirrors, toothbrush holders, and drinking-glass niches were mounted into the wall above the sink.

Living with Old-Styled Sinks

If you'd like to include "period" sinks as part of your restoration, the first step is to decide on the type and style most appropriate to the era of your particular house. Finding the right sink isn't too difficult—there are three primary sources: salvage, reproductions, and adaptive reuse.

Architectural salvage dealers are excellent sources for finding old kitchen and bathroom sinks. Check your local Yellow Pages under "Salvage," "Junk Dealers," or "Plumbing Fixtures & Supplies," or refer to the list of salvage dealers in *The Old-House Journal Buyer's Guide Catalog,* to see if there's anyone near you. Here are some things to look for when selecting a sink from a salvager:

• Be sure the sink will fit in the space you allot for it.

• Check the basin for cracks and chips that can cause leaks—fill the bowl with water, if possible. Cracks in the pedestal of a lavatory may present a structural problem, but minor chips and cracks are often only aesthetic flaws.

• Check the finish. Worn or discolored enamel can be professionally repaired, but it can be expensive. Blemishes on the finishes shouldn't dissuade you from considering a sink you really like, however.

• Try to get as complete a sink as possible, including all the original fixtures, fittings, and hardware. Fitting sizes have changed over the years, so it may be difficult to get new ones that will fit an old sink. Try to find an old sink that retains its connections, particularly the original supply stem nuts.

• *Be sure* the mounting tabs on the back of wall-hung sinks are intact and sturdy.

Installing Salvaged Sinks

In addition to your back issues of *OHJ,* consult *Salvaged Treasures* by Michael Litchfield and Rosmarie Haucherr (New York: Van Nostrand Reinhold, 1983) to learn how to install old sinks. Most of the procedures in installing old sinks fall within the range of common plumbing practices, but there are a few points to note:

• You'll probably have to use a number of adapters to make the fittings of the old sink connect to your modern plumbing system. Don't despair—a well-stocked plumbing-supply house should have a variety of them.

• Old faucets and drains, because of their age, may be leaky. Usually this is easily alleviated by replacing the gaskets. But remember how you disassemble an old faucet, because many vintage models are put together differently from modern faucets.

• Do-it-yourself paint touch-ups for enamel finishes are available, but they're generally inadequate. Color matching is very difficult and the patched areas quickly wear off under normal use. Unless you're prepared for a complete but expensive reenameling job by a professional, it's probably best to live with a worn enamel finish—it makes no difference to the integrity of the sink. Many stains can be removed with common cleaning products.

• If the old sink is wall mounted, it is very important to attach the mounting bracket to a sturdy wall surface. If you aren't mounting a sink where a previous one was hung, reinforce the wall by introducing a horizontal wood block that spans two adjacent wall studs. Cut the plaster and lath back to the inside edge of the adjacent studs. Fasten 2 × 3 blocking to the studs. (If possible, use a screw gun to prevent plaster damage from hammering.) Mount the blocking far enough back so that when you screw a piece of plywood to the blocking and gypsum board to the plywood, the gypsum board is flush with plaster. Fasten the sink bracket through the gypsum board into the plywood.

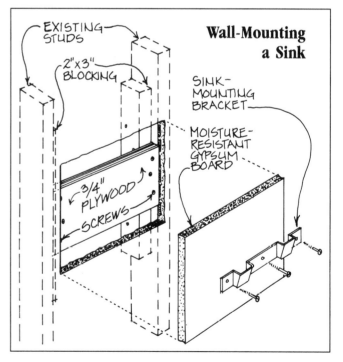

Reproduction Sinks

Most major sink manufacturers now produce at least one "antique-style" design as part of their line; several smaller companies specialize solely in period designs.

Also, any large plumbing-supply house should be able to order reproduction models for you. Remember to choose a design that's appropriate for your house—many Victorian-era sinks would be too fancy for an early twentieth-century house. The same is true for reproduction hardware (drains, knobs, faucets); earlier styles were more ornamental.

You'll find a variety of bathroom lavatory reproductions from which to choose, particularly attractive pedestal models. An even wider array of antique-style fixtures is available. However, very few old-style kitchen sink reproductions are available. Apparently, the more utilitarian look of an old kitchen sink has not yet found its way into our "nostalgic" hearts. One source, the Vermont Soapstone Company, makes an attractive soapstone kitchen model complete with a side drainboard. But perhaps your best source for old kitchen sinks will be salvage, not reproductions.

Adaptive Reuse

As previously mentioned, old washstands and dry sinks make good pieces for conversion to sinks. Fortunately, antique-style basins are readily available from many suppliers and come in a wide range of materials, including china, marble, enamel, copper, soapstone, cast iron, and stainless steel. The basins can be fitted into the top of a washstand in the same way as they would into a modern base cabinet.

Speaking of base cabinets, you don't have to settle for modern prefabricated designs. Anyone with reasonably competent skills can build custom base units which reflect the architectural character of your house. For example, narrow, beaded tongue-and-groove "matchboards" were a popular material for wainscotting in kitchens and bathrooms from Victorian times into this century, and they're still available today. A custom-made base cabinet

incorporating beaded boards as siding or in door panels would be an especially appropriate design. Other period details might include simple incised designs, glass knobs, paneled sides and doors, or natural wood finishes (especially oak). Look for design inspirations in the details of other antique furniture pieces such as Hoosier cabinets, old ice chests, pie safes, or linen chests.

Even a thoroughly modern sink can be made to appear more "old-fashioned" by simply replacing the fixtures with period reproductions. A wide variety is available, ranging from very expensive, solid-brass fixture sets to less-expensive, chrome- or nickel-plated models.

—————BATHROOMS—————

As early as 1850, a bathroom was an integral part of "grand" houses costing $10,000 or more. Then, shortly before the turn of the century, it was transformed from a luxury to a standard feature of even the cheapest "catalog" house. Fixtures were left exposed for a neat, sanitary appearance and easier cleaning, although the latter was often lost by over-ornamentation.

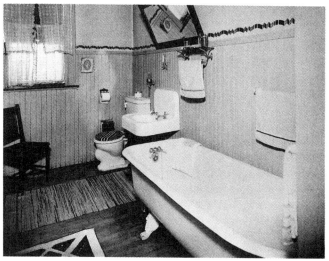

This turn-of-the-century bathroom still has tongue-and-groove boards and a wood floor instead of tiles.

From 1880 to 1900, embossed and surface decoration for bathroom fixtures was very elaborate, offered in as many varieties as wallpaper. These fixtures, usually made of cast iron coated with a porcelain glaze, were often painted to imitate wood, bronze, or gold. Even toilets were embossed or transfer-printed in designs suitable for the Colonial Revival, Aesthetic, or Art Nouveau styles.

At the same time, wood-encased washbasins gave way to open earthenware basins set on ornate cast-iron frames. These basins and their frames were often decorated to match the style chosen for the bathroom.

While every house had a toilet (often called the W.C. or water closet), and a sink, not all houses had an installed bath or shower. The hip bath was still in use up to about 1925. Many a grandparent can recall the cozy sight of a warm bedroom with a hip bath set on a waterproof sheet, hot-water cans gleaming in the light of a fire, and a thick

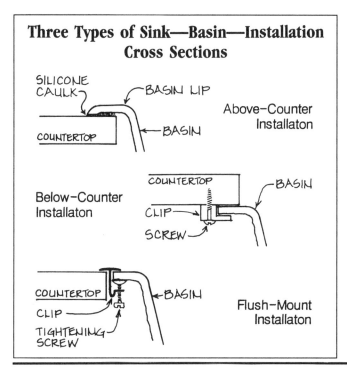

Three Types of Sink—Basin—Installation Cross Sections

SILICONE CAULK

BASIN LIP

COUNTERTOP

BASIN

Above-Counter Installaton

Below-Counter Installaton

COUNTERTOP

BASIN

CLIP

SCREW

COUNTERTOP

BASIN

CLIP

TIGHTENING SCREW

Flush-Mount Installaton

towel warming on the fireguard. While seemingly crude, hip baths were in fact covered with a bath sheet onto which water was poured. Thus, the occupant never saw (or felt) the basic metal container underneath.

Very early bathtubs were usually made of sheet metal, and often enclosed in the same wood wainscotting used to protect the walls. But by 1880, bathtubs, which had been encased in paneled woodwork with elaborate woodframes and tile splashbacks, were freestanding cast-iron forms with intricate, applied exterior decoration.

Wood wainscotting, no longer surrounding the tub, was still used on the walls. Moisture-resistant, embossed wallcoverings, such as Lincrusta, were often used above the wainscotting or in place of it. Hooded tubs, with a tall enclosure at one end, in such woods as mahogany, remained popular until about 1900.

When bathrooms became standard, they also got smaller—even for a large house, architects began to prefer several small bathrooms instead of one large one. Except for the occasional costly fantasy, even a bathroom in a large house was essentially the same as that in the smallest, newly built villa. By 1900, porcelain or vitreous china was commonly used for all fixtures; the various styles were discarded in favor of a plain, white, sanitary atmosphere.

Woodwork, curtains, carpets, and elaborate decorations began to disappear. In their place came white enamel fixtures, and polished brass and nickel-plating. (Maybe not as impressive but certainly more practical, especially for a house without servants.) Now and then, through the use of colored tiles, the walls and floors were often as elaborately decorated as any other room in the house. But small hexagonal, large square, or rectangular tiles, usually all in white, were the most popular. Often, a single course of patterned or colored tiles (such as glossy black) was inserted one course below or at the top of the dado, which was about four-feet high. Floor tiles were generally solid colors (usually white) with perhaps a sim-

ple border near the wall. Diamond and mosaic patterns were also used.

Toilets in the mid to late 1800s were a complex system of noisy pipes. By 1900, the syphonic toilet was developed (a model similar to the one we use today), bringing a peaceful and simple unit to the American bathroom. This advance in plumbing brought about first the high-tank, and then the low-tank, toilet. The toilet was made of china or porcelain and featured an oak tank with a matching toilet seat. By 1927, all the fixtures in the bathroom were available only in white china or porcelain. The toilet seat then was made of birch—hand-rubbed until it was ivory white for the ultimate sanitary effect.

The shower/bath also saw dramatic changes around 1900. A shower enclosure was often a semicylinder of

One-piece built-in bathtubs were still to come when this photo was taken, c.1910.

sheet zinc, double-shelled, and perforated inside to give a fine spray, an alternative to the overhead shower, also available by 1900. Showers as separate, freestanding units, or as cylindrical rings hung from the ceiling over the tub, were common features by 1910.

Freestanding tubs with stout legs were available in the Sears Catalog as early as 1902. By 1908, these legs had developed into ball & claw feet (sometimes whimsically gilded). These tubs were replaced, about 1913, by a tub similar to the one we use today. A cast-iron, double-shelled, 5-foot 6-inch-long tub, porcelain-enameled inside and out, was put into quantity production. It was a standard feature of every new house, often built into the

A toilet, c.1890, in the Kohler Museum in Kohler, Wisconsin. In period bathrooms the wooden tank was wall-mounted.

wall of the sanitary, compact bathroom, and available at a price everyone could afford to pay.

In 1900, sinks were one-piece basins made of fireclay or whiteware—what we now call china or porcelain. They often featured a recess for soap and were attached to the wall with brackets and later thin, porcelain legs. (Occasionally, wood cabinets were built to surround or support them.) By 1910, pedestal sinks, always in white, were a standard bathroom fixture. Lever faucet handles were followed by cross or "spoke" handles. Initially, they were made of brass or nickel-plated; later, porcelain became popular. At this time (in keeping with the trend for smaller, compact bathrooms), corner sinks and medicine cabinets became popular.

BATHTUBS

The first permanently sited bathtubs appeared just before the Civil War. Constructed of sheet metal, they resembled open coffins, especially as they were encased in wooden frames. The frame was designed to suit the architecture of the house, but its real purpose was to support the sheet-metal tub. Though tubs were made of lead, zinc, and copper, copper proved more durable than the other two metals. Plumbing manuals of the period recommended that the copper's weight be at least sixteen ounces to the square foot, the usual gauge for roof flashing. Anything less would buckle or "cockle" from expansion caused by hot water.

The design of the basic sheet-metal tub was fairly uniform from manufacturer to manufacturer, and not totally dissimilar from modern tubs. The wooden frame was rectangular, but the tub usually had one rounded end that sloped downward. The square, flat end was fitted with a drain and water spigots. Some versions featured a niche at the supply end in which a standpipe would serve as an overflow valve and bottom drain.

Copper tubs came in a variety of standard sizes. Lengths ranged from 4 1/2 feet to about 6 feet, and internal width and depth tended to be 20 to 25 inches. For an additional price, plumbing-supply manufacturers would provide longer tubs and shower units built into the basic tub. These units consisted of a copper hood at the supply end, supported by a wood frame. The shower plumbing was customized to the owner's requirements, but it usually included an overhead showerhead and side needle sprays with spray attachments aimed at the liver, as well as douche attachments.

Attractive when first installed, copper-and-wood baths were a housekeeper's nightmare. The copper dented easily and was almost impossible to repair. Riveted sheet-metal joints tended to give way after a few years of hard use, and the wood frame eventually suffered from water damage and became unsightly.

By the 1890s, the footed cast-iron porcelain tub dominated most catalogs, but sheet-metal tubs with copper linings on feet got a few listings. The 1898 catalog of the Buick and Sherwood Company of Detroit illustrates several steel bathtubs with galvanized and enameled interiors. In the course of claiming superior durability for the line at the lowest cost, the catalog noted that the steel bathtub was "especially suited for rough usage in tenement houses where people are known to use bathtubs as a receptacle for ice and wood."

All-copper tubs continued to be manufactured, but as one solid sheet rather than by the older method of riveting several together. An innovative material and rare example discussed in Lawler's 1896 American Sanitary Plumbing is an aluminum tub. Lawler described it in glowing terms because of its light weight, durability, and beautiful finish. It was, however, a rare and expensive bathroom feature because aluminum was a new metal in manufacture.

Cast-Iron Tubs

The winning alternative to the sheet-metal tub appeared in the 1860s. Made as a free-standing unit, the cast-iron tub is the familiar, footed fixture associated with the old-fashioned bathroom. In all likelihood, the design can be attributed to the J. L. Mott Iron Works of New York City. Their patented overflow bathtub shows up in trade catalogs of the late 1860s. The 1888 Mott catalog (reproduced today by Dover Publications) illustrates the cast-iron tub as well as a complete line of the older copper tubs.

The sloping shape of one end—that convenient backrest so characteristic of iron tubs—is functional. A quiet, efficient, sanitary drain requires a fair amount of water pressure to operate properly; this shape (and the narrower bottom) helped promote water flow to flush early soil lines clear of bathroom wastes.

The relative location of water inlets and the overflow drain (if any) also became a sanitary concern. While some pioneer manufacturers placed the inlets on the tub bottom, most were mounted higher on the tub wall to reduce the chances that soiled water might be drawn into the freshwater supply and contaminate the system. Even so, some older bathtubs designed without overflow drains were filled from inlets located below the tub rim, an arrangement that fails modern plumbing-code requirements. (Modifying hardware is usually available for these tubs to bring them up to code.)

Positioning the water supply at one end of the tub has always been the most popular layout, but it was not the only choice. By the 1870s, manufacturers were also offering models with the supply and drain fittings sited at the side of the tub. In print, some "sanitarians" felt that the side position was more convenient for the user and tub-scrubber because pipes could be hidden in the wall rather than hung on the tub. It was, however, more expensive, requiring additional carpentry and plaster work. The position of the fittings went hand in hand with the two major tub shapes, which catalogs labeled as "French" pattern (single sloping end) or "Roman" pattern (sloping at both ends).

Although the cast-iron tub was stronger and more durable than the copper tub, it too had several drawbacks.

Before the advent of porcelain coating, the metal had to be kept well painted or it would rust. The painted surface made the tub interior difficult to clean and its design as an elevated, freestanding unit meant that dirt and water could accumulate under and behind the tub.

Although the open area under the tub, the exposed pipes, and the attendant sanitation problems do not seem to have concerned tub manufacturers, it was a serious issue for plumbing-manual authors. Advice columns in both women's magazines and plumbers' annuals cautioned against neglecting regular cleaning of the entire bathroom. While these authors criticized the raised, footed bathtub, manufacturers saw the need to produce a sturdy, durable product and to give homeowners what they wanted. Catalogs demonstrate that the buying public preferred the footed tub well into the twentieth century.

In 1873, the Mott Iron Works produced America's first cast-iron tub with an enameled (porcelain) interior. The design was the same as the cast-iron tub, but the innovation of the interior finish—easy to maintain as it could be wiped clean after each use—made the bathtub a practical household item. The finish did not chip and crack (especially after initial technical problems such as delaminating were worked out), and thus did not need refinishing every few years as did the painted-interior cast-iron bathtub. By the 1920s, the shape of cast-iron bathtubs began changing to the tub-on-base and built-in designs, which led the way to the modern one-piece tub. Footed bathtubs, the most popular product up to World War I, were pushed further and further back in catalogs and advertised as suitable for tenements and inexpensive homes. Manufacturers and designers had been experimenting with built-in tubs since the 1910s; the first versions were freestanding tubs tiled in place. Later, flat aprons were welded onto the tub rim, and by the 1930s tubs cast in one piece were advertised heavily despite the Depression and a stalled house-construction industry.

Porcelain Tubs

Early on, the English sanitary-ware industry had solved many of the technical problems associated with producing large bathroom fixtures, and had been exporting products to America since the second quarter of the nineteenth century—among them bathtubs made completely of porcelain. These were prized above all others for American bathrooms, but their high cost and awesome weight made them impractical for most homes. The all-porcelain tub absorbed a great deal of the bathwater heat, while at the same time remaining colder due to the great mass of porcelain. The tub and water would eventually equalize their temperatures, but there was concern among some plumbing-manual authors that the temperature difference could be annoying. One writer, architect J. Pickering Putnam, went so far as to suggest in 1887 that the shock of different temperatures would be too much for delicate individuals. The first practical American clay porcelain tubs were produced in the 1870s. The Trenton Fire Clay and Porcelain Company made their version with a base of clay (the same used for firebrick) covered with a china glaze. At about the same time, an Englishman, Thomas Maddock, became associated with another Trenton pottery to make tubs, toilet bowls, and sinks "in the English manner."

Both the English and American all-porcelain tubs were similar in design to the footed bath. They were elevated on either four or two support rails with decorative ends. Drain and water-supply pipes were interchangeable between the all-clay, the copper, and the cast-iron tubs.

The all-porcelain tub did not differ in any great detail from the footed tub until the beginning of the twentieth century, when bases began to appear as an alternative to detachable feet. This eliminated a major objection to the footed tub—that of dirt and grime collecting around the tub. The tub-on-base scheme also provided a tidy place for the pipes. Design evolved until the tub was built in as a permanent part of the wall. The base and tub were constructed in one piece with a flat end and side. The flat ends were placed up against a tiled wall and secured with mounting bolts. The tub was usually grouted into the tile wall. By the time of Trenton Potteries Company's 1915 catalog, only two of the fifteen tub designs had feet. Most were designed to sit on a base of porcelain or to be a solid unit. Either way, they were tiled into the floor and wall.

In spite of its sanitary advantages, the all-porcelain tub remained an expensive luxury. The 1900 catalog of Crook, Horner & Co. of Baltimore lists a 5 1/2-foot, all-porcelain tub (the "Nero") for $200. By contrast, the 5 1/2-foot

The cast-iron bathtub feet are bronzed, as is the radiator.

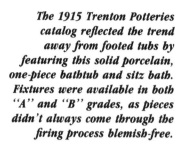

The 1915 Trenton Potteries catalog reflected the trend away from footed tubs by featuring this solid porcelain, one-piece bathtub and sitz bath. Fixtures were available in both "A" and "B" grades, as pieces didn't always come through the firing process blemish-free.

porcelain-enameled, cast-iron "Bard" with wood rim was $34.75. All-porcelain tubs were also extremely heavy and vulnerable to cracking, and required special care to ship and install. In time, these drawbacks doomed the tub. The 1925 Sears plumbing and heating catalog and the 1939 Kohler catalog contain no all-porcelain tubs. Today they are no longer produced.

FIXING UP YOUR OLD ──BATHROOM──

Put away that wrecking bar! Even the most horrendous bathroom can be made shiny and sanitary, usually without the expense of new fixtures or tiles. In many cases a rubber bucket, latex gloves, a scrub brush, and steel wool are the only restoration tools you'll need—along with a healthy measure of old-fashioned elbow grease!

Wall Tiles

In most old houses, bathroom tile was professionally installed by skilled masons and should last for many generations. The majority of tiles will be securely fixed to the wall; it's rare that you'll have to reset more than a few tiles. The first step is to clean any mold, mildew, and soap scum off the tile, so you can better appraise the situation.

Almost anything will clean glazed wall tile. To remove built-up scum, blobs of paint and caulk, and greasy dirt, methodically and gently scrape each tile with a single-edge razor in a holder. Then rinse with ammonia in water.

For heavy-duty cleaning of glazed wall tile, use a non-abrasive scouring agent like Bon Ami or Ajax Liquid with a sponge and hot water. Then thoroughly rinse off the scouring agent with a lot of water. Wipe dry with a terry-cloth towel.

For a super-neglected glazed tile surface, the Ceramic Tile Institute recommends this four-step poultice method: First, coat the tile with an undiluted neutral soap (animal fat soap, for example). Allow to dry and stand for several hours. Next, mix additional soap with warm water, and wet down the tile. While still wet, sprinkle with nonabrasive scouring powder and scrub with a stiff brush. Rinse thoroughly with water, and dry with a terrycloth towel.

Grout lines will probably still be dark with mold and mildew. Household bleach kills these fungi. Mix bleach and hot water and apply to the grout with a stiff old toothbrush. Choose a dilution depending upon the degree of mildew, the amount of ventilation available, and your ability to breathe chlorine. A good solution is one part Clorox to three parts hot water, but you may have to tolerate a 1:1 mixture. A cup of trisodium phosphate (TSP) and 1/2 cup detergent added for every gallon of bleach solution will accelerate its action. *Note:* Never mix bleach and ammonia as the combination produces toxic gases.

While you're scrubbing mold and mildew off the grout, keep a dental pick, awl, or similar tool handy. As soon as you notice any loose grout, dig it out. It's easier to remove it now than to search for it later. After you've thoroughly washed the tiles and removed all the loose grout, vacuum

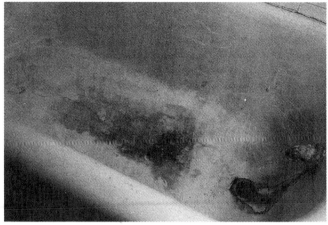

Though it looks hopeless, this tub can be cleaned.

all the open joints left between the tiles. (Use the crevice attachment.) Loose bits of old grout will mar the finish of new grout.

Tile Repair

Before regrouting areas of tile that need it, you have to replace any broken or missing tiles. Also check for any tiles that may be a little loose; subsequent movement of the tiles could spoil the appearance of your new grout.

Modern glues and adhesives won't work well for tiles set in cement. A good material for resetting such tiles is Structolite. Mix the Structolite to a fairly thick consistency, so you can easily set the tile to the proper depth. After the Structolite sets up a little, but before it's completely hard, clean any excess material from between the joints. Now you're ready to grout.

Fixtures

Old neglected bathroom fixtures can be especially grungy. Hard-water deposits, ground-in dirt, and rust stains make them appear unsalvageable. Worse, the porcelain finish may be scratched, gouged, or partially worn through. Damaged fixtures won't look as offensive after a good cleaning, so the first step is to remove dirt and stains.

Scrub the fixtures with Bon Ami, Liquid Ajax, or other nonabrasive cleanser and hot water. This will remove all the surface grime and give you a clearer picture of the filth that remains. Follow with full-strength vinegar on hard-water deposits, and a thorough rinse.

For really resilient, ground-in grime, you'll have to use a mildly abrasive cleaner like Ajax or Comet. Sprinkle the powder all over the fixtures, and wet with just enough water to form a thick paste. This acts as a poultice, bleaching the porcelain and drawing out stains. Allow to stand for several hours, keeping it moist. Then add some more cleanser and water, and scrub the dickens out of the sink, tub, or toilet with a stiff-bristle scrub brush. Rinse thoroughly with plenty of warm water.

After you've used these cleaning procedures, you may still be dissatisfied with the appearance of your bathroom fixtures. Abuse, repeated abrasive cleaning, or a constant drip may have worn away some of the porcelain, permitting deep penetration of rust stains. Crazed or chipped enamel may have allowed dirt to work its way down into the iron or clay body underneath, turning the cracks or chips dirty brown. Often these problem areas can be cleaned, but some of the methods may be damaging to the already-worn porcelain. So when it's time to bring on the artillery, always test its destructiveness in a small, inconspicuous area before proceeding.

Most rust stains can be removed with readily available commercial products sold in most hardware stores. Stay away from the sodium hydroxide crystals or other caustics packaged as rust removers; we've yet to find one that works effectively on stains (although they will do a job on your nasal passages). Naval jelly, muriatic acid, and dilute phosphoric acid are all quite effective for removing stubborn rust stains. Any chemical that will remove rust deposits deserves special respect and appropriate care when handling. Also, these preparations are not to be poured all over your fixtures just before you take off for the weekend: You don't want to leave them on your porcelain one second longer than is necessary to remove the stain.

Resurfacing Fixtures

Refinishing a bathroom fixture does carry some risk of failure. This is absolutely not a do-it-yourself proposition; we're talking about professional "reglazing" using polyurethane-based coatings. You may ultimately decide to buy a reproduction fixture rather than have the existing sink or tub refinished.

Bathtub refinishing has gotten a lot of bad press, much of it deserved. Ten or fifteen years ago, site-mixed two-part epoxy paints were used; these failed more often than was tolerable. Fly-by-night contractors sprang up, painted a lot of tubs, took the money, and left town before the new finishes started to peel. Some of those contractors were downright fraudulent opportunists. Others were well-intentioned businesspeople who lacked either expertise or proper materials.

Today, you can find well-trained, reputable contractors

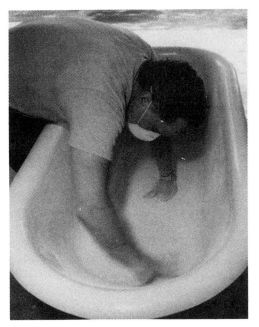

One part of the cleaning involves
wet-sanding the tub with 600-grit sandpaper.

mask or clean up—but you'll save money only if *you* can haul the fixture to and from the shop.

There are two basic processes used by national refinishing services. The only major difference is in how the paint is bonded to the surface. *Acid etching* creates a mechanical bond between the porcelain and the new coating. *Chemical bonding,* as the name suggests, uses a bonding agent that chemically connects the new coating to the porcelain. Cleaning, filling, sanding, painting, and polishing are all done in the same way for both processes.

The refinishers will disconnect all fittings and plumbing connections so that there will be a continuous coating on the fixture. (Painting around fittings would leave an edge—and that's where the coating could begin to fail.) A good scrubbing with a commercial detergent removes all surface oils and soapy residue. Then a wash with a proprietary phosphoric-acid cleaner removes scale and rust stains. The acid is often applied with 100-grit wet-or-dry sandpaper to make rust removal faster. The fixture is then rinsed with clear water, followed by an acetone wash. Finally, the fixture is allowed to dry thoroughly.

Once the piece is clean, nicks, gouges, and scratches are filled in and sanded smooth. This procedure is much like auto-body repair. Damaged areas are sanded with coarse sandpaper to rough up the surface to provide keying for the filler. A fiber filler is applied to the imperfections with a Teflon applicator, then wet-sanded smooth with a progression of grits once it sets up.

At this point the procedure differs depending on whether the contractor is using acid etching or chemical bonding to promote adhesion of the new coating. With

who use high-tech coatings to produce long-lasting finishes on old fixtures. While the process does have its limitations—paint doesn't perform like porcelain—you can expect to get a finish that will last ten years or more.

Fixture refinishing is a painting process. Even if the name of the product includes words like glass, glazing, porcelain or enamel, it's still paint. (We're often asked if it's possible to have a fixture reporcelainized and refired. In practice, we know of no such service.)

Refinishing lets you get fancy, by the way. You can choose almost any color or you can have the fixture poly-chromed or stenciled.

If you have an irreplaceable, one-of-a-kind fixture, the choice is clear: Have it refinished. Refinishing is sensible, too, if replacing the fixture would mean ripping up the whole bathroom. But if you have a more pedestrian piece, like a standard pedestal sink, consider buying a reproduction. A reproduction pedestal sink can be had for about $450 (and lasts 40 plus years). Refinishing an old one costs $150 (and lasts 10 to 15 years). A clawfoot tub sells for about $1500 brand new. You can have the old one refinished for about $450.

Of course, a new fixture will last longer than a refinished one. On the other hand, a new fixture may have attendant plumbing and tile work costs. When getting bids, please remember that you get what you pay for. If someone offers to paint your tub for fifty bucks, it will look great only until you fill it with water.

Most professional refinishers offer both on-site and in-shop service. If you're doing a major bathroom remodeling project, the contractor will advise you to remove the fixtures for refinishing in the shop. A shop environment is more controlled than your bathroom. Dust can be kept to a minimum, temperature and humidity set, the cat won't wander in. . . . Also, the contractor won't have to

REFINISHING SERVICES

There are many reputable, independently owned refinishing contractors in the Yellow Pages. Another place to start is with the companies listed below; they can give you the name of their authorized dealer nearest you. These local services are still independently owned, but they use the parent company's materials and methods, and have received training from the national chain.

Bathmasters International
1595 Miller Road
Imperial, MO 63052
(314)464-3242

DuraGlaze Service
  Corporation
2825 Bransford Avenue,
  Dept. OHJ
Nashville, TN 37204
(615)298-1787

Miracle Method
701 Center Street, Dept.
  OHJ
Ludlow, MA 01056
(413)589-0769

Perma Ceram
65 Smithtown Boulevard
Smithtown, NY 11788
(800)645-5039

Perma Glaze
1638 Research Loop Road,
  No. 160
P.O. Box 18377
Tucson, AZ 85710
(800)332-7397

Polyurethane paint is sprayed on the carefully prepared tub in several applications.

Outsides are typically rough-cast and pitted—but they can be skim-coated.

the acid-etching technique, the fixture receives a hydro-fluoric-acid wash. The acid etches the surface of the porcelain to allow the new coating to mechanically bond to the porcelain. With the chemical-bonding technique, the refinisher applies a liquid bonding agent.

After this painstaking preparation, the refinisher uses a spray gun to apply several coats of a high-gloss, polyurethane-based finish. Frequently, an infrared heat lamp is used to speed curing of the new coating. Once the finish has completely cured, dust particles and other foreign material are polished out of the surface by wet-sanding with 1200-grit sandpaper, followed by polishing with rubbing compound. (If the environment was especially dusty, it may be necessary for the contractor to start with 600- or even 400-grit wet-or-dry paper during polishing.)

To maintain your refinished fixture, don't use Ajax or Comet. Those cleansers are quite abrasive and will wear away the coating in no time. Use a liquid bathroom cleaner like SoftScrub. When necessary, you can resort to a nonabrasive powder such as Bon Ami.

Don't worry that you won't be able to adequately clean

the sink or tub. Refinished pieces have very smooth, high-gloss surfaces, and will clean up easily without any need of abrasive scrubbing.

Tile Floors

The standard solution for a dirty or damaged floor is to cover it with linoleum or vinyl tiles—a temporary remedy, at best. Most of the time it's just as easy to clean and repair tile floors as it is to cover them up with whatever is on sale at the home center. Original tile floors are worth saving; not only are they attractive and historically appropriate, but they're also long wearing and, when properly repaired, watertight.

The first step in restoring a tile floor may be finding the darned thing. It's not unusual for the floor to be hidden under half a dozen layers of linoleum. Removing the offensive layers is usually no problem. Linoleum does not stay put very well once water has gotten underneath it, so if you can lift one corner, you may be able to roll the whole floor up in one sheet. If it resists, gentle prying with a wide-blade putty knife should do the trick.

The finished tub: a blue exterior and a glossy white inside. Some folks get extravagant and have the feet highlighted with gold leaf.

A handpainted Blue Willow design was added to this antique tub during repainting. Fancy painting and colored "glaze" are refinishing options.

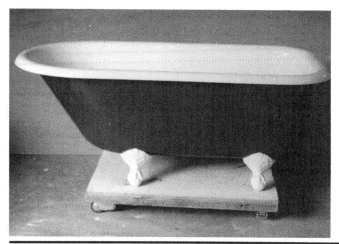

If the linoleum resists your efforts, try using a heat gun. The heat will penetrate the linoleum and soften the mastic (glue) that holds it down. If you move the heat gun along slowly, you should be able to lift the linoleum in small sections with a wide putty knife. A wallpaper steamer may also be used for this purpose. After the mastic cools, most of it can be removed from the tile by knocking it free with a putty knife, or scraping it off with a single-edge razor blade.

When you first examine your tile floor, you may consider covering it back up. Resist the temptation; after a good scrubbing you'll see that it's worth saving.

Here's the procedure for cleaning a heavily stained and soiled tile floor:

1. Vacuum thoroughly, then remove surface dirt with a quick detergent-and-hot-water mopping.

2. Scrub the floor with scouring powder, hot water, and scrub brush. Use 00 steel wool wherever gummy deposits exist. Rinse well with water and repeat process on bad areas. This step should take at least an hour for a small bathroom.

3. Mix Clorox and hot water 1:1 and spread evenly over the floor. Let stand until it has evaporated. This will bleach the floor and fade deeply imbedded stains. (Bathroom floor tile is unglazed to keep it nonslippery, but it does stain.) Rinse with clear water.

4. If necessary, scrub the grout with a stiff old toothbrush dipped in muriatic acid. Be sure to wear goggles and rubber gloves, and provide adequate ventilation. Completely rinse muriatic acid off the grout immediately. Muriatic acid works by dissolving some of the grout, so it's important not to let it stand any longer than necessary.

If stains and discolorations remain after such a thorough cleaning, you may be able to remove them with a poultice; one that works well on stubborn stains in floor tile is made of lacquer thinner and cornstarch. (*Warning:* Lacquer thinner is extremely flammable.) Pour lacquer thinner over a small section of the floor, and sprinkle cornstarch on it. Mush together to form a wet paste. The cornstarch draws the solvent up out of the tile, taking the stain with it. You'll see the snowy-white cornstarch turn gray-brown as it absorbs the stain and dries. Pick up the dry powder with a wide putty knife and dispose of it.

Regrouting may be necessary. Regrouting a floor is identical to grouting wall tiles—actually it's a little easier because you're working on a horizontal surface. Be sure to follow the manufacturer's instructions for mixing and curing the grout.

Cement patches may exist around toilets and tubs—plumbers fixing a leak are generally unconcerned about the damage they do to tiles. Fortunately, insensitive patchwork is usually confined to inconspicuous areas behind fixtures. If the tiles and patch are approximately the same color, just paint false grout lines on the patch. If not, smooth the patch level with a cold chisel and paint in false tiles. Sure, close inspection will reveal your time-saving trick—but few will notice at first glance.

Caulking

You need a flexible sealant around fixtures and in corners. Movement between fixtures and walls, and between tiles set in two different planes, will cause grout to fail in very short order.

Before caulking, thoroughly clean the joint. Remove all loose grout, caulk, soap film, and mildew. Use an elastic, nonporous, high-quality silicone sealant from a major manufacturer.

When sealing around a bathtub, first fill the tub with water, so the joint is at its maximum width. Apply the sealant by pushing the nozzle along the joint rather than pulling it. Dip your finger in water and use it to smooth the bead. Be careful not to get the stuff near your eyes, and wash thoroughly after handling the sealant. Clean up any blobs or drips with a razor blade after the caulk has set.

Cleanliness goes a long way toward making an old bathroom look like a well-cared-for antique. There are also several low-cost things you can do to spruce it up a little. For instance, replacing that gaudy 1960s light fixture with something more suitable can make a tremendous difference. A bright shower curtain will draw your attention away from the minor nicks and stains left in the bathtub. If you use a pipe collar to cover that gaping hole where the water feed passes through the floor, you'll improve the appearance of the entire room.

The important thing at this point is to look for low-cost measures that improve the general appearance of the bathroom. Painting the trim or stripping the door, replacing the broken cover plates, buying a new mirror or hanging a thick, colorful towel on a handsome towel rack will help the room a lot, yet may require less than $20 worth of materials.

PLAYING IT SAFE

• *Never* mix bleach and ammonia! When mixed, the two produce toxic gases. The fumes from these gases are insidious and can be fatal.

• Fumes from bleach, ammonia, and other cleaning preparations can be very damaging when inhaled. Always provide ample ventilation when handling these cleansers. If this isn't possible, wear a close-fitting respirator rated for organic solvents.

• Bathroom cleansers and stain removers can be very rough on your skin, and can permanently damage your eyes. Rubber gloves and safety glasses or goggles will save much discomfort.

• Solvents, like lacquer thinner and mineral spirits, are highly flammable. Provide plenty of ventilation when using these materials, and never use them in combination with a power tool.

• Grout and silicone caulks can be very damaging to your eyes. Wear proper protective gear and clean your hands thoroughly after handling these products.

• Inhalation of grout can cause extreme discomfort in allergic or asthmatic people. Even if you're not allergic, it will burn like the devil if it gets in your nose. Wear a dust mask when using any cement-based product.

APPENDIX 1

RENOVATOR'S LIBRARY

I. GENERAL REPAIR & MAINTENANCE

The Book of Home Restoration by John McGowan & Roger DuBern. New York: Gallery Books, 1985

Landmark Yellow Pages Washington, D.C.: Preservation Press, 1990

Modern Carpentry by Willis H. Wagner. South Holland, Ill.: Goodheart-Willcox, 1983

Old House Woodwork Restoration by Ed Johnson. Englewood Cliffs, N.J.: Prentice-Hall, 1983

Plastering Skills by F. Van Den Branden & Thomas L. Hartsell. Homewood, Ill.: American Technical, 1984

II. HOUSE STYLES

The American House by Mary Mix Foley. New York: Harper & Row, 1980

American Shelter by Lester Walker. Woodstock, N.Y.: Overlook, 1981

The Comfortable House by Alan Gowans. Cambridge, Mass.: MIT Press, 1987

A Field Guide to American Architecture by Carol Rifkind. New York: New American Library, 1980

A Field Guide to American Houses by Virginia & Lee McAlester. New York: Knopf, 1989

III. SYSTEMS

Electrical Wiring: Third Edition by Thomas S. Colvin. Athens, Ga.: AAVIM, 1991

Modern Roofing by Donald L. Meyers. Passaic, N.J.: Creative Homeowner Press, 1981

Plumbing for Old and New Houses by Jay Hedden. Passaic, N.J.: Creative Homeowner Press, 1981

Plumbing for Dummies by Don Frederiksson. New York: Bobbs-Merrill, 1983

Wiring: Basic Repairs by Mort Schultz. Passaic, N.J.: Creative Homeowner Press, 1981

IV. PERIOD DECORATING

American Interiors by Harold L. Peterson. New York: Charles Scribner's Sons, 1971

A Documentary History of American Interiors by Edgar Mayhew & Minor Myers. New York: Charles Scribner's Sons, 1980

Style Traditions by Stephen Calloway & Stephen Jones. New York: Rizzoli, 1990

Three Centuries of American Furniture by Oscar P. Fitzgerald. Englewood Cliffs, N.J.: Prentice-Hall, 1982

Victorian Interior Decoration by Roger Moss & Gail Winkler. New York: Holt, 1986

APPENDIX 2

SOURCES

CHAPTER 1

Architectural Services—Consulting Services & Historical Research

Alvin Holm, A.I.A. Architects
2014 Sansom Street, Dept. OHJ
Philadelphia, PA 19103
(215)963-0747
Design and consultation, preservation, adaptive re-use, appropriate additions. Also historic structures reports, systems analysis, National Register nominations.

Office of Allen Charles Hill AIA
25 Englewood Road, Dept. OHJ
Winchester, MA 01890
(617)729-0748
Architectural services for restoration, conservation, replication, and addition; building evaluation, analysis, technical assistance, and troubleshooting; research, consultation, and historic structures reports; lectures and workshops.

Archeological Surveys

Behre & McCabe, P.C.
43 Trinity Street, Dept. OHJ
Newton, NJ 07860
(201)579-2525
Preservation planning, historical research, National Register nominations, historic site surveys, adaptive re-use and restoration projects, grant proposals, building inspections, historic district ordinances, site interpretation, and Tax Act certifications.

National Preservation Institute
401 F Street, NW Dept. OHJ
Washington, DC 20001
(202)393-0038
Technical services include: preservation development and marketing strategies, reuse-feasibility analysis, tax-certification for historic rehabilitation, preservation and maintenance plans, and archeology surveys.

House Plans, Period Designs

Cross Country, Inc.
PO Box 15026, Dept. OHJ
Savannah, GA 31416
(912)354-2677
Traditionally styled, comfortable floor plans range from 1,260 to 3,760 square feet. AIA architecturally drafted, builder tested, construction drawings are available.

W.S. Lockhart
112 South Warren Street, Dept. OHJ
Timmonsville, SC 29161
(803)346-3531
Offering over 1,600 home plan designs and the blueprints.

CHAPTER 2

Contracting Services, Restoration

Restorations Unlimited, Inc.
24 West Main Street, Dept. OHJ
Elizabethville, PA 17023
(717)362-3477
General contractor specializing in the restoration of old houses.

George Yonnone Restorations
RD #2, West Center Road, Dept. OHJ
W. Stockbridge, MA 01266
(413)232-7060
A full-service company specializing in antique home and barn repair, restoration, and relocating. Offering a national consulting service focusing on difficult structural repairs to timber frames and antique structures damaged by natural disasters.

Heritage Restoration
122 South Church Avenue, Dept. OHJ
Bozeman, MT 05715
(406)587-1082
A design, consulting, and construction management firm specializing in historically sensitive remodeling and the acquisition of materials and labor for old-house restoration.

House-Inspection Services

Building Inspection Services Inc.
12813 Prestwick Drive, Dept. OHJ
Ft. Washington, MD 20744
(301)292-1299
Professional home inspectors and building consultants. Fax: (301)292-3730. Free literature.

Homecheck Building Inspections
PO Box 9614, Dept. OHJ
Fort Collins, CO 80525
(303)482-1976
Written reports based on physical evaluations and detail defects are provided, as well as prescribed remedies and estimate costs to cure. Specialists in older residential and commercial properties, and qualified asbestos and environmental inspectors.

HouseMaster of America
421 W. Union Avenue, Dept. OHJ
Bound Brook, NJ 08805
(800)526-3939
Home inspections performed for either the buyer or the seller to determine the condition of the house prior to sale.

CHAPTER 3

Architectural Services—Restoration Design

The Aachen Designers
22 West University Avenue, Dept. OHJ
Gainesville, FL 32601
(904)372-5056
Architectural and interior design firm: commercial and residential adaptive reuse, period design, restorations, measured drawings, programming, basic services (AIAB141), consulting, expert witness.

Douglas Gest Restorations Inc.
Box 832, Dept. OHJ
Norwich, VT 05055
(802)649-2928
A complete architectural restoration firm offering a full range of services.

The Image Group
398 So. Grant Avenue, Dept. OHJ
Columbus, OH 43215
(614)221-1016
Architectural and interior design services in the area of building rehabilitation and restoration.

Training Courses & Workshops

Architectural Resources Group
Pier 9, The Embarcadero, Dept. OHJ
San Francisco, CA 94111
(415)421-1680
Specialists in historic preservation with over 10 years experience.

Preservation Associates, Inc.
117 South Potomac Street, Dept. OHJ
Hagerstown, MD 21740
(301)791-7880

A nationally oriented firm providing a broad range of preservation consulting, educational and rehabilitation services relating specifically to older buildings.

Yestermorrow Design/Build School
PO Box 344, Dept. OHJ
Warren, VT 05674
(802)496-5545
Offering 1-week, 2-week, and 6-week courses teaching the homeowner or lay person how to design and build his home, complete a renovation, or build custom cabinetry.

Conservator's Tools

Conservation Materials, Ltd.
1165 Marietta Way, Dept. OHJ
Sparks, NV 89431
(702)331-0582
Suppliers of products and tools for professional conservation work.

TALAS
213 West 35th Street, Dept. OHJ
New York, NY 10001
(212)736-7744
Selling supplies to conservators and art restorers.

Architectural Salvage

Art Directions, Inc.
6120 Delmar Boulevard, Dept. OHJ
St. Louis, MO 63112
(314)863-1895
In the architectural salvage business since 1972. Specialists in restored lighting fixtures for both commercial and residential use, stained and beveled glass doors and windows, and other architectural pieces.

Philadelphia Architectural Salvage Ltd.
1214 North 26th Street, Dept. OHJ
Philadelphia, PA 19121
(215)236-9339
Non-profit suppliers of affordable, re-usable building materials. Product line includes mantels, columns, bars, roofing materials, architectural artifacts, and vintage furniture.

Salvage One Architectural Artifacts
1524 S. Sangamon Street, Dept. OHJ
Chicago, IL 60608
(312)733-0098
The midwest's largest source for architectural artifacts. Specialists in American and Continental artifacts from the 19th through the early 20th centuries.

United House Wrecking, Inc.
535 Hope Street, Dept. OHJ
Stamford, CT 06906
(203)348-5371
Connecticut's largest antique store and emporium. 30,000 square feet of unique antiques, nostalgia, architectural artifacts, memorabilia, furniture, fine stained glass, old lighting and plumbing fixtures, unusual wall decorations, fancy doors and windows, marble and wood mantels, French doors, ironwork, Victorian gingerbread, plumbing fixtures, fencing, lighting fixtures. Also butcher blocks, baker's racks, and marine and subway treasures.

Renovation Supply Stores

Cumberland General Store, Inc.
Route 3, Box 81, Dept. OHJ
Crossville, TN 38555
(800)334-4640
Complete outfitters: goods in endless variety for man and beast. From chamber pots to covered wagons—over 10,000 items available.

Renovation Concepts, Inc.
213 Washington Avenue, North, Dept. OHJ
Minneapolis, MN 55401
(612)333-5766
Distributors of unique and decorative architectural products for 12 years. Materials include columns and pedestals, mouldings and fretwork, tin ceilings, brass railings, door locksets and trim, pedestal sinks and faucets as well as lighting fixtures.

The Renovator's Supply
7594 Renovator's Old Mill, Dept. OHJ
Millers Falls, MA 01349
(413)659-2211
Suppliers of a wide selection of unique items such as bath fixtures and accessories, brass and chrome faucets, brass railings, ceiling medallions, solid-brass door and cabinet hardware, exterior and interior doors, ceramic and marble flooring, kitchen sinks and faucets, lighting fixtures, stair rods, switchplates, wallcoverings, and weathervanes.

CHAPTER 4

Power Tools

Addkison Hardware Co., Inc.
126 E. Amite Street, PO Box 102, Dept. OHJ
Jackson, MS 39205
(800)821-2750
A large stock of professional power tools is available for the builder and woodworking trades.

Milwaukee Electric Tool Corporation
13135 West Lisbon Road, Dept. OHJ
Brookfield, WI 53005
(414)781-3600
Manufacturer of portable electric tools such as drills, saws, grinders, hoists, routers, shears, vacuum cleaners, and much more.

Skil Corporation
4300 West Peterson Avenue, Dept. OHJ
Chicago, IL 60646
(312)286-7330
Manufacturers of a complete line of portable power tools and accessories including cordless products.

Wedge Innovations
2040 Fortune Drive, Dept. OHJ
San Jose, CA 95131
(800)762-7853
Developers and manufacturers of high-quality electronic hand and power tools for professional contractors and do-it-yourself users.

Adzes, Froes & Hand-Hewing Tools

Albert Constantine & Son, Inc.
2050 Eastchester Road, Dept. OHJ
Bronx, NY 10461
(212)792-1600
A retail and mail-order distributor of quality woodworking equipment and supplies.

Garrett Wade Company
161 Avenue of the Americas, Dept. OHJ
New York, NY 10013
(212)807-1155
A comprehensive selection of quality hand woodworking and carving tools, many imported from Western Europe and Japan.

Iron Horse Antiques, Inc.
PO Box 4001, Dept. OHJ
Pittsford, VT 05763
(802)483-2111
Publishers of The Fine Tool Journal, *a quarterly magazine devoted to fine hand tools, whether antique, obsolete, or modern.*

Safety Equipment

Direct Safety Company
7815 South 46th Street, Dept. OHJ
Phoenix, AZ 85044
(800)528-7405
A large assortment of mail-order safety equipment from goggles to leak detectors to asbestos-removal gloves.

Roofmaster Products Company
750 Monterey Pass Road, Dept. OHJ
Monterey Park, CA 91754
(213)261-5122
A large source for the industry's roofing equipment, tools, and accessory products, from safety products to hand tools.

CHAPTER 5

Masonry Patching & Restoration Materials

Abatron, Inc.
33 Center Drive, Dept. OHJ
Gilberts, IL 60136
(708)426-2200

Manufacturers of patching and resurfacing compounds for structural and decorative restoration.

Lehigh Portland Cement Company
718 Hamilton Mall, Dept. OHJ
Allentown, PA 18105
(215)776-2600
Producers of a complete line of gray portland and masonry cements for use in general concrete and masonry construction.

Tuff-Kote Company, Inc.
210 Seminary Avenue, Dept. OHJ
Woodstock, IL 60098
(815)338-2006
Manufacturers of quality interior and exterior building repair products to prime, patch, and seal roofs, gutters, chimneys, weathered wood, and masonry.

Mortar Analysis

Hayes & Associates Restoration
Route 12, Box 48, Dept. OHJ
Dothan, AL 36303
(205)692-3078
Exterior restoration (especially of masonry buildings). Mortar-matched experts.

Masonry Ink
PO Box 514, M.U. 18, Dept. OHJ
Yelm, WA 98597
(206)458-6777
Custom mortar and restorations. Mortar color matching through the mail and on site.

SPNEA Conservation Center
185 Lyman Street, Dept. OHJ
Waltham, MA 02154
(617)891-1985
Providing technical expertise for the conservation of original or period finishes: paint, wood, plaster, and stone.

Basement Waterproofing

Basement Water Control Corp.
1375 Laurel Avenue, Dept. OHJ
St. Paul, MN 55104
(612)646-7444

Makers of the Beaver Drain Systems.

Hancor, Inc.
401 Olive Street, Dept. OHJ
Findlay, OH 45840
(419)422-6521
Makers of the Channel Drain.

Thoro System Products
7800 NW 38th Street, Dept. OHJ
Miami, FL 33166
(305)592-2081
This business unit of ICI Specialty Chemicals is an international manufacturer of products formulated to waterproof, protect, decorate, and restore concrete and masonry.

Turnbuckle Stars

Clarksville Foundry, Inc.
PO Box 786, Dept. OHJ
Clarksville, TN 37040
(615)647-1538
Producers of a wide range of rough and finished castings in volumes of one piece to several hundred.

G. Krug & Son, Inc.
415 West Saratoga Street, Dept. OHJ
Baltimore, MD 21201
(301)752-3166
Manufacturers since 1810 of custom artistic ironwork.

Windy Hill Forge
3824 Schroeder Avenue, Dept. OHJ
Perry Hall, MD 21128
(410)256-5890
Builder hardware.

CHAPTER 6

Specialty Roofers

C&H Roofing, Inc.
PO Box 2105, Dept. OHJ
Lake City, FL 32056
(800)327-8115
Encompassing every phase of roofing: design, manufacturing, and installation.

C.H.S. Roofing, Inc.
272 Old Wells Road, Dept. OHJ
Easton, PA 18042
(215)252-0230

Roofing contractors specializing in the repair of existing clay, concrete, and slate roofs. Installers of new roofs of concrete, clay, slate, or copper.

South Side Roofing & Sheet Metal Company, Inc.
290 Hanley Industrial Court, Dept. OHJ
Saint Louis, MO 63144
(314)968-4800
Specialists in repair and restoration of slate and tile roofing. Custom metal fabrication of all types for roofing, guttering, etc.

Clay Tile Roofing

CertainTeed Corporation
17199 Laurel Park Drive, No. #201, Dept. OHJ
Livonia, MI 48152
(800)233-8990
A leading manufacturer of building materials including clay roof tiles and attic ventilation.

Ludowici-Celadon Inc.
PO Box 69, Dept. OHJ
New Lexington, OH 43764
(614)342-1995
Manufacturers of clay roof tiles for some of the nation's most well-known architecturally designed buildings.

TileSearch
PO Box 580, 216 James Street, Dept. OHJ
Roanoke, TX 76262
(817)491-2444
A computerized listing and selling service that provides all brands and shapes of the world's finest previously used clay roof tiles.

Vande Hey-Raleigh Manufacturing, Inc.
1665 Bohm Drive, Dept. OHJ
Little Chute, WI 54140
(800)236-8453
Roof tile available in shake, slate, hand brushed, Spanish, staggered, Cotswold stone, Riviera, or turret styles. Over 60 standard colors are available, as well as custom matching of any request, no matter the age of the tile.

Fiber/Cement Tile Roofing

Elk Corporation
14643 Dallas Parkway, Dept. OHJ
Dallas, TX 75240
(214)851-0400
Manufacturers of fiberglass roofing shingles.

IKO Manufacturing, Inc.
120 Hay Road, Dept. OHJ
Wilmington, DE 19809
(302)764-3100
A quality manufacturer of residential and commercial asphalt roofing products.

Supradur Manufacturing
Corporation
PO Box 908, Dept. OHJ
Rye, NY 10580
(800)223-1948
Manufacturers of 7 different styles of fiber-cement roofing shingles including slate substitutes, shake substitutes, deep grain staggered edge shingles, and replicas of historic shingle designs.

Metal Roofing

Conklin Metal Industries
PO Box 1858, Dept. OHJ
Atlanta, GA 30301
(404)688-4510
Manufacturers of metal roofing shingles, including one pattern typical of late 19th-century houses. Available in galvanized steel, copper, TCS, or terne.

Follansbee Steel
PO Box 610, Dept. OHJ
Follansbee, WV 26037
(304)527-1260
A leading producer of terne and terne-coated stainless roofing materials.

W.F. Norman Corporation
PO Box 323, 214 N. Cedar,
Dept. OHJ
Nevada, MO 64772
(800)641-4038
The nation's most complete collection of architectural sheet metal, including metal roof shingles.

Slate Roofing

Buckingham-Virginia Slate
Corporation
PO Box 8, Dept. OHJ
Arvonia, VA 23004
(804)581-1132

Excellent quality Virginia-region slate. Roofing slate available. Out-of-state shipping possible on orders.

H.B. Slate
RD 2, Box 131, Dept. OHJ
Granville, NY 12832
(518)642-2894
Manufacturers of slate products including colored flagstone, slate tile, veneer stone, and roofing slate.

The Structural Slate Company
222 E. Main Street, PO Box
187, Dept. OHJ
Pen Argyl, PA 18072
(215)863-4141
Flooring, roofing, fireplace facings and hearths, and other items made from slate.

Wood-Shingle Roofing

Granville Manufacturing Co.
Inc.
Route 100, PO Box 15, Dept.
OHJ
(802)767-4747
Manufacturer and wholesaler of specialty wood products for the building industry. Specialists in exterior siding products for new construction and restoration work.

Liberty Cedar
535 Liberty Lane, Dept. OHJ
W. Kingston, RI 02892
(401)789-6626
A lumber yard specializing in western red cedar, redwood, mahogany, and exterior wood products, especially wood roofs for historical applications.

South Coast Shingle
Company, Inc.
2220 East South Street, Dept.
OHJ
Long Beach, CA 90805
(213)634-7100
An old family business manufacturing fancy-cut wood shingles.

Slate Roofing Tools

Acme Construction, Inc.
PO Box 327, Dept. OHJ
Leeds, NY 12451
(518)945-2575
Specialists in exterior restoration, as well as slate, tile, and metal roofing.

Sonneborn Building Products
7711 Computer Avenue,
Dept. OHJ
Minneapolis, MN 55435
(612)835-3434
Complete line of quality products including roofing tools.

Slate Tools

Lehman Hardware &
Appliances
PO Box 41J, Dept. OHJ
Kidron, OH 44636
(216)857-5441
Old-fashioned, but still useful appliances and tools from the Amish/Mennonite community, including slater's and blacksmith's tools.

John Stortz & Son, Inc.
210 Vine Street, Dept. OHJ
Philadelphia, PA 19106
(215)627-3855
Manufacturers of a line of hand tools for the building trade, including slater's tools.

Wood Shakes & Shingles—For Siding

Mad River Woodworks
189 Taylor Way, PO Box
1067, Dept. OHJ
Blue Lake, CA 95525
(707)668-5671
Respected millwork shop providing quality turn-of-the-century and custom millwork in redwood and select hardwoods, including shingles.

Vintage Wood Works
Hwy. 34 South, PO Box R,
Dept. 2161
Quinlan, TX 75474
(903)356-2158
Major supplier of authentic Victorian and country millwork for interior and exterior.

West Forest Wood Products
PO Box 1500, Dept. OHJ
Coos Bay, OR 97420
(503)269-9597
Producers of mainly western red cedar shakes and shingles. Hand split, resawn 3/4-inch, 1/2-inch, and jumbo. Shingles: 5/8- and 7/8-inch. Special orders are welcome.

Handmade Nails

Iron Intentions Forge
1112 Lucabaugh Mill Road,
Dept. OHJ
Westminster, MD 21157
(410)876-6299
Reproduction 18th-century restoration hardware built to customers' specifications. All items from nails to fences, in both classic and contemporary style.

Manasquan Premium
Fasteners
PO Box 669, Dept. OHJ
Allenwood, NJ 08720
(800)542-1979
A national mail-order house supplying stainless steel fasteners. The product line includes stainless steel nails, screws, framing connectors, staples, and collated nails for pneumatic nailers.

Tremont Nail Company
PO Box 111, Dept. OHC92
Wareham, MA 02571
(508)295-0038
The world's oldest cut nail manufacturer. Manufacturers of twenty different patterns of cut nails for restoration work and Colonial effect.

Gutters, Leaders, & Leaderboxes

Jeff Alte Roofing, Inc.
PO Box 639, Dept. OHJ
Somerville, NJ 08876
(908)526-2111
Expertise and equipment to handle copper gutters, leaders, and built-in gutters. The metal shop can fabricate gutters, ridge caps, etc.

Inner Harbor Lumber &
Hardware
900 Fleet Street, Dept. OHJ
Baltimore, MD 21202
(301)837-0202
A renovation products center. Stock includes structural as well as decorative materials, including gutters and plumbing items.

Yost Manufacturing & Supply
Inc.
1018 Hartford Tpke., Rt. 85,
Dept. OHJ
Waterford, CT 06385
(800)872-9678

Roof Balustrades

Empire Woodworks
PO Box 717, Dept. OHJ
Blanco, TX 78606
(512)833-2116
Full line of Victorian wood products including brackets, corbels, spandrels, gable trim, porch posts, balustrades, and more.

Mansion Industries, Inc.
14425 E. Clark Avenue, PO Box 2220, Dept. OHJ
City of Industry, CA 91746
(818)968-9501
Manufacturer of wood products such as roof balustrades.

Roof Cresting

Adornments for Architecture
309 Hollow Road, Dept. OHJ
Staatsburg, NY 12580
(914)889-8390
Designers, fabricators, and suppliers of architectural ornaments.

Stewart Iron Works Company
PO Box 2612, Dept. OHJ
Covington, KY 41012
(606)431-1985
A manufacturer of ornamental iron products since 1886, including roof cresting.

Cupolas & Roof Vents

Cape Cod Cupola Company, Inc.
78 State Road, Dept. OHJ
North Dartmouth, MA 02747
(508)994-2119
Offering one of the largest selections of cupolas.

Classic Architectural Specialties
3223 Canton Street, Dept. OHJ
Dallas, TX 75223
(214)748-1668
One stop source for uncommon architectural ornamentation, including cupolas.

Midget Louver Company
800 Main Avenue, Dept. OHJ
Norwalk, CT 06851
(203)866-2342
Louvers that are excellent for venting moisture, air, and heat. They are round, all aluminum, in sizes 1–6

inches and are available in several styles.

Period Skylights

Fisher Skylights, Inc.
50 Snake Hill Road, Dept. OHJ
West Nyack, NY 10994
(914)358-9000
Designers, manufacturers, and installers of custom metal framed and glass skylights.

Albert J. Wagner & Son, Inc.
3762 North Clark Street, Dept. OHJ
Chicago, IL 60641
(312)935-1414
Fabrication and local installation of copper and glass skylights; gable and hip styles, cornice moulding and inlaid gutters.

Weather Shield Mfg., Inc.
531 North 8th Street, Dept. OHJ
Medford, WI 54451
(800)477-6808
Manufacturer of top quality, energy efficient wood windows and skylights.

Chimney Brushes

Ace Wire Brush Company Inc.
30 Henry Street, Dept. OHJ
Brooklyn, NY 11201
(718)624-8032
Manufacturers of all types of brushes and brooms. Chimney brushes and rod handles are also available.

Mazzeo's Chimney Sweep Suppliers
RFD 1, Box 1245, Dept. OHJ
Rockland, ME 04841
(207)596-6496
Supplying homeowners with all the necessary tools for cleaning their chimneys such as brushes, chimney rods, etc.

Chimney Linings

Ahrens Chimney Technique Inc.
2000 Industrial Avenue, Dept. OHJ
Sioux Falls, SD 57104
(605)334-2827

Manufacturers of a cast-in-place, UL-listed chimney lining system. Cerama-Flue ceramic liner is also offered. Both lining systems are listed for use with gas, wood, coal and oil, and are listed for use in chimneys with zero-clearance to combustible materials.

National Supaflu Systems, Inc.
PO Box 89, Industrial Park, Dept. OHJ
Walton, NY 13856
(800)788-7636
Supaflu in-place chimney lining/relining for restoration and repair.

ProTech Systems, Inc.
PO Box 1743, Dept. OHJ
Albany, NY 12201
(518)463-7284
The product marketing and development firm representing the BOA Ventinox lining systems for masonry chimneys. UL-listed lining systems for solid, liquid, and gas fuels.

Fireplace & Chimney Restoration

August West Systems, Inc.
38 Austin Street, PO Box 658, Dept. OHJ
Worcester, MA 01601-0658
(800)225-4016
Chimney-service technicians.

Buckley Rumford Fireplace Co.
PO Box 21131, Dept. OHJ
Columbus, OH 43221
(614)221-6131
Specializing in the building and restoration of Rumford fireplaces. Nationwide construction services as well as the sale of components (throats, dampers, and smoke chambers).

Certified Chimney Contractors Inc.
PO Box 222, Dept. OHJ
Hasbrouck Heights, NJ 07604
(201)478-7718
A full-service, year-round cleaning and restoration company. From the simple cleaning to complete renovations of chimneys for fireplaces, furnaces, and stoves (wood, coal, etc.).

Exterior Cornices

American Architectural Art Company
PO Box 904, Dept. OHJ
Adamstown, PA 19501
(215)775-8876
Professional artists and craftsmen custom sculpting and fabricating cornices in lightweight polymerized fiberglass, reinforced gypsum, or fiberglass-reinforced polyester.

American Custom Millwork, Inc.
3904 Newton Road, PO Box 3608, Dept. OHJ
Albany, GA 31706
(912)888-3303
A prime source for embossed architectural wood mouldings and custom millwork, including beautifully detailed cornices.

Chelsea Decorative Metal Co.
9603 Moonlight Drive, Dept. OHJ
Houston, TX 77096
(713)721-9200
Metal cornice comes in 4-foot lengths with varying widths.

Fireplace Surrounds

Fourth Bay
Box 287, Dept. OHJ
Garrettsville, OH 44231
(216)527-4343
Manufacturers and importers of elegant historic ceramic tile and cast-iron fireplaces for residential and commercial use. Complete tile selection includes tiles from various historic periods, complementary solid color tiles and trim pieces.

Starbuck Goldner Tile
315 West Fourth Street, Dept. OHJ
Bethlehem, PA 18015
(215)866-6321
Designers and producers of handmade ceramic tile, fireplace surrounds.

Sun House Tiles/Fergene Studios
9986 Happy Acres West, Dept. OHJ
Bozeman, MT 59715
(406)587-3651
Making custom embossed and plain tiles for period fireplaces.

Helen Williams, Antique
    Delft Tiles
12643 Hortense Street, Dept.
    OHJ
Studio City, CA 91604
(818)761-2756
*Importer of antique tiles
since 1953 including
seventeenth-century Dutch
firebacks.*

Custom-Built Fireplaces

Air Heat & Clean Sweep
PO Box 696, Dept. OHJ
New Providence, NJ 07974
(908)771-9137
*Specialists in masonry
restoration, new chimneys,
and the repair and cleaning
of old chimneys.*

Green Mountain Stoneworks
PO Box 26, Dept. OHJ
Williamstown, VT 05679
(802)433-6632
*Specialists in the creative
design and construction of
walls, fireplaces, walks,
foundations, patios, and
virtually anything
imaginable in slate, mica
schists, and granite.*

Halsted Welles Associates
287 East Houston Street,
    Dept. OHJ
New York, NY 10002
(212)777-5440
*Offering a full range of
fireplace services, including
renovation of existing period
fireplaces, design, and
construction of new models.*

Mantels

Maizefield Mantels
PO Box 336, Dept. OHJ
Port Townsend, WA 98368
(206)385-6789
*Specialists in the design,
fabrication, and installation
of architectural woodwork,
with an emphasis on mantels
and staircases. Custom styles
are developed upon request
and comprise 50 percent of
the work.*

Piedmont Mantel & Millwork
4320 Interstate Drive, Dept.
    OHJ
Macon, GA 31210
(912)477-7536
*Offering Colonial mantels in
walnut, cherry, oak,
mahogany, and antique
pine.*

Readybuilt Products
    Company
1701 McHenry Street, Box
    4425, Dept. OHJ
Baltimore, MD 21223
(301)233-5833
*More than 40 different styles
of hand-crafted ready-to-
install wood mantels for
built-in masonry fireplaces or
factory built metal units.*

CHAPTER 7

Lumber

Craftsman Lumber Company
436 Main Street, Dept. OHJ
Groton, MA 01450
(508)448-6336
*Perfectly straight boards,
properly graded and kiln
dried. Milled to any
specification.*

Mountain Lumber Company
PO Box 289, Route 606,
    Dept. OHJ
Ruckersville, VA 22968
(800)445-2671
*Manufacturers of antique
heart pine products.*

Sandy Pond Hardwoods
921-A Lancaster Pike, Dept.
    OHJ
Quarryville, PA 17566
(717)284-5030
*Specialists in tiger and
bird's-eye maple lumber and
flooring, as well as flame
yellow birch, and other
native American hardwoods.*

Salvaged Lumber

Albany Woodworks, Inc.
PO Box 729, Dept. OHJ
Albany, LA 70711
(504)567-1155
*Specialists in antique
building materials newly
milled from reclaimed virgin
growth heart pine and heart
cypress.*

Sylvan Brandt, Inc.
651 East Main Street, Dept.
    OHJ
Lititz, PA 17543
(717)626-4520
*Attic flooring and reworked
tung-and-groove flooring
4-foot to 16-foot sawed from
hand-hewn logs.*

The Woods Company
2357 Boteler Road, Dept.
    OHJ
Brownsville, MD 21715
(301)432-8419
*Specialty supplier of antique
wood flooring, mouldings,
millwork, and beams.*

Clapboards & Siding

Granville Manufacturing Co.
    Inc.
Route 100, PO Box 15, Dept.
    OHJ
Granville, VT 05747
(802)767-4747
*Suppliers of a complete
exterior siding and trim
package.*

Sky Lodge Farm
46 Wendell Road, Dept. OHJ
Shutesbury, MA 01072
(413)259-1271
*Manufacturers of radially
sawn, 100-percent vertical
grain clapboards.*

Ward Clapboard Mill, Inc.
PO Box 1030, Dept. OHJ
Waitsfield, VT 05660
(802)496-3581
*Family-owned and operated
mill for over one hundred
years, manufacturing and
supplying quartersawn
spruce, vertical grain
clapboard siding.*

Beaded-Edge & Old-Fashioned Clapboards

Donnell's Clapboard Mill
RR 1, Box 1560, Dept. OHJ
Sedgwick, ME 04676
(207)359-2036
*With nineteenth-century
clapboard machinery,
specialists in authentic
eighteenth- and
nineteenth-century radial cut
or quartersawn pine
clapboard in traditional 4
1/2-foot and 5 1/2-foot sizes.*

Harmony Exchange, Inc.
Rt. 2, Box 843, Dept. OHJ
Boone, NC 28607
(704)264-2314
*Specialty building materials
for log, timber, and exposed
beam construction.*

Rot Patching & Restoration Materials

Allied Resin Corporation
Weymouth Industrial Park,
    Dept. OHJ
East Weymouth, MA 02189
(617)337-6070
*A mail-order source for
epoxies, polyester resins,
silicones, and
pressure-sensitive tapes.*

Gougeon Brothers, Inc
PO Box 908, 100 Patterson
    Avenue, Dept. OHJ
Bay City, MI 48707
(517)684-7286
*West System Brand Epoxy
additives and application
tools, a versatile solution to
dryrot.*

T Distributing
24 St. Henry Court, Dept.
    OHJ
St. Charles, MO 63301
(314)724-1065
*Packagers and sellers of Kwik
Poly, a product which can be
used to restore just about
anything.*

Exterior Paint Strippers

Benco Sales Inc.
123 Stout Drive, PO Box
    1215, Dept. OHJ
Crossville, TN 38557
(800)854-4874
*Manufacturer of paint
strippers and paint-stripping
equipment.*

Creative Technologies Group
    Inc.
300 NCNB Place, 7 N.
    Laurens Street, Dept. OHJ
Greenville, SC 29601
(803)271-9194
*Manufacturers and
marketers of Woodfinisher's
Pride paint- and
varnish-stripping gels.*

Wash America Mobile Power
    Wash Inc.
943 Taft Vineland Road, Suite
    A, Dept. OHJ
Orlando, FL 32824
(800)331-7765
*Specialists in brick
restoration, multilayer paint
stripping, and waterproofing.
Eighty-one owner/operators
in thirty-one states and three
countries.*

Paint-Stripping Tools

Embee Corp.
552 W. State Street, PO Box 1268, Dept. OHJ
Springfield, OH 45501
(513)323-3795
Manufacturers of professional painter and stripping tools.

Hyde Manufacturing Company
54 Eastford Road, Dept. OHJ
Southbridge, MA 01550
(508)764-4344
Manufacturers of more than 800 different durable, high-quality tools for painting, decorating, and stripping.

Old-House Journal
2 Main Street
Gloucester, MA 01930
(508)283-3200
Suppliers of the Heavy-Duty Master Heat Gun and the Warner Heat Plate. Ideal for stripping paint when large areas are involved.

Paint-Stripping Services

Allstrip, Inc.
71 Third Street, Dept. OHJ
Brooklyn, NY 11231
(718)596-7823
A licensed restoration contractor specializing in, but not limited to, paint removal and wood refinishing.

Anderson Building Restoration
923 Marion Avenue, Dept. OHJ
Cincinnati, OH 45229
(513)281-5258
Exterior restoration contractors specializing in chemical paint removal and chemical cleaning of historic masonry structures.

Wayne Towle Inc.
8 Thayer Street, Dept. OHJ
Boston, MA 02118
(617)423-2902
Offering comprehensive on-site architectural wood stripping and finishing services.

Commercial Paints in Period Colors (Exterior)

Benjamin Moore & Company
51 Chestnut Ridge Road, Dept. OHJ
Montvale, NJ 07645
(800)344-0400
Documented Interior/Exterior Historical Color Collection card is available.

Janovic/Plaza, Inc.
30-35 Thomson Avenue, Dept. OHJ
Long Island City, NY 11101
(718)786-4444
Suppliers of a large stock of specialty paint, brushes, and decorating materials.

Martin-Senour Paints
101 Prospect Avenue, Dept. OHJ
Cleveland, OH 44115
(800)542-8468
Manufacturer of quality interior and exterior paints. The exclusive manufacturer of Colonial Williamsburg Colors.

Exterior Stains

Cabot Stains
100 Hale Street, Dept. OHJ
Newburyport, MA 01950
(508)465-1900
Developers and manufacturers of superior quality stains uniquely suited for every type of application, from exterior siding shakes and shingles, to decking; from fencing and pressure-treated wood surfaces, to interior walls and furniture.

United Gilsonite Laboratories (UGL)
PO Box 70, Dept. OHJ
Scranton, PA 18501
(717)344-1202
Manufacturers of over 80 home improvement products including Zar wood stains and clear finishes.

Waterlox Chemical & Coating Corp.
9808 Meech Avenue, Dept. OHJ
Cleveland, OH 44105
(216)641-4877
A 75-year-old paint and varnish manufacturer specializing in tung-oil-based coatings and other specialty-type coatings.

Paint & Varnish Brushes

Bay City Paint Company
2279 Market Street, Dept. OHJ
San Francisco, CA 94114
(415)431-4914
Since 1937, suppliers to professional painters, artists, finishers, and do-it-yourselfers, with specialty paints and brushes.

Epifanes USA
1218 SW 1st Avenue, Dept. OHJ
Fort Lauderdale, FL 33315
(305)467-8325
Imported from Holland, a full line of coatings and accessories including European-style brushes.

Liberty Paint Catalogue, Inc.
PO Box 1248, Dept. OHJ
Hudson, NY 12534
Not only a catalogue, but a resource book of methods, tools, and tradition, based on extensive research, historical documentation and application. Everything in the line of fancy painting, tole, gilding, Japan and marble work, and specialty brushes.

CHAPTER 8

Porch Parts

Architectural Cataloguer, USA
PO Box 8270, Dept. OHJ
Galveston, TX 77553
(409)763-4969
A one-stop mail-order source for a wide selection of period architectural elements, including porch parts.

Bruce Post Company, Inc.
PO Box 332, Dept. OHJ
Chestertown, MD 21620
(301)778-6181
Manufacturers of center-drilled, all-heart redwood turned newel posts. Excellent for decks and stoops.

Jeffries Wood Works, Inc.
8807 Valgro Road, Dept. OHJ
Knoxville, TN 37920
(615)573-5876
Faithfully reproducing missing turnings, matching existing and creating new pieces, including finials, spindles, balusters, newels, porch posts, and columns.

Architectural Millwork

Cumberland Woodcraft Co., Inc.
PO Drawer 609, 10 Stover Drive, Dept. OHJ
Carlisle, PA 17013
(717)243-0063
Leading manufacturer of Victorian millwork faithfully duplicates the intricate designs of the Victorian era. Providers of millwork to duplicate any period decor.

Detail Millwork Inc.
160 Riverview Avenue, Dept. OHJ
Waltham, MA 02154
(617)893-2241
Manufacturer of custom and historical reproduction woodwork of all kinds.

Silverton Victorian Millworks
PO Box 2987, Dept. OJL6
Durango, CO 81302
(800)933-3930
A complete source for top-quality millwork in pine and oak.

Porch Swings

Alfresco Porch Swing Company
PO Box 1336, Dept. OHJ
Durango, CO 81302
(303)247-9739
Suppliers of very comfortable porch swings. Available in standard 4-foot or 5 1/2-foot lengths of solid redwood. Custom lengths and hardwoods are also available.

Grand Era Reproductions
PO Box 1026, Dept. OHJ
Lapeer, MI 48446
(313)664-1756
Wooden and wicker porch swings.

Silver Creek Mill
Englers Block, 1335 W. Hwy. 76, Dept. OHJ
Branson, MO 65616
(417)335-6645
Woodland Series garden gates, swings, lawn and porch furniture.

Rustic Furniture

Adirondack Store & Gallery
109 Saranac Avenue, Dept.
OHJ
Lake Placid, NY 12946
(518)523-2646
Gifts, accessories, artwork, and furniture inspired by the great camps of the Adirondacks, including many unique and specialized items, such as balsam pillows, birch bark baskets, pinecone china, and rustic twig furniture.

La Lune Collection
930 E. Burleigh, Dept. OHJ
Milwaukee, WI 53212
(414)263-5300
Offering a wide selection of bent willow furniture, available in 15 finishes. Sofas, chaises lounges, chairs, tables, beds, chests, cabinets, and bar stools.

Daniel Mack Rustic
   Furnishings
3280 Broadway, Third Floor,
   Dept. OHJ
New York, NY 10027
(914)986-7293
A small custom woodworking shop making furniture in natural form materials.

Wicker Furniture

Michael's Classic Wicker
620-1/2 Westknoll Drive,
   Dept. OHJ
W. Hollywood, CA 90069
(213)854-6035
Manufacturer of reproduction Victorian wicker furniture. Featuring bedroom sets, including headboards, dressers, vanity tables, armoires, nightstands, and lamps.

Wicker Fixer
Route 1, Box 349, Dept. OHJ
Ozark, MO 65721
(417)485-6148
Sixteen years of experience in expert restoration; minor to major surgery. Over one hundred pieces of antique wicker are available.

The Wicker Garden
1318 Madison Avenue (at
   93rd Street), Dept. OHJ
New York, NY 10128
(212)410-7000
Specialists in antique

American wicker furniture from the 1880s through the 1920s.

Railings, Balconies, & Window Grilles

Architectural Iron Company
PO Box 126, Schocopee
   Road, Dept. OHJ
Milford, PA 18337
(717)296-7722
A full-service restoration company specializing in eighteenth- and nineteenth-century cast- and wrought-iron work.

Wood's Metal Studios
6945 Fishburg Road, Dept.
   OHJ
Huber Heights, OH 45424
(513)233-6751
A custom shop that deals with one-of-a-kind pieces, all hand wrought of iron or any other metals.

Exterior Columns & Capitals

Chadsworth Incorporated
PO Box 53268, Dept. OHJ
Atlanta, GA 30355
(404)876-5410
The architectural grandeur of ancient Greece and Rome lives again in classically designed, crafted wooden columns. These columns follow the specifications derived from the 15th-century Renaissance master architect Vignola. Architectural stock Tuscan, Contemporary, and Art Deco wooden columns are also available.

Classic Architectural
   Specialties
3223 Canton Street, Dept.
   OHJ
Dallas, TX 75223
(214)748-1668
One-stop source for uncommon architectural ornamentation for new construction and restoration/renovation, including capitals and columns.

A.F. Schwerd Manufacturing
   Co.
3215 McClure Avenue, Dept.
   OHJ
Pittsburgh, PA 15212
(412)766-6322

Manufacturers since 1860 of wood columns in Tuscan, Greek, and Roman orders, fluted, plain, round, square. Manufacturing columns and pilasters to stock designs or to your specifications. Ten styles of ornamental capitals are available.

Exterior Mouldings

Bendix Mouldings, Inc.
37 Ramland Road, South,
   Dept. OHJ
Orangeburg, NY 10962
(800)526-0240
Carved and embossed decorative mouldings, crown and chair rail mouldings, embossed wood ornaments, rope and beaded mouldings.

Governor's Antiques &
   Architectural Materials
6240 Meadowbridge Road,
   Dept. OHJ
Mechanicsville, VA 23111
(804)746-1030
A large architectural antique complex with over one million antiques, collectibles, and furniture. Focal Point mouldings are also available.

The Joinery Company
Parkhill Mall, PO Box 518,
   Dept. OHJ
Tarboro, NC 27886
(919)823-3306
A complete in-house handbuilding company specializing in antique resawn heart pine products and other antique woods. Old world standards produce the finest in flooring, mouldings, and cabinets, as well as many other items.

Cast Ironwork

Elm Industries
1539 Race Street, Dept. OHJ
Cincinnati, OH 45210
(513)241-7927
Custom-crafted ironwork.

FABCOR, Inc.
442 East 3rd Street, Dept.
   OHJ
Minster, OH 45865
(419)628-3891
Custom metal fabricators.

Robinson Iron Corporation
PO Box 1119, Robinson
   Road, Dept. OHJ
Alexander City, AL 35010
(205)329-8486
Reproduction or custom cast metals including iron, aluminum, and bronze.

Wrought Ironwork

Cambridge Smithy
RR 1, Box 1280, Dept. OHJ
Cambridge, VT 05444
(802)644-5358
Metalworker for over twenty years. Working with architects, interior designers, and individuals, creating for them those special items, such as wrought iron hardware and copper weathervanes. Call or write for more information.

Schwartz's Forge &
   Metalworks Inc.
Route 315, PO Box 205,
   Dept. OHJ
Deansboro, NY 13328
(315)841-4477
Designing and creating custom forged architectural metal work.

Star Metal
974 Grand Street, Dept. OHJ
Brooklyn, NY 11211
(718)384-2766
Custom architectural metalwork. Specialists in forged ironwork.

CHAPTER 9

Masonry Repair & Cleaning

Downstate Restorations
1944 West Superior, Dept.
   OHJ
Chicago, IL 60622
(312)738-3256
Building restoration firm specializing in facade restoration. Extensive masonry-cleaning experience.

Dan Haines Construction
   Company, Inc.
915 East Daley Street, Dept.
   OHJ
Indianapolis, IN 46202
(317)635-5858
One of the oldest and largest masonry restoration companies in Indiana;

family owned and operated since 1936. Specialties include building cleaning, tuckpointing, and all types of masonry repairing.

Trow & Holden Company, Inc.
45-57 South Main Street, Dept. OHJ
Barre, VT 05641
(802)476-7221
Manufacturers of hand and power tools for the stoneworking and masonry industry. Restoration tools for repair of stone, repointing brick, and cutting of new stone are a specialty.

Exterior Masonry Cleaners

American Building Restoration
9720 South 60th Street, Dept. OHJ
Franklin, WI 53132
(800)346-7532
Manufacturer of restoration products. Specializing in masonry cleaners.

Bioclean
1512 North Second Street, Dept. OHJ
Philadelphia, PA 19122
(215)739-6061
Restorers of historic building facades with special care to match the original craftsmanship. All aspects of exterior restoration and maintenance are completed by in-house craftsmen.

Masonry Tools

Goldblatt Tool Company
511 Osage, PO Box 2929, Dept. OHJ
Kansas City, KS 66110
(913)621-3010
Manufacturer of tools and related equipment items for concrete finishing, masonry, and drywall/plaster finishing.

Marshalltown Trowel
PO Box 738, Dept. OHJ
Marshalltown, IA 50158
(515)753-5999
Manufacturer of all types of trowels, including brick/block, concrete finishing, plastering, drywall, tiling, and eifs. Related hand tools are also available.

C.S. Osborne & Company
146 Jersey Street, Dept. OHJ
Harrison, NJ 07029
(201)483-3232
Manufacturers of specialty tools for masonry.

Handmade Bricks

The Brickyard, Inc.
PO Box A, Dept. OHJ
Harrisonville, MO 64701
(816)887-3366
Authentic, decades-old, unused clinker brick recovered from an abandoned brickyard.

Cushwa Brick, Inc.
PO Box 160, Dept. OHJ
Williamsport, MD 21795
(301)223-7700
Manufacturers of machine-moulded and handmade brick for residential, commercial, and landscaping purposes.

Old Carolina Brick Company
475 Majolica Road, Dept. OHJ
Salisbury, NC 28144
(704)636-8850
One of the country's largest producers of handmade brick.

Stone

Bergen Bluestone Company, Inc.
404 Rt. 17, PO Box 67, Dept. OHJ
Paramus, NJ 07652
(201)261-1903
Suppliers and contractors of natural stone, including granite, marble, travertine, limestone, slate, sandstone, and quartzite.

Delaware Quarries, Inc.
River Road, Dept. OHJ
Lumberville, PA 18933
(215)297-5647
Producers of an extensive line of building stone. Specialists in the matching of stone from old, unavailable sources. Custom fabrication of slate, limestone, granite, and sandstone is available for a variety of uses in the home.

Pasvalco
100 Bogert Street, Dept. OHJ
Closter, NJ 07624
(800)222-2133
Suppliers of all types of natural building stone. Custom stone fabrication and historic restoration available.

Sandstone & Brownstone Repair

ABCO Restoration Company
318 East 70th Street, Dept. OHJ
New York, NY 10021
(212)879-2602
Dedicated to properly restoring historic buildings by strictly adhering to New York City Landmark restoration techniques.

Exterior Masonry Paints

California Products Corp.
169 Waverly Street, Dept. OHJ
Cambridge, MA 02139
(617)547-5300
Manufacturers of masonry paints.

Pratt & Lambert
75 Tonawanda Street, Dept. OHJ
Buffalo, NY 14207
(716)873-6000
Manufacturers of exterior masonry paints.

Preserva-Products Inc.
Box 744, Dept. OHJ
Tahoe City, CA 96145
(916)583-0177
Manufacturers and distributors of proprietary products for use on wood and concrete masonry.

CHAPTER 10

Bathroom Accessories, Faucets, & Fittings

A-Ball Plumbing Supply
1703 West Burnside Street, Dept. OHJ
Portland, OR 97209
(503)228-0026
Various plumbing supplies and hardware, including shower set-ups, high-tank toilets, faucets, waste and overflow, metal and tile cleaners, epoxy tub-resurfacing kits, cast

aluminum reproduction grates, old-fashioned soap dishes, customized shower rings and rods, hand-held showers, and safety rails for clawfoot tubs.

Mac The Antique Plumber
885 57th Street, Dept. OHJ
Sacramento, CA 95819
(916)454-4507
Carrying a large selection of antique plumbing supplies, including leg-tub shower enclosures, high- and low-tank toilets, sinks, a variety of bathroom accessories, light fixtures, and hardware.

Urban Archaeology
285 Lafayette Street, Dept. OHJ
New York, NY 10012
(212)431-6969
Architectural antiques dealer, with reproduction bathroom fixtures available.

Lighting Fixtures Restoration & Wiring

Antique Lamp Parts & Service
218 North Foley Avenue, Dept. OHJ
Freeport, IL 61032
(815)232-8968
Lamp repair and wiring, brass and metal refurbishing, lamps made from all items, replacement of all missing lamp parts, old chandeliers restored, oil and gas lamps converted to electric, all parts for old and new lamps.

Conant Custom Brass, Inc.
270 Pine Street, Dept. OHJ
Burlington, VT 05401
(802)658-4482
The restoration and manufacturing divisions combine to offer one of the country's most diversified lighting shops.

Historic Lighting Restoration Service & Sales
10341 Jewell Lake Court, Dept. OHJ
Fenton, MI 48430
(313)629-4934
Restoration of lighting fixtures of all types. Manufacturers of lighting fixtures. Specialists in restoration and repairs by mail.

Museum Quality Restorations
PO Box 402, Dept. OHJ
Palmyra, NJ 08065
(609)829-4615
Specialists in historic lighting including restoration work.

Lighting Fixtures & Lamps—Antique & Reproduction

Ball and Ball
463 West Lincoln Highway, Dept. OHJ
Exton, PA 19341
(215)363-7330
Manufacturers of quality lighting fixtures, stock or made to order.

Brass Reproductions
9711 Canoga Avenue, Dept. OHJ
Chatsworth, CA 91311
(818)709-7844
Manufacturers of solid brass Victorian and Traditional lighting. Over 160 high-quality chandeliers, sconces, and floor and table lamp designs are available. Hand-crafted lighting made in the USA and UL listed.

City Lights
2226 Massachusetts Avenue, Dept. OHJ
Cambridge, MA 02140
(617)547-1490
Restored antique lighting fixtures dating 1850–1930. All styles available: Mission, Eastlake, Victorian, Renaissance revival, Georgian, French empire, Louis XV.

C. Neri, Antiques
313 South Street, Dept. OHJ
Philadelphia, PA 19147
(215)923-6669
Suppliers of fine antique furniture, and a large selection of American antique lighting fixtures.

Ocean View Lighting
2743 Ninth Street, Dept. OHJ92
Berkeley, CA 94710
(415)841-2937
Offering a complete line of handcrafted period lighting by Classic Illumination, Inc. Each lamp is made to the customer's specification with regard to finish, length, and choice of shade. The line encompasses Victorian, Art

Deco, and contemporary designs, with potential for custom modifications.

Period-Design Switch Plates

Acorn Manufacturing Company Inc.
457 School Street, Dept. OHJ
Mansfield, MA 02048
(800)835-0121
Manufacturer of forged-iron builders' and home hardware.

Classic Accents, Inc.
PO Box 1181, Dept. OHJ
Southgate, MI 48195
(313)282-5525
Offering push button light switches. Now featuring push button dimmer switches. Custom solid brass cover plates and wall outlet plates are also supplied.

Triarco, Inc.
317 E. Adrian Street, PO Box 66, Dept. OHJ
Blissfield, MI 49228
(517)486-4581
A variety of solid wood corner beads is offered.

Electric Candles

Authentic Designs Inc.
42 The Mill Road, Dept. OHJ
West Rupert, VT 05776
(802)394-7713
Handcrafted reproductions of eighteenth- and nineteenth-century lighting fixtures, such as chandeliers, sconces, and table lamps. Fixtures are available electrified or fitted for candle.

Elcanco, Ltd.
PO Box 682, Dept. OHJ
Westford, MA 01886
(508)392-0830
Custom manufacturer of handcrafted electric wax candles and beeswax candlecovers. Manufacturer of the Candlewick Bulb, a 1-candlepower bulb for use in Starlite candles.

The Lightsmith
5606 East Street, Rt. 37, Dept. OHJ
Delaware, OH 43015
(614)369-1817

A complete and authentic line of lighting, from window lights to table lamps and chandeliers. Manufacturer of a candlelight bulb that realistically creates the illusion of a lighted candle.

Period-Style Lampshades

Birds of Paradise Lampshades
114 Sherbourne Street, Dept. OHJ
Toronto, ON M5A 2R2 Canada
(416)366-4067
High-quality, custom lampshade studio. Lampshades in mica, parchment, hardback, and natural fiber (cotton, linen, and silk), created by hand in styles ranging from Victorian through Art Deco, as well as Traditional.

Lampshades of Antique
PO Box 2, Dept. 8
Medford, OR 97501
(503)826-9737
Designers and manufacturers of elegant lampshades for restaurants, hotels, theaters, casinos, antique and lighting stores.

Shady Lady
418 East 2nd Street, Dept. OHJ
Loveland, CO 80537
(303)669-1080
Handmade lampshade business growing consistently since 1978.

Gem Monogram & Cut Glass Corp.
628 Broadway, 3rd Floor, Dept. OHJ
New York, NY 10012
(212)674-8960
Specialists in the design and construction of crystal chandeliers since 1940. A quantity of parts is available for wall sconces and chandeliers.

Lamp Glass
2230 Massachusetts Avenue, Dept. OHJ
Cambridge, MA 02140
(617)497-0770
Specialists in replacement glass lampshades and parts.

Luigi Crystal
7332 Frankford Avenue, Dept. OHJ
Philadelphia, PA 19136
(215)338-2978
A unique collection of handmade crystal hurricane and buffet lamps and all-crystal chandeliers. All work is done by old world craftsmen and manufactured in-house. Suppliers of replacement prisms and bobeches.

Lighting-Fixture Parts, Metal

B&P Lamp Supply, Inc.
843 Old Morrison Highway, Dept. OHJ
McMinnville, TN 37110
(615)473-3016
Wholesale lamp parts supplier specializing in replacement parts for antique and early style lighting.

Roy Electric Company, Inc.
1054 Coney Island Avenue, Dept. OHJ
Brooklyn, NY 11230
(718)434-7002
Manufacturers of Victorian gas and early electric lighting. A source for original gas lighting through the Art Deco period. Restorers of original fixtures. Repairing is available.

The Tin Bin
20 Valley Road, Dept. OHJ
Neffsville, PA 17601
(717)569-6210
Specialists in reproductions of eighteenth- and nineteenth-century interior and exterior lighting devices and accessories for the home, handcrafted in tin, copper, and brass.

CHAPTER 11

Weatherstripping Products

Pemko Manufacturing Company
4226 Transport Street, Dept. OHJ
Ventura, CA 93003
(805)642-2600
Manufacturers and suppliers of weatherstripping and threshold products.

Zero International Inc.
415 Concord Avenue, Dept. OHJ
Bronx, NY 10455
(212)585-3230
Manufacturers of seals for doors and windows.

Central Heating Systems

Air Heat & Clean Sweep
PO Box 696, Dept. OHJ
New Providence, NJ 07974
(908)771-9137
Mechanical servicers, installers, and repairers of heating systems fired by wood, gas, or combination.

Heatway, Inc.
3131 W. Chestnut Expressway, Dept. OHJ
Springfield, MO 65802
(417)864-6108
Manufacturers and suppliers of Hydronic Radiant Floors and Snowmelting systems.

Radiant Systems Technology Inc.
19-B Thompson Street, Dept. OHJ
Dedham, MA 02026
(800)243-0089
Suppliers of specialty hot water heating products and high-velocity air-conditioning.

Furnace Parts

Heckler Bros.
4105 Steubenville Pike, Dept. OHJ
Pittsburgh, PA 15205
(412)922-6811
Suppliers of coal heating stove parts, coal cook stove parts, furnace repair parts, firebricks, and boiler parts.

Stoves & Heaters— Period Designs

Barnstable Stove Shop, Inc.
Box 472, Route 149, Dept. OHJ
W. Barnstable, MA 02668
(508)362-9913
Buyers, sellers, and restorers of antique stoves (wood, coal, and gas). A large selection of stoves and parts in old and new castings is available, as well as in nickel plating.

Heat-N-Glo Fireplace Products
6665 West Highway 13, Dept. OHJ
Savage, MN 55378
(800)669-4328
Manufacturer of quality, energy-efficient wood and gas fireplace products.

Woodstock Soapstone Company Inc.
Airpark Road, Box 37H, Dept. OHJ
West Lebanon, NH 03784
(800)866-4344
Manufacturers of premium woodstoves made of cast-iron and soapstone.

Storm Windows

Libby Owens Ford
PO Box 799, Dept. OHJ
Toledo, OH 43695
Storm panels with Energy Advantage Low-E Glass offer significant energy performance improvements in a variety of storm window and door applications.

Ray Tenebruso, Cabinetmaker
2842 Gaston Road, Dept. OHJ
Cottage Grove, WI 53527
(608)839-4012
Shutters, entry doors, passage doors, screen and storm doors, sash, and window storms and screens.

Vintage Storm Window Company
6755 8th NW, Dept. OHJ
Seattle, WA 98117
(206)782-5656
Storm windows, made with 1 3/8-inch clearfir, custom fitted, sealed, and installed creating a double window system.

Period-Style Radiators

A.A. Used Boiler Supply Co.
8720 Ditmas Avenue, Dept. OHJ
Brooklyn, NY 11236
(718)385-2111
All types and sizes of cast-iron steam and hot water radiators.

Enerjee Int'l
32 South Lafayette Avenue, Dept. OHJ
Morrisville, PA 19067
(215)295-0557
Specialists in hydronic heating systems, including radiators, radiant floor heating, outdoor reset controls, valves, and related equipment.

H.C. Oswald Supply Company Inc.
120 East 124th Street, Dept. OHJ
New York, NY 10035
(212)722-7000
Manufacturers of obsolete heating and boiler repair parts. Distributors of numerous boiler heating manufacturers' repair parts. Various sizes of push nipples for old cast-iron radiators are in stock (samples required).

CHAPTER 12

Hand-Hewn Beams

The Barn People, Inc.
PO Box 217, Dept. OHJ
Windsor, VT 05089
(802)674-5778
A source for antique building materials and producers of new hand-hewn beams, barn frames, and structural components.

Broad-Axe Beam Company
RD 2, Box 417, Dept. OHJ
Brattleboro, VT 05301
(802)257-0064
Producers of hand-hewn beams and wide pine flooring.

Carlisle Restoration Lumber
HCR 32, Box 679, Dept. OHJ
Stoddard, NH 03464
(603)446-3937
A source of hand-hewn beams.

Stair Rods

Heritage Brass Company
414 East Main Street, Dept. OHJ
Smethport, PA 16749
(814)887-6032
Suppliers of solid-brass stair rods with a choice of three finials: urn, pineapple, or ball. The fasteners are traditional eye screws. Custom lengths are available.

M. Wolchonok & Son, Inc.
155 East 52 Street, Dept. OHJ
New York, NY 10023
(212)755-2168
Extensive line of reproduction hardware, including decorative carpet rods.

Spiral Staircases

The Iron Shop
PO Box 547, 400 Reed Road, Dept. OHJ
Broomall, PA 19008
(215)544-7100
Offering three types of spiral stair kits: steel spiral stairs with oak and brass options, oak spiral stairs, and the new cast Victorian style.

Spiral Manufacturing Inc.
17251 Jefferson Highway, Dept. OHJ
Baton Rouge, LA 70817
(800)535-9956
Manufacturers of wood spiral and curved stair kits. A line of steel and aluminum spiral stairs is also available for exterior or interior use.

Steptoe & Wife Antiques Ltd.
322 Geary Avenue, Dept. OHJ
Toronto, ON M6H 2C7 Canada
(416)530-4200
Extensive restoration/renovation products including spiral and straight cast-iron Victorian stairs.

Wood Staircases

American Stair Builder
190 Highland Place, Dept. OHJ
Brooklyn, NY 11208
(718)647-5600
Suppliers of stairs of all types. Also offering a large selection of stair replacement parts. Restoration of old staircases is available.

Dahlke Stair Company
PO Box 418, Dept. OHJ
Hadlyme, CT 06439
(203)434-3589
Custom fabricated staircases. Catalogue, $5.

D.S. Nelson Company, Inc.
64 Halsey Street, Dept. OHJ
Newport, RI 02840
(401)847-8240
*Custom monumental stair
builders. Reproducing of old
staircases is available.*

Wood Staircase Parts

Tim Brennan Woodworking
4 N. Oakwood Terrace, Dept.
  OHJ
New Paltz, NY 12561
(914)255-3125
*Architectural woodworking
and cabinetry with an
emphasis on stairbuilding.*

Pagliacco Turning & Milling
PO Box 225, Dept. OHJ
Woodacre, CA 94973
(415)488-4333
*Over 150 stock designs of
balusters, newel posts,
railings.*

Turncraft
PO Box 2429, Dept. OHJ
White City, OR 97503
(503)826-2911
*A turning manufacturer of
quality products, including
spindles and balustrades.*

Iron Staircase Parts

J.G. Braun Company
7540 McCormick Boulevard,
  Dept. OHJ
Skokie, IL 60076
(312)761-4600
*Suppliers of aluminum
extrusions, bronze
extrusions, metal handrail
systems and their component
parts.*

Mylen Industries
650 Washington Street, Dept.
  OHJ
Peekskill, NY 10566
(800)431-2155
*A leading manufacturer of
spiral and specialty stairs
including adjustable steel
and all-oak spirals.*

CHAPTER 13

Metal Window Frames
& Sash

American Steel Window
  Service
108 West 17th Street, Dept.
  OHJ
New York, NY 10011
(212)242-8131

*Supplying obsolete
replacement parts for steel
casement window hardware.
Parts for new windows are
also available.*

Hope's Landmark Products,
  Inc.
84 Hopkins Avenue, Dept.
  OHJ
Jamestown, NY 14701
(716)665-5124
*Manufacturer of a complete
line of quality steel windows.*

Torrance Steel Window
  Company
1819 Abalone Avenue, Dept.
  OHJ
Torrance, CA 90501
(213)775-6195
*Active in residential
replacement and new
installations of windows with
snap-on glazing, similar to
putty.*

Wood Window Frames
& Sash

Andersen Windows, Inc.
PO Box 3900, Dept. OHJ
Peoria, IL 61614
(800)426-4261
*The nation's largest
manufacturer of stock wood
windows.*

Caradco, An Alcoa Company
905 Lakeside Drive, Dept.
  IMS OHJAA
Gurnee, IL 60031
(217)893-4444
*Crafting quality wood
windows for over 125 years
for both new construction
and remodeling projects.*

Marvin Windows
PO Box 100, Dept. OHJ
Warroad, MN 56763
(800)346-5128
*Creating made-to-order wood
windows in over 8,000
standard sizes and a
virtually unlimited number
of custom shapes and sizes.*

Wood Window Workshop
432 Lafayette Street, PO Box
  310, Dept. OHJ
Utica, NY 13503
(315)732-6767
*Specialists at making
windows look and perform
better than ever, whether it
means restoring them,
rebuilding them, or replacing
them altogether.*

Handmade Window
Glass, Clear

S.A. Bendheim Company,
  Inc.
61 Willett Street, Dept. OHJ
Passaic, NJ 07055
(800)221-7379
*Supplier for replacement
Colonial-type window glass
including mouth-blown
panes. Also imported and
domestic stained glass,
rondells, crown bullions,
bull's-eye, etc.*

Blenko Glass Company, Inc.
PO Box 67, Dept. OHJ
Milton, WV 25541
(304)743-9081
*Suppliers of hand-blown,
antique sheet glass. Panes
are available cut to size or as
full sheets.*

Golden Age Glassworks
339 Bellvale Road, Dept. OHJ
Warwick, NY 10990
(914)986-1487
*Custom designs in any style,
restorations, repairs,
alterations, museum-quality
work.*

Window-Sash Weights

Blaine Window Hardware,
  Inc.
1919 Blaine Drive, Dept. OHJ
Hagerstown, MD 21740
(800)678-1919
*Since 1954, a leading
manufacturer and
distributor of current and
obsolete hardware for
windows.*

Pullman Manufacturing Corp.
77 Commerce Drive, Dept.
  OHJ
Rochester, NY 14623
(716)334-1350
*Specialists in counterbalances
for windows, doors,
industrial equipment,
product end uses, custom
metal fabrication, and
vacuum formed plastics.*

Windows—Special
Architectural Shapes

Architectural Components
  Inc.
26 North Leverett Road,
  Dept. OHJ
Montague, MA 01351
(413)367-9441

*A variety of custom-made
window sashes, frames, and
pediments.*

Pella/Rolscreen Company
102 Main Street, Dept. OHJ
Pella, IA 50219
(515)628-1000
*Manufacturers of the Pella®
line of windows, doors,
sunrooms, and skylights.*

Pozzi Wood Windows
PO Box 5249, Dept. OHJ
Bend, OR 97708
(503)382-4411
*Manufacturers of high-end
wood windows, including a
clad line.*

Leaded-Glass Restoration

Art Glass Unlimited, Inc.
412 N. Euclid, Dept. OHJ
St. Louis, MO 63108
(314)361-0474
*Quality restorations and
repairs.*

Curran Art Glass Inc.
4125 N. Kostner, Dept. OHJ
Chicago, IL 60641
(312)777-2444
*Duplication of existing glass
is available, as well as
restoration of existing
decorative glass.*

Stained Glass Associates
PO Box 1531, Dept. OHJ
Raleigh, NC 27545
(919)266-2493
*Specialists in restoration of
leaded glass.*

Interior Doors

Lamson-Taylor Custom
  Doors
Tucker Road, Dept. OHJ
South Acworth, NH 03607
(603)835-2992
*A small custom door shop
specializing in
energy-efficient doors of
native woods to complement
any architectural style.
Traditional panel doors,
sidelights, and transoms.*

Pinecrest
2118 Blaisdell Avenue, Dept.
  OHJ
Minneapolis, MN 55404
(612)871-7071
*Custom manufacturers of
doors with hand-carved
leaded glass, raised panels,
and decorative metal.*

Simpson Door Company
PO Box 210, Dept. OHJ
McCleary, WA 98557
(206)495-3291
A leading manufacturer of stile and rail doors crafted from select vertical grain douglas fir or western hemlock.

Door Framing & Entryways— Reproduction

Kenmore Industries
One Thompson Square, Dept. OHJ
Boston, MA 02129
(617)242-1711
Offering a line of 50 doorways of the Federal and Georgian styles.

Reliance Industries, Inc.
PO Box 129, Dept. OHJ
Richland, IA 52585
(319)456-6030
Manufacturers of fine hardwood mouldings including door casing.

Jack Wallis Doors
Route 1, Box 22A, Dept. OHJ
Murray, KY 42071
(502)489-2613
Custom manufacturers of any type of door or entryway.

Door Hardware

Englewood Hardware Company Inc.
25 North Dean, Dept. OHJ
Englewood, NJ 07631
(201)568-1937
Distributors of decorative cabinet and door hardware.

Ryobi America Corporation
1424 Pearman Dairy Road, Dept. OHJ
Anderson, SC 29625
(803)226-6511
A complete line of door closers and builders' hardware is available.

Southeast Hardware Mfg. (SECO)
14060 S. Anderson Street, Dept. OHJ
Paramount, CA 90723
(213)231-9301
Artisan-crafted, custom door hardware.

Wrought-Iron Door Latches

18th Century Hardware Co., Inc.
131 East Third Street, Dept. OHJ
Derry, PA 15627
(412)694-2708
Reproduction hardware in brass, porcelain, and black iron, covering the Early American and Victorian periods. Pulls, knobs, casters, hinges, hooks, latches, door knockers, and other brass accessories.

Kayne & Son Custom Hardware
76 Daniel Ridge Road, Dept. OHJ
Candler, NC 28715
(704)667-8868
Custom wrought-iron hinges, thumb latches, bolts, hooks.

Williamsburg Blacksmiths, Inc.
Rt. 9, PO Box 1776, Dept. OHJ
Williamsburg, MA 01096
(413)268-7341
Manufacturers of authentic reproductions of Early American wrought-iron hardware suitable for use throughout period homes. Door latches now include both Suffolk and Norfolk styles.

Stock Antique Hardware

Architectural Elements
Rt. 2, Box 275, Dept. OHJ
Amery, WI 54004
(715)268-2694
Specialists in hardware.

Liz's Antique Hardware
704 J Street, Dept. OHJ
San Diego, CA 92116
(619)284-1075
Specialist in period hardware from 1850 to 1950.

Ole Fashion Things
402 SW Evangeline Thruway, Dept. OHJ
Lafayette, LA 70501
(800)228-4967
Architectural antiques including hardware.

Brass & Bronze Hardware

Bathroom Machineries
PO Box 1020, 495 Main Street, Dept. OHJ
Murphys, CA 95247
(209)728-2031
Product line includes solid brass, reproduction-Victorian door and cabinet hardware.

Cirecast, Inc.
380 7th Street, Dept. OHJ
San Francisco, CA 94103
(415)863-8319
Quality custom hardware manufacturer catering to architects and designers throughout the United States.

Brian Leo, Custom Hardware
7532 Columbus Avenue, South, Dept. OHJ
Minneapolis, MN 55423
(612)861-1473
Domestic and commercial hardware available in a wide variety of styles, periods, and sizes.

Sliding-Door Hardware

JGR Enterprises, Inc.
PO Box 49, 536 E. Poplar Street, Dept. OHJ
McConnellsburg, PA 17233
(800)223-7112
Manufacturers of Kennaframe hardware for sliding and folding doors (by-fold, by-pass, and pocket doors).

Merit Metal Products Corporation
242 Valley Road, Dept. OHJ
Warrington, PA 18976
(215)343-2500
Offering a complete selection of brass door, cabinet, and window hardware.

Window Hardware

Crown City Hardware
1047 N. Allen Avenue, Dept. OHJ
Pasadena, CA 91104
Suppliers of scarce decorative hardware for doors, windows, furniture, and cabinets.

Decorum Hardware Specialties
235 Commercial Street, Dept. OHJ
Portland, ME 04101
(207)775-3346

Large retail showroom of high-quality, traditional-style hardware.

Whitco/Vincent Whitney Company
60 Liberty Ship Way, Dept. OHJ
Sausalito, CA 94966
(800)332-3286
Manufacturers of hardware for wood sash windows. Clerestory operators for awning and casement windows available in hand-operated models.

CHAPTER 14

Plaster Patching Materials

Master of Plaster
PO Box 304, Dept. OHJ
Essex, NY 12936
(800)352-5915
A revolutionary new pre-mixed, two-coat system, giving a hard polished plaster surface with the ease of joint compound. No sanding, no bonding agents, no mixing (not even water). This system can be used over existing plaster, sheetrock, blueboard, even plywood.

Rutland Fire Clay Company (DBA Rutland Products)
PO Box 340, Dept. OHJ
Rutland, VT 05702
(802)775-5519
High-temperature refractory cements, fireplace mortar, furnace cement, creosote removers, stove polishes, gasketing materials, high-temperature silicone sealants, caulking materials, glazing compound, patching plasters, hydraulic cement, powder wood putty, roof cements, aluminum asphalt cement and coating, and more.

Tuff-Kote Company, Inc.
210 Seminary Avenue, Dept. OHJ
Woodstock, IL 60098
(815)338-2006
Manufacturers of quality interior and exterior building repair products since 1950. The exterior products are used to prime, patch, and seal roofs, gutters, chimneys, weathered wood, and masonry.

Plaster Washers

Charles Street Supply Company
54–56 Charles Street, Dept. OHJ
Boston, MA 02114
(617)367-9046
A True Value retail hardware store that additionally manufactures and sells plaster washers (ceiling buttons, plaster buttons) at retail and wholesale levels.

Fastenation Company
PO Box 1364, Dept. OHJ
Marblehead, MA 01945
(617)846-6444
Manufacturer and distributor of "ceiling buttons" (a.k.a. plaster washers). Made in Massachusetts from the finest sheet steel and plated in a special zinc chromate to prevent bleeding. Ceiling buttons are a quick fix for failing ceilings and walls.

Plastering & Masonry Tools

Bon Tool Company
4430 Gibsonia Road, Dept. OHJ
Gibsonia, PA 15044
(412)443-7080
Manufacturer and distributor of over 3,000 tools and related equipment for trowel trades and others. Popular restoration tools such as edgers, groovers, specialty jointers, brick trowels, and more.

Sculpture House
30 East 30th Street, Dept. OHJ
New York, NY 10016
(212)679-7474
Manufacturers of handmade tools for working in plaster, ceramics, and stone.

Ornamental Plastering

Felber Studios, Inc.
110 Ardmore Avenue, Dept. OHJ
Ardmore, PA 19003
(215)642-4710
Specializing in custom ornamental plaster work. Restoration, renovation and new construction, residential and commercial.

David Flaharty, Sculptor
402 Magazine Road, RD 2, Dept. OHJ
Green Lane, PA 18054
(215)234-8242
Specialist in the reproduction and restoration of architectural details and ornaments, especially in plaster.

C.G. Girolami & Sons
944 N. Spaulding Avenue, Dept. OHJ
Chicago, IL 60651
(312)227-1959
Restoring, reproducing, and redesigning turn-of-the-century plaster architectural work since 1913, including cornices, mouldings, rosettes, reliefs, and ornamental cast stone.

Ceiling Medallions

The Balmer Studios Inc.
9 Codeco Court, Dept. OHJ
Don Mills, ON M3A 1B6
Canada
(416)449-2155
Manufacturer of high-quality interior plaster mouldings and ceiling medallions.

Fischer & Jirouch Company
4821 Superior Avenue, NE, Dept. OHJ
Cleveland, OH 44103
(216)361-3840
One of the largest manufacturers of architectural plaster ornaments in the U.S. with over 1,500 designs. The product is made of fibrous plaster mixed with industrial P.C. reinforced with sisal and steel rods. Designs include Gothic, Victorian, Renaissance, English, and modern.

Hampton Decor
30 Fisk Street, Dept. OHJ
Jersey City, NJ 07305
(201)433-9002
Offering a large selection of classic architectural ornaments including ceiling medallions. All items are high-quality polyurethane, with excellent detailing, and are easily installed with liquid adhesive.

Moulding & Casting Supplies

PRG
PO Box 1768, Dept. OHJ
Rockville, MD 20849
(301)309-2222
Offering instruments, tools, and field-related products and books (including ICCROM books from Italy and other hard-to-find publications) for those concerned with the evaluation, preservation, conservation, and restoration of architecture and objects.

USG Corporation
101 South Wacker Drive, Dept. OHJ
Chicago, IL 60606
(312)606-4122
Producers of construction products including plaster, veneer plaster, patching materials, drywall, drywall primer paint, lightweight joint compound, gypsum, wood preservatives, waterproofing paints, glazing compounds, caulks and sealants, tintable wood putty, acoustic ceiling panels and grids, ceramic tile cement backer board, and wood stove backer board. Free literature.

Decorative Ceilings

AA Abbingdon Affiliates, Inc.
2149 Utica Avenue, Dept. OHJ
Brooklyn, NY 11234
(718)258-8333
Twenty-two Victorian and Art Deco tin ceiling patterns available in 2 × 4-foot and 2 × 8-foot nail up and 2 × 4-foot lay in. Copper and brass-plated sheets now available by special order in 2 × 2-foot or 2 × 4-foot sizes.

Classic Ceilings
902 E. Commonwealth Avenue, Dept. OHJ
Fullerton, CA 92631
(800)992-8700
Importer of the Anaglypta/Lincrusta line of embossed wallcoverings. This line includes friezes, wainscottings, and full wallcoverings; all are paintable. Distributors of W.F. Norman tin ceilings in

California, Nevada, and Arizona.

Entol Industries, Inc.
8180 NW 36th Avenue, Dept. OHJ
Miami, FL 33147
(305)696-0900
Manufacturers of decorative architectural products in polyurethane and in a fiberglass-reinforced gypsum. Over 150 ceiling designs are offered, as well as a full line of coordinated mouldings.

Wallcoverings Other Than Wallpaper

Bentley Brothers
2709 South Park Road, Dept. OHJ
Louisville, KY 40219
(800)824-4777
Distributor of Anaglypta® and Lincrusta® embossed, paintable wallcoverings from England, as well as Carton Pierre® embossed, paintable ornaments.

Colonial Wallcovering
707 East Passyunk Avenue, Dept. OHJ
Philadelphia, PA 19147
(215)351-9300
Victorian and Early American wallpapers including Crown Anaglypta and Lincrusta. Currently designing and printing original wallcoverings and fabric.

Crown Corporation, NA (Mile Hi Crown, Inc.)
1801 Wynkoop Street, Suite 235, Dept. OHJ
Denver, CO 80202
(300)292-1313
Importer and distributor of embossed wallcoverings from England (trade names: Anaglypta and Lincrusta wallcoverings).

Historical Wallpaper

Bradbury & Bradbury Wallpapers
PO Box 155B, Dept. OHJ
Benicia, CA 94510
(707)746-1900
Designers and handprinters of Victorian- and Edwardian-style wallpapers for decorators, homeowners, museums, and commercial interiors. A small firm willing to work directly with clients.

Handprinting of reasonably priced, hard-to-find specialties: borders, friezes, ceiling decorations, multi-design roomsets, and Morris papers.

J.R. Burrows & Company
PO Box 522, Dept. OHJ
Rockland, MA 02370
(617)982-1812
Documentary reproductions of Victorian wallpapers.

Richard E. Thibaut, Inc.
706 South 21st Street, Dept. OHJ
Irvington, NJ 07111
(201)399-7888
Textile and wallpaper converting company, producing exclusive Thibaut fabrics and wallcoverings.

Wallpapering & Decorating Tools

Colonial Company
7315 Hazeltine Boulevard, Dept. OHJ
Excelsior, MN 55331
(612)474-2610
Manufacturers and suppliers of electric wallpaper steamers.

E.L. Hilts & Company
2551 Hwy. 70 West, PO Box 1789, Dept. OHJ
Hickory, NC 28603
(800)354-4587
Serving the construction industry since 1945 with quality wholesale products.

CHAPTER 15

Wood Flooring

Coastal Millworks, Inc.
1335 Marietta Boulevard, NW, Dept. OHJ
Atlanta, GA 30318
(404)351-8400
A fifteen-year-old company specializing in the manufacturing of resawn/remilled pre-1900 antique heart pine flooring.

Historic Floors of Oshkosh
1107 Algoma Boulevard, Dept. OHJ
Oshkosh, WI 54901
(414)233-0075
Reproduction hardwood flooring in authentic parquet

borders, strips and full floor plans.

Pine Plains Woodworking Inc.
RR 1, Box 74C, Dept. OHJ
Pine Plains, NY 12567
(518)398-7665
A hardwood milling company with a 20,000-square-foot modern plant for producing all kinds of flooring from all domestic hardwoods: oak, cherry, maple, hickory, ash, etc. Specialists in wideboard (to 10-inch) hardwood floors.

Painted Floorcloths

Good & Co. Floorclothmakers
Box 497, Dept. OHJ
Dublin, NH 03444
(603)563-8021
Painters of one-of-a-kind, traditional, designer floorcloths.

Patterson, Flynn & Martin Inc.
979 Third Avenue, Dept. OHJ
New York, NY 10022
(212)688-7700
Offering a wide selection of broadlooms, needlepoints, braided rugs, orientals, handwovens, contemporary, and traditional floor-coverings.

Sunflower Studio
2851 Road B1/2, Dept. OHJ
Grand Junction, CO 81503
(303)242-3883
Producer of U.S.A. handwoven and hand-dyed fabrics. 39 different standard seventeenth-, eighteenth-, and early nineteenth-century fabrics and carpetings are made by custom order (minimum 20 yards).

Linoleum

Bangor Cork Company, Inc.
William & D Streets, Dept. OHJ
Pen Argyl, PA 18013
(215)863-9041
Selling battleship linoleum since 1938.

Linoleum City, Inc.
5657 Santa Monica Boulevard, Dept. OHJ
Hollywood, CA 90038
(213)469-0063

Specialists in old-fashioned marbleized linoleum products (sheet goods, tiles) which are natural products, cork floor tiles, and uniquely different floorcoverings.

Stone & Ceramic Flooring

Hoboken Flooring Corporation
70 Demarest Drive, Dept. OHJ
Wayne, NJ 07470
(201)694-2888

Summitville Tiles, Inc.
PO Box 73, Dept. OHJ
Summitville, OH 43962
(215)223-1511
Manufacturer of quarry tile for floors.

Tatko Bros. Slate Company
PO Box 198, Dept. OHJ
Middle Granville, NY 12849
(518)642-1640
Manufacturers of slate floor tile for interior and exterior installation.

Vinyl Flooring—Period Patterns

Europort-Marburger Inc.
933 East Orange Street, Dept. OHJ
Lancaster, PA 17602
(717)392-4199
A distributor to the flooring, entertainment, and production supply industries.

Floortown
26 Union Street, Dept. OHJ
Lynn, MA 01902
(617)599-6544
Specializing in carpet, vinyl, wood, and ceramic flooring for over forty years.

Rugs & Carpets

Family Heir-Loom Weavers
RD #3, Box 59E, Dept. OHJ
Red Lion, PA 17356
(717)246-2431
Ingrain carpets in historically accurate patterns.

Jan's Antique Studio
1065 West Madison, Dept. OHJ
Chicago, IL 60607
(312)243-1129
Oriental rugs.

Langhorne Carpet Company, Inc.
PO Box 7175, Dept. OHJ
Penndel, PA 19047
(215)757-5155
Manufacturer of Jacquard Wilton woven carpet.

Folk Rugs

Heritage Rugs
PO Box 404, Dept. OHJ
Lahaska, PA 18931
(215)343-5196
Designers and weavers of wool-rag rugs on nineteenth-century looms, in a very wide variety of colors, patterns, and sizes.

Thos. K. Woodard American Antiques & Quilts
835 Madison Avenue, Dept. OHJ
New York, NY 10021
(212)988-2906
A line of new woven carpets, Woodard Weave, which are cotton rugs copied from old American rag carpets, are available retail and to the trade, and are carried in about twenty-five showrooms throughout the country.

Country Braid House
Clark Road, Dept. OHJ
Tilton, NH 03276
(603)286-4511
Specialists in custom wool braided rugs.

CHAPTER 16

Finish Revivers

Daly's Wood Finishing Products
3525 Stoneway North, Dept. OHJ
Seattle, WA 98103
(206)633-4200
Specializing in wood finishing systems for refinishing and restoration projects, as well as finishing new woods.

Formby's Workshop
825 Crossover Lane #240, Dept. OHJ
Memphis, TN 38117
(800)367-6297
Manufacturers of complete systems for refinishing and maintaining wood furniture.

The Hope Company, Inc.
12777 Pennridge Drive, PO
Box 749, Dept. OHJ
Bridgeton, MO 63044
(314)739-7254
Manufacturers of refinishing products.

Decorative Finish Supplies

Johnson Paint Co. Inc.
355 Newbury Street, Dept.
OHJ
Boston, MA 02115
(617)536-4838
Boston's oldest paint and paint-specialty store, catering to the decorative painter. Suppliers of hard-to-find paint-related materials such as calcimine, dry pigments, and a complete line of decorative paintbrushes and tools for the faux finish market.

M. Swift & Sons, Inc.
10 Love Lane, Dept. OHJ
Hartford, CT 06141
(800)262-9620
A 100-year-old company manufacturing gold and silver leaf.

Wood Finishing Supply Co.
Inc.
100 Throop Street, Dept. OHJ
Palmyra, NY 14522
(315)597-3743
A mail-order company supplying all types of finishes for finishing or refinishing, as well as tools for the task.

Veneers & Inlays

Artistry in Veneers, Inc.
450 Oak Tree Avenue, Dept.
OHJ
S. Plainfield, NJ 07080
(908)668-1430
Suppliers of architectural domestic and exotic veneers, dyed veneers, burls, butts, crotches, swirls, precomposed veneers, fancy faces, inlay borders, flexible veneers, doorskins, edgebanding materials, marquetry kits, instructional books, and tools.

Homecraft Veneer
901 West Way, Dept. OHJ
Latrobe, PA 15650
(412)537-8435
Suppliers of fine-quality domestic and imported veneers in 1/28-inch to

1/40-inch thickness and widths from 4-inch to 18-inch, depending on the type of wood.

The Woodworker's Store
21801 Industrial Boulevard,
Dept. OHJ
Rogers, MN 55374
(612)428-4101
Domestic and exotic hardwoods, veneers, wood parts, specialty hardware, kitchen accessories, finishing supplies, tools, books, and plans.

Wood-Finishing Products

Barnard Products, Inc.
PO Box 1105, Dept. OHJ
Covina, CA 91722
(818)331-1223
Manufacturers and distributors of fire-retardant paints, varnishes, penetrants, mastics, and epoxies.

Eco Design Company (The
Natural Catalog)
1365 Rufina Circle, Dept.
OHJ
Santa Fe, NM 87501
(505)438-3448
Providers of old-fashioned, natural, and low-toxic paints with the pleasant fragrance of tree resins and plant oils. Superb colors from organic earth pigments provide U.V. protection for exterior stains and a wide variety of tints for interior wallpaints. Cleaners, polishers, and many other products are available for a healthy home and garden.

William Zinsser & Company
Inc.
39 Belmont Drive, Dept. OHJ
Somerset, NJ 08875
(908)469-8100
Shellac, the original finish in your old house. Always all-natural, environmentally safe, and nontoxic, shellac is the modern miracle discovered three hundred years ago.

Woodworking Tools

Channellock Inc.
1306 South Main Street, Dept.
OHJ
Meadville, PA 16335
(814)724-8700

Hand tools such as pliers, wrenches, screwdrivers, and nut drivers.

Frog Tool Company, Ltd.
700 West Jackson Boulevard,
Dept. OHJ
Chicago, IL 60661
(312)648-1270
Suppliers of hand woodworking tools of all kinds.

Williams & Hussey Machine
Co. Inc.
Riverview Mill, PO Box 1149,
Dept. 5625
Wilton, NH 03086
(603)654-6828
Manufacturers of woodworking equipment for over thirty-five years.

Woodcraft Supply Corp.
210 Wood County Industrial
Park, Dept. 92WY0
Parkersburg, WV 26102
(800)542-9115
Offering a complete full-line woodworking tool catalog, featuring over four thousand fine-quality woodworking tools, books, and supplies.

Corner Bead Moulding

Crawford's Old House Store
550 Elizabeth Street, Dept.
OHJ
Waukesha, WI 53186
(800)556-7878
A wide variety of old-house items including corner beads.

Maple Grove Restorations
PO Box 9194, Dept. OHJ
Bolton, CT 06043
(203)742-5432
A New England company specializing in interior raised-panel shutters, wainscotting, corner bead moulding, and raised-panel walls for the Colonial through late Victorian home.

Wood Moulding & Millwork
Producers Association
PO Box 25278, Dept. OHJ
Portland, OR 97225
(503)292-9288
The national trade association for manufacturers of wood mouldings, door jambs, door frames, plank paneling, and related wood products.

Interior Mouldings & Cornices, Stock

Classic Mouldings Inc.
155 Toryork Drive, Unit 1,
Dept. OHJ
Weston, ON M9L 1X9
Canada
(416)745-5560
Manufacturer and distributor of precast ornamental plaster mouldings.

Towne House Restorations
475 Keap Street, Dept. OHJ
Brooklyn, NY 11211
(718)599-4520
A custom moulding fabrication studio and manufacturing facility.

Worthington Group, Ltd.
PO Box 53101, Dept. OHJ
Atlanta, GA 30355
(800)872-1608
Offering a wide range of luxury architectural products, including mouldings.

Interior Mouldings & Trim, Wood

Arvid's Historic Woods
2820 Rucker Avenue, Dept.
OHJ
Everett, WA 98201
(800)627-8437
Offering over one thousand moulding profiles ranging from historic reproductions to custom designed contemporary. Custom moulding profiles are offered as well as the reproduction of mouldings.

Colorado Counter Moldings
PO Box 218, Dept. OHJ
Snowmass, CO 81654
(303)927-9427
Suppliers of Marteau Molding™, "the perfect edge for all countertops." This unique, no-drip moulding adds a custom look to any kitchen or bath cabinetry.

Haas Wood & Ivory Works,
Inc.
64 Clementina Street, Dept.
OHJ
San Francisco, CA 94105
(415)421-8273
A 103-year-old custom wood shop specializing in wood turning and straight and curved mouldings.

Wood Stains, Specialty

Bona Kemi USA, Inc.
14805 E. Moncrieff Place, Dept. OHJ
Aurora, CO 80011
(303)371-1411
Manufacturers of environmentally sound and technologically advanced hardwood floor stains and finishes. Many of these products are waterborne, which avoids the use of solvents found in many other stains and finishes.

Reliable Finishing Products
2625 Greenleaf Avenue, Dept. OHJ
Elk Grove Vllg., IL 60007
(708)228-7667
Manufacturer of finishing products for the restoration and antique market. Removers, finishes, nonpigmented stains, tung oils, etc.

CHAPTER 17

Kitchen Cabinets

Homecrest Corporation
1002 Eisenhower Drive, North, Dept. OHJ
Goshen, IN 46526
(219)533-9571
A leading manufacturer of kitchen cabinets, offering 26 different styles including standard wood and contemporary frameless cabinetry.

Quaker Maid/Div. of WCI Inc.
Route 61, PO Box H, Dept. OHJ
Leesport, PA 19533
(215)926-3011
A leading designer and manufacturer in the custom cabinet industry since 1950. Offering Classic, Q2000, and Coronado cabinets for the kitchen, bath, and other rooms.

Rutt
PO Box 129, 1564 Main Street, Dept. OHJ
Goodville, PA 17528
(215)445-6751
Manufacturer of custom cabinetry for kitchens, baths, and dens, for home and office applications.

Old-Style Kitchen Faucets & Fittings

Antique Baths & Kitchens
2220 Carlton Way, Dept. OHJ
Santa Barbara, CA 93109
(805)962-8598
Specialists in quality bath and kitchen fixtures. For the kitchen: copper sinks, cast-iron sinks, and faucets.

Restoration Works, Inc.
810 Main Street, Dept. OHJ
Buffalo, NY 14202
(800)735-3535
Supplier of decorative hardware, plumbing fixtures, kitchen accessories.

George Taylor Specialties Company
187 Lafayette Street, Dept. OHJ
New York, NY 10013
(212)226-5369
Specialists in rebuilding antique plumbing since 1896. Complete repair parts for all faucets are stocked, as well as a wide variety of antique and porcelain faucets, fittings, and accessories. Also on the premises is a machine shop to make obsolete parts while you wait. Reproduction faucets available. Custom orders are welcome.

Old-Style Kitchen Sinks

Antique Emporium
7805 Loraine Avenue, Dept. OHJ
Cleveland, OH 44102
(216)651-5480
Specialists in fine antique architectural fixtures, cabinetry, and accessories. All styles for bath and kitchen. Design and installation services available.

Porcher, Inc.
13-160 Merchandise Mart, Dept. OHJ
Chicago, IL 60654
(312)923-0995
France's leading manufacturer of fine fixtures and faucetry for the kitchen and bath is offering the American home true European styling, practicality, and stunning diversity.

Stove & Heaters, Cooking—Period Designs

AGA Cookers, Cooper & Torner Inc.
17 Towne Farm Lane, Dept. OHJ
Stowe, VT 05672
(802)253-9727
The legendary AGA Cooker combines classic design and superior cooking results.

House of Webster
PO Box 488, Dept. OHJ
Rogers, AR 72757
(501)636-4640
Manufacturer of electric cast-iron cook stoves that look like old-fashioned wood-burning stoves. Wall ovens, cast-iron electric skillets, and bean pots are available.

Viking Range Corporation
PO Drawer 956, Dept. OHJ
Greenwood, MS 38930
(601)453-8777
Providing the discriminating cook with the performance of professional cooking equipment in a restaurant-style range designed exclusively for home use.

Stove Parts & Repair

Brunelle Enterprises, Inc.
82 Union Road, Dept. OHJ
Wales, MA 01081
(413)245-7396
Buying, selling, and restoring antique wood, coal, and gas stoves. Parts are available for some models.

Portland Stove Company
Box 37, Fickett Road, Dept. OHJ
N. Pownal, ME 04069
(207)688-2254
Manufacturers of cookstoves. Antique stove restorations are available, as well as recastings of grates and liners. Specialists in cookstoves, parlor heaters, box heaters, and upright cylindrical parlor stoves (wood or coal). Supplier of parts for all Atlantic brand stoves.

Preston's
Old Route 28, PO Box 369, Dept. OHJ
Ossipee Village, NH 03864
(603)539-2807
Family business established in the 1800s dealing with heating and cooking equipment as well as accessories.

Macy's Texas Stove Works
5515 Almeda Road, Dept. OHJ
Houston, TX 77004
(713)521-0934
Supplier of ranges, parts, and services for vintage ranges, gas and electric. Cleaning and reconditioning is available for persons wishing to have their vintage range in the best possible working order.

Bathroom Accessories

Besco Plumbing
729 Atlantic Avenue, Dept. OHJ
Boston, MA 02111
(617)423-4535
Suppliers of hundreds of bathroom renovation items such as faucets, tubs, pedestal sinks, toilets, and shower systems. Specialists in porcelain, brass, nickel, and marble renovation products. Custom manufacturing of products to fit unusual specifications is available, as well as restoration of your antique fittings.

Bona Decorative Hardware
3073 Madison Road, Dept. OHJ
Cincinnati, OH 45245
(513)321-7877
Decorative hardware, mostly formal French and English in style. Bathroom fittings and accessories appropriate for period houses.

Watercolors Inc.
Dept. OHJ
Garrison, NY 10524
(914)424-3327
Exclusive importers and distributors of authentic English and French Edwardian bathroom fixtures and other traditional faucet and accessory designs. Complete fittings for U.S. specifications.

Bathroom Fixture Resurfacing

Hiles Plating Company, Inc.
2030 Broadway, Dept. OHJ
Kansas City, MO 64108
(816)421-6450
Specialists in silver, gold, brass, copper, and nickel plating. Brass, silver, copper, and pewter polishing is also done, as well as polishing of plumbing fixtures. Gold and nickel plating of tub clawfeet is also available.

Miracle Method Bathroom Restoration
701 Center Street, Dept. OHJ
Ludlow, MA 01056
(413)589-0769
Refinishing of clawfoot tubs and pedestal sinks using the Miracle Method bathroom restoration system. Reproduction faucets and hardware are available.

Perma Ceram Enterprises, Inc.
65 Smithtown Boulevard, Dept. OHJ
Smithtown, NY 11788
(800)645-5039
A large in-home bathroom resurfacing company with an exclusive formula to resurface bathtubs, sinks, and tile. Applied only by authorized factory-trained technicians. Available in all decorator colors. Work done is fully guaranteed.

Perma-Glaze, Inc.
1638 S. Research Loop Road #160, Dept. OHJ
Tucson, AZ 85710
(800)332-7397
Restoration and refinishing of bathroom and kitchen fixtures such as bathtubs, sinks, and ceramic wall tiles. Materials that can be refinished include porcelain, fiberglass, acrylic cultured marble, formica, kitchen appliances, whirlpool tubs, shower enclosures, and most building materials. Service includes chip repair, fiberglass and acrylic spa repairs, and restoration and reglazing of fixtures.

Bathroom Sinks, Toilets & Tubs

Antique Hardware Store
RD 2, Box A, Rt. 611, Dept. OHJ
Kintnersville, PA 18930
(800)422-9982
You'll find great prices on clawfoot bathtubs, shower conversions, faucets, sinks, high-tank toilets, and much more. 100 percent satisfaction guaranteed.

DuraGlaze Service Corp.
2825 Bransford Avenue, Dept. OHJ
Nashville, TN 37204
(615)298-1787
Antique bathtubs, sinks and plumbing for sale. Porcelain refinishing for antique tubs, sinks, and ceramic tile.

Kohler Company
444 Highland Drive, Dept. OHJ
Kohler, WI 53044
(414)457-4441
Manufacturing a broad array of plumbing fixtures, faucets, and accessories in a variety of styles for residential, commercial, industrial, and institutional uses.

Ohmega Salvage
2407 San Pablo Avenue, Dept. OHJ
Berkeley, CA 94702
(510)843-7368
Architectural details of all kinds including antique plumbing fixtures (rebuilt and guaranteed), tubs, sinks, hardware, and old wrought iron.

Sign of the Crab
3756 Omec Circle, Dept. OHJ
Rancho Cordova, CA 95742
(916)638-2722
A source for all renovation plumbing and hardware. Many designs of reproduction faucets are available, along with truly authentic door hardware and bath accessories.

Cabinetmaking & Fine Woodworking

J&M Custom Cabinets & Millworks
2750 North Bauer Road, Dept. OHJ
St. Johns, MI 48879
(517)593-2244
Builders of custom kitchens and cabinets for thirty-five years. Specialty millwork, such as Victorian trim and panel doors, is available.

The Kennebec Company
One Front Street, Dept. OHJ
Bath, ME 04530
(207)443-2131
A team of architectural designers and craftsmen specializing in country- and shaker-style cabinetry for kitchens. Services include design consultations nationwide, complete design, and custom-built cabinetry, paneling, furniture, and built-in wall sections handcrafted to exacting detail.

States Industries, Inc.
29545 Enid Rd. E., PO Box 7037, Dept. OHJ
Eugene, OR 97401
(503)688-7871
Manufacturers of a variety of hardwood plywood, and hardwood overlayed panel products, including stock panels for cabinets, furniture, prefinished interior wall panels, architectural panels, and furniture component parts.

Cabinet & Furniture Hardware

Baldwin Hardware Corporation
PO Box 15048, Dept. OHJ
Reading, PA 19612
(215)777-7811
A leading manufacturer of solid brass architectural hardware, decorative hardware, and bath accessories. Offering eighteenth-century door hardware designs and Victorian-designed bath accessories made of hot forged brass for finish perfection and crisp detail.

Hardware Plus, Inc.
701 E. Kingsley Road, Dept. OHJ
Garland, TX 75041
(214)271-0319
A mail-order source for all types of house and furniture hardware.

Paxton Hardware, Ltd.
7818 Bradshaw Road, PO Box 256, Dept. OHJ
Upper Falls, MD 21156
(301)592-8505
Suppliers of a wide selection of period brass furniture hardware such as pulls, locks, hinges, knobs, supports, table and deck hardware, and much more.

INDEX

C

D

F

lath, 257
neat plaster, 257, 270
and ornamental plaster, 270, 280
ready-mixed plaster, 257
wood-fibered plaster, 257
Gypsumboard
base, 253
laminating walls with, 268

Hacksaw, 81, 133, 308
    mini, 108
Hair
    for mortar, 162n, 162
    for plaster, 257
Half-lap joints, 241
Half-timbered dwellings, 13
Hall, 14
"Hall-and-parlor" floor plan, 14, 323
Hammer, 260
    clawhammer, 306, 308
    mason's, 157
    slater's, 78
    staple, 55
Hand finishes, 266
Handhewn boards, 283
Hand pumps, 331
Handrails, 233
    repairing, 232
Hand-rubbed finish, 316–19
Hardwall plaster, 257
Hardware
    installation, 42
    pocket door, 251, 252
    reproduction, 334–35
    sink, 334–35
    and stripping woodwork, 305
    suppliers, 320
    window, 242
Hardwood, 232
    floor, 220, 286, 292, 293, 325
    in kitchen, 232
    trim, stripping, 301
    wedges, 100
Hatchet, 56
Haucherr, Rosmarie, 334
Hawk, 155, 257, 260, 261, 262
    defined, 257
Hazardous waste, 165, 302, 303, 306
Header
    repair, 216–18
    over windows, 50
Head joints, 153
Health
    hazards, 39
    and lead pipes, 171
    and planning restoration, 40
    and "Swedish" finishes, 293
Heartwood floor, 290
Heat gun, 120, 121, 146, 238, 243, 298, 301, 343
Heat plate, 120, 301
Heat pump, 204
Heat stripping, 243, 300–01
    hazards, 120

tools, 120, 243
Heat systems
    electrical load, 179
    and energy costs, 35, 40, 193, 200–07
    imbalance, 204
    inspection checklist, 34–35, 36
    and planning restoration, 40, 42
    and "the Standards," 28
    See also Boiler; Energy; Furnace
Heat (thermal) storage, 205, 206–07
Heat transfer, 205
Hemlock, 104, 283
Hemp, 142, 291
Hepplewhite, 330
Hidden nail method, 81
High gloss exterior paints, 98
High-intensity "torch" lamps, 120
High-Lime Mortar formula, 161
High-resistance short circuit, 181
Hinges, 245, 246
Hip, defined, 76
Hip bath, 335
Hipped gable end, 14
Hipped roofs, 14, 16, 18, 21, 22, 23, 24
Historical designations
    and building permits, 27
    getting property listed, 25–26, 29
    and preservation regulations, 25
    and tax breaks and incentives, 25–30
Historical heritage, 3
    and bathrooms, 335–39
    and decorative details added after
        construction date, 28
    and exterior colors, 121, 122–25
    of floors, 282–86, 291, 293
    and kitchens, 321–27, 330–33
    and natural vs. painted woodwork,
        298, 300
    and porches, 129–31
    researching, 5–6
    securing elements against loss or
        damage, 39
    and sinks, 330–33, 334–35
    and textured plaster finishes, 266
    See also Styles
Historically significant houses, 10
Historical registers, 25
Historical restoration
    defined, 8
    vs. sensitive rehabilitation, 7, 7–8
Historical society, 5
Historic Architectural Review Board
        (HARB), 31
Historic district
    building and repair permits, 27
    "contributing element," 26, 27, 29
    preservation regulations, 30–31
Historic-resources surveys, 26
Hog bristles, 117
Holes and notches
    damage caused by, 50, 216, 222
    how tos, for rafters and joists, 218
    tools for boring, 55
Holesaws, 218
    bimetal, 55
Holland plaster, 265
"Holy stoning" floors, 283
Homeowner's insurance, 75
Homestead style, 23

Hoosier cupboard, 324, 327, 335
Hope's, 295
Horizontal siding, 18
Horse, 274
    defined, 272
    making, 272, 276
Hose connections, 171
Hot-dipped, galvanized nails, 81, 96, 108
Hot- or forced-air heat, 35, 184, 199
    register, checking, 36
Hot tank, 303, 305
Hot-water heat systems, 35, 331. See
        also Boiler; Radiators
Housewrap, 82
Hudson River School, 19
Hue, 122
Humidity, 209, 283
    and door swelling, 242–43
    and floor repair, 288–89, 290
    and plaster walls, 253–54
    See also Condensation; Moisture or
        dampness; Water penetration
        and damage
Husk, 190
Hybrid heat pump, 205
Hydrated lime
    applying, 262
    defined, 257, 258
    double, 260
    materials for, 260
    types, 257
Hydraulic cement, 60, 62
Hydraulic pressure, 60
Hydrostatic pressure, 60, 63, 68
Hyphens, 15

Illinois, 16
Imitation brick/stone/tile, 265
Incannel gouge, 230
Indiana, 16
Indirect lighting, 190, 327
Ingrain carpets, 285
Inner-City Ventures Fund, 30
Insects, 152
    and basement repair, 208
    checking for signs of, 208, 213
    control, 214
    damage to porch, 132
    protecting roof vents from, 83
    and synthetic siding, 102
    and treating wood before painting,
        115
    types defined, 211–14
    and wood decay, 49, 64
    See also Decay; Rot
Insl-X's Aqualock, 263
Inspection
    checklist, 25, 31–37
    columns, 137–38
    cornice, 98
    energy efficiency, 193
    masonry, 151, 153, 156, 157–58
    porch, 132

O

P

S

Waterproofing, 41, 59–60, 68, 108, 132, 133
  opaque, for sandblasted, 158
  paint for wet basement, 210
  sealers, clear, 209
  systems for basement, 210–11
Water pump, 179
  pliers, 173
Water repellent (WR), 133, 150
  homemade, 133
  preservative (WRP), 117, 133
  for sandblasted brick, 158–59
Water-soluble stains, 315
Watertable, colors, 121
Watt, defined, 180
Wattage, combined, 178
  calculating, 179, 180, 183
Wax finishes
  for floors, 282, 284, 292
  for woodwork
    cleaning, 295
    defined, 315
    for hand-rubbed finish, 320
Wayne Towle, Inc., 303
WD-40, 239
Weatherboards, 13, 103, 108
  defined, 105
Weathered wood
  painting, 115
  sealing before painting, 242
  staining, 127
Weatherface exposure, on clapboards, 106
Weathering
  of masonry, 151–52
  stain, 126, 127
Weatherizing, 193–98, 201, 241–42
  caulking, 113, 115
  and wall insulation, 199–200
Weatherproof glue, 139
Weatherstripping, 40
  door, 196–97
  windows, 197, 201, 236, 241–42
Wedges
  door, 246, 247
  stair, 226–30
Wedge slides, 140, 141
Weed killer, 163
Weep holes, 211
Weight, adding to house, 51
Weights, window
  defined, 235
  matching and replacing, 235
  repairing, 239–40
  suppliers, 236
Welder, 100
Welding, ironwork, 149
Weldwood phenol resorcinol, 96, 107
Well pump, 179
West Coast woods, in siding, 104, 106
White, color, 126
White coat, 277
White glue, 290, 308, 310
White neutra oil, 425
White pine, 104, 283
White spruce, 283
Whitewash
  brushes, 118, 156
  defined, 118

stripping, 302
Wicker furnishings, 131
WilsonArt, 327
Wilton carpets, 285
Window
  casings, 102, 243
  decorative parts, repair standards, 28
  jamb, 242, 268
  lintels, 152
  sill
    removing, 307
    stripping, 243
    and wood rot, 240
  See also Windowpanes; Windows
Windowpanes
  Colonial Revival, 21
  Federal and Georgian, 16
  Gothic Revival, 18, 19
  inspection checklist, 33
  loose or broken, 238
  painting technique, 119
  Prairie School style, 22
  repair and replacement standards, 28
  and window stripping, 243
  See also Glazing
Window putty, 238
Windows
  arch trouble, 100–02
  caulking, 114, 158, 196, 236, 241, 242
  clapboards under, 107
  Colonial, 14
  Colonial Revival, 22
  Cottage, 24
  double-hung
    taking apart, 237
    weatherstripping, 241
  drafty, 241–42
  enlarging, 50
  exterior colors, 121–23
  Federal and Georgian, 16
  Foursquare, 24
  Greek Revival, 18
  how they work, 234–36
  inspection checklist, 33, 36
  leaks, 99
  painting
    brushes for sashes, 118
    technique, 119, 242
  and passive solar methods, 205
  and planning restoration, 40, 41, 42
  Prairie School, 22
  Queen Anne, 21
  removing woodwork trim, 306–07
  repairing, 234–43
    epoxy, 110, 112
    standards, 28
  replacement
    and energy costs, 40, 193, 196
    standards, 31
  running wiring through, 186
  Second Empire/Mansard, 20
  stripping, 243
  stuck, 238
  suppliers, 236
  weatherizing, 196, 197–99, 200–01, 241–42
Winkler, Gail Caskey, 286
Wire
  brush, 146

cutter, 260
lath, 257
#12, 178
#14 AWG, 178
Wiring, 169
  current-carrying capacity of, 178
  defective, 180–84
  repairing improper, 39, 183–84
  routing, 184–86
  types defined, 174–78
  See also Electrical system
Wisconsin, 16
Wisteria, 131
Wolfe, Elsie de, 190
Wolf Paints, 319
Wolmanized wood, 217
Wood
  bare, treating before painting, 115, 243
  bleach, 313
  caulk and putty for exterior, 98
  clapboard repair, 107–09
  in Colonial houses, 13
  columns, 216
  countertops, 329
  decay, 94, 96, 138
    and cracks, 49, 68
    probing for, 138
    in windows, 240
  and differential settlement cracks, 47
  in Federal and Georgian houses, 16
  fillets, 291
  in Gothic Revival houses, 18–19
  grades, for floor lumber, 290
  gutters, 86
  inspection checklist, 32–33
  for kitchens, 323
  mouldings, and wiring, 176
  patches, 96
    clapboard, 108
    for window, 240
  patching and repair of exterior, 96–98
  pile or raft foundations, 48
  and planning restoration, 41
  plug repairs, 138–39
  porch, repairing, 137–45
  in Prairie School style, 22
  sagging, 46
  in Second Empire/Mansard house, 21
  siding, 20
  splice, 107
  storm windows, 198
  strips, 291
  trim, 28
  type
    in floors, 283
    and staining, 127
  using epoxy to repair
    column decay, 139–40
    rotted exterior, 108–12
    rotted window, 240–41
  window sash, 28
  See also Floors and flooring;
    Moulding; Trim; Wood shakes;
    Wood Shingles; Woodwork;
    specific parts made of wood;
    and specific types of wood
Wooden
  cleats, 174

ILLUSTRATION CREDITS

Chapter 1: p. 11 (*top*) John Slobodnik; p. 11 (*bottom*) Marilyn Loehr; p. 12 (*top left*) Laurence Sommer; p. 12 (*top right*) Donald Randazzo; p. 12 (*far left*) Gerald R. Mosher; p. 12 (*bottom*) Allyn S. Feinberg; p. 12 (*bottom right*) Cathy Anderson; p. 13, HABS; p. 17, HABS. **CHAPTER 2:** p. 26, Ridgley Ochs & Robert Tiernan; p. 28, James C. Massey. **CHAPTER 3:** pp. 43–50, William Ward Bucher. **CHAPTER 5:** p. 60, Phillip Marshall; p. 62, William Ward Bucher; pp. 62–67, Jonathan Poore; p. 67 (*bottom*) William Ward Bucher. **CHAPTER 6:** p. 69 (*left*) Jonathan Poore; p. 69 (*right*) Russell Gilmore; p. 72, Jonathan Poore; p. 75, Leo Blackman; p. 76, Creative Homeowner Press; p. 81 (*top*) Jeff Wilkinson; p. 81 (*bottom*) Cedar by Coleman; p. 85 (*bottom*) Leo Blackman; p. 86, Joseph F. Cempa; pp. 88–90, Jonathan Poore; p. 90, Jonathan Poore; p. 91 (*top*) International Society of Fire Service Instructors; p. 91 (*bottom*) Goldblatt Tool Company; p. 92 (*top*) Jonathan Poore; p. 93, Larry Jones; p. 94 (*bottom*) Larry Jones; p. 96, Larry Jones; p. 97 (*bottom right*) Larry Jones. **CHAPTER 7:** pp. 99–102, William Ward Bucher; p. 103 (*top left*) Kendall Atchison; p. 103 (*top right*) Ridgley Ochs & Robert Tiernan; p. 103 (*bottom right*) Jonathan Poore; p. 104 (*top left*) Jonathan

Poore; pp. 105–106 (*illustrations*) Jonathan Poore; p. 107 (*photo*) Bryan Butts; p. 107 (*right*) Larry Jones; p. 108, Larry Jones; p. 109 (*left*) Jonathan Poore; p. 109 (*right*) John Leeke; p. 110, John Leeke; pp. 113–114, Jonathan Poore; pp. 118–119, Jonathan Poore; p. 122, Restoration Graphics; pp. 123, 125, Charles Eanet. **CHAPTER 8:** p. 129, *Old-House Journal*; p. 130 (*illustration*) Stephanie Croce; p. 130 (*top photo*) Jeff Wilkinson; p. 131 (*top left*) Jeff Wilkinson; p. 132 (*photos*) Jerry Trescott; p. 132 (*illustration*) Larry Jones; p. 133, John Leeke; p. 134 (*photos*) John Leeke; p. 135 (*illustration*) Jeff Wilkinson; p. 135 (*photos at left*) John Leeke; p. 136, Gordon Bock; p. 137 (*illustrations*) Jonathan Poore; p. 137 (*photos*) John Leeke; p. 138 (*photos*) John Leeke; pp. 138–139 (*illustrations*) Jonathan Poore; p. 139 (*photos*) John Leeke; p. 140 (*illustration*) Jonathan Poore; p. 140 (*photos*) John Leeke; pp. 141–144, Kenneth D. Collister; p. 147, Jonathan Poore; p. 149, Tom Flagg. **CHAPTER 9:** p. 160, Jonathan Poore; p. 161, Larry Jones. **CHAPTER 10:** pp. 184–189, Jonathan Poore. **CHAPTER 11:** pp. 194–195, Jonathan Poore; p. 196 (*photo*) Andy Wallace; pp. 196–197 (*illustrations*) Jonathan Poore; pp. 198–200, Andy Wallace; p. 201 (*illustration*) Jonathan

Poore; p. 201 (*photo*) Andy Wallace; p. 202, Jonathan Poore; pp. 204–207, Jonathan Poore. **CHAPTER 12:** p. 210 (*left*) Jonathan Poore; p. 210 (*right top & bottom*) Larry Jones; p. 211, Jonathan Poore; p. 212 (*top*) Jonathan Poore; pp. 215–217, William Ward Bucher; pp. 218–233, Jonathan Poore. **CHAPTER 13:** pp. 237–242 (*illustrations*) Jonathan Poore; pp. 244–252, Jonathan Poore. **CHAPTER 14:** p. 255 (*left*) Larry Jones; p. 255 (*right*) Jonathan Poore; p. 259 (*right*) Jonathan Poore; p. 259 (*left*) Larry Jones; pp. 268–269 (*illustrations*) Jonathan Poore. **CHAPTER 15:** p. 282, Courtesy of The Brooklyn Museum; p. 283, Jonathan Poore; p. 284, The Joinery; pp. 286–289, Jonathan Poore; p. 289 (*bottom right*) Jeff Wilkinson. **CHAPTER 16:** p. 296, Jonathan Poore; p. 302, Bix Process Systems; p. 302 (*bottom right*) *Old-House Journal*; pp. 310–312, Jonathan Poore. **CHAPTER 17:** p. 323, Jonathan Poore; p. 324, Ken & Deborah Buck; p. 326 (*illustration*) Jonathan Poore; p. 329, Ken & Deborah Buck; pp. 331–333, Bekka Lindstrom; pp. 334–335 (*illustrations*) Jonathan Poore; p. 335 (*photo*) Kohler Company; p. 336, Kohler Company; p. 338, Kristan Del Sordo.